CLASSICS
OF THE
RENAISSANCE
THEATER
SEVEN ENGLISH PLAYS

EDITED BY

J. Dennis Huston

YALE UNIVERSITY

Alvin B. Kernan

YALE UNIVERSITY

HARCOURT, BRACE & WORLD, INC.
New York / Chicago / San Francisco / Atlanta

CLASSICS OF THE RENAIS- SANCE THEATER

SEVEN ENGLISH PLAYS

CLASSICS OF THE RENAISSANCE THEATER
SEVEN ENGLISH PLAYS
J. Dennis Huston / Alvin B. Kernan

© 1969 by Harcourt, Brace & World, Inc.

Library of Congress Catalog Card Number: 79–76617

Printed in the United States of America

Volpone (text and notes), edited by Alvin B. Kernan, is reprinted by permission of the publisher, Yale University Press. Copyright © 1962 by Yale University Press.

PREFACE

THIS BOOK OFFERS SEVEN OF THE MOST important and most frequently taught non-Shakespearean plays of the English Renaissance, which in combination make up a history of the development of drama in this period. The texts, all newly or recently edited from the first printed forms of the plays, are designed to provide the student with versions that are at once accurate renderings of the originals and readable playscripts that he can follow without confusion. Editorial additions, such as stage directions, are enclosed in brackets, and all emendations and significant variants are given in the notes. Punctuation has been modernized only where necessary to make the sense clear, but modern practices in spelling, capitalization, and italicization have been followed throughout, except where they would change the original meaning.

The language of these plays is frequently difficult for the modern student, and even for the specialist. We believe, however, that it is best to encourage the student to pursue the exact meaning of even the most difficult passages, and have therefore provided generous glosses that attempt to give the simple sense of unfamiliar words and tangled lines. We hope that the fullness of the notes will give the student enough help with the literal reading of the plays that class time can be spent on interpretation rather than on simple definition. In addition, we have included notes that call attention to certain salient themes—for example, the spacious geography of *Tamburlaine,* the frequent references to playing and imposture in *Volpone,* the submerged flow of sexual references in *The Changeling*—that are central to the meanings of the plays.

The Introduction takes the form of a general essay on the nature and progression of English Renaissance drama, focusing attention on the way in which the playwright of this period used acting and the theater as metaphors for the ambitions of his great heroes and the inevitability of their fates. A description and discussion of the physical structure of the Elizabethan theater is included in the Introduction and is supported by the illustrations preceding the plays. A short introduction at the beginning of each play offers information about the author and his works, the edition of the play on which our text is based, and some of the characteristics of the drama of this period that are evident in the play.

J. DENNIS HUSTON

ALVIN B. KERNAN

CONTENTS

CLASSICS
OF THE
RENAISSANCE
THEATER
SEVEN ENGLISH PLAYS

INTRODUCTION

THE BASIC THEATER HAS BEEN APTLY DEFINED as "two boards and a passion"—a stage and an actor—but historical development, cultural variation, and technical change have tended to obscure the enduring presence of these theatrical essentials. Over the last several thousand years the "boards" have developed into elaborate stages in complex theaters, enhanced by all the subtle arts of scenic design. During this time, the "passion" has found expression in costumes, masks, mime, dance, and poetry, all of which have combined to create hero, complex character, and *dramatis personae*. The great dramatists of all ages have, however, never failed to understand the fundamentals of the theatrical medium, and have never failed to realize that stage and actor are not only their basic tools but also the basic subject matter of drama.

No group of dramatists has ever been so intensely, almost obsessively, self-conscious about the nature of their craft as those English dramatists who wrote for the London theater between 1588 and 1640, the great age of Renaissance drama. Most obviously, these dramatists were creators of great passions, embodied in heroic characters whose voices filled the theaters with magnificent poetry expressing perfectly the grandeur of the Renaissance imagination. The heroic figure, "the Overreacher," who dominates this period of English drama from its Elizabethan beginning to its Caroline conclusion, is so self-assured, so certain of his own power, that he recognizes no reality outside his own mind and no law outside his own will.

Tamburlaine, Hieronimo, Volpone, Vindici, the Duchess of Malfi, De Flores, and Giovanni are all perfect instances of those "outstretched heroes" of whom Hamlet speaks so feelingly. Each of them is an absolutist in some area of life: in love, in politics, in pleasure, or in revenge. None can imagine that the world should not conform to his own desire, and each ruthlessly and recklessly oversteps the boundaries set by law and custom in order to achieve what it is his nature to desire. But the precise meaning of these willful thrusts for power and of this disdain for traditional social restraints is revealed in its purest, its archetypal form in Christopher Marlowe's hero Tamburlaine.

To the modern reader Marlowe's language may sound crude and overdone, his subject matter seem an incredible mixture of the naive and the melodramatic, and his dramaturgy appear awkward. Only ten

years after the play appeared, *Tamburlaine* already sounded all huff and
rant to the Elizabethans, who considered Marlowe, along with Thomas
Kyd, one of the primitives of their theater. But at least one writer, the
poet-playwright Michael Drayton, understood that a primitive writer
like Marlowe has some advantages over his more sophisticated
successors:

> Neat Marlowe, bathed in the *Thespian* springs,
> Had in him those brave translunary things
> That the first Poets had; his raptures were
> All ayre, and fire, which made his verses cleere,
> For that fine madnes still he did retaine,
> Which rightly should possesse a Poet's braine.

In speaking of "those brave translunary things" and in comparing
Marlowe to the first poets, Drayton is pointing to a quality in Marlowe's
writing that we should now call archetypal or mythic. That is, instead
of presenting life in a realistic way, Marlowe's oversize characters,
flamboyant style, and exaggerated plot offer open, undisguised images
of Renaissance man's recently acquired sense of unlimited powers,
abilities, and force.

Tamburlaine's physical power and majesty exceed realistic possibility, but they convey perfectly the new, idealized sense of the beauty
and strength of man.

> Of stature tall, and straightly fashionèd,
> Like his desire, lift upwards and divine,
> So large of limbs, his joints so strongly knit,
> Such breadth of shoulders as might mainly bear
> Old Atlas' burden. 'Twixt his manly pitch,
> A pearl more worth than all the world is placed,
> Wherein by curious sovereignty of art
> Are fixed his piercing instruments of sight,
> Whose fiery circles bear encompassèd
> A heaven of heavenly bodies in their spheres,
> That guides his steps and actions to the throne
> Where honor sits invested royally.
> Pale of complexion, wrought in him with passion,
> Thirsting with sovereignty, with love of arms,
> His lofty brows in folds do figure death,

And in their smoothness amity and life.
About them hangs a knot of amber hair,
Wrappèd in curls, as fierce Achilles' was,
On which the breath of heaven delights to play,
Making it dance with wanton majesty.
His arms and fingers, long and sinewy,
Betokening valor and excess of strength—
In every part proportioned like the man
Should make the world subdued to Tamburlaine.

(II.1.7–30)

In this portrait of vitality, of striving reach, of elevation, two details stand out particularly. First, the "long and sinewy" arms and hands of the figure suggest, as do several other physical details in the description, the statue of David by Michelangelo. The huge hands of both David and Tamburlaine image power and a delight in the physical world, the things that can be touched, but they also hint at a potentially tragic "excess of strength." Second, though this portrait of Tamburlaine emphasizes a powerful expansive movement, upward and outward, as if man, even at rest, were threatening to fill the entire universe, it also depicts a simultaneous countermovement of withdrawal into the self and hints at the existence there, in the human psyche, of a new world, a new reality. Tamburlaine's eyes are fiery circles that "bear encompassèd," i.e. surrounded, "a heaven of heavenly bodies in their spheres." These words seem to mean no more than that Tamburlaine's eyes shine brightly, but taken at full metaphoric value they suggest that reality no longer exists entirely outside the self. The bright spheres of the whirling universe will continue to turn, but there is now within the human mind a competing universe, a reality, as bright and powerful as that of nature. This essentially Romantic view of reality is expressed briefly and sharply by William Blake in one of the "Proverbs of Hell": "Everything possible to be believed is an image of truth."

The description of Tamburlaine's eyes directs us inward to his mind, where the full nature of his powers and passions is revealed.

Nature, that framed us of four elements
Warring within our breasts for regiment,
Doth teach us all to have aspiring minds.

Our souls, whose faculties can comprehend
The wondrous architecture of the world
And measure every wandering planet's course,
Still climbing after knowledge infinite,
And always moving as the restless spheres,
Wills us to wear ourselves and never rest,
Until we reach the ripest fruit of all,
That perfect bliss and sole felicity,
The sweet fruition of an earthly crown.

(II.7.18–29)

In Marlowe's dramatic world all of man's being is concentrated and
summed up in a drive for sovereignty. Nature, at every level, down to
the atoms and up to the universe, is war, a struggle, a process of the
survival of the fittest. Nature red in tooth and claw is now a familiar
concept, but the Elizabethans, though they had their doubts, still largely
believed that true nature was properly harmonious and kind. The
orthodox view was that anything truly *natural* sought and maintained
its proper place within a much larger scheme: within an already
established hierarchy, within a moral order, within a society, within a
family. But Tamburlaine speaks for a new way of thinking about man
and about life. He speaks not for social man, who subordinates himself
to an order outside himself, but for the unique individual whose goal in
life, whose every effort, is directed toward the achievement of his
singular desires and the establishment of his superiority over all other
men. Tamburlaine not only expresses these views in his person and his
words, he achieves them by his actions. Born a poor shepherd, he rises
by his courage and his brilliant use of words to marriage with the most
beautiful woman in the world, the divine Zenocrate. By force of arms
and power of will this great warrior overthrows, one after another,
the established, hereditary rulers of the world.

Marlowe goes far beyond revealing incipient democratic tenden-
cies, to create in the clearest and largest terms possible the drives and
assumptions that motivate the unique individual. Tamburlaine's
essential drive is "to be a king," and he states this openly after he has
helped the noble Cosroe wrest the throne of Persia from his legitimate
but weak brother Mycetes. Cosroe leaves to be crowned in the capital,
and as he departs, one of his attendants describes the coming coronation

in characteristically rich terms—nothing is ever described by Tamburlaine or his followers in mean terms. Cosroe goes, we are told, to "ride in triumph through Persepolis," and as the attendant speaks, the new King's entourage passes over the stage, leaving only Tamburlaine and his generals behind. Picking up the words of the previous speaker, Tamburlaine exclaims half in dream, half in certainty,

> TAMBURLAINE   "And ride in triumph through Persepolis!"
>   Is it not brave to be a king, Techelles?
>   Usumcasane and Theridamas,
>   Is it not passing brave to be a king,
>   And ride in triumph through Persepolis?
> TECHELLES   O, my lord, 'tis sweet and full of pomp.
> USUMCASANE   To be a king is half to be a god.
> THERIDAMAS   A god is not so glorious as a king.
>   I think the pleasure they enjoy in heaven
>   Cannot compare with kingly joys in earth:
>   To wear a crown enchased with pearl and gold,
>   Whose virtues carry with it life and death;
>   To ask and have, command and be obeyed;
>   When looks breed love, with looks to gain the prize,
>   Such power attractive shines in princes' eyes.
>
>   (II.5.50–64)

The word "king" has lost its magic for us, suggesting today only some hemophilic exile at Monte Carlo. It was, however, still one of the crucial words and one of the key ideas of the Renaissance, and the drama of this period is filled with kings, with struggles for kingdoms, with thrones, with crowns. But the word "king" was highly ambivalent. On one hand, it represented the old order and hierarchical ways of thinking, social systems in which the king under God, and man under king, subjected themselves to the rule of the established order. On the other, "king" meant what it means to Tamburlaine and his generals: absolute power to have one's will.

  Marlowe's plays are almost a catalogue of the ways in which the Renaissance man sought this power. In *Doctor Faustus* power is sought through learning, through magic and science; in *The Jew of Malta* power is achieved by means of wealth and political cunning; in *Tamburlaine* however, the principal means to power are courage and force of arms, and Tamburlaine satisfies his appetite for domination by the almost boringly repetitive conquest of larger and larger realms. But Tamburlaine is a great poet and orator as well as a great warrior. To speak poorly in this play, as Mycetes does, is to signal inadequacy in all activities of life, while the ability to speak magnificently, to use "working words," reflects all kinds of power. Words and style directly express the will and the power of the characters, and a brief examination of Marlowe's markedly personal style reveals in another way the full meaning of what his heroic characters seek.

The chief characteristics of the Marlovian heroic style are (1) the steady, heavy beat of "Marlowe's mighty line," which suggests authority, determination, and steady onward movement; (2) the consistent choice of present participles over adjectives—"shining" for "bright," "rising" for "high"—to suggest a nature always active and always aspiring, never at rest; (3) the repeated use of hyperbole to convey a constant striving for a condition beyond any known in this world—"lovelier than the love of Jove," "fairer than the whitest snow on Scythian hills," and "swifter than Pegasus"; (4) the consistent use of parataxis, the joining of several phrases and clauses by "and"—and . . . and . . . and—to create a sense of endless ongoing, of constant striving; (5) the use of the privative suffix after words that define limits—"topless," "quenchless," "endless"; and (6) the frequent use of exotic proper names and references to faraway, romantic places to suggest the grandeur, the wideness, and the richness of the world.[1]

But the stylistic device that summarizes all the other elements of the Marlovian style is what we might call "the pathetic fallacy in the imperative mood." The "pathetic fallacy" is a linguistic expression of anthropomorphism: man assumes that nature feels what he feels, that the earth *sorrows,* brooks *run,* and trees *sigh.* By shifting from the indicative to the imperative mood, man commands nature, and even the gods themselves, to share his feelings and obey his wishes. This is Tamburlaine's regular mode of address to the world: he praises Zenocrate's beauty and asserts that it will "clear the darkened sky / And calm the rage of thundering Jupiter"; or he asserts that this human

---

[1]A more complete treatment of these elements of the Marlovian style is to be found in Harry Levin, *The Overreacher, A Study of Christopher Marlowe* (Harvard University Press, 1952), where the details of this style were first worked out. The term "overreacher" is an English translation of the rhetorical figure hyperbole.

loveliness will "scale the icy mountains' lofty tops" and melt the eternal snows with its radiance. In moments of the highest passion, he commands the gods themselves to destroy his enemies and the heavens and the earth to be desolate and bare in sympathy with his sorrow.

Taken together, the elements of Marlowe's style provide a perfect example of language as action. In his use of words, Tamburlaine is not merely talking, he is doing; and what he is doing is manifesting and implementing his nature, which drives him toward "the sweet fruition of an earthly crown." His words and sentences constantly strive upward, remake the world to fit the grandeur of his own imagination, and reshape nature to his own will.

What Marlowe is dramatizing in Tamburlaine, then, is not merely man's thirst for political power or for kingship; kingship itself, with its thrones, scepters, and crowns, is only the symbolic representation of a more transcendent appetite for what is finally no less than recreation. The actual world may have a shape and nature of its own, but man has in his imagination a new idea of reality that he tries to impose on nature:

> A heaven of heavenly bodies in their spheres,
> That guides his steps and actions to the throne.

The throne that Tamburlaine seeks is no less than the absolute throne. He is storming the heavens—as he frequently boasts he will—overthrowing the old gods and *their* creation, and setting himself up as the creator of a new world shaped in accord with the forms of human imagination.

Presented here in its most open terms, this is the characteristic motive of the great heroes of English Renaissance drama. Each insists that he is a god who can remake the old, traditional world to suit his own desire. Hieronimo in *The Spanish Tragedy* and Vindici in *The Revenger's Tragedy,* refusing to accept the injustice of the world and the ancient order of the law, divine and social, which prohibits murder, impose their interpretation of justice on the world by means of revenge. De Flores and Beatrice in *The Changeling* and Giovanni in *'Tis Pity She's a Whore,* refusing to accept the traditional social and religious prohibitions that surround and limit love, follow the wild desire of their own hearts to its strange satisfaction in adultery, incest, and death.

Volpone and Mosca, in Jonson's *Volpone,* create a new world that turns around gold and pleasure and mocks all the old pieties—the play could be described as a series of black Masses. They seek by means of acting to create a world of perpetual delight and power for themselves.

These attempts to make the world conform to the desires of the mind meet with varying degrees of success. Tamburlaine is apparently the most successful, though there are ominous notes. But in Marlowe's sequel, *Tamburlaine, Part Two,* outer reality forces itself on Tamburlaine in a painful way. He continues in conquest after conquest, but total power, godlike power, eludes him: a son turns out to be cowardly and effeminate; the beautiful Zenocrate dies; other wills refuse to be broken to Tamburlaine's; and finally he too dies, planning to storm the citadel of the heavens and set his black battle flags in the firmament.

Marlowe draws no easy conclusion from all this, no sad, sub-servient moral to warn us that since man is mortal and life is short, man should submit and prepare for death. Rather, he sets up an unalterable opposition: on one side an external reality that eludes and eventually destroys man; on the other the human imagination and will that refuse to settle for any less than a complete conquest of reality. On one side the stage, on the other side the heroic character. It was this conflict which the Renaissance drama was to explore and refine, once Marlowe had set the dramatic terms.

In the modern realistic theater—and in the movie-house—when the house lights go out and the actors step onto the stage, the audience, by convention, agrees to pretend for the duration of the performance that the theater has vanished. The stage, disguised by the art of scene design, magically ceases to be a stage and becomes for a few hours an actual place—an orchard on a Russian estate or the house of a salesman in Brooklyn—and the performers cease to be actors playing a part and become the characters they are representing—a stoker on an ocean liner or the king of England. Modern dramatists have, at least until quite recently, strengthened this paradoxical "illusion of reality" by avoiding any words, actions, or settings that by straining credibility or conflicting with our common sense of reality would remind us that we are in a theater. These modern theatrical conventions are now taken as normal and "natural," but they are, in fact, peculiar to the modern age. In the Elizabethan public theater, performances took place in the after-noon, in daylight, so that the theater was never obscured, and the absence of all but the most rudimentary scenery and props left the fact of the stage nakedly open.

This theater, which was large enough to hold between two and three thousand people, was lavishly ornamented, but its fundamental physical features were quite simple.[2] It was a round or polygonal structure, open in the center, with several tiers of galleries built into the outside wall. A large gate served as an entrance to the open center, or "pit," where the "groundlings" stood for a penny. Additional payment provided admission to the galleries where there were seats and shelter from the rain. Opposite the entrance gate the large platform stage (approximately 25 feet by 40 feet) jutted out into the pit from the wall of the theater. In this wall there were probably two large doors, one on either side, through which the players entered and exited from the dressing rooms backstage. Between the doors there was most likely a recessed area, the "inner stage," or some small structure that served for scenes of privacy—for example, a bedroom, a study, a tomb. Above the stage on the rear wall was a gallery extending the width of the stage that provided an upper playing level, which served as a balcony, a battlement, a mountain, or whatever elevated place the play might call for. The greater part of the playing area was covered with a "shadow" or forward-sloping roof, the underside of which—the "heavens"—was painted to represent the stars and the firmament.

If we add a few simple sound-effect machines, a small group of musicians, some gorgeous costumes, and one or two trap doors to permit access to the "hell" underneath the stage, we have the major elements of the Elizabethan public theater. It was a simple and a very functional theater; but its technical functionalism should not obscure its symbolic nature. The most noted theater of the time was called "The Globe," and the Elizabethan theater was just that: a model in timber and plaster of the world as late medieval and early Renaissance society conceived it. The heavens above, hell below; the large playing area of the platform stage, on which great public actions take place, opening out from the inner stage, the small area of private life behind; the high

---

[2]There were in fact two types of Elizabethan theaters, the public and the private. The private theaters were smaller, indoor theaters, with rather different stage arrangements from those of the public theaters, and they catered to a different clientele. The theater described here is a typical public theater of the kind in which most of the plays in this volume were first performed.

places of the gallery and the low places of the stage where man plays out his assigned parts; the onlookers from the pit and galleries watching the great actors strutting and fretting their hour upon the stage; and all enclosed in the unmoving containing round of the exterior walls, with the enduring sky visible above.

The type of theater built by each culture is a model of that culture's view of the elemental arrangements of the world, of man's place in the universe. This arrangement suggests that the theater is like the world, but it also suggests that the world is like a stage. In the Elizabethan theater, whether the scene of a play was vaguely located in Rome or on the seacoast of Bohemia, in Elsinore or the Forest of Arden, the ultimate setting was always the theater, which remained constantly visible behind the pretense of the play. Unlike the modern realistic dramatist, the Renaissance dramatist did not try to hide the fact that his setting was a theater and his play a play; rather, he drew attention to this fact by frequent use of a great many self-conscious references to the theater—for example, plays-within-plays, scenes in which actors discuss their roles and the play they are about to perform, direct addresses to the audience by the players, and imagery that compares men to actors and their world to theaters.

Among the Renaissance dramatists, Thomas Kyd was not the greatest, but he shared fully his betters' self-consciousness about being writers of plays for a theater. So persistent is the theatrical metaphor in *The Spanish Tragedy* that the play seems to be constantly attempting to slough off any pretense of reality and declare itself openly as "play." There is the dumb show in Act I, Scene 3, in which Hieronimo presents the spectacle of the three knights taking the crowns from the three kings; the scene in which Balthazar and Lorenzo watch from above, like spectators, while Horatio and Bel-imperia play out their love below; the masque of the wedding; the play-within-the-play that concludes the plot; and, besides all these, the overall dramatic framework provided by the constant presence on stage of two spectators, Don Andrea and the character of Revenge, who sit and watch and occasionally comment, as the entire play works toward its necessary conclusion, the revenge of Don Andrea's death.

Each of these devices suggests the "play" quality of the action, suggests that life is like a play, but it is the last device that provides the key to the meaning of the insistent theatrical metaphor. Having been killed in a great battle between Spain and Portugal, Don Andrea descends for judgment to the underworld, a pagan not a Christian underworld, where he is promised that he shall have absolute justice, that his murderer, Don Balthazar, the Prince of Portugal, shall render up an eye for an eye and a tooth for a tooth. Led by Revenge, Don Andrea returns to the great stage of the world and proceeds to watch the bitter workings of absolute justice. Within this mythological framework, which suggests the inevitability of revenge for all murders, Kyd gives the process of revenge realistic motivation by constructing a linked series of psychologically probable, but no less inevitable, human desires for revenge. Andrea's beloved, Bel-imperia, gives her love to Horatio because he was Andrea's friend and because she wishes to revenge herself on Andrea's murderer, Balthazar, who now loves her. Balthazar finds his revenge for this slight by joining with Lorenzo, who wishes to revenge himself for a stain on his honor by killing Horatio. And finally Hieronimo, Horatio's father, seeks and eventually accomplishes his revenge by killing Balthazar and Lorenzo, as well as Lorenzo's father.

Thus, the plot of the play is the slow but inevitable working out of the revenge for Andrea's death, though none of the characters is aware that he is merely a cog in what G. K. Hunter has aptly termed "the justice machine." Each thinks he is pursuing some personal goal, such as love, or honor, or revenge for some immediate harm. But the constant brooding presence of Andrea and Revenge on stage as spectators of the action continually reminds us that "—the characters of the play, scheming, complaining, and hoping—are not to be taken by the audience as the independent and self-willed individuals they suppose themselves to be, but in fact only as the puppets of a predetermined and omnicompetent justice that they (the characters) cannot see and never really understand."[3] They are, in short, no more than actors in a play, whose author is the universal desire for revenge. Unwittingly, of course, they explicitly acknowledge their position as players when they become actors in "Soliman and Perseda," that brief play which has so much in common with *The Spanish Tragedy,* and literally *lock* themselves in the theater. Kyd's point seems to be that murder is inevitably

[3]G. K. Hunter, "Ironies of Justice in *The Spanish Tragedy,*" in S. Schoenbaum, ed., *Renaissance Drama,* VIII (Northwestern University Press, 1965), p. 93.

punished because of an innate human desire for revenge for harms, but the human beings involved are seldom themselves aware of the fact that they are merely instruments of an absolute justice that is beyond their control. This ironic and dramatic view of life is intensified in *The Spanish Tragedy* by the peculiarly inefficient and wasteful ways in which revenge works. Like those machines of Rube Goldberg's, which go through an infinite number of elaborate steps to perform some quite simple operation, the "justice machine" grinds up Lorenzo, Horatio, Serberine, Pedringano, Isabella, Hieronimo, Castile, and Bel-imperia before Don Andrea is revenged on Balthazar. Even the ghost of Andrea is bewildered by the eccentric way in which the mill of the gods turns, and he complains to Revenge,

> Broughtst thou me hither to increase my pain?
> I looked that Balthazar should have been slain;
> But 'tis my friend Horatio that is slain,
> And they abuse fair Bel-imperia,
> On whom I doted more than all the world,
> Because she loved me more than all the world.
>
> (II.Chorus.1–11)

Though Kyd's apparent subject is the relation of revenge to justice, the dramatic center of his play is the sense of man's helplessness against the great undertow of fate, or history, and his own psychological make-up. This understanding of the human condition squares so perfectly with the view of the world as theater, life as play, and character as role, that we can say that in *The Spanish Tragedy* content and form are not only in agreement, they are one.

As perfect as is Kyd's understanding of the view of life dictated by the theatrical mode, he was not as aware of the full range and subtlety of his medium as were some of his successors. Among the Renaissance dramatists, Ben Jonson was unusually sensitive to the nature of his art, particularly in *Volpone*. Here the metaphors of "playing" and "acting" are used with the utmost subtlety, and the perception that "life is a play" is developed in quite a different and more complex way than in *The Spanish Tragedy*.

Nearly every character in *Volpone* is an actor, pretending to be virtuous, honest, and wise, when in fact he is wicked, greedy, and stupid. In a world where pretending is *the* way of life, the greatest heroes are, of course, the greatest actors, and they are thoroughly aware of their skill. The vocabulary of Volpone and Mosca is thick with theatrical terms, and both play a variety of parts. Volpone plays, most obviously, a sick and dying man throughout the play; he also plays a mountebank and a clownish sergeant of the court. Mosca, an even more adept actor, can be at one moment a humble servant, anxious to help and please, and at the next moment a smiling pander, an injured friend of virtue, or a sober magnifico. He can, indeed, as he claims, "change a visor, swifter, than a thought."

Under the pressure of this persistent theatrical conception of character, the scene of the play at times becomes overtly a theater: in the two interludes acted out by Volpone's antic fools; in the mountebank scene on the public square; and in Act V, Scene 3, where a curtain is strung across the stage to conceal Volpone as he watches Mosca soberly pretending to be the heir, inventorying his goods, and putting each of the fools out of his humor as they rush in to demand what is coming to them. Even Volpone's great bed, its curtain drawn and opened at appropriate moments, is a small theater in which, expertly made up and costumed to simulate a dying man, the great pretender lies and acts out his marvelous scenes of sickness.

For Volpone and Mosca the art of acting, which recognizes the potential theater inhering in almost any situation, is not only a means of deception for mulcting the citizens of Venice; it is also the "cockering up" of their essential genius, a very way of life in which both "live free / To all delights." Their exhilaration in their acting powers is evident: neither of them can resist the opportunity to play a new role, and both delight in critical discussions of their art after some particularly skillful piece of acting. At times their pleasure in their skill soars to such a pitch that they think themselves godlike. Mosca feels he can "skip" out of his skin, rise and fall like an arrow, shoot through the air like a star, and, ultimately, "be here, / And there, and here, and yonder, all at once." Volpone is no less exuberant than his larcenous Ariel. "In varying figures," he tells Celia, he "would have contended / With the blue Proteus," with the ever-changing ocean itself, to win her love. And that love, rather than suffering the limitations and satiation of mortal love, is to be raised and kept at Jovian heights by the divine power of acting. "We shall," he tells her,

> in changèd shapes, act Ovid's tales,
> Thou like Europa now, and I like Jove,
> Then I like Mars, and thou like Erycine;
> So of the rest, till we have quite run through,
> And wearied all the fables of the gods.
> Then will I have thee in more modern forms,
> Attirèd like some sprightly dame of France,
> Brave Tuscan lady, or proud Spanish beauty;
> Sometimes unto the Persian Sophy's wife,
> Or the Grand Signior's mistress; and, for a change,
> To one of our most artful courtesans,
> Or some quick Negro, or cold Russian;
> And I will meet thee in as many shapes;
> Where we may, so, transfuse our wand'ring souls
> Out at our lips and score up sums of pleasures,
> > That the curious shall not know
> > How to tell them as they flow;
> > And the envious, when they find
> > What their number is, be pined.

> (III.7.221–39)

Each of the characters of the play is constantly pretending to be something that he is not, and usually the pretense is an effort to transform by means of acting something that is base and ignoble into something virtuous and valuable. These attempts are all summed up and defined in *Volpone* by the ultimate masquerade, the substitution of gold for all other values and virtues. This great imposture takes place in symbolic terms in the opening action of the play: Volpone rises, greets the sun perfunctorily, and turns quickly to revel in his treasure. He raises a large gold coin above his head and hails "the world's soul and mine." Then he goes on to detail the powers and history of this golden sun and golden god, which have replaced both the sun itself and the light that on the first day of creation brought order out of chaos. Gold was the pillar of fire that led the Israelites out of the desert into the Promised Land. Gold is "the best of things," which far transcends "all style of joy in children, parents, friends." Gold is the essence of love, the new god who while doing nothing "yet mak'st men do all things."

It is, finally,

> virtue, fame,
> Honor, and all things else. Who can get thee,
> He shall be noble, valiant, honest, wise—
>
> (I.1.25–27)

Volpone is the prophet of this golden god and the harbinger of the gold-centered world created by the new god. All Venice circles around gold, and for it men will give anything: honor, virtue, decency, even their humanity. Learning, law, love, and friendship can all be bought. Celia's beauty can find no greater praise in Mosca's mouth than to be styled "bright as your gold, and lovely as your gold"; and her concern for her virtue when she resists bedding with Volpone can be discredited by her husband's conclusive argument, "What! is my gold the worse for touching?" Gold, in Venice, replaces grace in a Christian society and finally knows no limit to its powers:

> Why, your gold
> Is such another med'cine, it dries up
> All those offensive savors! It transforms
> The most deformèd, and restores 'em lovely
> As 'twere the strange poetical girdle. Jove
> Could not invent t' himself a shroud more subtle
> To pass Acrisius' guards. It is the thing
> Makes all the world her grace, her youth, her beauty.
>
> (V.2.98–105)

Before the play is over, gold has been substituted for every traditional value, and the only measure of merit has become, "How much is it worth?"

In Act II, Scene 2, Volpone appears in the public square of Venice dressed as a mountebank, mounts his trestle stage, and delivers a spiel on the virtues of his medicinal oil, *oglio del Scoto*. As Scoto ascends the stage, he is followed by his zany, otherwise Nano the dwarf. The word "zany" nowadays means no more than "idiot," but, more specifically, a zany is the shadow figure, the eternal clown who haunts all human efforts at skill or nobility: the bumbling personification of awkwardness who stands behind the acrobats and cautiously tries a few tricks of his own, only to fall flat on his face; the parody who stands behind the orator and silently mocks his gestures and delivery. In short, he is a living form of the satiric and comic visions, which see the hero as braggart warrior, the romantic lover as cuckold, and reverend age as Pantaloon. Both as zany and as dwarf, Nano is a mockery of Scoto, and Scoto the mountebank, the mere street-corner peddler of worthless nostrums, is in turn a mockery of Volpone the magnifico.

The scene in the public square, the mountebank with his zany behind him, is a revelation in small of the central reality of *Volpone*. The faces that stare out from the stage are human in form, but just behind them, in their names and in their actions, are their zanies, the animal world: Volpone the fox, Mosca the fly, Voltore the vulture, Sir Pol the parrot, Corvino and Corbaccio the ravens. Behind a few pretenses, Volpone's household is a zany form of the family: instead of a servant there is a slavish parasite who flatters and tricks; instead of children there are sports of nature, the dwarf Nano, the hermaphrodite Androgyno, and the eunuch Castrone, who were begotten by Volpone in drunkenness and lust upon the beggars of the street and are now kept only for entertainment. To this house come "friends" pretending to visit a fellow citizen in his sickness, but each visitor is a scavenger of carrion, eager for and willing to hurry the departure of life from the carcass.

In *Volpone* a zany world lurks just behind all such august institutions as marriage, the family, the law—institutions which traditionally embody the most sacred human values. A father, so old and decrepit himself that life may go at any moment, disinherits his son in order to be named the heir of a man younger than himself. A husband so jealous of his wife that he threatens to lock her in a chastity belt and wall up her windows lest the "bawdy light" reach her, calls her "a whore" because she resists his attempts to deliver her into the bed of a dying man. A court of law, conducted in all solemnity and with the utmost formality, frees the guilty and condemns the innocent of the very crimes committed against them. Perhaps the summary image of this zany shadow world appears in Act I, Scene 2, where Volpone's three grotesques act out a little play written by Mosca. Their subject is the history of the world, and they cynically reduce all the heroism and grandeur of the past to camp.

As the play proceeds, the zany world ceases to lurk threateningly in the background, a grim reminder of what man might fall to. In Volpone's Venice the zany world comes to be the real world: magnificos *are* mountebanks, citizens *are* flesh-eating animals, and homes *are* zoos. But the great irony, the pivot on which *Volpone* turns, is that the characters, by acting, make themselves into their own zanies. Each is a great pretender, a talented actor, who uses his skill to cheat others and considers his ability to construct scenes and play roles as his supreme virtue. But each act, each pretense, instead of disguising the ghastly truth, actually reveals it. When Volpone disguises himself as a mountebank, or when Voltore pretends that he is possessed by an evil spirit, the "acting" proclaims a truth unknown to the actors. This pattern can be traced most specifically in the stages of degeneration through which Volpone passes in his simulated sickness, during which he strips himself, one by one, of all human attributes. His highest faculties, his understanding of values and his ability to reason validly, are destroyed in the opening scene, where he chooses gold over all traditional values. His senses deteriorate next. Sight, the highest of the senses in the Aristotelian scale, is gone by Act I, Scene 3, and shortly afterward he is left with only touch, the lowest of the senses. Corvino must place the pearl he has brought into Volpone's hand because

> 'tis only there
> He apprehends, he has his feeling yet.
> See how he grasps it!
>
> (I.5.18–20)

Soon his memory is gone:

> He knows no man,
> No face of friend, nor name of any servant,
> Who 't was that fed him last, or gave him drink;
> Not those he hath begotten, or brought up,
> Can he remember.
>
> (I.5.39–43)

Reproductive faculties disappear by III.6.64, where Mosca assures Corvino that there is no danger in giving Celia to Volpone because "a long forgetfulness hath seized that part." This "old, decrepit wretch" even loses the ability to nourish himself:

> That has no sense, no sinew; takes his meat
> With others' fingers; only knows to gape
> When you do scald his gums; a voice, a shadow.

(III.7.43–45)

Death inevitably follows, and by Act V, Scene 2, Volpone is pretending to be dead, a corrupted carcass that Mosca has to bury hastily.

Each of these diseases is, of course, a mere pretense used to implement the great swindle perpetrated by Volpone, who remains physically vital. But these symptoms mirror perfectly the stages in the oncoming death of Volpone's spirit, caused by his greedy desire for gold and power. On the spiritual plane, he is indeed blind and unable to apprehend anything he cannot touch, he has indeed forgotten the meaning of such ideals as friendship or parenthood, and his spirit is indeed unable to nurture itself or reproduce its light in the world. Volpone has with great cunning made himself his own zany in a most systematic manner.

Working in these ways, Jonson carefully constructs and keeps in constant interplay two, possibly three worlds. At the first level we have the boisterous, bubbling, comic world of Renaissance Venice, where a pair of clever entrepreneurs work a beautifully managed swindle on a bunch of grave and greedy citizens. Amoral perhaps, but not terribly sinister. But through this bright comic surface, the zany world juts up with great power and insistence. A group of men visiting a dying friend suddenly become carrion birds circling a dying fox, around whom the flesh fly is already buzzing. The faces of animals swim into focus through human features. The life-giving sun and its light fade away to a great gold coin dully glittering. Secular and sacred history take the shape of a downward spiral, a bad joke endlessly repeated to the accompaniment of a cynical cackle. A vibrantly healthy and vital man changes into a piece of decaying meat, grasping blindly at stage gim-cracks and paste jewels. The great bustle of life suddenly becomes no more real than a play, men no more real than actors. Only dimly, beyond and through this grotesque world, do we catch glimpses of an older, ideal world where *Fiat lux* banished chaos and darkness, where the real sun brought light and fertility to the earth, where honor and virtue were practiced and respected, where citizens concerned themselves with civic welfare, where courts administered justice, and where households cherished life.

The irony of *The Spanish Tragedy,* where the characters play assigned parts without knowing they do, is intensified in *Volpone,* where the characters quite consciously play parts but fail to realize that their make-believe becomes in time their reality. Where Kyd treated the theater as the inescapable scene of human life, Jonson offers it as a mode of being that men choose for themselves and, by following their appetites rather than their reasons and traditions, eventually transform into their own desperate reality. Volpone and his chums turn away from truth to make themselves and the world take the shape of their desires. They give up *being* for *acting, what is* for *theater,* and in doing so they trap themselves: their chosen roles become their prisons.

At the end of *The Spanish Tragedy,* Hieronimo locks all the actors in the theater, as if to acknowledge that there is no escape from the theatrical condition, and bites out his tongue, as if to accept the dramatic view that he is what he has done—no explanations, no revelations of personal feelings, are any longer pertinent. At the end of *Volpone,* the characters who were not forced to accept their roles, but gleefully chose them, are locked forever in what they thought was only make-believe: Mosca is sentenced to the galleys for life as the slave he is; Volpone is cramped in irons where his body will take forever the grotesque shape he has assumed in the play; Voltore is disbarred and sent into permanent exile to become the outlaw he has long truly been; Corbaccio is secured in the stocks, pelted with garbage, and mocked as the ass he has made of himself.

A good deal of the theatrical self-consciousness of the Renaissance dramatists was perhaps little more than fashion, but in the greatest plays of the age the self-consciousness about working in the dramatic mode is functional, and each reminder that the play *is* a play helps to establish the theater as the chief metaphor for life. Life in this drama is viewed not so much *sub specie aeternitatis,* under the aspect of eternity, as *sub specie ludi,* under the aspect of playing; and man is seen not so much as *Homo sapiens,* reasoning man, as *Homo ludens,* acting man.

Placed in the perspective of theater, great characters are only actors, and their courts and kingdoms are only pretenses existing for a brief moment within the enduring reality of the playhouse. The greatest and the most theatrically self-conscious of Elizabethan dramatists spells out the implications of presenting man as a player in a theater:

> These our actors,
> As I foretold you, were all spirits, and
> Are melted into air, into thin air.
> And, like the baseless fabric of this vision,
> The cloud-capped towers, the gorgeous palaces,
> The solemn temples, the great globe itself—
> Yea, all which it inherit—shall dissolve
> And, like this insubstantial pageant faded,
> Leave not a rack behind. We are such stuff
> As dreams are made on, and our little life
> Is rounded with a sleep.

> (*The Tempest,* IV.1.148–58)

Uncertainty, impermanence, mystery, smallness, inability to order and control destiny: these are the qualities of life seen *sub specie ludi.* The great dramatists of the age were so totally sensitive to the values implicit in dramatic form that even when they are not explicitly showing man as player and his world as theater, their standard dramatic techniques contain implicitly the theatrical perspective: dramatic irony puts the character, who speaks and acts with more significance than he comprehends, in the situation of an actor performing a part in a play he did not create and cannot control; "mirror scenes," where characters see themselves and their conditions reflected in others, suggest that the characters are not real persons, as they think, but are themselves in turn only mirrors held up to the audience; double plots, in which the parallel second and third plots reflect in brief form the action of the main plot, emphasize the theatrical nature of the main plot; the violation of the unities of time and place cram whole lifetimes into the two hours' traffic of the stage—to the disgust of critics trained in the classics—and thus suggest, by foreshortening, that the passage of time the characters take to be real is no longer than the fleeting moments of theatrical time; sudden reversals of fortune and abrupt changes of character suggest that the human personality is no more constant or durable than the various roles an actor plays. These are all staples of the English drama of the Renaissance, and all manifest and extend the meaning of the theatrical perspective on life.

But this drama, while it explores the meaning of presenting man as a player in a theater, also creates characters of such strength of will and power of imagination that they cannot conceive of themselves as anything less than totally "real" and cannot think of themselves as living in any world which they do not control or create. A character like Tamburlaine is, we might say, a determined realist who would find ridiculous the idea that he is no more free than an actor, that his world is no more real than a stage, and that his life is finally no more than a part in a play written by someone else. But even as he makes his boasts, the theater is always there, visible in the background, silently questioning the character's claim to permanence, to reality, to control over the shape of the world and the order of life.

It is this tension between character and stage, between poetry and scene, between self-confident hero and a world not entirely within his control, between pretense and reality, which the English dramatists of the Renaissance drew to the breaking point. They play so many variations on the dramatic perspective and explore man in the context of theater so persistently that the history of Renaissance drama is almost a history of the meanings inherent in dramatic form. Not every play in this collection contains a play-within-a-play, and not every one makes heavy use of overtly theatrical imagery, but all see life from the theatrical perspective, and all make use of techniques that suggest how much life is like a play. In *Tamburlaine,* for example, the scene of the fierce Bajazeth locked in his iron cage and butting his brains out on the bars is very close to being a dramatization of Tamburlaine's own situation: he is locked in a world, and a theater, that will never yield entirely to his desire to impose his will on everything that exists. In *The Changeling,* De Flores' simple statement to the murderous Beatrice, "Y'are the deed's creature," expresses perfectly that ultimate theatrical perspective on life which, because it views man from a distance, discounts motives and ignores any personal sense of righteousness, making man the product only of what he does. De Flores is the living embodiment of this dramatic point of view, and his plain, unemotional acceptance of his passionate love for Beatrice, his knowledge that it can only lead to disaster, and his unmoved encounter with his fate mark him as a man who knows human life is like a play and human character a role forced on man by circumstances outside his control. Beatrice, on the other hand, feels that she is completely free to control events and deny her status of actor by "writing her own play."

In other plays in this collection the theatrical metaphor is used as overtly as in *The Spanish Tragedy*. The revenge masque that concludes *'Tis Pity She's a Whore* and the playlet of the "Bony Lady" in *The Revenger's Tragedy*, in which Vindici shows the Duke the skull beneath the skin of lust, are excellent examples of the use of theater as a metaphor for life. In *'Tis Pity* the final masque depicts the sad fact, which the play dramatizes in a number of other ways, that in the end the lovers, who have dared everything to satisfy their own peculiar desires, cannot escape acting in the great play of nature and society, cannot help but be drawn into and forced to conform to the ancient established patterns of crime and punishment. In *The Revenger's Tragedy* the point is quite different. Here the frequent overt admissions that the play *is* a play seem to be demonstrating that a character's surrender to some over-whelming demonic passion, whether it be lust or revenge, strips him of true reality and makes him no more than a puppet manipulated by his passion, an actor in a play whose plot is controlled not by mind but by obsession.

English Renaissance drama constantly explored and refined this great opposition between the determined hero and his stage world, chiefly by a deeper and deeper penetration into the human mind and by an ever increasing awareness of what it means to be an actor in the great theater of the world. The seven plays in this volume constitute a history of that exploration, and nowhere is the antagonism between man and theater more perfectly realized than in *The Duchess of Malfi*, where Bosola presents a little play, a dance of the madmen, for the Duchess, who is about to die. The play tells the Duchess of all the hopelessness, idiocy, disorder, and terror of the world—but let Bosola interpret for us:

> Thou art a box of worm seed, at best but a salvatory of green mummy What's this flesh: a little cruded milk, fantastical puff-paste: our bodies are weaker than those paper prisons boys use to keep flies in, more contemptible—since ours is to preserve earth-worms. Didst thou ever see a lark in a cage? such is the soul in the body: this world is like her little turf of grass and the heaven o'er our heads, like her looking-glass, only gives us a miserable knowledge of the small compass of our prison.

(IV.2.117–24)

In his comparison of the soul in the body to a lark in a cage, Bosola is viewing life from the perspective of the theater; but in the Duchess' calm answer, "I am Duchess of Malfi still," she is refusing to bite out her tongue as Hieronimo did, refusing to accept the obliteration of her unique humanity in the scheme of the theater. In this play, the Duchess alone cares for life and love, and she is in the fullness of her humanity the only character who seems ultimately and meaningfully real. Although she dies, she endures in the person of her child and in the echoes of history that come back from the ruins of the old monastery. The other characters have no more permanence than actors in a play:

> These wretched, eminent things
> Leave no more fame behind 'em, than should one
> Fall in a frost and leave his print in snow:
> As soon as the sun shines, it ever melts
> Both form and matter.

> (V.5.111–15)

If the basic theater is "two boards and a passion," then Renaissance drama is a continuing statement of the ineradicable enmity between those boards and that passion. The seven plays in this volume have been chosen not only because they are excellent pieces of literature but because they form a history of the struggle between character and theater and create the fullest and clearest images, outside Shakespeare, of this great opposition.

TAMBUR-
LAINE
THE GREAT

PART ONE

(1588)

*Christopher
Marlowe*

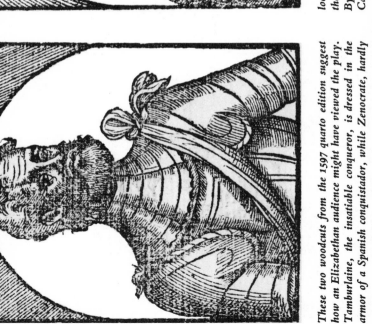

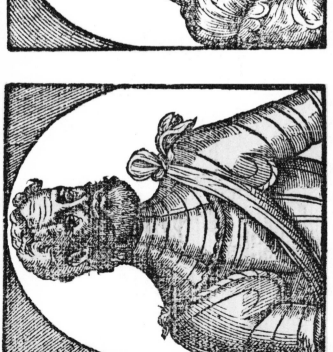

These two woodcuts from the 1597 quarto edition suggest how an Elizabethan audience might have viewed the play. Tamburlaine, the insatiable conqueror, is dressed in the armor of a Spanish conquistador, while Zenocrate, hardly looking like the daughter of an Egyptian Soldan, wears the elegant clothes of an English noblewoman of the day. By permission of The Huntington Library, San Marino, California.

C HRISTOPHER MARLOWE WAS A SHOEMAKER'S son from Canterbury, who became a prize scholar at Cambridge and then a spy for the head of Elizabeth's secret service, Sir Francis Walsingham. He was an atheist, a blasphemer, probably a homosexual, and, in general, a tough-minded rebel. Involved with suspect intellectual groups during most of his life, he was more or less constantly in trouble with the authorities. On the whole, he closely resembled his own heroic image of the Renaissance individual: tough, intelligent, bold, and adventuresome in ideas and acts.

Born in 1564, the same year as Shakespeare, Marlowe was killed in a tavern brawl early in 1593, in an argument apparently over paying the bill. But between the years 1588 and 1593 he wrote several of the most bizarre and interesting plays in English drama. Marlowe's dramatic subject was the new, Renaissance individual, restlessly seeking power and control over all the world, and in each of his major plays he traced the search in a different area. In the two parts of Tamburlaine (1588–89) the hero is a warrior and orator; in The Jew of Malta (1589), a great merchant and politician; in Doctor Faustus (1590–93), a learned philosopher-magician; and in Edward II (1592), a sybarite and seeker of pleasure. The remainder of Renaissance drama, Shakespeare included, is in many ways a continuing exploration of the types of human activity first dramatized on the mythic scale by Christopher Marlowe.

The two parts of Tamburlaine were printed together in a black-letter octavo in 1590. Several subsequent Elizabethan quarto editions were based on the 1590 octavo, which forms the basis of the text printed here.

To the
Gentlemen Readers and Others
That Take Pleasure in
Reading Histories

Gentlemen and courteous readers whosoever, I have here published in   5
print for your sakes the two tragical discourses of the Scythian shepherd
Tamburlaine, that became so great a conqueror and so mighty a
monarch. My hope is that they will be now no less acceptable unto you
to read after your serious affairs and studies than they have been lately
delightful for many of you to see when the same were showed in   10
London upon stages. I have purposely omitted and left out some fond
and frivolous gestures, digressing and, in my poor opinion, far unmeet
for the matter, which I thought might seem more tedious unto the wise
than any way else to be regarded, though haply they have been of some
vain, conceited fondlings greatly gaped at, what times they were showed 15
upon the stage in their graced deformities. Nevertheless, now to be
mixtured in print with such matter of worth, it would prove a disgrace
to so honorable and stately a history. Great folly were it in me to
commend unto your wisdoms either the eloquence of the author that
writ them or the worthiness of the matter itself. I, therefore, leave unto 20
your learned censures both the one and the other and myself, the poor
printer of them, unto your most courteous and favorable protection,
which if you vouchsafe to accept, you shall evermore bind me to
employ what travail and service I can to the advancing and pleasuring
of your excellent degree.   25

Yours, most humble at commandment,
R[ICHARD] J[ONES], Printer

Printer's Letter   6 *Scythian*   the name of a tribe of nomads that inhabited Eastern
Europe and parts of Asia. The Elizabethans mistakenly identified them with a region
always cold and snow-covered.   6–7 *shepherd Tamburlaine*   a Mongol conqueror of the
fourteenth century, famed for deeds of cruelty. Though European historians of Marlowe's
time claimed that he was of low birth, he seems in actuality to have been a descendant of
Genghis Khan.   11–16 *I . . . deformities*   It is not known whether these deletions were
merely bits of improvised stage business inserted by the actors for humor or comic
episodes written by Marlowe, but since Jones did retain some comic interludes, it seems
likely that his excisions did not extend to the text itself.   21 *censures*   judgment.

{DRAMATIS PERSONAE}

MYCETES, *King of Persia*
COSROE, *his brother*
MEANDER
THERIDAMAS
ORTYGIUS } *Persian lords*
CENEUS
MENAPHON
TAMBURLAINE, *a Scythian shepherd*
TECHELLES
USUMCASANE } *his followers*
BAJAZETH, *Emperor of the Turks*
KING OF FEZ
KING OF MOROCCO
KING OF ARGIER

KING OF ARABIA
SOLDAN OF EGYPT
GOVERNOR OF DAMASCUS
AGYDAS
MAGNETES } *Median lords*
CAPOLIN, *an Egyptian*
PHILEMUS
BASSOES, LORDS, CITIZENS, MOORS, SOLDIERS *and* ATTENDANTS
ZENOCRATE, *daughter of the Soldan of Egypt*
ANIPPE, *her maid*
ZABINA, *wife of Bajazeth*
EBEA, *her maid*
VIRGINS OF DAMASCUS }

Dramatis Personae *Bassoes* Turkish lords.

THE PROLOGUE

From jigging veins of rhyming mother wits,
And such conceits as clownage keeps in pay,
We'll lead you to the stately tent of war,
Where you shall hear the Scythian Tamburlaine
Threat'ning the world with high astounding terms   5
And scourging kingdoms with his conquering sword.
View but his picture in this tragic glass,
And then applaud his fortunes as you please.

ACT I
Scene 1   {*Persia*}

[*Enter*] MYCETES, COSROE, MEANDER, ORTYGIUS, CENEUS, [MENAPHON,]
with others.

MYCETES   Brother Cosroe, I find myself aggrieved,
        Yet insufficient to express the same,
        For it requires a great and thund'ring speech.
        Good brother, tell the cause unto my lords;
        I know you have a better wit than I.   5
COSROE   Unhappy Persia, that in former age
        Hast been the seat of mighty conquerors,
        That in their prowess and their policies
        Have triumphed over Afric and the bounds
        Of Europe, where the sun dares scarce appear   10

Prologue   1 *From . . . wits* away from the jig-like doggerel of unimaginative
rhymesters. **2** *conceits* low-minded ideas. **7** *glass* mirror.
🦋 **ACT I, Scene 1.   SD** In the first octavo edition (1590), act and scene divisions are
printed in Latin. **2** *insufficient* unable.

For freezing meteors and congealèd cold,
Now to be ruled and governed by a man
At whose birthday Cynthia with Saturn joined,
And Jove, the sun, and Mercury denied
To shed their influence in his fickle brain!   15
Now Turks and Tartars shake their swords at thee,
Meaning to mangle all thy provinces.

MYCETES   Brother, I see your meaning well enough,
And through your planets I perceive you think
I am not wise enough to be a king.   20
But I refer me to my noblemen,
That know my wit and can be witnesses.
I might command you to be slain for this.
Meander, might I not?

MEANDER   Not for so small a fault, my sovereign lord.   25

MYCETES   I mean it not, but yet I know I might.
Yet live, yea, live; Mycetes wills it so.
Meander, thou, my faithful counselor,
Declare the cause of my conceivèd grief,
Which is, God knows, about that Tamburlaine,   30
That, like a fox in midst of harvest-time,
Doth prey upon my flocks of passengers,
And, as I hear, doth mean to pull my plumes.
Therefore, 'tis good and meet for to be wise.

MEANDER   Oft have I heard your majesty complain   35
Of Tamburlaine, that sturdy Scythian thief
That robs your merchants of Persepolis
Treading by land unto the Western Isles,
And in your confines with his lawless train
Daily commits uncivil outrages,   40

---

11 *For* because of. ***freezing meteors*** Marlowe's concern here is not with scientific
fact, but with dramatic effect: so great is the cold of Northern Europe that even the
meteors there are made of ice.   **13 *Cynthia*** the moon.   **13–14 *Cynthia, Saturn, Jove,
sun, Mercury*** Marlowe associates these with the qualities they were thought to produce
in men: giddiness, stupidity, wisdom, beauty, and quick-wittedness, respectively.
16 *Tartars* warlike people who overran parts of Asia and Europe between the thirteenth
and fourteenth centuries. In this play, however, Marlowe uses Tartar and Scythian
interchangeably.   **19 *planets*** astrological calculations.   **32 *passengers*** travelers along
the trade routes.   **33 *pull my plumes*** take away my royal dress (and power).   **34 *meet***
proper.   **37 *Persepolis*** the capital of the ancient Persian empire.   **38 *Treading*** The
second octavo edition (1592–93) reads "trading." But whether the word is "treading" or
"trading," it modifies "merchants," not Tamburlaine.   ***Western Isles*** British Isles.

Hoping, misled by dreaming prophecies,
To reign in Asia, and with barbarous arms
To make himself the monarch of the East.
But ere he march in Asia, or display
His vagrant ensign in the Persian fields,   45
Your grace hath taken order by Theridamas,
Charged with a thousand horse, to apprehend
And bring him captive to your highness' throne.
MYCETES   Full true thou speakst, and like thyself, my lord,
Whom I may term a Damon for thy love.   50
Therefore 'tis best, if so it like you all,
To send my thousand horse incontinent
To apprehend that paltry Scythian.
How like you this, my honorable lords?
Is it not a kingly resolution?   55
COSROE   It cannot choose, because it comes from you.
MYCETES   Then hear thy charge, valiant Theridamas,
The chiefest captain of Mycetes' host,
The hope of Persia, and the very legs
Whereon our state doth lean, as on a staff   60
That holds us up and foils our neighbor foes.
Thou shalt be leader of this thousand horse,
Whose foaming gall, with rage and high disdain,
Have sworn the death of wicked Tamburlaine.
Go frowning forth, but come thou smiling home,   65
As did Sir Paris with the Grecian dame.
Return with speed; time passeth swift away.
Our life is frail, and we may die today.
THERIDAMAS   Before the moon renew her borrowed light,
Doubt not, my lord and gracious sovereign,   70
But Tamburlaine and that Tartarian rout
Shall either perish by our warlike hands
Or plead for mercy at your highness' feet.
MYCETES   Go, stout Theridamas; thy words are swords,
And with thy looks thou conquerest all thy foes.   75
I long to see thee back return from thence,

---

41 dreaming foolish.   **46 taken order by** issued an order for.   **47 Charged with**
commanding.   **horse** armed horsemen.   **52 incontinent** immediately.   **56 choose** be
otherwise.   **66 As ... dame** Mycetes fails to see that Paris' abduction of Helen was only
a temporary victory: the angry Greeks besieged Troy and eventually destroyed the entire
city.   **71 Tartarian rout** Scythian horde.

That I may view these milk-white steeds of mine
All laden with the heads of killèd men,
And from their knees even to their hoofs below
Besmeared with blood; that makes a dainty show.   80
THERIDAMAS   Then now, my lord, I humbly take my leave.   *Exit.*
MYCETES   Theridamas, farewell ten thousand times.
   Ah, Menaphon, why stayst thou thus behind
   When other men press forward for renown?
   Go, Menaphon, go into Scythia,   85
   And foot by foot follow Theridamas.
COSROE   Nay, pray you, let him stay. A greater [task]
   Fits Menaphon than warring with a thief.
   Create him prorex of [all] Africa,
   That he may win the Babylonians' hearts,   90
   Which will revolt from Persian government
   Unless they have a wiser king than you.
MYCETES   Unless they have a wiser king than you?
   These are his words. Meander, set them down.
COSROE   And add this to them: that all Asia   95
   Lament to see the folly of their king.
MYCETES   Well, here I swear by this my royal seat—
COSROE   [*Aside.*] You may do well to kiss it, then.
MYCETES   Embossed with silk as best beseems my state,
   To be revenged for these contemptuous words!   100
   O, where is duty and allegiance now?
   Fled to the Caspian or the ocean main?
   What shall I call thee? Brother?—No, a foe,
   Monster of nature, shame unto thy stock,
   That darst presume thy sovereign for to mock.   105
   Meander, come. I am abused, Meander.
      Exit [MYCETES *with his followers*]. COSROE *and* MENAPHON *remain.*
MENAPHON   How now, my lord? What, mated and amazed
   To hear the King thus threaten like himself?
COSROE   Ah, Menaphon, I pass not for his threats.
   The plot is laid by Persian noblemen   110
   And captains of the Median garrisons

---

80 *dainty*   pleasing—an example of Mycetes' simple-minded cruelty.   **89** *prorex*
viceroy.   **90** *Babylonians*   The Babylonian empire, which extended outward from the
Euphrates River, had been conquered by the Persian king Cyrus in 538 B.C.   **99** *Embossed* adorned.   **107** *mated* thwarted.   **108** *like himself* like a king.   **109** *pass* care.
111 *Media*   an ancient country of Western Asia, annexed to the Persian empire by Cyrus.

To crown me emperor of Asia.
But this it is that doth excruciate
The very substance of my vexèd soul:
To see our neighbors that were wont to quake   115
And tremble at the Persian monarch's name
Now sit and laugh our regiment to scorn;
And that which might resolve me into tears,
Men from the farthest equinoctial line
Have swarmed in troops into the Eastern India,   120
Lading their ships with gold and precious stones,
And made their spoils from all our provinces.
MENAPHON   This should entreat your highness to rejoice,
Since Fortune gives you opportunity
To gain the title of a conqueror   125
By curing of this maimèd empery.
Afric and Europe bordering on your land
And continent to your dominions,
How easily may you with a mighty host
Pass into Graecia, as did Cyrus once,   130
And cause them to withdraw their forces home,
Lest you subdue the pride of Christendom.

[*Trumpet within.*]

COSROE   But, Menaphon, what means this trumpet's sound?
MENAPHON   Behold, my lord, Ortygius and the rest
Bringing the crown to make you emperor!   135

Enter ORTYGIUS *and* CENEUS, *bearing a crown, with others.*

ORTYGIUS   Magnificent and mighty Prince Cosroe,
We, in the name of other Persian states
And commons of this mighty monarchy,
Present thee with th'imperial diadem.
CENEUS   The warlike soldiers and the gentlemen,   140
That heretofore have filled Persepolis
With Afric captains taken in the field,
Whose ransom made them march in coats of gold,
With costly jewels hanging at their ears

118 *resolve me into*   reduce me to.   119 *farthest . . . line*   southern provinces near
the equator.   126 *maimèd empery*   crumbling empire.   128 *continent*   next to.
130 *Graecia*   Greek possessions around Constantinople.   *Cyrus*   the most successful
conqueror among the Persian kings.   132 *pride of Christendom*   Constantinople.
137 *states*   lords.   138 *commons*   common people.

And shining stones upon their lofty crests,   145
Now living idle in the wallèd towns,
Wanting both pay and martial discipline,
Begin in troops to threaten civil war
And openly exclaim against the King.
Therefore, to stay all sudden mutinies,   150
We will invest your highness emperor,
Whereat the soldiers will conceive more joy
Than did the Macedonians at the spoil
Of great Darius and his wealthy host.
COSROE   Well, since I see the state of Persia droop   155
And languish in my brother's government,
I willingly receive th'imperial crown
And vow to wear it for my country's good,
In spite of them shall malice my estate.
ORTYGIUS   And, in assurance of desired success,   160
We here do crown thee monarch of the East,
Emperor of Asia and of Persia,
Great lord of Media and Armenia,
Duke of Africa and Albania,
Mesopotamia and of Parthia,   165
East India and the late-discovered isles,
Chief lord of all the wide, vast Euxine Sea,
And of the ever-raging Caspian lake.
Long live Cosroe, mighty emperor!
COSROE   And Jove may never let me longer live   170
Than I may seek to gratify your love,
And cause the soldiers that thus honor me
To triumph over many provinces!
By whose desires of discipline in arms
I doubt not shortly but to reign sole king,   175
And with the army of Theridamas,
Whither we presently will fly, my lords,
To rest secure against my brother's force.
ORTYGIUS   We knew, my lord, before we brought the crown,
Intending your investiòn so near   180

---

147 Wanting lacking. **150 sudden** incipient. **153-54 Than ... host** Alexander's
Macedonian troops defeated the forces of King Darius of Persia in 333 B.C. in a battle that
helped to extend the widest conquest of ancient times. **159 shall** who shall. **166 late-
discovered isles** the Americas (?). **167 Euxine Sea** Black Sea. **180 investiòn**
crowning.

The residence of your despisèd brother,
The lords would not be too exasperate
To injure or suppress your worthy title.
Or if they would, there are in readiness
Ten thousand horse to carry you from hence   185
In spite of all suspected enemies.

COSROE   I know it well, my lord, and thank you all.

ORTYGIUS   Sound up the trumpets, then. God save the King!

                                                       [Exeunt.]

ACT I
Scene 2   ⟩{*Scythia*}⟨

[*Enter*] TAMBURLAINE *leading* ZENOCRATE, TECHELLES, USUMCASANE,
[MAGNETES, AGYDAS, *and*] *other* LORDS *and* SOLDIERS, *laden with*
treasure.

TAMBURLAINE   Come lady, let not this appall your thoughts;
The jewels and the treasure we have ta'en
Shall be reserved, and you in better state
Than if you were arrived in Syria,
Even in the circle of your father's arms,   5
The mighty Soldan of Egyptia.

ZENOCRATE   Ah, shepherd, pity my distressèd plight—
If, as thou seemst thou art so mean a man—
And seek not to enrich thy followers
By lawless rapine from a silly maid,   10
Who, traveling with these Median lords
To Memphis from my uncle's country of Media,
Where all my youth I have been governèd,
Have passed the army of the mighty Turk,
Bearing his privy signet and his hand   15
To safe conduct us thorough Africa.

182–83 *would . . . to* would not be so angry as to.
🕮 ACT I, Scene 2. 3 *reserved* protected. *in . . . state* more highly honored.
8 *mean* lowly. 10 *silly* innocent. 13 *governèd* kept under the care of a governess.
15 *privy . . . hand* letters signed with his official seal.

MAGNETES   And since we have arrived in Scythia,
    Besides rich presents from the puissant Cham,
    We have his highness' letters to command
    Aid and assistance if we stand in need.   20
TAMBURLAINE   But now you see these letters and commands
    Are countermanded by a greater man,
    And through my provinces you must expect
    Letters of conduct from my mightiness,
    If you intend to keep your treasure safe.   25
    But since I love to live at liberty,
    As easily may you get the Soldan's crown
    As any prizes out of my precinct.
    For they are friends that help to wean my state,
    Till men and kingdoms help to strengthen it,   30
    And must maintain my life exempt from servitude.
    But tell me, madam, is your grace betrothed?
ZENOCRATE   I am, my lord—for so you do import.
TAMBURLAINE   I am a lord, for so my deeds shall prove,
    And yet a shepherd by my parentage.   35
    But, lady, this fair face and heavenly hue
    Must grace his bed that conquers Asia
    And means to be a terror to the world,
    Measuring the limits of his empery
    By east and west, as Phoebus doth his course.   40
    Lie here, ye weeds that I disdain to wear!
    This complete armor and this curtal ax
    Are adjuncts more beseeming Tamburlaine.
    And madam, whatsoever you esteem
    Of this success and loss unvaluèd,   45
    Both may invest you empress of the East.
    And these, that seem but silly country swains,
    May have the leading of so great an host
    As with their weight shall make the mountains quake,
    Even as when windy exhalations,   50
    Fighting for passage, tilt within the earth.
TECHELLES   As princely lions when they rouse themselves,

---

18 Cham Emperor of Tartary.   **29 to . . . state** to make my state grow.   **33 for . . .
import** for you carry yourself as if you were a lord.   **40 Phoebus** the sun.   **41 weeds**
his shepherd's clothes.   **42 curtal ax** cutlass.   **45 this** my.   **loss unvaluèd** your
small loss.   **46 invest** make.   **47 silly** simple.   **50 windy exhalations** subterranean
winds.   **51 passage** escape.

Stretching their paws and threat'ning herds of beasts,
So in his armor looketh Tamburlaine.
Methinks I see kings kneeling at his feet,   55
And he with frowning brows and fiery looks
Spurning their crowns from off their captive heads.
USUMCASANE   And making thee and me, Techelles, kings,
That even to death will follow Tamburlaine.
TAMBURLAINE   Nobly resolved, sweet friends and followers!   60
These lords perhaps do scorn our estimates,
And think we prattle with distempered spirits,
But since they measure our deserts so mean,
That in conceit bear empires on our spears,
Affecting thoughts coequal with the clouds,   65
They shall be kept our forcèd followers
Till with their eyes they view us emperors.
ZENOCRATE   The gods, defenders of the innocent,
Will never prosper your intended drifts,
That thus oppress poor friendless passengers.   70
Therefore, at least admit us liberty,
Even as thou hop'st to be eternizèd
By living Asia's mighty emperor.
AGYDAS   I hope our lady's treasure and our own
May serve for ransom to our liberties.   75
Return our mules and empty camels back,
That we may travel into Syria,
Where her betrothèd lord, Alcidamus,
Expects th'arrival of her highness' person.
MAGNETES   And wheresoever we repose ourselves,   80
We will report but well of Tamburlaine.
TAMBURLAINE   Disdains Zenocrate to live with me?
Or you, my lords, to be my followers?
Think you I weigh this treasure more than you?
Not all the gold in India's wealthy arms   85
Shall buy the meanest soldier of my train.
Zenocrate, lovelier than the love of Jove,

---

61 *estimates* evaluations of the situation. **62** *prattle . . . spirits* jabber as if we were mad. **63** *measure . . . mean* think we are of so little worth. **64** *conceit* imagination. **65** *Affecting* harboring. **69** *intended drifts* plans. **70** *passengers* travelers. **73** *living* living to become. **85** *in . . . arms* encompassed in India's wealthy land. **87** *love of Jove* probably Hera, queen of the gods, but Tamburlaine could mean any of Jove's many loves.

Brighter than is the silver Rhodope,
Fairer than whitest snow on Scythian hills,
Thy person is more worth to Tamburlaine   90
Than the possession of the Persian crown,
Which gracious stars have promised at my birth.
A hundred Tartars shall attend on thee,
Mounted on steeds swifter than Pegasus.
Thy garments shall be made of Median silk   95
Enchased with precious jewels of mine own,
More rich and valurous than Zenocrate's.
With milk-white harts upon an ivory sled,
Thou shalt be drawn amidst the frozen pools,
And scale the icy mountains' lofty tops,   100
Which with thy beauty will be soon resolved.
My martial prizes, with five hundred men
Won on the fifty-headed Volga's waves,
Shall all we offer to Zenocrate,
And then myself to fair Zenocrate.   105

TECHELLES   What now?—in love?

TAMBURLAINE   Techelles, women must be flatterèd,
But this is she with whom I am in love.

Enter a SOLDIER.

SOLDIER   News, news!

TAMBURLAINE   How now? What's the matter?   110

SOLDIER   A thousand Persian horsemen are at hand,
Sent from the King to overcome us all.

TAMBURLAINE   How now, my lords of Egypt and Zenocrate?
Now must your jewels be restored again,
And I that triumphed so be overcome?   115
How say you, lordlings? Is not this your hope?

AGYDAS   We hope yourself will willingly restore them.

TAMBURLAINE   Such hope, such fortune, have the thousand horse.
Soft ye, my lords and sweet Zenocrate,
You must be forcèd from me ere you go.   120
A thousand horsemen! We five hundred foot!
An odds too great for us to stand against.

---

88 *silver Rhodope* a mountain range in Thrace, famous for its silver mines.   **94** *Pegasus*
a winged horse, symbol of poetry.   **96** *Enchased* adorned.   **97** *valurous* valuable.
98 *upon* pulling.   **101** *resolved* melted.   **103** *fifty-headed Volga* The Volga River
had many tributaries.

But are they rich? And is their armor good?

SOLDIER   Their plumèd helms are wrought with beaten gold,
Their swords enameled, and about their necks   125
Hang massy chains of gold down to the waist,
In every part exceeding brave and rich.

TAMBURLAINE   Then shall we fight courageously with them,
Or look you I should play the orator?

TECHELLES   No—cowards and faint-hearted runaways   130
Look for orations when the foe is near.
Our swords shall play the orators for us.

USUMCASANE   Come, let us meet them at the mountain foot,
And with a sudden and an hot alarm
Drive all their horses headlong down the hill.   135

TECHELLES   Come, let us march.

TAMBURLAINE   Stay, Techelles. Ask a parley first.

The SOLDIERS *enter.*

Open the mails, yet guard the treasure sure.
Lay out our golden wedges to the view,
That their reflections may amaze the Persians,   140
And look we friendly on them when they come.
But if they offer word or violence,
We'll fight, five hundred men-at-arms to one,
Before we part with our possession.
And 'gainst the general we will lift our swords   145
And either lance his greedy, thirsting throat,
Or take him prisoner, and his chain shall serve
For manacles till he be ransomed home.

TECHELLES   I hear them come. Shall we encounter them?

TAMBURLAINE   Keep all your standings, and not stir a foot;   150
Myself will bide the danger of the brunt.

Enter THERIDAMAS, *with others.*

THERIDAMAS   Where is this Scythian, Tamburlaine?

TAMBURLAINE   Whom seekst thou, Persian? I am Tamburlaine.

---

125 enameled brightly adorned.   **127 brave** splendid.   **129 Or . . . orator** Or do you
think that I should deliver a long battle oration?   **134 hot alarm** concentrated attack.
137 parley different from the oration suggested in line 129.   **138 mails** trunks, bag-
gage.   **sure** with care.   **139 golden wedges** the treasures carried by Zenocrate's party,
now to be used to impress the Persians.   **143 five hundred . . . one** to the last man.
147 chain the long gold chains mentioned in line 126.   **151 Myself . . . brunt** I will
stand at the front of the phalanx.

THERIDAMAS   Tamburlaine! A Scythian shepherd so embellishèd
    With nature's pride and richest furniture!   155
    His looks do menace heaven and dare the gods.
    His fiery eyes are fixed upon the earth
    As if he now devised some stratagem,
    Or meant to pierce Avernus' darksome vaults
    To pull the triple-headed dog from hell.   160
TAMBURLAINE   Noble and mild this Persian seems to be,
    If outward habit judge the inward man.
TECHELLES   His deep affections make him passionate.
TAMBURLAINE   With what a majesty he rears his looks!
    In thee, thou valiant man of Persia,   165
    I see the folly of thy emperor.
    Art thou but captain of a thousand horse,
    That by characters graven in thy brows
    And by thy martial face and stout aspect,
    Deservst to have the leading of an host?   170
    Forsake thy king and do but join with me,
    And we will triumph over all the world.
    I hold the Fates bound fast in iron chains,
    And with my hand turn Fortune's wheel about,
    And sooner shall the sun fall from his sphere   175
    Than Tamburlaine be slain or overcome.
    Draw forth thy sword, thou mighty man-at-arms,
    Intending but to raze my charmèd skin,
    And Jove himself will stretch his hand from heaven
    To ward the blow and shield me safe from harm.   180

---

155 *furniture* attributes.   **159** *Avernus* a dark lake in southern Italy thought to lead to
the Underworld (cf. *Aeneid,* VI).   **160** *triple-headed dog* Cerberus, three-headed watchdog at the entrance to hell.   **162** *habit* appearance.   **163** *affections* feelings.
168 *characters* Moslems believed that Allah inscribed a man's fate in invisible characters
on his forehead.   **173** *Fates* in classical mythology, the women who controlled man's
destiny by spinning out the thread of his life and cutting it off wherever they chose.
174 *Fortune's wheel* Fortune was traditionally thought of as a blind goddess who spun a
wheel bringing good fortune to those at the top and bad to those at the bottom. Because
she kept the wheel spinning, men's fortunes changed suddenly and arbitrarily. Here, by
suggesting that he controls, and is not controlled by, Fortune's wheel, Tamburlaine gives
consummate expression to one of the defining characteristics of the Renaissance—the
belief that man was the measure of his own excellence and achievements.
175 *sun . . . sphere* The sun was thought to be set in a concentric, spherical shell through
which it moved about the earth.

See how he rains down heaps of gold in showers,
As if he meant to give my soldiers pay;
And as a sure and grounded argument
That I shall be the monarch of the East,
He sends this soldan's daughter, rich and brave,   185
To be my queen and portly emperess.
If thou wilt stay with me, renownèd man,
And lead thy thousand horse with my conduct,
Besides thy share of this Egyptian prize,
Those thousand horse shall sweat with martial spoil   190
Of conquered kingdoms and of cities sacked.
Both we will walk upon the lofty cliffs,
And Christian merchants, that with Russian stems
Plough up huge furrows in the Caspian Sea,
Shall vail to us as lords of all the lake.   195
Both we will reign as consuls of the earth,
And mighty kings shall be our senators.
Jove sometimes maskèd in a shepherd's weed,
And by those steps that he hath scaled the heavens,
May we become immortal like the gods.   200
Join with me now in this my mean estate—
I call it mean because, being yet obscure,
The nations far removed admire me not—
And when my name and honor shall be spread
As far as Boreas claps his brazen wings   205
Or fair Boötes sends his cheerful light,
Then shalt thou be competitor with me,
And sit with Tamburlaine in all his majesty.
THERIDAMAS   Not Hermes, prolocutor to the gods,
Could use persuasions more pathetical.   210
TAMBURLAINE   Nor are Apollo's oracles more true
Than thou shalt find my vaunts substantial.

181–82 *he . . . pay* a reference to the gold captured from travelers. 185 *brave* beautiful. 186 *portly* of noble bearing. 188 *with my conduct* under my leadership.
193 *stems* ships. 194 *Caspian Sea* used as a trade route to the East. 195 *vail* lower
their topsails in respect. 198 *shepherd's weed* one of the many disguises Jove assumed
in order to carry out his illicit love affairs. 205 *Boreas* the North Wind. *clap . . .
wings* blasts his piercing cold. 206 *Boötes* a northern constellation containing the
bright star Arcturus. 207 *competitor* partner. 290 *prolocutor* spokesman. Hermes
was the god of eloquence as well as messenger for the gods. 210 *pathetical* emotionally
moving. 211 *Apollo's oracles* predicted the future to those blessed with the capacity
to interpret them.

TECHELLES   We are his friends, and if the Persian king
    Should offer present dukedoms to our state,
    We think it loss to make exchange for that   215
    We are assured of by our friend's success.

USUMCASANE   And kingdoms, at the least, we all expect,
    Besides the honor in assured conquests,
    Where kings shall crouch unto our conquering swords
    And hosts of soldiers stand amazed at us,   220
    When with their fearful tongues they shall confess
    These are the men that all the world admires.

THERIDAMAS   What strong enchantments tice my yielding soul!
    Are these resolvèd, noble Scythians!
    But shall I prove a traitor to my king?   225

TAMBURLAINE   No, but the trusty friend of Tamburlaine.

THERIDAMAS   Won with thy words and conquered with thy looks,
    I yield myself, my men, and horse to thee:
    To be partaker of thy good or ill,
    As long as life maintains Theridamas.   230

TAMBURLAINE   Theridamas, my friend, take here my hand,
    Which is as much as if I swore by heaven
    And called the gods to witness of my vow.
    Thus shall my heart be still combined with thine,
    Until our bodies turn to elements,   235
    And both our souls aspire celestial thrones.
    Techelles and Casane, welcome him.

TECHELLES   Welcome, renownèd Persian, to us all.

USUMCASANE   Long may Theridamas remain with us.

TAMBURLAINE   These are my friends, in whom I more rejoice   240
    Than doth the King of Persia in his crown;
    And by the love of Pylades and Orestes,
    Whose statues we adore in Scythia,
    Thyself and them shall never part from me
    Before I crown you kings in Asia.   245
    Make much of them, gentle Theridamas,
    And they will never leave thee till the death.

THERIDAMAS   Nor thee, nor them, thrice-noble Tamburlaine,

---

214 *to our state* to us. **221** *fearful* full of fear. **223** *tice* tempt. **224** *Are these* these are. **235** *elements* earth, air, fire, and water, which the world was believed to be composed of. **236** *aspire* soar to. **242** *Pylades and Orestes* Pylades helped Orestes avenge his father's murder and later endured exile with him. **243** *statues* The 1590 octavo reads "statutes." **246** *gentle* noble, gentlemanly.

Shall want my heart to be with gladness pierced,
To do you honor and security.   250
TAMBURLAINE   A thousand thanks, worthy Theridamas.
And now, fair madam and my noble lords,
If you will willingly remain with me,
You shall have honors as your merits be.
Or else you shall be forced with slavery.   255
AGYDAS   We yield unto thee, happy Tamburlaine.
TAMBURLAINE   For you then, madam, I am out of doubt.
ZENOCRATE   I must be pleased perforce. Wretched Zenocrate!

                                                 Exeunt.

ACT II

Scene I   ⟨*Somewhere between Persia and Scythia*⟩

[*Enter*] COSROE, MENAPHON, ORTYGIUS, CENEUS, *with other* SOLDIERS.

COSROE   Thus far are we towards Theridamas
And valiant Tamburlaine, the man of fame,
The man that in the forehead of his fortune
Bears figures of renown and miracle.
But tell me, that hast seen him, Menaphon,   5
What stature wields he, and what personage?
MENAPHON   Of stature tall, and straightly fashionèd,
Like his desire, lift upwards and divine,
So large of limbs, his joints so strongly knit,
Such breadth of shoulders as might mainly bear   10
Old Atlas' burden. 'Twixt his manly pitch,

---

249 *want* lack. **256** *happy* blessed by fortune (hap). **257** *I . . . doubt* I no longer need doubt (your loyalty).
🦌 **ACT II, Scene I. 5** *that . . . him* Since Tamburlaine always offered opposing armies the same choice—surrender before battle or annihilation—Menophon could not very well ever have seen Tamburlaine and lived to tell about it. But dramatic effectiveness, not logic, is Marlowe's chief concern. He succeeds in emphasizing Tamburlaine's impressiveness by providing the sincere testimony of a leader of the *opposing* camp: even Tamburlaine's enemies acknowledge his greatness. **11** *Old . . . burden* Atlas was punished for his part in the revolt of the Titans by being condemned to hold the world upon his shoulders. *pitch* the breadth of his shoulders.

A pearl more worth than all the world is placed,
Wherein by curious sovereignty of art
Are fixed his piercing instruments of sight,
Whose fiery circles bear encompassèd   15
A heaven of heavenly bodies in their spheres,
That guides his steps and actions to the throne
Where honor sits invested royally.
Pale of complexion, wrought in him with passion,
Thirsting with sovereignty, with love of arms,   20
His lofty brows in folds do figure death,
And in their smoothness amity and life.
About them hangs a knot of amber hair,
Wrappèd in curls, as fierce Achilles' was,
On which the breath of heaven delights to play,   25
Making it dance with wanton majesty.
His arms and fingers, long and sinewy,
Betokening valor and excess of strength—
In every part proportioned like the man
Should make the world subdued to Tamburlaine.   30
COSROE   Well hast thou portrayed in thy terms of life
The face and personage of a wondrous man.
Nature doth strive with Fortune and his stars
To make him famous in accomplished worth;
And well his merits show him to be made   35
His fortune's master and the king of men,
That could persuade, at such a sudden pinch,
With reasons of his valor and his life,
A thousand sworn and overmatching foes.
Then, when our powers in points of swords are joined,   40
And closed in compass of the killing bullet,
Though strait the passage and the port be made
That leads to palace of my brother's life,
Proud is his fortune if we pierce it not.
And when the princely Persian diadem   45

---

12 *pearl* his head.   **15–18** *Whose ... royally* The fiery brightness in his eyes proclaims his destiny as a royal leader of men.   **21** *in folds* furrowed.   **27** *sinewy* The 1590 octavo reads "snowy," probably a typesetter's error.   **31** *of life* lively.   **33** *stars* fate. **38** *life* destined life.   **40** *our* Tamburlaine's and mine.   **41** *in . . . bullet* within range (of Mycetes).   **42** *port* entrance.   **43** *palace . . . life* Mycetes' body (which would be protected in battle by his guards).   **44** *Proud* lucky.   *it* his body, and also his life.

Shall overweigh his weary, witless head
And fall, like mellowed fruit, with shakes of death,
In fair Persia noble Tamburlaine
Shall be my regent, and remain as king.
ORTYGIUS   In happy hour we have set the crown   50
Upon your kingly head, that seeks our honor
In joining with the man ordained by heaven
To further every action to the best.
CENEUS   He that with shepherds and a little spoil
Durst, in disdain of wrong and tyranny,   55
Defend his freedom 'gainst a monarchy,
What will he do supported by a king,
Leading a troop of gentlemen and lords,
And stuffed with treasure for his highest thoughts?
COSROE   And such shall wait on worthy Tamburlaine.   60
Our army will be forty thousand strong,
When Tamburlaine and brave Theridamas
Have met us by the river Araris;
And all conjoined to meet the witless king
That now is marching near to Parthia,   65
And with unwilling soldiers faintly armed,
To seek revenge on me and Tamburlaine,
To whom, sweet Menaphon, direct me straight.
MENAPHON   I will, my lord.   *Exeunt.*

ACT II
Scene 2   *Near Parthia*

[*Enter*] MYCETES, MEANDER, *with other* LORDS *and* SOLDIERS.

MYCETES   Come, my Meander, let us to this gear.
I tell you true, my heart is swoll'n with wrath
On this same thievish villain, Tamburlaine,
And of that false Cosroe, my traitorous brother.

---

47 *with shakes* in the throes.   **59 *for*** equal to the desires.   **63 *Araris*** · No such river
is known. Perhaps Marlowe is thinking of the Araxis River, which flowed through
Armenia to the Caspian Sea.   **65 *Parthia*** an ancient country of Asia, southeast of the
Caspian Sea.   **66 *faintly*** weakly.
ACT II, Scene 2.   **1 *gear*** business.   **3 *On*** against.

Would it not grieve a king to be so abused   5
And have a thousand horsemen ta'en away?
And—which is worse—to have his diadem
Sought for by such scald knaves as love him not?
I think it would. Well then, by heavens, I swear
Aurora shall not peep out of her doors,   10
But I will have Cosroe by the head
And kill proud Tamburlaine with point of sword.
Tell you the rest, Meander, I have said.

MEANDER   Then, having passed Armenian deserts now,
And pitched our tents under the Georgian hills,   15
Whose tops are covered with Tartarian thieves
That lie in ambush, waiting for a prey,
What should we do but bid them battle straight
And rid the world of those detested troops?
Lest, if we let them linger here a while,   20
They gather strength by power of fresh supplies.
This country swarms with vile, outrageous men
That live by rapine and by lawless spoil—
Fit soldiers for the wicked Tamburlaine.
And he that could with gifts and promises   25
Inveigle him that led a thousand horse,
And make him false his faith unto his king,
Will quickly win such as are like himself.
Therefore, cheer up your minds; prepare to fight.
He that can take or slaughter Tamburlaine   30
Shall rule the province of Albania.
Who brings that traitor's head, Theridamas,
Shall have a government in Media,
Beside the spoil of him and all his train.
But if Cosroe—as our spials say,   35
And as we know—remains with Tamburlaine,
His highness' pleasure is that he should live
And be reclaimed with princely lenity.

[*Enter a* SPY.]

SPY   An hundred horsemen of my company,
Scouting abroad upon these champion plains,   40

---

8 *scald* contemptible.   10 *Aurora* goddess of dawn.   15 *Georgian hills* Caucasus
Mountains.   22 *outrageous* those who commit outrages.   28 *such . . . himself* thieves
and cutthroats.   35 *spials* spies.   40 *champion* level.

Have viewed the army of the Scythians,
Which make reports it far exceeds the King's.
MEANDER   Suppose they be in number infinite,
Yet being void of martial discipline,
All running headlong after greedy spoils,   45
And more regarding gain than victory,
Like to the cruel brothers of the earth,
Sprung of the teeth of dragons venomous,
Their careless swords shall lance their fellows' throats
And make us triumph in their overthrow.   50
MYCETES   Was there such brethren, sweet Meander, say,
That sprung of teeth of dragons venomous?
MEANDER   So poets say, my lord.
MYCETES   And 'tis a pretty toy to be a poet.
Well, well, Meander, thou art deeply read,   55
And having thee, I have a jewel sure.
Go on, my lord, and give your charge, I say.
Thy wit will make us conquerors today.
MEANDER   Then, noble soldiers, to entrap these thieves,
That live confounded in disordered troops,   60
If wealth or riches may prevail with them,
We have our camels laden all with gold,
Which you that be but common soldiers
Shall fling in every corner of the field;
And while the base-born Tartars take it up,   65
You, fighting more for honor than for gold,
Shall massacre those greedy-minded slaves.
And when their scattered army is subdued,
And you march on their slaughtered carcasses,
Share equally the gold that bought their lives,   70
And live like gentlemen in Persia.
Strike up the drum and march courageously.
Fortune herself doth sit upon our crests.
MYCETES   He tells you true, my masters; so he does.
Drums, why sound ye not when Meander speaks?   *Exeunt.*   75

---

42 Which the hundred scouts.   **47-49 Like . . . throats** At Athena's instruction,
Cadmus planted the teeth of a dragon that had devoured his companions. From these teeth,
armed warriors sprang up and fought one another until only five remained; these helped
found the city of Thebes.   **49 careless** undisciplined.   **54 pretty toy** foolishness.
57 charge speech to the troops.   **75 Drums . . . speaks** an indication of the lack of
enthusiasm in Mycetes' army.

ACT II

Scene 3   *Beside the Araris River*

[*Enter*] COSROE, TAMBURLAINE, THERIDAMAS, TECHELLES, USUM-
CASANE, ORTYGIUS, *with others.*

COSROE Now, worthy Tamburlaine, have I reposed
 In thy approvèd fortunes all my hope.
 What thinkst thou, man, shall come of our attempts?
 For even as from assurèd oracle,
 I take thy doom for satisfaction.   5

TAMBURLAINE And so mistake you not a whit, my lord,
 For fates and oracles [of] heaven have sworn
 To royalize the deeds of Tamburlaine,
 And make them blessed that share in his attempts.
 And doubt you not but, if you favor me   10
 And let my fortunes and my valor sway
 To some direction in your martial deeds,
 The world will strive with hosts of men-at-arms
 To swarm unto the ensign I support.
 The hosts of Xerxes, which by fame is said   15
 To drink the mighty Parthian Araris,
 Was but a handful to that we will have.
 Our quivering lances shaking in the air
 And bullets like Jove's dreadful thunderbolts,
 Enrolled in flames and fiery smoldering mists,   20
 Shall threat the gods more than Cyclopian wars;
 And with our sun-bright armor, as we march,
 We'll chase the stars from heaven and dim their eyes
 That stand and muse at our admirèd arms.

THERIDAMAS You see, my lord, what working words he hath,   25
 But when you see his actions top his speech,
 Your speech will stay or so extol his worth
 As I shall be commended and excused
 For turning my poor charge to his direction.

❧ ACT II, Scene 3. **5** *doom* opinion. *satisfaction* certainty. **11–12** *sway . . .
direction* lead you. **16** *drink . . . Araris* According to Herodotus, Xerxes' army,
perhaps the largest of ancient times, drank all but the major rivers dry. **19** *bullets* Here
and below Marlowe means cannon shot. **21** *Shall . . . wars* The Titans, who attempted
to overthrow Jove, were sometimes identified with the Cyclops. **25** *working* effective.

And these, his two renownèd friends, my lord,   30
Would make one thrust and strive to be retained
In such a great degree of amity.
TECHELLES   With duty and with amity we yield
Our utmost service to the fair Cosroe.
COSROE   Which I esteem as portion of my crown.   35
Usumcasane and Techelles both,
When she that rules in Rhamnis' golden gates
And makes a passage for all prosperous arms
Shall make me solely emperor of Asia,
Then shall your meeds and valors be advanced   40
To rooms of honor and nobility.
TAMBURLAINE   Then haste, Cosroe, to be king alone,
That I with these my friends and all my men
May triumph in our long expected fate.
The King, your brother, is now hard at hand;   45
Meet with the fool, and rid your royal shoulders
Of such a burden as outweighs the sands
And all the craggy rocks of Caspea.

[*Enter a* MESSENGER.]

MESSENGER   My lord, we have discoverèd the enemy
Ready to charge you with a mighty army.   50
COSROE   Come, Tamburlaine, now whet thy wingèd sword,
And lift thy lofty arm into the clouds,
That it may reach the King of Persia's crown
And set it safe on my victorious head.
TAMBURLAINE   See where it is, the keenest curtal ax   55
That e'er made passage thorough Persian arms.
These are the wings shall make it fly as swift
As doth the lightning or the breath of heaven,
And kill as sure as it swiftly flies.
COSROE   Thy words assure me of kind success.   60
Go, valiant soldier, go before and charge
The fainting army of that foolish king.
TAMBURLAINE   Usumcasane and Techelles, come.

---

31 *would . . . thrust*   would act as one with Tamburlaine (?); would make one gigantic
effort (?).   **35** *as*   as much as a.   **37** *she*   Nemesis, Greek goddess of retribution.
Rhamnis' golden gates   a temple built in her honor at Rhamnus, in Attica.   **38** *And . . .*
arms   and makes the losers fall before victorious armies.   **40** *meeds*   deservings.
41 *rooms*   positions.   **57** *These . . . wings*   his arms.   **62** *fainting*   faint-hearted.

We are enough to scare the enemy,
And more than needs to make an emperor.   [*Exeunt.*]   65

ACT II

Scene 4   *The battlefield*

[SOLDIERS *rush*] *to the battle and* [*then exeunt*]. MYCETES *comes out alone
with a crown in his hand, offering to hide it.*

MYCETES   Accursed be he that first invented war!
    They knew not—ah, they knew not, simple men—
    How those were hit by pelting cannon shot
    Stand staggering, like a quivering aspen leaf
    Fearing the force of Boreas' boisterous blasts.   5
    In what a lamentable case were I
    If nature had not given me wisdom's lore,
    For kings are clouts that every man shoots at,
    Our crown the pin that thousands seek to cleave.
    Therefore, in policy I think it good   10
    To hide it close—a goodly stratagem,
    And far from any man that is a fool.
    So shall not I be known, or if I be,
    They cannot take away my crown from me.
    Here will I hide it in this simple hole.   15

    Enter TAMBURLAINE.

TAMBURLAINE   What, fearful coward! Straggling from the camp,
    When kings themselves are present in the field?
MYCETES   Thou liest.
TAMBURLAINE   Base villain, darst thou give the lie?
MYCETES   Away! I am the king. Go! Touch me not!   20
    Thou breakst the law of arms unless thou kneel
    And cry me, "Mercy, noble King!"
TAMBURLAINE   Are you the witty king of Persia?
MYCETES   Ay, marry, am I. Have you any suit to me?

🦗 ACT II, Scene 4.   **5** *Boreas* the North Wind.   **8** *clouts* bull's-eye on an archery
target.   **9** *pin* exact center of the bull's-eye.   **11** *close* in a safe place.   **19** *give the
lie* prove it.   **23** *witty* wise (Tamburlaine is, of course, being sarcastic).

TAMBURLAINE   I would entreat you to speak but three wise words.   25
MYCETES   So I can, when I see my time.
TAMBURLAINE   Is this your crown?
MYCETES   Ay. Didst thou ever see a fairer?
TAMBURLAINE   You will not sell it, will ye?
MYCETES   Such another word, and I will have thee executed.   30
    Come, give it me.
TAMBURLAINE   No; I took it prisoner.
MYCETES   You lie; I gave it you.
TAMBURLAINE   Then 'tis mine.
MYCETES   No; I mean I let you keep it.   35
TAMBURLAINE   Well, I mean you shall have it again.
    Here, take it for a while: I lend it thee
    Till I may see thee hemmed with armèd men.
    Then shalt thou see me pull it from thy head;
    Thou art no match for mighty Tamburlaine.   [*Exit.*]   40
MYCETES   O gods, is this Tamburlaine the thief?
    I marvel much he stole it not away.
    Sound trumpets to the battle, and he runs in.

ACT II
Scene 5   *The same*

[*Enter*] COSROE, TAMBURLAINE, THERIDAMAS, MENAPHON, MEANDER,
ORTYGIUS, TECHELLES, USUMCASANE, *with others.*

TAMBURLAINE   Hold thee, Cosroe; wear two imperial crowns.
    Think thee invested now as royally,
    Even by the mighty hand of Tamburlaine,
    As if as many kings as could encompass thee,
    With greatest pomp, had crowned thee emperor.   5
COSROE   So do I, thrice renownèd man-at-arms,
    And none shall keep the crown but Tamburlaine.
    Thee do I make my regent of Persia
    And general lieutenant of my armies.
    Meander, you that were our brother's guide   10

26 *see my time* choose to do so.
🏵 **ACT II, Scene 5.   7 *keep*** protect.

And chiefest counselor in all his acts,
Since he is yielded to the stroke of war,
On your submission we with thanks excuse
And give you equal place in our affairs.

MEANDER   Most happy Emperor, in humblest terms   15
I vow my service to your majesty,
With utmost virtue of my faith and duty.

COSROE   Thanks, good Meander. Then, Cosroe, reign
And govern Persia in her former pomp.
Now send embassage to thy neighbor kings,   20
And let them know the Persian king is changed
From one that knew not what a king should do
To one that can command what 'longs thereto.
And now we will to fair Persepolis
With twenty thousand expert soldiers.   25
The lords and captains of my brother's camp
With little slaughter take Meander's course
And gladly yield them to my gracious rule.
Ortygius and Menaphon, my trusty friends,
Now will I gratify your former good   30
And grace your calling with a greater sway.

ORTYGIUS   And as we ever aimed at your behoof,
And sought your state all honor it deserved,
So will we with our powers and our lives
Endeavor to preserve and prosper it.   35

COSROE   I will not thank thee, sweet Ortygius;
Better replies shall prove my purposes.
And now, Lord Tamburlaine, my brother's camp
I leave to thee and to Theridamas,
To follow me to fair Persepolis.   40
Then will we march to all those Indian mines
My witless brother to the Christians lost,
And ransom them with fame and usury.
And till thou overtake me, Tamburlaine,
Staying to order all the scattered troops,   45
Farewell, lord regent and his happy friends.
I long to sit upon my brother's throne.

MENAPHON   Your majesty shall shortly have your wish,

---

31 *sway* power.   **32** *behoof* advance, profit.   **41** *Indian mines* gold mines near the Indus River.   **43** *usury* interest. (We will win back our earlier loss, and more besides).

And ride in triumph through Persepolis.
        Exeunt [all but] TAMBURLAINE, TECHELLES, THERIDAMAS, [*and*]
                        USUMCASANE.

TAMBURLAINE   "And ride in triumph through Persepolis!"   50
   Is it not brave to be a king, Techelles?
   Usumcasane and Theridamas,
   Is it not passing brave to be a king,
   And ride in triumph through Persepolis?
TECHELLES   O, my lord, 'tis sweet and full of pomp.   55
USUMCASANE   To be a king is half to be a god.
THERIDAMAS   A god is not so glorious as a king.
   I think the pleasure they enjoy in heaven
   Cannot compare with kingly joys in earth:
   To wear a crown enchased with pearl and gold,   60
   Whose virtues carry with it life and death;
   To ask and have, command and be obeyed;
   When looks breed love, with looks to gain the prize,
   Such power attractive shines in princes' eyes.
TAMBURLAINE   Why say, Theridamas, wilt thou be a king?   65
THERIDAMAS   Nay, though I praise it, I can live without it.
TAMBURLAINE   What says my other friends? Will you be kings?
TECHELLES   Ay, if I could, with all my heart, my lord.
TAMBURLAINE   Why, that's well said, Techelles; so would I.
   And so would you, my masters, would you not?   70
USUMCASANE   What then, my lord?
TAMBURLAINE   Why then, Casane, shall we wish for aught
   The world affords in greatest novelty
   And rest attemptless, faint and destitute?
   Methinks we should not. I am strongly moved,   75
   That if I should desire the Persian crown,
   I could attain it with a wondrous ease;
   And would not all our soldiers soon consent,
   If we should aim at such a dignity?
THERIDAMAS   I know they would with our persuasions.   80
TAMBURLAINE   Why then, Theridamas, I'll first assay
   To get the Persian kingdom to myself.
   Then thou for Parthia; they for Scythia and Media;
   And if I prosper, all shall be as sure

---

51 *brave* splendid.   **59** *in* on.   **64** ***power attractive*** power that attracts (prizes).
73 *in . . . novelty* very rarely.   **80** ***with our persuasions*** just as we have consented.

As if the Turk, the Pope, Afric, and Greece   85
Came creeping to us with their crowns apiece.

TECHELLES   Then shall we send to this triumphing king,
And bid him battle for his novel crown?

USUMCASANE   Nay, quickly then, before his room be hot.

TAMBURLAINE   'Twill prove a pretty jest, in faith, my friends.   90

THERIDAMAS   A jest to charge on twenty thousand men?
I judge the purchase more important far.

TAMBURLAINE   Judge by thyself, Theridamas, not me,
For presently Techelles here shall haste
To bid him battle ere he pass too far   95
And lose more labor than the gain will quite.
Then shalt thou see the Scythian Tamburlaine
Make but a jest to win the Persian crown.
Techelles, take a thousand horse with thee,
And bid him turn his back to war with us,   100
That only made him king to make us sport.
We will not steal upon him cowardly,
But give him warning and more warriors.
Haste thee, Techelles; we will follow thee.   [*Exit* TECHELLES.]
What saith Theridamas?   105

THERIDAMAS   Go on, for me.   *Exeunt.*

ACT II
Scene 6   *On the way to Persepolis*

[*Enter*] COSROE, MEANDER, ORTYGIUS, MENAPHON, *with other*
SOLDIERS.

COSROE   What means this devilish shepherd to aspire
With such a giantly presumption,
To cast up hills against the face of heaven,
And dare the force of angry Jupiter?

---

85 *the Turk . . . Greece* the four most powerful rulers in the world at that time.
86 *apiece* The 1590 octavo reads "apace." **89** *before . . . hot* before he is settled in
his new position. **92** *purchase* undertaking. **96** *quite* justify. **106** *for me* as far
as I am concerned.
ACT II, Scene 6. **3** *To . . . heaven* as the Titans did warring against Jove.

But as he thrust them underneath the hills,   5
And pressed out fire from their burning jaws,
So will I send this monstrous slave to hell,
Where flames shall ever feed upon his soul.
MEANDER   Some powers divine, or else infernal, mixed
Their angry seeds at his conception,   10
For he was never sprung of human race,
Since with the spirit of his fearful pride,
He dares so doubtlessly resolve of rule,
And by profession be ambitious.
ORTYGIUS   What god, or fiend, or spirit of the earth,   15
Or monster turnèd to a manly shape,
Or of what mold or mettle he be made,
What star or state soever govern him,
Let us put on our meet encountering minds,
And in detesting such a devilish thief,   20
In love of honor and defense of right
Be armed against the hate of such a foe,
Whether from earth, or hell, or heaven he grow.
COSROE   Nobly resolved, my good Ortygius,
And since we all have sucked one wholesome air,   25
And with the same proportion of elements
Resolve, I hope we are resembled,
Vowing our loves to equal death and life.
Let's cheer our soldiers to encounter him,
That grievous image of ingratitude,   30
That fiery thirster after sovereignty,
And burn him in the fury of that flame
That none can quench but blood and empery.
Resolve, my lords and loving soldiers, now
To save your king and country from decay.   35
Then strike up, drum; and all the stars that make
The loathsome circle of my dated life,
Direct my weapon to his barbarous heart,
That thus opposeth him against the gods,
And scorns the powers that govern Persia.   [Exeunt.]   40

---

5 them the Titans.   **12 fearful** fearsome.   **13-14 He . . . ambitious** He dares so self-
assuredly to desire to rule and announces his ambition.   **27 Resolve** dissolve into elements
(at death).   **resembled** in agreement.   **32 flame** ambition.   **37 circle** restrictions.
dated limited (in contrast to Tamburlaine's apparently charmed life).   **39 him** himself.

ACT II
Scene 7   *The same*

Enter [SOLDIERS] *to the battle, and after the battle enter* COSROE,
wounded, THERIDAMAS, TAMBURLAINE, TECHELLES, USUMCASANE, *with*
others.

COSROE   Barbarous and bloody Tamburlaine,
   Thus to deprive me of my crown and life!
   Treacherous and false Theridamas,
   Even at the morning of my happy state—
   Scarce being seated in my royal throne—   5
   To work my downfall and untimely end!
   An uncouth pain torments my grievèd soul,
   And death arrests the organ of my voice,
   Who, entering at the breach thy sword hath made,
   Sacks every vein and artier of my heart.   10
   Bloody and insatiate Tamburlaine!
TAMBURLAINE   The thirst of reign and sweetness of a crown,
   That caused the eldest son of heavenly Ops
   To thrust his doting father from his chair,
   And place himself in the imperial heaven,   15
   Moved me to manage arms against thy state.
   What better precedent than mighty Jove?
   Nature, that framed us of four elements
   Warring within our breasts for regiment,
   Doth teach us all to have aspiring minds.   20
   Our souls, whose faculties can comprehend
   The wondrous architecture of the world
   And measure every wandering planet's course,
   Still climbing after knowledge infinite,
   And always moving as the restless spheres,   25
   Will us to wear ourselves and never rest,
   Until we reach the ripest fruit of all,
   That perfect bliss and sole felicity,
   The sweet fruition of an earthly crown.
THERIDAMAS   And that made me to join with Tamburlaine.   30

ACT II, Scene 7.   7 *uncouth* unnatural. 9 *Who* death. 10 *artier* artery.
13 *eldest . . . Ops* Jove, who overthrew his father, Saturn, king of the old gods.
15 *imperial* "Empyreal" is also implied. 19 *regiment* rule.

For he is gross and like the massy earth
That moves not upwards, nor by princely deeds
Doth mean to soar above the highest sort.
TECHELLES   And that made us, the friends of Tamburlaine,
To lift our swords against the Persian king.   35
USUMCASANE   For as when Jove did thrust old Saturn down,
Neptune and Dis gained each of them a crown,
So do we hope to reign in Asia,
If Tamburlaine be placed in Persia.
COSROE   The strangest men that ever nature made!   40
I know not how to take their tyrannies.
My bloodless body waxeth chill and cold,
And with my blood my life slides through my wound.
My soul begins to take her flight to hell
And summons all my senses to depart.   45
The heat and moisture which did feed each other,
For want of nourishment to feed them both,
Is dry and cold; and now doth ghastly death
With greedy talents gripe my bleeding heart
And like a Harpy tires on my life.   50
Theridamas and Tamburlaine, I die—
And fearful vengeance light upon you both!

[*He dies.* TAMBURLAINE] *takes the crown and puts it on.*

TAMBURLAINE   Not all the curses which the Furies breathe
Shall make me leave so rich a prize as this.
Theridamas, Techelles, and the rest,   55
Who think you now is king of Persia?
ALL   Tamburlaine! Tamburlaine!
TAMBURLAINE   Though Mars himself, the angry god of arms,
And all the earthly potentates conspire
To dispossess me of this diadem,   60
Yet will I wear it in despite of them,
As great commander of this eastern world,
If you but say that Tamburlaine shall reign.
ALL   Long live Tamburlaine, and reign in Asia!

---

31 gross huge. **earth** heaviest of the "four elements" of line 18. **37 Neptune and
Dis** Jove's brothers, whom he made rulers of the sea and the Underworld. **46 heat
and moisture** qualities formerly carried in his blood. **47 nourishment** blood.
49 talents talons. **gripe** grip. **50 Harpy** noisome, ravenous birds with women's
faces that were believed to snatch away living souls. **53 Furies** avenging spirits.

TAMBURLAINE   So; now it is more surer on my head   65
    Than if the gods had held a parliament,
    And all pronounced me king of Persia.   [*Exeunt.*]

ACT III

Scene 1   ⟨*Near Constantinople*⟩

[*Enter*] BAJAZETH, *the* KINGS OF FEZ, MOROCCO, *and* ARGIER, *with others, in great pomp.*

BAJAZETH   Great Kings of Barbary and my portly bassoes,
    We hear the Tartars and the eastern thieves,
    Under the conduct of one Tamburlaine,
    Presume a bickering with your emperor,
    And think to rouse us from our dreadful siege   5
    Of the famous Grecian Constantinople.
    You know our army is invincible;
    As many circumcisèd Turks we have,
    And warlike bands of Christians renièd,
    As hath the ocean or the Terrene Sea   10
    Small drops of water when the moon begins
    To join in one her semicircled horns.
    Yet would we not be braved with foreign power
    Nor raise our siege before the Grecians yield
    Or breathless lie before the city walls.   15
KING OF FEZ   Renownèd Emperor and mighty General,
    What if you sent the bassoes of your guard
    To charge him to remain in Asia,
    Or else to threaten death and deadly arms
    As from the mouth of mighty Bajazeth?   20
BAJAZETH   Hie thee, my basso, fast to Persia.
    Tell him thy lord, the Turkish emperor,

❧ **ACT III, Scene 1.** **1** *portly* of noble bearing. *bassoes* Turkish lords. **4** *bickering* contention. **9** *Christians renièd* Christians who have renounced their faith. **10** *Terrene Sea* Mediterranean Sea. **11–12** *when . . . horns* when the moon is full (and tides are highest). **13** *braved* engaged in battle. **14** *Grecians* Byzantines. **15** *breathless* dead.

Dread lord of Afric, Europe, and Asia,
Great king and conqueror of Graecia,
The ocean, Terrene, and the coal-black sea,   25
The high and highest monarch of the world,
Wills and commands—for say not I entreat—
Not once to set his foot in Africa
Or spread his colors in Graecia,
Lest he incur the fury of my wrath.   30
Tell him I am content to take a truce,
Because I hear he bears a valiant mind;
But if, presuming on his silly power,
He be so mad to manage arms with me,
Then stay thou with him—say, I bid thee so—   35
And if, before the sun have measured heaven
With triple circuit, thou regreet us not,
We mean to take his morning's next arise
For messenger he will not be reclaimed,
And mean to fetch thee in despite of him.   40

BASSO   Most great and puissant monarch of the earth,
    Your basso will accomplish your behest
    And show your pleasure to the Persian,
    As fits the legate of the stately Turk.   *Exit* BASSO.

KING OF ARGIER   They say he is the King of Persia;   45
    But if he dare attempt to stir your siege,
    'Twere requisite he should be ten times more,
    For all flesh quakes at your magnificence.

BAJAZETH   True, Argier, and trembles at my looks.

KING OF MOROCCO   The spring is hindered by your smothering host,   50
    For neither rain can fall upon the earth,
    Nor sun reflex his virtuous beams thereon,
    The ground is mantled with such multitudes.

BAJAZETH   All this is true as holy Mahomet,
    And all the trees are blasted with our breaths.   55

KING OF FEZ   What thinks your greatness best to be achieved
    In pursuit of the city's overthrow?

BAJAZETH   I will the captive pioners of Argier
    Cut off the water that by leaden pipes

---

33 *silly* feeble. **34** *manage arms* engage in battle. **38** *his* the sun's. **39** *he* Tamburlaine. **47** *more* more the man. **52** *reflex* shine. **58** *will* order. *pioners* excavators. *Argier* Algeria.

Runs to the city from the mountain Carnon.   60
Two thousand horse shall forage up and down,
That no relief or succor come by land,
And all the sea my galleys countermand.
Then shall our footmen lie within the trench,
And with their cannons mouthed like Orcus' gulf,   65
Batter the walls, and we will enter in;
And thus the Grecians shall be conquerèd.   *Exeunt.*

ACT III

Scene 2   ⟨TAMBURLAINE'*s camp*⟩

[*Enter*] AGYDAS, ZENOCRATE, ANIPPE, *with others.*

AGYDAS   Madame Zenocrate, may I presume
To know the cause of these unquiet fits
That work such trouble to your wonted rest?
'Tis more than pity such a heavenly face
Should by heart's sorrow wax so wan and pale,   5
When your offensive rape by Tamburlaine,
Which of your whole displeasures should be most,
Hath seemed to be digested long ago.
ZENOCRATE   Although it be digested long ago,
As his exceeding favors have deserved,   10
And might content the queen of heaven as well
As it hath changed my first-conceived disdain;
Yet, since, a farther passion feeds my thoughts
With ceaseless and disconsolate conceits,
Which dyes my looks so lifeless as they are,   15
And might, if my extremes had full events,
Make me the ghastly counterfeit of death.
AGYDAS   Eternal heaven sooner be dissolved,
And all that pierceth Phoebe's silver eye,

---

60 mountain Carnon   geographically unidentifiable.   **63 countermand**   control.
65 Orcus' gulf   the opening to hell.
⚹ **ACT III, Scene 2.   6 rape**   seizure and abduction.   **7 Which...most**   which of all
your displeasures should be the most unpleasant.   **14 conceits**   imaginings.   **16 extremes**
passions.   *events*   expression.   **19 all...eye**   all that comes within the moon's vision
(i.e. the sublunary, change-governed world).

Before such hap fall to Zenocrate!   20
ZENOCRATE Ah, life and soul, still hover in his breast,
And leave my body senseless as the earth,
Or else unite you to his life and soul,
That I may live and die with Tamburlaine!

Enter [unseen] TAMBURLAINE, *with* TECHELLES, *and others.*

AGYDAS With Tamburlaine? Ah, fair Zenocrate,   25
Let not a man so vile and barbarous,
That holds you from your father in despite
And keeps you from the honors of a queen,
Being supposed his worthless concubine,
Be honored with your love but for necessity.   30
So, now the mighty Soldan hears of you,
Your highness needs not doubt but in short time
He will, with Tamburlaine's destruction,
Redeem you from this deadly servitude.
ZENOCRATE Leave to wound me with these words,   35
And speak of Tamburlaine as he deserves.
The entertainment we have had of him
Is far from villainy or servitude,
And might in noble minds be counted princely.
AGYDAS How can you fancy one that looks so fierce,   40
Only disposed to martial stratagems?
Who, when he shall embrace you in his arms,
Will tell how many thousand men he slew,
And, when you look for amorous discourse,
Will rattle forth his facts of war and blood,   45
Too harsh a subject for your dainty ears.
ZENOCRATE As looks the sun through Nilus' flowing stream,
Or when the morning holds him in her arms,
So looks my lordly love, fair Tamburlaine;
His talk much sweeter than the Muses' song   50
They sung for honor 'gainst Pierides,

---

35 *Leave . . . words* The line seems incomplete, for it is metrically deficient. It can be
"completed" by adding "Agydas" at the beginning as a direct address. **47 Nilus** Nile
River. **48 him** the sun. **50–51 His . . . Pierides** The Pierides, daughters of the
Macedonian king Pierus, foolishly challenged the nine Muses, goddesses of literature and
the arts, to a song contest; they were defeated and changed into magpies.

Or when Minerva did with Neptune strive;
And higher would I rear my estimate
Than Juno, sister to the highest god,
If I were matched with mighty Tamburlaine.   55
AGYDAS   Yet be not so inconstant in your love,
But let the young Arabian live in hope,
After your rescue to enjoy his choice.
You see, though first the King of Persia,
Being a shepherd, seemed to love you much,   60
Now, in his majesty, he leaves those looks,
Those words of favor, and those comfortings,
And gives no more than common courtesies.
ZENOCRATE   Thence rise the tears that so distain my cheeks,
Fearing his love through my unworthiness.   65

   TAMBURLAINE *goes to her, and takes her away lovingly by the hand,*
   looking wrathfully on AGYDAS, *and says nothing.* [*Exeunt all but*
   AGYDAS.]

AGYDAS   Betrayed by fortune and suspicious love,
Threat'nèd with frowning wrath and jealousy,
Surprised with fear of hideous revenge,
I stand aghast; but most astonièd
To see his choler shut in secret thoughts,   70
And wrapt in silence of his angry soul.
Upon his brows was portrayed ugly death,
And in his eyes the fury of his heart,
That shine as comets, menacing revenge,
And casts a pale complexion on his cheeks.   75
As when the seaman sees the Hyadès
Gather an army of Cimmerian clouds,
—Auster and Aquilon with wingèd steeds,

---

52 *Or . . . strive* Athena (who was later identified with Minerva by the Romans) and
Neptune engaged in a contest for control of the land of Attica, and it was decided that the
god who gave the more useful present to the inhabitants would be declared the victor.
Neptune struck a horse from the land with his trident; Athena presented an olive tree and
was judged the winner. At this victory the Muses sang with pleasure, because Athena is,
like them, a goddess associated with the arts.   **53** *rear my estimate* consider my condition.   **57** *young Arabian* to whom Zenocrate is betrothed.   **64** *distain* unnaturally
mark.   **65** *Fearing . . . unworthiness* fearing that I am not worthy of his love.
66 *suspicious* (Tamburlaine's) suspicious (love).   **69** *astonièd* astonished.   **76** *Hyadès*
a constellation which, if it rose with the sun, was thought to bring rain.   **77** *Cimmerian*
black.   **78** *Auster and Aquilon* the southwest and north winds.

All sweating, tilt about the watery heavens,
With shivering spears enforcing thunder claps,   80
And from their shields strike flames of lightning—
All-fearful folds his sails and sounds the main,
Lifting his prayers to the heavens for aid
Against the terror of the winds and waves,
So fares Agydas for the late-felt frowns   85
That sent a tempest to my daunted thoughts
And makes my soul divine her overthrow.

Enter TECHELLES *with a naked dagger* [*and* USUMCASANE].

TECHELLES   See you, Agydas, how the King salutes you.
He bids you prophesy what it imports.
AGYDAS   I prophesied before, and now I prove   90
The killing frowns of jealousy and love.
He needed not with words confirm my fear,
For words are vain where working tools present
The naked action of my threatened end.
It says, Agydas, thou shalt surely die,   95
And of extremities elect the least.
More honor and less pain it may procure,
To die by this resolvèd hand of thine
Than stay the torments he and heaven have sworn.
Then haste, Agydas, and prevent the plagues   100
Which thy prolongèd fates may draw on thee.
Go wander free from fear of tyrant's rage,
Removèd from the torments and the hell
Wherewith he may excruciate thy soul,
And let Agydas by Agydas die,   105
And with this stab slumber eternally.   [*Stabs himself.*]
TECHELLES   Usumcasane, see how right the man
Hath hit the meaning of my lord the King.
USUMCASANE   Faith and, Techelles, it was manly done;
And, since he was so wise and honorable,   110
Let us afford him now the bearing hence,
And crave his triple-worthy burial.
TECHELLES   Agreed, Casane; we will honor him.
                                   [*Exeunt, bearing out the body.*]

---

79 *watery* rain-filled.   **82 *sounds the main*** measures the depth of the sea.   **96 *ex-tremities*** painful deaths.   **99 *stay*** await.

ACT III
Scene 3   ⟨*The same*⟩

[*Enter*] TAMBURLAINE, TECHELLES, USUMCASANE, THERIDAMAS, BASSO, ZENOCRATE, [ANIPPE,] *with others.*

TAMBURLAINE   Basso, by this thy lord and master knows
    I mean to meet him in Bithynia.
    See how he comes! Tush, Turks are full of brags
    And menace more than they can well perform.
    He meet me in the field, and fetch thee hence!   5
    Alas, poor Turk, his fortune is too weak
    T'encounter with the strength of Tamburlaine.
    View well my camp, and speak indifferently:
    Do not my captains and my soldiers look
    As if they meant to conquer Africa?   10
BASSO   Your men are valiant, but their number few,
    And cannot terrify his mighty host.
    My lord, the great commander of the world,
    Besides fifteen contributory kings,
    Hath now in arms ten thousand janissaries,   15
    Mounted on lusty Mauritanian steeds,
    Brought to the war by men of Tripoli;
    Two hundred thousand footmen that have served
    In two set battles fought in Graecia;
    And for the expedition of this war,   20
    If he think good, can from his garrisons
    Withdraw as many more to follow him.
TECHELLES   The more he brings, the greater is the spoil:
    For when they perish by our warlike hands,
    We mean to set our footmen on their steeds,   25
    And rifle all those stately janissars.
TAMBURLAINE   But will those kings accompany your lord?
BASSO   Such as his highness please; but some must stay
    To rule the provinces he late subdued.
TAMBURLAINE   [*To his lieutenants.*] Then fight courageously; their   30
    crowns are yours.

🐉 **ACT III, Scene 3.**   **1** *this*   this time.   **2** *Bithynia*   an ancient country of north-west Asia, in what is now Turkey.   **8** *indifferently*   honestly.   **15** *janissaries*   Turkish soldiers.   **16** *Mauritanian*   from Mauritania, a region in North Africa.

This hand shall set them on your conquering heads,
That made me emperor of Asia.
USUMCASANE   Let him bring millions infinite of men,
Unpeopling Western Africa and Greece,
Yet we assure us of the victory.   35
THERIDAMAS   Even he, that in a trice vanquished two kings
More mighty than the Turkish emperor,
Shall rouse him out of Europe and pursue
His scattered army till they yield or die.
TAMBURLAINE   Well said, Theridamas! Speak in that mood,   40
For "will" and "shall" best fitteth Tamburlaine,
Whose smiling stars give him assurèd hope
Of martial triumph, ere he meet his foes.
I that am termed the scourge and wrath of God,
The only fear and terror of the world,   45
Will first subdue the Turk, and then enlarge
Those Christian captives which you keep as slaves,
Burdening their bodies with your heavy chains,
And feeding them with thin and slender fare,
That naked row about the Terrene Sea,   50
And, when they chance to breathe and rest a space,
Are punished with bastones so grievously
That they lie panting on the galley's side,
And strive for life at every stroke they give.
These are the cruel pirates of Argier,   55
That damnèd train, the scum of Africa,
Inhabited with straggling runagates,
That make quick havoc of the Christian blood.
But, as I live, that town shall curse the time
That Tamburlaine set foot in Africa.   60

Enter BAJAZETH *with his* BASSOES *and* CONTRIBUTORY KINGS [, ZABINA,
and EBEA].

BAJAZETH   Bassoes and janissaries of my guard,
Attend upon the person of your lord,
The greatest potentate of Africa.
TAMBURLAINE   Techelles and the rest, prepare your swords:
I mean t'encounter with that Bajazeth.   65

---

38 *him* Bajazeth.   **44** *scourge* whip, punishing instrument.   **46** *enlarge* free.
52 *bastones* cudgels.   **54** *they* their Turkish guards.   **57** *runagates* deserters (both
from military service and from the Christian religion).   **59** *that town* Argier.

BAJAZETH   Kings of Fez, Morocco, and Argier,
He calls me Bajazeth, whom you call lord!
Note the presumption of this Scythian slave!
I tell thee, villain, those that lead my horse
Have to their names titles of dignity,   70
And darst thou bluntly call me Bajazeth?
TAMBURLAINE   And know thou, Turk, that those which lead my horse
Shall lead thee captive thorough Africa,
And darst thou bluntly call me Tamburlaine?
BAJAZETH   By Mahomet, my kinsman's, sepulcher,   75
And by the holy Alcoran I swear,
He shall be made a chaste and lustless eunuch,
And in my sarell tend my concubines;
And all his captains, that thus stoutly stand,
Shall draw the chariot of my emperess,   80
Whom I have brought to see their overthrow.
TAMBURLAINE   By this my sword that conquered Persia,
Thy fall shall make me famous through the world.
I will not tell thee how I'll handle thee,
But every common soldier of my camp   85
Shall smile to see thy miserable state.
KING OF FEZ   What means the mighty Turkish emperor
To talk with one so base as Tamburlaine?
KING OF MOROCCO   Ye Moors and valiant men of Barbary,
How can ye suffer these indignities?   90
KING OF ARGIER   Leave words, and let them feel your lances' points,
Which glided through the bowels of the Greeks.
BAJAZETH   Well said, my stout contributory king!
Your threefold army and my hugy host
Shall swallow up these base-born Persians.   95
TECHELLES   Puissant, renowned, and mighty Tamburlaine,
Why stay we thus prolonging all their lives?
THERIDAMAS   I long to see those crowns won by our swords,
That we may reign as kings of Africa.
USUMCASANE   What coward would not fight for such a prize?   100
TAMBURLAINE   Fight all courageously, and be you kings.
I speak it, and my words are oracles.
BAJAZETH   Zabina, mother of three braver boys

---

76 *Alcoran* the Koran. 78 *sarell* harem. 94 *hugy* huge. 103 *braver* both more
handsome and more courageous.

Than Hercules, that in his infancy
Did pash the jaws of serpents venomous,   105
Whose hands are made to gripe a warlike lance,
Their shoulders broad, for complete armor fit,
Their limbs more large and of a bigger size
Than all the brats ysprung from Typhon's loins,
Who, when they come unto their father's age,   110
Will batter turrets with their manly fists—
Sit here upon this royal chair of state,
And on thy head wear my imperial crown,
Until I bring this sturdy Tamburlaine
And all his captains bound in captive chains.   115
ZABINA   Such good success happen to Bajazeth!
TAMBURLAINE   Zenocrate, the loveliest maid alive,
Fairer than rocks of pearl and precious stone,
The only paragon of Tamburlaine,
Whose eyes are brighter than the lamps of heaven   120
And speech more pleasant than sweet harmony,
That with thy looks canst clear the darkened sky
And calm the rage of thundering Jupiter,
Sit down by her, adornèd with my crown,
As if thou wert the empress of the world.   125
Stir not, Zenocrate, until thou see
Me march victoriously with all my men,
Triumphing over him and these his kings,
Which I will bring as vassals to thy feet.
Till then, take thou my crown, vaunt of my worth,   130
And manage words with her, as we will arms.
ZENOCRATE   And may my love, the King of Persia,
Return with victory and free from wound!
BAJAZETH   Now shalt thou feel the force of Turkish arms,
Which lately made all Europe quake for fear.   135
I have of Turks, Arabians, Moors, and Jews,
Enough to cover all Bithynia.
Let thousands die! Their slaughtered carcasses

104–5 *that . . . venomous* It was believed that Hercules as an infant, still in his cradle, strangled two poisonous snakes that Hera sent to kill him. **109** *ysprung* an archaic form of *sprung* (reduced from the Old English prefix "ge-"). *Typhon* a many-headed, many-handed monster who fathered a brood of ugly beasts, including Cerberus, the Hydra of Lerna, the Chimera, Geryon, and the Sphinx. **114** *sturdy* rash. **130** *vaunt* the outward show.

Shall serve for walls and bulwarks to the rest;
And as the heads of Hydra, so my power,   140
Subdued, shall stand as mighty as before.
If they should yield their necks unto the sword,
Thy soldiers' arms could not endure to strike
So many blows as I have heads for thee.
Thou knowst not, foolish-hardy Tamburlaine,   145
What 'tis to meet me in the open field,
That leaves no ground for thee to march upon.

TAMBURLAINE   Our conquering swords shall marshal us the way
We use to march upon the slaughtered foe,
Trampling their bowels with our horses' hoofs,   150
Brave horses bred on the white Tartarian hills.
My camp is like to Julius Caesar's host,
That never fought but had the victory;
Nor in Pharsalia was there such hot war
As these my followers willingly would have.   155
Legions of spirits, fleeting in the air,
Direct our bullets and our weapons' points,
And make our strokes to wound the senseless lure.
And when she sees our bloody colors spread,
Then Victory begins to take her flight,   160
Resting herself upon my milk-white tent.
But come, my lords, to weapons let us fall;
The field is ours, the Turk, his wife, and all.

Exit with his followers.

BAJAZETH   Come, Kings and Bassoes, let us glut our swords,
That thirst to drink the feeble Persians' blood.   165

Exit with his followers.

ZABINA   Base concubine, must thou be placed by me
That am the empress of the mighty Turk?

ZENOCRATE   Disdainful Turkess, and unreverend boss,
Callst thou me concubine, that am betrothed
Unto the great and mighty Tamburlaine?   170

ZABINA   To Tamburlaine, the great Tartarian thief!

ZENOCRATE   Thou wilt repent these lavish words of thine
When thy great basso master and thyself

---

140 *Hydra* a many-headed monster who grew new heads to replace ones that were cut off.   **154** *Pharsalia* the site of Caesar's defeat of Pompey in 48 B.C.   **158** *lure* meat used to recall a falcon to his perch. Tamburlaine implies that Bajazeth's soldiers are little more than meat for his own men to feed on.   **168** *boss* a gross, fat woman.

Must plead for mercy at his kingly feet,
And sue to me to be your advocates[s].   175
ZABINA   And sue to thee? I tell thee, shameless girl,
Thou shalt be laundress to my waiting-maid.
How likst thou her, Ebea? Will she serve?
EBEA   Madam, she thinks perhaps she is too fine,
But I shall turn her into other weeds   180
And make her dainty fingers fall to work.
ZENOCRATE   Hear'st thou, Anippe, how thy drudge doth talk,
And how my slave, her mistress, menaceth?
Both for their sauciness shall be employed
To dress the common soldiers' meat and drink,   185
For we will scorn they should come near ourselves.
ANIPPE   Yet sometimes let your highness send for them
To do the work my chambermaid disdains.
                            They sound the battle within.
ZENOCRATE   Ye gods and powers that govern Persia,
And made my lordly love her worthy king,   190
Now strengthen him against the Turkish Bajazeth,
And let his foes, like flocks of fearful roes
Pursued by hunters, fly his angry looks,
That I may see him issue conqueror.
ZABINA   Now, Mahomet, solicit God himself,   195
And make him rain down murdering shot from heaven
To dash the Scythians' brains, and strike them dead
That dare to manage arms with him
That offered jewels to thy sacred shrine
When first he warred against the Christians.   200

To the battle again.

ZENOCRATE   By this the Turks lie weltering in their blood,
And Tamburlaine is lord of Africa.
ZABINA   Thou art deceived. I heard the trumpets sound
As when my emperor overthrew the Greeks
And led them captive into Africa.   205
Straight will I use thee as thy pride deserves;
Prepare thyself to live and die my slave.
ZENOCRATE   If Mahomet should come from heaven and swear
My royal lord is slain or conquerèd,
Yet should he not persuade me otherwise   210

180 weeds clothes.   **185 dress** prepare.

But that he lives and will be conqueror.

[*Enter* BAJAZETH, *with* TAMBURLAINE *in pursuit.* They fight and]
BAJAZETH *is overcome.*

TAMBURLAINE   Now, king of bassoes, who is conqueror?
BAJAZETH   Thou, by the fortune of this damnèd soil.
TAMBURLAINE   Where are your stout contributory kings?

Enter TECHELLES, THERIDAMAS, [*and*] USUMCASANE.

TECHELLES   We have their crowns; their bodies strow the field.   215
TAMBURLAINE   Each man a crown? Why, kingly fought, i'faith.
Deliver them into my treasury.
ZENOCRATE   Now let me offer to my gracious lord
His royal crown again, so highly won.
TAMBURLAINE   Nay, take the Turkish crown from her, Zenocrate,   220
And crown me emperor of Africa.
ZABINA   No, Tamburlaine; though now thou gat the best,
Thou shalt not yet be lord of Africa.
THERIDAMAS   Give her the crown, Turkess, you were best.

He takes it from her and gives it [*to*] ZENOCRATE.

ZABINA   Injurious villains, thieves, runagates,   225
How dare you thus abuse my majesty?
THERIDAMAS   [*To* ZENOCRATE] Here, madam, you are empress; she is
none.
TAMBURLAINE   Not now, Theridamas; her time is past.
The pillars that have bolstered up those terms
Are fall'n in clusters at my conquering feet.   230
ZABINA   Though he be prisoner, he may be ransomèd.
TAMBURLAINE   Not all the world shall ransom Bajazeth.
BAJAZETH   Ah, fair Zabina, we have lost the field,
And never had the Turkish emperor
So great a foil by any foreign foe.   235
Now will the Christian miscreants be glad,
Ringing with joy their superstitious bells,
And making bonfires for my overthrow.

---

213 soil This word is usually emended to "foil," meaning defeat, but the correction
seems unnecessary: Bajazeth is probably cursing the bad luck that he thinks has accompanied his decision to fight at a location selected by Tamburlaine (cf. III.3.2). **220 her**
Zabina. **222 thou gat** you have gotten. **224 you were best** It would be best for you.
228 Not now (How right you are that she is) not now empress. **229 pillars** the contributory kings and their armies. **terms** titles. **235 foil** defeat. **236 Christian
miscreants** false-believing Christians (because they do not embrace the Turkish religion).

But ere I die, those foul idolaters
Shall make me bonfires with their filthy bones;   240
For though the glory of this day be lost,
Afric and Greece have garrisons enough
To make me sovereign of the earth again.

TAMBURLAINE   Those wallèd garrisons will I subdue,
And write myself great lord of Africa.   245
So from the East unto the furthest West
Shall Tamburlaine extend his puissant arm.
The galleys and those pilling brigandines,
That yearly sail to the Venetian gulf
And hover in the straits for Christians' wrack,   250
Shall lie at anchor in the Isle Asant,
Until the Persian fleet and men-of-war,
Sailing along the oriental sea,
Have fetched about the Indian continent,
Even from Persepolis to Mexico,   255
And thence unto the Straits of Jubalter,
Where they shall meet and join their force in one,
Keeping in awe the Bay of Portingale
And all the ocean by the British shore;
And by this means I'll win the world at last.   260

BAJAZETH   Yet set a ransom on me, Tamburlaine.

TAMBURLAINE   What, thinkst thou Tamburlaine esteems thy gold?
I'll make the Kings of India, ere I die,
Offer their mines to sue for peace to me,
And dig for treasure to appease my wrath.   265
Come, bind them both, and one lead in the Turk;
The Turkess let my love's maid lead away.

They bind them.

BAJAZETH   Ah, villains, dare you touch my sacred arms?
O Mahomet! O sleepy Mahomet!

ZABINA   O cursèd Mahomet, that makst us thus   270
The slaves to Scythians rude and barbarous!

TAMBURLAINE   Come, bring them in, and for this happy conquest,
Triumph and solemnize a martial feast.   *Exeunt.*

---

248 pilling brigandines pillaging warships.   **250 for**   for the purpose of working.
251 Isle Asant   the island of Zante, just off the coast of Greece.   **255 Even . . . Mexico**
across the Pacific.   **256 Jubalter** Gibraltar.   **258 Portingale** Portugal (Bay of Biscay).
266 one someone.   **269 sleepy** unresponsive.

ACT IV

Scene 1   ⟨*Memphis*⟩

[*Enter the*] SOLDAN OF EGYPT, *with three or four* LORDS, CAPOLIN[, *and
a* MESSENGER].

SOLDAN   Awake, ye men of Memphis! Hear the clang
  Of Scythian trumpets! Hear the basilisks,
  That roaring shake Damascus' turrets down!
  The rogue of Volga holds Zenocrate,
  The Soldan's daughter, for his concubine,   5
  And with a troop of thieves and vagabonds,
  Hath spread his colors to our high disgrace,
  While you faint-hearted, base Egyptians,
  Lie slumbering on the flowery banks of Nile,
  As crocodiles that unaffrighted rest   10
  While thundering cannons rattle on their skins.
MESSENGER   Nay, mighty Soldan, did your greatness see
  The frowning looks of fiery Tamburlaine,
  That with his terror and imperious eyes
  Commands the hearts of his associates,   15
  It might amaze your royal majesty.
SOLDAN   Villain, I tell thee, were that Tamburlaine
  As monstrous as Gorgon, prince of hell,
  The Soldan would not start a foot from him.
  But speak, what power hath he?   20
MESSENGER   Mighty lord,
  Three hundred thousand men in armor clad,
  Upon their prancing steeds, disdainfully
  With wanton paces trampling on the ground;
  Five hundred thousand footmen threat'ning shot, 25
  Shaking their swords, their spears, and iron bills,
  Environing their standard round, that stood
  As bristle-pointed as a thorny wood;
  Their warlike engines and munition
  Exceed the forces of their martial men.   30

❧ ACT IV, Scene 1.   2 *basilisks* cannons.   4 *rogue of Volga* The Soldan identifies
Tamburlaine's birthplace as the area north of the Caspian Sea.   18 *Gorgon* This mythical beast turned any beholder to stone. The Soldan confuses it with the Demogorgon,
one of the princes of hell.   26 *bills* pikes.

SOLDAN   Nay, could their numbers countervail the stars,
   Or ever-drizzling drops of April showers,
   Or withered leaves that autumn shaketh down,
   Yet would the Soldan by his conquering power
   So scatter and consume them in his rage,   35
   That not a man should live to rue their fall.
CAPOLIN   So might your highness, had you time to sort
   Your fighting men and raise your royal host,
   But Tamburlaine by expedition
   Advantage takes of your unreadiness.   40
SOLDAN   Let him take all th'advantages he can.
   Were all the world conspired to fight for him,
   Nay, were he devil, as he is no man,
   Yet in revenge of fair Zenocrate,
   Whom he detaineth in despite of us,   45
   This arm should send him down to Erebus,
   To shroud his shame in darkness of the night.
MESSENGER   Pleaseth your mightiness to understand,
   His resolution far exceedeth all.
   The first day when he pitcheth down his tents,   50
   White is their hue, and on his silver crest
   A snowy feather, spangled white he bears,
   To signify the mildness of his mind
   That, satiate with spoil, refuseth blood;
   But when Aurora mounts the second time,   55
   As red as scarlet is his furniture;
   Then must his kindled wrath be quenched with blood,
   Not sparing any that can manage arms;
   But if these threats move not submission,
   Black are his colors, black pavilion;   60
   His spear, his shield, his horse, his armor, plumes,
   And jetty feathers menace death and hell:
   Without respect of sex, degree, or age,
   He razeth all his foes with fire and sword.
SOLDAN   Merciless villain, peasant ignorant   65
   Of lawful arms or martial discipline!
   Pillage and murder are his usual trades.

---

31 *countervail* equal. **39** *expedition* prompt action. **46** *Erebus* a region of primeval darkness between the earth and hell. **49** *resolution* unalterable determination. **56** *furniture* military array. **60** *pavilion* tent.

The slave usurps the glorious name of war.
See Capolin—the fair Arabian king,
That hath been disappointed by this slave   70
Of my fair daughter and his princely love—
May have fresh warning to go war with us,
And be revenged for her disparagement.   [*Exeunt.*]

ACT IV

Scene 2   {*Before the gates of Damascus*}

[*Enter*] TAMBURLAINE, TECHELLES, THERIDAMAS, USUMCASANE,
ZENOCRATE, ANIPPE, *two* MOORS *drawing* BAJAZETH *in his cage, and
his wife following him.*

TAMBURLAINE   Bring out my footstool.

They take BAJAZETH *out of the cage.*

BAJAZETH   Ye holy priests of heavenly Mahomet,
That, sacrificing, slice and cut your flesh,
Staining his altars with your purple blood,
Make heaven to frown and every fixèd star   5
To suck up poison from the moorish fens,
And pour it in this glorious tyrant's throat!

TAMBURLAINE   The chiefest god, first mover of that sphere
Enchased with thousands ever-shining lamps,
Will sooner burn the glorious frame of heaven   10
Than it should so conspire my overthrow.
But, villain, thou that wishest this to me,
Fall prostrate on the low, disdainful earth,
And be the footstool of great Tamburlaine,
That I may rise into my royal throne.   15

BAJAZETH   First shalt thou rip my bowels with thy sword
And sacrifice my heart to death and hell,
Before I yield to such a slavery.

TAMBURLAINE   Base villain, vassal, slave to Tamburlaine,
Unworthy to embrace or touch the ground   20

72 *warning* notice.
❧ ACT IV, Scene 2.   7 *glorious* boastful.

That bears the honor of my royal weight,
Stoop, villain, stoop! Stoop, for so he bids
That may command thee piecemeal to be torn,
Or scattered like the lofty cedar trees
Struck with the voice of thundering Jupiter.   25

BAJAZETH   Then as I look down to the damnèd fiends,
Fiends, look on me! And thou, dread god of hell,
With ebon scepter strike this hateful earth,
And make it swallow both of us at once!

[TAMBURLAINE] *gets up upon him to his chair.*

TAMBURLAINE   Now clear the triple region of the air,   30
And let the majesty of heaven behold
Their scourge and terror tread on emperors.
Smile stars that reigned at my nativity,
And dim the brightness of their neighbor lamps;
Disdain to borrow light of Cynthia,   35
For I, the chiefest lamp of all the earth,
First rising in the east with mild aspect,
But fixèd now in the meridian line,
Will send up fire to your turning spheres
And cause the sun to borrow light of you.   40
My sword struck fire from his coat of steel,
Even in Bithynia, when I took this Turk,
As when a fiery exhalation,
Wrapped in the bowels of a freezing cloud,
Fighting for passage, makes the welkin crack   45
And casts a flash of lightning to the earth.
But ere I march to wealthy Persia,
Or leave Damascus and th'Egyptian fields,
As was the fame of Clymene's brain-sick son
That almost brent the axle-tree of heaven,   50
So shall our swords, our lances, and our shot
Fill all the air with fiery meteors.
Then, when the sky shall wax as red as blood,

---

28 *ebon* ebony. **30** *triple . . . air* The air was thought to be divided into an upper, a middle, and a lower region. **38** *meridian line* the equator (i.e. the high point of his fortunes). **39** *your* the stars'. **45** *welkin* sky. **49** *Clymene's . . . son* Phaëthon, son of Clymene and Apollo, tried to drive his father's sun-chariot across the sky but was unable to control the horses, which bolted and almost burned up the earth. **50** *brent* burned. *axle-tree of heaven* the axis on which the spheres of the universe were thought to turn.

It shall be said I made it red myself,
To make me think of naught but blood and war.   55
ZABINA   Unworthy King, that by thy cruelty
    Unlawfully usurpst the Persian seat,
    Darst thou, that never saw an emperor
    Before thou met my husband in the field,
    Being thy captive, thus abuse his state,   60
    Keeping his kingly body in a cage,
    That roofs of gold and sun-bright palaces
    Should have prepared to entertain his grace?
    And treading him beneath thy loathsome feet,
    Whose feet the kings of Africa have kissed?   65
TECHELLES   You must devise some torment worse, my lord,
    To make these captives rein their lavish tongues.
TAMBURLAINE   Zenocrate, look better to your slave.
ZENOCRATE   She is my handmaid's slave, and she shall look
    That these abuses flow not from her tongue.   70
    Chide her, Anippe.
ANIPPE   Let these be warnings for you then, my slave,
    How you abuse the person of the King;
    Or else I swear to have you whipped stark naked.
BAJAZETH   Great Tamburlaine, great in my overthrow,   75
    Ambitious pride shall make thee fall as low,
    For treading on the back of Bajazeth,
    That should be horsèd on four mighty kings.
TAMBURLAINE   Thy names and titles and thy dignities
    Are fled from Bajazeth and remain with me,   80
    That will maintain it against a world of kings.
    Put him in again.

    [*They put him into the cage.*]

BAJAZETH   Is this a place for mighty Bajazeth?
    Confusion light on him that helps thee thus.
TAMBURLAINE   There, while he lives, shall Bajazeth be kept,   85
    And where I go be thus in triumph drawn;
    And thou, his wife, shalt feed him with the scraps
    My servitors shalt bring thee from my board;
    For he that gives him other food than this
    Shall sit by him and starve to death himself.   90
    This is my mind, and I will have it so.

84 *him*   probably Techelles.   *thee*   Tamburlaine.   **88** *board*   table.

Not all the kings and emperors of the earth,
If they would lay their crowns before my feet,
Shall ransom him or take him from his cage.
The ages that shall talk of Tamburlaine,   95
Even from this day to Plato's wondrous year,
Shall talk how I have handled Bajazeth.
These Moors, that drew him from Bithynia
To fair Damascus, where we now remain,
Shall lead him with us wheresoe'er we go.   100
Techelles, and my loving followers,
Now may we see Damascus' lofty towers,
Like to the shadows of Pyramidès
That with their beauties graced the Memphian fields.
The golden stature of their feathered bird,   105
That spreads her wings upon the city walls,
Shall not defend it from our battering shot.
The townsmen mask in silk and cloth of gold,
And every house is as a treasury;
The men, the treasure, and the town is ours.   110
THERIDAMAS Your tents of white now pitched before the gates,
And gentle flags of amity displayed,
I doubt not but the Governor will yield,
Offering Damascus to your majesty.
TAMBURLAINE So shall he have his life, and all the rest.   115
But if he stay until the bloody flag
Be once advanced on my vermilion tent,
He dies, and those that kept us out so long.
And when they see me march in black array,
With mournful streamers hanging down their heads,   120
Were in that city all the world contained,
Not one should 'scape, but perish by our swords.
ZENOCRATE Yet would you have some pity for my sake,
Because it is my country's and my father's.
TAMBURLAINE Not for the world, Zenocrate, if I have sworn.   125
Come, bring in the Turk.   *Exeunt.*

---

96 Plato's . . . year The hypothetical year when all irregularities in the universal
motions would be regularized so that "all the eight revolutions [of the spheres], having
their relative degrees of swiftness, are accomplished together and attain their completion
at the same time . . ." (*Timaeus,* 39d, Jowett translation). **105 stature** statue. *feathered*
bird the Ibis, sacred to the Egyptians.

ACT IV

Scene 3   {*Between Memphis and Damascus*}

[*Enter*] SOLDAN, [KING OF] ARABIA, CAPOLIN, *with streaming colors, and* SOLDIERS.

SOLDAN   Methinks we march as Meleager did,
    Environèd with brave Argolian knights,
    To chase the savage Calydonian boar,
    Or Cephalus, with lusty Theban youths,
    Against the wolf that angry Themis sent   5
    To waste and spoil the sweet Aonian fields.
    A monster of five hundred thousand heads,
    Compact of rapine, piracy, and spoil,
    The scum of men, the hate and scourge of God,
    Raves in Egyptia and annoyeth us.   10
    My lord, it is the bloody Tamburlaine,
    A sturdy felon, and a base-bred thief,
    By murder raisèd to the Persian crown,
    That dares control us in our territories.
    To tame the pride of this presumptuous beast,   15
    Join your Arabians with the Soldan's power;
    Let us unite our royal bands in one
    And hasten to remove Damascus' siege.
    It is a blemish to the majesty
    And high estate of mighty emperors,   20
    That such a base, usurping vagabond
    Should brave a king or wear a princely crown.
KING OF ARABIA   Renownèd Soldan, have ye lately heard
    The overthrow of mighty Bajazeth

🐾 **ACT IV, Scene 3.   1** *Meleager*   prince of Calydon; with a band of heroes from Argos, he killed a giant boar sent by Artemis to ravage the land.   **4** *Cephalus*   a Greek hunter who owned a spear that never missed the mark and a hound that always caught its quarry. When Cephalus and his hound joined a group of Thebans who were hunting an uncatchable wolf that was ravaging the countryside, Zeus turned both the charmed dog and the wolf into stone.   **5** *Themis*   one of Zeus' officers; also a personification of justice.   **6** *Aonia*   Boetia, a region of ancient Greece north of the Gulf of Corinth, whose capital was Thebes.   **7** *A monster . . . heads*   Tamburlaine's army.   **9** *scourge of God* The Soldan twists Tamburlaine's ambiguous phrase; for him the conqueror is not God's instrument of justice but a defamer and rebel against Him.   **12** *sturdy*   rash.   **22** *brave* defy.

About the confines of Bithynia?   25
The slavery wherewith he persecutes
The noble Turk and his great emperess?
SOLDAN   I have, and sorrow for his bad success.
But, noble lord of great Arabia,
Be so persuaded that the Soldan is   30
No more dismayed with tidings of his fall,
Than in the haven when the pilot stands
And views a stranger's ship rent in the winds
And shiverèd against a craggy rock.
Yet in compassion of his wretched state,   35
A sacred vow to heaven and him I make,
Confirming it with Ibis' holy name,
That Tamburlaine shall rue the day, the hour,
Wherein he wrought such ignominious wrong
Unto the hallowed person of a prince,   40
Or kept the fair Zenocrate so long,
As concubine, I fear, to feed his lust.
KING OF ARABIA   Let grief and fury hasten on revenge.
Let Tamburlaine for his offenses feel
Such plagues as heaven and we can pour on him.   45
I long to break my spear upon his crest
And prove the weight of his victorious arm;
For fame, I fear, hath been too prodigal
In sounding through the world his partial praise.
SOLDAN   Capolin, hast thou surveyed our powers?   50
CAPOLIN   Great Emperors of Egypt and Arabia,
The number of your hosts united is
A hundred and fifty thousand horse,
Two hundred thousand foot, brave men-at-arms,
Courageous and full of hardiness,   55
As frolic as the hunters in the chase
Of savage beasts amid the desert woods.
KING OF ARABIA   My mind presageth fortunate success,
And, Tamburlaine, my spirit doth foresee
The utter ruin of thy men and thee.   60
SOLDAN   Then rear your standards; let your sounding drums
Direct our soldiers to Damascus' walls.
Now, Tamburlaine, the mighty Soldan comes

28 *success* fortune.   **49** *partial* partisan.   **56** *frolic* enthusiastic.

And leads with him the great Arabian king
To dim thy baseness and obscurity,   65
Famous for nothing but for theft and spoil;
To raze and scatter thy inglorious crew
Of Scythians and slavish Persians.   *Exeunt.*

ACT IV

Scene 4   {*Outside the walls of Damascus*}

The banquet and to it cometh TAMBURLAINE, *all in scarlet,* [ZENOCRATE,]
THERIDAMAS, TECHELLES, USUMCASANE, *the* TURK, [*drawn in his cage,*
ZABINA,] *with others.*

TAMBURLAINE   Now hang our bloody colors by Damascus,
      Reflexing hues of blood upon their heads,
      While they walk quivering on their city walls,
      Half dead for fear before they feel my wrath.
      Then let us freely banquet and carouse   5
      Full bowls of wine unto the god of war,
      That means to fill your helmets full of gold,
      And make Damascus' spoils as rich to you
      As was to Jason Colchos' golden fleece.
      And now, Bajazeth, hast thou any stomach?   10
BAJAZETH   Ay, such a stomach, cruel Tamburlaine, as I could willingly
      feed upon thy blood-raw heart.
TAMBURLAINE   Nay, thine own is easier to come by. Pluck out that, and
      'twill serve thee and thy wife. Well, Zenocrate, Techelles, and the
      rest, fall to your victuals.   15
BAJAZETH   Fall to, and never may your meat digest!
      Ye Furies, that can mask invisible,
      Dive to the bottom of Avernus' pool,
      And in your hands bring hellish poison up,
      And squeeze it in the cup of Tamburlaine!   20

---

65 obscurity   blackness (of purpose).
✻ ACT IV, Scene 4.   **2 Reflexing**   reflecting.   **5 carouse**   drink joyously and deeply.
9 As . . . fleece   Jason was a Greek hero who sailed with fifty noble companions in the
ship Argos to Colchos in an attempt to recover the golden fleece, the inestimably valuable
magic fleece of a ram. After numerous adventures, the group succeeded in obtaining the
prize and returned it to Pelias, King of Iolcus.   **10 stomach**   appetite; also, courage.

Or, wingèd snakes of Lerna, cast your stings,
And leave your venoms in this tyrant's dish!
ZABINA   And may this banquet prove as ominous
As Progne's to th'adulterous Thracian king
That fed upon the substance of his child.   25
ZENOCRATE   My lord, how can you suffer these
Outrageous curses by these slaves of yours?
TAMBURLAINE   To let them see, divine Zenocrate,
I glory in the curses of my foes,
Having the power from the imperial heaven   30
To turn them all upon their proper heads.
TECHELLES   I pray you, give them leave, madam; this speech is a goodly
refreshing to them.
THERIDAMAS   But, if his highness would let them be fed, it would do
them more good.   35
TAMBURLAINE   Sirrah, why fall you not to? Are you so daintily brought
up, you cannot eat your own flesh?
BAJAZETH   First, legions of devils shall tear thee in pieces.
USUMCASANE   Villain, knowest thou to whom thou speakest?
TAMBURLAINE   Oh, let him alone. Here, eat, sir. Take it from my   40
sword's point, or I'll thrust it to thy heart.

[BAJAZETH] *takes [the food] and stamps upon it.*

THERIDAMAS   He stamps it under his feet, my lord.
TAMBURLAINE   Take it up, villain, and eat it, or I will make thee slice
the brawns of thy arms into carbonadoes and eat them.
USUMCASANE   Nay, 'twere better he killed his wife, and then she shall   45
be sure not to be starved, and he be provided for a month's victual
beforehand.
TAMBURLAINE   Here is my dagger. Dispatch her while she is fat, for if
she live but a while longer, she will fall into a consumption with
fretting, and then she will not be worth the eating.   50
THERIDAMAS   Dost thou think that Mahomet will suffer this?
TECHELLES   'Tis like he will, when he cannot let it.
TAMBURLAINE   Go to; fall to your meat. What, not a bit? Belike he
hath not been watered today; give him some drink.

---

21 *wingèd . . . Lerna*   The Hydra, a many-headed reptile, was reputed to live in the
marshes of Lerna, near Argos.   **23–25** *And . . . child*   Progne sought revenge on her
husband Tereus, King of Thrace, for his rape of her sister Philomela, by murdering their
child and serving it to him at a banquet.   **30** *imperial*   "Empyreal" is also implied.
31 *proper*   own.   **33** *refreshing*   refreshment.   **44** *carbonadoes*   thin strips of meat.
52 *let*   prevent.   **53** *not a bit?*   Not at all hungry?   *Belike*   probably.

They give him water to drink, and he flings it on the ground.

Fast, and welcome, sir, while hunger make you eat. How now,   55
Zenocrate, doth not the Turk and his wife make a goodly show at
a banquet?

ZENOCRATE Yes, my lord.

THERIDAMAS Methinks 'tis a great deal better than a consort of music.

TAMBURLAINE Yet music would do well to cheer up Zenocrate. Pray   60
thee, tell why art thou so sad? If thou wilt have a song, the Turk
shall strain his voice. But why is it?

ZENOCRATE My lord, to see my father's town besieged,
The country wasted, where myself was born,
How can it but afflict my very soul?   65
If any love remain in you, my lord,
Or if my love unto your majesty
May merit favor at your highness' hands,
Then raise your siege from fair Damascus' walls,
And with my father take a friendly truce.   70

TAMBURLAINE Zenocrate, were Egypt Jove's own land,
Yet would I with my sword make Jove to stoop.
I will confute those blind geographers
That make a triple region in the world,
Excluding regions which I mean to trace,   75
And with this pen reduce them to a map,
Calling the provinces, cities, and towns
After my name and thine, Zenocrate.
Here at Damascus will I make the point
That shall begin the perpendicular.   80
And wouldst thou have me buy thy father's love
With such a loss? Tell me, Zenocrate.

ZENOCRATE Honor still wait on happy Tamburlaine;
Yet give me leave to plead for him, my lord.

TAMBURLAINE Content thyself: his person shall be safe,   85
And all the friends of fair Zenocrate,
If with their lives they will be pleased to yield
Or may be forced to make me emperor;

---

55 *while* until. **59** *consort* group of musicians playing or, perhaps, a concert.
74 *triple region* In Tamburlaine's time the world was thought to comprise three
continents: Africa, Europe, and Asia. **75-76** *which ... map* which I mean to discover
and to control. **76** *this pen* his sword. **79-80** *point ... perpendicular* the place
from which all longitude is reckoned, the very center of the world he intends to conquer.
83 *still* forever. *happy* blessed by fortune.

For Egypt and Arabia must be mine.

[*To* BAJAZETH.] Feed, you slave; thou mayst think thyself happy to   90
be fed from my trencher.

BAJAZETH   My empty stomach, full of idle heat,
Draws bloody humors from my feeble parts,
Preserving life by hasting cruel death.
My veins are pale, my sinews hard and dry,   95
My joints benumbed; unless I eat, I die.

ZABINA   Eat, Bajazeth. Let us live in spite of them, looking some happy
power will pity and enlarge us.

TAMBURLAINE   Here, Turk; wilt thou have a clean trencher?

BAJAZETH   Ay, tyrant, and more meat.   100

TAMBURLAINE   Soft, sir, you must be dieted; too much eating will
make you surfeit.

THERIDAMAS   So it would, my lord, 'specially having so small a walk
and so little exercise.

Enter a second course, of crowns.

TAMBURLAINE   Theridamas, Techelles, and Casane, here are the cates   105
you desire to finger, are they not?

THERIDAMAS   Ay, my lord, but none save kings must feed with these.

TECHELLES   'Tis enough for us to see them, and for Tamburlaine only
to enjoy them.

TAMBURLAINE   Well, here is now to the Soldan of Egypt, the King of   110
Arabia, and the Governor of Damascus. Now, take these three
crowns, and pledge me, my contributory kings. I crown you here,
Theridamas, King of Argier; Techelles, King of Fez; and Usumcasane, King of Morocco. How say you to this, Turk? These are
not your contributory kings.   115

BAJAZETH   Nor shall they long be thine, I warrant them.

TAMBURLAINE   Kings of Argier, Morocco, and of Fez,
You that have marched with happy Tamburlaine
As far as from the frozen place of heaven
Unto the wat'ry morning's ruddy bower,   120
And thence by land unto the torrid zone,

---

91 *trencher* wooden platter. **92** *idle heat* excessive anger. **97** *looking* hoping.
SD *crowns* As if they were delicacies to be eaten, crowns are now brought before
Tamburlaine. **105** *cates* delicacies. **116** *warrant* warn. **119-21** *As . . . zone*
The Elizabethans thought of Scythia as a cold, snowy region; these lines imply that
Tamburlaine's lieutenants have marched with him from the north to the east and then to
the south. **120** *Unto . . . bower* to the seas of the East (principally the Black Sea).

Deserve these titles I endow you with
By valor and by magnanimity.
Your births shall be no blemish to your fame:
For virtue is the fount whence honor springs,   125
And they are worthy she investeth kings.

THERIDAMAS   And since your highness hath so well vouchsafed,
If we deserve them not with higher meeds
Than erst our states and actions have retained,
Take them away again, and make us slaves.   130

TAMBURLAINE   Well said, Theridamas. When holy Fates
Shall 'stablish me in strong Egyptia,
We mean to travel to th'antarctic pole,
Conquering the people underneath our feet,
And be renowned as never emperors were.   135
Zenocrate, I will not crown thee yet,
Until with greater honors I be graced.   [*Exeunt.*]

ACT V

Scene 1   {*Within Damascus*}

[*Enter*] *the* GOVERNOR OF DAMASCUS *with three or four* CITIZENS, *and
four* VIRGINS, *with branches of laurel in their hands.*

GOVERNOR   Still doth this man, or rather god, of war,
Batter our walls and beat our turrets down;
And to resist with longer stubbornness
Or hope of rescue from the Soldan's power,
Were but to bring our wilful overthrow,   5
And make us desp'rate of our threatened lives.
We see his tents have now been alterèd
With terrors to the last and cruel'st hue.
His coal-black colors, everywhere advanced,
Threaten our city with a general spoil.   10
And if we should with common rites of arms
Offer our safeties to his clemency,

126 *they are* those who are.   128 *meeds* merits.   129 *erst* formerly.   132 *strong*
rich, powerful.

I fear the custom proper to his sword,
Which he observes as parcel of his fame,
Intending so to terrify the world,   15
By any innovation or remorse
Will never be dispensed with till our deaths.
Therefore, for these our harmless virgins' sakes,
Whose honors and whose lives rely on him,
Let us have hope that their unspotted prayers,   20
Their blubbered cheeks, and hearty humble moans
Will melt his fury into some remorse,
And use us like a loving conqueror.
FIRST VIRGIN   If humble suits or imprecations—
Uttered with tears of wretchedness and blood   25
Shed from the heads and hearts of all our sex,
Some made your wives, and some your children—
Might have entreated your obdurate breasts
To entertain some care of our securities
Whiles only danger beat upon our walls,   30
These more-than-dangerous warrants of our death
Had never been erected as they be,
Nor you depend on such weak helps as we.
GOVERNOR   Well, lovely virgins, think our country's care,
Our love of honor, loath to be enthralled   35
To foreign powers and rough imperious yokes,
Would not with too much cowardice or fear,
Before all hope of rescue were denied,
Submit yourselves and us to servitude.
Therefore, in that your safeties and our own,   40
Your honors, liberties, and lives were weighed
In equal care and balance with our own,
Endure as we the malice of our stars,
The wrath of Tamburlaine and power of wars,
Or be the means the overweighing heavens   45
Have kept to qualify these hot extremes,
And bring us pardon in your cheerful looks.
SECOND VIRGIN   Then here, before the majesty of heaven

ACT V, Scene I. 13 *proper to* characteristic of. 14 *parcel* an important part.
16 *innovation* change of heart. 21 *blubbered* tear-stained. 23 *loving* merciful.
24 *imprecations* entreaties. 25 *blood* passionate intensity. 31 *warrants* both warnings and decrees (in the colors of Tamburlaine's regalia). 38 *rescue* by the Soldan.
40 *in that* since. 46 *qualify* moderate.

And holy patrons of Egyptia,
With knees and hearts submissive we entreat   50
Grace to our words and pity to our looks—
That this device may prove propitious,
And through the eyes and ears of Tamburlaine
Convey events of mercy to his heart.
Grant that these signs of victory we yield   55
May bind the temples of his conquering head
To hide the folded furrows of his brows,
And shadow his displeasèd countenance
With happy looks of ruth and lenity.
Leave us, my lord, and loving countrymen: 60
What simple virgins may persuade, we will.
GOVERNOR   Farewell, sweet virgins, on whose safe return
Depends our city, liberty, and lives.

Exeunt [all but the VIRGINS].

ACT V

Scene 2   {*Outside the walls of Damascus*}

[*Enter*] TAMBURLAINE, TECHELLES, THERIDAMAS, USUMCASANE, *with
others;* TAMBURLAINE *all in black, and very melancholy.*

TAMBURLAINE   What, are the turtles frayed out of their nests?
Alas, poor fools! Must you be first shall feel
The sworn destruction of Damascus?
They know my custom. Could they not as well
Have sent ye out when first my milk-white flags,   5
Through which sweet Mercy threw her gentle beams,
Reflexing them on your disdainful eyes,
As now when fury and incensèd hate
Flings slaughtering terror from my coal-black tents,
And tells for truth submission comes too late?   10
FIRST VIRGIN   Most happy King and Emperor of the earth,
Image of honor and nobility,

_____

54 *events* effects.   55 *signs of victory* the laurel branches.   59 *happy* fortunate
(for us).
⁊ ACT V, Scene 2.   1 *turtles* turtledoves.   *frayed* frightened.   10 *for truth* truly.

For whom the powers divine have made the world
And on whose throne the holy Graces sit;
In whose sweet person is comprised the sum   15
Of nature's skill and heavenly majesty,
Pity our plights! O, pity poor Damascus!
Pity old age, within whose silver hairs
Honor and reverence evermore have reigned.
Pity the marriage-bed, where many a lord,   20
In prime and glory of his loving joy,
Embraceth now with tears of ruth and blood
The jealous body of his fearful wife,
Whose cheeks and hearts, so punished with conceit
To think thy puissant never-stayèd arm   25
Will part their bodies and prevent their souls
From heavens of comfort yet their age might bear,
Now wax all pale and withered to the death,
As well for grief our ruthless governor
Have thus refused the mercy of thy hand—   30
Whose scepter angels kiss and Furies dread—
As for their liberties, their loves, or lives.
Oh, then, for these, and such as we ourselves,
For us, for infants, and for all our bloods,
That never nourished thought against thy rule,   35
Pity, O pity, sacred Emperor,
The prostrate service of this wretched town;
And take, in sign thereof, this gilded wreath,
Whereto each man of rule hath given his hand,
And wished, as worthy subjects, happy means   40
To be investers of thy royal brows
Even with the true Egyptian diadem.
TAMBURLAINE   Virgins, in vain ye labor to prevent
That which mine honor swears shall be performed.
Behold my sword: What see you at the point?   45
FIRST VIRGIN   Nothing but fear and fatal steel, my lord.
TAMBURLAINE   Your fearful minds are thick and misty then,
For there sits Death; there sits imperious Death,

---

14 *holy Graces*   three goddesses usually thought to serve some greater god; they were
associated with splendor and grace.   15 *whose*   Tamburlaine's.   23 *jealous*   jealous of
the life she fears Tamburlaine will take from them both.   24 *conceit*   imaginings.
27 *yet . . . bear*   that they might yet attain.   34 *bloods*   progeny.   37 *service*   servitude.   39 *Whereto*   to the making of which.

Keeping his circuit by the slicing edge.
But I am pleased you shall not see him there.   50
He now is seated on my horsemen's spears,
And on their points his fleshless body feeds.
Techelles, straight go charge a few of them
To charge these dames and show my servant, Death,
Sitting in scarlet on their armèd spears.   55
VIRGINS Oh, pity us!
TAMBURLAINE Away with them, I say, and show them Death.

They take them away.

I will not spare these proud Egyptians,
Nor change my martial observations
For all the wealth of Gihon's golden waves,   60
Or for the love of Venus, would she leave
The angry god of arms and lie with me.
They have refused the offer of their lives,
And know my customs are as peremptory
As wrathful planets, death or destiny.   65

Enter TECHELLES.

What, have your horsemen shown the virgins Death?
TECHELLES They have, my lord, and on Damascus' walls
Have hoisted up their slaughtered carcasses.
TAMBURLAINE A sight as baneful to their souls, I think,
As are Thessalian drugs or mithridate.   70
But go, my lords, put the rest to the sword.
                              Exeunt [all but TAMBURLAINE].
Ah, fair Zenocrate! Divine Zenocrate!
Fair is too foul an epithet for thee,
That in thy passion for thy country's love,
And fear to see thy kingly father's harm,   75
With hair disheveled wip'st thy watery cheeks;
And, like to Flora in her morning's pride,
Shaking her silver tresses in the air,
Rainst on the earth resolvèd pearl in showers,

---

49 *circuit* sphere of rule. 53 *charge* command. 56 *Virgins* The 1590 octavo reads "omnes." 59 *observations* decrees. 60 *Gihon* one of the four rivers of Eden. 61 *would she* even if she would. 62 *god of arms* Mars, Venus' paramour. 70 *Thessalian . . . mithridate* forms of poison. (Thessaly was traditionally thought of as a land of witchcraft and magicians). 77 *Flora* goddess of flowers. 79 *resolvèd pearl* tears.

And sprinklest sapphires on thy shining face,   80
Where Beauty, mother to the Muses, sits
And comments volumes with her ivory pen,
Taking instructions from thy flowing eyes;
Eyes, when that Ebena steps to heaven,
In silence of thy solemn evening's walk,   85
Making the mantle of the richest night—
The moon, the planets, and the meteors—light.
There angels in their crystal armors fight
A doubtful battle with my tempted thoughts
For Egypt's freedom and the Soldan's life: 90
His life that so consumes Zenocrate,
Whose sorrows lay more siege unto my soul
Than all my army to Damascus' walls;
And neither Persians' sovereign nor the Turk
Troubled my senses with conceit of foil   95
So much by much as doth Zenocrate.
What is beauty, saith my sufferings, then?
If all the pens that ever poets held
Had fed the feeling of their masters' thoughts,
And every sweetness that inspired their hearts,   100
Their minds, and muses on admirèd themes;
If all the heavenly quintessence they still
From their immortal flowers of poesy—
Wherein, as in a mirror, we perceive
The highest reaches of a human wit—   105
If these had made one poem's period,
And all combined in beauty's worthiness,
Yet should there hover in their restless heads
One thought, one grace, one wonder, at the least,
Which into words no virtue can digest.   110
But how unseemly is it for my sex,
My discipline of arms and chivalry,
My nature, and the terror of my name,
To harbor thoughts effeminate and faint!

---

84 *when that* that when. **Ebena** a deity of night and darkness that Marlowe may have
invented. **86–87** *Making . . . light* adding light even to the brightest nights. **88** *There*
in her eyes. **91** *consumes* preoccupies. **95** *conceit of foil* thoughts of defeat.
102 *still* distill. **106** *If . . . period* if all these had been united in one poem.

Save only that in beauty's just applause,   115
With whose instinct the soul of man is touched;
And every warrior that is rapt with love
Of fame, of valor, and of victory,
Must needs have beauty beat on his conceits.
I thus conceiving and subduing both,   120
That which hath stopped the tempest of the gods,
Even from the fiery, spangled veil of heaven,
To feel the lovely warmth of shepherds' flames
And march in cottages of strowèd weeds,
Shall give the world to note, for all my birth,   125
That virtue solely is the sum of glory,
And fashions men with true nobility.
Who's within there?

Enter two or three [ATTENDANTS].

Hath Bajazeth been fed today?
ATTENDANT   Ay, my lord.   130
TAMBURLAINE   Bring him forth. And let us know if the town be ran-
sacked.   [*Exeunt* ATTENDANTS.]

Enter TECHELLES, THERIDAMAS, USUMCASANE, *and others.*

TECHELLES   The town is ours, my lord, and fresh supply
Of conquest and of spoil is offered us.
TAMBURLAINE   That's well, Techelles. What's the news?   135
TECHELLES   The Soldan and the Arabian king together
March on us with such eager violence
As if there were no way but one with us.
TAMBURLAINE   No more there is not, I warrant thee, Techelles.

They bring in the TURK [*in his cage, and* ZABINA].

THERIDAMAS   We know the victory is ours, my lord,   140
But let us save the reverend Soldan's life

---

115 *Save . . . applause*   The rest of Tamburlaine's speech here seems to be textually
corrupt because this sentence, abruptly cut off by the interpolation of lines 117–19, is
unfinished.   119 *conceits* imaginings.   120-25 *I . . . give*   This passage, extremely
difficult and perhaps corrupt, may be paraphrased: "Thus both conceiving and subduing
beauty—which has shown the power to calm tempests ordered by the gods and to cause
these gods, even from their distant positions in the brightly starred heavens, to feel the
lovely warmth of shepherds' loves (and way of living) and, as a consequence of this
feeling, to enter in disguise a shepherd's cottage—I shall give. . . ."   125 *for . . . birth*
in spite of my humble birth.   138 *As . . . us*   as if they had no choice but to meet us
head-on.

For fair Zenocrate that so laments his state.

TAMBURLAINE   That will we chiefly see unto, Theridamas,
    For sweet Zenocrate, whose worthiness
    Deserves a conquest over every heart.   145
    And now, my footstool, if I lose the field,
    You hope of liberty and restitution.
    Here let him stay, my masters, from the tents,
    Till we have made us ready for the field.
    Pray for us, Bajazeth; we are going.   150
                            Exeunt [all but BAJAZETH *and* ZABINA].

BAJAZETH   Go, never to return with victory!
    Millions of men encompass thee about,
    And gore thy body with as many wounds!
    Sharp, forkèd arrows light upon thy horse!
    Furies from the black Cocytus lake,   155
    Break up the earth, and with their firebrands
    Enforce thee run upon the baneful pikes!
    Volleys of shot pierce through thy charmèd skin,
    And every bullet dipped in poisoned drugs!
    Or roaring cannons sever all thy joints,   160
    Making thee mount as high as eagles soar!

ZABINA   Let all the swords and lances in the field
    Stick in his breast as in their proper rooms!
    At every pore let blood come dropping forth,
    That lingering pains may massacre his heart   165
    And madness send his damnèd soul to hell!

BAJAZETH   Ah, fair Zabina, we may curse his power,
    The heavens may frown, the earth for anger quake,
    But such a star hath influence in his sword
    As rules the skies and countermands the gods   170
    More than Cimmerian Styx or Destiny.
    And then shall we in this detested guise,
    With shame, with hunger, and with horror—ay,
    Griping our bowels with retorquèd thoughts—
    And have no hope to end our ecstasies.   175

ZABINA   Then is there left no Mahomet, no God,
    No fiend, no fortune, nor no hope of end

---

148 *from* away from. **155** *Cocytus* One of the rivers of the Underworld. **163** *proper rooms* own places. **165** *massacre* mutilate. **171** *Cimmerian* black. *Styx* the main river of the Underworld. **174** *Griping* eating at. *retorquèd* frustrating, convoluted. **175** *ecstasies* deposition and exile.

To our infamous, monstrous slaveries?
Gape earth, and let the fiends infernal view
A hell as hopeless and as full of fear   180
As are the blasted banks of Erebus,
Where shaking ghosts with ever-howling groans
Hover about the ugly ferryman
To get a passage to Elysium.
Why should we live? Oh, wretches, beggars, slaves!   185
Why live we, Bajazeth, and build up nests
So high within the region of the air,
By living long in this oppression,
That all the world will see and laugh to scorn
The former triumphs of our mightiness   190
In this obscure infernal servitude?

BAJAZETH   O life, more loathsome to my vexèd thoughts
Than noisome parbreak of the Stygian snakes,
Which fills the nooks of hell with standing air,
Infecting all the ghosts with cureless griefs!   195
O dreary engines of my loathèd sight,
That sees my crown, my honor, and my name
Thrust under yoke and thralldom of a thief,
Why feed ye still on day's accursèd beams,
And sink not quite into my tortured soul?   200
You see my wife, my queen, and emperess,
Brought up and proppèd by the hand of Fame,
Queen of fifteen contributory queens,
Now thrown to rooms of black abjection,
Smeared with blots of basest drudgery,   205
And villeiness to shame, disdain, and misery.
Accursèd Bajazeth, whose words of ruth,
That would with pity cheer Zabina's heart,
And make our souls resolve in ceaseless tears,
Sharp hunger bites upon and gripes the root   210
From whence the issues of my thoughts do break.
O poor Zabina! O my Queen, my Queen!
Fetch me some water for my burning breast,

---

183 *ferryman*   Charon, who ferried the souls of the dead across the river Styx to Hades.
186–87 *build . . . air*   make our ignominy so conspicuous by nurturing high hopes of
escape.   **191** *obscure*   dark, black.   **193** *parbreak . . . snakes*   vomit of hell's serpents.
194 *standing*   stagnant.   **196** *engines*   his eyes.   **200** *quite*   both "fully" and "quiet."
206 *villeiness*   servant.   **209** *resolve*   dissolve.   **210** *gripes*   afflicts.

To cool and comfort me with longer date,
That in the shortened sequel of my life   215
I may pour forth my soul into thine arms
With words of love, whose moaning intercourse
Hath hitherto been stayed with wrath and hate
Of our expressless banned inflictions.

ZABINA Sweet Bajazeth, I will prolong thy life   220
As long as any blood or spark of breath
Can quench or cool the torments of my grief.   *She goes out.*

BAJAZETH Now, Bajazeth, abridge thy baneful days,
And beat thy brains out of thy conquered head,
Since other means are all forbidden me,   225
That may be ministers of my decay.
O highest lamp of ever-living Jove,
Accursèd day, infected with my griefs,
Hide now thy stainèd face in endless night,
And shut the windows of the lightsome heavens.   230
Let ugly Darkness with her rusty coach
Engirt with tempests, wrapped in pitchy clouds,
Smother the earth with never-fading mists,
And let her horses from their nostrils breathe
Rebellious winds and dreadful thunder claps,   235
That in this terror Tamburlaine may live,
And my pined soul, resolved in liquid air,
May still excruciate his tormented thoughts!
Then let the stony dart of senseless cold
Pierce through the center of my withered heart   240
And make a passage for my loathèd life!
                              He brains himself against the cage.

Enter ZABINA.

ZABINA What do mine eyes behold? My husband dead!
His skull all riven in twain, his brains dashed out!
The brains of Bajazeth, my lord and sovereign!
O, Bajazeth, my husband and my lord!   245
O Bajazeth! O Turk! O Emperor!
Give him his liquor? Not I. Bring milk and fire, and my blood I

---

214 *date* duration (of life). **219** *expressless* inexpressible. **banned** binding.
227 *highest lamp* the sun. **231** *rusty* because the sky is often red at sundown.
238 *still* forever.

bring him again. Tear me in pieces. Give me the sword with a ball
of wild-fire upon it. Down with him! Down with him! Go to, my
child. Away, away, away! Ah, save that infant! Save him, save   250
him! I, even I, speak to her. The sun was down—streamers white,
red, black. Here, here, here! Fling the meat in his face! Tamburlaine, Tamburlaine! Let the soldiers be buried. Hell, death,
Tamburlaine, hell! Make ready my coach, my chair, my jewels.
I come, I come, I come!   255

She runs against the cage and brains herself.

[*Enter*] ZENOCRATE *with* ANIPPE.

ZENOCRATE Wretched Zenocrate, that livest to see
Damascus' walls dyed with Egyptian blood—
Thy father's subjects and thy countrymen;
Thy streets strowed with disseuered joints of men,
And wounded bodies gasping yet for life;   260
But most accursed, to see the sun-bright troop
Of heavenly virgins and unspotted maids,
Whose looks might make the angry god of arms
To break his sword and mildly treat of love,
On horsemen's lances to be hoisted up,   265
And guiltlessly endure a cruel death.
For every fell and stout Tartarian steed,
That stamped on others with their thundering hoofs,
When all their riders charged their quivering spears,
Began to check the ground and rein themselves,   270
Gazing upon the beauty of their looks.
Ah, Tamburlaine, wert thou the cause of this,
That termst Zenocrate thy dearest love?
Whose lives were dearer to Zenocrate
Than her own life, or aught save thine own love?—   275
But see, another bloody spectacle!
Ah, wretched eyes, the enemies of my heart,
How are ye glutted with these grievous objects,
And tell my soul more tales of bleeding ruth!
See, see, Anippe, if they breathe or no.   280

248–55 Give . . . come Tormented by grief at her husband's death, which adds an
intolerable burden to the strain produced by her earlier downfall, imprisonment, and
afflictions, Zabina goes mad, and in her madness, relives the horrible events of her recent
past (not all reported in the play)—the loss of her child, the mayhem of battle, the violent
hatred and defiance she feels for Tamburlaine, and the torturing recollection of her past
glory. **269 charged** attacked with. **270 check** stamp.

ANIPPE   No breath, nor sense, nor motion in them both.
　　　Ah, madam, this their slavery hath enforced,
　　　And ruthless cruelty of Tamburlaine.
ZENOCRATE   Earth, cast up fountains from thy entrails,
　　　And wet thy cheeks for their untimely deaths.   285
　　　Shake with their weight in sign of fear and grief.
　　　Blush heaven, that gave them honor at their birth
　　　And let them die a death so barbarous.
　　　Those that are proud of fickle empery
　　　And place their chiefest good in earthly pomp,   290
　　　Behold the Turk and his great emperess!
　　　Ah, Tamburlaine my love, sweet Tamburlaine,
　　　That fights for scepters and for slippery crowns,
　　　Behold the Turk and his great emperess!
　　　Thou, that in conduct of thy happy stars,   295
　　　Sleep'st every night with conquest on thy brows,
　　　And yet wouldst shun the wavering turns of war,
　　　In fear and feeling of the like distress,
　　　Behold the Turk and his great emperess!
　　　Ah, mighty Jove and holy Mahomet,   300
　　　Pardon my love! Oh, pardon his contempt
　　　Of earthly fortune and respect of pity,
　　　And let not conquest, ruthlessly pursued,
　　　Be equally against his life incensed
　　　In this great Turk and hapless emperess!   305
　　　And pardon me that was not moved with ruth
　　　To see them live so long in misery!
　　　Ah, what may chance to thee, Zenocrate?
ANIPPE   Madam, content yourself, and be resolved.
　　　Your love hath Fortune so at his command,   310
　　　That she shall stay and turn her wheel no more,
　　　As long as life maintains his mighty arm
　　　That fights for honor to adorn your head.

　　　Enter [PHILEMUS,] *a messenger.*

ZENOCRATE   What other heavy news now brings Philemus?
PHILEMUS   Madam, your father and th'Arabian king,   315
　　　The first affecter of your excellence,

---

289 *empery* imperial rule. **297** *wavering turns* ups and downs. **298** *feeling* fore-
warning. **302** *Of . . . fortune* of changes in earthly fortune. *respect of pity* (contempt for) any respect of pity. **304–5** *incensed in* aroused to anger, as in the case of.

    Comes now, as Turnus 'gainst Aeneas did,
    Armèd with lance into the Egyptian fields,
    Ready for battle 'gainst my lord the King.
ZENOCRATE Now shame and duty, love and fear present   320
    A thousand sorrows to my martyred soul.
    Whom should I wish the fatal victory,
    When my poor pleasures are divided thus,
    And racked by duty from my cursèd heart?
    My father and my first-betrothèd love   325
    Must fight against my life and present love,
    Wherein the change I use condemns my faith
    And makes my deeds infamous through the world.
    But as the gods, to end the Trojans' toil,
    Prevented Turnus of Lavinia   330
    And fatally enriched Aeneas' love,
    So, for a final issue to my griefs,
    To pacify my country and my love,
    Must Tamburlaine by their resistless powers,
    With virtue of a gentle victory,   335
    Conclude a league of honor to my hope;
    Then, as the powers divine have pre-ordained,
    With happy safety of my father's life
    Send like defense of fair Arabia.

    They sound to the battle. And TAMBURLAINE *enjoys the victory; after,*
    ARABIA *enters wounded.*

KING OF ARABIA What cursèd power guides the murdering hands   340
    Of this infamous tyrant's soldiers,
    That no escape may save their enemies,
    Nor fortune keep themselves from victory?
    Lie down Arabia, wounded to the death,
    And let Zenocrate's fair eyes behold   345
    That, as for her thou bear'st these wretched arms,
    Even so for her thou diest in these arms,
    Leaving thy blood for witness of thy love.

---

317 *as . . . did* Turnus was Aeneas' principal enemy because the Trojan prince married Lavinia, Turnus' betrothed. **324** *racked* put on the rack. **327** *change I use* change of my allegiance (from father and first-betrothed to Tamburlaine). **329–31** *But . . . love* Although Turnus was the noblest of Lavinia's suitors in Latium, her father the King had been divinely ordered to marry her to a stranger who would come into the land. Thus when an embassy was sent to him by Aeneas, the King willingly offered his daughter's hand to the Trojan prince. **331** *fatally* by the decree of the Fates. **332** *issue* conclusion. **334** *their* the gods'. **336** *to my hope* in accordance with my hopes.

ZENOCRATE   Too dear a witness for such love, my lord.
          Behold Zenocrate, the cursed object   350
          Whose fortunes never masterèd her griefs.
          Behold her wounded in conceit for thee,
          As much as thy fair body is for me!
KING OF ARABIA   Then shall I die with full contented heart,
          Having beheld divine Zenocrate,   355
          Whose sight with joy would take away my life,
          As now it bringeth sweetness to my wound,
          If I had not been wounded as I am—
          Ah, that the deadly pangs I suffer now
          Would lend an hour's license to my tongue,   360
          To make discourse of some sweet accidents
          Have chanced thy merits in this worthless bondage,
          And that I might be privy to the state
          Of thy deserved contentment and thy love.
          But, making now a virtue of thy sight   365
          To drive all sorrow from my fainting soul,
          Since death denies me further cause of joy,
          Deprived of care, my heart with comfort dies,
          Since thy desired hand shall close mine eyes.   [*He dies.*]

          Enter TAMBURLAINE, *leading the* SOLDAN; TECHELLES, THERIDAMAS,
          USUMCASANE, *with others.*

TAMBURLAINE   Come, happy father of Zenocrate,   370
          A title higher than thy Soldan's name.
          Though my right hand have thus enthrallèd thee,
          Thy princely daughter here shall set thee free,
          She that hath calmed the fury of my sword,
          Which had ere this been bathed in streams of blood   375
          As vast and deep as Euphrates or Nile.
ZENOCRATE   O sight thrice-welcome to my joyful soul,
          To see the King my father issue safe
          From dangerous battle of my conquering love!
SOLDAN   Well met, my only dear Zenocrate,   380
          Though with the loss of Egypt and my crown.
TAMBURLAINE   'Twas I, my lord, that gat the victory,
          And therefore grieve not at your overthrow,
          Since I shall render all into your hands,

---

352 *conceit* imagination. **362 *Have . . . bondage*** which thy merits have chanced to
bring into this worthless bondage of my life (?). **370 *happy*** fortunate. **379 *of*** against.

And add more strength to your dominions   385
Than ever yet confirmed th'Egyptian crown.
The god of war resigns his room to me,
Meaning to make me general of the world.
Jove, viewing me in arms, looks pale and wan,
Fearing my power should pull him from his throne.   390
Where'er I come the Fatal Sisters sweat,
And grisly Death, by running to and fro
To do their ceaseless homage to my sword.
And here in Afric, where it seldom rains,
Since I arrived with my triumphant host,   395
Have swelling clouds, drawn from wide-gasping wounds,
Been oft resolved in bloody purple showers,
A meteor that might terrify the earth,
And make it quake at every drop it drinks.
Millions of souls sit on the banks of Styx,   400
Waiting the back-return of Charon's boat;
Hell and Elysium swarm with ghosts of men
That I have sent from sundry foughten fields
To spread my fame through hell and up to heaven—
And see, my lord, a sight of strange import,   405
Emperors and kings lie breathless at my feet.
The Turk and his great empress, as it seems,
Left to themselves while we were at the fight,
Have desperately dispatched their slavish lives;
With them Arabia too hath left his life: 410
All sights of power to grace my victory.
And such are objects fit for Tamburlaine,
Wherein, as in a mirror, may be seen
His honor, that consists in shedding blood
When men presume to manage arms with him.   415
SOLDAN   Mighty hath God and Mahomet made thy hand,
Renownèd Tamburlaine, to whom all kings
Of force must yield their crowns and emperies;
And I am pleased with this my overthrow,
If, as beseems a person of thy state,   420
Thou hast with honor used Zenocrate.

---

386 *confirmed* was commanded by. **387** *room* place or station. **392** *And . . . Death*
also governed by the verb "sweat." **398–99** *meteor . . . drinks* The lines are in appo-
sition with "sword" above. **402** *Elysium* that part of the Underworld where noble
souls live in bliss. **403** *foughten fields* battlegrounds.

TAMBURLAINE Her state and person want no pomp, you see,
    And for all blot of foul unchastity,
    I record heaven, her heavenly self is clear.
    Then let me find no further time to grace   425
    Her princely temples with the Persian crown;
    But here these kings that on my fortunes wait,
    And have been crowned for provèd worthiness
    Even by this hand that shall establish them,
    Shall now, adjoining all their hands with mine,   430
    Invest her here my queen of Persia.
    What saith the noble Soldan and Zenocrate?
SOLDAN I yield with thanks and protestations
    Of endless honor to thee for her love.
TAMBURLAINE Then doubt I not but fair Zenocrate   435
    Will soon consent to satisfy us both.
ZENOCRATE Else should I much forget myself, my lord.
THERIDAMAS Then let us set the crown upon her head,
    That long hath lingered for so high a seat.
TECHELLES My hand is ready to perform the deed,   440
    For now her marriage-time shall work us rest.
USUMCASANE And here's the crown, my lord; help set it on.
TAMBURLAINE Then sit thou down, divine Zenocrate,
    And here we crown thee queen of Persia,
    And all the kingdoms and dominions   445
    That late the power of Tamburlaine subdued.
    As Juno, when the giants were suppressed
    That darted mountains at her brother Jove,
    So looks my love, shadowing in her brows
    Triumphs and trophies for my victories;   450
    Or as Latona's daughter, bent to arms,
    Adding more courage to my conquering mind.
    To gratify thee, sweet Zenocrate,
    Egyptians, Moors, and men of Asia,
    From Barbary unto the Western Indie,   455
    Shall pay a yearly tribute to thy sire;
    And from the bounds of Afric to the banks
    Of Ganges shall his mighty arm extend.

---

422 want lack. **425 find ... time** wait no longer. **447–50 As ... victories** There is no such description of Juno in the classical accounts of Jove's war with the Titans. **451 Latona's daughter** the goddess Diana, who was a hunter, not a warrior. **bent** inclined.

And now, my lords and loving followers,
That purchased kingdoms by your martial deeds,   460
Cast off your armor, put on scarlet robes,
Mount up your royal places of estate,
Environèd with troops of noble men,
And there make laws to rule your provinces.
Hang up your weapons on Alcides' post,   465
For Tamburlaine takes truce with all the world.
Thy first-betrothèd love, Arabia,
Shall we with honor, as beseems, entomb
With this great Turk and his fair emperess.
Then, after all these solemn exequies,   470
We will our rites of marriage solemnize.   [*Exeunt.*]

---

465 *Alcides' post*   the doorpost of Hercules' temple.   470 *exequies*   funeral rites.

THE SPANISH TRAGEDY

(1589?)

Thomas Kyd

Like billboards outside a modern movie theater, this woodcut, which appeared on the title page of the 1615 edition, gives promise of the violence to be found within. Conflating different moments from II.4, the artist presents both Hieronimo's discovery of his son's body and Bel-imperia's earlier call for help. He underscores Lorenzo's malevolence by presenting him as a Moor. The Folger Shakespeare Library, Washington, D. C.

THE REPUTATION OF THOMAS KYD (1558–94) rests entirely on The Spanish Tragedy. *He apparently wrote a play dealing with Hamlet—the "Ur-Hamlet"—but no version survives. Besides* The Spanish Tragedy *his only extant works are a few pamphlets and a poor translation of a contemporary French tragedy.*

Of his life and literary career little is known. A Londoner, Kyd drifted into writing for the theater in the late 1580's and did considerable hack work, writing on any subject or in any vein that was popular. In 1593 he was arrested on suspicion of treason and atheism and was imprisoned and racked. Under torture he apparently tried to prove his innocence by stating that the seditious and atheistical pamphlets found in a search of his papers belonged to Christopher Marlowe, with whom he had once shared rooms. What effect this accusation had on Marlowe is not known.

Shortly after his release from prison, Kyd died in unknown circumstances. He was not a great poet but only a literary journeyman who managed, in a way that can only be wondered at, to write a limited masterpiece.

The date of composition of The Spanish Tragedy is not entirely certain; the first extant edition of the play appeared without date, probably in 1592, and subsequent editions were printed in 1594, 1599, and 1602. In preparing our text we have tried to follow the 1592 edition wherever possible, choosing alternative readings from later texts only when the early version seemed clearly wrong. We have italicized and included within the body of the text itself several long, interpolated passages that first appeared in the 1602 edition and may have been written by Ben Jonson.

⊰{DRAMATIS PERSONAE}⊱

GHOST OF ANDREA, *a Spanish courtier* ⎫
REVENGE ⎬ *Chorus*
⎭

KING OF SPAIN

DON CYPRIAN, DUKE OF CASTILE, *his brother*

LORENZO, *the Duke's son*

BEL-IMPERIA, *Lorenzo's sister*

VICEROY OF PORTUGAL

BALTHAZAR, *his son*

DON PEDRO, *the Viceroy's brother*

HIERONIMO, *Marshal of Spain*

ISABELLA, *his wife*

HORATIO, *their son*

SPANISH GENERAL

DEPUTY

DON BAZULTO, *an old man*

THREE CITIZENS

PORTUGUESE AMBASSADOR

ALEXANDRO ⎫ *Portuguese*
VILLUPPO ⎬ *noblemen*

TWO PORTUGUESE

PEDRINGANO, *Bel-imperia's servant*

CHRISTOPHIL, *Bel-imperia's custodian*

LORENZO'S PAGE

SERBERINE, *Balthazar's servant*

ISABELLA'S MAID

MESSENGER

HANGMAN

SOLIMAN, *Sultan of Turkey (Balthazar)* ⎫
ERASTUS, *Knight of Rhodes (Lorenzo)* ⎬ *In Hieronimo's play*
THE BASHAW *(Hieronimo)* ⎪
PERSEDA *(Bel-imperia)* ⎭

THREE KINGS *and* THREE KNIGHTS *in the first dumb show*

HYMEN *and two torchbearers in the second*

BAZARDO, *a painter* ⎫
PEDRO *and* JAQUES, *Hieronimo's servants* ⎬ *In the additions to the play*
⎭

ARMY, ROYAL SUITES, NOBLEMEN, HALBERDIERS, OFFICERS, THREE WATCHMEN, SERVANTS, ETC.

ACT I
⁌{Induction}⁍

Enter the GHOST OF ANDREA, *and with him* REVENGE.

GHOST When this eternal substance of my soul
    Did live imprisoned in my wanton flesh,
    Each in their function serving other's need,
    I was a courtier in the Spanish court.
    My name was Don Andrea; my descent,   5
    Though not ignoble, yet inferior far
    To gracious fortunes of my tender youth:
    For there in prime and pride of all my years,
    By duteous service and deserving love,
    In secret I possessed a worthy dame,   10
    Which hight sweet Bel-imperia by name.
    But in the harvest of my summer joys
    Death's winter nipped the blossoms of my bliss,
    Forcing divorce betwixt my love and me.
    For in the late conflict with Portingale   15
    My valor drew me into danger's mouth
    Till life to death made passage through my wounds.
    When I was slain, my soul descended straight
    To pass the flowing stream of Acheron;
    But churlish Charon, only boatman there,   20
    Said that, my rites of burial not performed,
    I might not sit amongst his passengers.

❧ **ACT I, Induction** In the 1592 edition of the play, act divisions are printed in Latin. **11 hight** One of the many deliberately archaic and exaggerated expressions that Kyd employs throughout the play. The archaic language, like the numerous references to classical mythology and like the technique of placing the action of the drama under the control of an all-knowing chorus, serves to distance the audience from the play. Because Kyd's art thus repeatedly calls attention to its identity as art, it demands a specific kind of critical response from its audience: they are asked to contemplate, from their position of detachment, the *meaning* of a particular event rather than—and this is the function of art that encourages emotional engagement—to share in the experiences and events that they watch. **14 divorce** separation. **15 Portingale** Portugal. **19–85 To . . . eye** This description of the Underworld is based on Book VI of the *Aeneid*. **19 Acheron** fiery river boundary of the Underworld. **20 Charon** the boatman who ferried the souls of the dead across the river to Hades.

Ere Sol had slept three nights in Thetis' lap
And slaked his smoking chariot in her flood,
By Don Horatio, our Knight Marshal's son,   25
My funerals and obsequies were done.
Then was the ferryman of hell content
To pass me over to the slimy strond
That leads to fell Avernus' ugly waves:
There, pleasing Cerberus with honeyed speech,   30
I passed the perils of the foremost porch.
Not far from hence, amidst ten thousand souls,
Sat Minos, Aeacus, and Rhadamanth;
To whom no sooner 'gan I make approach,
To crave a passport for my wand'ring ghost,   35
But Minos, in graven leaves of lottery
Drew forth the manner of my life and death.
"This knight," quoth he, "both lived and died in love,
And for his love tried fortune of the wars,
And by war's fortune lost both love and life."   40
"Why then," said Aeacus, "convey him hence,
To walk with lovers in our fields of love,
And spend the course of everlasting time
Under green myrtle trees and cypress shades."
"No, no," said Rhadamanth, "it were not well   45
With loving souls to place a martialist.
He died in war and must to martial fields,
Where wounded Hector lives in lasting pain,
And Achilles' Myrmidons do scour the plain."
Then Minos, mildest censor of the three,   50
Made this device to end the difference:
"Send him," quoth he, "to our infernal king,
To doom him as best seems his majesty."
To this effect my passport straight was drawn.
In keeping on my way to Pluto's court   55
Through dreadful shades of ever-glooming night,
I saw more sights than thousand tongues can tell,

---

23 *Thetis* sea nymph.   **28** *strond* shore.   **29** *fell* cruel, fierce.   *Avernus* a lake in
the Underworld.   **30** *Cerberus* three-headed dog who guarded the entrance to Hades.
33 *Minos . . . Rhadamanth* infallible judges of the Underworld, who won their positions
by leading just lives on earth.   **36–37** The judge draws from an urn slips on which the
events of Andrea's life are written.   **49** *Myrmidons* Achilles' soldiers.   *scour* to hurry
about.

Or pens can write, or mortal hearts can think.
Three ways there were: that on the right-hand side
Was ready way unto the 'foresaid fields,   60
Where lovers live, and bloody martialists;
But either sort contained within his bounds.
The left-hand path, declining fearfully,
Was ready downfall to the deepest hell,
Where bloody Furies shake their whips of steel,   65
And poor Ixion turns an endless wheel;
Where usurers are choked with melting gold,
And wantons are embraced with ugly snakes,
And murderers groan with never-killing wounds,
And perjured wights scalded in boiling lead,   70
And all foul sins with torments overwhelmed.
'Twixt these two ways I trod the middle path,
Which brought me to the fair Elysian green,
In midst whereof there stands a stately tower,
The walls of brass, the gates of adamant.   75
Here finding Pluto with his Proserpine,
I showed my passport, humbled on my knee;
Whereat fair Proserpine began to smile,
And begged that only she might give my doom.
Pluto was pleased and sealed it with a kiss.   80
Forthwith, Revenge, she rounded thee in th'ear,
And bade thee lead me through the Gates of Horn,
Where dreams have passage in the silent night.
No sooner had she spoke, but we were here—
I wot not how—in twinkling of an eye.   85
REVENGE   Then know, Andrea, that thou art arrived
Where thou shalt see the author of thy death,
Don Balthazar, the Prince of Portingale,
Deprived of life by Bel-imperia.
Here sit we down to see the mystery,   90
And serve for chorus in this tragedy.

---

66 Ixion in Greek mythology, a wrong-doer punished for his crimes by being bound in Hades on an ever-turning wheel.   **73 Elysian green** the place in the Underworld where those favored by the gods live in joy, after death.   **76 Proserpine** maiden of spring, who was abducted by Pluto.   **81 rounded** whispered.   **82 Gates of Horn** according to *Aeneid*, VI, one of the two Gates of Sleep. Through the Gates of Horn are sent visions which the future will prove true in the light of day.   **85 wot** know.   **90 Here . . . down** Andrea and Revenge remain on stage, perhaps on an upper balcony, during the whole play.

ACT I

Scene 1   *The Spanish court*

Enter SPANISH KING, GENERAL, CASTILE, [*and*] HIERONIMO.

KING   Now say, Lord General, how fares our camp?

GENERAL   All well, my sovereign liege, except some few
    That are deceased by fortune of the war.

KING   But what portends thy cheerful countenance,
    And posting to our presence thus in haste?   5
    Speak, man, hath fortune given us victory?

GENERAL   Victory, my liege, and that with little loss.

KING   Our Portingals will pay us tribute then?

GENERAL   Tribute and wonted homage therewithal.

KING   Then blessed be heaven and guider of the heavens,   10
    From whose fair influence such justice flows.

CASTILE   *O multum dilecte Deo, tibi militat aether,*
    Et conjuratae curvato poplite gentes
    Succumbunt: recti soror est victoria juris.

KING   Thanks to my loving brother of Castile.   15
    But, General, unfold in brief discourse
    Your form of battle and your war's success,
    That, adding all the pleasure of thy news
    Unto the height of former happiness,
    With deeper wage and greater dignity   20
    We may reward thy blissful chivalry.

GENERAL   Where Spain and Portingale do jointly knit
    Their frontiers, leaning on each other's bound,
    There met our armies in their proud array:
    Both furnished well, both full of hope and fear,   25
    Both menacing alike with daring shows,
    Both vaunting sundry colors of device,
    Both cheerly sounding trumpets, drums, and fifes,
    Both raising dreadful clamors to the sky,
    That valleys, hills, and rivers made rebound,   30
    And heaven itself was frighted with the sound.
    Our battles both were pitched in squadron form,

🔖 ACT I, Scene 1.   12–14 *O . . . juris* O one much beloved of God, for you heaven
fights, and the conspiring nations fall on bended knee: victory is the sister of just law.
20 *wage* reward.   27 *colors of device* heraldic banners.

Each corner strongly fenced with wings of shot;
But ere we joined and came to push of pike,
I brought a squadron of our readiest shot   35
From out our rearward to begin the fight:
They brought another wing t'encounter us.
Meanwhile, our ordnance played on either side,
And captains strove to have their valors tried.
Don Pedro, their chief horsemen's colonel,   40
Did with his cornet bravely make attempt
To break the order of our battle ranks;
But Don Rogero, worthy man of war,
Marched forth against him with our musketeers,
And stopped the malice of his fell approach.   45
While they maintain hot skirmish to and fro,
Both battles join, and fall to handy blows,
Their violent shot resembling th'ocean's rage,
When, roaring loud and with a swelling tide,
It beats upon the rampiers of huge rocks,   50
And gapes to swallow neighbor-bounding lands.
Now, while Bellona rageth here and there,
Thick storms of bullets rain like winter's hail,
And shivered lances dark the troubled air.
Pede pes et cuspide cuspis;   55
Arma sonant armis, vir petiturque viro.
On every side drop captains to the ground,
And soldiers, some ill-maimed, some slain outright:
Here falls a body scindred from his head,
There legs and arms lie bleeding on the grass,   60
Mingled with weapons and unboweled steeds,
That scattering overspread the purple plain.
In all this turmoil, three long hours and more,
The victory to neither part inclined,
Till Don Andrea with his brave lanciers   65
In their main battle made so great a breach,
That, half dismayed, the multitude retired;
But Balthazar, the Portingals' young prince,

---

33 *wings of shot* troops with firearms.   **34** *push of pike* hand-to-hand combat.
41 *cornet* squad of cavalry.   **47** *handy* hand-to-hand.   **50** *rampiers* fortifications.
52 *Bellona* Roman goddess of war.   **55-56** *Pede . . . viro* foot to foot and lance to
lance, arms resound against arms, and man is attacked by man.   **59** *scindred* sundered.
(Cf. Latin *scindere,* to cleave.) The 1602 text alters to "sundered."

Brought rescue and encouraged them to stay.
Here-hence the fight was eagerly renewed,   70
And in that conflict was Andrea slain—
Brave man-at-arms, but weak to Balthazar.
Yet while the Prince, insulting over him,
Breathed out proud vaunts, sounding to our reproach,
Friendship and hardy valor, joined in one,   75
Pricked forth Horatio, our Knight Marshal's son,
To challenge forth that Prince in single fight.
Not long between these twain the fight endured,
But straight the Prince was beaten from his horse
And forced to yield him prisoner to his foe.   80
When he was taken, all the rest they fled,
And our carbines pursued them to the death,
Till, Phoebus waving to the western deep,
Our trumpeters were charged to sound retreat.

KING   Thanks, good Lord General, for these good news;   85
And for some argument of more to come,
Take this and wear it for thy sovereign's sake.

Gives him his chain.

But tell me now, hast thou confirmed a peace?

GENERAL   No peace, my liege, but peace conditional,
That if with homage tribute be well paid,   90
The fury of your forces will be stayed;
And to this peace their viceroy hath subscribed,

Gives the KING *a paper.*

And made a solemn vow that during life
His tribute shall be truly paid to Spain.

KING   These words, these deeds, become thy person well.   95
But now, Knight Marshal, frolic with thy king,
For 'tis thy son that wins this battle's prize.

HIERONIMO   Long may he live to serve my sovereign liege,
And soon decay, unless he serve my liege.

A tucket afar off.

KING   Nor thou, nor he, shall die without reward.   100
What means this warning of this trumpet's sound?

---

70 Here-hence as a result of this.   **76 Pricked** rode.   **83 *waving*** settling down into the waves; also, bidding adieu. The 1602 text alters to "waning."   **SD *tucket*** a flourish of trumpets.

GENERAL   This tells me that your grace's men of war,
         Such as war's fortune hath reserved from death,
         Come marching on towards your royal seat
         To show themselves before your majesty;   105
         For so I gave in charge at my depart.
         Whereby by demonstration shall appear
         That all, except three hundred or few more,
         Are safe returned, and by their foes enriched.

         The ARMY *enters;* BALTHAZAR *between* LORENZO *and* HORATIO, *captive.*

KING   A gladsome sight! I long to see them here.   110

         They enter and pass by.

         Was that the warlike Prince of Portingale,
         That by our nephew was in triumph led?
GENERAL   It was, my liege, the Prince of Portingale.
KING   But what was he that on the other side
         Held him by th'arm as partner of the prize?   115
HIERONIMO   That was my son, my gracious sovereign;
         Of whom though from his tender infancy
         My loving thoughts did never hope but well,
         He never pleased his father's eyes till now,
         Nor filled my heart with over-cloying joys.   120
KING   Go, let them march once more about these walls,
         That, staying them, we may confer and talk
         With our brave prisoner and his double guard. [*Exit a* MESSENGER.]
         Hieronimo, it greatly pleaseth us
         That in our victory thou have a share,   125
         By virtue of thy worthy son's exploit.

         Enter [*the victorious* ARMY] *again.*

         Bring hither the young Prince of Portingale.
         The rest march on, but ere they be dismissed,
         We will bestow on every soldier
         Two ducats, and on every leader ten,   130
         That they may know our largess welcomes them.
                 Exeunt all [*the* ARMY] *but* BALTHAZAR, LORENZO *and* HORATIO.
         Welcome, Don Balthazar! Welcome, nephew!
         And thou, Horatio, thou art welcome too.
         Young Prince, although thy father's hard misdeeds,
         In keeping back the tribute that he owes,
         Deserve but evil measure at our hands,
         Yet shalt thou know that Spain is honorable.

BALTHAZAR   The trespass that my father made in peace
           Is now controlled by fortune of the wars;
           And cards once dealt, it boots not ask why so.   140
           His men are slain, a weakening to his realm;
           His colors seized, a blot unto his name;
           His son distressed, a corsive to his heart:
           These punishments may clear his late offense.
KING   Ah, Balthazar, if he observe this truce,   145
       Our peace will grow the stronger for these wars.
       Meanwhile live thou, though not in liberty,
       Yet free from bearing any servile yoke;
       For in our hearing thy deserts were great,
       And in our sight thyself art gracious.   150
BALTHAZAR   And I shall study to deserve this grace.
KING   But tell me—for their holding makes me doubt—
       To which of these twain art thou prisoner?
LORENZO   To me, my liege.
HORATIO   To me, my sovereign.
LORENZO   This hand first took his courser by the reins.   155
HORATIO   But first my lance did put him from his horse.
LORENZO   I seized his weapon and enjoyed it first.
HORATIO   But first I forced him lay his weapons down.
KING   Let go his arm, upon our privilege.

       [*They*] *let him go.*

       Say, worthy Prince, to whether didst thou yield?   160
BALTHAZAR   To him in courtesy, to this perforce.
           He spake me fair, this other gave me strokes;
           He promised life, this other threatened death;
           He wan my love, this other conquered me,
           And truth to say, I yield myself to both.   165
HIERONIMO   But that I know your grace for just and wise,
            And might seem partial in this difference,
            Enforced by nature and by law of arms,
            My tongue should plead for young Horatio's right.
            He hunted well that was a lion's death,   170

---

140 *boots* rewards. 143 *corsive* corrosive. 157 *enjoyed* possessed. 160 *whether*
which of these two. 161 *him* Lorenzo. *this* this other one (Horatio). 164 *wan*
won. 167 *And . . . partial* and because I also know that any comment from me might
seem partial.

Not he that in a garment wore his skin;
So hares may pull dead lions by the beard.
KING   Content thee, Marshal, thou shalt have no wrong;
And for thy sake thy son shall want no right.
Will both abide the censure of my doom?   175
LORENZO   I crave no better than your grace awards.
HORATIO   Nor I, although I sit beside my right.
KING   Then by my judgment, thus your strife shall end:
You both deserve, and both shall have reward.
Nephew, thou tookst his weapon and his horse: 180
His weapons and his horse are thy reward.
Horatio, thou didst force him first to yield:
His ransom therefore is thy valor's fee;
Appoint the sum, as you shall both agree.
But, nephew, thou shalt have the Prince in guard,   185
For thine estate best fitteth such a guest:
Horatio's house were small for all his train.
Yet, in regard thy substance passeth his,
And that just guerdon may befall desert,
To him we yield the armor of the Prince.   190
How likes Don Balthazar of this device?
BALTHAZAR   Right well, my liege, if this proviso were,
That Don Horatio bear us company,
Whom I admire and love for chivalry.
KING   Horatio, leave him not that loves thee so.   195
Now let us hence to see our soldiers paid,
And feast our prisoner as our friendly guest.   *Exeunt.*

ACT I

Scene 2   *Portugal: the* VICEROY's *palace*

Enter VICEROY, ALEXANDRO, VILLUPPO[, *and* ATTENDANTS].

VICEROY   Is our ambassador despatched for Spain?
ALEXANDRO   Two days, my liege, are past since his depart.
VICEROY   And tribute payment gone along with him?

175 *censure . . . doom* my judgment.   177 *sit . . . right* lose what is rightfully mine.
188 *in regard* because.   189 *guerdon* reward.   190 *him* Horatio.   191 *device* plan
((devising).

ALEXANDRO   Ay, my good lord.

VICEROY   Then rest we here awhile in our unrest,   5
    And feed our sorrows with some inward sighs,
    For deepest cares break never into tears.
    But wherefore sit I in a regal throne?
    This better fits a wretch's endless moan.

    [*Kneels.*]

    Yet this is higher than my fortunes reach,   10
    And therefore better than my state deserves,

    Falls to the ground.

    Ay, ay, this earth, image of melancholy,
    Seeks him whom fates adjudge to misery.
    Here let me lie; now am I at the lowest.
    Qui jacet in terra, non habet unde cadat.   15
    In me consumpsit vires fortuna nocendo;
    Nil superest ut jam possit obesse magis.
    Yes, Fortune may bereave me of my crown.
    Here, take it now; let Fortune do her worst,
    She will not rob me of this sable weed.   20
    O no, she envies none but pleasant things:
    Such is the folly of despiteful chance!
    Fortune is blind and sees not my deserts;
    So is she deaf and hears not my laments;
    And could she hear, yet is she willful-mad,   25
    And therefore will not pity my distress.
    Suppose that she could pity me, what then?
    What help can be expected at her hands,
    Whose foot [is] standing on a rolling stone,
    And mind more mutable than fickle winds?   30
    Why wail I, then, where's hope of no redress?
    O yes, complaining makes my grief seem less.
    My late ambition hath distained my faith;
    My breach of faith occasioned bloody wars.
    Those bloody wars have spent my treasure,   35
    And with my treasure my people's blood;

🔆 ACT I, Scene 2.   **12** *image of melancholy*   because earth's baseness seems to confirm Hieronimo's pessimistic view of the world.   **15–17** *Qui ... magis*   He who lies on the ground cannot fall further. Fortune has used up its power to do me harm. Nothing remains that is able to harm me more.   **20** *weed*   garment.   **31** *where's*   where there is.   **33** *distained*   sullied.

And with their blood, my joy and best beloved,
My best beloved, my sweet and only son.
O, wherefore went I not to war myself?
The cause was mine; I might have died for both.   40
My years were mellow, his but young and green;
My death were natural, but his was forced.
ALEXANDRO   No doubt, my liege, but still the Prince survives.
VICEROY   Survives! Ay, where?
ALEXANDRO   In Spain, a prisoner by mischance of war.   45
VICEROY   Then they have slain him for his father's fault.
ALEXANDRO   That were a breach to common law of arms.
VICEROY   They reck no laws that meditate revenge.
ALEXANDRO   His ransom's worth will stay from foul revenge.
VICEROY   No, if he lived, the news would soon be here.   50
ALEXANDRO   Nay, evil news fly faster still than good.
VICEROY   Tell me no more of news, for he is dead.
VILLUPPO   My sovereign, pardon the author of ill news,
And I'll bewray the fortune of thy son.
VICEROY   Speak on, I'll guerdon thee, whate'er it be.   55
Mine ear is ready to receive ill news;
My heart grown hard 'gainst mischief's battery.
Stand up, I say, and tell thy tale at large.
VILLUPPO   Then hear that truth which these mine eyes have seen.
When both the armies were in battle joined,   60
Don Balthazar, amidst the thickest troops,
To win renown did wondrous feats of arms.
Amongst the rest, I saw him, hand to hand,
In single fight with their lord general;
Till Alexandro, that here counterfeits   65
Under the color of a duteous friend,
Discharged his pistol at the Prince's back
As though he would have slain their general;
But therewithal Don Balthazar fell down;
And when he fell, then we began to fly.   70
But had he lived, the day had sure been ours.
ALEXANDRO   O wicked forgery! O traitorous miscreant!
VICEROY   Hold thou thy peace! But now, Villuppo, say
Where then became the carcass of my son?
VILLUPPO   I saw them drag it to the Spanish tents.   75

40 both both of us.   **48 reck** recognize.   **74 Where...became** what then became of.

VICEROY   Ay, ay, my nightly dreams have told me this.
    Thou false, unkind, unthankful, traitorous beast,
    Wherein had Balthazar offended thee,
    That thou shouldst thus betray him to our foes?
    Was't Spanish gold that bleared so thine eyes   80
    That thou couldst see no part of our deserts?
    Perchance, because thou art Terceira's lord,
    Thou hadst some hope to wear this diadem,
    If first my son and then myself were slain;
    But thy ambitious thought shall break thy neck.   85
    Ay, this was it that made thee spill his blood;

    Take the crown and put it on again.

    But I'll now wear it till thy blood be spilt.
ALEXANDRO   Vouchsafe, dread sovereign, to hear me speak.
VICEROY   Away with him! His sight is second hell.
    Keep him till we determine of his death.   [*He is led off, captive.*]   90
    If Balthazar be dead, he shall not live.
    Villuppo, follow us for thy reward.   *Exit* VICEROY.
VILLUPPO   Thus have I with an envious, forged tale
    Deceived the King, betrayed mine enemy,
    And hope for guerdon of my villany.   *Exit.*   95

ACT I
Scene 3   *The Spanish court*

Enter HORATIO *and* BEL-IMPERIA.

BEL-IMPERIA   Signior Horatio, this is the place and hour.
    Wherein I must entreat thee to relate
    The circumstance of Don Andrea's death,
    Who, living, was my garland's sweetest flower,
    And in his death hath buried my delights.   5
HORATIO   For love of him and service to yourself,
    I nill refuse this heavy doleful charge;

82 *Terceira*   an island in the Azores exploited by Portugal.
ACT I, Scene 3.   7 *nill*   will not.

Yet tears and sighs, I fear, will hinder me.
When both our armies were enjoined in fight,
Your worthy chevalier amidst the thickest,   10
For glorious cause still aiming at their fairest,
Was at the last by young Don Balthazar
Encountered hand to hand. Their fight was long,
Their hearts were great, their clamors menacing,
Their strength alike, their strokes both dangerous.   15
But wrathful Nemesis, that wicked power,
Envying at Andrea's praise and worth,
Cut short his life, to end his praise and worth.
She, she herself, disguised in armor's mask,
As Pallas was before proud Pergamus,   20
Brought in a fresh supply of halberdiers,
Which paunched his horse, and dinged him to the ground.
Then young Don Balthazar with ruthless rage,
Taking advantage of his foe's distress,
Did finish what his halberdiers begun,   25
And left not till Andrea's life was done.
Then, though too late, incensed with just remorse,
I with my band set forth against the Prince,
And brought him prisoner from his halberdiers.
BEL-IMPERIA   Would thou hadst slain him that so slew my love!   30
But then was Don Andrea's carcass lost?
HORATIO   No, that was it for which I chiefly strove,
Nor stepped I back till I recovered him.
I took him up, and wound him in mine arms,
And welding him unto my private tent,   35
There laid him down, and dewed him with my tears,
And sighed and sorrowed as became a friend.
But neither friendly sorrow, sighs, nor tears
Could win pale Death from his usurpèd right.
Yet this I did, and less I could not do: 40

10 **chevalier** horseman, knight. 11 **For . . . fairest** driven by the glorious cause (of your love) to perform the most impressive deeds in battle. 16 **Nemesis** goddess of divine retribution, who personified the gods' resentment at man's attempts to become godlike. 20 **Pergamus** Trojan citadel. The reference here is to *Aeneid*, II. 615–16: granted a vision of the gods' destruction of Troy, Aeneas sees on its highest towers Pallas Athena, resplendent in a garment of cloud, with the image of a gorgon's head on her breast. 21 **halberdiers** soldiers armed with halberds, weapons having a battleax and a pike mounted on a single long shaft. 22 **paunched** stabbed in the belly. **dinged** knocked. 35 **welding** carrying.

I saw him honored with due funeral.
This scarf I plucked from off his liveless arm,
And wear it in remembrance of my friend.
BEL-IMPERIA   I know the scarf; would he had kept it still!
   For had he lived, he would have kept it still,   45
   And worn it for his Bel-imperia's sake:
   For't was my favor at his last depart.
   But now wear thou it both for him and me;
   For after him thou hast deserved it best.
   But for thy kindness in his life and death,   50
   Be sure, while Bel-imperia's life endures,
   She will be Don Horatio's thankful friend.
HORATIO   And, madam, Don Horatio will not slack
   Humbly to serve fair Bel-imperia.
   But now if your good liking stand thereto,   55
   I'll crave your pardon to go seek the Prince;
   For so the Duke, your father, gave me charge.   *Exit.*
BEL-IMPERIA   Ay, go, Horatio, leave me here alone;
   For solitude best fits my cheerless mood.
   Yet what avails to wail Andrea's death,   60
   From whence Horatio proves my second love?
   Had he not loved Andrea as he did,
   He could not sit in Bel-imperia's thoughts.
   But how can love find harbor in my breast
   Till I revenge the death of my beloved?   65
   Yes, second love shall further my revenge!
   I'll love Horatio, my Andrea's friend,
   The more to spite the prince that wrought his end;
   And where Don Balthazar, that slew my love,
   Himself now pleads for favor at my hands,   70
   He shall, in rigor of my just disdain,
   Reap long repentance for his murd'rous deed.
   For what was't else but murd'rous cowardice,
   So many to oppress one valiant knight,
   Without respect of honor in the fight?   75
   And here he comes that murdered my delight.

   Enter LORENZO *and* BALTHAZAR.

LORENZO   Sister, what means this melancholy walk?
BEL-IMPERIA   That for a while I wish no company.
LORENZO   But here the Prince is come to visit you.
BEL-IMPERIA   That argues that he lives in liberty.   80

BALTHAZAR   No, madam, but in pleasing servitude.
BEL-IMPERIA   Your prison then, belike, is your conceit.
BALTHAZAR   Ay, by conceit my freedom is enthralled.
BEL-IMPERIA   Then with conceit enlarge yourself again.
BALTHAZAR   What, if conceit have laid my heart to gage?   85
BEL-IMPERIA   Pay that you borrowed, and recover it.
BALTHAZAR   I die if it return from whence it lies.
BEL-IMPERIA   A heartless man, and live? A miracle!
BALTHAZAR   Ay, lady, love can work such miracles.
LORENZO   Tush, tush, my lord! Let go these ambages,   90
          And in plain terms acquaint her with your love.
BEL-IMPERIA   What boots complaint, when there's no remedy?
BALTHAZAR   Yes, to your gracious self must I complain,
          In whose fair answer lies my remedy,
          On whose perfection all my thoughts attend,   95
          On whose aspect mine eyes find beauty's bower,
          In whose translucent breast my heart is lodged.
BEL-IMPERIA   Alas, my lord, these are but words of course,
          And but device to drive me from this place.

          She, in going in, lets fall her glove, which HORATIO, *coming out, takes up.*

HORATIO   Madam, your glove.   100
BEL-IMPERIA   Thanks, good Horatio; take it for thy pains.
BALTHAZAR   Signior Horatio stooped in happy time!
HORATIO   I reaped more grace than I deserved or hoped.
LORENZO   My lord, be not dismayed for what is past:
          You know that women oft are humorous.   105
          These clouds will overblow with little wind;
          Let me alone, I'll scatter them myself.
          Meanwhile, let us devise to spend the time
          In some delightful sports and reveling.
HORATIO   The King, my lords, is coming hither straight,   110
          To feast the Portingal ambassador;
          Things were in readiness before I came.
BALTHAZAR   Then here it fits us to attend the King,
          To welcome hither our ambassador
          And learn my father and my country's health.   115

---

82 belike most likely. **conceit** imagination. **84 enlarge** free. **85 to gage** as a
pledge. **90 ambages** indirect ways of speaking. **98 words of course** conventional
phrases. **99 but device** only a device. **105 humorous** subject to various whims, or
humors.

Enter the banquet, trumpets, the KING, *and* AMBASSADOR.

KING   See, Lord Ambassador, how Spain entreats
    Their prisoner Balthazar, thy Viceroy's son.
    We pleasure more in kindness than in wars.
AMBASSADOR   Sad is our king, and Portingale laments,
    Supposing that Don Balthazar is slain.   120
BALTHAZAR   So am I slain, by beauty's tyranny!
    You see, my lord, how Balthazar is slain:
    I frolic with the Duke of Castile's son,
    Wrapped every hour in pleasures of the court,
    And graced with favors of his majesty.   125
KING   Put off your greetings, till our feast be done;
    Now come and sit with us, and taste our cheer.

Sit to the banquet.

    Sit down, young Prince, you are our second guest;
    Brother, sit down; and, nephew, take your place.
    Signior Horatio, wait thou upon our cup,   130
    For well thou hast deserved to be honored.
    Now, lordings, fall to; Spain is Portugal,
    And Portugal is Spain; we both are friends;
    Tribute is paid, and we enjoy our right.
    But where is old Hieronimo, our marshal?   135
    He promised us, in honor of our guest,
    To grace our banquet with some pompous jest.

Enter HIERONIMO, *with a drum, three* KNIGHTS, *each* [*with*] *his* [*own*]
scutcheon; then he fetches three KINGS; *they take their crowns and them
captive.*

    Hieronimo, this masque contents mine eye,
    Although I sound not well the mystery.
HIERONIMO   The first armed knight, that hung his scutcheon up,   140

He takes the scutcheon and gives it to the KING.

    Was English Robert, Earl of Gloucester,
    Who, when King Stephen bore sway in Albion,

---

137 *pompous jest* impressive entertainment. **139 *mystery*** meaning. **140–67 The . . .
prisoner** At the very least, Hieronimo's accounts of the English triumphs over Portugal are
glorified. English soldiers did help to seize Lisbon in 1147, but Robert of Gloucester is
never mentioned in the historical accounts of the battle; Edmund Langley, Earl of Kent,
in 1381–82 *aided* the King of Portugal against Spain; and John of Gaunt led expeditions
to Spain in 1367 and in 1386–87, but he failed both times in his attempt to seize the
Spanish throne.

Arrived with five and twenty thousand men
In Portingale, and by success of war
Enforced the King, then but a Saracen,   145
To bear the yoke of the English monarchy.
KING   My Lord of Portingale, by this you see
That which may comfort both your king and you,
And make your late discomfort seem the less.
But say, Hieronimo, what was the next?   150
HIERONIMO   The second knight, that hung his scutcheon up,

He doth as he did before.

Was Edmund Earl of Kent in Albion,
When English Richard wore the diadem.
He came likewise, and razèd Lisbon walls,
And took the King of Portingale in fight;   155
For which, and other such-like service done,
He after was created Duke of York.
KING   This is another special argument,
That Portingale may deign to bear our yoke
When it by little England hath been yoked.   160
But now, Hieronimo, what were the last?
HIERONIMO   The third and last, not least, in our account,

Doing as before.

Was, as the rest, a valiant Englishman,
Brave John of Gaunt, the Duke of Lancaster,
As by his scutcheon plainly may appear.   165
He with a puissant army came to Spain,
And took our King of Castile prisoner.
AMBASSADOR   This is an argument for our viceroy
That Spain may not insult for her success,
Since English warriors likewise conquered Spain,   170
And made them bow their knees to Albion.
KING   Hieronimo, I drink to thee for this device,
Which hath pleased both the Ambassador and me:
Pledge me, Hieronimo, if thou love the King.

Takes the cup of HORATIO.

My lord, I fear we sit but overlong,   175
Unless our dainties were more delicate;

175–76 *we . . . delicate* The time we have taken over this meal would be justified only if
the banquet were considerably richer.

But welcome are you to the best we have.
Now let us in, that you may be despatched;
I think our council is already set.   *Exeunt omnes.*

ACT I
Chorus

ANDREA   Come we for this from depth of underground,
    To see him feast that gave me my death's wound?
    These pleasant sights are sorrow to my soul:
    Nothing but league, and love, and banqueting!
REVENGE   Be still, Andrea; ere we go from hence,   5
    I'll turn their friendship into fell despite,
    Their love to mortal hate, their day to night,
    Their hope into despair, their peace to war,
    Their joys to pain, their bliss to misery.

ACT II
Scene 1   *The* DUKE'*s castle*

Enter LORENZO *and* BALTHAZAR.

LORENZO   My lord, though Bel-imperia seem thus coy,
    Let reason hold you in your wonted joy;
    In time the savage bull sustains the yoke,

🐾 **ACT II, Scene 1.**   3–10 *In . . . wall*   These verses are based on Sonnet 47 in Thomas
Watson's *Hecatompathia,* which was entered in the Stationers' Register on March 31, 1582.
The pertinent lines of the sonnet (1–6) read:
    In time the Bull is brought to weare the yoake;
    In time all haggred Haukes will stoope the Lures;
    In time small wedge will cleaue the sturdiest Oake;
    In time the Marble weares with weakest shewres:
      More fierce is my sweete loue, more hard withall,
      Then Beast, or Birde, then Tree, or Stony wall.

In time all haggard hawks will stoop to lure,
In time small wedges cleave the hardest oak,   5
In time the flint is pierced with softest shower,
And she in time will fall from her disdain,
And rue the sufferance of your friendly pain.
BALTHAZAR   No, she is wilder, and more hard withal,
Than beast, or bird, or tree, or stony wall.   10
But wherefore blot I Bel-imperia's name?
It is my fault, not she, that merits blame.
My feature is not to content her sight;
My words are rude and work her no delight.
The lines I send her are but harsh and ill,   15
Such as do drop from Pan and Marsyas' quill.
My presents are not of sufficient cost,
And being worthless, all my labor's lost.
Yet might she love me for my valiancy:
Ay, but that's slandered by captivity.   20
Yet might she love me to content her sire:
Ay, but her reason masters his desire.
Yet might she love me as her brother's friend:
Ay, but her hopes aim at some other end.
Yet might she love me to uprear her state: 25
Ay, but perhaps she hopes some nobler mate.
Yet might she love me as her beauty's thrall:
Ay, but I fear she cannot love at all.
LORENZO   My lord, for my sake leave these ecstasies,
And doubt not but we'll find some remedy.   30
Some cause there is that lets you not be loved;
First that must needs be known, and then removed.
What, if my sister love some other knight?
BALTHAZAR   My summer's day will turn to winter's night.
LORENZO   I have already found a stratagem   35
To sound the bottom of this doubtful theme.
My lord, for once you shall be ruled by me;
Hinder me not, whate'er you hear or see.
By force or fair means will I cast about

---

4 *haggard* untamed. *stoop to lure* return to a perch for food. 16 *Pan and Marsyas*
satyrs who challenged Apollo to flute-playing contests and lost. 27 *beauty's* The 1592
edition reads "beauteous." 29 *ecstasies* literally, "being outside of oneself" (see John
Donne's *The Extasie*) and, by implication, debilitating passions. 37 *for once* in this
instance.

To find the truth of all this question out.   40
Ho, Pedringano!

PEDRINGANO   *Signior!*

LORENZO   *Vien qui presto.*

Enter PEDRINGANO.

PEDRINGANO   Hath your lordship any service to command me?

LORENZO   Ay, Pedringano, service of import;
And, not to spend the time in trifling words,
Thus stands the case: it is not long, thou knowst,   45
Since I did shield thee from my father's wrath,
For thy conveyance in Andrea's love,
For which thou wert adjudged to punishment.
I stood betwixt thee and thy punishment,
And since, thou knowst how I have favored thee.   50
Now to these favors will I add reward,
Not with fair words, but store of golden coin,
And lands and living joined with dignities,
If thou but satisfy my just demand.
Tell truth, and have me for thy lasting friend.   55

PEDRINGANO   Whate'er it be your lordship shall demand,
My bounden duty bids me tell the truth,
If case it lie in me to tell the truth.

LORENZO   Then, Pedringano, this is my demand:
Whom loves my sister Bel-imperia?   60
For she reposeth all her trust in thee.
Speak, man, and gain both friendship and reward.
I mean, whom loves she in Andrea's place?

PEDRINGANO   Alas, my lord, since Don Andrea's death,
I have no credit with her as before,   65
And therefore know not, if she love or no.

LORENZO   Nay, if thou dally, then I am thy foe,

[*Draws his sword.*]

And fear shall force what friendship cannot win.
Thy death shall bury what thy life conceals:
Thou diest for more esteeming her than me.   70

PEDRINGANO   O, stay, my lord!

LORENZO   Yet speak the truth, and I will guerdon thee,

---

41 *Vien qui presto* (Italian) Come here quickly. **47 *conveyance*** actions as a go-between. **58 *If case*** if it is the case that. **67 *dally*** act foolishly (by trying to deceive me).

And shield thee from whatever can ensue,
And will conceal whate'er proceeds from thee.
But if thou dally once again, thou diest.   75
PEDRINGANO   If madam Bel-imperia be in love—
LORENZO   What, villain! If's and and's?

[*Offers to kill him.*]

PEDRINGANO   O, stay, my lord! She loves Horatio.

BALTHAZAR *starts back.*

LORENZO   What, Don Horatio, our Knight Marshal's son?
PEDRINGANO   Even him, my lord.   80
LORENZO   Now say but how knowst thou he is her love,
And thou shalt find me kind and liberal.
Stand up, I say, and fearless tell the truth.
PEDRINGANO   She sent him letters, which myself perused,
Full-fraught with lines and arguments of love,   85
Preferring him before Prince Balthazar.
LORENZO   Swear on this cross that what thou sayst is true,
And that thou wilt conceal what thou hast told.
PEDRINGANO   I swear to both, by Him that made us all.
LORENZO   In hope thine oath is true, here's thy reward;   90

[*Gives gold.*]

But if I prove thee perjured and unjust,
This very sword whereon thou tookst thine oath
Shall be the worker of thy tragedy.
PEDRINGANO   What I have said is true, and shall—for me—
Be still concealed from Bel-imperia.   95
Besides, your honor's liberality
Deserves my duteous service, even till death.
LORENZO   Let this be all that thou shalt do for me:
Be watchful when and where these lovers meet,
And give me notice in some secret sort.   100
PEDRINGANO   I will, my lord.
LORENZO   Then shalt thou find that I am liberal.
Thou knowst that I can more advance thy state
Than she; be therefore wise, and fail me not.
Go and attend her, as thy custom is,   105
Lest absence make her think thou dost amiss.   *Exit* PEDRINGANO.

---

87 *cross* sword hilt.   **94** *for me* by me.   **100** *sort* way.

Why so, *tam armis quam ingenio:*
Where words prevail not, violence prevails;
But gold doth more than either of them both.
How likes Prince Balthazar this stratagem?   110
BALTHAZAR   Both well and ill; it makes me glad and sad:
Glad, that I know the hinderer of my love;
Sad, that I fear she hates me whom I love;
Glad, that I know on whom to be revenged;
Sad, that she'll fly me, if I take revenge.   115
Yet must I take revenge, or die myself,
For love resisted grows impatient.
I think Horatio be my destined plague:
First in his hand he brandishèd a sword,
And with that sword he fiercely wagèd war,   120
And in that war he gave me dangerous wounds,
And by those wounds he forcèd me to yield,
And by my yielding I became his slave.
Now in his mouth he carries pleasing words,
Which pleasing words do harbor sweet conceits,   125
Which sweet conceits are limed with sly deceits,
Which sly deceits smooth Bel-imperia's ears,
And through her ears dive down into her heart,
And in her heart set him where I should stand.
Thus hath he ta'en my body by his force,   130
And now by sleight would captivate my soul;
But in his fall I'll tempt the destinies,
And either lose my life, or win my love.
LORENZO   Let's go, my lord; your staying stays revenge.
Do you but follow me and gain your love: 135
Her favor must be won by his remove.   *Exeunt.*

---

107 tam . . . ingenio as much by power as by cleverness. **126 limed** trapped (a
metaphor derived from the practice of trapping birds by smearing trees with a sticky
substance called birdlime).

ACT II

Scene 2   *The* DUKE'*s castle*

Enter HORATIO *and* BEL-IMPERIA.

HORATIO   Now, madam, since by favor of your love
Our hidden smoke is turned to open flame,
And that with looks and words we feed our thought
(Two chief contents, where more cannot be had);
Thus, in the midst of love's fair blandishments,   5
Why show you sign of inward languishments?

PEDRINGANO *showeth all to the* PRINCE *and* LORENZO, *placing them in
secret.*

BEL-IMPERIA   My heart, sweet friend, is like a ship at sea:
She wisheth port, where, riding all at ease,
She may repair what stormy times have worn,
And leaning on the shore, may sing with joy   10
That pleasure follows pain, and bliss annoy.
Possession of thy love is th'only port,
Wherein my heart, with fears and hopes long tossed,
Each hour doth wish and long to make resort,
There to repair the joys that it hath lost,   15
And, sitting safe, to sing in Cupid's choir
That sweetest bliss is crown of love's desire.

BALTHAZAR [*and* LORENZO] *above.*

BALTHAZAR   O sleep, mine eyes, see not my love profaned;
Be deaf, my ears, hear not my discontent;
Die, heart; another joys what thou deservst.   20

LORENZO   Watch still, mine eyes, to see this love disjoined;
Hear still, mine ears, to hear them both lament;
Live, heart, to joy at fond Horatio's fall.

BEL-IMPERIA   Why stands Horatio speechless all this while?

HORATIO   The less I speak, the more I meditate.   25

BEL-IMPERIA   But whereon dost thou chiefly meditate?

ACT II, Scene 2.   1 *favor* indulgence. **7–17** *My . . . desire* The metaphors
Bel-imperia uses were conventional in the Elizabethan sonnet sequences of the 1590's
but were usually the stock-in-trade of the male lover; by giving them to Bel-imperia,
Kyd suggests that she is assuming the active, or male, role in this affair. **20** *joys* enjoys.
23 *fond* infatuated.

HORATIO   On dangers past, and pleasures to ensue.

BALTHAZAR   On pleasures past, and dangers to ensue.

BEL-IMPERIA   What dangers and what pleasures dost thou mean?

HORATIO   Dangers of war, and pleasures of our love.   30

LORENZO   Dangers of death, but pleasures none at all.

BEL-IMPERIA   Let dangers go, thy war shall be with me:
    But such a war as breaks no bond of peace.
    Speak thou fair words, I'll cross them with fair words;
    Send thou sweet looks, I'll meet them with sweet looks;   35
    Write loving lines, I'll answer loving lines;
    Give me a kiss, I'll countercheck thy kiss:
    Be this our warring peace, or peaceful war.

HORATIO   But, gracious madam, then appoint the field,
    Where trial of this war shall first be made.   40

BALTHAZAR   Ambitious villain, how his boldness grows!

BEL-IMPERIA   Then be thy father's pleasant bower the field,
    Where first we vowed a mutual amity:
    The court were dangerous; that place is safe.
    Our hour shall be, when Vesper 'gins to rise,   45
    That summons home distressful travelers.
    There none shall hear us but the harmless birds;
    Happily the gentle nightingale
    Shall carol us asleep, ere we be ware,
    And, singing with the prickle at her breast,   50
    Tell our delight and mirthful dalliance.
    Till then each hour will seem a year and more.

HORATIO   But, honey-sweet and honorable love,
    Return we now into your father's sight;
    Dangerous suspicion waits on our delight.   55

LORENZO   Ay, danger mixed with jealous despite
    Shall send thy soul into eternal night.   *Exeunt.*

---

45 *Vesper* the evening star.   **46** *travelers* both wanderers and laborers ("travailers").
50 *prickle* thorn (of sorrow?). The apparent contradiction in this passage may be
intentional complexity. Out of the loss of a loved one, the nightingale makes a beautiful
song and eventually finds delight in the song itself. Similarly, Bel-imperia has, out of the
loss of one lover, found a new delight—Horatio. The parallel is not exact, of course,
because delighting in a song of sorrow is not the same as delighting in love or in the
pronouncements of it, as Bel-imperia seems to be doing here. But Kyd's imagery is rarely
exact, and here, as elsewhere, he seems most concerned with the *general* expression of an
idea—in this instance, that the potential for beauty inheres even in agony.

ACT II
Scene 3   *The Spanish court*

Enter KING OF SPAIN, PORTINGALE AMBASSADOR, DON CYPRIAN, *etc.*

KING   Brother of Castile, to the Prince's love
    What says your daughter Bel-imperia?

CYPRIAN   Although she coy it, as becomes her kind,
    And yet dissemble that she loves the Prince,
    I doubt not, I, but she will stoop in time.
    And were she froward, which she will not be,   5
    Yet herein shall she follow my advice,
    Which is to love him, or forgo my love.

KING   Then, Lord Ambassador of Portingale,
    Advise thy king to make this marriage up,   10
    For strengthening of our late-confirmèd league;
    I know no better means to make us friends.
    Her dowry shall be large and liberal.
    Besides that she is daughter and half-heir
    Unto our brother here, Don Cyprian,   15
    And shall enjoy the moiety of his land,
    I'll grace her marriage with an uncle's gift,
    And this it is: in case the match go forward,
    The tribute which you pay, shall be released;
    And if by Balthazar she have a son,   20
    He shall enjoy the kingdom after us.

AMBASSADOR   I'll make the motion to my sovereign liege,
    And work it if my counsel may prevail.

KING   Do so, my lord, and if he give consent,
    I hope his presence here will honor us   25
    In celebration of the nuptial day;
    And let himself determine of the time.

AMBASSADOR   Will't please your grace command me aught beside?

KING   Commend me to the King, and so farewell.
    But where's Prince Balthazar to take his leave?   30

AMBASSADOR   That is performed already, my good lord.

KING   Amongst the rest of what you have in charge,

🐉 **ACT II, Scene 3. 3 *coy it*** appears shy. ***kind*** sex. **4 *dissemble . . . loves***
disguises her love for. **16 *moiety*** half.

The Prince's ransom must not be forgot:
That's none of mine, but his that took him prisoner;
And well his forwardness deserves reward.   35
It was Horatio, our Knight Marshal's son.
AMBASSADOR   Between us there's a price already pitched,
And shall be sent with all convenient speed.
KING   Then once again farewell, my lord.
AMBASSADOR   Farewell, my Lord of Castile and the rest.   *Exit.*   40
KING   Now, brother, you must take some little pains
To win fair Bel-imperia from her will.
Young virgins must be rulèd by their friends.
The Prince is amiable and loves her well;
If she neglect him and forgo his love,   45
She both will wrong her own estate and ours.
Therefore, whiles I do entertain the Prince
With greatest pleasure that our court affords,
Endeavor you to win your daughter's thought:
If she give back, all this will come to naught.   *Exeunt.*   50

ACT II

Scene 4   HIERONIMO's *garden*

Enter HORATIO, BEL-IMPERIA, *and* PEDRINGANO.

HORATIO   Now that the night begins with sable wings
To overcloud the brightness of the sun,
And that in darkness pleasures may be done,
Come, Bel-imperia, let us to the bower,
And there in safety pass a pleasant hour.   5
BEL-IMPERIA   I follow thee, my love, and will not back,
Although my fainting heart controls my soul.
HORATIO   Why, make you doubt of Pedringano's faith?
BEL-IMPERIA   No, he is as trusty as my second self.
Go, Pedringano, watch without the gate,   10
And let us know if any make approach.

---

37 *pitched*   settled.   **50** *give back*   give us her back (i.e. refuse).
ACT II, Scene 4.   7 *controls*   contradicts the inclinations of.

PEDRINGANO   [*Aside*]. Instead of watching, I'll deserve more gold
    By fetching Don Lorenzo to this match.   *Exit* PEDRINGANO.
HORATIO   What means thy love?
BEL-IMPERIA   I know not what myself;
    And yet my heart foretells me some mischance.   15
HORATIO   Sweet, say not so; fair fortune is our friend,
    And heavens have shut up day to pleasure us.
    The stars, thou seest, hold back their twinkling shine,
    And Luna hides herself to pleasure us.
BEL-IMPERIA   Thou hast prevailed; I'll conquer my misdoubt,   20
    And in thy love and counsel drown my fear.
    I fear no more; love now is all my thoughts.
    Why sit we not? for pleasure asketh ease.
HORATIO   The more thou sittst within these leafy bowers,
    The more will Flora deck it with her flowers.   25
BEL-IMPERIA   Ay, but if Flora spy Horatio here,
    Her jealous eye will think I sit too near.
HORATIO   Hark, madam, how the birds record by night,
    For joy that Bel-imperia sits in sight.
BEL-IMPERIA   No, Cupid counterfeits the nightingale,   30
    To frame sweet music to Horatio's tale.
HORATIO   If Cupid sing, then Venus is not far;
    Ay, thou art Venus, or some fairer star.
BEL-IMPERIA   If I be Venus, thou must needs be Mars;
    And where Mars reigneth, there must needs be wars.   35
HORATIO   Then thus begin our wars: put forth thy hand,
    That it may combat with my ruder hand.
BEL-IMPERIA   Set forth thy foot to try the push of mine.
HORATIO   But first my looks shall combat against thine.
BEL-IMPERIA   Then ward thyself: I dart this kiss at thee.   40
HORATIO   Thus I retort the dart thou threwst at me.
BEL-IMPERIA   Nay then, to gain the glory of the field,
    My twining arms shall yoke and make thee yield.

---

25 *Flora* Roman goddess of flowers.   **28 *record*** sing.   **30 *Cupid*** the Roman boy-
god of love and the son and emissary of Venus. Perhaps his most important appearance
in literature is in the first book of the *Aeneid* where, disguised as Ascanius, Aeneas' son,
he arouses Dido's love for Aeneas. It is certainly to this incident that Bel-imperia indirectly
refers in lines 30–31 when by inference she suggests her own resemblance to Dido—because
she too is victimized by Cupid in disguise and won over by the story of a hero's adventures. A variation on this theme is adumbrated by the ghost at the end of the play when
(IV.Chorus.227) he compares Bel-imperia to Dido.   **33 *fairer star*** Venus is the brightest
of the planets.   **34 *Mars*** Venus' lover.

HORATIO   Nay then, my arms are large and strong withal:
　　Thus elms by vines are compassed, till they fall.   45
BEL-IMPERIA   O, let me go; for in my troubled eyes
　　Now mayst thou read that life in passion dies.
HORATIO   O, stay a while, and I will die with thee;
　　So shalt thou yield, and yet have conquered me.
BEL-IMPERIA   Who's there, Pedringano? We are betrayed!   50

Enter LORENZO, BALTHAZAR, SERBERINE, PEDRINGANO, *disguised.*

LORENZO   My lord, away with her, take her aside.—
　　O sir, forbear; your valor is already tried.
　　Quickly despatch, my masters.

They hang him in the arbor.

HORATIO   What, will you murder me?
LORENZO   Ay, thus, and thus: these are the fruits of love.   55

They stab him.

BEL-IMPERIA   O save his life, and let me die for him!
　　O save him, brother; save him, Balthazar:
　　I loved Horatio; but he loved not me.
BALTHAZAR   But Balthazar loves Bel-imperia.
LORENZO   Although his life were still ambitious, proud,   60
　　Yet is he at the highest now he is dead.
BEL-IMPERIA   Murder! Murder! Help, Hieronimo, help!
LORENZO   Come, stop her mouth; away with her.
　　　　　Exeunt[, but they leave the body hanging in the arbor].

Enter HIERONIMO *in his shirt, etc.*

HIERONIMO   What outcries pluck me from my naked bed,
　　And chill my throbbing heart with trembling fear,   65
　　Which never danger yet could daunt before?
　　Who calls Hieronimo? Speak, here I am.
　　I did not slumber; therefore, 'twas no dream.
　　No, no, it was some woman cried for help,
　　And here within this garden did she cry,   70
　　And in this garden must I rescue her.—
　　But stay, what murd'rous spectacle is this?
　　A man hanged up, and all the murderers gone!

47–48 Now . . . thee   This exchange includes the usual Renaissance pun on the word "die"—to experience sexual orgasm.   **52 tried**   both "proven" and "uselessly employed."   **53 despatch**   carry out the murder.

And in my bower, to lay the guilt on me!
This place was made for pleasure, not for death.   75

He cuts him down.

Those garments that he wears I oft have seen—
Alas, it is Horatio, my sweet son!
O no, but he that whilom was my son!
O, was it thou that calledst me from my bed?
O speak, if any spark of life remain!   80
I am thy father. Who hath slain my son?
What savage monster, not of human kind,
Hath here been glutted with thy harmless blood,
And left thy bloody corpse dishonored here,
For me, amidst these dark and deathful shades,   85
To drown thee with an ocean of my tears?
O heavens, why made you night to cover sin?
By day this deed of darkness had not been.
O earth, why didst thou not in time devour
The vild profaner of this sacred bower?   90
O poor Horatio, what hadst thou misdone
To leese thy life, ere life was new begun?
O wicked butcher, whatsoe'er thou wert,
How could thou strangle virtue and desert?
Ay me most wretched, that have lost my joy   95
In leesing my Horatio, my sweet boy!

Enter ISABELLA.

ISABELLA   My husband's absence makes my heart to throb!—
Hieronimo!
HIERONIMO   Here, Isabella, help me to lament,
For sighs are stopped, and all my tears are spent.   100
ISABELLA   What world of grief—My son Horatio!
O, where's the author of this endless woe?
HIERONIMO   To know the author were some ease of grief,
For in revenge my heart would find relief.
ISABELLA   Then is he gone? And is my son gone too?   105
O gush out, tears, fountains and floods of tears;
Blow, sighs, and raise an everlasting storm:
For outrage fits our cursèd wretchedness.

---

78 whilom formerly.   **90 vild** vile.   **92 leese** lose.   **new begun** hardly begun.

[*Ay me, Hieronimo, sweet husband, speak!*
HIERONIMO   *He supped with us tonight, frolic and merry.*   110
     And said he would go visit Balthazar
     At the Duke's palace: there the Prince doth lodge.
     He had no custom to stay out so late.
     He may be in his chamber; some go see.
     Roderigo, ho!   115

     Enter PEDRO and JAQUES.

ISABELLA   *Ay me, he raves! Sweet Hieronimo!*
HIERONIMO   *True, all Spain takes note of it.*
     Besides, he is so generally beloved:
     His majesty the other day did grace him
     With waiting on his cup. These be favors,   120
     Which do assure me he cannot be short-lived.
ISABELLA   *Sweet Hieronimo!*
HIERONIMO   *I wonder how this fellow got his clothes?*
     Sirrah, sirrah, I'll know the truth of all.
     Jaques, run to the Duke of Castile's presently,   125
     And bid my son Horatio to come home:
     I and his mother have had strange dreams tonight.
     Do ye hear me, sir?
JAQUES   *Ay, sir.*
HIERONIMO   *Well, sir, be gone.*
     Pedro, come hither. Knowst thou who this is?
PEDRO   *Too well, sir.*   130
HIERONIMO   *Too well! Who, who is it? Peace, Isabella!*
     Nay, blush not, man.

109–62 The bracketed lines comprise the first of five sets of additions which originally appeared in the 1602 edition. The author of these additional verses is not known for certain, and different scholars have suggested different probable authors. On the basis of historical evidence, the best argument can be made for Ben Jonson, who in 1601 was paid two pounds by Philip Henslowe for "his adicions in geronymo." But in spite of this apparently incontrovertible bit of historical evidence, Jonson is not the most likely author, for at least three reasons. First, the sum Henslowe records is, by Elizabethan standards, much too great a payment for a mere three-hundred-and-some-odd lines—Henslowe usually paid only six pounds for a *complete* play. Second, John Marston seems to have parodied the fourth addition in the painter scene of his *Antonio and Mellida,* a play whose composition date is thought to be 1599, two years before Jonson received payment from Henslowe. And third, the style of the additions is not very Jonsonian. In fact, stylistically, the additions, particularly the painter scene, seem Shakespearean—though Webster and Dekker have also been suggested as possible authors. Whoever the author of these additions may be, however, one fact seems undeniable: they sometimes attain an emotional pitch beyond the reach of Thomas Kyd.   **114** *some* someone.   **123** *his* Horatio's.

PEDRO   *It is my lord Horatio.*

HIERONIMO   *Ha, ha, St. James! But this doth make me laugh,*
  That there are more deluded than myself.

PEDRO   *Deluded?*   135

HIERONIMO   *Ay! I would have sworn myself, within this hour,*
  That this had been my son Horatio:
  His garments are so like.
  Ha! Are they not great persuasions?

ISABELLA   *O, would to God it were not so!*   140

HIERONIMO   *Were not, Isabella? Dost thou dream it is?*
  Can thy soft bosom entertain a thought
  That such a black deed of mischief should be done
  On one so pure and spotless as our son?
  Away, I am ashamèd.

ISABELLA   *Dear Hieronimo,*   145
  Cast a more serious eye upon thy grief:
  Weak apprehension gives but weak belief.

HIERONIMO   *It was a man, sure, that was hanged up here:*
  A youth, as I remember; I cut him down.
  If it should prove my son now after all—   150
  Say you? say you?—Light! Lend me a taper!
  Let me look again!—O God!
  Confusion, mischief, torment, death, and hell,
  Drop all your stings at once in my cold bosom,
  That now is stiff with horror; kill me quickly!   155
  Be gracious to me, thou infective night,
  And drop this deed of murder down on me.
  Gird in my waste of grief with thy large darkness,
  And let me not survive to see the light
  May put me in the mind I had a son.   160

ISABELLA   *O sweet Horatio! O my dearest son!*

HIERONIMO   *How strangely had I lost my way to grief.*]
  Sweet, lovely rose, ill-pluckt before thy time.
  Fair, worthy son, not conquered but betrayed,
  I'll kiss thee now, for words with tears are stayed.   165

ISABELLA   And I'll close up the glasses of his sight,
  For once these eyes were only my delight.

HIERONIMO   Seest thou this handkercher besmeared with blood?
  It shall not from me, till I take revenge.
  Seest thou those wounds that yet are bleeding fresh?   170

---

160 May ... mind that may show me that.   **165 stayed** The 1592 text reads "stained."

I'll not entomb them, till I have revenged.
Then will I joy amidst my discontent;
Till then my sorrow never shall be spent.

ISABELLA   The heavens are just; murder cannot be hid.
Time is the author both of truth and right,   175
And time will bring this treachery to light.

HIERONIMO   Meanwhile, good Isabella, cease thy plaints,
Or, at the least, dissemble them awhile;
So shall we sooner find the practice out,
And learn by whom all this was brought about.   180
Come, Isabel, now let us take him up,

They take him up.

And bear him in from out this cursèd place.
I'll say his dirge; singing fits not this case.
        O aliquis mihi quas pulchrum ver educat herbas,

HIERONIMO *sets his breast unto his sword.*

        Misceat, et nostro detur medicina dolori;   185
        Aut, si qui faciunt annorum oblivia, succos
        Praebeat; ipse metam magnum quaecunque per orbem
        Gramina Sol pulchras effert in luminis oras;
        Ipse bibam quicquid meditatur saga veneni,
        Quicquid et herbarum vi caeca nenia nectit: 190
        Omnia perpetiar, lethum quoque, dum semel omnis
        Noster in extincto moriatur pectore sensus.
        Ergo tuos oculos nunquam, mea vita, videbo,
        Et tua perpetuus sepelivit lumina somnus?
        Emoriar tecum: sic, sic juvat ire sub umbras.   195
        At tamen absistam properato cedere letho,
        Ne mortem vindicta tuam tam nulla sequatur.

Here he throws it from him and bears the body away.

---

179 practice evildoing.   **184–97 O . . . sequatur** The Latin in the 1592 text is faulty
throughout and has been corrected by modern editors. This passage may be translated:
"O, let someone mix for me those herbs which beautiful spring brings forth, and let a
medicine be administered for our pain; or else let someone offer potions, if there be any,
which bring forgetfulness of years. I myself shall collect, from all over the great world,
whatever herbs the sun brings up into the bright realms of light. I also shall drink whatever poison the sorceress prepares and whatever herbs her incantation joins together by
secret power. I shall endure all things, even death, until all feeling dies, once and for all,
in my breast. Shall I never again, my life, see your eyes? And has everlasting sleep put an
end to your light? I shall die with you: so, so would it be pleasing to go to the place of
shades. But nevertheless I shall abstain from submitting to a hasty death lest there be no
revenge following your decease."

ACT II
Chorus

ANDREA   Broughtst thou me hither to increase my pain?
     I looked that Balthazar should have been slain;
     But 'tis my friend Horatio that is slain,
     And they abuse fair Bel-imperia,
     On whom I doted more than all the world,   5
     Because she loved me more than all the world.
REVENGE   Thou talkst of harvest, when the corn is green.
     The end is crown of every work well done:
     The sickle comes not, till the corn be ripe.
     Be still; and ere I lead thee from this place,   10
     I'll show thee Balthazar in heavy case.

ACT III

Scene 1   *The Portuguese court*

Enter VICEROY OF PORTINGALE, NOBLES, VILLUPPO.

VICEROY   Infortunate condition of kings,
     Seated amidst so many helpless doubts!
     First we are placed upon extremest height,
     And oft supplanted with exceeding heat,
     But ever subject to the wheel of chance: 5
     And at our highest never joy we so
     As we both doubt and dread our overthrow.
     So striveth not the waves with sundry winds
     As Fortune toileth in th'affairs of kings,
     That would be feared, yet fear to be beloved,   10

ACT II, Chorus   2 *looked*   expected.   **5** *On*   The 1592 edition reads "Or."
11 *in . . . case*   a pun, meaning both "in a burdensome situation" and "in a casket."
ACT III, Scene 1.   4 *heat*   the heat from being too near the sun (kings are "placed upon extremest height") and, metaphorically, of others' passionate jealousy (of the king's elevated position).

Sith fear or love to kings is flattery.
For instance, lordings, look upon your king,
By hate deprivèd of his dearest son,
The only hope of our successive line.

NOBLEMAN   I had not thought that Alexandro's heart   15
Had been envenomed with such extreme hate;
But now I see that words have several works,
And there's no credit in the countenance.

VILLUPPO   No; for, my lord, had you beheld the train
That feignèd love had colored in his looks,   20
When he in camp consorted Balthazar,
Far more inconstant had you thought the sun,
That hourly coasts the center of the earth,
Than Alexandro's purpose to the Prince.

VICEROY   No more, Villuppo, thou hast said enough,   25
And with thy words thou slayst our wounded thoughts.
Nor shall I longer dally with the world.
Procrastinating Alexandro's death.
Go some of you and fetch the traitor forth,
That as he is condemnèd, he may die.   30

Enter ALEXANDRO *with a* NOBLEMAN *and halberts.*

NOBLEMAN   In such extremes will nought but patience serve.

ALEXANDRO   But in extremes what patience shall I use?
Nor discontents it me to leave the world,
With whom there nothing can prevail but wrong.

NOBLEMAN   Yet hope the best.

ALEXANDRO   'Tis heaven is my hope.   35
As for the earth, it is too much infect
To yield me hope of any of her mold.

VICEROY   Why linger ye? Bring forth that daring fiend,
And let him die for his accursèd deed.

ALEXANDRO   Not that I fear the extremity of death   40
(For nobles cannot stoop to servile fear)
Do I, O King, thus discontented live.

---

11 *Sith* since.   17 *works* meanings.   19 *train* deceit.   19–22 *had . . . sun* The
confusion in this metaphor is the result of Kyd's periodic imprecision of expression. He
means to have Villuppo say, "Had you beheld the apparent love that his skill in deceit
enabled him to paint on his face, then you would have thought the sun more inconstant
than his love."   21 *consorted* accompanied as a friend.   23 *hourly coasts* hour by
hour continues its constant journey around.   SD *halberts* halberdiers.

But this, O this, torments my laboring soul:
That thus I die suspected of a sin
Whereof, as heavens have known my secret thoughts,   45
So am I free from this suggestion.
VICEROY   No more, I say! To the tortures! When?
Bind him, and burn his body in those flames

They bind him to the stake.

That shall prefigure those unquenchèd fires
Of Phlegethon, preparèd for his soul.   50
ALEXANDRO   My guiltless death will be avenged on thee,
On thee, Villuppo, that hath maliced thus,
Or for thy meed hast falsely me accused.
VILLUPPO   Nay, Alexandro, if thou menace me,
I'll lend a hand to send thee to the lake   55
Where those thy words shall perish with thy works,
Injurious traitor! Monstrous homicide!

Enter AMBASSADOR.

AMBASSADOR   Stay, hold a while,
And here—with pardon of his majesty—
Lay hands upon Villuppo.
VICEROY   Ambassador,   60
What news hath urged this sudden entrance?
AMBASSADOR   Know, sovereign lord, that Balthazar doth live.
VICEROY   What sayst thou? Liveth Balthazar our son?
AMBASSADOR   Your highness' son, Lord Balthazar, doth live;
And, well entreated in the court of Spain,   65
Humbly commends him to your majesty.
These eyes beheld; and these my followers,
With these, the letters of the King's commends,

Gives him letters.

Are happy witnesses of his highness' health.

The KING *looks on the letters, and proceeds.*

VICEROY   "Thy son doth live; your tribute is received;   70
Thy peace is made, and we are satisfied.

---

47 *When* an expression of impatience. **50** *Phlegethon* a fiery river in Hades.
52 *maliced* plotted with such malice. **53** *meed* reward. **55** *lake* the lake of fire
and brimstone in hell, where, according to the Bible, evildoers suffer eternal punishment
(see particularly Revelations 19:20 and 20:10–15). **65** *entreated* treated. **68** *commends* greetings.

The rest resolve upon as things proposed
For both our honors and thy benefit."
AMBASSADOR   These are his highness' farther articles.

He gives him more letters.

VICEROY   Accursèd wretch, to intimate these ills   75
Against the life and reputation
Of noble Alexandro! Come, my lord, unbind him.
Let him unbind thee that is bound to death,
To make a quital for thy discontent.

They unbind him.

ALEXANDRO   Dread lord, in kindness you could do no less   80
Upon report of such a damnèd fact;
But thus we see our innocence hath saved
The hopeless life which thou, Villuppo, sought
By thy suggestions to have massacred.
VICEROY   Say, false Villuppo! wherefore didst thou thus   85
Falsely betray Lord Alexandro's life?
Him whom thou knowst that no unkindness else
But even the slaughter of our dearest son
Could once have moved us to have misconceived.
ALEXANDRO   Say, treacherous Villuppo, tell the King: 90
Or wherein hath Alexandro used thee ill?
VILLUPPO   Rent with remembrance of so foul a deed,
My guilty soul submits me to thy doom;
For not for Alexandro's injuries,
But for reward and hope to be preferred,   95
Thus have I shamelessly hazarded his life.
VICEROY   Which, villain, shall be ransomed with thy death;
And not so mean a torment as we here
Devised for him who, thou saidst, slew our son,
But with the bitt'rest torments and extremes   100
That may be yet invented for thine end.

ALEXANDRO *seems to entreat.*

Entreat me not; go, take the traitor hence.
                                        Exit VILLUPPO[, *under guard*].
And, Alexandro, let us honor thee

---

72 The rest the following articles. **78 him** Villuppo. **79 To . . . quital** to pay
dearly. **80 in kindness** naturally. **88 But even** except. **91 Or wherein** or else
tell the King wherein. **98 mean** moderate.

With public notice of thy loyalty.
To end those things articulated here   105
By our great lord, the mighty King of Spain,
We with our council will deliberate.
Come, Alexandro, keep us company.   *Exeunt.*

ACT III

Scene 2   *Spain: near the* DUKE's *castle*

Enter HIERONIMO.

HIERONIMO   O eyes! no eyes, but fountains fraught with tears;
            O life! no life, but lively form of death;
            O world! no world, but mass of public wrongs,
            Confused and filled with murder and misdeeds!
            O sacred heavens! If this unhallowed deed,   5
            If this inhuman and barbarous attempt,
            If this incomparable murder thus
            Of mine, but now no more my son,
            Shall unrevealèd and unrevengèd pass,
            How should we term your dealings to be just,   10
            If you unjustly deal with those that in your justice trust?
            The night, sad secretary to my moans,
            With direful visions wake my vexèd soul,
            And with the wounds of my distressful son
            Solicit me for notice of his death.   15
            The ugly fiends do sally forth of hell,
            And frame my steps to unfrequented paths,
            And fear my heart with fierce inflamèd thoughts.
            The cloudy day my discontents records,
            Early begins to register my dreams   20
            And drive me forth to seek the murderer.
            Eyes, life, world, heavens, hell, night, and day,
            See, search, shew, send some man, some mean, that may—
            A letter falleth.

🐉 **ACT III, Scene 2.   12** *secretary*   listener.   **16** *of*   from out of.   **18** *fear*   put fear
into.

What's here? A letter? Tush, it is not so!—
A letter written to Hieronimo!   25

Red ink.

"For want of ink, receive this bloody writ.
Me hath my hapless brother hid from thee;
Revenge thyself on Balthazar and him:
For these were they that murderèd thy son.
Hieronimo, revenge Horatio's death,   30
And better fare than Bel-imperia doth."
What means this unexpected miracle?
My son slain by Lorenzo and the Prince!
What cause had they Horatio to malign?
Or what might move thee, Bel-imperia,   35
To accuse thy brother, had he been the mean?
Hieronimo, beware! Thou art betrayed;
And to entrap thy life this train is laid.
Advise thee therefore, be not credulous.
This is devisèd to endanger thee,   40
That thou, by this, Lorenzo shouldst accuse:
And he, for thy dishonor done, should draw
Thy life in question and thy name in hate.
Dear was the life of my beloved son,
And of his death behoves me be revenged;   45
Then hazard not thine own, Hieronimo,
But live t'effect thy resolution.
I, therefore, will by circumstances try
What I can gather to confirm this writ;
And, heark'ning near the Duke of Castile's house,   50
Close, if I can, with Bel-imperia,
To listen more, but nothing to bewray.

Enter PEDRINGANO.

Now, Pedringano!
PEDRINGANO   Now, Hieronimo!

26–31 *For . . . doth* In the 1592 edition this speech is assigned to Bel-imperia; it
is possible, though improbable, that she delivered it herself from off-stage. The effect
thereby achieved would be not unlike that of many contemporary melodramatic movies
when a character's disembodied voice is similarly used to reveal the contents of a letter
he has written. **34** *malign* plot maliciously against. **36** *mean* agent of death.
38 *train* trap. **48** *by circumstances* by paying careful attention to circumstances.
51 *Close* meet inconspicuously. **52** *bewray* divulge.

HIERONIMO   Where's thy lady?
PEDRINGANO   I know not; here's my lord.

Enter LORENZO.

LORENZO   How now, who's this? Hieronimo?
HIERONIMO   My lord.   55
PEDRINGANO   He asketh for my lady Bel-imperia.
LORENZO   What to do, Hieronimo? The Duke my father hath
   Upon some disgrace awhile removed her hence;
   But if it be aught I may inform her of,
   Tell me, Hieronimo, and I'll let her know it.   60
HIERONIMO   Nay, nay, my lord, I thank you; it shall not need.
   I had a suit unto her, but too late,
   And her disgrace makes me unfortunate.
LORENZO   Why so, Hieronimo? Use me.
HIERONIMO   O no, my lord, I dare not; it must not be.   65
   I humbly thank your lordship.
[HIERONIMO   *Who? You, my lord?*
   I reserve your favor for a greater honor;
   This is a very toy, my lord, a toy.
LORENZO   *All's one, Hieronimo, acquaint me with it.*
HIERONIMO   *I' faith, my lord, it is an idle thing,*   70
   I must confess: I ha' been too slack, too tardy,
   Too remiss unto your honor.
LORENZO   *How now, Hieronimo?*
HIERONIMO   *In troth, my lord, it is a thing of nothing:*
   The murder of a son, or so—
   A thing of nothing, my lord!]
LORENZO   Why then, farewell.   75
HIERONIMO   My grief no heart, my thoughts no tongue can tell.
                                        Exit.
LORENZO   Come hither, Pedringano, seest thou this?
PEDRINGANO   My lord, I see it, and suspect it too.
LORENZO   This is that damnèd villain Serberine
   That hath, I fear, revealed Horatio's death.   80
PEDRINGANO   My lord, he could not; 'twas so lately done.
   And since, he hath not left my company.

---

62 *suit* request. **64 *Use me*** make use of me to answer your request. **66–75 *Who
. . . lord*** The second addition would replace lines 65–66. **68 *toy*** something of small
consequence. **69 *All's one*** just the same. **79 *Serberine*** Balthazar's servant.

LORENZO   Admit he have not, his condition's such,
   As fear or flattering words may make him false.
   I know his humor, and therewith repent   85
   That e'er I used him in this enterprise.
   But, Pedringano, to prevent the worst,
   And 'cause I know thee secret as my soul,
   Here, for thy further satisfaction, take thou this,

   Gives him more gold.

   And hearken to me; thus it is devised: 90
   This night thou must (and, prithee, so resolve),
   Meet Serberine at Saint Luigi's Park—
   Thou knowst 'tis here hard by behind the house—
   There take thy stand, and see thou strike him sure,
   For die he must, if we do mean to live.   95
PEDRINGANO   But how shall Serberine be there, my lord?
LORENZO   Let me alone; I'll send to him to meet
   The Prince and me, where thou must do this deed.
PEDRINGANO   It shall be done, my lord; it shall be done.
   And I'll go arm myself to meet him there.   100
LORENZO   When things shall alter, as I hope they will,
   Then shalt thou mount for this. Thou knowst my mind.
                                  Exit PEDRINGANO.

   Che le Ieron!

   Enter PAGE.

PAGE   My lord?
LORENZO   Go, sirrah, to Serberine,
   And bid him forthwith meet the Prince and me
   At Saint Luigi's Park, behind the house—   105
   This evening, boy!
PAGE   I go, my lord.
LORENZO   But, sirrah, let the hour be eight o'clock.
   Bid him not fail.
PAGE   I fly, my lord.   *Exit.*
LORENZO   Now to confirm the complot thou hast cast
   Of all these practices, I'll spread the watch,   110
   Upon precise commandment from the King,

---

83 *Admit* even admitting. **102** *mount* Lorenzo purposely uses a word that is ambiguous, meaning either "you will be promoted" or "you will be hanged." **103** *Che le Ieron* gibberish; perhaps a corruption of the page's name. **109** *complot* conspiracy.
110 *practices* schemes.

Strongly to guard the place where Pedringano
This night shall murder hapless Serberine.
Thus must we work that will avoid distrust;
Thus must we practice to prevent mishap,   115
And thus one ill another must expulse.
This sly enquiry of Hieronimo
For Bel-imperia breeds suspicion,
And this suspicion bodes a further ill.
As for myself, I know my secret fault,   120
And so do they; but I have dealt for them.
They that for coin their souls endangerèd,
To save my life, for coin shall venture theirs;
And better it's that base companions die
Than by their life to hazard our good haps.   125
Nor shall they live, for me to fear their faith:
I'll trust myself, myself shall be my friend;
For die they shall—
Slaves are ordainèd to no other end.   *Exit.*

ACT III

Scene 3   *Saint Luigi's Park*

Enter PEDRINGANO, *with a pistol.*

PEDRINGANO   Now, Pedringano, bid thy pistol hold,
And hold on, Fortune! Once more favor me;
Give but success to mine attempting spirit,
And let me shift for taking of mine aim.
Here is the gold: this is the gold proposed;   5
It is no dream that I adventure for,
But Pedringano is possessed thereof.
And he that would not strain his conscience
For him that thus his liberal purse hath stretched,
Unworthy such a favor, may he fail,   10
And, wishing, want when such as I prevail.
As for the fear of apprehension,

🎋 **ACT III, Scene 3.** 4 *And . . . aim* and I will handle the task of aiming the pistol
myself.

I know, if need should be, my noble lord
Will stand between me and ensuing harms.
Besides, this place is free from all suspect.   15
Here, therefore, will I stay and take my stand.

Enter the WATCH.

FIRST WATCH   I wonder much to what intent it is
That we are thus expressly charged to watch.
SECOND WATCH   'Tis by commandment in the King's own name.
THIRD WATCH   But we were never wont to watch and ward   20
So near the Duke his brother's house before.
SECOND WATCH   Content yourself, stand close, there's somewhat in't.

Enter SERBERINE.

SERBERINE   Here, Serberine, attend and stay thy pace;
For here did Don Lorenzo's page appoint
That thou by his command shouldst meet with him.   25
How fit a place—if one were so disposed—
Methinks this corner is to close with one.
PEDRINGANO   Here comes the bird that I must seize upon.
Now, Pedringano, or never! Play the man!
SERBERINE   I wonder that his lordship stays so long,   30
Or wherefore should he send for me so late?
PEDRINGANO   For this, Serberine! And thou shalt ha't.

Shoots the dag.

So, there he lies; my promise is performed.

The WATCH.

FIRST WATCH   Hark, gentlemen, this is a pistol shot.
SECOND WATCH   And here's one slain; stay the murderer.   35
PEDRINGANO   Now by the sorrows of the souls in hell,

He strives with the WATCH.

Who first lays hand on me, I'll be his priest.
THIRD WATCH   Sirrah, confess, and therein play the priest,
Why has thou thus unkindly killed the man?
PEDRINGANO   Why? Because he walked abroad so late.   40
THIRD WATCH   Come, sir, you had been better kept your bed,
Than have committed this misdeed so late.
SECOND WATCH   Come, to the Marshal's with the murderer!

---

27 *close with* close in upon.   **SD** *dag* pistol.   **37** *be his priest* serve him at the moment of death (i.e. kill him).

FIRST WATCH   On to Hieronimo's! Help me here
 To bring the murdered body with us too.   45
PEDRINGANO   Hieronimo? Carry me before whom you will.
 Whate'er he be, I'll answer him and you.
 And do your worst, for I defy you all.   *Exeunt.*

ACT III
Scene 4   *The* DUKE'*s castle*

Enter LORENZO *and* BALTHAZAR.

BALTHAZAR   How now, my lord, what makes you rise so soon?
LORENZO   Fear of preventing our mishaps too late.
BALTHAZAR   What mischief is it that we not mistrust?
LORENZO   Our greatest ills we least mistrust, my lord,
 And inexpected harms do hurt us most.   5
BALTHAZAR   Why, tell me, Don Lorenzo, tell me, man,
 If aught concerns our honor and your own.
LORENZO   Nor you nor me, my lord, but both in one;
 For I suspect—and the presumption's great—
 That by those base confederates in our fault,   10
 Touching the death of Don Horatio,
 We are betrayed to old Hieronimo.
BALTHAZAR   Betrayed, Lorenzo? Tush, it cannot be.
LORENZO   A guilty conscience, urgèd with the thought
 Of former evils, easily cannot err.   15
 I am persuaded—and dissuade me not—
 That all's revealèd to Hieronimo.
 And therefore know that I have cast it thus—

Enter PAGE.

 But here's the page. How now? What news with thee?
PAGE   My lord, Serberine is slain.   20
BALTHAZAR   Who? Serberine, my man?
PAGE   Your highness' man, my lord.
LORENZO   Speak, page, who murdered him?
PAGE   He that is apprehended for the fact.
LORENZO   Who?   25

🦌 ACT III, Scene 4.   10 *fault*   villainy.   24 *fact*   deed.

PAGE   Pedringano.

BALTHAZAR   Is Serberine slain, that loved his lord so well?
Injurious villain, murderer of his friend!

LORENZO   Hath Pedringano murdered Serberine?
My lord, let me entreat you to take the pains   30
To exasperate and hasten his revenge
With your complaints unto my lord the King.
This their dissension breeds a greater doubt.

BALTHAZAR   Assure thee, Don Lorenzo, he shall die,
Or else his highness hardly shall deny.   35
Meanwhile I'll haste the marshal-sessions,
For die he shall for this his damnèd deed.   *Exit* BALTHAZAR.

LORENZO   Why so, this fits our former policy,
And thus experience bids the wise to deal.
I lay the plot; he prosecutes the point.   40
I set the trap; he breaks the worthless twigs
And sees not that wherewith the bird was limed.
Thus hopeful men, that mean to hold their own,
Must look like fowlers to their dearest friends.
He runs to kill whom I have holp to catch,   45
And no man knows it was my reaching fatch.
'Tis hard to trust unto a multitude,
Or any one, in mine opinion,
When men themselves their secrets will reveal.

Enter a MESSENGER *with a letter.*

Boy!   50

PAGE   My lord.

LORENZO   What's he?

MESSENGER   I have a letter to your lordship.

LORENZO   From whence?

MESSENGER   From Pedringano that's imprisoned.

LORENZO   So he is in prison then?

MESSENGER   Ay, my good lord.

---

31 *exasperate* make severe. **35** *hardly . . . deny* shall refuse me only with great
difficulty. **36** *marshal-sessions* trial. **42** *limed* caught. **44** *fowlers* Lorenzo implies that in order to succeed in the world men must resort to deception like the hunters
of fowl, who catch their prey with harmless-looking sticky lime. But, like most of
Lorenzo's statements, this one is ambiguous: punning on "fowlers," he suggests that men
do not hesitate to double-cross, and thus become "foulers" to "their dearest friends."
46 *reaching fatch* carefully planned stratagem. **47–49** *'Tis . . . reveal* Lorenzo's
excuse for more villainy. He plans to eliminate his fellow conspirators so that they will
not tell what they know about him ("their secrets").

LORENZO   What would he with us?—He writes us here,   55
        To stand good lord and help him in distress.
        Tell him I have his letters, know his mind;
        And what we may, let him assure him of.
        Fellow, begone; my boy shall follow thee.   *Exit* MESSENGER.
        This works like wax; yet once more try thy wits.   60
        Boy, go, convey this purse to Pedringano;
        Thou knowst the prison; closely give it him,
        And be advised that none be there about.
        Bid him be merry still, but secret;
        And though the marshal-sessions be today,   65
        Bid him not doubt of his delivery.
        Tell him his pardon is already signed,
        And thereon bid him boldly be resolved:
        For, were he ready to be turnèd off—
        As 'tis my will the uttermost be tried—   70
        Thou with his pardon shalt attend him still.
        Show him this box; tell him his pardon's in't.
        But open't not, and if thou lovst thy life,
        But let him wisely keep his hopes unknown:
        He shall not want while Don Lorenzo lives.   75
        Away!
PAGE   I go, my lord, I run.
LORENZO   But, sirrah, see that this be cleanly done.   *Exit* PAGE.
        Now stands our fortune on a tickle point,
        And now or never ends Lorenzo's doubts.
        One only thing is uneffected yet,   80
        And that's to see the executioner.
        But to what end? I list not trust the air
        With utterance of our pretense therein,
        For fear the privy whisp'ring of the wind
        Convey our words amongst unfriendly ears,   85
        That lie too open to advantages.
        E quel che voglio io, nessun lo sa;
        Intendo io: quel mi basterà.   *Exit.*

---

60 This . . . wax This plan takes shape easily. **62 closely** secretly. **69 turnèd off**
hanged. **70 As . . . tried** since I have resolved to exert my influence to its utmost.
(Lorenzo is characteristically ambiguous.) **73 and if** if. **77 cleanly** cleverly.
78 tickle precarious. **82 list** dare. **83 pretense** intention. **87–88 E . . . basterà**
(Italian) And what I want, no one knows; I understand: that is enough for me.

ACT III
Scene 5   *A street*

Enter BOY *with the box.*

BOY My master hath forbidden me to look in this box, and by my
troth 'tis likely, if he had not warned me, I should not have had
so much idle time; for we men's-kind in our minority are like
women in their uncertainty: that they are most forbidden, they
will soonest attempt; so I now. [*He opens the box.*] By my bare   5
honesty, here's nothing but the bare empty box! Were it not sin
against secrecy, I would say it were a piece of gentlemanlike
knavery. I must go to Pedringano, and tell him his pardon is in
this box; nay, I would have sworn it, had I not seen the contrary.
I cannot choose but smile to think how the villain will flout the   10
gallows, scorn the audience, and descant on the hangman, and all
presuming of his pardon from hence. Will't not be an odd jest for
me to stand and grace every jest he makes, pointing my finger at
this box, as who would say, "Mock on, here's thy warrant." Is't
not a scurvy jest that a man should jest himself to death? Alas!   15
poor Pedringano, I am in a sort sorry for thee; but if I should be
hanged with thee, I cannot weep.   *Exit.*

ACT III
Scene 6   *The Court of Justice*

Enter HIERONIMO *and the* DEPUTY.

HIERONIMO   Thus must we toil in other men's extremes,
That know not how to remedy our own;
And do them justice, when unjustly we,
For all our wrongs, can compass no redress.
But shall I never live to see the day,   5
That I may come, by justice of the heavens,
To know the cause that may my cares allay?

🦜 **ACT III, Scene 5.   11** *descant*   comment.   **16-17** *but . . . thee*   but because I
might be hanged with thee if I showed this sorrow (and gave away Lorenzo's villainy).

This toils my body, this consumeth age:
That only I to all men just must be,
And neither gods nor men be just to me.   10
DEPUTY   Worthy Hieronimo, your office asks
A care to punish such as do transgress.
HIERONIMO   So is't my duty to regard his death
Who, when he lived, deserved my dearest blood.
But come: for that we came for, let's begin,   15
For here lies that which bids me to be gone.

Enter OFFICERS, BOY, *and* PEDRINGANO, *with a letter in his hand, bound.*

DEPUTY   Bring forth the prisoner, for the court is set.
PEDRINGANO   Gramercy, boy, but it was time to come;
For I had written to my lord anew
A nearer matter that concerneth him,   20
For fear his lordship had forgotten me.
But sith he hath rememb'red me so well—
Come, come, come on, when shall we to this gear?
HIERONIMO   Stand forth, thou monster, murderer of men,
And here, for satisfaction of the world,   25
Confess thy folly and repent thy fault;
For there's thy place of execution.
PEDRINGANO   This is short work. Well, to your marshalship
First I confess—nor fear I death therefore—
I am the man: 'twas I slew Serberine.   30
But, sir, then you think this shall be the place,
Where we shall satisfy you for this gear?
DEPUTY   Ay, Pedringano.
PEDRINGANO   Now I think not so.
HIERONIMO   Peace, impudent; for thou shalt find it so:
For blood with blood shall, while I sit as judge,   35
Be satisfied, and the law discharged.
And though myself cannot receive the like,
Yet will I see that others have their right.
Despatch; the fault's approvèd and confessed,
And by our law he is condemned to die.   40
[*Enter* HANGMAN.]
HANGMAN   Come on, sir, are you ready?

🎋 **ACT III, Scene 6.   16** *here* in his heart, which he probably touches.   **18** *Gramercy* an expression of gratitude (contracted from "grand mercy").   **23** *gear* business. **39** *approvèd* proven.

PEDRINGANO   To do what, my fine, officious knave?

HANGMAN   To go to this gear.

PEDRINGANO   O sir, you are too forward: thou wouldst fain furnish
   me with a halter, to disfurnish me of my habit. So I should go out   45
   of this gear, my raiment, into that gear, the rope. But, hangman,
   now I spy your knavery, I'll not change without boot, that's flat.

HANGMAN   Come, sir.

PEDRINGANO   So, then, I must up?

HANGMAN   No remedy.   50

PEDRINGANO   Yes, but there shall be for my coming down.

HANGMAN   Indeed, here's a remedy for that.

PEDRINGANO   How? Be turned off?

HANGMAN   Ay, truly. Come, are you ready? I pray, sir, despatch; the
   day goes away.   55

PEDRINGANO   What, do you hang by the hour? If you do, I may chance
   to break your old custom.

HANGMAN   Faith, you have reason; for I am like to break your young
   neck.

PEDRINGANO   Dost thou mock me, hangman? Pray God, I be not   60
   preserved to break your knave's pate for this.

HANGMAN   Alas, sir! You are a foot too low to reach it, and I hope
   you will never grow so high while I am in the office.

PEDRINGANO   Sirrah, dost see yonder boy with the box in his hand?

HANGMAN   What, he that points to it with his finger?   65

PEDRINGANO   Ay, that companion.

HANGMAN   I know him not; but what of him?

PEDRINGANO   Dost thou think to live till his old doublet will make
   thee a new truss?

HANGMAN   Ay, and many a fair year after, to truss up many an honester   70
   man than either thou or he.

PEDRINGANO   What hath he in his box, as thou thinkst?

HANGMAN   Faith, I cannot tell, nor I care not greatly; methinks you
   should rather hearken to your soul's health.

PEDRINGANO   Why, sirrah, hangman, I take it that that is good for the   75
   body is likewise good for the soul; and it may be, in that box is
   balm for both.

---

45 habit The hangman was traditionally given the clothes of those he executed.
47 boot additional payment. **53 Be . . . off** You mean my fall, and my life, will be
ended (turned off) by a length of rope? **66 companion** fellow. **70 truss** trousers or
breeches, but the word also means "hang"; this meaning is the basis of the hangman's
pun in his next speech.

HANGMAN   Well, thou art even the merriest piece of man's flesh that
    e'er groaned at my office door!

PEDRINGANO   Is your roguery become an office with a knave's name?   80

HANGMAN·   Ay, and that shall all they witness that see you seal it with a
    thief's name.

PEDRINGANO   I prithee, request this good company to pray with me.

HANGMAN   Ay, marry, sir, this is a good motion. My masters, you see
    here's a good fellow.   85

PEDRINGANO   Nay, now I remember me, let them alone till some other
    time; for now I have no great need.

HIERONIMO   I have not seen a wretch so impudent!
    O monstrous times, where murder's set so light,
    And where the soul, that should be shrined in heaven,   90
    Solely delights in interdicted things,
    Still wand'ring in the thorny passages,
    That intercepts itself of happiness.
    Murder! O bloody monster! God forbid
    A fault so foul should 'scape unpunishèd.   95
    Despatch, and see this execution done!
    This makes me to remember thee, my son.

                                    Exit HIERONIMO.

PEDRINGANO   Nay, soft, no haste.

DEPUTY   Why, wherefore stay you? Have you hope of life?

PEDRINGANO   Why, ay!   100

HANGMAN   As how?

PEDRINGANO   Why, rascal, by my pardon from the King.

HANGMAN   Stand you on that? Then you shall off with this.

    He turns him off.

DEPUTY   So, executioner, convey him hence;
    But let his body be unburièd: 105
    Let not the earth be chokèd or infect
    With that which heaven contemns, and men neglect.   *Exeunt.*

---

80 *Is . . . name*   Hasn't your roguery corrupted the reputation of your office so much
that it will hereafter be thought suitable only for a knave?   **91** *interdicted*   forbidden.
93 *intercepts . . . of*   cuts itself off from.

ACT III

{ Scene 7   HIERONIMO's *house* }

Enter HIERONIMO.

HIERONIMO   Where shall I run to breathe abroad my woes,
My woes, whose weight hath wearièd the earth?
Or mine exclaims, that have surcharged the air
With ceaseless plaints for my deceasèd son?
The blust'ring winds, conspiring with my words,   5
At my lament have moved the leaveless trees,
Disrobed the meadows of their flowered green,
Made mountains marsh with spring-tides of my tears,
And broken through the brazen gates of hell.
Yet still tormented is my tortured soul   10
With broken sighs and restless passions,
That, wingèd, mount, and, hovering in the air,
Beat at the windows of the brightest heavens,
Soliciting for justice and revenge.
But they are placed in those imperial heights,   15
Where, countermured with walls of diamond,
I find the place impregnable; and they
Resist my woes, and give my words no way.

Enter HANGMAN *with a letter.*

HANGMAN   O lord, sir! God bless you, sir! The man, sir, Petergade,
sir—he that was so full of merry conceits—   20
HIERONIMO   Well, what of him?
HANGMAN   O lord, sir, he went the wrong way; the fellow had a fair
commission to the contrary. Sir, here is his passport; I pray you,
sir, we have done him wrong.
HIERONIMO   I warrant thee; give it me.   25
HANGMAN   You will stand between the gallows and me?
HIERONIMO   Ay, ay.
HANGMAN   I thank your lord worship.   *Exit* HANGMAN.
HIERONIMO   And yet, though somewhat nearer me concerns,
I will, to ease the grief that I sustain,   30

🎋 **ACT III, Scene 7.   15** *imperial*   The homonym "empyreal" is also implied.
16 *countermured*   reinforced by double walls.   **29** *somewhat . . . concerns*   Something
nearer (my own heart) concerns me.

Take truce with sorrow while I read on this.
"My lord, I write, as mine extremes required,
That you would labor my delivery:
If you neglect, my life is desperate,
And in my death I shall reveal the troth.   35
You know, my lord, I slew him for your sake,
And was confed'rate with the Prince and you;
Won by rewards and hopeful promises,
I holp to murder Don Horatio too."
Holp he to murder mine Horatio?   40
And actors in th'accursèd tragedy
Wast thou, Lorenzo, Balthazar and thou,
Of whom my son, my son, deserved so well?
What have I heard? What have mine eyes beheld?
O sacred heavens, may it come to pass   45
That such a monstrous and detested deed,
So closely smothered, and so long concealed,
Shall thus by this be vengèd or revealed?
Now see I what I durst not then suspect—
That Bel-imperia's letter was not feigned,   50
Nor feignèd she, though falsely they have wronged
Both her, myself, Horatio, and themselves.
Now may I make compare 'twixt hers and this,
Of every accident: I ne'er could find
Till now—and now I feelingly perceive—   55
They did what heaven unpunished would not leave.
O false Lorenzo! Are these thy flattering looks?
Is this the honor that thou didst my son?
And Balthazar—bane to thy soul and me!—
Was this the ransom he reserved thee for?   60
Woe to the cause of these constrainèd wars!
Woe to thy baseness and captivity,
Woe to thy birth, thy body, and thy soul,
Thy cursèd father, and thy conquered self!
And banned with bitter execrations be   65
The day and place where he did pity thee!

---

32 lord Lorenzo. **53–56 Now . . . leave** Now I can verify all the facts by comparing Bel-imperia's letter with Pedringano's. Until now—when I see the truth feelingly—I could not know for certain of this villainy, which heaven has brought to light so that the murderers may be punished. **60 he** Horatio.

But wherefore waste I mine unfruitful words,
When nought but blood will satisfy my woes?
I will go plain me to my lord the King,
And cry aloud for justice through the court,   70
Wearing the flints with these my withered feet;
And either purchase justice by entreats,
Or tire them all with my revenging threats.   *Exit.*

ACT III
Scene 8   *The same*

Enter ISABELLA *and her* MAID.

ISABELLA   So that you say this herb will purge the eye,
And this, the head?
Ah, but none of them will purge the heart!
No, there's no medicine left for my disease,
Nor any physic to recure the dead.   5

She runs lunatic.

Horatio! O, where's Horatio?
MAID   Good madam, affright not thus yourself
With outrage for your son Horatio;
He sleeps in quiet in the Elysian fields.
ISABELLA   Why, did I not give you gowns and goodly things,   10
Bought you a whistle and a whipstalk too,
To be revengèd on their villainies?
MAID   Madam, these humors do torment my soul.
ISABELLA   My soul? Poor soul, thou talks of things
Thou knowst not what—my soul hath silver wings,   15
That mounts me up unto the highest heavens;
To heaven! Ay, there sits my Horatio,
Backed with a troop of fiery cherubims,
Dancing about his newly healèd wounds,
Singing sweet hymns and chanting heavenly notes,   20
Rare harmony to greet his innocence,
That died, ay died, a mirror in our days.

69 *plain me*   present my complaint.
❧ ACT III, Scene 8.   **5** *recure* revive.   **11** *whipstalk*   whip handle.   **13** *humors*
quick and unpredictable changes of mood.   **22** *mirror*   a mirror (of perfection).

But say, where shall I find the men, the murderers,
That slew Horatio? Whither shall I run
To find them out that murderèd my son?   *Exeunt.*   25

ACT III
Scene 9   *The* DUKE's *castle*

BEL-IMPERIA *at a window*[, *on the upper stage*].

BEL-IMPERIA   What means this outrage that is offered me?
    Why am I thus sequestered from the court?
    No notice! Shall I not know the cause
    Of these my secret and suspicious ills?
    Accursèd brother, unkind murderer,   5
    Why bends thou thus thy mind to martyr me?
    Hieronimo, why writ I of thy wrongs,
    Or why art thou so slack in thy revenge?
    Andrea, O Andrea! that thou sawest
    Me for thy friend Horatio handled thus,   10
    And him for me thus causeless murderèd!—
    Well, force perforce, I must constrain myself
    To patience, and apply me to the time,
    Till heaven, as I have hoped, shall set me free.
    Enter CHRISTOPHIL.

CHRISTOPHIL   Come, Madam Bel-imperia, this may not be.   *Exeunt.*   15

ACT III
Scene 10   *A room in the castle*

Enter LORENZO, BALTHAZAR, *and the* PAGE.

LORENZO   Boy, talk no further; thus far things go well.
    Thou art assured that thou sawest him dead?
PAGE   Or else, my lord, I live not.
LORENZO   That's enough.

🐾 **ACT III, Scene 9. 3** *notice* information. **13** *apply . . . time* submit myself to
the circumstances.

As for his resolution in his end,
Leave that to Him with whom he sojourns now.   5
Here, take my ring and give it Christophil,
And bid him let my sister be enlarged,
And bring him hither straight.—   *Exit* PAGE.
This that I did was for a policy,
To smooth and keep the murder secret,   10
Which, as a nine-days' wonder, being o'erblown,
My gentle sister will I now enlarge.

BALTHAZAR   And time, Lorenzo, for my lord the Duke,
You heard, enquirèd for her yesternight.

LORENZO   Why, and my lord, I hope you heard me say   15
Sufficient reason why she kept away;
But that's all one. My lord, you love her?

BALTHAZAR   Ay.

LORENZO   Then in your love beware; deal cunningly:
Salve all suspicions, only soothe me up;
And if she hap to stand on terms with us—   20
As for her sweetheart and concealment so—
Jest with her gently; under feignèd jest
Are things concealed that else would breed unrest.
But here she comes.

Enter BEL-IMPERIA.

                    Now, sister,—

BEL-IMPERIA   Sister? No!
Thou art no brother, but an enemy;   25
Else wouldst thou not have used thy sister so:
First, to affright me with thy weapons drawn,
And with extremes abuse my company;
And then to hurry me, like whirlwind's rage,
Amidst a crew of thy confederates,   30
And clap me up where none might come at me,
Nor I at any to reveal my wrongs.
What madding fury did possess thy wits?
Or wherein is't that I offended thee?

🦎 ACT III, Scene 10.   11 *nine-days' wonder*   an object or event that creates a short-
lived sensation.   19 *soothe me up*   corroborate my story.   20 *stand on terms*   make
things difficult.   21–22 *As . . . gently*   Lorenzo considers murder a privilege that
naturally accompanies his high social rank; therefore, his reference to Horatio's death and
Bel-imperia's imprisonment, however frighteningly casual, is nevertheless perfectly consistent with his perversely self-interested philosophy.   28 *company*   companion.

LORENZO   Advise you better, Bel-imperia,   35
    For I have done you no disparagement;
    Unless, by more discretion than deserved,
    I sought to save your honor and mine own.
BEL-IMPERIA   Mine honor! Why, Lorenzo, wherein is't
    That I neglect my reputation so,   40
    As you, or any, need to rescue it?
LORENZO   His highness and my father were resolved
    To come confer with old Hieronimo
    Concerning certain matters of estate
    That by the Viceroy was determinèd.   45
BEL-IMPERIA   And wherein was mine honor touched in that?
BALTHAZAR   Have patience, Bel-imperia; hear the rest.
LORENZO   Me, next in sight, as messenger they sent
    To give him notice that they were so nigh:
    Now when I came, consorted with the Prince,   50
    And unexpected in an arbor there
    Found Bel-imperia with Horatio—
BEL-IMPERIA   How then?
LORENZO   Why, then, remembering that old disgrace,
    Which you for Don Andrea had endured,   55
    And now were likely longer to sustain,
    By being found so meanly accompanied,
    Thought rather—for I knew no readier mean—
    To thrust Horatio forth my father's way.
BALTHAZAR   And carry you obscurely somewhere else,   60
    Lest that his highness should have found you there.
BEL-IMPERIA   Even so, my lord? And you are witness
    That this is true which he entreateth of?
    You, gentle brother, forged this for my sake,
    And you, my lord, were made his instrument?   65
    A work of worth, worthy the noting too!
    But what's the cause that you concealed me since?
LORENZO   Your melancholy, sister: since the news
    Of your first favorite Don Andrea's death,
    My father's old wrath hath exasperate.   70

---

37 than deserved than (you) deserved. **45 That . . . determinèd** that the Viceroy was giving up his claim to. **48 next in sight** both "nearby" and "next in line for the estate" (as the Duke's son). **50 consorted with** accompanied by. **57 meanly accompanied** Horatio, son of a court official, was of a lower social class than Bel-imperia, daughter of a duke. **59 forth** out of. **70 exasperate** grown more severe.

BALTHAZAR   And better was't for you, being in disgrace,
    To absent yourself, and give his fury place.
BEL-IMPERIA   But why had I no notice of his ire?
LORENZO   That were to add more fuel to your fire,
    Who burnt like Aetna for Andrea's loss.   75
BEL-IMPERIA   Hath not my father then enquired for me?
LORENZO   Sister, he hath, and thus excused I thee.

    He whispereth in her ear.

    But Bel-imperia, see the gentle Prince;
    Look on thy love; behold young Balthazar,
    Whose passions by thy presence are increased,   80
    And in whose melancholy thou mayst see
    Thy hate, his love; thy flight, his following thee.
BEL-IMPERIA   Brother, you are become an orator—
    I know not, I, by what experience—
    Too politic for me, past all compare,   85
    Since last I saw you; but content yourself:
    The Prince is meditating higher things.
BALTHAZAR   'Tis of thy beauty, then, that conquers kings;
    Of those thy tresses, Ariadne's twines,
    Wherewith my liberty thou hast surprised;   90
    Of that thine ivory front, my sorrow's map,
    Wherein I see no haven to rest my hope.
BEL-IMPERIA   To love and fear, and both at once, my lord,
    In my conceit, are things of more import
    Than women's wits are to be busied with.   95
BALTHAZAR   'Tis I that love.
BEL-IMPERIA   Whom?
BALTHAZAR   Bel-imperia.
BEL-IMPERIA   But I that fear.
BALTHAZAR   Whom?
BEL-IMPERIA   Bel-imperia.

---

89 *Ariadne's twines*   Kyd again seems confused here, for Balthazar implies that he is
held in bondage by Bel-imperia's hair, and Ariadne is never in classical mythology associated with any deprivation of liberty. Because she held the thread which guided Theseus
through the tortuous passages of the labyrinth, she would more logically be associated
with freedom from imprisonment. Perhaps Kyd confused her with Arachne, a weaver
who was metamorphosed into a spider; or, more probably, feeling that Ariadne's general
association with twine justified the reference, he may not have worried about the *specific*
implications of the myth.   **91** *front*   forehead.   **94** *conceit*   opinion.

LORENZO   Fear yourself?
BEL-IMPERIA   Ay, brother.
LORENZO   How?
BEL-IMPERIA   As those
 That what they love are loath and fear to lose.
BALTHAZAR   Then, fair, let Balthazar your keeper be.   100
BEL-IMPERIA   No, Balthazar doth fear as well as we:
 Et tremulo metui pavidum iunxere timorem—
 Est vanum stolidae proditionis opus.
LORENZO   Nay, and you argue things so cunningly,
 We'll go continue this discourse at court.   105
BALTHAZAR   Led by the lodestar of her heavenly looks,
 Wends poor, oppressèd Balthazar,
 As o'er the mountains walks the wanderer,
 Incertain to effect his pilgrimage.   *Exeunt.*

ACT III
Scene 11 *A street*

Enter TWO PORTINGALES, *and* HIERONIMO *meets them.*

FIRST PORTINGALE   By your leave, sir.
HIERONIMO   [*'Tis neither as you think, nor as you think,*
 Nor as you think; you're wide all.
 These slippers are not mine, they were my son Horatio's.
 My son! And what's a son? A thing begot   5
 Within a pair of minutes—thereabout;
 A lump bred up in darkness, and doth serve
 To ballace these light creatures we call women;
 And, at nine months' end, creeps forth to light.
 What is there yet in a son   10
 To make a father dote, rave, or run mad?
 Being born, it pouts, cries, and breeds teeth.
 What is there yet in a son? He must be fed,
 Be taught to go, and speak. Ay, or yet?

102–3 *Et . . . opus*   And I was afraid to add terrible fear to one already quaking. The work of foolish treachery is vain.

🦆 **ACT III, Scene 11.**   **3** *wide*   far from the mark.   **8** *ballace*   ballast.   **14** *Ay, or yet*   a modified rhetorical repetition of the question "What is there yet in a son . . .?"

Why might not a man love a calf as well?   15
Or melt in passion o'er a frisking kid,
As for a son? Methinks, a young bacon
Or a fine little smooth horse colt
Should move a man as much as doth a son.
For one of these, in very little time,   20
Will grow to some good use; whereas a son,
The more he grows in stature and in years,
The more unsquared, unbeveled, he appears,
Reckons his parents among the rank of fools,
Strikes care upon their heads with his mad riots,   25
Makes them look old before they meet with age.
This is a son! And what a loss were this,
Considered truly?—O, but my Horatio
Grew out of reach of these insatiate humors:
He loved his loving parents;   30
He was my comfort, and his mother's joy,
The very arm that did hold up our house:
Our hopes were storèd up in him,
None but a damned murderer could hate him.
He had not seen the back of nineteen year,   35
When his strong arm unhorsed
The proud Prince Balthazar, and his great mind,
Too full of honor, took him unto mercy,
That valiant but ignoble Portingale!
Well, heaven is heaven still!   40
And there is Nemesis, and Furies,
And things called whips,
And they sometimes do meet with murderers:
They do not always 'scape, that's some comfort.
Ay, ay, ay; and then time steals on,   45
And steals, and steals, till violence leaps forth
Like thunder wrapt in a ball of fire,
And so doth bring confusion to them all.]
Good leave have you; nay, I pray you go,
For I'll leave you, if you can leave me so.   50

17 *bacon*   pig.

SECOND PORTINGALE   Pray you, which is the next way to my lord the
　　Duke's?
HIERONIMO   The next way from me.
FIRST PORTINGALE   To his house, we mean.
HIERONIMO   O, hard by: 'tis yon house that you see.   55
SECOND PORTINGALE   You could not tell us if his son were there?
HIERONIMO   Who, my Lord Lorenzo?
FIRST PORTINGALE   Ay, sir.

He [HIERONIMO] *goeth in at one door and comes out at another.*

HIERONIMO   O, forbear!
　　For other talk for us far fitter were.   60
　　But if you be importunate to know
　　The way to him, and where to find him out,
　　Then list to me, and I'll resolve your doubt.
　　There is a path upon your left-hand side
　　That leadeth from a guilty conscience   65
　　Unto a forest of distrust and fear—
　　A darksome place, and dangerous to pass.
　　There shall you meet with melancholy thoughts,
　　Whose baleful humors if you but uphold,
　　It will conduct you to despair and death;   70
　　Whose rocky cliffs when you have once beheld,
　　Within a hugy dale of lasting night,
　　That, kindled with the world's iniquities,
　　Doth cast up filthy and detested fumes.
　　Not far from thence, where murderers have built   75
　　A habitation for their cursèd souls,
　　There, in a brazen caldron fixed by Jove
　　In his fell wrath, upon a sulphur flame,
　　Yourselves shall find Lorenzo bathing him
　　In boiling lead and blood of innocents.   80
FIRST PORTINGALE   Ha, ha, ha!
HIERONIMO   Ha, ha, ha! Why, ha, ha, ha! Farewell, good ha, ha, ha!
　　　　　　　　　　　　　　　　　　　　　　　　Exit.
SECOND PORTINGALE   Doubtless this man is passing lunatic,
　　Or imperfection of his age doth make him dote.
　　Come, let's away to seek my lord the Duke.   [*Exeunt.*]   85

51–53 **Pray . . . me**   Hieronimo interprets the phrase "my lord the Duke's" as des-
criptive of a state of mind, not of a place. Since the Duke's fortune is good and Hieronimo's
is bad, the way to "my lord the Duke's" (state of mind) is the one that leads away from
("the next way from") Hieronimo's. **51 next** nearest. **69 uphold** continue to
follow. **72 hugy** huge. **79 him** himself.

ACT III

Scene 12   *The Spanish court*

Enter HIERONIMO, *with a poniard in one hand and a rope in the other.*

HIERONIMO   Now, sir, perhaps I come and see the King;
    The King sees me, and fain would hear my suit.
    Why, is not this a strange and seld-seen thing,
    That standers-by with toys should strike me mute?
    Go to, I see their shifts, and say no more.   5
    Hieronimo, 'tis time for thee to trudge.
    Down by the dale that flows with purple gore
    Standeth a fiery tower; there sits a judge
    Upon a seat of steel and molten brass,
    And 'twixt his teeth he holds a firebrand,   10
    That leads unto the lake where hell doth stand.
    Away, Hieronimo; to him be gone:
    He'll do thee justice for Horatio's death.
    Turn down this path; thou shalt be with him straight;
    Or this, and then thou needst not take thy breath: 15
    This way, or that way?—Soft and fair, not so!
    For if I hang or kill myself, let's know
    Who will revenge Horatio's murder then?
    No, no! fie, no! Pardon me, I'll none of that.

He flings away the dagger and halter.

    This way I'll take, and this way comes the King: 20

He takes them up again.

    And here I'll have a fling at him, that's flat;
    And, Balthazar, I'll be with thee to bring,
    And thee, Lorenzo! Here's the King—nay, stay;
    And here, ay here—there goes the hare away.

Enter KING, AMBASSADOR, CASTILE, *and* LORENZO.

KING   Now show, Ambassador, what our Viceroy saith.   25
    Hath he received the articles we sent?

🦂 **ACT III, Scene 12.   SD** *poniard . . . rope* conventional stage properties of a man
contemplating suicide.   **3** *seld-seen* rare.   **4** *toys* vain trifles.   **5** *shifts* tricks.
6 *trudge* get moving.   **13** *do* give.   **16** *This . . . way* Shall I kill myself with the
knife or the rope?   *Soft and fair* at a leisurely pace, gently.   **21** *flat* settled.   **22** *I'll
. . . bring* I'll get even with you.   **24** *there . . . away* The chase has begun.

HIERONIMO   Justice! O justice to Hieronimo!
LORENZO   Back! Seest thou not the King is busy?
HIERONIMO   O, is he so?
KING   Who is he that interrupts our business?   30
HIERONIMO   Not I. Hieronimo, beware! Go by, go by!
AMBASSADOR   Renownèd King, he hath received and read
    Thy kingly proffers, and thy promised league;
    And, as a man extremely overjoyed
    To hear his son so princely entertained,   35
    Whose death he had so solemnly bewailed,
    This, for thy further satisfaction
    And kingly love, he kindly lets thee know:
    First, for the marriage of his princely son
    With Bel-imperia, thy beloved niece,   40
    The news are more delightful to his soul,
    Than myrrh or incense to the offended heavens.
    In person, therefore, will he come himself,
    To see the marriage rites solemnized,
    And, in the presence of the court of Spain,   45
    To knit a sure, inexplicable band
    Of kingly love and everlasting league
    Betwixt the crowns of Spain and Portingale.
    There will he give his crown to Balthazar,
    And make a queen of Bel-imperia.   50
KING   Brother, how like you this our Viceroy's love?
CASTILE   No doubt, my lord, it is an argument
    Of honorable care to keep his friend,
    And wondrous zeal to Balthazar his son;
    Nor am I least indebted to his grace,   55
    That bends his liking to my daughter thus.
AMBASSADOR   Now last, dread lord, here hath his highness sent
    (Although he send not that his son return)
    His ransom due to Don Horatio.
HIERONIMO   Horatio! Who calls Horatio?   60
KING   And well remembered; thank his majesty.
    Here, see it given to Horatio.
HIERONIMO   Justice! O, justice, justice, gentle King!
KING   Who is that? Hieronimo?

---

31 Go ... by Be careful. **46 inexplicable** unbreakable. **62 Here ... Horatio** The King does not know about Horatio's death simply because the plot demands his ignorance; there is no *logical* reason why he should not have heard of the murder.

HERONIMO   Justice, O, justice! O my son, my son!   65
    My son, whom naught can ransom or redeem!
LORENZO   Hieronimo, you are not well-advised.
HIERONIMO   Away, Lorenzo, hinder me no more;
    For thou hast made me bankrupt of my bliss.
    Give me my son! You shall not ransom him!   70
    Away! I'll rip the bowels of the earth,

    He diggeth with his dagger.

    And ferry over to th'Elysian plains,
    And bring my son to show his deadly wounds.
    Stand from about me!
    I'll make a pickax of my poniard,   75
    And here surrender up my marshalship;
    For I'll go marshal up the fiends in hell,
    To be avengèd on you all for this.
KING   What means this outrage?
    Will none of you restrain his fury?   80
HIERONIMO   Nay, soft and fair! You shall not need to strive.
    Needs must he go that the devils drive.   *Exit.*
KING   What accident hath happed Hieronimo?
    I have not seen him to demean him so.
LORENZO   My gracious lord, he is with extreme pride—   85
    Conceived of young Horatio his son—
    And covetous of having to himself
    The ransom of the young prince Balthazar,
    Distract, and in a manner lunatic.
KING   Believe me, nephew, we are sorry for't;   90
    This is the love that fathers bear their sons.
    But, gentle brother, go give to him this gold,
    The Prince's ransom; let him have his due.
    For what he hath, Horatio shall not want;
    Haply Hieronimo hath need thereof.   95
LORENZO   But if he be thus helplessly distract,
    'Tis requisite his office be resigned,
    And given to one of more discretion.
KING   We shall increase his melancholy so.
    'Tis best that we see further in it first,   100

---

83 *happed* happened to.   **86** *Conceived of* growing out of (the deeds of).   **94–95** *For
... thereof* for Horatio will not lack what his father has; and perchance Hieronimo is in
need now (?).

Till when, ourself will exempt the place.
And, brother, now bring in th'Ambassador,
That he may be a witness of the match
'Twixt Balthazar and Bel-imperia,
And that we may prefix a certain time,   105
Wherein the marriage shall be solemnized,
That we may have thy lord, the Viceroy, here.

AMBASSADOR   Therein your highness highly shall content
His majesty, that longs to hear from hence.

KING   On, then, and hear you, Lord Ambassador.   *Exeunt.*   110

ACT III
Scene 13   HIERONIMO's *garden*

[Enter JAQUES and PEDRO.

JAQUES   *I wonder, Pedro, why our master thus*
At midnight sends us with our torches' light,
When man and bird and beast are all at rest,
Save those that watch for rape and bloody murder?

PEDRO   *O Jaques, know thou that our master's mind*   5
Is much distraught since his Horatio died,
And—now his agèd years should sleep in rest,
His heart in quiet—like a desperate man,
Grows lunatic and childish for his son.
Sometimes, as he doth at his table sit,   10
He speaks as if Horatio stood by him;
Then, starting in a rage, falls on the earth,
Cries out, "Horatio! Where is my Horatio?"
So that with extreme grief and cutting sorrow
There is not left in him one inch of man.   15
See, where he comes.

Enter HIERONIMO.

HIERONIMO   *I pry through every crevice of each wall,*
Look on each tree, and search through every brake,

---

101 *exempt*   refrain from appointing another to.
🦌 **ACT III, Scene 13.   18** *brake*   thicket.

Beat at the bushes, stamp our grandam earth,
Dive in the water, and stare up to heaven,   20
Yet cannot I behold my son Horatio.
How now, who's there? Sprites? sprites?

PEDRO   *We are your servants that attend you, sir.*

HIERONIMO   *What make you with your torches in the dark?*

PEDRO   *You bid us light them, and attend you here.*   25

HIERONIMO   *No, no, you are deceived! Not I—you are deceived!*
Was I so mad to bid you light your torches now?
Light me your torches at the mid of noon,
Whenas the sun god rides in all his glory;
Light me your torches then.

PEDRO   *Then we burn daylight.*   30

HIERONIMO   *Let it be burnt; night is a murderous slut,*
That would not have her treasons to be seen;
And yonder pale-faced Hecate there, the moon,
Doth give consent to that is done in darkness;
And all those stars that gaze upon her face,   35
Are aglets on her sleeve, pins on her train;
And those that should be powerful and divine
Do sleep in darkness when they most should shine.

PEDRO   *Provoke them not, fair sir, with tempting words;*
The heavens are gracious, and your miseries   40
And sorrow make you speak you know not what.

HIERONIMO   *Villain, thou liest! And thou dost nought*
But tell me I am mad. Thou liest, I am not mad!
I know thee to be Pedro, and he Jaques.
I'll prove it to thee; and were I mad, how could I?   45
Where was she that same night when my Horatio
Was murdered? She should have shone; search thou the book.
Had the moon shone, in my boy's face there was a kind of grace,
That I know—nay, I do know—had the murderer seen him,
His weapon would have fall'n and cut the earth,   50
Had he been framed of naught but blood and death.
Alack, when mischief doth it knows not what,
What shall we say to mischief?

Enter ISABELLA.

ISABELLA   *Dear Hieronimo, come in a-doors;*
O, seek not means so to increase thy sorrow.   55

---

19 grandam old mother. **22 Sprites** spirits. **29 Whenas** when. **30 burn** waste.
33 Hecate a goddess of the moon and of witchcraft. **36 aglets** metal ornaments.

HIERONIMO   *Indeed, Isabella, we do nothing here;*
  I do not cry—ask Pedro, and ask Jaques—
  Not I indeed; we are very merry, very merry.
ISABELLA   *How? Be merry here, be merry here?*
  Is not this the place, and this the very tree,   60
  Where my Horatio died, where he was murdered?
HIERONIMO   *Was—do not say what: let her weep it out.*
  This was the tree; I set it of a kernel;
  And when our hot Spain could not let it grow,
  But that the infant and the human sap   65
  Began to wither, duly twice a morning
  Would I be sprinkling it with fountain water.
  At last it grew and grew, and bore and bore,
  Till at the length
  It grew a gallows, and did bear our son;   70
  It bore thy fruit and mine—O wicked, wicked plant!

 One knocks within at the door.

 See who knocks there.

PEDRO   *It is a painter, sir.*
HIERONIMO   *Bid him come in, and paint some comfort,*
  For surely there's none lives but painted comfort.
  Let him come in! One knows not what may chance: 75
  God's will that I should set this tree!—But even so
  Masters ungrateful servants rear from nought,
  And then they hate them that did bring them up.

 Enter the PAINTER.

PAINTER   *God bless you, sir.*
HIERONIMO   *Wherefore? Why, thou scornful villain?*   80
  How, where, or by what means should I be blessed?
ISABELLA   *What wouldst thou have, good fellow?*
PAINTER   *Justice, madam.*
HIERONIMO   *O ambitious beggar!*
  Wouldst thou have that that lives not in the world?
  Why, all the undelved mines cannot buy   85
  An ounce of justice, 'tis a jewel so inestimable.
  I tell thee,
  God hath engrossed all justice in his hands,
  And there is none but what comes from him.

63 *I . . . kernel*   I grew it from a seed.   **74** *painted*   false.

PAINTER   *O, then I see*   90
    That God must right me for my murdered son.
HIERONIMO   *How, was thy son murdered?*
PAINTER   *Ay, sir; no man did hold a son so dear.*
HIERONIMO   *What, not as thine? That's a lie,*
    As massy as the earth. I had a son   95
    Whose least unvalued hair did weigh
    A thousand of thy sons; and he was murdered.
PAINTER   *Alas, sir, I had no more but he.*
HIERONIMO   *Nor I, nor I; but this same one of mine*
    Was worth a legion. But all is one.   100
    Pedro, Jaques, go in a-doors; Isabella, go,
    And this good fellow here and I
    Will range this hideous orchard up and down,
    Like to two lions reav'd of their young.
    Go in a-doors, I say.   Exeunt [ISABELLA, PEDRO, JAQUES].   105
    The PAINTER and he sit down.
    Come, let's talk wisely now. Was thy son murdered?
PAINTER   *Ay, sir.*
HIERONIMO   *So was mine. How dost take it? Art thou not sometimes mad?*
    Is there no tricks that comes before thine eyes?
PAINTER   *O Lord, yes, sir.*   110
HIERONIMO   *Art a painter? Canst paint me a tear, or a wound, a groan, or*
    a sigh? Canst paint me such a tree as this?
PAINTER   *Sir, I am sure you have heard of my painting: my name's Bazardo.*
HIERONIMO   *Bazardo! Afore God, an excellent fellow! Look you, sir, do you*
    see? I'd have you paint me [in] my gallery, in your oil colors matted,   115
    and draw me five years younger than I am—do ye see, sir, let five years
    go; let them go like the Marshal of Spain—my wife Isabella standing by
    me, with a speaking look to my son Horatio, which should intend to this
    or some such like purpose: "God bless thee, my sweet son," and my hand
    leaning upon his head, thus, sir; do you see? May it be done?   120
PAINTER   *Very well, sir.*
HIERONIMO   *Nay, I pray, mark me, sir. Then, sir, would I have you paint*
    me this tree, this very tree. Canst paint a doleful cry?

---

109 *tricks* illusory visions. **115** *matted* dulled. **117** *like . . . Spain* There are at
least two possible interpretations. Hieronimo may mean, "Let five years go, just as
the Lord Marshal can let five years of a man's sentence go," or, more probably, he may
be expressing his despair by saying, "Let five years be lost ("go") just as the Marshal of
Spain—whose son is dead, whose legal power is gone, and whose world is given over to
chaos—is lost."

PAINTER   *Seemingly, sir.*

HIERONIMO   *Nay, it should cry; but all is one. Well, sir, paint me a youth*   125
run through and through with villains' swords, hanging upon this tree.
Canst thou draw a murderer?

PAINTER   *I'll warrant you, sir; I have the pattern of the most notorious*
villains that ever lived in all Spain.

HIERONIMO   *O, let them be worse, worse; stretch thine art, and let their*   130
beards be of Judas his own color; and let their eyebrows jutty over: in any
case observe that. Then, sir, after some violent noise bring me forth in my
shirt, and my gown under mine arm, with my torch in my hand, and my
sword reared up, thus—and with these words:
      "What noise is this? Who calls Hieronimo?"   135
   May it be done?

PAINTER   *Yea, sir.*

HIERONIMO   *Well, sir, then bring me forth; bring me through alley and alley,*
still with a distracted countenance going along, and let my hair heave up
my nightcap. Let the clouds scowl, make the moon dark, the stars extinct,   140
the winds blowing, the bells tolling, the owls shrieking, the toads
croaking, the minutes jarring, and the clock striking twelve. And then at
last, sir, starting, behold a man hanging, and tottering and tottering, as
you know the wind will weave a man, and I with a trice to cut him down.
And looking upon him by the advantage of my torch, find it to be my son   145
Horatio. There you may [show] a passion; there you may show a
passion! Draw me like old Priam of Troy, crying, "The house is afire,
the house is afire, as the torch over my head!" Make me curse, make me
rave, make me cry, make me mad, make me well again, make me curse
hell, invocate heaven, and in the end, leave me in a trance—and so forth.   150

PAINTER   *And is this the end?*

HIERONIMO   *O no, there is no end; the end is death and madness! As I am*
never better than when I am mad, then methinks I am a brave fellow,
then I do wonders; but reason abuseth me, and there's the torment,
there's the hell. At the last, sir, bring me to one of the murderers: were he   155
as strong as Hector, thus would I tear and drag him up and down.

He beats the PAINTER in, then comes out again, with a book in his
hand.]

---

131 *Judas . . . color* red (symbolic of his association with the devil). **131** *jutty*
over project out. **142** *jarring* ticking. **144** *weave* sway back and forth. *with a*
trice with a sudden jerk (i.e. quickly). **147** *Priam* King of Troy at the time of its
defeat by the Greeks. **156** *Hector* greatest Trojan warrior.

ACT III

Scene 14   HIERONIMO's *house*

Enter HIERONIMO, *with a book in his hand.*

HIERONIMO   *Vindicta mihi!*
Ay, heaven will be revenged of every ill,
Nor will they suffer murder unrepaid.
Then stay, Hieronimo, attend their will:
For mortal men may not appoint their time.   5
Per scelus semper tutum est sceleribus iter.
Strike, and strike home, where wrong is offered thee;
For evils unto ills conductors be,
And death's the worst of resolution.
For he that thinks with patience to contend   10
To quiet life, his life shall easily end.
Fata si miseros juvant, habes salutem;
Fata si vitam negant, habes sepulchrum:
"If destiny thy miseries do ease,
Then hast thou health, and happy shalt thou be;   15
If destiny deny thee life, Hieronimo,
Yet shalt thou be assurèd of a tomb."
If neither, yet let this thy comfort be:
Heaven covereth him that hath no burial.
And, to conclude, I will revenge his death!   20
But how? Not as the vulgar wits of men,
With open, but inevitable ills,
As by a secret, yet a certain mean,
Which under kindship will be cloakèd best.
Wise men will take their opportunity,   25
Closely and safely fitting things to time.
But in extremes advantage hath no time;
And, therefore, all times fit not for revenge.
Thus, therefore, will I rest me in unrest,
Dissembling quiet in unquietness—   30
Not seeming that I know their villainies,

🏶 ACT III, Scene 14.   1 *Vindicta mihi* Vengeance is mine.   6 *Per . . . iter* For crime, the safe way is always through crime (from Seneca's *Agamemnon*).   12–13 *Fata . . . sepulchrum* Hieronimo translates this quotation from Seneca's *Troades* in the next four lines.   22 *inevitable* inescapable.   24 *kindship* kindness.

That my simplicity may make them think
That ignorantly I will let all slip;
For ignorance, I wot, and well they know,
Remedium malorum iners est.   35
Nor aught avails it me to menace them,
Who, as a wintry storm upon a plain,
Will bear me down with their nobility.
No, no, Hieronimo, thou must enjoin
Thine eyes to observation, and thy tongue   40
To milder speeches than thy spirit affords,
Thy heart to patience, and thy hands to rest,
Thy cap to courtesy, and thy knee to bow,
Till to revenge thou know when, where, and how.
A noise within.

How now, what noise? What coil is that you keep?   45

Enter a SERVANT.

SERVANT   Here are a sort of poor petitioners
That are importunate, and it shall please you, sir,
That you should plead their cases to the King.
HIERONIMO   That I should plead their several actions?
Why, let them enter, and let me see them.   50

Enter THREE CITIZENS *and an* OLD MAN.

FIRST CITIZEN   So, I tell you this: for learning and for law,
There is not any advocate in Spain
That can prevail, or will take half the pain
That he will, in pursuit of equity.
HIERONIMO   Come near, you men, that thus importune me.   55
[*Aside.*] Now must I bear a face of gravity;
For thus I used, before my marshalship,
To plead in causes as corregidor.
Come on, sirs, what's the matter?
SECOND CITIZEN   Sir, an action.
HIERONIMO   Of battery?
FIRST CITIZEN   Mine of debt.
HIERONIMO   Give place.   60
SECOND CITIZEN   No, sir, mine is an action of the case.

---

34 *wot* know. **35** *Remedium . . . est* is a useless remedy for ills. **45** *coil* disturbance. *keep* make. **46** *sort* group. **58** *corregidor* advocate. **61** *action . . . case*
a legal action needing a special writ because it is not technically within the jurisdiction
of the Common Pleas.

THIRD CITIZEN   Mine an *ejectione firmae* by a lease.

HIERONIMO   Content you, sirs; are you determined
    That I should plead your several actions?

FIRST CITIZEN   Ay, sir, and here's my declaration.   65

SECOND CITIZEN   And here is my band.

THIRD CITIZEN   And here is my lease.

    They give him papers.

HIERONIMO   But wherefore stands yon silly man so mute,
    With mournful eyes and hands to heaven upreared?
    Come hither, father, let me know thy cause.

SENEX   O worthy sir, my cause, but slightly known,   70
    May move the hearts of warlike Myrmidons,
    And melt the Corsic rocks with ruthful tears.

HIERONIMO   Say, father, tell me, what's thy suit?

SENEX   No, sir, could my woes
    Give way unto my most distressful words,   75
    Then should I not in paper, as you see,
    With ink bewray what blood began in me.

HIERONIMO   What's here? "The humble supplication
    Of Don Bazulto for his murdered son."

SENEX   Ay, sir.

HIERONIMO   No, sir, it was my murdered son: 80
    O my son, my son, O my son Horatio!
    But mine, or thine, Bazulto, be content.
    Here, take my handkercher and wipe thine eyes,
    Whiles wretched I, in thy mishaps, may see
    The lively portrait of my dying self.   85

    He draweth out a bloody napkin.

    O no, not this! Horatio, this was thine;
    And when I dyed it in thy dearest blood,
    This was a token 'twixt thy soul and me,
    That of thy death revengèd I should be.

---

62 *ejectione firmae*   a writ to eject a tenant before his lease expires.   **66** *band*   bond.
67 *silly*   pitiable.   **71** *Myrmidons*   Achilles' soldiers. The specific reference is to
Aeneid, II.6–8.   **72** *Corsic*   of Corsica.   **74–77** *could . . . me*   If my woes ended with
my cries of distress, then I would not divulge, in the cold ink of a legal document, the
anger I feel welling within me.

But here, take this, and this—what, my purse?—   90
Ay, this, and that, and all of them are thine;
For all as one are our extremities.
FIRST CITIZEN   O, see the kindness of Hieronimo!
SECOND CITIZEN   This gentleness shows him a gentleman.
HIERONIMO   See, see, O see thy shame, Hieronimo!   95
See here a loving father to his son!
Behold the sorrows and the sad laments,
That he delivereth for his son's decease!
If love's effects so strive in lesser things,
If love enforce such moods in meaner wits,   100
If love express such power in poor estates,
Hieronimo, as when a raging sea,
Tossed with the wind and tide, o'erturneth then
The upper billows, course of waves to keep,
Whilst lesser waters labor in the deep,   105
Then sham'st thou not, Hieronimo, to neglect
The sweet revenge of thy Horatio?
Though on this earth justice will not be found,
I'll down to hell, and in this passion
Knock at the dismal gates of Pluto's court,   110
Getting by force, as once Alcides did,
A troop of Furies and tormenting hags
To torture Don Lorenzo and the rest.

90–91 *But . . . thine*   It is, of course, impossible to determine the exact references for
the relative pronouns here; each would have to be decided by the actor and director.
The general situation, however, is clear: Hieronimo, like King Lear (III.4), despairingly
thinks all worldly goods are superfluous and tries to give away everything of this world
that he has about him—his purse, his seal of office, his legal papers, and perhaps even
particular articles of his clothing.   **102–7** *as . . . Horatio*   This passage is probably the
most difficult in the entire play, and it will not sustain a close reading. Perhaps the text
is corrupt (the 1592 edition reads "when as" instead of "as when" and "ore turnest then"
instead of "o'erturneth then"), or perhaps Kyd was again more concerned with a general
effect than with the consistency of specific elements. At any rate, two basic ideas are
developed by the simile: first, that order has yielded to chaos, as when the normal condition of the sea is unsettled by a violent storm; and, second, that in this disorder, love
has moved Don Bazulto, a man supposedly less sensitive and intelligent than Hieronimo,
to struggle desperately and nobly against great forces ("lesser waters labor in the deep"),
while Hieronimo, experiencing the same storm, is failing to resist it as he should,—that
is, by seeking revenge.   **111** *Alcides*   The reference is to Heracles, the most famous of
the Greek heroes, who in performing his twelfth and greatest labor, captured and bound
Cerberus, the watchdog of Hades. To accomplish this deed, he had, of course, to knock
at the gates of Pluto's court and display his immense power.

Yet lest the triple-headed porter should
Deny my passage to the slimy strand,   115
The Thracian poet thou shalt counterfeit.
Come on, old father, be my Orpheus,
And if thou canst no notes upon the harp,
Then sound the burden of thy sore heart's grief,
Till we do gain that Proserpine may grant   120
Revenge on them that murderèd my son.
Then will I rent and tear them, thus and thus,
Shivering their limbs in pieces with my teeth.

Tear the papers.

FIRST CITIZEN   O sir, my declaration!   *Exit* HIERONIMO, *and they after.*
SECOND CITIZEN   Save my bond!

Enter HIERONIMO.

SECOND CITIZEN   Save my bond!   125
THIRD CITIZEN   Alas, my lease! It cost me ten pound
And you, my lord, have torn the same.
HIERONIMO   That cannot be; I gave it never a wound.
Show me one drop of blood fall from the same!
How is it possible I should slay it then?   130
Tush, no; run after, catch me if you can.

Exeunt all but the OLD MAN.

BAZULTO *remains till* HIERONIMO *enters again, who, staring him in the
face, speaks.*

HIERONIMO   And art thou come, Horatio, from the depth,
To ask for justice in this upper earth?
To tell thy father thou art unrevenged?
To wring more tears from Isabella's eyes,   135
Whose lights are dimmed with overlong laments?
Go back, my son, complain to Aeacus,
For here's no justice; gentle boy, begone,
For justice is exiled from earth:
Hieronimo will bear thee company.   140
The mother cries on righteous Rhadamanth
For just revenge against the murderers.

---

114 triple-headed porter Cerberus. **116 *Thracian poet*** Orpheus, a legendary, pre-
Homeric poet who played so skillfully on his lyre that he induced Proserpine, Queen of
the Underworld, to allow his dead wife to return from Hades. **137 *Aeacus,* 141
*Rhadamanth*** infallible judges of the dead.

SENEX   Alas, my lord, whence springs this troubled speech?
HIERONIMO   But let me look on my Horatio.
    Sweet boy, how art thou changed in death's black shade!   145
    Had Proserpine no pity on thy youth,
    But suffered thy fair crimson-colored spring
    With withered winter to be blasted thus?
    Horatio, thou art older than thy father.
    Ah, ruthless fate, that favor thus transforms!   150
SENEX   Ah, my good lord, I am not your young son.
HIERONIMO   What, not my son? Thou then a Fury art,
    Sent from the empty kingdom of black night
    To summon me to make appearance
    Before grim Minos and just Rhadamanth,   155
    To plague Hieronimo that is remiss,
    And seeks not vengeance for Horatio's death.
SENEX   I am a grievèd man, and not a ghost,
    That came for justice for my murdered son.
HIERONIMO   Ay, now I know thee, now thou nam'st thy son: 160
    Thou art the lively image of my grief;
    Within thy face my sorrows I may see.
    Thy eyes are gummed with tears, thy cheeks are wan,
    Thy forehead troubled, and thy mutt'ring lips
    Murmur sad words abruptly broken off   165
    By force of windy sighs thy spirit breathes;
    And all this sorrow riseth for thy son:
    And selfsame sorrow feel I for my son.
    Come in, old man, thou shalt to Isabel.
    Lean on my arm; I thee, thou me, shalt stay,   170
    And thou, and I, and she will sing a song,
    Three parts in one, but all of discords framed—
    Talk not of chords, but let us now be gone,
    For with a cord Horatio was slain.   *Exeunt.*

---

150 *favor*   both "appearance" and "good fortune."   155 *Minos*   another judge in the
Underworld.

ACT III

{ Scene 15   *The Spanish court* }

Enter KING OF SPAIN, *the* DUKE, VICEROY, *and* LORENZO, BALTHAZAR,
DON PEDRO, *and* BEL-IMPERIA.

KING   Go, brother, it is the Duke of Castile's cause;
    Salute the Viceroy in our name.
CASTILE   I go.
VICEROY   Go forth, Don Pedro, for thy nephew's sake,
    And greet the Duke of Castile.
PEDRO   It shall be so.
KING   And now to meet these Portuguese,   5
    For as we now are, so sometimes were these:
    Kings and commanders of the western Indies.
    Welcome, brave Viceroy, to the court of Spain,
    And welcome, all his honorable train!
    'Tis not unknown to us for why you come,   10
    Or have so kingly crossed the seas.
    Sufficeth it, in this we note the troth
    And more than common love you lend to us.
    So is it that mine honorable niece
    (For it beseems us now that it be known)   15
    Already is betrothed to Balthazar;
    And by appointment and our condescent
    Tomorrow are they to be marrièd.
    To this intent we entertain thyself,
    Thy followers, their pleasure, and our peace.   20
    Speak, men of Portingale, shall it be so?
    If ay, say so; if not, say flatly no.
VICEROY   Renownèd King, I come not, as thou thinkst,
    With doubtful followers, unresolvèd men,
    But such as have upon thine articles   25
    Confirmed thy motion and contented me.
    Know, sovereign, I come to solemnize
    The marriage of thy beloved niece,
    Fair Bel-imperia, with my Balthazar,
    With thee, my son; whom sith I live to see,   30

🦚 ACT III, Scene 15.   17 *condescent*   consent.

Here take my crown, I give it her and thee;
And let me live a solitary life,
In ceaseless prayers,
To think how strangely heaven hath thee preserved.
KING   See, brother, see, how nature strives in him!   35
Come, worthy Viceroy, and accompany
Thy friend with thine extremities;
A place more private fits this princely mood.
VICEROY   Or here, or where your highness thinks it good.
                              Exeunt all but CASTILE *and* LORENZO.
CASTILE   Nay, stay, Lorenzo, let me talk with you.   40
Seest thou this entertainment of these kings?
LORENZO   I do, my lord, and joy to see the same.
CASTILE   And knowst thou why this meeting is?
LORENZO   For her, my lord, whom Balthazar doth love,
And to confirm their promised marriage.   45
CASTILE   She is thy sister?
LORENZO   Who, Bel-imperia?
Ay, my gracious lord, and this is the day,
That I have longed so happily to see.
CASTILE   Thou wouldst be loth that any fault of thine
Should intercept her in her happiness?   50
LORENZO   Heavens will not let Lorenzo err so much.
CASTILE   Why then, Lorenzo, listen to my words:
It is suspected, and reported too,
That thou, Lorenzo, wrongst Hieronimo,
And in his suits towards his majesty   55
Still keeps him back, and seeks to cross his suit.
LORENZO   That I, my lord—?
CASTILE   I tell thee, son, myself have heard it said,
When to my sorrow I have been ashamed
To answer for thee, though thou art my son.   60
Lorenzo, knowst thou not the common love
And kindness that Hieronimo hath won
By his deserts within the court of Spain?
Or seest thou not the King my brother's care
In his behalf, and to procure his health?   65
Lorenzo, shouldst thou thwart his passions,

---

35 *how . . . him* how natural feelings of happiness overwhelm his formal reserve.
37 *extremities* intense emotions.   **39** *Or . . . or* either . . . or.

And he exclaim against thee to the King,
What honor were't in this assembly,
Or what a scandal were't among the kings
To hear Hieronimo exclaim on thee?   70
Tell me—and look thou tell me truly too—
Whence grows the ground of this report in court?

LORENZO   My lord, it lies not in Lorenzo's power
To stop the vulgar liberal of their tongues.
A small advantage makes a water-breach,   75
And no man lives that long contenteth all.

CASTILE   Myself have seen thee busy to keep back
Him and his supplications from the King.

LORENZO   Yourself, my lord, hath seen his passions,
That ill beseemed the presence of a king;   80
And for I pitied him in his distress,
I held him thence with kind and courteous words
As free from malice to Hieronimo
As to my soul, my lord.

CASTILE   Hieronimo, my son, mistakes thee then.   85

LORENZO   My gracious father, believe me, so he doth.
But what's a silly man, distract in mind
To think upon the murder of his son?
Alas, how easy is it for him to err!
But for his satisfaction and the world's,   90
'Twere good, my lord, that Hieronimo and I
Were reconciled, if he misconster me.

CASTILE   Lorenzo, thou hast said, it shall be so.
Go one of you, and call Hieronimo.

Enter BALTHAZAR *and* BEL-IMPERIA.

BALTHAZAR   Come, Bel-imperia, Balthazar's content,   95
My sorrow's ease and sovereign of my bliss,
Sith heaven hath ordained thee to be mine.
Disperse those clouds and melancholy looks,
And clear them up with those thy sun-bright eyes,
Wherein my hope and heaven's fair beauty lies.   100

BEL-IMPERIA   My looks, my lord, are fitting for my love,
Which, new-begun, can show no brighter yet.

---

74 *vulgar liberal* common overuse.   **75** *small . . . water-breach* Like water rushing
against cracks in a dam, rumor enlarges small weaknesses.   **81** *And for* because.
85 *mistakes* misunderstands.   **87** *silly* pathetic, in need of compassion.   **92** *misconster* misinterpret.

BALTHAZAR   New-kindled flames should burn as morning sun.
BEL-IMPERIA   But not too fast, lest heat and all be done.
    I see my lord my father.
BALTHAZAR   Truce, my love;   105
    I will go salute him.
CASTILE   Welcome, Balthazar.
    Welcome, brave Prince, the pledge of Castile's peace!
    And welcome, Bel-imperia!—How now, girl?
    Why comst thou sadly to salute us thus?
    Content thyself, for I am satisfied: 110
    It is not now as when Andrea lived;
    We have forgotten and forgiven that,
    And thou art gracèd with a happier love.
    But, Balthazar, here comes Hieronimo;
    I'll have a word with him.   115

    Enter HIERONIMO *and a* SERVANT.

HIERONIMO   And where's the Duke?
SERVANT   Yonder.
HIERONIMO   Even so.—
    What new device have they devisèd, trow?
    Pocas palabras! Mild as the lamb!
    Is't I will be revenged? No, I am not the man.
CASTILE   Welcome, Hieronimo.   120
LORENZO   Welcome, Hieronimo.
BALTHAZAR   Welcome, Hieronimo.
HIERONIMO   My lords, I thank you for Horatio.
CASTILE   Hieronimo, the reason that I sent
    To speak with you is this:
HIERONIMO   —What, so short?   125
    Then I'll be gone, I thank you for't.
CASTILE   Nay, stay, Hieronimo! Go call him, son.
LORENZO   Hieronimo, my father craves a word with you.
HIERONIMO   With me, sir? Why, my lord, I thought you had done.
LORENZO   No. [*Aside.*] Would he had!
CASTILE   Hieronimo, I hear   130
    You find yourself aggrievèd at my son,
    Because you have not access unto the King;
    And say 'tis he that intercepts your suits.

117 *trow* I wonder. **118** *Pocas palabras* (Spanish) few words. **119** *I . . . man* I am
not the man (who is courageous enough to carry out his revenge).

HIERONIMO   Why, is not this a miserable thing, my lord?
CASTILE   Hieronimo, I hope you have no cause,   135
      And would be loath that one of your deserts
      Should once have reason to suspect my son,
      Considering how I think of you myself.
HIERONIMO   Your son Lorenzo! Whom, my noble lord?
      The hope of Spain, mine honorable friend?   140
      Grant me the combat of them, if they dare;

      Draws out his sword.

      I'll meet him face to face, to tell me so!
      These be the scandalous reports of such
      As love not me, and hate my lord too much.
      Should I suspect Lorenzo would prevent   145
      Or cross my suit, that loved my son so well?
      My lord, I am ashamed it should be said.
LORENZO   Hieronimo, I never gave you cause.
HIERONIMO   My good lord, I know you did not.
CASTILE   There then pause;
      And for the satisfaction of the world,   150
      Hieronimo, frequent my homely house,
      The Duke of Castile, Cyprian's ancient seat;
      And where thou wilt, use me, my son, and it.
      But here, before Prince Balthazar and me,
      Embrace each other, and be perfect friends.   155
HIERONIMO   Ay, marry, my lord, and shall.
      Friends, quoth he? See, I'll be friends with you all:
      Especially with you, my lovely lord;
      For divers causes it is fit for us
      That we be friends: the world is suspicious,   160
      And men may think what we imagine not.
BALTHAZAR   Why, this is friendly done, Hieronimo.
LORENZO   And that I hope: old grudges are forgot.
HIERONIMO   What else? It were a shame it should not be so.
CASTILE   Come on, Hieronimo, at my request;   165
      Let us entreat your company today.   *Exeunt [all but* HIERONIMO].
HIERONIMO   Your lordship's to command.—Pha! keep your way:
      Chi mi fa piú carezze che non suole,
      Tradito mi ha, o tradir mi vuole.

---

136 *of . . . deserts*   so deserving as you.   **151** *homely*   hospitable.   **158** *lovely*   meriting
love (because of moral worth).   **168–69** *Chi . . . vuole*   (Italian) He who shows me more
affection than usual either has betrayed me or wants to do so.

{ ACT III }
Chorus

GHOST [*of* ANDREA] *and* REVENGE.

GHOST   Awake, Erichtho! Cerberus, awake!
Solicit Pluto, gentle Proserpine!
To combat, Acheron and Erebus!
For ne'er, by Styx and Phlegethon in hell,
Nor ferried Charon to the fiery lakes   5
Such fearful sights, as poor Andrea sees.
Revenge, awake!
REVENGE   Awake? For why?
GHOST   Awake, Revenge; for thou art ill-advised
To sleep away what thou art warned to watch!
REVENGE   Content thyself, and do not trouble me.   10
GHOST   Awake, Revenge, if love—as love hath had—
Have yet the power or prevalence in hell!
Hieronimo with Lorenzo is joined in league,
And intercepts our passage to revenge.
Awake, Revenge, or we are woebegone!   15
REVENGE   Thus worldlings ground what they have dreamed upon.
Content thyself, Andrea; though I sleep,
Yet is my mood soliciting their souls.
Sufficeth thee that poor Hieronimo
Cannot forget his son Horatio.   20
Nor dies Revenge, although he sleep awhile;
For in unquiet, quietness is feigned,
And slumb'ring is a common worldly wile.
Behold, Andrea, for an instance, how
Revenge hath slept, and then imagine thou   25
What 'tis to be subject to destiny.

Enter a dumb show.

GHOST   Awake, Revenge; reveal this mystery.
REVENGE   The two first, the nuptial torches bore,

🐾 **ACT III, Chorus   I *Erichtho*** a sorceress. **3 *Erebus*** primeval darkness. **5–7
*Nor . . . awake*** These lines are corrupt, and what is here presented is a text emended by
modern editors. **16 *ground*** base their impressions upon. **18 *mood soliciting*** anger
taking control of. **27 *mystery*** the meaning of the dumb show.

As brightly burning as the midday's sun;
But after them doth Hymen hie as fast,   30
Clothed in sable and a saffron robe,
And blows them out, and quencheth them with blood,
As discontent that things continue so.

GHOST   Sufficeth me; thy meaning's understood,
And thanks to thee and those infernal powers   35
That will not tolerate a lover's woe.
Rest thee, for I will sit to see the rest.

REVENGE   Then argue not, for thou hast thy request.   *Exeunt.*

ACT IV

{Scene 1   *The* DUKE'*s castle*}

Enter BEL-IMPERIA *and* HIERONIMO.

BEL-IMPERIA   Is this the love thou bearst Horatio?
Is this the kindness that thou counterfeits?
Are these the fruits of thine incessant tears?
Hieronimo, are these thy passions,
Thy protestations and thy deep laments,   5
That thou wert wont to weary men withal?
O unkind father! O deceitful world!
With what excuses canst thou show thyself
From this dishonor and the hate of men,
Thus to neglect the loss and life of him   10
Whom both my letters and thine own belief
Assures thee to be causeless slaughterèd?
Hieronimo, for shame, Hieronimo,
Be not a history to aftertimes
Of such ingratitude unto thy son.   15
Unhappy mothers of such children then!
But monstrous fathers to forget so soon

---

30 Hymen   god of marriage.
🦚 **ACT IV, Scene 1.   8–9 With . . . men**   After line 8 of the 1592 edition there is an
extraneous verse which combines lines 8 and 9: "With what dishonor and the hate of
men."

The death of those whom they with care and cost
Have tendered so, thus careless should be lost.
Myself, a stranger in respect of thee,   20
So loved his life, as still I wish their deaths.
Nor shall his death be unrevenged by me,
Although I bear it out for fashion's sake;
For here I swear, in sight of heaven and earth,
Shouldst thou neglect the love thou shouldst retain,   25
And give it over and devise no more,
Myself should send their hateful souls to hell
That wrought his downfall with extremest death.

HIERONIMO   But may it be that Bel-imperia
Vows such revenge as she hath deigned to say?   30
Why, then I see that heaven applies our drift,
And all the saints do sit soliciting
For vengeance on those cursèd murderers.
Madam, 'tis true—and now I find it so—
I found a letter, written in your name,   35
And in that letter, how Horatio died.
Pardon, O pardon, Bel-imperia,
My fear and care in not believing it;
Nor think I thoughtless think upon a mean
To let his death be unrevenged at full.   40
And here I vow—so you but give consent,
And will conceal my resolution—
I will ere long determine of their deaths
That causeless thus have murderèd my son.

BEL-IMPERIA   Hieronimo, I will consent, conceal,   45
And aught that may effect for thine avail,
Join with thee to revenge Horatio's death.

HIERONIMO   On, then. Whatsoever I devise,
Let me entreat you, grace my practices,
For why the plot's already in mine head.   50
Here they are.

Enter BALTHAZAR *and* LORENZO.

---

19 *thus . . . lost*   The phrase modifies children of "unhappy mothers" and "monstrous fathers."   **20** *stranger . . . thee*   a stranger to Horatio when compared to you, his father.   **23** *bear it out*   pretend not to think about his death or revenge.   **31** *applies our drift* directs our courage.   **39–40** *Nor . . . full*   Do not think that I thoughtlessly plan to let his death pass unrevenged.   **50** *For why*   because.

BALTHAZAR   How now, Hieronimo?
   What, courting Bel-imperia?
HIERONIMO   Ay, my lord;
   Such courting as, I promise you,
   She hath my heart, but you, my lord, have hers.
LORENZO   But now, Hieronimo, or never,   55
   We are to entreat your help.
HIERONIMO   My help?
   Why, my good lords, assure yourselves of me;
   For you have given me cause,—ay, by my faith have you!
BALTHAZAR   It pleased you, at the entertainment of the Ambassador,
   To grace the King so much as with a show.   60
   Now, were your study so well furnishèd,
   As, for the passing of the first night's sport,
   To entertain my father with the like,
   Or any such like pleasing motion,
   Assure yourself, it would content them well.   65
HIERONIMO   Is this all?
BALTHAZAR   Ay, this is all.
HIERONIMO   Why then, I'll fit you; say no more.
   When I was young, I gave my mind
   And plied myself to fruitless poetry;
   Which though it profit the professor naught,   70
   Yet is it passing pleasing to the world.
LORENZO   And how for that?
HIERONIMO   Marry, my good lord, thus—
   And yet methinks, you are too quick with us—
   When in Toledo there I studièd,
   It was my chance to write a tragedy,   75
   See here, my lords,

   He shows them a book.

   Which, long forgot, I found this other day.
   Now would your lordships favor me so much
   As but to grace me with your acting it—
   I mean each one of you to play a part—   80
   Assure you it will prove most passing strange,

---

60 *as with* with.   **64** *motion* entertainment.   **67** *I'll fit you* a pun, meaning both "I'll oblige you" and "I'll pay you what you deserve." For a modern reference to the ambiguity in this passage, see T. S. Eliot's *The Wasteland,* v.431.   **73** *quick* impatient.

And wondrous plausible to that assembly.

BALTHAZAR   What, would you have us play a tragedy?

HIERONIMO   Why, Nero thought it no disparagement,
And kings and emperors have ta'en delight   85
To make experience of their wits in plays.

LORENZO   Nay, be not angry, good Hieronimo;
The Prince but asked a question.

BALTHAZAR   In faith, Hieronimo, and you be in earnest,
I'll make one.

LORENZO   And I another.   90

HIERONIMO   Now, my good lord, could you entreat
Your sister Bel-imperia to make one?
For what's a play without a woman in it?

BEL-IMPERIA   Little entreaty shall serve me, Hieronimo;
For I must needs be employed in your play.   95

HIERONIMO   Why, this is well. I tell you, lordings,
It was determined to have been acted
By gentlemen and scholars too,
Such as could tell what to speak.

BALTHAZAR   And now

It shall be played by princes and courtiers,   100
Such as can tell how to speak
If, as it is our country manner,
You will but let us know the argument.

HIERONIMO   That shall I roundly. The chronicles of Spain
Record this written of a knight of Rhodes: 105
He was betrothed, and wedded at the length
To one Perseda, an Italian dame,
Whose beauty ravished all that her beheld,
Especially the soul of Soliman,
Who at the marriage was the chiefest guest.   110
By sundry means sought Soliman to win
Perseda's love, and could not gain the same.
Then 'gan he break his passions to a friend,
One of his bashaws, whom he held full dear.

---

82 plausible another pun, meaning both "worthy of applause" and "convincingly realistic" (because the murders will actually occur). **84 Nero** Emperor of Rome from A.D. 54–68, who prided himself on his artistic talents. He, like Hieronimo in this instance, delighted in conceiving brutal and spectacular public displays. **89 and** and if. **97 determined** intended. **103 argument** plot. **104 roundly** without delay. **114 bashaws** men of high rank or office in Turkey.

Her had this bashaw long solicited,   115
And saw she was not otherwise to be won,
But by her husband's death, this knight of Rhodes,
Whom presently by treachery he slew.
She, stirred with an exceeding hate therefore,
As cause of this slew Soliman,   120
And, to escape the bashaw's tyranny,
Did stab herself; and this the tragedy.

LORENZO   O excellent!

BEL-IMPERIA   But say, Hieronimo,
    What then became of him that was the bashaw?

HIERONIMO   Marry, thus: moved with remorse of his misdeeds,   125
    Ran to a mountain top, and hung himself.

BALTHAZAR   But which of us is to perform that part?

HIERONIMO   O, that will I, my lords; make no doubt of it.
    I'll play the murderer, I warrant you;
    For I already have conceited that.   130

BALTHAZAR   And what shall I?

HIERONIMO   Great Soliman, the Turkish emperor.

LORENZO   And I?

HIERONIMO   Erastus, the knight of Rhodes.

BEL-IMPERIA   And I?

HIERONIMO   Perseda, chaste and resolute.
    And here, my lords, are several abstracts drawn,   135
    For each of you to note your parts,
    And act it, as occasion's offered you.
    You must provide a Turkish cap,
    A black mustachio and a fauchion;

Gives a paper to BALTHAZAR.

    You with a cross, like to a knight of Rhodes;   140

Gives another to LORENZO.

    And, madam, you must attire yourself

He giveth BEL-IMPERIA *another.*

    Like Phoebe, Flora, or the huntress,
    Which to your discretion shall seem best.

---

118 *he* the bashaw.   **130** *conceited* conceived of.   **139** *fauchion* a broad-bladed,
slightly curved sword.   **142** *Phoebe* a goddess of the moon. *the huntress* Diana,
the goddess of chastity.

And as for me, my lords, I'll look to one,
And, with the ransom that the Viceroy sent,   145
So furnish and perform this tragedy,
As all the world shall say, Hieronimo
Was liberal in gracing of it so.

BALTHAZAR   Hieronimo, methinks a comedy were better.

HIERONIMO   A comedy?   150
Fie! comedies are fit for common wits;
But to present a kingly troop withal,
Give me a stately-written tragedy;
Tragoedia cothurnata, fitting kings,
Containing matter, and not common things.   155
My lords, all this must be performed,
As fitting for the first night's reveling.
The Italian tragedians were so sharp of wit,
That in one hour's meditation
They would perform anything in action.   160

LORENZO   And well it may; for I have seen the like
In Paris 'mongst the French tragedians.

HIERONIMO   In Paris? mass! And well rememberèd!
There's one thing more that rests for us to do.

BALTHAZAR   What's that, Hieronimo? Forget not anything.   165

HIERONIMO   Each one of us must act his part
In unknown languages,
That it may breed the more variety:
As you, my lord, in Latin, I in Greek,
You in Italian; and for because I know   170
That Bel-imperia hath practiced the French,
In courtly French shall all her phrases be.

BEL-IMPERIA   You mean to try my cunning then, Hieronimo?

BALTHAZAR   But this will be a mere confusion
And hardly shall we all be understood.   175

HIERONIMO   It must be so; for the conclusion

---

144 I'll . . . one I'll act, and provide the costume for, one part myself. **148 gracing**
producing. **154 Tragoedia cothurnata** the buskined, formal tragedy of the Greek
theater. **160 They** This reference is probably not to Italian "tragedians," as Hieronimo
says, but rather to the actors of Italian *commedia dell'arte*, where much of the action was
spontaneously developed out of situations involving stock comic characters. **163 mass**
an exclamation of surprise (contracted from "by the mass!"). **173 cunning** a pun,
meaning both "aptitude for learning" and "skill in trickery." **175 hardly** with
difficulty.

Shall prove the invention and all was good;
And I myself in an oration,
And with a strange and wondrous show besides,
That I will have there behind a curtain,   180
Assure yourself, shall make the matter known;
And all shall be concluded in one scene,
For there's no pleasure ta'en in tediousness.

BALTHAZAR [*Aside to* LORENZO.] How like you this?
LORENZO [*Aside to* BALTHAZAR.] Why, thus my lord: 185
  We must resolve to soothe his humors up.
BALTHAZAR On then, Hieronimo; farewell till soon.
HIERONIMO You'll ply this gear?
LORENZO   I warrant you.
                        Exeunt all but HIERONIMO.
HIERONIMO   Why so!

Now shall I see the fall of Babylon,
Wrought by the heavens in this confusion.   190
And if the world like not this tragedy,
Hard is the hap of old Hieronimo.   *Exit.*

ACT IV

Scene 2   HIERONIMO'*s garden*

Enter ISABELLA *with a weapon*[, *a knife*].

ISABELLA Tell me no more! O monstrous homicides!
  Since neither piety nor pity moves
  The King to justice or compassion,
  I will revenge myself upon this place,
  Where thus they murdered my beloved son.   5

---

177 *invention . . . good* the imaginative artistry of the play's plot and all (the writing and acting) that goes with it. 186 *soothe . . . up* humor him. 188 *ply this gear* employ yourself at this business (of preparing for the play). 189 *Babylon* The kingdom of Babylon serves repeatedly in the Bible as a symbol of man's commitment to the ungodly: it is a city of material splendor, lust, and corruption; and the practices of its inhabitants are constantly denounced by the prophets. In Revelations, Chapter 18, its final destruction is announced and described. In addition, the word Babylon ("confusion") is associated with the Tower of Babel, a reference which Hieronimo is also making here— since his players are theoretically going to speak in different languages.

She cuts down the arbor.

Down with these branches and these loathsome boughs
Of this unfortunate and fatal pine!
Down with them, Isabella; rent them up,
And burn the roots from whence the rest is sprung!
I will not leave a root, a stalk, a tree,   10
A bough, a branch, a blossom, nor a leaf,
No, not an herb within this garden plot—
Accursèd complot of my misery!
Fruitless forever may this garden be,
Barren the earth, and blissless whosoever   15
Imagines not to keep it unmanured!
An eastern wind, commixed with noisome airs,
Shall blast the plants and the young saplings;
The earth with serpents shall be pesterèd,
And passengers, for fear to be infect,   20
Shall stand aloof, and, looking at it, tell:
"There, murdered, died the son of Isabel."
Ay, here he died, and here I him embrace;
See, where his ghost solicits with his wounds
Revenge on her that should revenge his death.   25
Hieronimo, make haste to see thy son:
For sorrow and despair hath cited me
To hear Horatio plead with Rhadamanth.
Make haste, Hieronimo, to hold excused
Thy negligence in pursuit of their deaths   30
Whose hateful wrath bereaved him of his breath.
Ah, nay, thou dost delay their deaths,
Forgives the murderers of thy noble son,
And none but I bestir me—to an end!
And as I curse this tree from further fruit,   35
So shall my womb be cursèd for his sake;
And with this weapon will I wound the breast,

She stabs herself.

The hapless breast, that gave Horatio suck.   [*She exits, dying.*]

🦋 ACT IV, Scene 2. SD *cuts down* Isabella probably hacks at the tree with the
"weapon." 8 *rent* tear. 13 *complot* conspirator. 16 *unmanured* uncultivated.
20 *passengers* those who pass by. 27 *cited* called me forth (incited). 29 *hold
excused* find excuse for.

ACT IV
Scene 3   *The* DUKE'*s castle*

Enter HIERONIMO; *he knocks up the curtain[in order to conceal* HORATIO'*s body]. Enter the* DUKE OF CASTILE.

CASTILE   How now, Hieronimo, where's your fellows,
That you take all this pain?
HIERONIMO   O sir, it is for the author's credit
To look that all things may go well.
But, good my lord, let me entreat your grace   5
To give the King the copy of the play:
This is the argument of what we show.
CASTILE   I will, Hieronimo.
HIERONIMO   One thing more, my good lord.
CASTILE   What's that?
HIERONIMO   Let me entreat your grace   10
That, when the train are passed into the gallery,
You would vouchsafe to throw me down the key.
CASTILE   I will, Hieronimo.   *Exit* CASTILE.
HIERONIMO   What, are you ready, Balthazar?
Bring a chair and a cushion for the King.   15

Enter BALTHAZAR, *with a chair.*

Well done, Balthazar! Hang up the title:
Our scene is Rhodes. What, is your beard on?
BALTHAZAR   Half on; the other is in my hand.
HIERONIMO   Despatch for shame; are you so long?   *Exit* BALTHAZAR.
Bethink thyself, Hieronimo,   20
Recall thy wits, recompt thy former wrongs
Thou hast received by murder of thy son,
And lastly, not least, how Isabel,
Once his mother and thy dearest wife,
All woebegone for him, hath slain herself.   25
Behoves thee then, Hieronimo, to be revenged!

🦌 **ACT IV, Scene 3.   SD** *knocks up* probably "puts up hastily."   **7** *argument* summary of the play.   **11** *train . . . into* when the procession has entered.   *gallery* the audience of the play-within-the-play, probably seated on the main stage and partly encircling the actors of Hieronimo's production.   **16** *title* title board, containing essential information about the scene and time of the play.   **21** *recompt* tabulate again.

The plot is laid of dire revenge.
On, then, Hieronimo, pursue revenge.
For nothing wants but acting of revenge!   *Exit* HIERONIMO.

ACT IV
Scene 4   *The same*

Enter SPANISH KING, VICEROY, *the* DUKE OF CASTILE, *and their train.*

KING   Now, Viceroy, shall we see the tragedy
Of Soliman, the Turkish emperor,
Performed of pleasure by your son the Prince,
My nephew Don Lorenzo, and my niece.

VICEROY   Who? Bel-imperia?

KING   Ay, and Hieronimo, our marshal,   5
At whose request they deign to do't themselves.
These be our pastimes in the court of Spain.
Here, brother, you shall be the bookkeeper:
This is the argument of that they show.

He giveth him a book.

Gentlemen, this play of HIERONIMO, *in sundry languages, was thought*   10
good to be set down in English, more largely, for the easier understanding
to every public reader.

Enter BALTHAZAR, BEL-IMPERIA, *and* HIERONIMO.

BALTHAZAR   Bashaw, that Rhodes is ours, yield heavens the honor,
And holy Mahomet, our sacred prophet!
And be thou graced with every excellence   15
That Soliman can give, or thou desire.
But thy desert in conquering Rhodes is less
Than in reserving this fair Christian nymph,
Perseda, blissful lamp of excellence,
Whose eyes compel, like powerful adamant,   20
The warlike heart of Soliman to wait.

KING   See, Viceroy, that is Balthazar, your son,

🦊 ACT IV, Scene 4. 8 *bookkeeper* prompter. 10–12 *Gentlemen . . . reader*
perhaps the printer's note or a modification of a prologue spoken by Hieronimo.

That represents the emperor Soliman:
How well he acts his amorous passion!
VICEROY   Ay, Bel-imperia hath taught him that.   25
CASTILE   That's because his mind runs all on Bel-imperia.
HIERONIMO   Whatever joy earth yields, betide your majesty.
BALTHAZAR   Earth yields no joy without Perseda's love.
HIERONIMO   Let then Perseda on your grace attend.
BALTHAZAR   She shall not wait on me, but I on her: 30
   Drawn by the influence of her lights, I yield.
   But let my friend, the Rhodian knight, come forth,
   Erasto, dearer than my life to me,
   That he may see Perseda, my beloved.

   Enter ERASTO.

KING   Here comes Lorenzo: look upon the plot,   35
   And tell me, brother, what part plays he?

BEL-IMPERIA   Ah, my Erasto, welcome to Perseda.
LORENZO   Thrice happy is Erasto that thou livst;
   Rhodes' loss is nothing to Erasto's joy;
   Sith his Perseda lives, his life survives.   40
BALTHAZAR   Ah, bashaw, here is love between Erasto
   And fair Perseda, sovereign of my soul.
HIERONIMO   Remove Erasto, mighty Soliman,
   And then Perseda will be quickly won.
BALTHAZAR   Erasto is my friend; and while he lives,   45
   Perseda never will remove her love.
HIERONIMO   Let not Erasto live to grieve great Soliman.
BALTHAZAR   Dear is Erasto in our princely eye.
HIERONIMO   But if he be your rival, let him die.
BALTHAZAR   Why, let him die: so love commandeth me.   50
   Yet grieve I that Erasto should so die.
HIERONIMO   Erasto, Soliman saluteth thee,
   And lets thee wit by me his highness' will,
   Which is, thou shouldst be thus employed. *Stab him.*
BEL-IMPERIA   Ay me!
   Erasto! See, Soliman, Erasto's slain!   55
BALTHAZAR   Yet liveth Soliman to comfort thee.
   Fair queen of beauty, let not favor die,
   But with a gracious eye behold his grief,
   That with Perseda's beauty is increased,
   If by Perseda his grief be not released.   60

31 *lights* eyes.   53 *wit* know.

BEL-IMPERIA   Tyrant, desist soliciting vain suits;
  Relentless are mine ears to thy laments,
  As thy butcher is pitiless and base,
  Which seized on my Erasto, harmless knight.
  Yet by thy power thou thinkest to command,   65
  And to thy power Perseda doth obey;
  But, were she able, thus she would revenge
  Thy treacheries on thee, ignoble Prince:
  Stab him.
  And on herself she would be thus revenged.   *Stab herself.*

KING   Well said!—Old Marshal, this was bravely done! 70
HIERONIMO   But Bel-imperia plays Perseda well!
VICEROY   Were this in earnest, Bel-imperia,
  You would be better to my son than so.
KING   But now what follows for Hieronimo?
HIERONIMO   Marry, this follows for Hieronimo: 75
  Here break we off our sundry languages,
  And thus conclude I in our vulgar tongue.
  Haply you think—but bootless are your thoughts—
  That this is fabulously counterfeit,
  And that we do as all tragedians do,   80
  To die today, for fashioning our scene,
  The death of Ajax or some Roman peer,
  And in a minute starting up again,
  Revive to please tomorrow's audience.
  No, Princes; know I am Hieronimo,   85
  The hopeless father of a hapless son,
  Whose tongue is tuned to tell his latest tale,
  Not to excuse gross errors in the play.
  I see, your looks urge instance of these words;
  Behold the reason urging me to this!   90
  Shows his dead son.

  See here my show, look on this spectacle!
  Here lay my hope, and here my hope hath end;
  Here lay my heart, and here my heart was slain;
  Here lay my treasure, here my treasure lost;
  Here lay my bliss, and here my bliss bereft;   95

70 *bravely* making a fine show or display. **82 *death of Ajax*** the subject of a tragedy
by Sophocles. **89 *instance*** evidence.

But hope, heart, treasure, joy, and bliss,
All fled, failed, died, yea, all decayed with this.
From forth these wounds came breath that gave me life;
They murdered me that made these fatal marks.
The cause was love, whence grew this mortal hate: 100
The hate, Lorenzo and young Balthazar,
The love, my son to Bel-imperia.
But night, the coverer of accursèd crimes,
With pitchy silence hushed these traitors' harms,
And lent them leave, for they had sorted leisure   105
To take advantage in my garden plot
Upon my son, my dear Horatio.
There merciless they butchered up my boy,
In black, dark night, to pale, dim, cruel death.
He shrieks; I heard—and yet, methinks, I hear—   110
His dismal outcry echo in the air.
With soonest speed I hasted to the noise,
Where hanging on a tree I found my son,
Through-girt with wounds, and slaught'red as you see.
And grieved I, think you, at this spectacle?   115
Speak, Portuguese, whose loss resembles mine:
If thou canst weep upon thy Balthazar,
'Tis like I wailed for my Horatio.
And you, my lord, whose reconcilèd son
Marched in a net, and thought himself unseen,   120
And rated me for brainsick lunacy,
With "God amend that mad Hieronimo!"—
How can you brook our play's catastrophe?
And here behold this bloody handkercher,
Which at Horatio's death I weeping dipped   125
Within the river of his bleeding wounds:
It as propitious, see, I have reserved,
And never hath it left my bloody heart,
Soliciting remembrance of my vow
With these, O, these accursèd murderers,   130
Which now performed, my heart is satisfied.
And to this end the bashaw I became
That might revenge me on Lorenzo's life,

---

105 *sorted* chosen.   **114** *Through-girt* pierced through.   **120** *Marched . . . net*
acted deceitfully.   **121** *rated* berated.

Who therefore was appointed to the part,
And was to represent the knight of Rhodes,   135
That I might kill him more conveniently.
So, Viceroy, was this Balthazar, thy son,
That Soliman which Bel-imperia,
In person of Perseda, murderèd;
Solely appointed to that tragic part   140
That she might slay him that offended her.
Poor Bel-imperia missed her part in this:
For though the story saith she should have died,
Yet I of kindness, and of care to her,
Did otherwise determine of her end;   145
But love of him whom they did hate too much
Did urge her resolution to be such.
And, Princes, now behold Hieronimo,
Author and actor in this tragedy,
Bearing his latest fortune in his fist;   150
And will as resolute conclude his part,
As any of the actors gone before.
And, gentles, thus I end my play;
Urge no more words; I have no more to say.

He runs to hang himself.

KING   O hearken, Viceroy! Hold, Hieronimo!   155
Brother, my nephew and thy son are slain!
VICEROY   We are betrayed! My Balthazar is slain!
Break ope the doors; run, save Hieronimo.

[*They break in and hold* HIERONIMO.]

Hieronimo, do but inform the King of these events;
Upon mine honor, thou shalt have no harm.   160
HIERONIMO   Viceroy, I will not trust thee with my life,
Which I this day have offered to my son.
Accursèd wretch!
Why stayst thou him that was resolved to die?
KING   Speak, traitor! Damnèd, bloody murd'rer, speak!   165
For now I have thee, I will make thee speak.
Why hast thou done this undeserving deed?
VICEROY   Why has thou murderèd my Balthazar?
CASTILE   Why hast thou butchered both my children thus?

---

150 his . . . fortune   the rope with which he intends to hang himself.

HIERONIMO   O, good words!   170
   As dear to me was my Horatio
   As yours, or yours, or yours, my lord, to you.
   My guiltless son was by Lorenzo slain,
   And by Lorenzo and that Balthazar
   Am I at last revengèd thoroughly,   175
   Upon whose souls may heavens be yet avenged
   With greater far than these afflictions.
CASTILE   But who were thy confederates in this?
VICEROY   That was thy daughter Bel-imperia;
   For by her hand my Balthazar was slain: 180
   I saw her stab him.
KING   Why speakst thou not?
HIERONIMO   What lesser liberty can kings afford
   Than harmless silence? Then afford it me.
   Sufficeth, I may not, nor I will not tell thee.
KING   Fetch forth the tortures; traitor as thou art,   185
   I'll make thee tell.
HIERONIMO   Indeed,
   Thou mayst torment me as his wretched son
   Hath done in murd'ring my Horatio;
   But never shalt thou force me to reveal
   The thing which I have vowed inviolate.   190
   And therefore, in despite of all thy threats,
   Pleased with their deaths, and eased with their revenge,
   First take my tongue, and afterwards my heart.
[HIERONIMO   *But are you sure they are dead?*
CASTILE   *Ay, slave, too sure.*
HIERONIMO   *What, and yours too?*   195
VICEROY   *Ay, all are dead; not one of them survive.*
HIERONIMO   *Nay, then I care not; come, and we shall be friends.*
   Let us lay our heads together:
   See, here's a goodly noose will hold them all.
VICEROY   *O damnèd devil, how secure he is!*   200
HIERONIMO   *Secure? Why, dost thou wonder at it?*
   I tell thee, Viceroy, this day I have seen revenge,
   And in that sight am grown a prouder monarch,
   Than ever sat under the crown of Spain.

194–243 *But . . . heart*   The fifth set of additions replaces lines 170–93.   **200** *secure* self-assured.

    Had I as many lives as there be stars,   205
    As many heavens to go to, as those lives,
    I'd give them all, ay, and my soul to boot,
    But I would see thee ride in this red pool.
CASTILE   But who were thy confederates in this?
VICEROY   That was thy daughter Bel-imperia;   210
    For by her hand my Balthazar was slain:
    I saw her stab him.
HIERONIMO   O, good words!
    As dear to me was my Horatio,
    As yours, or yours, or yours, my lord, to you.   215
    My guiltless son was by Lorenzo slain,
    And by Lorenzo and that Balthazar
    Am I at last revengèd thoroughly,
    Upon whose souls may heavens be yet revenged
    With greater far than these afflictions.   220
    Methinks, since I grew inward with revenge,
    I cannot look with scorn enough on death.
KING   What, dost thou mock us, slave? Bring tortures forth!
HIERONIMO   Do, do, do; and meantime I'll torture you.
    You had a son, as I take it; and your son   225
    Should ha' been married to your daughter.
    Ha, was it not so?—You had a son too.
    He was my liege's nephew; he was proud
    And politic; had he lived, he might ha' come
    To wear the crown of Spain, I think 'twas so.   230
    'Twas I that killed him; look you, this same hand.
    'Twas it that stabbed his heart—do ye see? this hand—
    For one Horatio, if you ever knew him: a youth,
    One that they hanged up in his father's garden;
    One that did force your valiant son to yield,   235
    While your more valiant son did take him prisoner.
VICEROY   Be deaf, my senses; I can hear no more.
KING   Fall, heaven, and cover us with thy sad ruins.
CASTILE   Roll all the world within thy pitchy cloud.
HIERONIMO   Now do I applaud what I have acted.   240
    Nunc iners cadat manus!

---

221 grew ... with became familiar with. **225–26 your ... daughter** Hieronimo turns
from the Viceroy to the Duke as he talks. **241 Nunc . . . manus** My hand now falls
idle.

Now to express the rupture of my part:
First take my tongue, and afterward my heart.]

He bites out his tongue.

KING   O monstrous resolution of a wretch!
    See, Viceroy, he hath bitten forth his tongue,   245
    Rather than to reveal what we required.
CASTILE   Yet can he write.
KING   And if in this he satisfy us not,
    We will devise th'extremest kind of death
    That ever was invented for a wretch.   250

Then he make[s] signs for a knife to mend his pen.

CASTILE   O, he would have a knife to mend his pen.
    Here, and advise thee that thou write the troth.—
    Look to my brother! Save Hieronimo!

He with a knife stabs the DUKE *and himself.*

KING   What age hath ever heard such monstrous deeds?
    My brother, and the whole succeeding hope   255
    That Spain expected after my decease!
    Go, bear his body hence, that we may mourn
    The loss of our belovèd brother's death,
    That he may be entombed whate'er befall.
    I am the next, the nearest, last of all.   260
VICEROY   And thou, Don Pedro, do the like for us:
    Take up our hapless son, untimely slain;
    Set me with him, and he with woeful me,
    Upon the mainmast of a ship unmanned,
    And let the wind and tide haul me along   265
    To Scylla's barking and untamèd gulf,
    Or to the loathsome pool of Acheron,
    To weep my want for my sweet Balthazar:
    Spain hath no refuge for a Portingale.

The trumpets sound a dead march, the KING OF SPAIN *mourning after*
his brother's body, and the KING OF PORTINGAL *bearing the body of his*
                                    son.

---

257 *his* the Duke's.   **266 *Scylla*** a mythological monster which captured and devoured
sailors who passed by its cave.

ACT IV
Chorus

Enter GHOST [*of* ANDREA] *and* REVENGE.

GHOST Ay, now my hopes have end in their effects,
When blood and sorrow finish my desires:
Horatio murdered in his father's bower;
Vild Serberine by Pedringano slain;
False Pedringano hanged by quaint device;   5
Fair Isabella by herself misdone;
Prince Balthazar by Bel-imperia stabbed;
The Duke of Castile and his wicked son
Both done to death by old Hieronimo;
My Bel-imperia fall'n as Dido fell,   10
And good Hieronimo slain by himself:
Ay, these were spectacles to please my soul!
Now will I beg at lovely Proserpine
That, by the virtue of her princely doom,
I may consort my friends in pleasing sort,   15
And on my foes work just and sharp revenge.
I'll lead my friend Horatio through those fields,
Where never-dying wars are still inured;
I'll lead fair Isabella to that train,
Where pity weeps, but never feeleth pain;   20
I'll lead my Bel-imperia to those joys
That vestal virgins and fair queens possess;
I'll lead Hieronimo where Orpheus plays,
Adding sweet pleasure to eternal days.
But say, Revenge, for thou must help, or none,   25
Against the rest how shall my hate be shown?
REVENGE This hand shall hale them down to deepest hell,
Where none but Furies, bugs, and tortures dwell.
GHOST Then, sweet Revenge, do this at my request:

🐎 ACT IV, Chorus   10 She killed herself after Aeneas abandoned her (cf. *Aeneid,* IV).
15 *consort* associate with.   18 *inured* carried on.   19 *train* procession of mourners.
23 *Orpheus* the most skilled of musicians.   28 *bugs* frightening objects, bugbears.

Let me be judge, and doom them to unrest.   30
Let loose poor Tityus from the vulture's gripe,
And let Don Cyprian supply his room;
Place Don Lorenzo on Ixion's wheel,
And let the lover's endless pains surcease
(Juno forgets old wrath, and grants him ease);   35
Hang Balthazar about Chimaera's neck,
And let him there bewail his bloody love,
Repining at our joys that are above;
Let Serberine go roll the fatal stone,
And take from Sisyphus his endless moan;   40
False Pedringano, for his treachery,
Let him be dragged through boiling Acheron,
And there live, dying still in endless flames,
Blaspheming gods and all their holy names.
REVENGE   Then haste we down to meet thy friends and foes: 45
To place thy friends in ease, the rest in woes;
For here though death hath end their misery,
I'll there begin their endless tragedy.   *Exeunt.*

---

31 **Tityus** in Greek mythology, a giant imprisoned in Hades and tortured by having
his liver constantly consumed by vultures. **gripe** grip. 33 **Ixion** As punishment
for attempting to seduce Juno, he was bound in Hades on an ever-turning wheel.
36 **Chimaera** a mythical monster, with the head of a lion, body of a goat, and tail of
a dragon. 40 **Sisyphus** a mythical king of Corinth who, for his misdeeds on earth,
was condemned in Hades eternally to roll to the top of a hill a large stone, which then
immediately rolled back down to the bottom.

VOLPONE,
OR
THE FOX
(1605)

Ben Jonson

This woodcut from Giacomo Franco's Habiti d'Huomeni et Donne Venetiane (1609 ?)
shows the various kinds of entertainment that one might find in a Venetian piazza. In the
foreground, a snake charmer, a troubadour, and actors from the commedia dell' arte perform before a cosmopolitan crowd. In the background, a small group is singing at the left,
while at the right a mountebank and his assistants, like Volpone before Celia's window,
peddle their miraculous elixirs. The Folger Shakespeare Library, Washington, D. C.

BEN JONSON (1572–1637) IS THE GREATEST OF the English comic dramatists, standing to the tragedy of his time as Aristophanes stood to the tragedy of Aeschylus, Sophocles, and Euripides. The posthumous son of a minister, Jonson attended Westminster School, where his master was the great classicist and English historian William Camden. He failed to win a university scholarship and was instead apprenticed as a bricklayer, a craft that may have contributed to the meticulous construction of his plays. He fought in the wars in the Low Countries, and upon his return to England became an actor. His most famous part was apparently that of Hieronimo in The Spanish Tragedy. From acting he drifted into writing plays, and by the late 1590's he was offering plays on the London stage and was deeply engaged in what was to be his chief activity throughout the remainder of his life.

Throughout these busy years—which included killing a better actor in a duel—Jonson continued his studies of the classics, and by the early 1600's he was known as one of the great English scholars. He conceived of his mission as the reform of the theaters and the restoration to drama of the classical virtues of simplicity, directness, morality, and order. This evangelical classicism was the literary form taken by his innate conservatism. In an age in which a great many men thought, with Tamburlaine, that man was capable of remaking the world to suit his own desires, Jonson looked on mankind with a comical and cynical eye. His plays dramatize the Renaissance dream of infinite power, infinite wealth, infinite pleasure. But while the dream is there in Volpone's delight in his limitless freedom and Sir Epicure Mammon's vision of life as unending pleasure and joy, it is presented by Jonson not in the heroic vein of Marlowe but in a comic and satiric vein. The great dreamers turn out to be only rascals and cheats; their aims are shown to be finally no higher than amassing money and seducing women, and their fates are not to storm the firmament but to end by revealing themselves as fools who have, by trying the impossible, cheated themselves of the very things they sought.

These comic treatments of the Marlovian subject matter reached their high point in the middle of Jonson's life in a series of plays beginning with Volpone *in 1604 and extending through* Epicoene *(1609) and* The Alchemist *(1610) to* Bartholomew Fair *(1614).*

For the rest of his life, Jonson was busily employed as a poet, playwright, critic, writer of court masques, translator, and general arbiter of poetic matters in London. After 1615, however, his dramatic genius never struck the same sparks again, and he died in 1637 after a long illness, poor and with his children dead before him. But despite the many trials and confusions of his life, Jonson never relinquished his idea of himself as a great poet and a great playwright. In an age when plays were considered not quite literature, writing for money not quite decent, and publication not quite respectable, Jonson gathered together his own plays written for the public stage and arranged for their publication in a grand manner befitting the most serious kind of writing. The first volume of his collected works, Opera, *was published in 1616, after Jonson carefully prepared the manuscript for the printer and then did something unheard of: proofreading and overseeing the printing. As a result, the texts of the plays printed in the 1616 volume are the only ones from a great age of drama where we can be certain that we have what the author intended us to have. The present text of* Volpone *is based on this 1616 folio.*

To the

Most Noble and Most Equal Sisters,

The Two Famous Universities,

for Their

Love and Acceptance Shown to His Poem   5

in the Presentation;

Ben. Jonson,

the Grateful Acknowledger,

Dedicates Both It and Himself.

There follows an Epistle, if   10

you dare venture on the length.

Never, most equal Sisters, had any man a wit so presently excellent as
that it could raise itself; but there must come both matter, occasion,
commenders, and favorers to it. If this be true, and that the fortune of all
writers doth daily prove it, it behooves the careful to provide well   15
toward these accidents, and, having acquired them, to preserve that part
of reputation most tenderly wherein the benefit of a friend is also
defended. Hence is it that I now render myself grateful and am studious
to justify the bounty of your act, to which, though your mere authority
were satisfying, yet, it being an age wherein poetry and the professors of   20
it hear so ill on all sides, there will a reason be looked for in the subject.
It is certain, nor can it with any forehead be opposed, that the too much
license of poetasters in this time hath much deformed their mistress,
that, every day, their manifold and manifest ignorance doth stick

Epistle   **2 Equal**   of equal merit, and in the Latin sense: *aequus,* just.   **3 Two . . .
Universities**   Oxford and Cambridge.   **6 Presentation**   At some time after *Volpone* had
been played in London by the King's Men (Shakespeare's company) in the winter of
1605–6, the play was presented at Oxford and Cambridge. The probable date of these
performances is the summer of 1606.   **10–11 There . . . length**   in quarto only.   **12 wit**
intelligence.   **presently**   immediately.   **13 matter**   subject matter.   **14 that**   that it be
the truth.   **16 toward**   for.   **accidents**   chance occurrences, incidental additions to wit
rather than innate characteristics.   **17 benefit**   kindness, i.e. the love and acceptance shown
to his poem.   **19 mere**   absolute.   **20 satisfying**   sufficient.   **professors**   practitioners.
21 hear so ill   are spoken of in such an ill manner.   **22 forehead**   assurance, command
of countenance.   **23 poetasters**   petty poets.   **mistress**   the poetic muse, i.e. poetry.

unnatural reproaches upon her; but for their petulancy it were an act of   25
the greatest injustice either to let the learned suffer, or so divine a skill
(which indeed should not be attempted with unclean hands) to fall
under the least contempt. For, if men will impartially, and not asquint,
look toward the offices and function of a poet, they will easily conclude
to themselves the impossibility of any man's being the good poet   30
without first being a good man. He that is said to be able to inform
young men to all good disciplines, inflame grown men to all great
virtues, keep old men in their best and supreme state, or, as they decline
to childhood, recover them to their first strength; that comes forth the
interpreter and arbiter of nature, a teacher of things divine no less than   35
human, a master in manners; and can alone, or with a few, effect the
business of mankind: this, I take him, is no subject for pride and
ignorance to exercise their railing rhetoric upon. But it will here be
hastily answered that the writers of these days are other things: that not
only their manners, but their natures, are inverted, and nothing   40
remaining with them of the dignity of poet but the abused name, which
every scribe usurps; that now, especially in dramatic, or, as they term it,
stage poetry, nothing but ribaldry, profanation, blasphemy, all license
of offense to God and man is practiced. I dare not deny a great part of
this, and am sorry I dare not, because in some men's abortive features   45
(and would they had never boasted the light) it is overtrue; but that all
are embarked in this bold adventure for hell is a most uncharitable
thought, and, uttered, a more malicious slander. For my particular, I
can, and from a most clear conscience, affirm, that I have ever trembled
to think toward the least profaneness, have loathed the use of such foul   50
and unwashed bawdry as is now made the food of the scene. And,
howsoever I cannot escape, from some, the imputation of sharpness, but

---

25 for because of. **petulancy** insolence. **31 inform** form, mold. **36–37 effect
. . . mankind** perform the proper functions of man. **37 I take him** as I understand it.
38 railing abusive. **42–44** Blasphemy, obscenity, and lack of moral purpose were the
standard charges leveled by the Puritans in their continuing war against the theaters. By
1606 there was some substance to their accusations, as Jonson admits, for in the sensational
plays of some writers like John Marston and Thomas Middleton there is a pronounced
tendency to seek out the obscene for its own sake. The best description of this new sensationalism in the theater is to be found in Alfred Harbage, *Shakespeare and the Rival
Tradition*, New York, 1952. Jonson in the Induction to *Every Man out of His Humor*
describes more fully the poetic practices to which he objects. **45 abortive features**
premature and malformed plays—plays are here considered the offspring of the poet.
51 food substance.

that they will say I have taken a pride, or lust, to be bitter, and not my
youngest infant but hath come into the world with all his teeth; I would
ask of these supercilious politics, what nation, society, or general order,   55
or state I have provoked? what public person? whether I have not in all
these preserved their dignity, as mine own person, safe? My works are
read, allowed (I speak of those that are entirely mine); look into them.
What broad reproofs have I used? where have I been particular? where
personal? except to a mimic, cheater, bawd, or buffoon, creatures for   60
their insolencies worthy to be taxed? Yet to which of these so pointingly
as he might not either ingenuously have confessed or wisely dissembled
his disease? But it is not rumor can make men guilty, much less entitle
me to other men's crimes. I know that nothing can be so innocently
writ or carried, but may be made obnoxious to construction; marry,   65
whilst I bear mine innocence about me, I fear it not. Application is now
grown a trade with many, and there are that profess to have a key for
the deciphering of everything; but let wise and noble persons take heed
how they be too credulous, or give leave to these invading interpreters
to be overfamiliar with their fames, who cunningly, and often, utter   70
their own virulent malice under other men's simplest meanings. As for
those that will (by faults which charity hath raked up, or common
honesty concealed) make themselves a name with the multitude, or (to
draw their rude and beastly claps) care not whose living faces they
entrench with their petulant styles, may they do it without a rival, for   75

---

53 lust liking. **54 youngest infant** Jonson's recent play, *Sejanus,* which had caused
him some difficulty with the authorities. **with . . . teeth** capable of biting, satiric.
Richard III was popularly believed to have been born with a full set of teeth, and Shakespeare, following tradition, makes of this a fearful omen of Richard's later unnatural
behavior. See *Richard III,* II.4. **55 politics** shrewd persons, with the additional sense
of cunning contrivers. **58 allowed** Licensed for public production by the Master of
the Revels, a court official who acted as censor in Elizabethan times. This power later
passed to the Lord Chamberlain, who, through a deputy called the censor, still exercises
it. **those . . . mine** Jonson was the part author of a number of plays, among them
Eastward Ho (1604), which he wrote with Chapman and Marston. This play, though it
was produced, was definitely not allowed, and Jonson went to jail, along with Chapman
and Marston, for certain passages in it which offended King James. **59 broad** indecent.
60 mimic actor or perhaps plagiarist. **61 taxed** censured. **pointingly** specifically.
65 carried managed. **to construction** by interpretation. **66 Application** specific
identification (of persons and events in plays). **67 there are** there are those. **70 utter**
used in the special sense of circulating false money. **72 raked up** covered over.
73 make . . . name by insisting that they are caricatured in some play. **74 claps**
applause. **75 entrench** mark.

me. I choose rather to lie graved in obscurity than share with them in so preposterous a fame. Nor can I blame the wishes of those severe and wiser patriots, who, providing the hurts these licentious spirits may do in a state, desire rather to see fools, and devils, and those antique relics of barbarism retrieved, with all other ridiculous and exploded follies,   80 than behold the wounds of private men, of princes, and nations. For, as Horace makes Trebatius speak, among these,

   —*Sibi quisque timet, quamquam est intactus, et odit.*

And men may justly impute such rages, if continued, to the writer, as his sports. The increase of which lust in liberty, together with the   85 present trade of the stage, in all their misc'line interludes, what learned or liberal soul doth not already abhor? where nothing but the filth of the time is uttered, and that with such impropriety of phrase, such plenty of solecisms, such dearth of sense, so bold prolepses, so racked metaphors, with brothelry able to violate the ear of a pagan, and   90 blasphemy to turn the blood of a Christian to water. I cannot but be serious in a cause of this nature, wherein my fame and the reputations of divers honest and learned are the question; when a name so full of

---

78 patriots those concerned for the nation's welfare. ***providing*** foreseeing. **79 fools, and devils** The reference here is to the old-fashioned morality plays and early Elizabethan drama modeled on these, in which fools of the slapstick variety, clowning devils, and melodramatic Vices were stocks in trade. The playwrights of the early seventeenth century, and Jonson particularly, were extremely self-conscious of writing a more sophisticated type of play, and they looked back with tolerant scorn on earlier plays, "antique relics of barbarism," and even on such recent drama of the ranting variety as Kyd's *The Spanish Tragedy* and Marlowe's *Tamburlaine*. For an example of Jonson's amused treatment of devils and the older type play see the opening scene of *The Devil Is an Ass*. **antique** grotesque. **80 exploded** literally "to clap and hoot off the stage" (OED). **83 Sibi . . . odit** "Although he is uninjured, everyone fears for himself and is angry" (Horace, *Sermones* 2.1.23). **84 the writer** The sense of this entire passage is somewhat difficult because Jonson leaps from subject to subject. Here it is necessary to realize that "the writer" and the man who considers that some foolish character in a play is a caricature of himself are one and the same. Jonson has in mind the so-called "War of the Theaters" in which he is supposed to have caricatured John Marston and Thomas Dekker. These writers took their revenge by putting Jonson in a play. The alternating process went on for several years. Jonson is here objecting that he never really meant to satirize any particular person, and arguing, in the age-old manner of satirists, that by being angry, the victim identifies himself with the fool in the play. **85 lust** pleasure. **liberty** unrestrained freedom. **86 misc'line** mixed, jumbled. **93 question** topic. **a name** Horace. Thomas Dekker in his play *Satiromastix* (1601) presented Jonson, in a ridiculous manner, under the name of Horace. Jonson had previously used Horace as the satirist in his *Poetaster*.

authority, antiquity, and all great mark, is, through their insolence, become the lowest scorn of the age; and those men subject to the 95 petulancy of every vernaculous orator that were wont to be the care of kings and happiest monarchs. This it is that hath not only rapt me to present indignation, but made me studious heretofore, and by all my actions to stand off from them; which may most appear in this my latest work—which you, most learned Arbitresses, have seen, judged, 100 and, to my crown, approved—wherein I have labored, for their instruction and amendment, to reduce not only the ancient forms, but manners of the scene: the easiness, the propriety, the innocence, and last, the doctrine, which is the principal end of poesie, to inform men in the best reason of living. And though my catastrophe may in the strict 105 rigor of comic law meet with censure, as turning back to my promise; I desire the learned and charitable critic to have so much faith in me to think it was done of industry: for with what ease I could have varied it nearer his scale (but that I fear to boast my own faculty) I could here insert. But my special aim being to put the snaffle in their mouths that 110 cry out: We never punish vice in our interludes, &c. I took the more liberty, though not without some lines of example, drawn even in the ancients themselves, the goings out of whose comedies are not always joyful, but oft times the bawds, the servants, the rivals, yea, and the masters are mulcted, and fitly, it being the office of a comic poet to 115 imitate justice, and instruct to life, as well as purity of language, or stir up gentle affections. To which I shall take the occasion elsewhere to speak. For the present, most reverenced Sisters, as I have cared to be thankful for your affections past, and here made the understanding

94 *mark* note. **96** *vernaculous* ill-bred, scurrilous. **97** *rapt* carried by force. **102** *reduce* bring back. **103** *innocence* harmlessness. **105** *catastrophe* climax of the play. **106** *as . . . promise* "because it fails to fulfill my promise (to reduce . . . the ancient forms)." According to the critics, comedy was supposed to end joyfully. This "comic law" was purportedly derived from the practice of classical comedy, but as Jonson points out a few lines later on, not all the plays of Aristophanes, Plautus, and Terence end on a happy note. **108** *of industry* purposely. **111** *We . . . interludes* another common Puritan complaint against the theater. *interludes* plays. **113** *goings out* conclusions. **116-17** *as . . . affections* Jonson's parallelism breaks down in the last two grammatical elements. *to* about. **117-18** *To . . . speak* Jonson probably refers to his commentary on Horace's *Ars Poetica,* on which he had announced a year or two before that he was working. The commentary does not survive, and it seems likely that it was lost when Jonson's library burned several years later. **119** *the understanding* the intelligent.

acquainted with some ground of your favors, let me not despair their   120
continuance, to the maturing of some worthier fruits; wherein, if my
muses be true to me, I shall raise the despised head of poetry again, and
stripping her out of those rotten and base rags wherewith the times have
adulterated her form, restore her to her primitive habit, feature, and
majesty, and render her worthy to be embraced and kissed of all the   125
great and master-spirits of our world. As for the vile and slothful, who
never affected an act worthy of celebration, or are so inward with their
own vicious natures, as they worthily fear her and think it a high point
of policy to keep her in contempt with their declamatory and windy
invectives; she shall out of just rage incite her servants (who are *genus*   130
irritabile) to spout ink in their faces that shall eat, farther than their
marrow, into their fames, and not Cinnamus the barber with his art
shall be able to take out the brands, but they shall live, and be read, till
the wretches die, as things worst deserving of themselves in chief, and
then of all mankind.   135

From my house in the Blackfriars,
this 11th day of February, 1607

---

124 *primitive* original, first. *habit* clothing. **132** *Cinnamus the barber* In Elizabethan days the barber often was a surgeon as well and would be called on to remove
such marks as Jonson, figuratively, plans to make on the poetasters who have whored
the Muse. Martial in one of his epigrams (6.64.26) mentions the skill of Cinnamus in removing "stigmata." **133** *brands* scars, marks. **134** *in chief* first of all. **136–37** *From
. . . 1607* in quarto only. **136** *Blackfriars* a fashionable residential area in the
heart of the City of London. Several indoor theaters were in this area.

THE PERSONS OF
THE PLAY

VOLPONE, *a magnifico*
MOSCA, *his parasite*
VOLTORE, *an advocate*
CORBACCIO, *an old gentleman*
CORVINO, *a merchant*
AVOCATORI, *four magistrates*
NOTARIO, *the register*
NANO, *a dwarf*
CASTRONE, *an eunuch*
[SIR] POLITIC WOULDBE, *a knight*
PEREGRINE, *a gent[leman]-traveler*

BONARIO, *a young gentleman*
  [*son of Corbaccio*]
FINE MADAME WOULDBE,
  the knight's wife
CELIA, *the merchant's wife*
COMMENDATORI, *officers*
MERCATORI, *three merchants*
ANDROGYNO, *a hermaphrodite*
SERVITORE, *a servant*
GREGE
WOMEN

The Scene   *Venice*

Persons of the Play   *Volpone*   At the basis of this play is a beast fable—much like those told by Aesop and retold with variations during the Middle Ages—in which the fox, pretending to be dying, attracts the birds of prey only to outwit them in the end. The names of the chief characters are forms of animal names: Volpone, the fox; Mosca, the fly; Voltore, the vulture; Corbaccio and Corvino, ravens; Sir Pol, the parrot; and Peregrine, a hunting hawk.   *magnifico*   rich and distinguished man.   *parasite*   a flatterer, hanger-on.   *advocate*   lawyer.   *register*   clerk of the court.   [*Sir*] *Politic*   "Politic" here has the meaning of crafty and skilled in diplomacy.   *Grege*   crowd.

Scene   *Venice*   In Jonson's time Venice was known not only for its connection with trade but also for its wealth, luxury, sophistication, and political cunning. The first act of *Othello* provides an excellent picture of what Venice meant to the Renaissance Englishman.

THE ARGUMENT

V olpone, childless, rich, feigns sick, despairs,
O ffers his state to hopes of several heirs,
L ies languishing; his Parasite receives
P resents of all, assures, deludes; then weaves
O ther cross plots, which ope themselves, are told.   5
N ew tricks for safety are sought; they thrive; when, bold,
E ach tempts th'other again, and all are sold.

PROLOGUE

Now, luck yet send us, and a little wit
    Will serve to make our play hit;
According to the palates of the season,
    Here is rhyme not empty of reason.
This we were bid to credit from our poet,   5
    Whose true scope, if you would know it,
In all his poems still hath been this measure:
    To mix profit with your pleasure;
And not as some, whose throats their envy failing,
    Cry hoarsely, "All he writes is railing,"   10
And when his plays come forth, think they can flout them,
    With saying, "He was a year about them."

The Argument 2 *state* property. **5** *ope* open. *told* exposed. **7** *sold* enslaved.
Prologue 5 *credit* believe, understand. **6** *scope* aim. **8** *To . . . pleasure* the
Horatian formula, *utile dulci,* which Jonson refers to frequently. **10** *railing* carping,
abusive language. **12** *"He . . . them"* It was one of Jonson's boasts that he was a
craftsman who worked and reworked his plays rather than turning them out hurriedly,
as most Elizabethan playwrights apparently did. In the satirical treatment of Jonson as
Horace in *Satiromastix* this boast is ridiculed (V.2.202).

To these there needs no lie but this his creature,
   Which was two months since no feature;
And though he dares give them five lives to mend it,   15
   'Tis known, five weeks fully penned it,
From his own hand, without a coadjutor,
   Novice, journeyman, or tutor.
Yet thus much I can give you as a token
   Of his play's worth: no eggs are broken,   20
Nor quaking custards with fierce teeth affrighted,
   Wherewith your rout are so delighted;

13 *To . . . creature* this play answers the charge. **14** *was . . . feature* was not begun two months ago. **17–18** *coadjutor . . . tutor* Elizabethan playing companies were repertory companies requiring vast numbers of plays. Plays were thus usually treated as mere commodities and were often written by factory methods. The various forms which this method could take are referred to in this list: *coadjutor,* a co-writer who wrote part of a play, as Jonson wrote part of *Eastward Ho; novice,* an apprentice doing parts under a master's direction—Richard Brome, later a dramatist in his own right, was Jonson's novice; *journeyman,* a specialist called in to repair plays and rewrite parts, as Jonson wrote additions to *The Spanish Tragedy; tutor,* a guide and corrector of what others wrote—in later life Jonson, whose reputation was by then assured, often performed this function for other poets and playwrights.

In this passage, and throughout the Epistle and the Prologue, Jonson is anxious to make it clear that he is a poet with the loftiest understanding of his art and not a mere writer of plays seeking to make a living by pleasing his audience. No doubt the length of Jonson's explanations was necessitated by the fact that the Elizabethans denied the elevated name of poet to mere playwrights, and that Jonson, from the time he began working in the theater, about 1598–99, had been engaged in all the activities he now scorns. At one time he was an actor and early in his career he worked as a play-patcher for the theatrical entrepreneur Philip Henslowe. He had undoubtedly engaged in personal quarrels with other playwrights, caricaturing them in his plays, and these satiric activities had recently been exposed in Dekker's *Satiromastix.* **21** *quaking custards* The usual explanation of this term is that it refers to a huge custard brought in at city feasts and made the source of many foolish tricks. But it is difficult to see how a custard can be "with fierce teeth affrighted." John Marston writes, "Let custards quake, my rage must freely run," in his satirical poem *The Scourge of Villainy* (1598–99), and the word "custards" refers to the bumbling fools whom he is prepared to attack in his fierce satiric style (Satire II, line 4). Jonson in his *Poetaster,* where he objects to the outlandish style of the verse satirists, makes Crispinus (Marston), the false poet, vomit up this term along with a number of others (V.3.525). In 1599, when the further printing of verse satire was forbidden, Marston carried his satiric style to the theater, where for a number of years his dramatic satirists proceeded with "fierce teeth" to frighten "quaking custards." It is, I believe, such satiric plays as Marston's *Histriomastix* and *The Malcontent* that Jonson is referring to here. **22** *rout* mob.

Nor hales he in a gull old ends reciting,
　To stop gaps in his loose writing,
With such a deal of monstrous and forced action,   25
　As might make Bedlam a faction;
Nor made he 'his play for jests stol'n from each table,
　But makes jests to fit his fable.
And so presents quick comedy refined,
　As best critics have designed;   30
The laws of time, place, persons he observeth,
　From no needful rule he swerveth.
All gall and copperas from his ink he draineth,
　Only a little salt remaineth,
Wherewith he'll rub your cheeks, till red with laughter,   35
　They shall look fresh a week after.

---

23 hales hauls. **gull** simple dupe. **old ends** bits and pieces of poetry. Shakespeare's Pistol is the most remarkable reciter of old ends in Elizabethan drama. **26 make . . . faction** add a new party to the madhouse. **Bedlam** St. Mary of Bethlehem, a religious institution which became the London insane asylum. **27–28 Nor . . . fable** He does not construct his plays to accommodate stolen jokes, but makes his own jokes to fit his plays. **27 stol'n . . . table** The comparison is to scraps stolen from a feast. The Elizabethan playwright was notorious for lifting material from the classics and from his contemporaries. Since no playwright borrowed from the classics more readily than Jonson—the present play is a tissue of lines and situations borrowed from every comic writer from Aristophanes to Erasmus—he must have in mind some distinction between the writer who simply lifts whole passages and the writer like himself, who reworks and recombines the old material into a new play. **28 fable** plot. **29 quick** lively. **31 laws . . . persons** During the sixteenth century a number of critics had set up from Aristotle's *Poetics* several laws supposed to govern dramatic representation. The law of time limited stage time to twenty-four hours; the law of place limited stage action to an area which could be realistically traveled in the space of time allowed; and the law of persons limited growth and change in characters to an amount that could realistically occur in twenty-four hours. Obviously the average Elizabethan playwright paid no attention to these "laws," but Jonson adhered to them rather closely. His qualification in line 32, "needful rule," suggests his basic attitude toward the "laws." **33 copperas** an acid.

ACT I

Scene 1 ⟨VOLPONE's *house*⟩

[VOLPONE] Good morning to the day; and next, my gold!
　　Open the shrine that I may see my saint.

[MOSCA *opens a curtain disclosing piles of gold.*]

　　Hail the world's soul, and mine! More glad than is
　　The teeming earth to see the longed-for sun
　　Peep through the horns of the celestial Ram,　　　　　　5
　　Am I, to view thy splendor darkening his;
　　That lying here, amongst my other hoards,
　　Showst like a flame by night, or like the day
　　Struck out of chaos, when all darkness fled
　　Unto the center. O thou son of Sol,　　　　　　　　　10
　　But brighter than thy father, let me kiss,
　　With adoration, thee, and every relic
　　Of sacred treasure in this blessed room.
　　Well did wise poets by thy glorious name
　　Title that age which they would have the best,　　　　　15
　　Thou being the best of things, and far transcending
　　All style of joy in children, parents, friends,
　　Or any other waking dream on earth.
　　Thy looks when they to Venus did ascribe,
　　They should have giv'n her twenty thousand cupids,　　　20
　　Such are thy beauties and our loves! Dear saint,

🦌 **ACT I, Scene 1.　1 *Volpone*** Jonson does not provide a speech ascription for the first speech in a scene but simply lists the characters present at the beginning of the scene. In this edition the lists of characters are deleted and the necessary speech ascription added, without further comment.　**4 *teeming*** filled with life and ready to bear.　**5 *Peep . . . Ram*** The Ram is the sign of Aries in the zodiac. The sun enters Aries on the 21st of March, the spring equinox, and from this time the "teeming" earth can look forward to increasing light, warmth, and growth.　**7 *That*** Gold is the understood subject of this clause.　**8–9 *day . . . chaos*** the day of creation.　**10 *center*** center of the earth.　***son of Sol*** In alchemy gold was considered the offspring of the sun.　**15 *that age*** A number of classical poets, Ovid particularly (see *Metamorphoses* 1.89–112), looked back to a mythical golden age when men lived simpler and more honest lives, and which, according to the myth, was distinguished by its lack of precious metals. The discovery of gold and jewels always brings about the transition from the age of gold to the ages of bronze, silver, and, at last, iron. Volpone completely misunderstands the metaphorical meaning of "gold" in the traditional term.　***have*** argue to be.　**17 *style*** form.　**19 *they . . . ascribe*** Venus was frequently styled "golden" (*aurea Venus*) by the Latin poets.

Riches, the dumb god that givst all men tongues,
That canst do nought, and yet mak'st men do all things;
The price of souls; even hell, with thee to boot,
Is made worth heaven! Thou art virtue, fame,   25
Honor, and all things else. Who can get thee,
He shall be noble, valiant, honest, wise—
MOSCA   And what he will, sir. Riches are in fortune
A greater good than wisdom is in nature.
VOLPONE   True, my belovèd Mosca. Yet, I glory   30
More in the cunning purchase of my wealth
Than in the glad possession, since I gain
No common way: I use no trade, no venture;
I wound no earth with ploughshares; fat no beasts
To feed the shambles; have no mills for iron,   35
Oil, corn, or men, to grind 'em into powder;
I blow no subtle glass; expose no ships
To threat'nings of the furrow-facèd sea;
I turn no monies in the public bank,
Nor usure private—
MOSCA   No, sir, nor devour   40
Soft prodigals. You shall ha' some will swallow
A melting heir as glibly as your Dutch
Will pills of butter, and ne'er purge for't;
Tear forth the fathers of poor families
Out of their beds, and coffin them, alive,   45
In some kind, clasping prison, where their bones

---

22 the dumb god "silence is golden." **28 what** whatever. **31 purchase** getting.
32 gain make money in. **33 common** ordinary. **use** employ. **venture** risky
business enterprise. **35 shambles** slaughterhouse. **36 corn** grain. **37 subtle** intri-
cately wrought. **39 turn** to keep passing in a course of exchange or traffic. **40 usure**
Volpone refers here to the practice of men loaning money at exorbitant rates to individuals in need, particularly to young men of fashion living beyond their means, the "soft
prodigals" of line 41. This entire passage through line 66 is a catalogue of the various
means by which the growing Elizabethan mercantile class made their fortunes. Although
Volpone disdains these "common" ways of making money, Jonson is not setting all these
business practices up as honest ways of life. Many of them are the comparatively new
methods of the entrepreneur who, in contrast to the medieval craftsmen, made money
by risking money rather than by making a product and then selling it. For a full description of the new economic practices Jonson refers to here and the older medieval practices
which are being silently invoked as a standard, see L. C. Knights, *Drama and Society in
the Age of Jonson*, London, 1937. **private** privately. **41 Soft prodigals** easy spend-
thrifts. **42–43 Dutch . . . butter** The Dutch were famous for their delight in eating
butter. **43 purge** take a laxative.

May be forthcoming, when the flesh is rotten.
But, your sweet nature doth abhor these courses;
You loathe the widow's or the orphan's tears
Should wash your pavements, or their piteous cries   50
Ring in your roofs, and beat the air for vengeance—
VOLPONE   Right, Mosca, I do loathe it.
MOSCA   And, besides, sir,
You are not like the thresher that doth stand
With a huge flail, watching a heap of corn,
And, hungry, dares not taste the smallest grain,   55
But feeds on mallows and such bitter herbs;
Nor like the merchant, who hath filled his vaults
With Romagnìa and rich Candian wines,
Yet drinks the lees of Lombard's vinegar.
You will not lie in straw, whilst moths and worms   60
Feed on your sumptuous hangings and soft beds.
You know the use of riches, and dare give, now,
From that bright heap, to me, your poor observer,
Or to your dwarf, or your hermaphrodite,
Your eunuch, or what other household trifle   65
Your pleasure allows maintenance—
VOLPONE   Hold thee, Mosca,

[*Gives him money.*]

Take, of my hand; thou strik'st on truth in all,
And they are envious term thee parasite.
Call forth my dwarf, my eunuch, and my fool,
And let 'em make me sport. What should I do   [*Exit* MOSCA.]   70
But cocker up my genius and live free
To all delights my fortune calls me to?
I have no wife, no parent, child, ally,
To give my substance to; but whom I make
Must be my heir, and this makes men observe me.   75

---

56 *mallows* a variety of coarse, harsh plants. **58** *Romagnìa* wine from Greece (Romanie) often referred to as "Rumney." Note accent on next to last syllable. *Candian wines* from Candy, i.e. Crete. **59** *Lombard's vinegar* cheap, acid wine from Lombardy. **68** *term* that term. **71** *cocker up* encourage. *genius* innate talents. **74** *whom I make* whomever I designate. **75** *observe* be obsequious to.

This draws new clients, daily, to my house,
Women and men of every sex and age,
That bring me presents, send me plate, coin, jewels,
With hope that when I die (which they expect
Each greedy minute) it shall then return   80
Tenfold upon them; whilst some, covetous
Above the rest, seek to engross me, whole,
And counterwork the one unto the other,
Contend in gifts, as they would seem in love.
All which I suffer, playing with their hopes,   85
And am content to coin 'em into profit,
And look upon their kindness, and take more,
And look on that; still bearing them in hand,
Letting the cherry knock against their lips,
And draw it by their mouths, and back again.   90
How now!

ACT I   Scene 2

[MOSCA *enters with* NANO, ANDROGYNO, *and* CASTRONE *prepared to put on an entertainment.*]

NANO   Now, room for fresh gamesters, who do will you to know,

---

76 clients Although Volpone uses the word in the general sense of "dependents," the word also looks back to the original Latin meaning: free men who, lacking Roman citizenship, placed themselves under the protection of a wealthy Roman who then became their "patron." Ideally the situation was one of mutual dependence and support, but under the Empire the arrangement degenerated into a nominal relationship between wealthy vanity on one side and servile, flattering poverty on the other. By use of the word "clients"—and Mosca's frequent use of the word "patron"—Jonson evokes another image of social degeneration. **78 plate** dishes and utensils made of silver or gold. **82 engross** to absorb entirely. **83 unto** against. **84 as . . . love** in order to try to show that they love me. **85 suffer** allow. **88 bearing . . . hand** leading them on.

⁂ ACT I, Scene 2. **1** The entertainment put on by Nano and Androgyno provides a good example of the complexity and range of Jonson's dramatic technique. Most immediately what we have here is a scene of sophisticated degeneracy: a dwarf and a hermaphrodite act out a dialogue in which such matters as souls, religion, war, and philosophy are treated in a mocking, cynical fashion. The scorn of these cynics for such matters is driven home by the use of the old-fashioned, stumbling, four-stress meter—the implication being that only in the crude, old-fashioned plays which employed this verse form were such matters as the soul taken seriously. Mosca, the author of the entertainment, derived much of this mock-history of the soul from another cynical and sophisticated author, the

They do bring you neither play nor university show;
And therefore do entreat you that whatsoever they rehearse,
May not fare a whit the worse, for the false pace of the verse.
If you wonder at this, you will wonder more ere we pass,   5
For know, here is enclosed the soul of Pythagoras,

[*Pointing to* ANDROGYNO.]

That juggler divine, as hereafter shall follow;
Which soul, fast and loose, sir, came first from Apollo,
And was breathed into Aethalides, Mercurius his son,
Where it had the gift to remember all that ever was done.   10
From thence it fled forth, and made quick transmigration
To goldy-locked Euphorbus, who was killed in good fashion,

second-century Greek satirist Lucian, in whose *Dream* or *Dialogue of the Cobbler and the Cock* a cock tells his owner, a poor cobbler, of the various transmigrations of soul which have brought him at last to the barnyard. But this tale of Lucian's has a point to which Mosca does not refer: the cobbler is eaten up with envy of a friend of his who has become wealthy, and the cock in the end succeeds in showing the cobbler what miserable lives the wealthy lead. The moral of the story thus has an immediate bearing on the events of the play and reflects back in an ironic fashion on the gold-worshiping household of Volpone. These clever people are condemning themselves from their own mouths.
The scene has, however, a third dimension. It is a brief announcement of the central theme of the play. We have here a short and irreverent history of the progressive degenera-tion of mankind—the soul which comes first from Apollo, ends at last in a fool and a hermaphrodite—and in the body of the play itself the characters pass through a variety of assumed shapes, ending in the forms of ridicule and sickness which the court forces them into at the end of the play. Volpone, for example, while imagining himself actually to be in his cleverness the "paragon of animals," passes successively through the shapes of a sick man, a mountebank, an "impotent," and finally an inmate of a prison for incurables. Harry Levin, "Jonson's Metempsychosis," *PQ 22,* 1943, compares this scene to other contemporary treatments of the theme of degeneration, such as Donne's *Anniversaries.* **2 *play . . . show*** Nano is pointing out—in mockingly humble tones—that his enter-tainment is a small affair and not to be judged by the standards applicable to a play put on in the public playhouses or to one of the learned productions of the students at the universities, where classical plays or strict imitations of the dramas of Seneca, Terence, and Plautus were often performed. **4 *false pace*** referring to the doggerel rhythms and forced rhymes of this speech. **6 *Pythagoras*** Greek philosopher of sixth century B.C., and founder of a school which had for one of its tenets a belief in transmigration, the passage of the soul from one body to another after death. **8 *fast and loose*** A gambling trick, somewhat like our "shell game," in which a leather belt was folded cleverly a number of times, and a dagger driven in between the folds. Bets were then made on whether the belt was fast or loose, i.e. around the dagger or free of it. **9 *Aethalides*** herald for Jason's Argonauts. ***Mercurius his*** a common Elizabethan form of third person singular possessive. **12 *Euphorbus*** the Trojan who first wounded Patroclus, *Iliad* XVIII.

At the siege of old Troy, by the cuckold of Sparta.
Hermotimus was next (I find it in my charta)
To whom it did pass, where no sooner it was missing,   15
But with one Pyrrhus of Delos it learned to go afishing;
And thence did it enter the sophist of Greece.
From Pythagore, she went into a beautiful piece,
Hight Aspasia, the meretrix; and the next toss of her
Was again of a whore, she became a philosopher,   20
Crates the Cynic, as itself doth relate it.
Since, kings, knights, and beggars, knaves, lords, and fools gat it,
Besides ox and ass, camel, mule, goat, and brock,
In all which it hath spoke, as in the Cobbler's cock.
But I come not here to discourse of that matter,   25
Or his one, two, or three, or his great oath, "By Quater!"
His musics, his trigon, his golden thigh,
Or his telling how elements shift; but I
Would ask, how of late thou hast suffered translation,
And shifted thy coat in these days of reformation?   30
ANDROGYNO   Like one of the reformèd, a fool, as you see,
Counting all old doctrine heresy.

NANO   But not on thine own forbid meats hast thou ventured?

ANDROGYNO   On fish, when first a Carthusian I entered.

---

13 *cuckold of Sparta* Menelaus, whose wife, Helen, was stolen by Paris.   **14 *Hermotimus*** a Greek philosopher of Claizomene who lived about 500 B.C.   ***charta*** paper; either the part he is reading or the source of this information, Lucian's *Dialogue of the Cobbler and the Cock*.   **16 *Pyrrhus of Delos*** This could be one of several classical philosophers.   **17 *sophist*** philosopher—Pythagoras is meant.   **19 *Aspasia*** the mistress of Pericles, leader of Athens in the fifth century.   ***meretrix*** courtesan.   **21 *Crates*** Crates of Thebes, a pupil of the Cynic philosopher Diogenes.   ***itself*** The neuter pronoun suggests that Nano may here point to Androgyno who is playing the part of the soul.   **23 *brock*** badger.   **24 *Cobbler's cock*** the cock who speaks in Lucian's dialogue. See note to line 1.   **26 *By Quater*** Pythagoras believed that number was the principle of harmony in the universe, and he therefore attached supernatural significance to the geometrical relationships. The "quater" referred to here is the triangle made with four as its base:

27 *trigon* triangle.   ***golden thigh*** Pythagoras was believed by his followers to have had a golden thigh.   **29 *translation*** change, transmigration.   **30 *reformation*** the Protestant Reformation.   **31 *reformèd*** Puritans.   **33 *forbid meats*** forbidden foods—the Pythagoreans did not eat fish.   **34 *Carthusian*** a religious order famed for the severity of its diet.

NANO   Why, then thy dogmatical silence hath left thee?   35
ANDROGYNO   Of that an obstreperous lawyer bereft me.
NANO   O wonderful change! When Sir Lawyer forsook thee,
    For Pythagore's sake, what body then took thee?
ANDROGYNO   A good, dull moyle.
NANO   And how! by that means
    Thou wert brought to allow of the eating of beans?   40
ANDROGYNO   Yes.
NANO   But from the moyle into whom didst thou pass?
ANDROGYNO   Into a very strange beast, by some writers called an ass;
    By others, a precise, pure, illuminate brother,
    Of those devour flesh, and sometimes one another,
    And will drop you forth a libel, or a sanctified lie,   45
    Betwixt every spoonful of a nativity pie.
NANO   Now quit thee, for heaven, of that profane nation,
    And gently report thy next transmigration.
ANDROGYNO   To the same that I am.
NANO   A creature of delight,
    And what is more than a fool, an hermaphrodite?   50
    Now, 'pray thee, sweet soul, in all thy variation,
    Which body wouldst thou choose to take up thy station?
ANDROGYNO   Troth, this I am in, even here would I tarry.
NANO   'Cause here the delight of each sex thou canst vary?
ANDROGYNO   Alas, those pleasures be stale and forsaken;   55
    No, 'tis your fool wherewith I am so taken,
    The only one creature that I can call blessèd,
    For all other forms I have proved most distressèd.
NANO   Spoke true, as thou wert in Pythagoras still.
    This learned opinion we celebrate will,   60
    Fellow eunuch, as behooves us, with all our wit and art,
    To dignify that whereof ourselves are so great and special a part.
VOLPONE   Now, very, very pretty! Mosca, this
    Was thy invention?
MOSCA   If it please my patron,
    Not else.

---

35 *silence* the Pythagoreans were bound to a five-year silence. **36** *obstreperous* in
the Latin sense, "to make a noise." **39** *moyle* mule. **43** *precise* Puritanical. *illumi-*
nate illuminated, i.e. one who has had a vision of religious truth. **46** *nativity pie*
Christmas pie. **47** *quit thee* get out. **52** *to . . . station* to stay in. **53** *Troth* in
truth. **62** *that* i.e. folly.

VOLPONE   It doth, good Mosca.

MOSCA   Then it was, sir.   65

                          Song

Fools, they are the only nation
Worth men's envy or admiration;
Free from care or sorrow-taking,
Selves and others merry making,
All they speak or do is sterling.   70
Your fool, he is your great man's dearling,
And your ladies' sport and pleasure;
Tongue and bable are his treasure.
E'en his face begetteth laughter,   75
And he speaks truth free from slaughter.
He's the grace of every feast,
And, sometimes, the chiefest guest:
Hath his trencher and his stool,
When wit waits upon the fool.   80
         O, who would not be
         Hee, hee, hee?

One knocks without.

VOLPONE   Who's that? Away! Look, Mosca.

MOSCA   Fool, begone!

         [*Exeunt* NANO, CASTRONE, ANDROGYNO.]

'Tis Signior Voltore, the advocate;
I know him by his knock.

VOLPONE   Fetch me my gown,   85
My furs, and night-caps; say my couch is changing,
And let him entertain himself awhile
Without i' th' gallery. [*Exit* MOSCA.] Now, now, my clients

---

66 Song Volpone and Mosca may join the three grotesques in this song, or the latter may sing it alone as a conclusion to their entertainment. **71 sterling** excellent. **72 dearling** darling. **74 bable** bauble, the mock scepter carried by a jester or professional fool—also slang for the male organ. The word also suggests "babble." **76 free from slaughter** without fear of consequences. The rhyme "laughter-slaughter" is a somewhat unusual one, and shortly after *Volpone* was played, John Marston, who had long engaged in satirical exchanges with Jonson (see above, note to Epistle), commented in his play *The Fawne* on the foolish critic who "vowed to get the consumption of the lungs, or to leave to posterity the true pronunciation and orthography of laughing" (IV.1). For a discussion of the various possibilities of rhyming these words see Helge Kökeritz, *Shakespeare's Pronunciation* (New Haven, 1953), pp. 183–84. **86 furs** warm robes worn by the sick man. **my . . . changing** My bed is being changed.

Begin their visitation! Vulture, kite,
Raven, and gorcrow, all my birds of prey,   90
That think me turning carcass, now they come.
I am not for 'em yet. [*Enter* MOSCA.] How now? the news?
MOSCA   A piece of plate, sir.
VOLPONE   Of what bigness?
MOSCA   Huge,
Massy, and antique, with your name inscribed,
And arms engraven.
VOLPONE   Good! and not a fox   95
Stretched on the earth, with fine delusive sleights
Mocking a gaping crow? ha, Mosca!
MOSCA   Sharp, sir.
VOLPONE   Give me my furs. Why dost thou laugh so, man?
MOSCA   I cannot choose, sir, when I apprehend
What thoughts he has, without, now, as he walks: 100
That this might be the last gift he should give;
That this would fetch you; if you died today,
And gave him all, what he should be tomorrow;
What large return would come of all his ventures;
How he should worshipped be, and reverenced;   105
Ride with his furs, and foot-cloths; waited on
By herds of fools and clients; have clear way
Made for his moyle, as lettered as himself;
Be called the great and learnèd advocate:
And then concludes, there's nought impossible.   110
VOLPONE   Yes, to be learnèd, Mosca.
MOSCA   O, no; rich
Implies it. Hood an ass with reverend purple,
So you can hide his two ambitious ears,
And he shall pass for a cathedral doctor.
VOLPONE   My caps, my caps, good Mosca. Fetch him in.   115
MOSCA   Stay, sir; your ointment for your eyes.
VOLPONE   That's true;
Dispatch, dispatch. I long to have possession

---

90 gorcrow carrion crow. **92 for 'em** ready for them, i.e. not yet "made up" as a
dying man. **104 ventures** business enterprises; specifically here, the gifts he has given
Volpone. **108 lettered** learned. **112 Hood . . . purple** the purple hood worn on the
academic gown by Doctors of Philosophy. **116 ointment . . . eyes** to make them look
rheumy. **117 Dispatch** hurry.

Of my new present.

MOSCA   That, and thousands more,
I hope to see you lord of.

VOLPONE   Thanks, kind Mosca.

MOSCA   And that, when I am lost in blended dust,   120
And hundreds such as I am, in succession—

VOLPONE   Nay, that were too much, Mosca.

MOSCA   You shall live
Still to delude these harpies.

VOLPONE   Loving Mosca!

[*Looking into a mirror.*]

'Tis well. My pillow now, and let him enter.   [*Exit* MOSCA.]
Now, my feigned cough, my phthisic, and my gout,   125
My apoplexy, palsy, and catarrhs,
Help, with your forcèd functions, this my posture,
Wherein, this three year, I have milked their hopes.
He comes, I hear him—uh! uh! uh! uh! O—

ACT I   Scene 3

[*Enter* MOSCA *with* VOLTORE. VOLPONE *in bed.*]

MOSCA   You still are what you were, sir. Only you,
Of all the rest, are he commands his love,

---

121 *in succession*   following me, i.e. other servants to Volpone.   **123** *Still*   always.
124 *'Tis . . . now*   Volpone is satisfied with the make-up and costume he
has, like an actor, been donning. He now settles into his sickbed. Throughout the
remainder of this scene Volpone remains in bed. The bed might have been placed in
a small curtained space at the rear of the platform stage, but since most of the action takes
place around the bed it would seem more likely that it was placed somewhere toward
the front, where the facial expression of the "sick man" could have been seen and his low,
faltering words heard. To meet this dramatic problem a bed could have been set up on
the stage proper or within a small tent, or "mansion," placed forward of the tiring-house
wall. For a description of these mansions and a discussion of their use see C. Walter
Hodges, *The Globe Restored* (New York, 1954), pp. 58–61. See also A. M. Nagler,
Shakespeare's Stage, New Haven, 1958.   **125–28** *Now . . . hopes*   These four lines constitute a mock invocation. Where the poet or petitioner usually calls on the gods for
inspiration, Volpone, abusing poetry as he abuses other institutions of mankind, calls on
sickness. For another example of Volpone's sacrilegious poetry see the mock aubade—song
to the dawn—with which the play begins.   **125** *phthisic*   consumption.   **127** *posture*
imposture.   **128** *this . . . year*   for three years.
🦊 **ACT I, Scene 3.   2** *are he*   are that man.

    And you do wisely to preserve it thus,
    With early visitation, and kind notes
    Of your good meaning to him, which, I know,   5
    Cannot but come most grateful. Patron, sir.
    Here's Signior Voltore is come—
VOLPONE [*Faintly.*]   What say you?
MOSCA   Sir, Signior Voltore is come this morning
    To visit you.
VOLPONE   I thank him.
MOSCA   And hath brought
    A piece of antique plate, bought of St. Mark,   10
    With which he here presents you.
VOLPONE   He is welcome.
    Pray him to come more often.
MOSCA   Yes.
VOLTORE   What says he?
MOSCA   He thanks you and desires you see him often.
VOLPONE   Mosca.
MOSCA   My patron?
VOLPONE   Bring him near, where is he?
    I long to feel his hand.
MOSCA   [*Directing* VOLPONE'*s groping hands.*] The plate is here, sir.   15
VOLTORE   How fare you, sir?
VOLPONE   I thank you, Signior Voltore.
    Where is the plate? mine eyes are bad.
VOLTORE   [*Putting it into his hands.*]   I'm sorry
    To see you still thus weak.
MOSCA   [*Aside.*] That he is not weaker.
VOLPONE   You are too munificent.
VOLTORE   No, sir; would to heaven
    I could as well give health to you as that plate!   20
VOLPONE   You give, sir, what you can. I thank you. Your love
    Hath taste in this, and shall not be unanswered.
    I pray you see me often.
VOLTORE   Yes, I shall, sir.
VOLPONE   Be not far from me.
MOSCA   [*To* VOLTORE.]   Do you observe that, sir?

---

5 good meaning well wishing. **10 of St. Mark** at a goldsmith's shop in the Square of St. Mark. **12 What . . . he** Throughout this scene Volpone speaks in a very low voice, and pretends that he can neither see nor hear very well. **21–22 Your . . . this** This (the plate) gives an idea of how much you love me. **22 unanswered** unrewarded.

VOLPONE   Hearken unto me still; it will concern you.   25
MOSCA   You are a happy man, sir; know your good.
VOLPONE   I cannot now last long—
MOSCA   You are his heir, sir.
VOLTORE   Am I?
VOLPONE   I feel me going, uh! uh! uh! uh!
    I am sailing to my port, uh! uh! uh! uh!
    And I am glad I am so near my haven.   30
MOSCA   Alas, kind gentleman. Well, we must all go—
VOLTORE   But, Mosca—
MOSCA   Age will conquer.
VOLTORE   Pray thee, hear me.
    Am I inscribed his heir for certain?
MOSCA   Are you?
    I do beseech you, sir, you will vouchsafe
    To write me i' your family. All my hopes   35
    Depend upon your worship. I am lost
    Except the rising sun do shine on me.
VOLTORE   It shall both shine and warm thee, Mosca.
MOSCA   Sir,
    I am a man that have not done your love
    All the worst offices. Here I wear your keys,   40
    See all your coffers and your caskets locked,
    Keep the poor inventory of your jewels,
    Your plate, and monies; am your steward, sir,
    Husband your goods here.
VOLTORE   But am I sole heir?
MOSCA   Without a partner, sir, confirmed this morning;   45
    The wax is warm yet, and the ink scarce dry
    Upon the parchment.
VOLTORE   Happy, happy me!
    By what good chance, sweet Mosca?
MOSCA   Your desert, sir;
    I know no second cause.
VOLTORE   Thy modesty
    Is loth to know it; well, we shall requite it.   50
MOSCA   He ever liked your course, sir; that first took him.
    I oft have heard him say how he admired

35 *To . . . family* make me a member of your household. 51 *course* manner of
acting. ***took him*** took his fancy.

Men of your large profession, that could speak
To every cause, and things mere contraries,
Till they were hoarse again, yet all be law;   55
That, with most quick agility, could turn,
And re-turn; make knots, and undo them;
Give forkèd counsel; take provoking gold
On either hand, and put it up. These men,
He knew, would thrive with their humility.   60
And, for his part, he thought he should be bless'd
To have his heir of such a suffering spirit,
So wise, so grave, of so perplexed a tongue,
And loud withal, that would not wag, nor scarce
Lie still, without a fee; when every word   65
Your worship but lets fall, is a chequin!

Another knocks.

Who's that? One knocks. I would not have you seen, sir.
And yet—pretend you came and went in haste;
I'll fashion an excuse. And, gentle sir,
When you do come to swim in golden lard,   70
Up to the arms in honey, that your chin
Is borne up stiff with fatness of the flood,
Think on your vassal; but remember me:
I ha' not been your worst of clients.
VOLTORE   Mosca—
MOSCA   When will you have your inventory brought, sir?   75
Or see a copy of the will? [*Calling out to the one knocking.*] Anon.
I'll bring 'em to you, sir. Away, be gone,
Put business i' your face.   [*Exit* VOLTORE.]
VOLPONE   Excellent, Mosca!
Come hither, let me kiss thee.
MOSCA   Keep you still, sir.
Here is Corbaccio.
VOLPONE   Set the plate away.   80
The vulture's gone, and the old raven's come.

---

53 *large* liberal. **53–54** *speak . . . contraries* defend any case and argue for exactly
opposite causes. **54** *mere* absolute. **58** *forkèd* fork-tongued. *provoking* "provoke
. . . To call to a judge or court to take up one's cause" (*OED*). **59** *put it up* pocket it.
63 *perplexed* intricate (in the sense of being double, speaking on either side). **66** *chequin*
a gold coin. **73** *but* simply. **78** *Put . . . face* Look as if you were here on a matter
of business.

ACT I   Scene 4

MOSCA   Betake you to your silence, and your sleep.

[*Sets the plate aside.*]

Stand there and multiply. Now shall we see
A wretch who is indeed more impotent
Than this can feign to be, yet hopes to hop
Over his grave. [*Enter* CORBACCIO.] Signior Corbaccio!   5
You're very welcome, sir.

CORBACCIO   How does your patron?

MOSCA   Troth, as he did, sir; no amends.

CORBACCIO   [*Cupping his ear.*]   What? mends he?

MOSCA   [*Shouting.*] No, sir. He is rather worse.

CORBACCIO   That's well. Where is he?

MOSCA   Upon his couch, sir, newly fall'n asleep.

CORBACCIO   Does he sleep well?

MOSCA   No wink, sir, all this night,   10
Nor yesterday, but slumbers.

CORBACCIO   Good! he should take
Some counsel of physicians. I have brought him
An opiate here, from mine own doctor—

MOSCA   He will not hear of drugs.

CORBACCIO   Why? I myself
Stood by while 't was made, saw all th'ingredients,   15
And know it cannot but most gently work.
My life for his, 'tis but to make him sleep.

VOLPONE   [*Aside.*] Ay, his last sleep, if he would take it.

MOSCA   Sir,
He has no faith in physic.

CORBACCIO   Say you, say you?

MOSCA   He has no faith in physic: he does think   20
Most of your doctors are the greater danger,
And worse disease t'escape. I often have
Heard him protest that your physician
Should never be his heir.

CORBACCIO   Not I his heir?

🦋 **ACT I, Scene 4.   4** *this* Volpone.   **11** *but slumbers* only dozes.   **19** *physic* medicine.   **21** *your* used not to refer to Corbaccio's doctor, but in vague and contemptuous reference to doctors in general.

MOSCA   Not your physician, sir.

CORBACCIO   O, no, no, no,   25
  I do not mean it.

MOSCA   No, sir, nor their fees
  He cannot brook; he says they flay a man
  Before they kill him.

CORBACCIO   Right, I do conceive you.

MOSCA   And then, they do it by experiment,
  For which the law not only doth absolve 'em,   30
  But gives them great reward; and he is loth
  To hire his death so.

CORBACCIO   It is true, they kill
  With as much license as a judge.

MOSCA   Nay, more;
  For he but kills, sir, where the law condemns,
  And these can kill him too.

CORBACCIO   Ay, or me,   35
  Or any man. How does his apoplex?
  Is that strong on him still?

MOSCA   Most violent.
  His speech is broken, and his eyes are set,
  His face drawn longer than 't was wont—

CORBACCIO   How! how!
  Stronger than he was wont?

MOSCA   No, sir; his face   40
  Drawn longer than 't was wont.

CORBACCIO   O, good.

MOSCA   His mouth
  Is ever gaping, and his eyelids hang.

CORBACCIO   Good.

MOSCA   A freezing numbness stiffens all his joints,
  And makes the color of his flesh like lead.

CORBACCIO   'Tis good.

MOSCA   His pulse beats slow and dull.

CORBACCIO   Good symptoms still.   45

---

26 mean intend. **27 flay** skin alive. **28 conceive** understand. **29 by experiment** by trying out various remedies on the patient.

MOSCA And from his brain—
CORBACCIO   Ha! How? not from his brain?
MOSCA Yes, sir, and from his brain—
CORBACCIO   I conceive you; good.
MOSCA Flows a cold sweat, with a continual rheum,
    Forth the resolvèd corners of his eyes.
CORBACCIO Is't possible? Yet I am better, ha!   50
    How does he with the swimming of his head?
MOSCA O, sir, 'tis past the scotomy; he now
    Hath lost his feeling, and hath left to snort;
    You hardly can perceive him that he breathes.
CORBACCIO Excellent, excellent; sure I shall outlast him!   55
    This makes me young again, a score of years.
MOSCA I was a-coming for you, sir.
CORBACCIO   Has he made his will?
    What has he given me?
MOSCA   No, sir.
CORBACCIO   Nothing? ha!
MOSCA He has not made his will, sir.
CORBACCIO   Oh, oh, oh.
    What then did Voltore, the lawyer, here?   60
MOSCA He smelled a carcass, sir, when he but heard
    My master was about his testament;
    As I did urge him to it for your good—
CORBACCIO He came unto him, did he? I thought so.
MOSCA Yes, and presented him this piece of plate.   65
CORBACCIO To be his heir?
MOSCA   I do not know, sir.
CORBACCIO   True,
    I know it too.
MOSCA [Aside.] By your own scale, sir.
CORBACCIO   Well,

---

46 *from his brain* Drainage of fluid from the brain was believed to be one of the final stages of the disease strong apoplexy, which Mosca is describing so carefully, symptom by symptom. Corbaccio's excited interruption at this point shows that he is fully aware of the significance of this symptom, and that he now believes his dearest hope is about to be realized. **49 *resolvèd*** relaxed. **52 *scotomy*** dimness of sight accompanied by dizziness. **53 *left*** ceased. **54 *perceive him that*** perceive that. **56 *This . . . years*** This news makes me feel twenty years younger. **66–67 *True . . . too*** Corbaccio pays no attention to what Mosca says, or does not hear him, and assumes that he has agreed that Voltore came to be made heir. **67 *By . . . scale*** measuring by your own standard.

I shall prevent him yet. See, Mosca, look,
Here I have brought a bag of bright chequins,
Will quite weigh down his plate.
MOSCA [*Taking the bag.*]   Yea, marry, sir.   70
This is true physic, this your sacred medicine;
No talk of opiates to this great elixir.
CORBACCIO 'Tis aurum palpabile, if not potabile.
MOSCA It shall be ministered to him, in his bowl?
CORBACCIO Ay, do, do, do.
MOSCA   Most blessed cordial!   75
This will recover him.
CORBACCIO   Yes, do, do, do.
MOSCA I think it were not best, sir.
CORBACCIO   What?
MOSCA   To recover him.
CORBACCIO O, no, no, no; by no means.
MOSCA   Why, sir, this
Will work some strange effect if he but feel it.
CORBACCIO 'Tis true, therefore forbear; I'll take my venture;   80
Give me't again.
MOSCA   At no hand. Pardon me.
You shall not do yourself that wrong, sir. I
Will advise you, you shall have it all.
CORBACCIO How?
MOSCA   All, sir; 'tis your right, your own; no man
Can claim a part; 'tis yours without a rival,   85
Decreed by destiny.
CORBACCIO   How, how, good Mosca?
MOSCA I'll tell you, sir. This fit he shall recover—
CORBACCIO I do conceive you.
MOSCA   And on first advantage
Of his gained sense, will I re-importune him
Unto the making of his testament,   90

68 *prevent* get ahead of—literally "come before." **70** *weigh down* outweigh in scales. *marry* indeed. **72** *No . . . to* There is no comparing other medicines to . . . *elixir* a drug supposed to be capable of prolonging life indefinitely. **73** *aurum palpabile* gold which can be felt. *potabile* drinkable. Medicine having gold as its principal ingredient was believed to be a sovereign remedy for all diseases, and it is this compound which Mosca and Corbaccio discuss in the following lines. **75** *cordial* a medicine which stimulates the heart. **80** *venture* i.e. the bag of gold. **87** *recover* recover from. **88** *first advantage* first opportunity. **89** *gained* regained.

And show him this. [*Points to the bag of gold.*]
CORBACCIO   Good, good.
MOSCA   'Tis better yet,
    If you will hear, sir.
CORBACCIO   Yes, with all my heart.
MOSCA   Now would I counsel you, make home with speed;
    There, frame a will whereto you shall inscribe
    My master your sole heir.
CORBACCIO   And disinherit   95
    My son?
MOSCA   O, sir, the better; for that color
    Shall make it much more taking.
CORBACCIO   O, but color?
MOSCA   This will, sir, you shall send it unto me.
    Now, when I come to enforce, as I will do,
    Your cares, your watchings, and your many prayers,   100
    Your more than many gifts, your this day's present,
    And, last, produce your will; where, without thought
    Or least regard unto your proper issue,
    A son so brave and highly meriting,
    The stream of your diverted love hath thrown you   105
    Upon my master, and made him your heir:
    He cannot be so stupid, or stone dead,
    But out of conscience and mere gratitude—
CORBACCIO   He must pronounce me his?
MOSCA   'Tis true.
CORBACCIO   This plot
    Did I think on before.
MOSCA   I do believe it.   110
CORBACCIO   Do you not believe it?
MOSCA   Yes, sir.
CORBACCIO   Mine own project.
MOSCA   Which, when he hath done, sir—
CORBACCIO   Published me his heir?
MOSCA   And you so certain to survive him—
CORBACCIO   Ay.

---

94 *frame* devise, write. *whereto* wherein. **96** *color* pretense, outward appearance
concealing truth. **97** *taking* attractive. *O, but color* O, is it only pretense?
99 *enforce* urge. **103** *proper issue* true child. **108** *mere* complete. **110** *think
on before* think of earlier.

MOSCA   Being so lusty a man—
CORBACCIO   'Tis true.
MOSCA   Yes, sir—
CORBACCIO   I thought on that too. See, how he should be   115
    The very organ to express my thoughts!
MOSCA   You have not only done yourself a good—
CORBACCIO   But multiplied it on my son?
MOSCA   'Tis right, sir.
CORBACCIO   Still my invention.
MOSCA   'Las, sir, heaven knows
    It hath been all my study, all my care,   120
    (I e'en grow grey withal) how to work things—
CORBACCIO   I do conceive, sweet Mosca.
MOSCA   You are he
    For whom I labor here.
CORBACCIO   Ay, do, do, do.
    I'll straight about it. [*Going.*]

    [MOSCA *now begins to bow and smile while speaking too softly for*
    CORBACCIO *to hear.*]

MOSCA   Rook go with you, raven!
CORBACCIO   I know thee honest.
MOSCA   You do lie, sir.
CORBACCIO   And—   125
MOSCA   Your knowledge is no better than your ears, sir.
CORBACCIO   I do not doubt to be a father to thee.
MOSCA   Nor I to gull my brother of his blessing.
CORBACCIO   I may ha' my youth restored to me, why not?
MOSCA   Your worship is a precious ass—
CORBACCIO   What sayst thou?   130
MOSCA   I do desire your worship to make haste, sir.
CORBACCIO   'Tis done, 'tis done, I go.   [*Exit.*]
VOLPONE   [*Leaping up.*]   O, I shall burst!

---

115 *See . . . be*   Look, and if he isn't . . .   116 *very organ*   exact instrument.   119 *Still my invention*   Again my idea! (?)   *'Las*   alas.   120 *study*   concern.   124 *straight*   at once.   *Rook . . . you*   May you be cheated (rooked).   126 *Your . . . ears*   Your understanding is no better than your hearing—referring to Corbaccio's deafness and perhaps suggesting that being an ass, he has the ears of that animal.   128 *gull*   cheat.   *my brother* Corbaccio's son. There is a glancing but significant reference here to the biblical story (Genesis 27) in which Jacob defrauds his brother Esau of Isaac's blessing by disguising himself in the skin of a goat.

Let out my sides, let out my sides.
MOSCA   Contain
Your flux of laughter, sir. You know this hope
Is such a bait it covers any hook.   135
VOLPONE   O, but thy working, and thy placing it!
I cannot hold; good rascal, let me kiss thee.
I never knew thee in so rare a humor.
MOSCA   Alas, sir, I but do as I am taught;
Follow your grave instructions; give 'em words;   140
Pour oil into their ears, and send them hence.
VOLPONE   'Tis true, 'tis true. What a rare punishment
Is avarice to itself!
MOSCA   Ay, with our help, sir.
VOLPONE   So many cares, so many maladies,
So many fears attending on old age.   145
Yea, death so often called on as no wish
Can be more frequent with 'em. Their limbs faint,
Their senses dull, their seeing, hearing, going,
All dead before them; yea, their very teeth,
Their instruments of eating, failing them.   150
Yet this is reckoned life! Nay, here was one,
Is now gone home, that wishes to live longer!
Feels not his gout, nor palsy; feigns himself
Younger by scores of years, flatters his age
With confident belying it; hopes he may   155
With charms, like Aeson have his youth restored;
And with these thoughts so battens, as if fate
Would be as easily cheated on as he,

Another knocks.

And all turns air! Who's that, there, now? a third?
MOSCA   Close to your couch again; I hear his voice.   160
It is Corvino, our spruce merchant.
VOLPONE   [*Lies down.*]   Dead.
MOSCA   Another bout, sir, with your eyes. Who's there?

---

134 *flux* flood—the word also means "dysentery." *this hope* i.e. to inherit Volpone's wealth. **138** *rare* excellent. *humor* fanciful mood. **140** *grave* wise. **141** *Pour . . . ears* flatter them with soft, easy words. **148** *going* ability to walk. **149** *before them* before they are. **156** *Aeson* The father of Jason, captain of the Argonauts, who was restored to youth by the black magic of Medea. **157** *battens* grows fat. **159** *all turns air* everything becomes nothing. **162** *bout* turn—Mosca again puts ointment in Volpone's eyes.

ACT I   Scene 5

[*Enter* CORVINO.]

MOSCA   Signior Corvino! come most wished for! O,
How happy were you, if you knew it, now!

CORVINO   Why? what? wherein?

MOSCA   The tardy hour is come, sir.

CORVINO   He is not dead?

MOSCA   Not dead, sir, but as good;
He knows no man.

CORVINO   How shall I do then?

MOSCA   Why, sir?   5

CORVINO   I have brought him here a pearl.

MOSCA   Perhaps he has
So much remembrance left as to know you, sir.
He still calls on you, nothing but your name
Is in his mouth. Is your pearl orient, sir?

CORVINO   Venice was never owner of the like.   10

VOLPONE   [*Faintly.*] Signior Corvino.

MOSCA   Hark.

VOLPONE   Signior Corvino.

MOSCA   He calls you; step and give it him. He is here, sir.
And he has brought you a rich pearl.

CORVINO   How do you, sir?
Tell him it doubles the twelfth caract.

MOSCA   Sir,
He cannot understand, his hearing's gone,   15
And yet it comforts him to see you—

CORVINO   Say
I have a diamond for him, too.

MOSCA   Best show 't, sir,
Put it into his hand; 'tis only there
He apprehends, he has his feeling yet.

[VOLPONE *seizes the pearl.*]

See how he grasps it!

CORVINO   'Las, good gentleman.   20

🦌 ACT I, Scene 5.   1 *come most* arrived, just when you are most . . .   9 *orient*
precious and lustrous.   14 *caract* carat.   17 *diamond* trisyllabic: di-a-mond.

How pitiful the sight is!
MOSCA   Tut, forget, sir.
   The weeping of an heir should still be laughter
   Under a visor.
CORVINO   Why, am I his heir?
MOSCA   Sir, I am sworn, I may not show the will
   Till he be dead. But here has been Corbaccio,   25
   Here has been Voltore, here were others too,
   I cannot number 'em, they were so many;
   All gaping here for legacies; but I,
   Taking the vantage of his naming you,
   "Signior Corvino, Signior Corvino," took   30
   Paper, and pen, and ink, and there I asked him
   Whom he would have his heir? *"Corvino."* Who
   Should be executor? *"Corvino."* And
   To any question he was silent to,
   I still interpreted the nods he made,   35
   Through weakness, for consent; and sent home th' others,
   Nothing bequeathed them but to cry and curse.

   They embrace.

CORVINO   O, my dear Mosca. Does he not perceive us?
MOSCA   No more than a blind harper. He knows no man,
   No face of friend, nor name of any servant,   40
   Who 't was that fed him last, or gave him drink;
   Not those he hath begotten, or brought up,
   Can he remember.
CORVINO   Has he children?
MOSCA   Bastards,
   Some dozen, or more, that he begot on beggars,
   Gypsies, and Jews, and black-moors when he was drunk.   45
   Knew you not that, sir? 'Tis the common fable,
   The dwarf, the fool, the eunuch are all his;
   He's the true father of his family,
   In all save me, but he has given 'em nothing.
CORVINO   That's well, that's well. Art sure he does not hear us?   50
MOSCA   Sure, sir? why, look you, credit your own sense.

   [*Shouts in* VOLPONE'*s ear.*]

23 *visor* mask. **30** *Signior Corvino* Mosca imitates Volpone's feeble voice. **35** *still*
continually. **39** *blind harper* proverbial term for member of a crowd. **46** *fable*
story—not used here in the modern sense of "something invented or made up."

The pox approach and add to your diseases,
If it would send you hence the sooner, sir,
For, your incontinence, it hath deserved it
Throughly and throughly, and the plague to boot.   55
You may come near, sir—Would you would once close
Those filthy eyes of yours that flow with slime
Like two frog-pits, and those same hanging cheeks,
Covered with hide instead of skin—Nay, help, sir—
That look like frozen dish-clouts set on end.   60

CORVINO   Or, like an old smoked wall, on which the rain
    Ran down in streaks.

MOSCA   Excellent, sir, speak out.
    You may be louder yet; a culverin
    Dischargèd in his ear would hardly bore it.

CORVINO   His nose is like a common sewer, still running.   65

MOSCA   'Tis good! And what his mouth?

CORVINO   A very draught.

MOSCA   O, stop it up— [*Starting to smother him.*]

CORVINO   By no means.

MOSCA   Pray you, let me.
    Faith I could stifle him rarely with a pillow,
    As well as any woman that should keep him.

CORVINO   Do as you will, but I'll be gone.

MOSCA   Be so.   70
    It is your presence makes him last so long.

CORVINO   I pray you, use no violence.

MOSCA   No, sir? why?
    Why should you be thus scrupulous, pray you, sir?

CORVINO   Nay, at your discretion.

MOSCA   Well, good sir, be gone.

CORVINO   I will not trouble him now to take my pearl?   75

MOSCA   Puh! nor your diamond. What a needless care

    [*Taking the jewels.*]

    Is this afflicts you! Is not all here yours?
    Am not I here, whom you have made? Your creature?

---

52 pox the great pox, i.e. syphilis.   **54 it . . . it** incontinence . . . the pox.
55 Throughly and throughly through and through.   **56 You . . . sir** Mosca speaks
here to Corvino.   **58 frog-pits** stagnant puddles in which frogs live.   **60 clouts** rags.
63 culverin musket or a cannon.   **68 rarely** excellently.   **73 scrupulous** overly nice.
75 pearl Volpone has the pearl and diamond clutched in his hand.

That owe my being to you?
CORVINO   Grateful Mosca!
Thou art my friend, my fellow, my companion,   80
My partner, and shalt share in all my fortunes.
MOSCA Excepting one.
CORVINO   What's that?
MOSCA   Your gallant wife, sir.
                              [*Exit* CORVINO *hurriedly*.]
Now is he gone; we had no other means
To shoot him hence but this.
VOLPONE   My divine Mosca!
Thou hast today outgone thyself. *Another knocks.* Who's there?   85
I will be troubled with no more. Prepare
Me music, dances, banquets, all delights;
The Turk is not more sensual in his pleasures
Than will Volpone. [*Exit* MOSCA.] Let me see: a pearl!
A diamond! plate! chequins! good morning's purchase.   90
Why, this is better than rob churches, yet,
Or fat, by eating once a month a man.

[*Enter* MOSCA.]

Who is't?
MOSCA   The beauteous Lady Wouldbe, sir,
Wife to the English knight, Sir Politic Wouldbe—
This is the style, sir, is directed me—   95
Hath sent to know how you have slept tonight,
And if you would be visited?
VOLPONE   Not now.
Some three hours hence.
MOSCA   I told the squire so much.
VOLPONE When I am high with mirth and wine, then, then.
'Fore heaven, I wonder at the desperate valor   100
Of the bold English, that they dare let loose
Their wives to all encounters!
MOSCA   Sir, this knight
Had not his name for nothing; he is *politic*,

---

88 *Turk* The Turks were noted for their extreme sensuality as well as their cruelty.
90 *purchase* catch. **92** *fat* grow fat. **95** *style* manner of speaking. *is directed me*
that I am ordered to use. **100-2** *'Fore . . . encounters* The English were much laughed
at abroad for the freedom with which they allowed their ladies to come and go as they
pleased and without supervision.

And knows, howe'er his wife affect strange airs,
She hath not yet the face to be dishonest.   105
But had she Signior Corvino's wife's face—
VOLPONE   Has she so rare a face?
MOSCA   O, sir, the wonder,
The blazing star of Italy, a wench
O' the first year! a beauty ripe as harvest!
Whose skin is whiter than a swan, all over!   110
Than silver, snow, or lilies! a soft lip,
Would tempt you to eternity of kissing!
And flesh that melteth in the touch to blood!
Bright as your gold! and lovely as your gold!
VOLPONE   Why had not I known this before?
MOSCA   Alas, sir,   115
Myself but yesterday discovered it.
VOLPONE   How might I see her?
MOSCA   O, not possible;
She's kept as warily as is your gold,
Never does come abroad, never takes air
But at a window. All her looks are sweet   120
As the first grapes or cherries, and are watched
As near as they are.
VOLPONE   I must see her—
MOSCA   Sir,
There is a guard, of ten spies thick, upon her;
All his whole household; each of which is set
Upon his fellow, and have all their charge,   125
When he goes out, when he comes in, examined.
VOLPONE   I will go see her, though but at her window.
MOSCA   In some disguise then.
VOLPONE   That is true. I must
Maintain mine own shape still the same: we'll think.   [*Exeunt.*]

---

105 *dishonest* unchaste.   **109 *O' the first year*** of the finest order.   **113 *to blood*** to
blushes.   **119 *abroad*** out of the house.   **122 *near*** closely.   **124–25 *set Upon*** set to
watch.   **125 *charge*** responsibility.   **126 *he*** On entering and leaving his house Corvino
questions his guards on each particular of their instructions. He has, the passage suggests,
turned his house into a fortress to guard his wife.   **129 *Maintain . . . shape*** In a play
in which changing shape—i.e. appearance—is a leading theme, this line is thoroughly
ambiguous; but Volpone's surface meaning is that he agrees with Mosca that he must
wear a disguise when he goes out, for if the bilking of the fools is to succeed he must
always be thought of as a dying man.

ACT II

Scene 1   { *The public square,*
           before CORVINO'*s house* }

[*Enter* POLITIC WOULDBE, PEREGRINE.]

SIR POLITIC   Sir, to a wise man, all the world's his soil.
   It is not Italy, nor France, nor Europe,
   That must bound me, if my fates call me forth.
   Yet, I protest, it is no salt desire
   Of seeing countries, shifting a religion,   5
   Nor any disaffection to the state
   Where I was bred, and unto which I owe
   My dearest plots, hath brought me out; much less
   That idle, antique, stale, grey-headed project
   Of knowing men's minds, and manners, with Ulysses;   10
   But a peculiar humor of my wife's,
   Laid for this height of Venice, to observe,
   To quote, to learn the language, and so forth.
   I hope you travel, sir, with license?
PEREGRINE   Yes.
SIR POLITIC   I dare the safelier converse. How long, sir,   15
   Since you left England?
PEREGRINE   Seven weeks.
SIR POLITIC   So lately!
   You ha' not been with my lord ambassador?
PEREGRINE   Not yet, sir.
SIR POLITIC   'Pray you, what news, sir, vents our climate?
   I heard, last night, a most strange thing reported

🦊 **ACT II, Scene 1.** **1** *soil* country. **4** *salt* keen. **6** *disaffection to* dissatisfaction with. **8** *plots* schemes, projects. **10** *Ulysses* Ulysses is described in the opening lines of *The Odyssey* as a man who "roamed the wide world and saw the cities of many peoples and learned their ways." He became for the Renaissance the prototype of the curious traveler and a model for the young men of fashion who completed their education with a journey abroad. Their purpose was, of course, to know "men's minds and manners," and Sir Politic reveals his own lack of sense in his scorn for this project. **11** *humor* passion. **12** *Laid . . . height* aimed for the latitude. Sir Politic uses an elaborate manner of speech, and avoids the plain word whenever he can. **13** *quote* note down (the peculiarities of the country). **14** *license* passport. **17** *my lord ambassador* Sir Henry Wotton, King James' ambassador at Venice, was himself a noted intriguer. **18** *vents our climate* comes from our country. Another of Sir Pol's circumlocutions.

By some of my lord's followers, and I long   20
To hear how 'twill be seconded.
PEREGRINE   What was't, sir?
SIR POLITIC   Marry, sir, of a raven, that should build
In a ship royal of the King's.
PEREGRINE   [*Aside.*] —This fellow,
Does he gull me, trow? or is gulled?—Your name, sir?
SIR POLITIC   My name is Politic Wouldbe.
PEREGRINE   [*Aside.*] —O, that speaks him—   25
A knight, sir?
SIR POLITIC   A poor knight, sir.
PEREGRINE   Your lady
Lies here, in Venice, for intelligence
Of tires, and fashions, and behavior
Among the courtesans? The fine Lady Wouldbe?
SIR POLITIC   Yes, sir, the spider and the bee ofttimes   30
Suck from one flower.
PEREGRINE   Good Sir Politic!
I cry you mercy; I have heard much of you.
'Tis true, sir, of your raven.
SIR POLITIC   On your knowledge?
PEREGRINE   Yes, and your lion's whelping in the Tower.
SIR POLITIC   Another whelp!
PEREGRINE   Another, sir.
SIR POLITIC   Now heaven!   35
What prodigies be these? The fires at Berwick!
And the new star! These things concurring, strange!
And full of omen! Saw you those meteors?

---

21 seconded confirmed.   **22 raven** bird of ill omen.   **should** used here to mark
reported speech.   **24 gull** fool.   **trow** a mild expletive.   **25 speaks** defines.   **27 Lies**
stays.   **intelligence** knowledge.   **28 tires** attires, clothes.   **29 courtesans** fashionable prostitutes. Venice was famous for its courtesans.   **32 cry you mercy** ask your
pardon (for not recognizing you).   **33 your** used indeterminately, or to mean roughly,
"that you know of."   **34 lion's . . . Tower** A lioness, Elizabeth, was at this time kept
in the Tower of London, and she produced cubs in 1604 and again in 1605.   **36 prodigies**
strange omens.   **36–37 fires . . . star** In 1604 there were reports of ghostly armies
fighting at Berwick, on the Scottish border, and Kepler discovered a new star in the
constellation Serpentarius. Mass hallucinations were very common in England during this
period, and there were many reports of battles in the clouds and other ominous sights.
37 concurring coinciding.   **38 meteors** Meteors, because they are a disruption of the
ordinary pattern of the heavens, were taken as ominous portents of impending social
disorder.

PEREGRINE   I did, sir.

SIR POLITIC   Fearful! Pray you, sir, confirm me,
   Were there three porpoises seen above the bridge,   40
   As they give out?

PEREGRINE   Six, and a sturgeon, sir.

SIR POLITIC   I am astonished!

PEREGRINE   Nay, sir, be not so;
   I'll tell you a greater prodigy than these—

SIR POLITIC   What should these things portend?

PEREGRINE   The very day
   (Let me be sure) that I put forth from London,   45
   There was a whale discovered in the river,
   As high as Woolwich, that had waited there,
   Few know how many months, for the subversion
   Of the Stode fleet.

SIR POLITIC   Is't possible? Believe it,
   'Twas either sent from Spain, or the Archduke's!   50
   Spinola's whale, upon my life, my credit!
   Will they not leave these projects? Worthy sir,
   Some other news.

PEREGRINE   Faith, Stone the fool is dead,
   And they do lack a tavern fool extremely.

SIR POLITIC   Is Mas' Stone dead?

PEREGRINE   He's dead, sir; why, I hope   55
   You thought him not immortal? [*Aside.*] —O, this knight,
   Were he well known, would be a precious thing
   To fit our English stage. He that should write
   But such a fellow, should be thought to feign
   Extremely, if not maliciously.—

SIR POLITIC   Stone dead!   60

PEREGRINE   Dead. Lord, how deeply, sir, you apprehend it!
   He was no kinsman to you?

SIR POLITIC   That I know of.

---

40 *the bridge* London Bridge. **41** *give out* report. **46** *whale* A whale did come
up the Thames at this time, within eight miles of London, and the fearful believed that
it intended to pump all the water from the river onto the land. **49** *Stode* city at the
mouth of the Elbe. **50** *Archduke* ruler of the Spanish Netherlands. **51** *Spinola* the
Spanish general in the Netherlands at this time. He was extremely successful and was
believed by the gullible in England to be fantastically clever in devising cunning schemes
and "secret weapons." **53** *Stone* a well-known London clown who had been flogged
not long before *Volpone* was written for making mocking speeches about the Lord
Admiral. **55** *Mas'* master. **61** *apprehend* both "feel" and "understand." **62** *That*
not that.

Well, that same fellow was an unknown fool.
PEREGRINE   And yet you know him, it seems?
SIR POLITIC   I did so. Sir,
   I knew him one of the most dangerous heads   65
   Living within the state, and so I held him.
PEREGRINE   Indeed, sir?
SIR POLITIC   While he lived, in action.
   He has received weekly intelligence,
   Upon my knowledge, out of the Low Countries,
   For all parts of the world, in cabbages;   70
   And those dispensed, again, t'ambassadors,
   In oranges, musk-melons, apricots,
   Lemons, pome-citrons, and suchlike; sometimes
   In Colchester oysters, and your Selsey cockles.
PEREGRINE   You make me wonder.
SIR POLITIC   Sir, upon my knowledge.   75
   Nay, I have observed him at your public ordinary
   Take his advertisement from a traveler,
   A concealed statesman, in a trencher of meat;
   And, instantly, before the meal was done,
   Convey an answer in a toothpick.
PEREGRINE   Strange!   80
   How could this be, sir?
SIR POLITIC   Why, the meat was cut
   So like his chàracter, and so laid as he
   Must easily read the cipher.
PEREGRINE   I have heard
   He could not read, sir.
SIR POLITIC   So 'twas given out,
   In policy, by those that did employ him;   85
   But he could read, and had your languages,

---

63 unknown misinterpreted.   **65 dangerous heads** subversive persons.   **67 action**
doing—i.e. he was an active spy, not merely passively unfriendly to the state.   **73 pome-
citrons** lemon-like fruit.   **76 ordinary** tavern.   **77 advertisement** information.
78 concealed statesman disguised agent.   **trencher** platter.   **80 toothpick** All of Sir
Politic's descriptions of plots, spies, and methods of espionage are burlesques not of
genuine activities but of those imagined by the foolish and timorous in the days immediately after the discovery of the Gunpowder Plot, a Catholic attempt to blow up King
James and the assembled Parliament on November 4, 1605.   **82 chàracter** handwriting,
code—accented on second syllable, cha-ràc-ter.   **85 policy** craft.   **86 had ... languages**
was a skilled linguist.

And to't, as sound a noddle—
PEREGRINE   I have heard, sir,
    That your baboons were spies, and that they were
    A kind of subtle nation near to China.
SIR POLITIC   Ay, ay, your Mamaluchi. Faith, they had   90
    Their hand in a French plot, or two; but they
    Were so extremely given to women as
    They made discovery of all; yet I
    Had my advices here, on Wednesday last,
    From one of their own coat, they were returned,   95
    Made their relations, as the fashion is,
    And now stand fair for fresh employment.
PEREGRINE   [*Aside.*] —'Heart!
    This Sir Pol will be ignorant of nothing—
    It seems, sir, you know all.
SIR POLITIC   Not all, sir. But
    I have some general notions; I do love   100
    To note and to observe: though I live out,
    Free from the active torrent, yet I'd mark
    The currents and the passages of things
    For mine own private use; and know the ebbs
    And flows of state.
PEREGRINE   Believe it, sir, I hold   105
    Myself in no small tie unto my fortunes
    For casting me thus luckily upon you,
    Whose knowledge, if your bounty equal it,
    May do me great assistance in instruction
    For my behavior, and my bearing, which   110
    Is yet so rude and raw.
SIR POLITIC   Why? came you forth
    Empty of rules for travel?
PEREGRINE   Faith, I had

---

87 to't in addition. **noddle** head, intelligence. **89 subtle** cunning and devious.
90 Mamaluchi plural form of "Mameluke," former Christian slaves of the Turks who
became rulers of Egypt during the thirteenth century. Sir Pol is simply seizing on any
rare word to support his pretense of knowing all about every matter of state. **92 given
to** fond of. **93 discovery** disclosure. **94 advices** dispatches. **95 coat** party,
faction. **96 relations** reports. **97 stand fair** are ready. **'Heart** God's heart; curses
were frequently formed in this manner, e.g. 'swounds, God's wounds. **101-2 though
. . . torrent** though I am not actively engaged in political affairs. **106 in . . . tie** much
obliged. **108 if . . . it** if you are as generous as you are wise.

Some common ones, from out that vulgar grammar,
Which he that cried Italian to me, taught me.
SIR POLITIC   Why, this it is that spoils all our brave bloods,   115
Trusting our hopeful gentry unto pedants,
Fellows of outside, and mere bark. You seem
To be a gentleman, of ingenuous race—
I not profess it, but my fate hath been
To be where I have been consulted with   120
In this high kind, touching some great men's sons,
Persons of blood and honor—
PEREGRINE   Who be these, sir?

ACT II   Scene 2

[*Enter* MOSCA *and* NANO, *disguised as mountebank's attendants, with materials to erect a scaffold stage. A crowd follows them.*]

MOSCA   Under that window, there't must be. The same.
SIR POLITIC   Fellows to mount a bank! Did your instructor

---

113 *vulgar grammar* ordinary grammar book.   **114** *cried* pronounced, i.e. taught.
115 *brave bloods* gallants, well-born young men.   **117** *outside . . . bark* mere show
and pretense—"bark" seems also to be a poor pun going back to "cried."   **118** *ingenuous
race* noble lineage.   **119** *I . . . it* It (the education of high-born young men) is not
my profession.   **121** *high kind* important matter.   *touching* bearing on.   **122** *blood*
nobility.
☙ **ACT II, Scene 2.**   **SD** There is no longer any exact equivalent of the mountebank
and his show, but the old-fashioned Indian medicine man with his traveling wagon, his
show, his "snake oil," and his "spiel" was in the direct line of descent from the mountebank. A picture of the type of stage referred to here is reproduced in P. L. Duchartre,
The Italian Comedy (1929), p. 63, where the crowd, including one figure called "Inglese,"
is gathered around stages set up in St. Mark's Square. The date of this print is 1610.
2 *bank* Sir Pol is apparently correct, for the accepted etymology of "mountebank" is the
Italian *monta in banco*. Bench (Italian, *banco*) here means the basic platform stage—simply
boards laid on trestles with perhaps a cloth backdrop. George Kernodle's recent theory
about this type of stage seems to fit the situation in *Volpone*. Kernodle first argued that the
physical details of the Elizabethan theater served as symbols of the social and cosmic order
and therefore the action in the plays always took place before concrete reminders of a solid,
unchanging reality. But, he continues: "The true historical prototype of the modern open
stage is . . . the mounte-bank theater that dates from the Middle Ages. That stage was free
and empty, uncluttered by symbols of social or cosmic order for the simple reason that the
medieval mountebank, peddling his snake oil and entertaining on the streets, was the first
completely isolated individual. He had no place in medieval society. He was an outcast,
a vagabond. Everyone else had a place—a set place—and all other stages of the time had

In the dear tongues, never discourse to you
Of the Italian mountebanks?

PEREGRINE   Yes, sir.

SIR POLITIC   Why,
Here shall you see one.

PEREGRINE   They are quacksalvers,   5
Fellows that live by venting oils and drugs.

SIR POLITIC   Was that the character he gave you of them?

PEREGRINE   As I remember.

SIR POLITIC   Pity his ignorance.
They are the only knowing men of Europe!
Great general scholars, excellent physicians,   10
Most admired statesmen, professed favorites
And cabinet counselors to the greatest princes!
The only languaged men of all the world!

PEREGRINE   And I have heard they are most lewd impostors,
Made all of terms and shreds; no less beliers   15
Of great men's favors than their own vile medicines;
Which they will utter upon monstrous oaths,
Selling that drug for twopence, ere they part,
Which they have valued at twelve crowns before.

SIR POLITIC   Sir, calumnies are answered best with silence.   20
Yourself shall judge. Who is it mounts, my friends?

MOSCA   Scoto of Mantua, sir.

SIR POLITIC   Is't he? Nay, then
I'll proudly promise, sir, you shall behold
Another man than has been phantasied to you.

---

elaborate scenic symbols of the temporal order." "The Open Stage: Elizabethan or
Existentialist?" *Shakespeare Survey,* 12 (1960), p. 3. The term "isolated individual"
describes Volpone perfectly, and his actions throughout the play are those of a man who
considers himself entirely free of the normal controls imposed by society or nature. It
should be noted, however, that Volpone's mountebank stage is a theater erected within a
theater—a play within a play—and that although he is unaware of the irony of his situation,
the stable order still stands unchanged in the details of the larger theater and mocks his
pretensions to absolute freedom. **3 dear** esteemed. **6 venting** vending. **12 cabinet
counselors** close advisers. **14 lewd** ignorant. **15 terms** technical expressions. **shreds**
bits and pieces of language such as proverbs, quotations from the classics. **15-16 beliers
. . . favors** men who lie about the esteem in which they are held by the great. **17 utter**
sell. **22 Scoto of Mantua** A sixteenth-century Italian actor and leader of a troupe of
players licensed by the Duke of Mantua. Scoto was a renowned juggler and sleight-of-
hand artist who appeared in England about 1576 and performed before the Queen and
her court. By the time *Volpone* was written Scoto's name had become, in England, synony-
mous with the skillful deceiver. **24 phantasied** fancied, presented to the imagination.

I wonder, yet, that he should mount his bank   25
Here, in this nook, that has been wont t'appear
In face of the Piazza! Here he comes.

[*Enter* VOLPONE, *disguised as a mountebank.*]

VOLPONE [*To* NANO.] Mount, zany.
GREGE Follow, follow, follow, follow, follow.

[VOLPONE *mounts the stage.*]

SIR POLITIC See how the people follow him! He's a man   30
May write ten thousand crowns in bank here. Note,
Mark but his gesture. I do use to observe
The state he keeps in getting up!
PEREGRINE   'Tis worth it, sir.
VOLPONE Most noble gentlemen, and my worthy patrons, it may
seem strange that I, your Scoto Mantuano, who was ever wont to   35
fix my bank in face of the public Piazza, near the shelter of the
Portico to the Procuratia, should now, after eight months' absence

---

27 *In face of* in the front, or main, part. 28 *zany* clown—see note to line 52 below.
33 *state* formality of bearing. 37 *Procuratia* residence, along the north side of the
Piazza del San Marco, for the Procurators, important civic officials. Here and in the
remainder of Scoto's speech the geographical details are quite correct, and the biographical
details, though no source is known for them, form a plausible enough description of the
life of a traveling actor and mountebank in sixteenth-century Italy. But certain details, both
geographical and biographical, suggest that under the cover of sixteenth-century Venice,
Jonson is talking about early seventeenth-century London and his own life as a playwright.
At least, the fortunes and character of Scoto and Ben Jonson are sufficiently similar to be
worthy of note. Scoto is now playing in an "obscure nook" after having usually played in
"face of the public Piazza"; Jonson was now presenting *Volpone* at the Globe Theater, on
the south bank of the Thames, after several years in which his plays, with one exception,
Sejanus, had been acted at Blackfriars, a private theater in the center of the city. Scoto
refers to false reports that he had been sent to the galleys recently for insulting Cardinal
Bembo; Jonson had actually been imprisoned in 1605 for his part in a play, *Eastward Ho,*
which contained passages offensive to King James. Scoto has only scorn for the common
mountebanks, ground *ciarlitani,* who take their stories from collections like Boccaccio's
Decameron and perform only for the delight of their vulgar audience, "your shriveled,
salad-eating artisans"; Jonson had from the beginning of his dramatic career been contemptuous of the petty playwrights of the day who borrowed liberally from other authors
to provide sensational theatrical fare for the groundlings, while he, like Scoto, had
followed the "craggy paths of study" to arrive at the "flowery plains of honor and
reputation." Sixpence is the final price of Scoto's elixir, and it may well have been the
price of admission to the earliest performances of *Volpone.* The Globe Theater, where the
play was first performed, was a public theater, where the standard admission fee was a
penny, with additional payments up to twopence for better seats. Herford and Simpson
(9, 196) note, however, a passage from Jasper Mayne, *Jonsonus Virbius* (1638), lines 67–68:

from this illustrious city of Venice, humbly retire myself into an
obscure nook of the Piazza.

SIR POLITIC   Did not I now object the same?

PEREGRINE   Peace, sir.   40

VOLPONE   Let me tell you: I am not, as your Lombard proverb saith,
cold on my feet, or content to part with my commodities at a
cheaper rate than I accustomed. Look not for it. Nor that the
calumnious reports of that impudent detractor, and shame to our
profession, Allessandro Buttone I mean, who gave out, in public,   45
I was condemned *a sforzato* to the galleys, for poisoning the
Cardinal Bembo's—cook, hath at all attached, much less dejected
me. No, no, worthy gentlemen; to tell you true, I cannot endure
to see the rabble of these ground *ciarlitani* that spread their cloaks
on the pavement as if they meant to do feats of activity, and then   50
come in lamely with their moldy tales out of Boccaccio, like stale
Tabarin, the fabulist: some of them discoursing their travels, and
of their tedious captivity in the Turk's galleys, when, indeed,

So when thy *Foxe* had ten times acted beene,
Each day was *first,* but that 'twas cheaper seene.

They consider this a reference to the "higher prices of earliest performances"; and if I am
correct about the parallel between Scoto of Mantua and Ben Jonson of London, it seems
likely that sixpence was the price of general admission to the first performances of *Volpone.*
Scoto-Volpone is, of course, a charlatan, the nostrum he sells worthless, and the
language he uses mere spiel; but Jonson is, I believe, working here in an ironic fashion, as
he does so regularly in this play. Just as Volpone's opening speech on gold calls our
attention to those vital natural and social forces which have been perverted by the sup-
stitution of a gold coin for the sun, so here our attention is focused on the nature of true
medicine, *and true playing,* by the distortion of both those arts wrought by greed and lust.
the moving powers behind Scoto-Volpone's performance. But Jonson's nostrum, his
satiric plays, are, the speech implies, the true moral medicine for a sick world, and they
represent the standard of playwrighting against which Scoto's false play is measured.
40 object bring before the eyes, visualize—another of Sir Pol's extravagant words.
42 cold on my feet *Aver freddo a 'piedi,* "to have cold at the feet," be forced to sell cheap.
45 Buttone a rival mountebank. **46 sforzato** galley slave. **47 Bembo's** The dash
suggests that Volpone is about to say "mistress." Cardinal Bembo (1470–1547) was a
famous Italian humanist noted for his pure Latin style and for the beautiful culminating
speech he delivers in Castiglione's *Il Cortegiano* (1528) on the progress from love of earthly
beauty to love of the spiritual. Castiglione's book was translated into English as *The Book
of the Courtier* by Sir Thomas Hoby in 1561 and became a handbook for the Renaissance
English gentleman. **attached** caused me to be arrested (?). **49 ground ciarlitani**
literally "ground charlatans," i.e. the poorer quacks who performed on the pavement
rather than on a platform. **50 feats of activity** tumbling. **51–52 Boccaccio ... fabulist**
Giovanni Boccaccio (1313?–75), whose collection of tales (fables) *The Decameron* was a
storehouse for later storytellers. **52 Tabarin** a famous zany in an Italian traveling
company of comedians—the name means "short cloak." **discoursing** talking of.

were the truth known, they were the Christian's galleys, where
very temperately they eat bread, and drunk water, as a whole-   55
some penance enjoined them by their confessors, for base pilferies.

SIR POLITIC   Note but his bearing and contempt of these.

VOLPONE   These turdy-facy-nasty-paty-lousy-fartical rogues, with one
poor groatsworth of unprepared antimony, finely wrapped up in
several *scartoccios,* are able, very well, to kill their twenty a week,   60
and play; yet these meager, starved spirits, who have half stopped
the organs of their minds with earthy oppilations, want not their
favorers among your shriveled salad-eating artisans, who are overjoyed that they may have their half-pe'rth of physic; though it
purge 'em into another world, 't makes no matter.   65

SIR POLITIC   Excellent! ha' you heard better language, sir?

VOLPONE   Well, let 'em go. And, gentlemen, honorable gentlemen,
know that for this time our bank, being thus removed from the
clamors of the *canaglia,* shall be the scene of pleasure and delight;
for I have nothing to sell, little or nothing to sell.   70

SIR POLITIC   I told you, sir, his end.

PEREGRINE   You did so, sir.

VOLPONE   I protest, I and my six servants are not able to make of this
precious liquor so fast as it is fetched away from my lodging by
gentlemen of your city, strangers of the Terra Firma, worshipful   75
merchants, ay, and senators too, who, ever since my arrival, have
detained me to their uses by their splendidous liberalities. And
worthily. For what avails your rich man to have his magazines
stuft with *moscadelli,* or of the purest grape, when his physicians
prescribe him, on pain of death, to drink nothing but water cocted   80
with aniseeds? O health! health! the blessing of the rich! the riches
of the poor! who can buy thee at too dear a rate, since there is no
enjoying this world without thee? Be not then so sparing of your
purses, honorable gentlemen, as to abridge the natural course of
life—   85

---

55 *eat* ate. **56 *enjoined them*** prescribed for them. **59 *unprepared*** not made fit
for human use. **60 *several*** separate. ***scartoccios*** papers—used to contain medicines,
but may here refer also to plays. See note to line 37. **61–62 *stopped . . . oppilations***
have become so concerned with gross, mundane activities that their minds have ceased to
work. ***oppilations*** obstructions. **63 *salad*** probably has meaning here of "raw, unprepared vegetables." ***artisans*** workers. **64 *half-pe'rth*** half-pennyworth. ***physic***
medicine. **69 *canaglia*** canaille, rabble. **75 *Terra Firma*** Venetian possessions
on the mainland. **78 *worthily*** properly. ***magazines*** storehouses. **79 *moscadelli***
muscatel wines. **80 *cocted*** boiled.

PEREGRINE   You see his end?

SIR POLITIC   Ay, is't not good?

VOLPONE   For, when a humid flux, or catarrh, by the mutability of air
   falls from your head into an arm or shoulder, or any other part,
   take you a ducat, or your chequin of gold, and apply to the place
   affected: see, what good effect it can work. No, no, 'tis this blessed   90
   unguento, this rare extraction, that hath only power to disperse all
   malignant humors that proceed either of hot, cold, moist, or
   windy causes—

PEREGRINE   I would he had put in dry too.

SIR POLITIC   'Pray you, observe.

VOLPONE   To fortify the most indigest and crude stomach, ay, were it   95
   of one that through extreme weakness vomited blood, applying
   only a warm napkin to the place, after the unction and fricace; for
   the vertigine in the head, putting but a drop into your nostrils,
   likewise behind the ears; a most sovereign and approved remedy:
   the *mal caduco*, cramps, convulsions, paralyses, epilepsies, *tremor*   100
   cordia, retired nerves, ill vapors of the spleen, stoppings of the
   liver, the stone, the strangury, *hernia ventosa, iliaca passio;* stops a

---

86 *end* goal. **87 *flux*** catarrh, discharge. Volpone's medicine throughout this speech
is based on the medieval and Renaissance theory of the four humors and the four elements,
which eventually goes back to Aristotelian physics. The four elements and their qualities
were: earth (cold, heavy, and dry), water (cold, heavy, and wet), air (warm, light, and
wet), and fire (hot, light, and dry). These four elements were the building blocks out of
which everything, including physical man, was believed to be constructed. In man the
elements took the form of humors or fluids, the four cardinal humors being blood, phlegm,
choler, and melancholy or black choler. In the healthy man the humors were, theoretically, balanced, but in the majority of men one humor predominated and determined a
man's "humor" or temperament: sanguine, phlegmatic, choleric, melancholic. When the
humors became seriously unbalanced, sickness resulted, and the "humid flux" Volpone
refers to is an excess of heavy wetness flowing out of the head into the body—we should
probably call it arthritis. In his earlier humor plays, *Every Man in His Humor* and *Every
Man out of His Humor,* Jonson had translated the concept of humors from the physical
to the psychic realm and had defined a humor as a situation in which,

> some one particular quality
> Doth so possess a man, that it doth draw
> All his affects, his spirits, and his powers,
> In their confluctions, all to run one way . . .
>   (*After the Second Sounding,* lines 105–8)

91 *unguento* salve. **92 *humors*** see note to line 87. **95 *crude*** sour. **97 *fricace***
massage. **98 *vertigine*** dizziness. Volpone is now simply reeling off medical jargon in the
manner of a pitchman. **100 *mal caduco*** epilepsy. **100–01 *tremor cordia*** palpitation of
the heart. **101 *retired nerves*** shrunken sinews. **102 *the stone*** kidney stone. ***strangury***
difficult urination. ***hernia ventosa*** tumor containing gas. ***iliaca passio*** cramps of
the small intestine.

dysenteria immediately; easeth the torsion of the small guts; and
cures *melancholia hypocondriaca,* being taken and applied according
to my printed receipt. (*Pointing to his bill and his glass.*) For, this is   105
the physician, this the medicine; this counsels, this cures; this
gives the direction, this works the effect; and, in sum, both
together may be termed an abstract of the theoric and practic in
the Aesculapian art. 'Twill cost you eight crowns. And, Zan
Fritada, pray thee sing a verse, extempore, in honor of it.   110

SIR POLITIC   How do you like him, sir?

PEREGRINE   Most strangely, I!

SIR POLITIC   Is not his language rare?

PEREGRINE   But alchemy
I never heard the like, or Broughton's books.

Song

Had old Hippocrates or Galen,   115
That to their books put med'cines all in,
But known this secret, they had never,
Of which they will be guilty ever,
Been murderers of so much paper,
Or wasted many a hurtless taper.   120
No Indian drug had e'er been famèd,
Tobacco, sassafras not namèd;
Ne yet of guacum one small stick, sir,
Nor Raymond Lully's great elixir.
Ne had been known the Danish Gonswart,   125
Or Paracelsus, with his long sword.

---

105 *receipt* recipe. **SD *bill*** prescription. ***glass*** bottle containing medicine.
106 *this . . . this* He points first to the bill and then to the glass. **108 *abstract***
compendium. ***theoric*** theory. ***practic*** practice. **109 *Aesculapian art*** medicine.
Aesculapius was the Roman god of medicine. **109–10 *Zan Fritada*** a famous Italian
comedian. The order is probably addressed to Nano, who is playing zany to Volpone's
mountebank. **112 *But*** except for. **113 *Broughton's books*** Hugh Broughton (1549–
1617) was a Puritan minister and scholar who wrote a number of strange books on religious
subjects. Jonson's intense dislike of the Puritans regularly finds expression in his plays.
115 *Hippocrates or Galen* two famous Greek physicians. **120 *hurtless*** harmless.
122 *Tobacco, sassafras* both used as medicines. **123 *Ne*** nor. ***guacum*** drug extracted
from resin of guaiacum tree. **124 *Raymond Lully*** renowned medieval alchemist supposed to have discovered the elixir. ***elixir*** a drug believed by alchemists to be capable
of prolonging life and health indefinitely. **125 *Gonswart*** identity not known certainly,
but perhaps the theologian Johannes Wessel of Gansfort (1420–89). **126 *Paracelsus . . .
sword*** Paracelsus was one of the strangest and most noted of the early Renaissance
physician-magicians. Alchemy and physic were for him but part of one subject. He was
supposed to have kept his secret "essences" in the handle of his sword.

PEREGRINE   All this, yet, will not do; eight crowns is high.

VOLPONE   No more. Gentlemen, if I had but time to discourse to you
the miraculous effects of this my oil, surnamed *Oglio del Scoto,*
with the countless catalogue of those I have cured of th'aforesaid,   130
and many more diseases; the patents and privileges of all the
princes and commonwealths of Christendom; or but the depositions of those that appeared on my part, before the signiory of the
Sanita and most learned college of physicians; where I was
authorized, upon notice taken of the admirable virtues of my   135
medicaments, and mine own excellency in matter of rare and
unknown secrets, not only to disperse them publicly in this
famous city, but in all the territories that happily joy under the
government of the most pious and magnificent states of Italy.
But may some other gallant fellow say, "O, there be divers that   140
make profession to have as good and as experimented receipts as
yours." Indeed, very many have assayed, like apes, in imitation of
that, which is really and essentially in me, to make of this oil;
bestowed great cost in furnaces, stills, alembics, continual fires,
and preparation of the ingredients (as indeed there goes to it six   145
hundred several simples, besides some quantity of human fat, for
the conglutination, which we buy of the anatomists), but, when
these practitioners come to the last decoction, blow, blow, puff,
puff, and all flies in fumo. Ha, ha, ha! Poor wretches! I rather pity
their folly and indiscretion than their loss of time and money; for   150
those may be recovered by industry; but to be a fool born is a
disease incurable. For myself, I always from my youth have
endeavored to get the rarest secrets, and book them, either in
exchange or for money; I spared nor cost nor labor where anything was worthy to be learned. And gentlemen, honorable   155
gentlemen, I will undertake, by virtue of chemical art, out of the
honorable hat that covers your head to extract the four elements,
that is to say, the fire, air, water, and earth, and return you your
felt without burn or stain. For, whilst others have been at the

---

129 *Oglio del Scoto*   Dr. Scoto's Oil.   **131** *patents*   official certificates confer-
ring certain rights.   *privileges*   special ordinance giving honors to an individual.
133–34 *signiory . . . Sanita*   Venetian board for granting medical licenses.   **140** *divers*
many.   **141** *experimented*   tested.   **144** *furnaces . . . alembics*   pieces of alchemical
equipment.   **146** *several simples*   separate herbs.   **148** *decoction*   boiling to extract the
essences.   *blow . . . puff*   Volpone is imitating the alchemist blowing on his fire to get
it to the proper heat.   **149** *fumo*   smoke.   **152** *from*   since.   **153** *book*   note.   **153–54** *in
exchange*   by trading (secret for secret).   **154** *nor . . . nor*   neither . . . nor.   **156** *chemical*
alchemical.   **157** *four elements*   See note to line 87 above.

balloo, I have been at my book, and am now past the craggy paths   160
of study, and come to the flowery plains of honor and reputation.

SIR POLITIC   I do assure you, sir, that is his aim.

VOLPONE   But to our price—

PEREGRINE   And that withal, Sir Pol.

VOLPONE   You all know, honorable gentlemen, I never valued this
ampulla, or vial, at less than eight crowns, but for this time I am   165
content to be deprived of it for six; six crowns is the price, and less
in courtesy I know you cannot offer me; take it or leave it, howsoever, both it and I am at your service. I ask you not as the value
of the thing, for then I should demand of you a thousand crowns;
so the Cardinals Montalto, Farnese, the great Duke of Tuscany,   170
my gossip, with divers other princes have given me; but I despise
money. Only to show my affection to you, honorable gentlemen,
and your illustrious state here, I have neglected the messages of
these princes, mine own offices, framed my journey hither, only to
present you with the fruits of my travels. [*To* NANO *and* MOSCA.]   175
Tune your voices once more to the touch of your instruments,
and give the honorable assembly some delightful recreation.

PEREGRINE   What monstrous and most painful circumstance
Is here, to get some three or four *gazets!*
Some threepence i' th' whole, for that 'twill come to.   180

                              Song

     You that would last long, list to my song,
     Make no more coil, but buy of this oil.
     Would you be ever fair? and young?
     Stout of teeth? and strong of tongue?   185
     Tart of palate? quick of ear?
     Sharp of sight? of nostril clear?
     Moist of hand? and light of foot?
     Or I will come nearer to't,
     Would you live free from all diseases?   190
     Do the act your mistress pleases,

---

160 balloo a Venetian game in which a large ball was tossed high in the air. **at my
book** in careful study. **163 withal** as well. **165 ampulla** container. **168 as the
value** as (the oil) is valued; what it is worth. **171 gossip** godfather. **174 offices**
duties. **framed** directed. **178 painful circumstance** careful arrangement of details,
i.e. setting the scene in preparation for the sale. **179 gazets** Venetian coin worth a
penny. **180 i' th' whole** altogether. **183 coil** row, fuss. **186 Tart** keen. **189 come
. . . to't** get down to what is most important.

Yet fright all aches from your bones?
Here's a med'cine for the nones.

VOLPONE Well, I am in a humor, at this time, to make a present of
the small quantity my coffer contains to the rich, in courtesy, and   195
to the poor, for God's sake. Wherefore, now mark: I asked you
six crowns, and six crowns at other times you have paid me; you
shall not give me six crowns, nor five, nor four, nor three, nor
two, nor one; nor half a ducat; no, nor a *moccenigo*. Six-pence it
will cost you, or six hundred pound—expect no lower price, for   200
by the banner of my front, I will not bate a bagatine; that I will
have, only, a pledge of your loves, to carry something from
amongst you to show I am not contemned by you. Therefore,
now, toss your handkerchiefs, cheerfully, cheerfully; and be
advertised that the first heroic spirit that deigns to grace me with a   205
handkerchief, I will give it a little remembrance of something
beside, shall please it better than if I had presented it with a double
pistolet.

PEREGRINE Will you be that heroic spark, Sir Pol?

CELIA *at the window throws down her handkerchief.*

O see! the window has prevented you.   210

VOLPONE Lady, I kiss your bounty, and for this timely grace you
have done your poor Scoto of Mantua, I will return you, over and
above my oil, a secret of that high and inestimable nature shall
make you forever enamored on that minute wherein your eye
first descended on so mean, yet not altogether to be despised, an   215
object. Here is a poulder concealed in this paper of which, if I
should speak to the worth, nine thousand volumes were but as
one page, that page as a line, that line as a word: so short is this
pilgrimage of man, which some call life, to the expressing of it.
Would I reflect on the price? Why, the whole world were but as   220
an empire, that empire as a province, that province as a bank, that
bank as a private purse to the purchase of it. I will, only, tell you:

---

192 *aches* disyllabic, "aitches." **193** *nones* nonce, occasion. **194** *humor* mood.
199 *moccenigo* small coin. **201** *banner ... front* the mountebank's banner displayed
before his stand which lists diseases and cures. *bate* abate, subtract. **202** *only* alone.
203 *contemned* despised. **204–05** *be advertised* understand. **206** *it* him. **207–
208** *double pistolet* valuable Spanish gold coin. **209** *spark* man of fashion. **SD** *Celia
at window* Celia is on the upper stage above and at the rear of the Elizabethan stage, or
at a windowed projection to the side of this balcony. **210** *prevented* literally "come
before," anticipated. **213** *shall* which shall—Jonson, like other Elizabethan writers,
frequently omits the relative pronoun. **216** *poulder* powder. **217** *to* of.

it is the poulder that made Venus a goddess (given her by Apollo), that kept her perpetually young, cleared her wrinkles, firmed her gums, filled her skin, colored her hair. From her derived to Helen, 225 and at the sack of Troy unfortunately lost; till now, in this our age, it was as happily recovered by a studious antiquary out of some ruins of Asia, who sent a moiety of it to the court of France (but much sophisticated), wherewith the ladies there now color their hair. The rest, at this present, remains with me; extracted to 230 a quintessence, so that wherever it but touches in youth it perpetually preserves, in age restores the complexion; seats your teeth, did they dance like virginal jacks, firm as a wall; makes them white as ivory, that were black as—

ACT II   Scene 3

[*Enter* CORVINO.]

CORVINO   Spite o' the devil, and my shame!
[*To* VOLPONE.]   Come down here;
Come down! No house but mine to make your scene?

He beats away the mountebank, &c.

Signior Flaminio, will you down, sir? down?
What, is my wife your Franciscina, sir?

225 **Helen** Helen of Troy. 227 **antiquary** scholar. 228 **moiety** part. 229 **sophisticated** adulterated. 230–31 **extracted . . . quintessence** refined to its pure essence. 233 **virginal jacks** The virginal was a small spinet without legs, and its "jack" was a board with quills which plucked the strings as the keys were played. But the reference here is probably to the keys, which resemble teeth.
🦌 **ACT II, Scene 3.** 1 *Spite . . . devil* manifestation of the devil's hatred of man, i.e. woman. 3 **scene** Renaissance critical theory prescribed as the proper setting or "scene" for comedy a public place backing on private houses. Although the literal meaning applies well enough here, the larger meaning of "scene" as "setting for a play" should not be overlooked, for Volpone has just acted out a play of his own devising. 3 *Flaminio,* 4 *Franciscina,* 8 *Pantalone* These are all names connected with the *commedia dell' arte,* the popular Italian street comedy of the sixteenth and seventeenth centuries. The plays, put on by traveling troupes playing on stages like those used by Scoto, were improvisations in which each actor played a stock role and put his part together out of memorized lines, speeches, and stage actions called *lazzi.* The plot was also improvised as the play proceeded. There have been references to the *commedia* throughout the mountebank's speech—"Zany," "Tabarin," "Zan Fritada"—and the names which Corvino rolls off show that he recognizes the similarity of the scene here

No windows on the whole Piazza, here,   5
To make your properties, but mine? but mine?
Heart! ere tomorrow I shall be new christened,
And called the Pantalone di Besogniosi
About the town.   [*Exit.*]
PEREGRINE   What should this mean, Sir Pol?
SIR POLITIC   Some trick of state, believe it. I will home.   10
PEREGRINE   It may be some design on you.
SIR POLITIC   I know not.
I'll stand upon my guard.
PEREGRINE   It is your best, sir.
SIR POLITIC   This three weeks all my advices, all my letters,
They have been intercepted.
PEREGRINE   Indeed, sir?
Best have a care.
SIR POLITIC   Nay, so I will. [*Exit.*]
PEREGRINE   This knight,   15
I may not lose him for my mirth, till night.   [*Exit.*]

ACT II

Scene 4   ⟨VOLPONE'*s house*⟩

[VOLPONE *and* MOSCA.]
VOLPONE   O, I am wounded!
MOSCA   Where, sir?
VOLPONE   Not without;
Those blows were nothing, I could bear them ever.
But angry Cupid, bolting from her eyes,

with one of the stock comic situations. Flaminio was a noted actor in the *commedia,*
Franciscina was a standard name for the amorous and witty servant girl, and Pantalone
was the name for the old Venetian merchant who is inevitably cuckolded.
    In the mountebank scene Jonson has combined three separate but related forms of
showmanship designed to gull the fools: the mountebank crying his wares, the alchemist
promising the elixir which will prolong life and beauty, and the street comedian.
6 *properties* stage properties, set.   **10 *home*** go home.   **11 *design*** plot.   **12 *It . . .
best*** You were best to do so.
🦊 **ACT II, Scene 4.   1 *without*** outside, on the body.   **2 *Those*** blows given him
by Corvino.   **3 *bolting*** springing, but also shooting. A bolt is an arrow, and "Cupid's
bolt" was a standard figure of speech.   ***her*** Celia's.

  Hath shot himself into me like a flame;
  Where, now, he flings about his burning heat,   5
  As in a furnace an ambitious fire
  Whose vent is stopped. The fight is all within me.
  I cannot live except thou help me, Mosca;
  My liver melts, and I, without the hope
  Of some soft air from her refreshing breath,   10
  Am but a heap of cinders.
MOSCA   'Las, good sir!
  Would you had never seen her!
VOLPONE   Nay, would thou
  Hadst never told me of her.
MOSCA   Sir, 'tis true;
  I do confess I was unfortunate,
  And you unhappy; but I'm bound in conscience,   15
  No less than duty, to effect my best
  To your release of torment, and I will, sir.
VOLPONE Dear Mosca, shall I hope?
MOSCA   Sir, more than dear,
  I will not bid you to despair of aught
  Within a human compass.
VOLPONE   O, there spoke   20
  My better angel. Mosca, take my keys,
  Gold, plate, and jewels, all's at thy devotion;
  Employ them how thou wilt; nay, coin me too,
  So thou in this but crown my longings—Mosca?
MOSCA Use but your patience.
VOLPONE   So I have.
MOSCA   I doubt not   25
  To bring success to your desires.
VOLPONE   Nay, then,
  I not repent me of my late disguise.
MOSCA If you can horn him, sir, you need not.
VOLPONE   True.
  Besides, I never meant him for my heir.

---

6 *ambitious* swelling. **9 *liver*** the supposed seat of violent passions such as love or
hate. **20 *compass*** reach, possibility of achievement. **22 *devotion*** use. **23 *coin***
mint, turn to gold—but the word often had the meaning of counterfeiting. **24 *crown***
satisfy, bring to fulfillment. A crown was also a coin. **—*Mosca?*** a delay is indicated
here; Mosca says nothing for a time until Volpone impatiently queries him. **27 *not***
do not. **28 *horn*** give him a pair of horns, i.e. cuckold him.

Is not the color o' my beard and eyebrows   30
To make me known?

MOSCA   No jot.

VOLPONE   I did it well.

MOSCA   So well, would I could follow you in mine,
With half the happiness; and yet, I would
Escape your epilogue.

VOLPONE   But were they gulled
With a belief that I was Scoto?

MOSCA   Sir,   35
Scoto himself could hardly have distinguished!
I have not time to flatter you now; we'll part,
And as I prosper, so applaud my art.   [*Exeunt.*]

ACT II

Scene 5   ❰CORVINO's *house*❱

[*Enter* CORVINO, CELIA.]

CORVINO   Death of mine honor, with the city's fool?
A juggling, tooth-drawing, prating mountebank?
And at a public window? where, whilst he,
With his strained action, and his dole of faces,
To his drug-lecture draws your itching ears,   5
A crew of old, unmarried, noted lechers
Stood leering up like satyrs: and you smile
Most graciously, and fan your favors forth,
To give your hot spectators satisfaction!
What, was your mountebank their call? their whistle?   10
Or were y'enamored on his copper rings?

30–31 *Is . . . known*   Will not the distinctive color [red] . . . identify me?   31 *No jot*
not a bit.   32 *mine*   my disguise and playing.   34 *your epilogue*   your end, i.e. the
beating. But Mosca's comment refers on another level to the "epilogue" he plans to all
Volpone's deception: bilking him of his fortune.   *gulled*   fooled, taken in.

❧ ACT II, Scene 5.   2 *tooth-drawing*   one of the major activities of itinerant quacks.
3 *public*   opening on the square.   4 *strained action*   overdone theatrical gestures.   *dole
of faces*   repertory of masks or facial expressions.   7 *satyrs*   mythological demigods
noted for their cruelty and lechery.   10 *call*   "a cry used to attract birds" (*OED*).
11–15 *copper . . . beard*   The mountebank then, like all pitchmen still, wore elaborate
costumes and make-up to attract his audience. Many believed that the toad had a jewel,

His saffron jewel, with the toad stone in't?
Or his embroidèred suit, with the cope-stitch,
Made of a hearse cloth? or his old tilt-feather?
Or his starched beard! Well, you shall have him, yes.   15
He shall come home and minister unto you
The fricace for the mother. Or, let me see,
I think you'd rather mount? would you not mount?
Why, if you'll mount, you may; yes truly, you may,
And so you may be seen, down to th' foot.   20
Get you a cittern, Lady Vanity,
And be a dealer with the virtuous man;
Make one. I'll but protest myself a cuckold,
And save your dowry. I am a Dutchman, I!
For if you thought me an Italian,   25
You would be damned ere you did this, you whore!
Thou'dst tremble to imagine that the murder
Of father, mother, brother, all thy race,
Should follow as the subject of my justice.

CELIA   Good sir, have patience!

CORVINO   What couldst thou propose   30
Less to thyself than in this heat of wrath,
And stung with my dishonor, I should strike

[*Waves his sword.*]

This steel into thee, with as many stabs
As thou wert gazed upon with goatish eyes?

CELIA   Alas, sir, be appeased! I could not think   35

---

toad stone, between his eyes which had magical properties. The exact meaning of **cope-stitch** is uncertain but doubtless it was a fancy, large stitch of some type which stood out on the ornate embroidered suit. The hearse was traditionally a framework over a tomb used to support rich hangings, **hearse cloths.** The implication here is probably that the mountebank has stolen, or at least bought secondhand, these funeral draperies for his clothes. The **tilt-feather** was a large, ornate feather or plume worn in helmets; and a **starched beard** was one of the extreme fashions of the time. **17 fricace . . . mother** massage for an attack of hysteria—perhaps a standard medical treatment, but Corvino is also suggesting that Volpone will seduce Celia. **18 mount** Corvino is again punning in an unpleasant manner. Celia, he suggests, may join the mountebank's troupe, mount the bank; and may also mount the mountebank. **21 cittern** zither. **Lady Vanity** stock character in English morality plays. **22 dealer** prostitute. **virtuous man** pun on "virtuoso." **23 Make one** make a bargain. **protest** declare. **24 save . . . dowry** By law if a husband could show that his wife had been unfaithful, he gained possession of her dowry, which otherwise remained in the wife's control during her lifetime. **24-25 Dutchman . . . Italian** By popular belief the Dutch were phlegmatic, while the Italians were quick to anger and terrible in revenge. **30-31 What . . . thyself** What less could you expect?

My being at the window should more now
Move your impatience than at other times.
CORVINO   No? not to seek and entertain a parley
With a known knave? before a multitude?
You were an actor with your handkerchief,   40
Which he, most sweetly, kissed in the receipt.
And might, no doubt, return it with a letter,
And point the place where you might meet: your sister's,
Your mother's, or your aunt's might serve the turn.
CELIA   Why, dear sir, when do I make these excuses?   45
Or ever stir abroad but to the church?
And that so seldom—
CORVINO   Well, it shall be less;
And thy restraint before was liberty
To what I now decree, and therefore mark me.
First, I will have this bawdy light dammed up;   50
And till't be done, some two, or three yards off
I'll chalk a line, o'er which if thou but chance
To set thy desp'rate foot, more hell, more horror,
More wild, remorseless rage shall seize on thee
Than on a conjurer that had heedless left   55
His circle's safety ere his devil was laid.
Then, here's a lock which I will hang upon thee,
And, now I think on't, I will keep thee backwards;
Thy lodging shall be backwards, thy walks backwards,
Thy prospect—all be backwards, and no pleasure,   60
That thou shalt know but backwards. Nay, since you force
My honest nature, know it is your own
Being too open makes me use you thus.
Since you will not contain your subtle nostrils
In a sweet room, but they must snuff the air   65
Of rank and sweaty passengers— *Knock within.*
                              One knocks.
Away, and be not seen, pain of thy life;
Not look toward the window; if thou dost—

---

38 *parley* conversation. **41** *in the receipt* when he received it. **43** *point* appoint.
44 *serve the turn* do the trick. **46** *abroad* out of doors. **49** *To* compared to.
mark pay close attention to. **53** *desp'rate* reckless, violent. **55–56** *conjurer . . . laid*
The conjurer (magician) who desired to raise a devil drew a magic circle within which
he was safe until the devil was returned to hell, i.e. "laid." **57** *lock* chastity belt.
60 *prospect* view. **64** *subtle* cunning (to smell out lust). **65** *air* odor. **66** *passengers* passers-by. **67** *pain* on pain. **68** *Not* do not.

[CELIA *starts to leave.*]

Nay, stay, hear this, let me not prosper, whore,
But I will make thee an anatomy,   70
Dissect thee mine own self, and read a lecture
Upon thee to the city, and in public.
Away! [*Exit* CELIA.] Who's there? [*Enter* SERVANT.]
SERVANT   'Tis Signior Mosca, sir.

ACT II   Scene 6

CORVINO   Let him come in, his master's dead. There's yet
Some good to help the bad. [*Enter* MOSCA.] My Mosca, welcome!
I guess your news.
MOSCA   I fear you cannot, sir.
CORVINO   Is't not his death?
MOSCA   Rather the contrary.
CORVINO   Not his recovery?
MOSCA   Yes, sir.
CORVINO   I am cursed,   5
I am bewitched, my crosses meet to vex me.
How? how? how? how?
MOSCA   Why, sir, with Scoto's oil!
Corbaccio and Voltore brought of it,
Whilst I was busy in an inner room—
CORVINO   Death! that damned mountebank! but for the law,   10
Now, I could kill the rascal; 't cannot be
His oil should have that virtue. Ha' not I
Known him a common rogue, come fiddling in
To th'*osterìa,* with a tumbling whore,
And, when he has done all his forced tricks, been glad   15
Of a poor spoonful of dead wine, with flies in't?
It cannot be. All his ingredients

---

70 make . . . anatomy   anatomize you, i.e. describe your moral character detail by detail. So great is Corvino's fury, however, that he is also threatening literal dissection.
☙ **ACT II, Scene 6.   6 crosses** troubles. **8 of** some of. **14 osterìa** inn. Scoto is now being described as an itinerant entertainer singing and performing for his supper. **tumbling whore** female acrobat and dancer. **15 forced** strained, awkwardly apparent. **17 It** Volpone's recovery by means of the oil.

Are a sheep's gall, a roasted bitch's marrow,
Some few sod earwigs, pounded caterpillars,
A little capon's grease, and fasting spittle;   20
I know 'em to a dram.

MOSCA   I know not, sir;
But some on't, there, they poured into his ears,
Some in his nostrils, and recovered him,
Applying but the fricace.

CORVINO   Pox o' that fricace.

MOSCA   And since, to seem the more officious   25
And flatt'ring of his health, there they have had,
At extreme fees, the college of physicians
Consulting on him how they might restore him;
Where one would have a cataplasm of spices,
Another a flayed ape clapped to his breast,   30
A third would ha' it a dog, a fourth an oil
With wild cats' skins. At last, they all resolved
That to preserve him was no other means
But some young woman must be straight sought out,
Lusty, and full of juice, to sleep by him;   35
And to this service, most unhappily
And most unwillingly, am I now employed,
Which here I thought to pre-acquaint you with,
For your advice, since it concerns you most,
Because I would not do that thing might cross   40
Your ends, on whom I have my whole dependence, sir.
Yet, if I do it not they may delate
My slackness to my patron, work me out
Of his opinion; and there all your hopes,
Ventures, or whatsoever, are all frustrate.   45
I do but tell you, sir. Besides, they are all
Now striving who shall first present him. Therefore,

---

19 sod earwigs boiled insects. The earwig was supposed to creep into the ear and the word came to have the figurative meaning of "flatterer." **20 fasting spittle** fasting man's saliva; the implication being that Scoto is starving and poverty-stricken. **22 on't** of it. **there** in Volpone's house. **24 Pox** the great pox, i.e. syphilis. **25 officious** dutiful. **27 extreme fees** enormous expense. **29 cataplasm** large plaster. **33 was** there was. **34 straight** instantly. **36 to** on. **41 ends** aims, intentions. **42 delate** report. **43–44 work . . . opinion** persuade him out of his high regard for me. **45 frustrate** frustrated. **46 I . . . sir** I only tell what *may* happen. **47 present him** i.e. with the young woman prescribed.

I could entreat you, briefly, conclude somewhat.
Prevent 'em if you can.
CORVINO   Death to my hopes!
This is my villainous fortune! Best to hire   50
Some common courtesan?
MOSCA   Ay, I thought on that, sir.
But they are all so subtle, full of art,
And age again doting and flexible,
So as—I cannot tell—we may perchance
Light on a quean may cheat us all.
CORVINO   'Tis true.   55
MOSCA No, no; it must be one that has no tricks, sir,
Some simple thing, a creature made unto it;
Some wench you may command. Ha' you no kinswoman?
God's so—Think, think, think, think, think, think, think, sir.
One o' the doctors offered there his daughter.   60
CORVINO How!
MOSCA   Yes, Signior Lupo, the physician.
CORVINO His daughter!
MOSCA   And a virgin, sir. Why, alas,
He knows the state of 's body, what it is;
That nought can warm his blood, sir, but a fever;
Nor any incantation raise his spirit;   65
A long forgetfulness hath seized that part.
Besides, sir, who shall know it? Some one or two—
CORVINO I pray thee give me leave.

[*Walks up and down and talks to himself.*]

                              If any man
But I had had this luck—The thing in't self,
I know, is nothing—Wherefore should not I   70
As well command my blood and my affections
As this dull doctor? In the point of honor
The cases are all one of wife and daughter.

---

48 briefly quickly. **conclude somewhat** decide something, form some plan.
49 Prevent in both the sense of "stop" and the literal meaning of "come before" or
"anticipate." **52 subtle** cunning, tricky. **art** wiles. **53 age again** old age on the
other hand. **flexible** pliable, gullible. **55 quean** whore. **57 made unto** forced to,
directed. **59 so** soul (?). Also a suggestion of Italian, *cazzo,* the male organ. **61 Lupo**
wolf. **68 give me leave** excuse me. **71 blood** spirit. **affections** feelings. **72 point**
matter. **73 cases . . . of** it is the same with.

MOSCA   [*Aside.*] I hear him coming.
CORVINO   She shall do't. 'Tis done.
   'Slight, if this doctor, who is not engaged,   75
   Unless't be for his counsel, which is nothing,
   Offer his daughter, what should I that am
   So deeply in? I will prevent him. Wretch!
   Covetous wretch! Mosca, I have determined.
MOSCA   How, sir?
CORVINO   We'll make all sure. The party you wot of   80
   Shall be mine own wife, Mosca.
MOSCA   Sir, the thing
   But that I would not seem to counsel you,
   I should have motioned to you at the first.
   And make your count, you have cut all their throats.
   Why, 'tis directly taking a possession!   85
   And in his next fit, we may let him go.
   'Tis but to pull the pillow from his head,
   And he is throttled; 't had been done before
   But for your scrupulous doubts.
CORVINO   Ay, a plague on't,
   My conscience fools my wit! Well, I'll be brief,   90
   And so be thou, lest they should be before us.
   Go home, prepare him, tell him with what zeal
   And willingness I do it; swear it was
   On the first hearing, as thou mayst do, truly,
   Mine own free motion.
MOSCA   Sir, I warrant you,   95
   I'll so possess him with it that the rest
   Of his starved clients shall be banished all;
   And only you received. But come not, sir,
   Until I send, for I have something else
   To ripen for your good, you must not know't.   100
CORVINO   But do not you forget to send now.
MOSCA   Fear not. [*Exit* MOSCA.]

---

74 coming coming round, taking the bait. **75 'Slight** God's light. *engaged* deeply involved. **79 determined** decided. **80 wot** know. **81 the thing** the very thing. **83 motioned** suggested. **84 make your count** inventory Volpone's goods which you are sure to get (?). **85 possession** in law "the detention or enjoyment of a thing by a person himself or another in his name" (*OED*). **87 'Tis but** we need only. *from* from under. **89 scrupulous** overly nice. **90 wit** reason. *brief* quick. **91 before** ahead of. **95 free motion** unprompted proposal.

ACT II   Scene 7

CORVINO   Where are you, wife? My Celia? wife? [*Enter* CELIA *crying.*]
                                                                            What, blubbering?
 Come, dry those tears. I think thou thoughtst me in earnest?
 Ha? by this light I talked so but to try thee.
 Methinks the lightness of the occasion
 Should ha' confirmed thee. Come, I am not jealous.

CELIA   No?   5

CORVINO   Faith I am not, I, nor never was;
 It is a poor unprofitable humor.
 Do not I know if women have a will
 They'll do 'gainst all the watches o' the world?
 And that the fiercest spies are tamed with gold?
 Tut, I am confident in thee, thou shalt see't;   10
 And see I'll give thee cause too, to believe it.
 Come, kiss me. Go, and make thee ready straight
 In all thy best attire, thy choicest jewels,
 Put 'em all on, and, with 'em, thy best looks.
 We are invited to a solemn feast   15
 At old Volpone's, where it shall appear
 How far I am free from jealousy or fear.   [*Exeunt.*]

ACT III

Scene 1   ⟨*A street*⟩

[MOSCA *alone.*]

MOSCA   I fear I shall begin to grow in love
 With my dear self and my most prosp'rous parts,
 They do so spring and burgeon; I can feel
 A whimsy i' my blood. I know not how,

❧ ACT II, Scene 7.   3 *try* test.   4 *lightness* triviality.   *occasion* i.e. leaning out
the window, dropping handkerchief.   5 *confirmed* reassured.   6 *Faith* in faith.
8 *will* sexual appetite.   9 *'gainst* despite.   *watches* precautions.   10 *tamed* bribed.
16 *solemn feast* formal banquet.
❧ ACT III, Scene 1.   2 *prosp'rous parts* flourishing talents.   4 *whimsy* dizziness,
whirling.

Success hath made me wanton. I could skip   5
Out of my skin, now, like a subtle snake,
I am so limber. O! your parasite
Is a most precious thing, dropped from above,
Not bred 'mongst clods and clodpolls, here on earth.
I muse the mystery was not made a science,   10
It is so liberally professed! Almost
All the wise world is little else in nature
But parasites or sub-parasites. And yet,
I mean not those that have your bare town-art,
To know who's fit to feed 'em; have no house,   15
No family, no care, and therefore mold
Tales for men's ears, to bait that sense; or get
Kitchen-invention, and some stale receipts
To please the belly, and the groin; nor those,
With their court-dog-tricks, that can fawn and fleer,   20
Make their revènue out of legs and faces,
Echo my lord, and lick away a moth.
But your fine, elegant rascal, that can rise
And stoop, almost together, like an arrow;
Shoot through the air as nimbly as a star;   25
Turn short as doth a swallow; and be here,
And there, and here, and yonder, all at once;
Present to any humor, all occasion;

---

5 wanton playful. **6 subtle** cunning; also dexterous, elusive. **9 clodpolls** dolts.
10 mystery craft. **science** A term formerly applied to certain philosophical studies
required for a degree in the School of *Literae Humaniores,* the Liberal Arts—see "liberally
professed" in line 11. Mosca is lamenting that the art of the flatterer should be considered
only a "mystery," i.e. a mechanical skill or trade, and he is proposing that in view of its
prevalence it be raised to the dignity of a science and made, like logic, a required study
for all educated men. **11 liberally professed** freely practiced. See note to line 10.
14 bare town-art i.e. crude skill. **16-17 mold Tales** invent gossip and slander.
18 Kitchen-invention recipes for elaborate dishes. **receipts** recipes. **19 groin** Mosca
implies that pandering, or perhaps, considering the word "receipts," retailing new varieties
of sensual pleasure, is among the activities of the "unattached" parasite who out of the
poverty of his imagination and his desperate condition is forced to these unworthy tricks
—unworthy of the master parasite like Mosca. **20 fleer** smile obsequiously. **21 revènue**
accented on second syllable. **legs and faces** bows and smirks. **22 lick . . . moth**
Mosca is carrying to the extreme that form of servility, common in all ages, in which the
flatterer picks threads or other objects from the coats of those he is trying to please.
"Moth" had until the eighteenth century the general meaning of "vermin." **28 Present
. . . occasion** ready to satisfy any whim and meet any situation.

And change a visor swifter than a thought,
This is the creature had the art born with him;   30
Toils not to learn it, but doth practice it
Out of most excellent nature: and such sparks
Are the true parasites, others but their zanies.

ACT III   Scene 2

[*Enter* BONARIO.]

MOSCA Who's this? Bonario? Old Corbaccio's son?
          The person I was bound to seek. Fair sir,
          You are happ'ly met.
BONARIO   That cannot be by thee.
MOSCA Why, sir?
BONARIO   Nay, 'pray thee know thy way and leave me:
          I would be loth to interchange discourse   5
          With such a mate as thou art.
MOSCA   Courteous sir,
          Scorn not my poverty.
BONARIO   Not I, by heaven;
          But thou shalt give me leave to hate thy baseness.
MOSCA Baseness?
BONARIO   Ay, answer me, is not thy sloth
          Sufficient argument? thy flattery?   10
          Thy means of feeding?
MOSCA   Heaven be good to me!
          These imputations are too common, sir,
          And eas'ly stuck on virtue when she's poor.
          You are unequal to me, and howe'er
          Your sentence may be righteous, yet you are not,   15
          That ere you know me, thus proceed in censure.
          St. Mark bear witness 'gainst you, 'tis inhuman.

          [*He cries.*]

BONARIO [*Aside.*] What? does he weep? the sign is soft and good.
          I do repent me that I was so harsh.

---

29 *visor* mask, i.e. personality. **33 *zanies*** clowns, assistants—see II.2, where Nano
plays Scoto's zany.
🐜 **ACT III, Scene 2. 2 *bound*** on my way. **6 *mate*** low person. **10 *argument***
reason. **14 *unequal*** unjust. ***howe'er*** no matter how much.

MOSCA   'Tis true that swayed by strong necessity,   20
        I am enforced to eat my carefull bread
        With too much obsequy; 'tis true, beside,
        That I am fain to spin mine own poor raiment
        Out of my mere observance, being not born
        To a free fortune; but that I have done   25
        Base offices, in rending friends asunder,
        Dividing families, betraying counsels,
        Whispering false lies, or mining men with praises,
        Trained their credulity with perjuries,
        Corrupted chastity, or am in love   30
        With mine own tender ease, but would not rather
        Prove the most rugged and laborious course,
        That might redeem my present estimation,
        Let me here perish, in all hope of goodness.
BONARIO [*Aside.*]—This cannot be a personated passion—   35
        I was to blame, so to mistake thy nature;
        Pray thee forgive me and speak out thy business.
MOSCA   Sir, it concerns you, and though I may seem
        At first to make a main offence in manners,
        And in my gratitude unto my master,   40
        Yet, for the pure love which I bear all right,
        And hatred of the wrong, I must reveal it.
        This very hour your father is in purpose
        To disinherit you—
BONARIO   How!
MOSCA   And thrust you forth
        As a mere stranger to his blood; 'tis true, sir.   45
        The work no way engageth me, but as
        I claim an interest in the general state
        Of goodness and true virtue, which I hear
        T'abound in you, and for which mere respect,
        Without a second aim, sir, I have done it.   50
BONARIO This tale hath lost thee much of the late trust
        Thou hadst with me; it is impossible.

---

20 *swayed* controlled. **21** *carefull* full of care, i.e. gotten with pain. **22** *obsequy* humility. **23** *fain* obliged. *spin . . . raiment* get clothing. **24** *mere observance* service alone. **28** *mining* undermining. **32** *Prove* endure. **33** *estimation* reputation. **35** *personated* pretended. *passion* strong feeling. **39** *main* great. **45** *mere* complete. **49** *for . . . respect* only for this reason. **50** *second aim* concealed purpose.

I know not how to lend it any thought
My father should be so unnatural.
MOSCA   It is a confidence that well becomes   55
Your piety, and formed, no doubt, it is
From your own simple innocence, which makes
Your wrong more monstrous and abhorred. But, sir,
I now tell you more. This very minute
It is, or will be doing; and if you   60
Shall be but pleased to go with me, I'll bring you,
I dare not say where you shall see, but where
Your ear shall be a witness of the deed;
Hear yourself written bastard and professed
The common issue of the earth.
BONARIO   I'm mazed!   65
MOSCA   Sir, if I do it not, draw your just sword
And score your vengeance on my front and face;
Mark me your villain. You have too much wrong,
And I do suffer for you, sir. My heart
Weeps blood in anguish—
BONARIO   Lead, I follow thee.   [*Exeunt.*]   70

ACT III
Scene 3   ⟨VOLPONE's *house*⟩

VOLPONE   Mosca stays long, methinks. Bring forth your sports
And help to make the wretched time more sweet.

[*Enter* NANO, CASTRONE, ANDROGYNO.]

NANO   Dwarf, fool, and eunuch, well met here we be.
A question it were now, whether of us three,
Being, all, the known delicates of a rich man,
In pleasing him, claim the precedency can?   5
CASTRONE   I claim for myself.
ANDROGYNO   And so doth the fool.

---

53 *lend . . . thought* believe it at all. **56** *piety* filial love (Latin, *pietas*). **64** *professed* proclaimed. **65** *common . . . earth* a man without family or position. *mazed* bewildered, confused. **67** *score* mark. *front* forehead.
❧ ACT III, Scene 3. **4** *whether* which. **5** *known delicates* acknowledged favorites.

NANO   'Tis foolish indeed, let me set you both to school.
  First for your dwarf, he's little and witty,
  And everything, as it is little, is pretty;   10
  Else, why do men say to a creature of my shape,
  So soon as they see him, "It's a pretty little ape"?
  And, why a pretty ape? but for pleasing imitation
  Of greater men's action, in a ridiculous fashion.
  Beside, this feat body of mine doth not crave   15
  Half the meat, drink, and cloth one of your bulks will have.
  Admit your fool's face be the mother of laughter,
  Yet, for his brain, it must always come after;
  And though that do feed him, it's a pitiful case
  His body is beholding to such a bad face.   20

  One knocks.

VOLPONE   Who's there? My couch, away, look, Nano, see;
  Give me my caps first—go, inquire.
         [*Exeunt* CASTRONE, ANDROGYNO.]
  [VOLPONE *lies down in his bed.*]
           Now Cupid
  Send it be Mosca, and with fair return.
NANO   It is the beauteous madam—
VOLPONE   Wouldbe—is it?
NANO   The same.
VOLPONE   Now, torment on me; squire her in,   25
  For she will enter, or dwell here forever.
  Nay, quickly, that my fit were past. I fear   [*Exit* NANO.]
  A second hell too: that my loathing this
  Will quite expel my appetite to the other.
  Would she were taking, now, her tedious leave.   30
  Lord, how it threats me, what I am to suffer!

---

8 *set . . . school* instruct. **10** *as* to the degree that. **15** *feat* elegant. **18** *come after* follow, i.e. be second, less important. **19** *that* i.e. the face, the mouth. **23** *fair return* good luck—the phrase has commercial suggestions: a "fair return" on a venture. **28** *this* Lady Wouldbe. **29** *other* Celia.

ACT III   Scene 4

[*Enter* NANO *with* LADY WOULDBE.]

LADY WOULDBE   [*To* NANO.] I thank you, good sir. Pray you signify
   Unto your patron I am here—This band
   Shows not my neck enough.—I trouble you, sir;
   Let me request you bid one of my women
   Come hither to me. In good faith, I am dressed   5
   Most favorably today! It is no matter;
   'Tis well enough. [*Enter* FIRST WOMAN.] Look, see these petulant
     things!
   How they have done this!
VOLPONE   [*Aside*.] —I do feel the fever
   Ent'ring in at mine ears. O for a charm
   To fright it hence—
LADY WOULDBE   Come nearer. Is this curl   10
   In his right place? or this? Why is this higher
   Than all the rest? You ha' not washed your eyes yet?
   Or do they not stand even i' your head?
   Where's your fellow? Call her. [*Exit* FIRST WOMAN.]
NANO   [*Aside*.] Now, St. Mark
   Deliver us! Anon she'll beat her women   15
   Because her nose is red.
        [*Re-enter* FIRST WOMAN *with* SECOND WOMAN.]
LADY WOULDBE   I pray you, view
   This tire, forsooth; are all things apt, or no?
FIRST WOMAN   One hair a little, here, sticks out, forsooth.
LADY WOULDBE   Dost so, forsooth? And where was your dear sight
   When it did so, forsooth? What now! Bird-eyed?   20
   And you too? Pray you both approach and mend it.
   Now, by that light, I muse you're not ashamed!
   I, that have preached these things, so oft, unto you,
   Read you the principles, argued all the grounds,
   Disputed every fitness, every grace,   25
   Called you to counsel of so frequent dressings—
NANO   [*Aside*.] More carefully than of your fame or honor.

🔏 ACT III, Scene 4. **2** *band* ruff.   **5-6** *I . . . favorably* ironic.   **12-13** *You . . .
head* Can't you see straight?   **17** *tire* hair arrangement.   **20** *Bird-eyed* frightened (?).
24 *grounds* fundamentals—dressing is treated here like a science or the art of government.
27 *fame* reputation.

LADY WOULDBE   Made you acquainted what an ample dowry
    The knowledge of these things would be unto you,
    Able, alone, to get you noble husbands   30
    At your return; and you, thus, to neglect it!
    Besides, you seeing what a curious nation
    Th' Italians are, what will they say of me?
    "The English lady cannot dress herself."
    Here's a fine imputation to our country!   35
    Well, go your ways, and stay i' the next room.
    This fucus was too coarse, too; it's no matter.
    Good sir, you'll give 'em entertainment? [*Exit* NANO *with* WOMEN.]
VOLPONE   The storm comes toward me.
LADY WOULDBE   How does my Volp?
VOLPONE   Troubled with noise, I cannot sleep; I dreamt   40
    That a strange fury entered, now, my house,
    And, with the dreadful tempest of her breath,
    Did cleave my roof asunder.
LADY WOULDBE   Believe me, and I
    Had the most *fearful* dream, could I remember't—
VOLPONE   [*Aside.*] Out on my fate! I ha' giv'n her the occasion   45
    How to torment me. She will tell me hers.
LADY WOULDBE   Methought the golden mediocrity,
    Polite, and delicate—
VOLPONE   Oh, if you do love me,
    No more; I sweat, and suffer, at the mention
    Of *any* dream; feel how I tremble yet.   50

    [*Placing her hand on his heart.*]

LADY WOULDBE   Alas, good soul! the passion of the heart,
    Seed-pearl were good now, boiled with syrup of apples,

---

31 *return*   i.e. to England.   **32** *curious*   particular in small details.   **37** *fucus*   cosmetic for covering up complexion, "pancake makeup."   **38** *give 'em entertainment*   look out for them.   **45** *occasion*   means and opportunity.   **47** *golden mediocrity*   Herford and Simpson (9, 715) refer to this phrase as "high sounding nonsense" which Lady Wouldbe invents on the spur of the moment. This is true, but the phrase operates—like most of the apparent nonsense spoken by Jonson's characters—to remind us of ideals being violated and to define the moral status of the characters and action. Here the ideal referred to is the "golden mean," that classic guide to conduct which dictates "nothing in excess," and which has been lost completely in Volpone's world where men pursue gold and power and lust to the exclusion of all else, becoming in the process "golden mediocrities." **51** *passion . . . heart*   stomach gas pressing on the heart.   **52–56** *Seed-pearl . . . muscadel* a catalogue of popular remedies.

Tincture of gold, and coral, citron-pills,
Your elecampane root, myrobalanes—
VOLPONE [*Aside.*] Ay me, I have ta'en a grasshopper by the wing!   55
LADY WOULDBE Burnt silk and amber. You have muscadel
Good in the house—
VOLPONE   You will not drink and part?
LADY WOULDBE No, fear not that. I doubt we shall not get
Some English saffron, half a dram would serve,
Your sixteen cloves, a little musk, dried mints,   60
Bugloss, and barley-meal—
VOLPONE   [*Aside.*] She's in again.
Before I feigned diseases, now I have one.
LADY WOULDBE And these applied with a right scarlet cloth.
VOLPONE [*Aside.*] Another flood of words! a very torrent!
LADY WOULDBE Shall I, sir, make you a poultice?
VOLPONE   No, no, no.   65
I'm very well, you need prescribe no more.
LADY WOULDBE I have, a little, studied physic; but now
I'm all for music, save, i' the forenoons
An hour or two for painting. I would have
A lady, indeed, to have all letters and arts,   70
Be able to discourse, to write, to paint,
But principal, as Plato holds, your music,
And so does wise Pythagoras, I take it,
Is your true rapture, when there is concent
In face, in voice, and clothes, and is, indeed,   75
Our sex's chiefest ornament.
VOLPONE   The poet
As old in time as Plato, and as knowing,
Says that your highest female grace is silence.
LADY WOULDBE Which o' your poets? Petrarch? or Tasso? or Dante?
Guarini? Ariosto? Aretine?   80
Cieco di Hadria? I have read them all.

---

55 grasshopper referring to constant whirring noise made by captive grasshoppers.
58 doubt fear. **63 right** true. **67 physic** medicine. **74 concent** agreement, harmony. **76 poet** Sophocles, *Ajax* 293. **80 Aretine, 81 Cieco di Hadria** The other names Lady Wouldbe reels off are major Italian poets, but Luigi Groto, known as Cieco di Hadria, is a distinctly minor writer, while Pietro Aretino was a writer of powerful but extremely scurrilous and obscene verses. By joining these names to those of the poets of the great tradition Lady Wouldbe betrays her lack of discrimination, her inability to distinguish in literature as in life the profound from the vulgar.

VOLPONE   [*Aside.*] Is everything a cause to my destruction?
LADY WOULDBE   I think I ha' two or three of 'em about me.
VOLPONE   [*Aside.*] The sun, the sea, will sooner both stand still
    Than her eternal tongue! Nothing can scape it.   85
LADY WOULDBE   Here's *Pastor Fido*—[*Producing a book.*]
VOLPONE   [*Aside.*] Profess obstinate silence;
    That's now my safest.
LADY WOULDBE   All our English writers,
    I mean such as are happy in th' Italian,
    Will deign to steal out of this author, mainly;
    Almost as much as from Montagniè.   90
    He has so modern and facile a vein,
    Fitting the time, and catching the court-ear.
    Your Petrarch is more passionate, yet he,
    In days of sonneting, trusted 'em with much.
    Dante is hard, and few can understand him.   95
    But for a desperate wit, there's Aretine!
    Only, his pictures are a little obscene—
    You mark me not.
VOLPONE   Alas, my mind's perturbed.
LADY WOULDBE   Why, in such cases, we must cure ourselves,
    Make use of our philosophy—
VOLPONE   O'y me!   100
LADY WOULDBE   And as we find our passions do rebel,
    Encounter 'em with reason, or divert 'em
    By giving scope unto some other humor
    Of lesser danger: as, in politic bodies
    There's nothing more doth overwhelm the judgment,   105
    And clouds the understanding, than too much
    Settling and fixing, and, as 'twere, subsiding
    Upon one object. For the incorporating

---

86 *Pastor Fido*   *The Faithful Shepherd* (1590), Guarini's pastoral play.   **88** *happy*   fluent.
90 *Montagniè*   Montaigne, the French essayist. Pronounced with four syllables here.
92 *court-ear*   ear of courtiers.   **93–94** *Petrarch . . . much*   Petrarch was most famous
for his love sonnets, which were imitated by generations of poets—Sidney's *Astrophel
and Stella* and Spenser's *Amoretti* were in this tradition—and this extensive imitation and
borrowing are perhaps the basis for the statement "trusted 'em with much."   **96** *desperate*   outrageous.   **97** *pictures*   Aretino wrote poems to accompany a series of obscene
drawings.   **102** *Encounter*   battle.   **103** *scope*   free play.   *humor*   desire.   **104** *politic
bodies*   kingdoms.

Of these same outward things into that part
Which we call mental, leaves some certain feces   110
That stop the organs, and, as Plato says,
Assassinates our knowledge.

VOLPONE   [*Aside.*] Now, the spirit
Of patience help me!

LADY WOULDBE   Come, in faith, I must
Visit you more adays and make you well;
Laugh and be lusty.

VOLPONE   [*Aside.*] My good angel save me!   115

LADY WOULDBE   There was but one sole man in all the world
With whom I e'er could sympathize; and he
Would lie you often, three, four hours together
To hear me speak, and be sometime so rapt,
As he would answer me quite from the purpose,   120
Like you, and you are like him, just. I'll discourse,
An't be but only, sir, to bring you asleep,
How we did spend our time and loves together,
For some six years.

VOLPONE   Oh, oh, oh, oh, oh, oh.

LADY WOULDBE   For we were *coaetanei*, and brought up—   125

VOLPONE   Some power, some fate, some fortune rescue me!

ACT III   Scene 5

[*Enter* MOSCA.]

MOSCA   God save you, madam!

LADY WOULDBE   Good sir.

VOLPONE   Mosca, welcome!
Welcome to my redemption.

MOSCA   Why, sir?

VOLPONE   Oh,

---

109 outward things the object on which the mind has fixed. Lady Wouldbe's psy-
chology is as crude, jargon-ridden, and jumbled as her medicine and her literary criticism,
but it does describe roughly what has happened to the characters of the play and the city
of Venice—she is using the commonplace Renaissance comparison of man the microcosm
and the state or body politic. Man and state in *Volpone* have chosen gold as their *idée
fixe,* and the result has been clouded understanding. **118 lie you** lie. **120 from the
purpose** nothing to the point. **125 coaetanei** of the same age.

Rid me of this my torture quickly, there,
My madam with the everlasting voice;
The bells in time of pestilence ne'er made   5
Like noise, or were in that perpetual motion!
The cock-pit comes not near it. All my house,
But now, steamed like a bath with her thick breath.
A lawyer could not have been heard; nor scarce
Another woman, such a hail of words   10
She has let fall. For hell's sake, rid her hence.

MOSCA   Has she presented?

VOLPONE   Oh, I do not care;
I'll take her absence upon any price,
With any loss.

MOSCA   Madam—

LADY WOULDBE   I ha' brought your patron
A toy, a cap here, of mine own work.

MOSCA   'Tis well.   15
I had forgot to tell you I saw your knight
Where you'd little think it.

LADY WOULDBE   Where?

MOSCA   Marry,
Where yet, if you make haste, you may apprehend him,
Rowing upon the water in a gondole,
With the most cunning courtesan of Venice.   20

LADY WOULDBE   Is't true?

MOSCA   Pursue 'em, and believe your eyes.
Leave me to make your gift. [*Exit* LADY WOULDBE.] I knew 'twould
   take.
For lightly, they that use themselves most license,
Are still most jealous.

VOLPONE   Mosca, hearty thanks
For thy quick fiction and delivery of me.   25
Now to my hopes, what sayst thou? [*Re-enter* LADY WOULDBE.]

LADY WOULDBE   But do you hear, sir?

VOLPONE   Again! I fear a paroxysm.

LADY WOULDBE   Which way

🎇 **ACT III, Scene 5.   5** *bells . . . pestilence*   The bells in London rang almost without
ceasing during times of the plague.   **7** *cock-pit*   where cock fights were put on.
12 *presented*   given a present.   **23** *lightly*   commonly.   *use . . . license*   are most free
(morally).   **24** *still*   always.

Rowed they together?

MOSCA   Toward the Rialto.

LADY WOULDBE   I pray you lend me your dwarf.

MOSCA   I pray you, take him.

                                           [*Exit* LADY WOULDBE.]

Your hopes, sir, are like happy blossoms: fair,   30
And promise timely fruit, if you will stay
But the maturing; keep you at your couch.
Corbaccio will arrive straight with the will;
When he is gone, I'll tell you more. [*Exit* MOSCA.]

VOLPONE   My blood,
My spirits are returned; I am alive;   35
And, like your wanton gamester at primero,
Whose thought had whispered to him, not go less,
Methinks I lie, and draw—for an encounter.

                             [*He draws the curtains across his bed.*]

ACT III   Scene 6

[MOSCA *leads* BONARIO *on stage and hides him.*]

MOSCA   Sir, here concealed you may hear all. But pray you

    One knocks.

Have patience, sir; the same's your father knocks.
I am compelled to leave you.

BONARIO   Do so. Yet
Cannot my thought imagine this a truth.

ACT III   Scene 7

[MOSCA *opens door and admits* CORVINO *and* CELIA.]

MOSCA   Death on me! you are come too soon, what meant you?
Did not I say I would send?

CORVINO   Yes, but I feared

---

36 wanton gamester reckless gambler. **primero** a popular card game of the day.
Volpone makes use of the technical terms of the game—"go less" (i.e. wager less), "draw"
and "encounter"—as metaphors for his coming meeting with Celia.
🦌 **ACT III, Scene 7. 2 send** send word when to come.

You might forget it, and then they prevent us.
MOSCA   Prevent! [*Aside.*]—Did e'er man haste so for his horns?
        A courtier would not ply it so for a place.—   5
        Well, now there's no helping it, stay here;
        I'll presently return. [*He moves to one side.*]
CORVINO   Where are you, Celia?
        You know not wherefore I have brought you hither?
CELIA   Not well, except you told me.
CORVINO   Now I will:
        Hark hither. [*He leads her aside and whispers to her.*]
MOSCA   [*To* BONARIO.] Sir, your father hath sent word,   10
        It will be half an hour ere he come;
        And therefore, if you please to walk the while
        Into that gallery—at the upper end
        There are some books to entertain the time.
        And I'll take care no man shall come unto you, sir.   15
BONARIO Yes, I will stay there. [*Aside.*] I do doubt this fellow. [*Exit.*]
MOSCA   There, he is far enough; he can hear nothing.
        And for his father, I can keep him off.

        [*Returns to* VOLPONE's *couch, opens the curtains, and whispers to him.*]

CORVINO   Nay, now, there is no starting back, and therefore
        Resolve upon it: I have so decreed.   20
        It must be done. Nor would I move't afore,
        Because I would avoid all shifts and tricks,
        That might deny me.
CELIA   Sir, let me beseech you,
        Affect not these strange trials; if you doubt
        My chastity, why, lock me up forever;   25
        Make me the heir of darkness. Let me live
        Where I may please your fears, if not your trust.
CORVINO   Believe it, I have no such humor, I.
        All that I speak I mean; yet I am not mad;
        Not horn-mad, see you? Go to, show yourself   30
        Obedient, and a wife.
CELIA   O heaven!
CORVINO   I say it,

---

3 *they* the other legacy hunters. 4 *horns* the symbol of the cuckold. 5 *ply . . .
place* work so hard for an office at court. 7 *presently* immediately. 9 *except*
except what. 14 *entertain* pass. 21 *move* suggest. 22 *shifts* evasions. 24 *Affect
. . . trials* Do not pretend to make such unusual tests (of her virtue). 30 *horn-mad*
with fear of being a cuckold.

Do so.

CELIA   Was this the train?

CORVINO   I've told you reasons:
What the physicians have set down; how much
It may concern me; what my engagements are;
My means, and the necessity of those means   35
For my recovery; wherefore, if you be
Loyal and mine, be won, respect my venture.

CELIA Before your honor?

CORVINO   Honor! tut, a breath.
There's no such thing in nature; a mere term
Invented to awe fools. What, is my gold   40
The worse for touching? clothes for being looked on?
Why, this 's no more. An old, decrepit wretch,
That has no sense, no sinew; takes his meat
With others' fingers; only knows to gape
When you do scald his gums; a voice, a shadow;   45
And what can this man hurt you?

CELIA   Lord, what spirit
Is this hath entered him?

CORVINO   And for your fame,
That's such a jig; as if I would go tell it,
Cry it, on the Piazza! Who shall know it
But he that cannot speak it, and this fellow,   50
Whose lips are i' my pocket, save yourself.
—If you'll proclaim't, you may—I know no other
Should come to know it.

CELIA   Are heaven and saints then nothing?
Will they be blind, or stupid?

CORVINO   How?

CELIA   Good sir,
Be jealous still, emulate them, and think   55
What hate they burn with toward every sin.

CORVINO I grant you. If I thought it were a sin
I would not urge you. Should I offer this
To some young Frenchman, or hot Tuscan blood

---

32 *train* trap. **34** *engagements* financial commitments. **35** *means* i.e. becoming
Volpone's heir. **36** *recovery* regaining financial stability. **37** *venture* commercial
enterprise. **43** *sense* sensory perception. **47** *fame* reputation. **48** *jig* farce. **51** *lips
. . . pocket* Mosca will not speak because Corvino owns him. **57** *I grant you* Agreed.

That had read Aretine, conned all his prints,   60
Knew every quirk within lust's labyrinth,
And were professed critic in lechery;
And I would look upon him, and applaud him,
This were a sin; but here, 'tis contrary,
A pious work, mere charity, for physic   65
And honest policy to assure mine own.

CELIA   O heaven! canst thou suffer such a change?

VOLPONE   Thou art mine honor, Mosca, and my pride,
My joy, my tickling, my delight! Go, bring 'em.

MOSCA   Please you draw near, sir.

CORVINO   Come on, what—   70

[*She hangs back.*]

You will not be rebellious? By that light—

[*He drags her to the bed.*]

MOSCA   [*To* VOLPONE.] Sir, Signior Corvino, here, is come to see you.

VOLPONE   Oh!

MOSCA   And hearing of the consultation had,
So lately, for your health, is come to offer,
Or rather, sir, to prostitute—

CORVINO   Thanks, sweet Mosca.   75

MOSCA   Freely, unasked, or unentreated—

CORVINO   Well.

MOSCA   As the true, fervent instance of his love,
His own most fair and proper wife, the beauty
Only of price in Venice—

CORVINO   'Tis well urged.

MOSCA   To be your comfortress, and to preserve you.   80

VOLPONE   Alas, I'm past already! Pray you, thank him
For his good care and promptness; but for that,
'Tis a vain labor e'en to fight 'gainst heaven;
Applying fire to a stone, uh, uh, uh, uh!
Making a dead leaf grow again. I take   85
His wishes gently, though; and you may tell him
What I've done for him. Marry, my state is hopeless!
Will him to pray for me, and t' use his fortune

---

60 *prints* the obscene pictures referred to above. **62** *professed critic* connoisseur.
63 *And* if. **66** *own* i.e. inheritance. **79** *Only of price* uniquely beautiful.
84 *Applying . . . stone* proverbial statement of absolute futility.

With reverence when he comes to't.

MOSCA   Do you hear, sir?

Go to him with your wife.

CORVINO   [*To* CELIA.]   Heart of my father!   90
Wilt thou persist thus? Come, I pray thee, come.
Thou seest 'tis nothing, Celia. By this hand

[*Raising his hand.*]

I shall grow violent. Come, do't, I say.

CELIA   Sir, kill me rather. I will take down poison,
Eat burning coals, do anything—

CORVINO   Be damned!   95
Heart! I will drag thee hence home by the hair,
Cry thee a strumpet through the streets, rip up
Thy mouth unto thine ears, and slit thy nose,
Like a raw rotchet!—Do not tempt me, come.
Yield, I am loth—Death! I will buy some slave   100
Whom I will kill, and bind thee to him, alive;
And at my window hang you forth, devising
Some monstrous crime, which I, in capital letters,
Will eat into thy flesh with aquafortis,
And burning cor'sives, on this stubborn breast.   105
Now, by the blood thou hast incensed, I'll do't!

CELIA   Sir, what you please, you may; I am your martyr.

CORVINO   Be not thus obstinate, I ha' not deserved it.
Think who it is entreats you. Pray thee, sweet;
Good faith, thou shalt have jewels, gowns, attires,   110
What thou wilt, think and ask. Do, but go kiss him.
Or touch him, but. For my sake. At my suit.
This once. [*She refuses.*] No? Not? I shall remember this.
Will you disgrace me thus? D' you thirst my undoing?

MOSCA   Nay, gentle lady, be advised.

CORVINO   No, no.   115
She has watched her time. God's precious, this is scurvy,
'Tis very scurvy; and you are—

MOSCA   Nay, good sir.

CORVINO   An errant locust, by heaven, a locust! Whore,

---

95 *Eat . . . coals* method of suicide used by Portia, Brutus' wife. 99 *rotchet* a variety
of fish. 104 *aquafortis* acid. 105 *cor'sives* corrosives. 115 *advised* persuaded by
the argument. 116 *watched her time* waited for her moment. 118 *errant* either
"far-roving" or a form of "arrant."

Crocodile, that hast thy tears prepared,
Expecting how thou'lt bid 'em flow.
MOSCA   Nay, pray you, sir!   120
She will consider.
CELIA   Would my life would serve
To satisfy.
CORVINO   'Sdeath! if she would but speak to him,
And save my reputation, 'twere somewhat;
But spitefully to effect utter ruin!
MOSCA   Ay, now you've put your fortune in her hands.   125
Why i' faith, it is her modesty, I must quit her.
If you were absent, she would be more coming;
I know it, and dare undertake for her.
What woman can before her husband? Pray you,
Let us depart and leave her here.
CORVINO   Sweet Celia,   130
Thou mayst redeem all yet; I'll say no more.
If not, esteem yourself as lost. [*She begins to leave with him.*] Nay,
       stay there.
                          [*Exit* MOSCA *and* CORVINO.]
CELIA   O God, and his good angels! whither, whither,
Is shame fled human breasts? that with such ease
Men dare put off your honors, and their own?   135
Is that, which ever was a cause of life,
Now placed beneath the basest circumstance,
And modesty an exile made, for money?
VOLPONE   Ay, in Corvino, and such earth-fed minds,

He leaps off from the couch.

That never tasted the true heaven of love.   140
Assure thee, Celia, he that would sell thee,
Only for hope of gain, and that uncertain,
He would have sold his part of Paradise
For ready money, had he met a cope-man.
Why art thou mazed to see me thus revived?   145
Rather applaud thy beauty's miracle;
'Tis thy great work, that hath, not now alone,

---

119 *Crocodile . . . tears* The crocodile was proverbially believed to shed tears in order
to lure his victims. **126 *quit*** excuse. **127 *coming*** agreeable. **128 *undertake for***
warrant. **135 *your*** i.e. God's and his angels'. **137 *circumstance*** matter of little
importance. **144 *cope-man*** merchant. **145 *mazed*** amazed.

But sundry times raised me in several shapes,
And, but this morning, like a mountebank,
To see thee at thy window. Ay, before   150
I would have left my practice for thy love,
In varying figures I would have contended
With the blue Proteus, or the hornèd flood.
Now, art thou welcome.

CELIA   Sir!
VOLPONE   Nay, fly me not.
Nor let thy false imagination   155
That I was bed-rid, make thee think I am so:
Thou shalt not find it. I am, now, as fresh,
As hot, as high, and in as jovial plight
As when in that so celebrated scene
At recitation of our comedy,   160
For entertainment of the great Valois,
I acted young Antinous, and attracted
The eyes and ears of all the ladies present,
T' admire each graceful gesture, note, and footing.
                    Song   165
         Come, my Celia, let us prove,
         While we can, the sports of love;
         Time will not be ours forever,
         He, at length, our good will sever;
         Spend not then his gifts in vain.   170

---

151 *practice* scheming. **152** *figures* shapes, disguises. **153** *blue . . . flood* Proteus
was the "old man of the sea" who could change himself at will into any shape—see
Odyssey, IV.456 ff., where Menelaus struggles with him in many forms. Blue is a translation of the Latin adjective *caerulus,* applied to anything connected with the sea. "Hornèd
flood" refers to the river Achelous—"hornèd" because it branches and roars—which
struggled with Hercules in three forms: bull, serpent, and man-ox. Volpone, it should be
noticed, here defines his genius as the ability to change shape at will, and so great is his
power, he feels, that he could contend with water itself, the very element of change.
158 *jovial plight* happy condition, but Jove and his love for earthly maidens is referred
to. **161** *great Valois* Henry of Valois, later Henry III of France, was magnificently
entertained in Venice in 1524. Plays were one of the standard features of such entertainments. **162** *Antinous* usually identified as the Roman Emperor Hadrian's favorite
courtier, noted for his physical beauty. **164** *footing* movement. **165** *Song* This is an
imitation of and partly translated from the famous fifth ode of Catullus, beginning
Vivamus, mea Lesbia, atque amemus. The song is lovely but it evokes here not so much an
image of a beautiful love seizing its moment, as of the ultimate faithlessness of Catullus'
Clodia, the Lesbia of the poem, and her degeneration into a sensuality as gross as Volpone's.
166 *prove* try, test.

        Suns that set may rise again;
        But if once we lose this light,
        'Tis with us perpetual night.
        Why should we defer our joys?
        Fame and rumor are but toys.   175
        Cannot we delude the eyes
        Of a few poor household spies?
        Or his easier ears beguile,
        Thus removèd by our wile?
        'Tis no sin love's fruits to steal,   180
        But the sweet thefts to reveal:
        To be taken, to be seen,
        These have crimes accounted been.
CELIA   Some serene blast me, or dire lightning strike
    This my offending face.
VOLPONE   Why droops my Celia?   185
    Thou hast in place of a base husband found
    A worthy lover; use thy fortune well,
    With secrecy and pleasure. See, behold,

    [*Pointing to his treasure.*]

    What thou art queen of; not in expectation,
    As I feed others, but possessed and crowned.   190
    See, here, a rope of pearl, and each more orient
    Than that the brave Egyptian queen caroused;
    Dissolve and drink 'em. See, a carbuncle
    May put out both the eyes of our St. Mark;
    A diamond would have bought Lollia Paulina   195
    When she came in like star-light, hid with jewels
    That were the spoils of provinces; take these,
    And wear, and lose 'em; yet remains an earring
    To purchase them again, and this whole state.

---

175 *toys* trifles. **184 *serene*** poisonous mist. **185 *offending*** i.e. because its beauty attracts Volpone. **191 *orient*** precious. **192 *Egyptian queen*** Cleopatra, who at an extravagant banquet drank pearls dissolved in vinegar. ***caroused*** drank. **193 *carbuncle*** rounded red gem, e.g. a ruby. **194 *May . . . St. Mark*** It may be that some image of St. Mark, the patron saint of Venice, had jewels for eyes, and that the jewel Volpone holds up makes them seem trivial, "puts out," by comparison. But at the same time, the jewel "puts out" or obliterates the eyes of the saint in the same way that Volpone's gold in the opening scene "darkens" the light of the sun (line 6). **195 *Lollia Paulina*** wife of a Roman governor of a province who covered herself with jewels taken from the province.

A gem but worth a private patrimony   200
Is nothing; we will eat such at a meal.
The heads of parrots, tongues of nightingales,
The brains of peacocks, and of estriches
Shall be our food, and, could we get the phoenix,
Though nature lost her kind, she were our dish.   205
CELIA   Good sir, these things might move a mind affected
With such delights; but I, whose innocence
Is all I can think wealthy, or worth th' enjoying,
And which, once lost, I have nought to lose beyond it,
Cannot be taken with these sensual baits.   210
If you have conscience—
VOLPONE   'Tis the beggar's virtue;
If thou hast wisdom, hear me, Celia.
Thy baths shall be the juice of July-flowers,
Spirit of roses, and of violets,
The milk of unicorns, and panthers' breath   215
Gathered in bags and mixed with Cretan wines.
Our drink shall be preparèd gold and amber,
Which we will take until my roof whirl round
With the vertigo; and my dwarf shall dance,
My eunuch sing, my fool make up the antic.   220
Whilst we, in changèd shapes, act Ovid's tales,
Thou like Europa now, and I like Jove,
Then I like Mars, and thou like Erycine;
So of the rest, till we have quite run through,
And wearied all the fables of the gods.   225

200 *private patrimony* single inheritance.   **204 *phoenix*** mythical bird. Only one was
believed to exist at a time, and from his ashes another was born.   **205 *nature . . . kind***
(The phoenix) became extinct.   **213 *July-flowers*** gillyflowers.   **215 *panthers' breath***
This is, of course, the supreme touch of rarity in Volpone's catalogue of sensual pleasures,
and it topples the speech into the ludicrous. But again the particular detail is meaningful:
panthers were popularly believed to have an extraordinarily sweet smell which attracted
their prey, like the tears of the crocodile referred to in the note to line 119 above. The
images which run through this speech, and through the play, are used unself-consciously
by the speakers, but they serve to identify the characters and their world. Mosca crying
for Bonario is the crocodile luring its prey with tears; Volpone tempting Celia with
"sensual baits" is the sweet-smelling panther; and the world he moves in is the same
world as that of Nero's Rome in which a province could be stripped by a Roman general
and all its treasures placed in gaudy and vulgar profusion on a woman, Lollia Paulina.
This ironic use of imagery is characteristic of Jonson's dramatic technique.   **220 *antic***
grotesque dance.   **221 *Ovid's tales*** *The Metamorphoses,* a series of stories dealing with
human transformations.   **223 *Erycine*** Venus.

Then will I have thee in more modern forms,
Attirèd like some sprightly dame of France,
Brave Tuscan lady, or proud Spanish beauty;
Sometimes unto the Persian Sophy's wife,
Or the Grand Signior's mistress; and, for change,   230
To one of our most artful courtesans,
Or some quick Negro, or cold Russian;
And I will meet thee in as many shapes;
Where we may, so, transfuse our wand'ring souls

[*Kissing her.*]

Out at our lips and score up sums of pleasures,   235
    That the curious shall not know
    How to tell them as they flow;
    And the envious, when they find
    What their number is, be pined.
CELIA   If you have ears that will be pierced, or eyes   240
    That can be opened, a heart may be touched,
Or any part that yet sounds man about you;
If you have touch of holy saints, or heaven,
Do me the grace to let me 'scape. If not,
Be bountiful and kill me. You do know   245
I am a creature hither ill betrayed
By one whose shame I would forget it were.
If you will deign me neither of these graces,
Yet feed your wrath, sir, rather than your lust,
It is a vice comes nearer manliness,   250
And punish that unhappy crime of nature,
Which you miscall my beauty: flay my face,
Or poison it with ointments for seducing
Your blood to this rebellion. Rub these hands
With what may cause an eating leprosy,   255
E'en to my bones and marrow; anything
That may disfavor me, save in my honor,
And I will kneel to you, pray for you, pay down

---

229 *Sophy* ruler. **230** *Grand Signior* Sultan of Turkey, noted for cruelty.
232 *quick* lively. **237** *tell* count. **239** *pined* eaten up with envy. **242** *sounds man* announces you to be a man (rather than beast). **254** *rebellion* because reason and virtue should control passion, "blood." **255** *leprosy* any serious disease of the skin. **257** *disfavor* make the face ugly.

A thousand hourly vows, sir, for your health;
Report, and think you virtuous—

CELIA   Think me cold,   260

VOLPONE
Frozen, and impotent, and so report me?
That I had Nestor's hernia thou wouldst think.
I do degenerate and abuse my nation
To play with opportunity thus long;
I should have done the act, and then have parleyed.   265
Yield, or I'll force thee. [*He seizes her.*]

CELIA   O! just God!

VOLPONE   In vain—

BONARIO   Forbear, foul ravisher! libidinous swine!

He leaps out from where MOSCA *had placed him.*

Free the forced lady, or thou diest, impostor.
But that I am loth to snatch thy punishment
Out of the hand of justice, thou shouldst yet   270
Be made the timely sacrifice of vengeance,
Before this altar, and this dross, thy idol.

[*Points to the gold.*]
Lady, let's quit the place, it is the den
Of villainy; fear nought, you have a guard;
And he ere long shall meet his just reward.   275

[*Exeunt* BONARIO *and* CELIA.]

VOLPONE   Fall on me, roof, and bury me in ruin!
Become my grave, that wert my shelter! O!
I am unmasked, unspirited, undone,
Betrayed to beggary, to infamy—

ACT III   Scene 8

[*Enter* MOSCA, *bleeding.*]

MOSCA   Where shall I run, most wretched shame of men,
To beat out my unlucky brains?

VOLPONE   Here, here.
What! dost thou bleed?

MOSCA   O, that his well-driven sword

---

262 Nestor's hernia Nestor is the very old and wise Greek of the *Iliad*—the hernia
suggests impotence.   **268 impostor** pretender; but see note to IV.6.24.   **275 he**
Volpone.

Had been so courteous to have cleft me down
Unto the navel, ere I lived to see   5
My life, my hopes, my spirits, my patron, all
Thus desperately engagèd by my error.

VOLPONE   Woe on thy fortune!

MOSCA   And my follies, sir.

VOLPONE   Th' hast made me miserable.

MOSCA   And myself, sir.
Who would have thought he would have hearkened so?   10

VOLPONE   What shall we do?

MOSCA   I know not; if my heart
Could expiate the mischance, I'd pluck it out.
Will you be pleased to hang me, or cut my throat?
And I'll requite you, sir. Let's die like Romans,
Since we have lived like Grecians. *They knock without.*

VOLPONE   Hark! who's there?   15
I hear some footing; officers, the *Saffi,*
Come to apprehend us! I do feel the brand
Hissing already at my forehead; now,
Mine ears are boring.

MOSCA   To your couch, sir; you
Make that place good, however. Guilty men   20

[VOLPONE *lies down.*]

Suspect what they deserve still. [MOSCA *opens door.*] Signior
    Corbaccio!

ACT III   Scene 9

[*Enter* CORBACCIO.]

CORBACCIO   Why, how now, Mosca?

MOSCA   O, undone, amazed, sir.
Your son, I know not by what accident,
Acquainted with your purpose to my patron,

🦗 ACT III, Scene 8.   **7** *engagèd* trapped.   **10** *he* Bonario.   *hearkened* listened.
14 *requite* do the same for.   *Romans* referring to Roman custom of committing
suicide in adversity.   **15** *Grecians* noted for dissolute living.   **16** *footing* footsteps.
Saffi police.   **17-19** *brand . . . boring* branding on the forehead and cutting the ears
was common punishment for criminals.   **20** *Make . . . however* Maintain your disguise
as a sick man whatever happens.
🦗 ACT III, Scene 9.   **1** *amazed* confused.   **3** *purpose* intention.

Touching your will, and making him your heir,
Entered our house with violence, his sword drawn,   5
Sought for you, called you wretch, unnatural,
Vowed he would kill you.

CORBACCIO   Me?

MOSCA   Yes, and my patron.

CORBACCIO   This act shall disinherit him indeed.
Here is the will.

MOSCA   'Tis well, sir.

CORBACCIO   Right and well.
Be you as careful now for me. [*Enter* VOLTORE *behind.*]

MOSCA   My life, sir,   10
Is not more tendered; I am only yours.

CORBACCIO   How does he? Will he die shortly, thinkst thou?

MOSCA   I fear
He'll outlast May.

CORBACCIO   Today?

MOSCA   [*Shouting.*]   No, last out May, sir.

CORBACCIO   Couldst thou not gi' him a dram?

MOSCA   O, by no means, sir.

CORBACCIO   Nay, I'll not bid you.

VOLTORE   [*Stepping forward.*]   This is a knave, I see.   15

MOSCA   [*Aside.*] How! Signior Voltore! Did he hear me?

VOLTORE   Parasite!

MOSCA   Who's that? O, sir, most timely welcome.

VOLTORE   Scarce
To the discovery of your tricks, I fear.
You are his, only? And mine, also, are you not?

[CORBACCIO *wanders to the side of the stage and stands there.*]

MOSCA   Who? I, sir?

VOLTORE   You, sir. What device is this   20
About a will?

MOSCA   A plot for you, sir.

VOLTORE   Come,
Put not your foists upon me; I shall scent 'em.

MOSCA   Did you not hear it?

VOLTORE   Yes, I hear Corbaccio
Hath made your patron, there, his heir.

MOSCA   'Tis true,

---

10 *careful* concerned for benefit. **11** *tendered* watched over. **14** *dram* drink (of
poison). **20** *device* scheme. **22** *foists* tricks, but word also means "odor."

By my device, drawn to it by my plot,   25
With hope—
VOLTORE   Your patron should reciprocate?
And you have promised?
MOSCA   For your good I did, sir.
Nay, more, I told his son, brought, hid him here,
Where he might hear his father pass the deed;
Being persuaded to it by this thought, sir: 30
That the unnaturalness, first, of the act,
And then his father's oft disclaiming in him,
Which I did mean t' help on, would sure enrage him
To do some violence upon his parent.
On which the law should take sufficient hold,   35
And you be stated in a double hope.
Truth be my comfort, and my conscience,
My only aim was to dig you a fortune
Out of these two old, rotten sepulchres—
VOLTORE I cry thee mercy, Mosca.
MOSCA   Worth your patience,   40
And your great merit, sir. And see the change!
VOLTORE Why, what success?
MOSCA   Most hapless! you must help, sir.
Whilst we expected th'old raven, in comes
Corvino's wife, sent hither by her husband—
VOLTORE What, with a present?
MOSCA   No, sir, on visitation;   45
I'll tell you how anon—and staying long,
The youth he grows impatient, rushes forth,
Seizeth the lady, wounds me, makes her swear—
Or he would murder her, that was his vow—
T' affirm my patron to have done her rape,   50
Which how unlike it is, you see! and hence,
With that pretext he's gone t' accuse his father,
Defame my patron, defeat you—
VOLTORE   Where's her husband?
Let him be sent for straight.
MOSCA   Sir, I'll go fetch him.

---

32 *oft . . . him* frequent denial of kinship. **35** *sufficient hold* punish him in such a way that he could not inherit. **36** *stated* settled. *double hope* inheriting Volpone's and Corbaccio's fortunes. **40** *cry . . . mercy* beg your pardon. **42** *success* result.

VOLTORE   Bring him to the *Scrutineo.*

MOSCA   Sir, I will.   55

VOLTORE   This must be stopped.

MOSCA   O, you do nobly, sir.
 Alas, 'twas labored all, sir, for your good;
 Nor was there want of counsel in the plot.
 But Fortune can, at any time, o'erthrow
 The projects of a hundred learned clerks, sir.   60

CORBACCIO   What's that?

 [*Suddenly becoming aware that others are present.*]

VOLTORE   [*To* CORBACCIO.]

      Will 't please you, sir, to go along?

      [*Exeunt* CORBACCIO *and* VOLTORE.]

MOSCA   [*To* VOLPONE.] Patron, go in and pray for our success.

VOLPONE   Need makes devotion; heaven your labor bless!

ACT IV

Scene 1   ⟨*A street in Venice*⟩

[*Enter* SIR POLITIC *and* PEREGRINE.]

SIR POLITIC   I told you, sir, it was a plot; you see
 What observation is! You mentioned me
 For some instructions: I will tell you, sir,
 Since we are met here in this height of Venice,
 Some few particulars I have set down   5
 Only for this meridian, fit to be known
 Of your crude traveler; and they are these.

---

55 *Scrutineo* law court in Senate House. **60 *clerks*** learned men.
🦊 **ACT IV, Scene 1. 1 *it*** Sir Pol apparently takes the entire mountebank scene as a
plot. **2 *observation*** careful scrutiny of events. ***mentioned*** In the advice to Peregrine
which Sir Politic delivers in the remainder of the scene he details the perfect formula for
becoming an arrant fop and fool. Concerned only with the outside of man, he makes
morality a matter of policy—"never speak a truth"—somewhat in the manner of Polonius
advising his son Laertes on how to conduct himself in Paris; religion a matter of fashion;
and places his major educational emphasis on table manners and mad schemes for getting
rich. **4 *height*** latitude.

I will not touch, sir, at your phrase, or clothes,
For they are old.
PEREGRINE   Sir, I have better.
SIR POLITIC   Pardon,
I meant as they are themes.
PEREGRINE   O, sir, proceed.   10
I'll slander you no more of wit, good sir.
SIR POLITIC   First, for your garb, it must be grave and serious,
Very reserved and locked; not tell a secret
On any terms, not to your father; scarce
A fable but with caution; make sure choice   15
Both of your company and discourse; beware
You never speak a truth—
PEREGRINE   How!
SIR POLITIC   Not to strangers,
For those be they you must converse with most;
Others I would not know, sir, but at distance,
So as I still might be a saver in 'em.   20
You shall have tricks, else, passed upon you hourly.
And then, for your religion, profess none,
But wonder at the diversity of all;
And, for your part, protest were there no other
But simply the laws o' th' land, you could content you.   25
Nick Machiavel and Monsieur Bodin both
Were of this mind. Then must you learn the use
And handling of your silver fork at meals,
The metal of your glass (these are main matters

---

8 *touch . . . at* deal with. *phrase* manner of speaking. 10 *themes* topics for discussion. 12 *garb* bearing. 13 *not* do not. 15 *fable* story. 19 *know* acknowledge. 20 *So . . . 'em* so I might retain their friendship (?). 24–25 *were . . . you* You
could be quite content if there were no religion, only the law. It should be remembered
that *Volpone* was written in a time of fierce religious quarrels between Protestant and
Catholic, and Protestant and Protestant; and the old angers had recently flared again in
England on the discovery of the Gunpowder Plot. In times of such trouble it was fashionable for some of the more skeptical and the more elegant to reject all churches and put
their trust in the state alone. Jonson was at this time a professed Catholic who held to his
religion under considerable pressure. 26 *Machiavel . . . Bodin* two advanced thinkers
of the age whose books were as popular among the intellectuals and their imitators as
Nietzsche and Freud are today. Niccolò Machiavelli was the author of *The Prince,* a handbook of *Realpolitik;* and Jean Bodin had argued in his writings for religious toleration on
the grounds that it was obviously impossible to achieve religious agreement. 28 *fork*
Forks were fairly common in Italy, but not in England, at this time. 29 *metal* material.
main primary.

With your Italian), and to know the hour   30
When you must eat your melons and your figs.
PEREGRINE   Is that a point of state too?
SIR POLITIC   Here it is.
For your Venetian, if he see a man
Preposterous in the least, he has him straight;
He has, he strips him. I'll acquaint you, sir.   35
I now have lived here 'tis some fourteen months;
Within the first week of my landing here,
All took me for a citizen of Venice,
I knew the forms so well—
PEREGRINE   [*Aside.*] And nothing else.
SIR POLITIC   I had read Contarini, took me a house,   40
Dealt with my Jews to furnish it with movables—
Well, if I could but find one man, one man
To mine own heart, whom I durst trust, I would—
PEREGRINE   What, what, sir?
SIR POLITIC   Make him rich, make him a fortune:
He should not think again. I would command it.   45
PEREGRINE   As how?
SIR POLITIC   With certain projects that I have,
Which I may not discover.
PEREGRINE   [*Aside.*] If I had
But one to wager with, I would lay odds, now,
He tells me instantly.
SIR POLITIC   One is, and that
I care not greatly who knows, to serve the state   50
Of Venice with red herrings for three years,
And at a certain rate, from Rotterdam,
Where I have correspondence. There's a letter

[*Showing a greasy sheet of paper.*]

Sent me from one o' th' States, and to that purpose;
He cannot write his name, but that's his mark.   55
PEREGRINE   He is a chandler?
SIR POLITIC   No, a cheesemonger.

---

34 *Preposterous* incorrect. ***straight*** at once. **40 *Contarini*** Cardinal Contarini
(1483–1542) wrote a book on Venice which was translated into English in 1599.
41 *movables* furnishings. **46 *projects*** Sir Politic is an example of the type of man
known as a projector, the idea man of his time who proposed schemes—projects—for
making money. **47 *discover*** disclose. **53 *correspondence*** commercial connections.
54 *States* Holland. ***that purpose*** i.e. selling herring to Venice. **56 *chandler*** seller
of candles. Peregrine is commenting on the greasiness of the paper.

There are some other too with whom I treat
About the same negotiation;
And I will undertake it: for 'tis thus
I'll do't with ease, I've cast it all. Your hoy   60
Carries but three men in her, and a boy;
And she shall make me three returns a year.
So, if there come but one of three, I save;
If two, I can defalk. But this is now
If my main project fail.
PEREGRINE   Then you have others?   65
SIR POLITIC   I should be loath to draw the subtle air
Of such a place without my thousand aims.
I'll not dissemble, sir; where'er I come
I love to be considerative, and 'tis true
I have at my free hours thought upon   70
Some certain goods unto the state of Venice,
Which I do call my cautions; and, sir, which
I mean, in hope of pension, to propound
To the Great Council, then unto the Forty,
So to the Ten. My means are made already—   75
PEREGRINE   By whom?
SIR POLITIC   Sir, one that though his place be obscure,
Yet he can sway, and they will hear him. He's
A *commendatore.*
PEREGRINE   What, a common sergeant?
SIR POLITIC   Sir, such as they are put it in their mouths
What they should say, sometimes, as well as greater.   80
I think I have my notes to show you— [*Searching his pockets.*]
PEREGRINE   Good sir.
SIR POLITIC   But you shall swear unto me, on your gentry,
Not to anticipate—
PEREGRINE   I, sir?
SIR POLITIC   Nor reveal
A circumstance—My paper is not with me.
PEREGRINE   O, but you can remember, sir.
SIR POLITIC   My first is   85

---

60 *cast* figured.   *hoy* small Dutch coastal boat.   **64** *defalk* retrench financially.
69 *considerative* inquiring and thoughtful.   **72** *cautions* precautions.   **73** *pension*
He hopes for a pension from the state as reward for his projects.   **74–75** *Great . . . Ten*
the ruling bodies of Venice in order of importance.   **80** *What . . . greater* Common
sergeants as well as more important people sometimes tell the powerful what to think
and say.

Concerning tinderboxes. You must know
No family is here without its box.
Now, sir, it being so portable a thing,
Put case that you or I were ill affected
Unto the state; sir, with it in our pockets   90
Might not I go into the Arsenal?
Or you? Come out again? And none the wiser?
PEREGRINE   Except yourself, sir.
SIR POLITIC   Go to, then. I therefore
Advertise to the state how fit it were
That none but such as were known patriots,   95
Sound lovers of their country, should be suffered
T'enjoy them in their houses; and even those
Sealed at some office, and at such a bigness
As might not lurk in pockets.
PEREGRINE   Admirable!
SIR POLITIC   My next is, how t'inquire, and be resolved   100
By present demonstration, whether a ship
Newly arrivèd from Syria, or from
Any suspected part of all the Levant,
Be guilty of the plague. And where they use
To lie out forty, fifty days, sometimes,   105
About the *Lazaretto* for their trial,
I'll save that charge and loss unto the merchant,
And in an hour clear the doubt.
PEREGRINE   Indeed, sir!
SIR POLITIC   Or—I will lose my labor.
PEREGRINE   My faith, that's much.
SIR POLITIC   Nay, sir, conceive me. 'Twill cost me, in onions,   110
Some thirty livres—
PEREGRINE   Which is one pound sterling.
SIR POLITIC   Beside my waterworks. For this I do, sir:
First, I bring in your ship 'twixt two brick walls—
But those the state shall venture. On the one
I strain me a fair tarpaulin, and in that   115
I stick my onions, cut in halves; the other

---

89 *Put case* Say for example.   **91** *Arsenal* famous Venetian building which housed
all their ships and weapons.   **94** *Advertise* make known.   **97** *them* tinderboxes.
101 *present demonstration* immediate experiment.   **104** *guilty of* infected with.
use are accustomed.   **106** *Lazaretto* a quarantine hospital.   **108** *clear the doubt*
make sure (whether they are infected).   **111** *livre* French coin.   **114** *venture* pay for.

Is full of loopholes, out at which I thrust
The noses of my bellows; and those bellows
I keep, with waterworks, in perpetual motion,
Which is the easiest matter of a hundred.   120
Now, sir, your onion, which doth naturally
Attract th' infection, and your bellows blowing
The air upon him, will show instantly
By his changed color if there be contagion,
Or else remain as fair as at the first.   125
Now 'tis known, 'tis nothing.
PEREGRINE   You are right, sir.
SIR POLITIC   I would I had my note. [*Searching his pockets.*]
PEREGRINE   Faith, so would I.
But you ha' done well for once, sir.
SIR POLITIC   Were I false,
Or would be made so, I could show you reasons
How I could sell this state, now, to the Turk—   130
Spite of their galleys, or their—[*Still frantically searching his pocket.*]
PEREGRINE   Pray you, Sir Pol.
SIR POLITIC   I have 'em not about me.
PEREGRINE   That I feared.
They're there, sir? [*Pulling a book from* SIR POL's *pocket.*]
SIR POLITIC   No, this is my diary,
Wherein I note my actions of the day.
PEREGRINE   Pray you let's see, sir. What is here?—"*Notandum,*   135
A rat had gnawn my spur leathers; notwithstanding,
I put on new and did go forth; but first
I threw three beans over the threshold. Item,
I went and bought two toothpicks, whereof one
I burst, immediately, in a discourse   140
With a Dutch merchant 'bout *ragion del stato.*
From him I went and paid a *moccenigo*

121–22 *naturally Attract* Onions were believed to collect plague infection. **128** *false* traitorous. **129** *reasons* feasible methods(?). **131** *their* i.e. the Venetians'. **133** *diary* Jonson is burlesquing the many travelers of his time who kept and published journals in which they noted every trivial detail of their journeys, like that meticulous observer of petty facts, Captain Lemuel Gulliver. **138** *three beans* According to Theophrastus in the "Superstitious Man," from which Jonson took this detail, gnawed spur leathers or any other commonplace happening was taken by the superstitious as having supernatural meaning. Beans were traditionally believed to have an expiatory value, something like "knocking on wood." **141** *ragion del stato* political affairs. **142** *moccenigo* coin of small value.

For piecing my silk stockings; by the way
I cheapened sprats, and at St. Mark's I urined."
Faith, these are politic notes!

SIR POLITIC   Sir, I do slip   145
No action of my life, thus but I quote it.

PEREGRINE   Believe me it is wise!

SIR POLITIC   Nay, sir, read forth.

ACT IV   Scene 2

[*Enter* LADY WOULDBE, NANO, *and two* WOMEN.]

LADY WOULDBE   Where should this loose knight be, trow? Sure, he's
          housed.

NANO   Why, then he's fast.

LADY WOULDBE   Ay, he plays both with me.
I pray you stay. This heat will do more harm
To my complexion than his heart is worth.
I do not care to hinder, but to take him.   5
How it comes off! [*Rubbing her make-up.*]

FIRST WOMAN   My master's yonder. [*Pointing.*]

LADY WOULDBE   Where?

SECOND WOMAN   With a young gentleman.

LADY WOULDBE   That same's the party!
In man's apparel! Pray you, sir, jog my knight.
I will be tender to his reputation,
However he demerit.

SIR POLITIC   My lady!

PEREGRINE   Where?   10

SIR POLITIC   'Tis she indeed; sir, you shall know her. She is,
Were she not mine, a lady of that merit
For fashion, and behavior, and for beauty
I durst compare—

PEREGRINE   It seems you are not jealous,
That dare commend her.

SIR POLITIC   Nay, and for discourse—   15

---

143 *piecing* mending. **144** *cheapened* bargained for. **145** *slip* allow to pass.
146 *thus but* but in this manner. *quote* note. **147** *forth* on.
❧ ACT IV, Scene 2. **1** *loose* lascivious. *housed* i.e. in a bawdy house. **2** *fast*
caught. *both* fast and loose; see note to I.2.8. **8** *jog* poke (?); remind. **10** *demerit*
does not deserve (care for his reputation). **15** *discourse* conversation.

PEREGRINE   Being your wife, she cannot miss that.

   [*The parties join.*]

SIR POLITIC   Madam,
   Here is a gentleman; pray you, use him fairly;
   He seems a youth, but he is—
LADY WOULDBE   None?
SIR POLITIC   Yes, one
   Has put his face as soon into the world—
LADY WOULDBE   You mean, as early? But today?
SIR POLITIC   How's this?   20
LADY WOULDBE   Why, in this habit, sir; you apprehend me!
   Well, Master Wouldbe, this doth not become you.
   I had thought the odor, sir, of your good name
   Had been more precious to you; that you would not
   Have done this dire massàcre on your honor,   25
   One of your gravity, and rank besides!
   But knights, I see, care little for the oath
   They make to ladies, chiefly their own ladies.
SIR POLITIC   Now, by my spurs, the symbol of my knighthood—
PEREGRINE   [*Aside.*] Lord, how his brain is humbled for an oath!   30
SIR POLITIC   I reach you not.
LADY WOULDBE   Right sir, your policy
   May bear it through thus. [*To* PEREGRINE.] Sir, a word with you,
   I would be loath to contest publicly
   With any gentlewoman, or to seem
   Froward, or violent, as *The Courtier* says.   35
   It comes too near rusticity in a lady,
   Which I would shun by all means. And, however
   I may deserve from Master Wouldbe, yet
   T' have one fair gentlewoman, thus, be made
   Th'unkind instrument to wrong another,   40
   And one she knows not, ay, and to persèver,

---

16 miss lack.   **21 habit** dress.   **25 massàcre** accented on second syllable.
30 humbled literally, brought low, i.e. all the way down to his spurs; past commentators
have found here a cutting reference to the cheapening of knighthood by King James,
who soon after he became king in 1603 created knights indiscriminately for political
reasons.   **31 reach** understand.   **policy** craft.   **32 bear it through** carry it off.
35 Froward perverse.   *The Courtier* (*Il Cortegiano,* 1528), by Baldassare Castiglione,
the most famous of the Renaissance handbooks on the conduct becoming to a gentleman,
or gentlewoman. Lady Wouldbe fails, of course, to meet any of the standards of gentility
laid down in this book.   **36 rusticity** country manners, vulgarity.   **41 persèver**
accented on second syllable.

In my poor judgment, is not warranted
From being a solecism in our sex,
If not in manners.

PEREGRINE   How is this!
SIR POLITIC   Sweet madam,
Come nearer to your aim.

LADY WOULDBE   Marry, and will, sir.   45
Since you provoke me with your impudence
And laughter of your light land-siren here,
Your Sporus, your hermaphrodite—

PEREGRINE   What's here?
Poetic fury and historic storms!

SIR POLITIC   The gentleman, believe it, is of worth,   50
And of our nation.

LADY WOULDBE   Ay, your Whitefriars nation!
Come, I blush for you, Master Wouldbe, ay;
And am ashamed you should ha' no more forehead
Than thus to be the patron, or St. George,
To a lewd harlot, a base fricatrice,   55
A female devil in a male outside.

SIR POLITIC   ⸝   Nay,
And you be such a one, I must bid adieu
To your delights. The case appears too liquid.   [*Exit.*]

LADY WOULDBE   Ay, you may carry't clear, with your state-face!

---

42 *warranted* guaranteed (against).   **43 *solecism . . . sex*** sexual impropriety—the lady's language is overcharged.   **45 *Come . . . aim*** Make your point more clearly.   **47 *light*** immoral.   **48 *Sporus*** a young man whom Nero fancied. He had him castrated and then married him with full ceremony. Volpone has Castrone in his private zoo.   **51 *Whitefriars nation*** Whitefriars was a "liberty" within the City of London, one of those areas exempted by Royal Charter in times past from the control of the town. In Jonson's day the outcasts and those fleeing the law who had taken refuge here had set up a state of their own, based on disorder, and even adopted an official thieves' language. The anarchic condition of Whitefriars suggests the new Venice being created by greed and foolishness in *Volpone*.   **53 *forehead*** shame.   **55 *fricatrice*** literally a massage, but also slang for whore.   **56–58 *Nay . . . liquid*** J. D. Rea suggests in his edition of *Volpone*, p. 214, that these lines are addressed to Peregrine. Sir Politic, Rea argues, is so obsessed with plots that he readily accepts his wife's explanation—though he has had considerable difficulty understanding it—that Peregrine is a disguised courtesan. "Liquid" would then mean "clearly to be seen," and "case" could mean, as it often does, "a mask." This explanation is interesting, but there is no way of proving it, and the lines may equally well be an ironic farewell to a crying ("liquid") Lady Wouldbe.   **59 *carry't clear*** carry on your pretense (of innocence).   ***state-face*** grave, official manner—Lady Wouldbe seems to take her husband's pretenses to statesmanship seriously.

But for your carnival concupiscence,   60
Who here is fled for liberty of conscience,
From furious persecution of the marshal,
Her will I disc'ple.

PEREGRINE   This is fine, i'faith!
And do you use this often? Is this part
Of your wit's exercise, 'gainst you have occasion?   65
Madam—

LADY WOULDBE   Go to sir.

PEREGRINE   Do you hear me, lady?
Why, if your knight have set you to beg shirts,
Or to invite me home, you might have done it
A nearer way by far.

LADY WOULDBE   This cannot work you
Out of my snare.

PEREGRINE   Why, am I in it, then?   70
Indeed, your husband told me you were fair,
And so you are; only your nose inclines—
That side that's next the sun—to the queen-apple.

LADY WOULDBE   This cannot be endured by any patience.

ACT IV   Scene 3

[*Enter* MOSCA.]

MOSCA   What's the matter, madam?

LADY WOULDBE   If the Senate
Right not my quest in this, I will protest 'em
To all the world no aristocracy.

MOSCA   What is the injury, lady?

LADY WOULDBE   Why, the callet
You told me of, here I have ta'en disguised.   5

MOSCA   Who? This! What means your ladyship? The creature

---

60 *carnival concupiscence* licentious wench—Lady Wouldbe is close to using malaprop-
isms. 61 *liberty of conscience* i.e. freedom to practice her bawdy trade. 62 *marshal*
court officer and keeper of prisons. 63 *disc'ple* discipline. 64 *use this* act in this way.
65 *'gainst* in preparation for a time when. *occasion* real need. 69 *nearer* more
direct. 71 *fair* light-complexioned—considered an attribute of beauty. 72 *inclines*
tends. 73 *queen-apple* i.e. bright red.
🙰 ACT IV, Scene 3. 2 *quest* petition. *protest* publish. 4 *callet* prostitute.

I mentioned to you is apprehended, now
Before the Senate. You shall see her—
LADY WOULDBE   Where?
MOSCA   I'll bring you to her. This young gentleman,
I saw him land this morning at the port.   10
LADY WOULDBE   Is't possible? How has my judgment wandered!
Sir, I must, blushing, say to you, I have erred;
And plead your pardon.
PEREGRINE   What, more changes yet?
LADY WOULDBE   I hope y' ha' not the malice to remember
A gentlewoman's passion. If you stay   15
In Venice, here, please you to use me, sir—
MOSCA   Will you go, madam?
LADY WOULDBE   Pray you, sir, use me. In faith,
The more you see me, the more I shall conceive
You have forgot our quarrel.
            [*Exeunt* LADY WOULDBE, MOSCA, NANO, *and* WOMEN.]
PEREGRINE   This is rare!
Sir Politic Wouldbe? No, Sir Politic Bawd,   20
To bring me, thus, acquainted with his wife!
Well, wise Sir Pol, since you have practiced thus
Upon my freshmanship, I'll try your salt-head,
What proof it is against a counterplot.   [*Exit.*]

ACT IV

Scene 4   ⟨*The Scrutineo, the Venetian court of law*⟩

[*Enter* VOLTORE, CORBACCIO, CORVINO, *and* MOSCA.]

VOLTORE   Well, now you know the carriage of the business,
Your constancy is all that is required,
Unto the safety of it.
MOSCA   Is the lie

---

16 *use* Employ, make use of in social matters; but the word has also a sexual meaning,
as does "conceive" in line 18, which Peregrine picks up quickly. Lady Wouldbe is as
clumsy as her husband in her choice of language. 20 *Bawd* pander. 21 *bring* make.
22 *practiced* intrigued. 23 *freshmanship* newness, greenness—Peregrine seems to
believe that Sir Pol has been having a joke at his expense. *salt-head* experienced in the
world—spoken ironically.
🦌 ACT IV, Scene 4. 1 *carriage* management, way of handling.

Safely conveyed amongst us? Is that sure?
Knows every man his burden?
CORVINO   Yes.
MOSCA   Then shrink not.   5
CORVINO   [*Aside to* MOSCA.] But knows the advocate the truth?
MOSCA   O sir,
By no means. I devised a formal tale
That salved your reputation. But be valiant, sir.
CORVINO   I fear no one but him, that this his pleading
Should make him stand for a co-heir—
MOSCA   Co-halter!   10
Hang him, we will but use his tongue, his noise,
As we do Croaker's here. [*Pointing to* CORBACCIO.]
CORVINO ·   Ay, what shall he do?
MOSCA   When we ha' done, you mean?
CORVINO   Yes.
MOSCA   Why, we'll think:
Sell him for mummia, he's half dust already.

[*Turns away from* CORVINO *and speaks to* VOLTORE.]

Do not you smile to see this buffalo,   15
How he doth sport it with his head?—I should,
If all were well and past. [*To* CORBACCIO.] Sir, only you
Are he that shall enjoy the crop of all,
And these not know for whom they toil.
CORBACCIO   Ay, peace.
MOSCA   [*To* CORVINO.] But you shall eat it.—Much!—
                            [*To* VOLTORE.] Worshipful sir,   20
Mercury sit upon your thund'ring tongue,
Or the French Hercules, and make your language
As conquering as his club, to beat along,
As with a tempest, flat, our adversaries;
But much more yours, sir.
VOLTORE   Here they come, ha' done.   25

---

4 conveyed spread to all. **5 burden** refrain in a song, i.e. what he is to say at the right
moment. **7 formal** "elaborately constructed, circumstantial" (*OED*). **8 salved** saved.
14 mummia The juice that oozes from embalmed human bodies. It was much prized
until fairly recent times as an ingredient for certain medicines. This passage is part of the
theme of cannibalism which runs through the play: e.g. I.1.36, "or men, to grind 'em
into powder," or I.5.92, "Or fat, by eating once a month a man." **15 buffalo** referring
to Corvino's horns. **16 sport . . . head** play about unconscious of his horns. **20 eat it**
enjoy all the gold. **Much** not at all. **21 Mercury** god of eloquence, but also of
thieves. **22 French Hercules** another symbol of eloquence.

MOSCA   I have another witness if you need, sir,
  I can produce.
VOLTORE   Who is it?
MOSCA   Sir, I have her.

ACT IV   Scene 5

[*Enter four* AVOCATORI, BONARIO, CELIA, NOTARIO, COMMENDATORI,
and OTHERS.]

FIRST AVOCATORE   The like of this the Sentate never heard of.
SECOND AVOCATORE   'Twill come most strange to them when we
  report it.
FOURTH AVOCATORE   The gentlewoman has been ever held
  Of unreprovèd name.
THIRD AVOCATORE   So the young man.
FOURTH AVOCATORE   The more unnatural part, that of his father.   5
SECOND AVOCATORE   More of the husband.
FIRST AVOCATORE   I not know to give
  His act a name, it is so monstrous!
FOURTH AVOCATORE   But the impostor, he is a thing created
  T'exceed example.
FIRST AVOCATORE   And all after-times!
SECOND AVOCATORE   I never heard a true voluptuary   10
  Described but him.
THIRD AVOCATORE   Appear yet those were cited?
NOTARIO   All but the old magnifico, Volpone.
FIRST AVOCATORE   Why is not he here?
MOSCA   Please your fatherhoods,
  Here is his advocate. Himself's so weak,
  So feeble—
FOURTH AVOCATORE   What are you?
BONARIO   His parasite,   15
  His knave, his pander! I beseech the court
  He may be forced to come, that your grave eyes
  May bear strong witness of his strange impostures.

---

27 her Lady Wouldbe.
✥ **ACT IV, Scene 5.   5 part** i.e. to disinherit his son.   **7 monstrous** trisyllabic:
mon-ster-ous.   **9 example** the outstanding instances provided by art and history.   **after-
times** the future.   **11 cited** summoned.   **12 magnifico** nobleman.

VOLTORE   Upon my faith and credit with your virtues,
 He is not able to endure the air.   20
SECOND AVOCATORE   Bring him, however.
THIRD AVOCATORE   We will see him.
FOURTH AVOCATORE   Fetch him.
VOLTORE   Your fatherhoods' fit pleasures be obeyed,
 But sure the sight will rather move your pities
 Than indignation. May it please the court,
 In the meantime he may be heard in me!   25
 I know this place most void of prejudice,
 And therefore crave it, since we have no reason
 To fear our truth should hurt our cause.
THIRD AVOCATORE   Speak free.
VOLTORE   Then know, most honored fathers, I must now
 Discover to your strangely abusèd ears   30
 The most prodigious and most frontless piece
 Of solid impudence, and treachery,
 That ever vicious nature yet brought forth
 To shame the state of Venice. This lewd woman,

 [*Pointing to* CELIA.]

 That wants no artificial looks or tears   35
 To help the visor she has now put on,
 Hath long been known a close adulteress
 To that lascivious youth, there; [*Pointing to* BONARIO.] not suspected,
 I say, but known, and taken, in the act,
 With him; and by this man, the easy husband,   40

 [*Pointing to* CORVINO.]

 Pardoned; whose timeless bounty makes him now
 Stand here, the most unhappy, innocent person
 That ever man's own goodness made accused.
 For these, not knowing how to owe a gift

---

22 fatherhoods This is a correct title of respect to apply to the venerable judges of
Venice, but Voltore makes good use of this fact. By his frequent references to the judges
as fathers he establishes a prejudice on their part for the outraged father, Corbaccio; makes
them feel the wrongs done Corbaccio the father are done to them, the fathers of the city.
Volpone, a splendid rhetorician himself, is properly appreciative of the fine points of
Voltore's art and comments particularly on this device, V.2.33–37.   **27 it**   to be heard.
31 frontless shameless.   **35 wants** lacks.   **36 visor** mask. Celia is crying and distraught, and Voltore is accusing her of pretending.   **37 close** secret.

Of that dear grace but with their shame, being placed   45
So above all powers of their gratitude,
Began to hate the benefit, and in place
Of thanks, devise t'extirp the memory
Of such an act. Wherein, I pray your fatherhoods
To observe the malice, yea, the rage of creatures   50
Discovered in their evils; and what heart
Such take, even from their crimes. But that anon
Will more appear. This gentleman, the father,

[*Pointing to* CORBACCIO.]

Hearing of this foul fact, with many others,
Which daily struck at his too tender ears,   55
And grieved in nothing more than that he could not
Preserve himself a parent (his son's ills
Growing to that strange flood) at last decreed
To disinherit him.

FIRST AVOCATORE   These be strange turns!
SECOND AVOCATORE   The young man's fame was ever fair and honest.   60
VOLTORE   So much more full of danger is his vice,
That can beguile so under shade of virtue.
But as I said, my honored sires, his father
Having this settled purpose—by what means
To him betrayed, we know not—and this day   65
Appointed for the deed, that parricide,
I cannot style him better, by confederacy
Preparing this his paramour to be there,
Entered Volpone's house—who was the man,
Your fatherhoods must understand, designed   70
For the inheritance—there sought his father.
But with what purpose sought he him, my lords?
I tremble to pronounce it, that a son
Unto a father, and to such a father,
Should have so foul, felonious intent: 75

---

45 *dear grace* rich value.   45–46 *being . . . gratitude* Forgiveness is so rare a virtue
that these base creatures cannot comprehend it and be grateful.   47 *benefit* Corvino's
forgiveness.   48 *extirp* eradicate.   54 *fact* crime—Latin *facinus*.   56 *grieved . . . more*
Nothing grieved him more.   57 *ills* wrongdoings.   58 *Growing . . . flood* increasing
to such great unnaturalness.   59 *turns* events.   60 *fame* reputation.   62 *shade* cover,
pretense.   65 *him* Bonario.   67 *confederacy* secret agreement.   70 *designed* des-
ignated.

It was, to murder him! When, being prevented
By his more happy absence, what then did he?
Not check his wicked thoughts? No, now new deeds—
Mischief doth ever end where it begins—
An act of horror, fathers! He dragged forth   80
The agèd gentleman, that had there lain bed-rid
Three years, and more, out off his innocent couch,
Naked, upon the floor, there left him; wounded
His servant in the face; and, with this strumpet,
The stale to his forged practice, who was glad   85
To be so active—I shall here desire
Your fatherhoods to note but my collections
As most remarkable—thought at once to stop
His father's ends, discredit his free choice
In the old gentleman, redeem themselves   90
By laying infamy upon this man,
To whom, with blushing, they should owe their lives.

FIRST AVOCATORE   What proofs have you of this?

BONARIO   Most honored fathers,
I humbly crave there be no credit given
To this man's mercenary tongue.

SECOND AVOCATORE   Forbear.   95

BONARIO   His soul moves in his fee.

THIRD AVOCATORE   O, sir!

BONARIO   This fellow,
For six sols more would plead against his Maker.

FIRST AVOCATORE   You do forget yourself.

VOLTORE   Nay, nay, grave fathers,
Let him have scope. Can any man imagine
That he will spare's accuser, that would not   100
Have spared his parent?

FIRST AVOCATORE   Well, produce your proofs.

CELIA   I would I could forget I were a creature!

VOLTORE   Signior Corbaccio!

FOURTH AVOCATORE   What is he?

VOLTORE   The father.

---

85 *stale* lure. *forged practice* contrived scheme. **87** *collections* conclusions.
89 *ends* intentions. **90** *In* of. *old gentleman* Volpone. **91** *this man* Corvino.
92 *owe* acknowledge due. **97** *sols* coins of small value. **99** *scope* freedom (to
insult).

SECOND AVOCATORE   Has he had an oath?
NOTARIO   Yes.
CORBACCIO   What must I do now?
NOTARIO   Your testimony's craved.
CORBACCIO   [*Cupping his ear.*]   Speak to the knave?   105
   I'll ha' my mouth first stopped with earth. My heart
   Abhors his knowledge. I disclaim in him.
FIRST AVOCATORE   But for what cause?
CORBACCIO   The mere portent of nature.
   He is an utter stranger to my loins.
BONARIO   Have they made you to this?
CORBACCIO   I will not hear thee,   110
   Monster of men, swine, goat, wolf, parricide!
   Speak not, thou viper.
BONARIO   Sir, I will sit down,
   And rather wish my innocence should suffer,
   Than I resist the authority of a father.
VOLTORE   Signior Corvino!
SECOND AVOCATORE   This is strange.
FIRST AVOCATORE   Who's this?   115
NOTARIO   The husband.
FOURTH AVOCATORE   Is he sworn?
NOTARIO   He is.
THIRD AVOCATORE   Speak, then.
CORVINO   This woman, please your fatherhoods, is a whore
   Of most hot exercise, more than a partridge,
   Upon recòrd—
FIRST AVOCATORE   No more.
CORVINO   Neighs like a jennet.
NOTARIO   Preserve the honor of the court.
CORVINO   I shall,   120
   And modesty of your most reverend ears.
   And, yet, I hope that I may say these eyes
   Have seen her glued unto that piece of cedar,
   That fine, well-timbered gallant; and that here
   [*Tapping his forehead.*]

---

107 *his knowledge* knowing him. *disclaim in him* deny kinship to him. **108** *mere portent* complete monster. **110** *made . . . this* wrought you to this shape (i.e. a parent denying his son). **118** *hot exercise* frequent and passionate activity. *partridge* believed to be an extremely lecherous bird. **119** *Upon recòrd* generally known and acknowledged. **124** *well-timbered gallant* handsome young man (i.e. Bonario).

The letters may be read, thorough the horn,   125
That make the story perfect.

MOSCA   Excellent, sir.

[MOSCA *and* CORVINO *whisper.*]

CORVINO   There is no shame in this now, is there?

MOSCA   None.

CORVINO   Or if I said I hoped that she were onward
To her damnation, if there be a hell
Greater than whore and woman; a good Catholic   130
May make the doubt.

THIRD AVOCATORE   His grief hath made him frantic.

FIRST AVOCATORE   Remove him hence. *She* [CELIA] *swoons.*

SECOND AVOCATORE   Look to the woman.

CORVINO   Rare!
Prettily feigned! Again!

FOURTH AVOCATORE   Stand from about her.

FIRST AVOCATORE   Give her the air.

THIRD AVOCATORE   [*To* MOSCA.]   What can you say?

MOSCA   My wound,
May't please your wisdoms, speaks for me, received   135
In aid of my good patron, when he missed
His sought-for father, when that well-taught dame
Had her cue given her to cry out a rape.

BONARIO   O most laid impudence! Fathers—

THIRD AVOCATORE   Sir, be silent,
You had your hearing free, so must they theirs.   140

SECOND AVOCATORE   I do begin to doubt th'imposture here.

FOURTH AVOCATORE   This woman has too many moods.

VOLTORE   Grave fathers,

---

125 *letters . . . horn* an elaborate but common play on the cuckold and his horns. The *letter* is the "V" which Corvino makes with his fingers on his forehead to manifest his horns. But the joke also involves the "hornbook," the Elizabethan primer from which the schoolboy learned his letters. These books were single printed sheets covered with thin, transparent horn to preserve them. The letters were thus read "thorough the horn." It should be noted that in this scene the animal imagery present throughout the play is greatly intensified. Not only is Corvino reduced to an ox by his own efforts but all the characters are brought down by the language and lies of the fools to the level of "jennet" or "swine, goat, wolf." **thorough** through. **126 *perfect*** complete. **128 *onward*** well along. **131 *make the doubt*** question (whether whore, woman, and hell be not equivalent). **136 *he*** Bonario. **139 *laid*** carefully planned. **140 *free*** without interference.

She is a creature of a most professed
And prostituted lewdness.

CORVINO   Most impetuous,
Unsatisfied, grave fathers!

VOLTORE   May her feignings   145
Not take your wisdoms; but this day she baited
A stranger, a grave knight, with her loose eyes
And more lascivious kisses. This man saw 'em
Together on the water in a gondola.

MOSCA   Here is the lady herself that saw 'em too,   150
Without; who, then, had in the open streets
Pursued them, but for saving her knight's honor.

FIRST AVOCATORE   Produce that lady. [MOSCA *beckons to the wings.*]

SECOND AVOCATORE   Let her come.

FOURTH AVOCATORE   These things.
They strike with wonder!

THIRD AVOCATORE   I am turned a stone!

ACT IV   Scene 6

[*Enter* LADY WOULDBE.]

MOSCA   Be resolute, madam.

LADY WOULDBE   [*Pointing to* CELIA.] Ay, this same is she.
Out, thou chameleon harlot! Now thine eyes
Vie tears with the hyena. Darst thou look

---

143 *professed* open. **146 *but*** only. ***baited*** enticed. **147 *loose*** lewd. **151 *Without*** outside.

❄ ACT IV, Scene 6. 2 *chameleon,* 3 *hyena* Lady Wouldbe is simply hurling insults, but here again is an excellent instance of Jonson's ironic use of imagery. The chameleon was considered a "fraudulent, ravening, and gluttonous beast," and was famed then as now for its ability to change color to suit its circumstances. The hyena was predominantly a symbol of treachery, but it was believed able to imitate the voices of human beings. Thus— like the animals mentioned earlier, the crocodile with its tears and the panther with its sweet smells—the images of hyena and chameleon define the activities of fools and villains in *Volpone:* they are basically "ravening and gluttonous" beasts who are able to change color like the chameleon and imitate the voices of men like the hyena. The most useful book of the period describing the strange natures of the animals as the Elizabethans and their predecessors understood them is Edward Topsell's *The Historie of the Foure-Footed Beastes,* London, 1607. Topsell describes one type of hyena, the Mantichora, who seems to resemble the characters of the play most closely: he has a face like a man, a treble row of teeth top and bottom, "His wildnes such as can never be tamed, and his appetite is especially to the flesh of man" (p. 437).

Upon my wrongèd face? I cry your pardons.
[*To the Court.*] I fear I have forgettingly transgressed   5
Against the dignity of the court—
SECOND AVOCATORE   No, madam.
LADY WOULDBE   And been exorbitant—
FOURTH AVOCATORE   You have not, lady.
These proofs are strong.
LADY WOULDBE   Surely, I had no purpose
To scandalize your honors, or my sex's.
THIRD AVOCATORE   We do believe it.
LADY WOULDBE   Surely, you may believe it.   10
SECOND AVOCATORE   Madam, we do.
LADY WOULDBE   Indeed, you may; my breeding
Is not so coarse—
FOURTH AVOCATORE   We know it.
LADY WOULDBE   To offend
With pertinacy—
THIRD AVOCATORE   Lady—
LADY WOULDBE   Such a presence.
No, surely,
FIRST AVOCATORE   We well think it.
LADY WOULDBE   You may think it.
FIRST AVOCATORE   Let her o'ercome. [*To* BONARIO.] What witnesses
have you   15
To make good your report?
BONARIO   Our consciences.
CELIA   And heaven, that never fails the innocent.
FOURTH AVOCATORE   These are no testimonies.
BONARIO   Not in your courts,
Where multitude and clamor overcomes.
FIRST AVOCATORE   Nay, then you do wax insolent.

VOLPONE *is brought in, as impotent.*

VOLTORE   Here, here,   20
The testimony comes that will convince,
And put to utter dumbness their bold tongues.
See here, grave fathers, here's the ravisher,

---

7 *exorbitant* disorderly.   **8** *These proofs* those offered for Celia and Bonario's guilt.
13 *pertinacy* pertinacity.   **15** *o'ercome* conquer (in exchange of formalities).   **16** *make good* verify.   **19** *multitude* the larger number (swearing the same story).   *clamor* loudness.   **SD** *impotent* completely disabled—he is presumably lying in a litter.

The rider on men's wives, the great impostor,
The grand voluptuary! Do you not think   25
These limbs should affect venery? Or these eyes
Covet a concubine? Pray you, mark these hands.
Are they not fit to stroke a lady's breasts?
Perhaps he doth dissemble!

BONARIO   So he does.
VOLTORE   Would you ha' him tortured?
BONARIO   I would have him proved.   30
VOLTORE   Best try him, then, with goads, or burning irons;
Put him to the strappado. I have heard
The rack hath cured the gout. Faith, give it him
And help him of a malady; be courteous.
I'll undertake, before these honored fathers,   35
He shall have yet as many left diseases
As she has known adulterers, or thou strumpets.
O my most equal hearers, if these deeds,

---

24 great impostor This term means no more literally than "pretender," but the "impostor" is a stock character of classical comedy, and it is of considerable interest that Jonson uses the term, and the related word "imposture," so frequently in connection with Volpone (e.g. III.7.268; IV.5.8, 18; IV.5.141; IV.6.24). According to the *Tractatus Coislinianus,* believed by some to be written by Aristotle, comedy has three types of characters: the *alazon* or impostor, the *eiron* or ironical type (Peregrine, Mosca) and the *bomolochos* or buffoon. The *alazon* is discussed in detail by F. M. Cornford, *The Origin of Attic Comedy* (London, 1914), Chapter 2, as he appears in the old comedy of Aristophanes and, perhaps, in the various dances and fertility rites from which, according to Cornford, literary comedy developed. In both rites and plays the impostors were, Cornford says, "unwelcome intruders," "impudent and absurd pretenders," as are the standard butts of comedy still familiar to us: the pedant, the minor official, the informer, the doctor, the lawyer. They always appeared at feasts or celebrations to which they had contributed nothing and insisted on sharing, but were always driven off by the hero or *eiron* with curses and blows. The obvious parallels in *Volpone* to the stock comic scene are V.3, where Mosca, acting for Volpone, drives the various minor impostors from the "feast" of Volpone's fortune; and V.4, where Peregrine drives Sir Politic from Venice and from any pretense of being a wise statesman. But Jonson's irony is double, at least, and the *eirons* of one scene, Volpone and Mosca, are revealed at the conclusion of the play as *impostors* on the larger scene of Venice, intruders on the feast of a society to which they contributed nothing. And so they, along with their dupes, are driven out of society by the court. The parallels between Jonson's play and the older forms of comedy are both interesting and critically useful, but it is impossible to say that Jonson was aware of the history of the word "impostor," even though his familiarity with Aristophanes and his enormous knowledge of the classics make it probable that he was. **26 affect venery** care for lust. **30 proved** tested. **32 strappado** a form of torture in which the victim is hoisted up by his arms, which are first tied behind him, and then dropped. **34 of** be rid of.

Acts of this bold and most exorbitant strain,
May pass with sufferance, what one citizen   40
But owes the forfeit of his life, yea, fame,
To him that dares traduce him? Which of you
Are safe, my honored fathers? I would ask,
With leave of your grave fatherhoods, if their plot
Have any face or color like to truth?   45
Or if, unto the dullest nostril here,
It smell not rank and most abhorrèd slander?
I crave your care of this good gentleman,
Whose life is much endangered by their fable;
And as for them, I will conclude with this: 50
That vicious persons when they are hot and fleshed
In impious acts, their constancy abounds:
Damned deeds are done with greatest confidence.

FIRST AVOCATORE   Take 'em to custody, and sever them.

                             [CELIA *and* BONARIO *are taken out.*]

SECOND AVOCATORE   'Tis pity two such prodigies should live.   55

FIRST AVOCATORE   Let the old gentleman be returned with care.
I'm sorry our credulity wronged him.

                            [*Exeunt* OFFICERS *with* VOLPONE.]

FOURTH AVOCATORE   These are two creatures!

THIRD AVOCATORE   I have an earthquake in me!

SECOND AVOCATORE   Their shame, even in their cradles, fled their faces.

FOURTH AVOCATORE   [*To* VOLTORE.] You've done a worthy service to
    the state, sir,   60
In their discovery.

FIRST AVOCATORE   You shall hear ere night
What punishment the court decrees upon 'em.

VOLTORE   We thank your fatherhoods.—[*Exeunt* COURT OFFICIALS.]
                    How like you it?

MOSCA   Rare.
I'd ha' your tongue, sir, tipped with gold for this;
I'd ha' you be the heir to the whole city;   65
The earth I'd have want men, ere you want living.
They're bound to erect your statue in St. Mark's.

---

39 *exorbitant strain* disordered type.   **40** *pass . . . sufferance* be permitted and
condoned.   **45** *face or color* appearance or seeming.   **49** *fable* falsehood.   **51** *fleshed*
hardened, confirmed.   **52** *constancy* firm determination.   **55** *prodigies* unnatural
creatures, monsters.   **66** *living* income.

[VOLTORE *moves to one side.*]

Signior Corvino, I would have you go
And show yourself, that you have conquered.

CORVINO   Yes.

MOSCA It was much better than you should profess   70
    Yourself a cuckold, thus, than that the other
    Should have been proved.

CORVINO   Nay, I considered that.
    Now, it is her fault.

MOSCA   Then, it had been yours.

CORVINO True. I do doubt this advocate still.

MOSCA   I'faith,
    You need not; I dare ease you of that care.   75

CORVINO I trust thee, Mosca.

MOSCA   As your own soul, sir. [*Exit* CORVINO.]

CORBACCIO   Mosca!

MOSCA Now for your business, sir.

CORBACCIO   How! Ha' you business?

MOSCA Yes, yours, sir.

CORBACCIO   O, none else?

MOSCA   None else, not I.

CORBACCIO Be careful then.

MOSCA   Rest you with both your eyes, sir.

CORBACCIO Dispatch it.

MOSCA   Instantly.

CORBACCIO   And look that all   80
    Whatever be put in: jewels, plate, moneys,
    Household stuff, bedding, curtains.

MOSCA   Curtain-rings, sir;
    Only the advocate's fee must be deducted.

CORBACCIO I'll pay him now; you'll be too prodigal.

MOSCA Sir, I must tender it.

CORBACCIO   Two chequins is well?   85

MOSCA No, six, sir.

CORBACCIO   'Tis too much.

MOSCA   He talked a great while,
    You must consider that, sir.

CORBACCIO   Well, there's three—

---

71 *other* i.e. that he was pander for his wife. **74** *doubt* suspect. **78** *None* no one.
79 *Rest . . . eyes* Don't worry about a thing. **80** *Dispatch* be quick about. **81** *in*
in the inventory of Volpone's goods. **85** *tender* give.

MOSCA   I'll give it him.

CORBACCIO   Do so, and there's for thee.

                                    [*Gives* MOSCA *money and exits.*]

MOSCA   Bountiful bones! What horrid, strange offense
   Did he commit 'gainst nature in his youth,   90
   Worthy this age? [*To* VOLTORE.] You see, sir, how I work
   Unto your ends; take you no notice.

VOLTORE   No,
   I'll leave you.

MOSCA   All is yours, [*Exit* VOLTORE.] —the devil and all,
   Good advocate!— [*To* LADY WOULDBE.] Madam, I'll bring you
     home.

LADY WOULDBE   No, I'll go see your patron.

MOSCA   That you shall not.   95
   I'll tell you why: my purpose is to urge
   My patron to reform his will, and for
   The zeal you've shown today, whereas before
   You were but third or fourth, you shall be now
   Put in the first; which would appear as begged   100
   If you were present. Therefore—

LADY WOULDBE   You shall sway me.   [*Exeunt.*]

ACT V

Scene 1   ⟨VOLPONE's *house*⟩

[*Enter* VOLPONE.]

VOLPONE   Well, I am here, and all this brunt is past.
   I ne'er was in dislike with my disguise
   Till this fled moment. Here, 'twas good, in private,
   But in your public—*Cavè,* whilst I breathe.
   'Fore God, my left leg 'gan to have the cramp,   5
   And I apprehended, straight, some power had struck me

89 Bountiful bones This may be an exclamation of surprise at the physical and moral ugliness of Corbaccio, or it may refer ironically to his stinginess.   **91 Worthy . . . age** to have justified his horrible state in old age.   **97 reform** rewrite.   **101 sway** persuade. ❧ **ACT V, Scene 1. 1 brunt** confusion, crisis.   **3 fled** past.   **4 Cavè** beware. **6 apprehended** felt.   **straight** at once.

With a dead palsy. Well, I must be merry
And shake it off. A many of these fears
Would put me into some villainous disease
Should they come thick upon me. I'll prevent 'em.   10
Give me a bowl of lusty wine to fright
This humor from my heart. Hum, hum, hum!

He drinks.

'Tis almost gone already; I shall conquer.
Any device, now, of rare, ingenious knavery
That would possess me with a violent laughter,   15
Would make me up again. So, so, so, so.

Drinks again.

This heat is life; 'tis blood by this time! Mosca!

ACT V   Scene 2

[*Enter* MOSCA.]

MOSCA   How now, sir? Does the day look clear again?
Are we recovered? and wrought out of error
Into our way, to see our path before us?
Is our trade free once more?
VOLPONE   Exquisite Mosca!
MOSCA   Was it not carried learnedly?
VOLPONE   And stoutly.   5
Good wits are greatest in extremities.
MOSCA   It were a folly beyond thought to trust
Any grand act unto a cowardly spirit.
You are not taken with it enough, methinks?
VOLPONE   O, more than if I had enjoyed the wench.   10
The pleasure of all womankind's not like it.

---

16 make me up restore me.   **17 heat . . . time** According to Renaissance physiology,
food was turned by the liver into the four humors (see above, note to II.2.87) balanced
in the blood. This blood then went to the heart where it created "vital heat." Volpone's
absolute equation of this heat with life is, however, a measure of his degeneration from
the proper state of man, for it was believed that this vital heat existed in man only to
nurture the brain and thus contribute to such higher human functions as understanding
and will.
✥ **ACT V, Scene 2.   6 extremities** dangerous situations.   **7 beyond thought** un-
thinkable.

MOSCA   Why, now you speak, sir! We must here be fixed;
        Here we must rest. This is our masterpiece;
        We cannot think to go beyond this.
VOLPONE   True,
        Th'ast played thy prize, my precious Mosca.
MOSCA   Nay, sir,   15
        To gull the court—
VOLPONE   And quite divert the torrent
        Upon the innocent.
MOSCA   Yes, and to make
        So rare a music out of discords—
VOLPONE   Right.
        That yet to me 's the strangest; how th'ast borne it!
        That these, being so divided 'mongst themselves,   20
        Should not scent somewhat, or in me or thee,
        Or doubt their own side.
MOSCA   True, they will not see't.
        Too much light blinds 'em, I think. Each of 'em
        Is so possessed and stuffed with his own hopes
        That anything unto the contrary,   25
        Never so true, or never so apparent,
        Never so palpable, they will resist it—
VOLPONE   Like a temptation of the devil.
MOSCA   Right, sir.
        Merchants may talk of trade, and your great signiors
        Of land that yields well; but if Italy   30
        Have any glebe more fruitful than these fellows,
        I am deceived. Did not your advocate rare?
VOLPONE   O—"My most honored fathers, my grave fathers,
        Under correction of your fatherhoods,
        What face of truth is here? If these strange deeds   35
        May pass, most honored fathers"—I had much ado
        To forbear laughing.
MOSCA   'T seemed to me you sweat, sir.
VOLPONE   In troth, I did a little.
MOSCA   But confess, sir;
        Were you not daunted?
VOLPONE   In good faith, I was

---

16 gull trick. **torrent** i.e. the law. **18 discords** referring to the various fools, each
striving to be sole heir. **19 borne** managed. **21 or . . . or** either . . . or. **23 light**
i.e. their greed and hopes. **31 glebe** land. **32 rare** rarely. **33–36** See note to IV.5.22.

A little in a mist, but not dejected;   40
Never but still myself.
MOSCA   I think it, sir.
Now, so truth help me, I must needs say this, sir,
And out of conscience for your advocate:
He's taken pains, in faith, sir, and deserved,
In my poor judgment, I speak it under favor,   45
Not to contrary you, sir, very richly—
Well—to be cozened.
VOLPONE   Troth, and I think so too,
By that I heard him in the latter end.
MOSCA   O, but before, sir, had you heard him first
Draw it to certain heads, then aggravate,   50
Then use his vehement figures—I looked still
When he would shift a shirt; and doing this
Out of pure love, no hope of gain—
VOLPONE   'Tis right.
I cannot answer him, Mosca, as I would,
Not yet; but for thy sake, at thy entreaty,   55
I will begin e'en now to vex 'em all,
This very instant.
MOSCA   Good, sir.
VOLPONE   Call the dwarf
And eunuch forth.
MOSCA   Castrone! Nano! [*Enter* CASTRONE *and* NANO.]
NANO   Here.
VOLPONE   Shall we have a jig now?
MOSCA   What you please, sir.
VOLPONE   Go,   60
Straight give out about the streets, you two,
That I am dead; do it with constancy,

---

40 mist dimness of eyesight caused by bodily disorders. **41 think** believe. **45 under favor** with permission. **47 cozened** bilked. **48 By . . . end** to judge by the latter part of his speech. Volpone was brought in halfway through Voltore's performance. **50 Draw . . . heads** gather his material into topics. ***aggravate*** emphasize. **51 vehement figures** powerful rhetorical tropes. **52 shift a shirt** So violent were the actions Voltore used to accompany his speech that Mosca humorously compares him to a man trying to change a shirt; or perhaps he means that Voltore worked up such a sweat that he needed to change his shirt. **54 answer** repay. **59 jig** literally a dance, but a trick is meant. Jigs were the stock-in-trade of the low comedians in the Elizabethan theater, where performances usually ended with a jig. **60 Straight** at once. **61 with constancy** firmly, i.e. seriously.

Sadly, do you hear? Impute it to the grief
Of this late slander.   [*Exeunt* CASTRONE *and* NANO.]
MOSCA   What do you mean, sir?
VOLPONE   O,
I shall have instantly my vulture, crow,
Raven, come flying hither on the news   65
To peck for carrion, my she-wolf and all,
Greedy and full of expectation—
MOSCA   And then to have it ravished from their mouths?
VOLPONE   'Tis true. I will ha' thee put on a gown,
And take upon thee as thou wert mine heir;   70
Show 'em a will. Open that chest and reach
Forth one of those that has the blanks. I'll straight
Put in thy name.
MOSCA   It will be rare, sir.
VOLPONE   Ay,
When they e'en gape, and find themselves deluded—
MOSCA   Yes.
VOLPONE   And thou use them scurvily! Dispatch,   75
Get on thy gown.
MOSCA   But what, sir, if they ask
After the body?
VOLPONE   Say it was corrupted.
MOSCA   I'll say it stunk, sir; and was fain t' have it
Coffined up instantly and sent away.
VOLPONE   Anything, what thou wilt. Hold, here's my will.   80
Get thee a cap, a count-book, pen and ink,
Papers afore thee; sit as thou wert taking
An inventory of parcels. I'll get up
Behind the curtain, on a stool, and hearken;
Sometime peep over, see how they do look,   85
With what degrees their blood doth leave their faces.
O, 'twill afford me a rare meal of laughter!

---

62 Sadly gravely.   **70 take . . . thee** assume such manners and airs.   **75 Dispatch**
hurry.   **78 was fain** It was necessary.   **81 count-book** ledger.   **83 parcels** parts (of
his possessions).   **84 curtain** In Scene 3 Jonson has the stage direction "Volpone peeps
from behind a traverse." Either he has retreated into an inner stage across which a curtain
is drawn, or a curtain is placed on a wire across part of the main stage. A "traverse" may
be, however, a movable screen of some variety. Whatever the arrangement, the "curtain"
is probably the same one used to cover the bed ordinarily, and the effect is once again to
create a stage on a stage, a theater within a theater.

MOSCA   Your advocate will turn stark dull upon it.

VOLPONE   It will take off his oratory's edge.

MOSCA   But your *clarissimo,* old round-back, he   90
    Will crump you like a hog-louse with the touch.

VOLPONE   And what Corvino?

MOSCA   O sir, look for him
    Tomorrow morning with a rope and dagger
    To visit all the streets; he must run mad.
    My lady too, that came into the court   95
    To bear false witness for your worship—

VOLPONE   Yes,
    And kissed me 'fore the fathers, when my face
    Flowed all with oils—

MOSCA   And sweat, sir. Why, your gold
    Is such another med'cine, it dries up
    All those offensive savors! It transforms   100
    The most deformèd, and restores 'em lovely
    As 'twere the strange poetical girdle. Jove   *Cestus.*
    Could not invent t' himself a shroud more subtle
    To pass Acrisius' guards. It is the thing
    Makes all the world her grace, her youth, her beauty.   105

VOLPONE   I think she loves me.

MOSCA   Who? The lady, sir?
    She's jealous of you.

VOLPONE   Dost thou say so? [*Knocking without.*]

MOSCA   Hark,
    There's some already.

VOLPONE   Look!

MOSCA   [*Peering out.*]   It is the vulture;
    He has the quickest scent.

VOLPONE   I'll to my place,

---

90 clarissimo Venetian of high rank.   **round-back** Corbaccio, who obviously stoops.
91 crump you curl up.   **93 rope and dagger** Carrying these props was probably a
standard symbol of extravagant madness on the Elizabethan stage. See *The Spanish
Tragedy,* IV.4, where Hieronimo runs mad. Jonson had once played Hieronimo's part.
See also *Faerie Queene,* I.9.29, and Skelton's *Magnyfycence,* lines 2312 ff.   **98 sweat** Mosca
will not allow Volpone to forget that he was nervous at the trial.   **102 girdle . . . Cestus**
Cestus was added by Jonson to the folio to explain the meaning of the "strange poetical
girdle." The reference is to the girdle of Venus, mentioned by Homer in *The Iliad,* into
which was woven "love, desire, sweetness, soft parley, gracefulness, persuasion, and all
the powers of Venus."   **102–4 Jove . . . guards** Acrisius was the father of Danaë whom
Jove visited in the form of a shower of gold.

Thou to thy posture.

MOSCA　　　　　　　　　I am set.

VOLPONE　　　　　　　　　　　　But Mosca, 110
Play the artificer now, torture 'em rarely.

ACT V　　Scene 3

[*Enter* VOLTORE.]

VOLTORE　How now, my Mosca?

MOSCA　[*Writing.*]　　　　　Turkey carpets, nine—

VOLTORE　Taking an inventory? That is well.

MOSCA　Two suits of bedding, tissue—

VOLTORE　　　　　　　　　Where's the will?
Let me read that the while.

[*Enter bearers carrying* CORBACCIO *in a chair.*]

CORBACCIO　　　　　　　So, set me down,
And get you home. [*Exeunt bearers.*]

VOLTORE　　　　　　Is he come now, to trouble us? 5

MOSCA　Of cloth of gold, two more—

CORBACCIO　　　　　　　　Is it done, Mosca?

MOSCA　Of several vellets, eight—

VOLTORE　　　　　　　　I like his care.

CORBACCIO　Dost thou not hear? [*Enter* CORVINO.]

CORVINO　　　　　　Ha! Is the hour come, Mosca?

VOLPONE　[*Aside.*] Ay, now they muster. *Peeps from behind a traverse.*

CORVINO　　　　　　What does the advocate here,
Or this Corbaccio?

CORBACCIO　　What do these here? [*Enter* LADY WOULDBE.]

LADY WOULDBE　　　　　　Mosca! 10
Is his thread spun?

MOSCA　　　　　Eight chests of linen—

VOLPONE　　　　　　[*Aside.*] O,

---

110 posture pretense, act. **111 artificer** player (?), maker of schemes.
🐝 **ACT V, Scene 3. 1 Turkey carpets** used during this period as table covers.
3 suits sets. **bedding** covers, hangings. **tissue** woven gold cloth. **4 the while**
during the time (the inventory continues). **7 several vellets** separate velvet hangings.
9 traverse see note to V.2.84. **11 thread spun** Lady Wouldbe can never abandon her
elaborate and "learned" phrasing. The myth referred to here is that of the three Fates.
The thread of a man's life was spun by Clotho, measured by Lachesis, and then cut by
Atropos.

My fine Dame Wouldbe, too!
CORVINO   Mosca, the will,
    That I may show it these and rid 'em hence.
MOSCA   Six chests of diaper, four of damask—There.

[*Gives them the will and continues to write.*]

CORBACCIO   Is that the will?
MOSCA   Down-beds, and bolsters—
VOLPONE   [*Aside.*] Rare!   15
    Be busy still. Now they begin to flutter;
    They never think of me. Look, see, see, see!
    How their swift eyes run over the long deed
    Unto the name, and to the legacies,
    What is bequeathed them there.
MOSCA   Ten suits of hangings—   20
VOLPONE   [*Aside.*] Ay, i' their garters, Mosca. Now their hopes
    Are at the gasp.
VOLTORE   Mosca the heir!
CORBACCIO   What's that?
VOLPONE   [*Aside.*] My advocate is dumb; look to my merchant.
    He has heard of some strange storm, a ship is lost,
    He faints; my lady will swoon. Old glazen-eyes   25
    He hath not reached his despair, yet.
CORBACCIO   All these
    Are out of hope; I'm sure the man.
CORVINO   But, Mosca—
MOSCA   Two cabinets—
CORVINO   Is this in earnest?
MOSCA   One
    Of ebony—
CORVINO   Or do you but delude me?
MOSCA   The other, mother of pearl—I am very busy.   30
    Good faith, it is a fortune thrown upon me—
    Item, one salt of agate—not my seeking.
LADY WOULDBE   Do you hear, sir?
MOSCA   A perfumed box—Pray you forbear,
    You see I'm troubled—made of an onyx—
LADY WOULDBE   How?

---

14 *diaper* cloth woven with reiterated pattern. **20–21** *hangings . . . garters* "Hang themselves in their own garters," a mocking formula for suicide. **22** *gasp* last gasp. **32** *salt* saltcellar.

MOSCA   Tomorrow, or next day, I shall be at leisure   35
 To talk with you all.
CORVINO   Is this my large hope's issue?
LADY WOULDBE   Sir, I must have a fairer answer.
MOSCA   Madam!
 Marry, and shall: pray you, fairly quit my house.
 Nay, raise no tempest with your looks; but hark you,
 Remember what your ladyship offered me   40
 To put you in an heir; go to, think on't.
 And what you said e'en your best madams did
 For maintenance, and why not you? Enough.
 Go home and use the poor Sir Pol, your knight, well,
 For fear I tell some riddles. Go, be melancholic.   45
         [*Exit* LADY WOULDBE.]
VOLPONE   [*Aside.*] O my fine devil!
CORVINO   Mosca, pray you a word.
MOSCA   Lord! Will not you take your dispatch hence yet?
 Methinks of all you should have been th'example.
 Why should you stay here? With what thought? What promise?
 Hear you: do not you know I know you an ass,   50
 And that you would most fain have been a wittol
 If fortune would have let you? That you are
 A declared cuckold, on good terms? This pearl,

[*Holding up jewels.*]

 You'll say, was yours? Right. This diamond?
 I'll not deny't, but thank you. Much here else?   55
 It may be so. Why, think that these good works
 May help to hide your bad. I'll not betray you,
 Although you be but extraordinary,
 And have it only in title, it sufficeth.
 Go home, be melancholic too, or mad.   [*Exit* CORVINO.]   60
VOLPONE   [*Aside.*] Rare, Mosca! How his villainy becomes him!
VOLTORE   Certain he doth delude all these for me.
CORBACCIO   Mosca the heir? [*Still straining to read the will.*]
VOLPONE   [*Aside.*] O, his four eyes have found it!

---

38 *fairly* This word has roughly the present-day sense of "just" in "just leave the house."
40 *Remember . . . me* Lady Wouldbe has obviously offered her favors to Mosca. This fact explains the tone of line IV.6.101. **47 *dispatch*** dismissal. **48 *example*** i.e. by leaving first show the others the way. **51 *wittol*** knowing cuckold. **55 *else*** otherwise. **58–59 *Although . . . sufficeth*** Although you are an unusual cuckold, being one in title but not in fact, this will do for you.

CORBACCIO   I'm cozened, cheated, by a parasite slave!
    Harlot, th'ast gulled me.
MOSCA   Yes, sir. Stop your mouth,   65
    Or I shall draw the only tooth is left.
    Are not you he, that filthy, covetous wretch
    With the three legs, that here, in hope of prey,
    Have, any time this three year, snuffed about
    With your most grov'ling nose, and would have hired   70
    Me to the pois'ning of my patron, sir?
    Are not you he that have, today, in court,
    Professed the disinheriting of your son?
    Perjured yourself? Go home, and die, and stink.
    If you but croak a syllable, all comes out.   75
    Away, and call your porters! Go, go, stink.   [*Exit* CORBACCIO.]
VOLPONE   [*Aside.*] Excellent varlet!
VOLTORE   Now, my faithful Mosca,
    I find thy constancy.
MOSCA   Sir?
VOLTORE   Sincere.
MOSCA   A table
    Of porphyry—I mar'l you'll be thus troublesome.
VOLTORE   Nay, leave off now, they are gone.
MOSCA   Why, who are you?   80
    What! Who did send for you? O, cry you mercy,
    Reverend sir! Good faith, I am grieved for you,
    That any chance of mine should thus defeat
    Your—I must needs say—most deserving travails.
    But I protest, sir, it was cast upon me,   85
    And I could, almost, wish to be without it,
    But that the will o' th' dead must be observed.
    Marry, my joy is that you need it not;
    You have a gift, sir—thank your education—
    Will never let you want while there are men   90
    And malice to breed causes. Would I had
    But half the like, for all my fortune, sir.
    If I have any suits—as I do hope,
    Things being so easy and direct, I shall not—

---

65 *Harlot* malicious fellow—originally applied to men.   **68** *three legs* Corbaccio uses
a cane.   **69** *any time* at any time.   **79** *mar'l* marvel.   **81** *cry you mercy* beg your
pardon.   **83** *chance* luck.   **91** *causes* lawsuits.   **94** *Things . . . direct* the will being
so clear and uncomplicated.

I will make bold with your obstreperous aid;   95
Conceive me, for your fee, sir. In meantime,
You that have so much law, I know ha' the conscience
Not to be covetous of what is mine.
Good sir, I thank you for my plate: 'twill help
To set up a young man. Good faith, you look   100
As you were costive; best go home and purge, sir.
                                        [*Exit* VOLTORE.]

VOLPONE   Bid him eat lettuce well! My witty mischief,

[*Coming from behind curtain.*]

Let me embrace thee. O that I could now
Transform thee to a Venus—Mosca, go,
Straight take my habit of *clarissimo,*   105
And walk the streets; be seen, torment 'em more.
We must pursue as well as plot. Who would
Have lost this feast?

MOSCA   I doubt it will lose them.

VOLPONE   O, my recovery shall recover all.
That I could now but think on some disguise   110
To meet 'em in, and ask 'em questions.
How I would vex 'em still at every turn!

MOSCA   Sir, I can fit you.

VOLPONE   Canst thou?

MOSCA   Yes, I know
One o' th' *commendatori,* sir, so like you;
Him will I straight make drunk, and bring you his habit. 115

VOLPONE   A rare disguise, and answering thy brain!
O, I will be a sharp disease unto 'em.

MOSCA   Sir, you must look for curses—

VOLPONE   Till they burst;
The fox fares ever best when he is cursed.   [*Exeunt.*]

---

95 obstreperous clamorous. **96 Conceive** understand. *for your fee* I will not ask
your services gratis but will pay the standard price. **97 have** know. **99 plate** the
one Voltore gave earlier as a present. **101 costive** constipated. **102 lettuce** a laxative.
105 habit robe. Special dress was decreed for various social orders. **108 lose** get rid
of. **113 fit you** find just what you want. **114 commendatori** sergeants, or minor
officials, of the court. **116 answering** resembling (the rareness of Mosca's brain).
117 sharp painful. **119 The . . . cursed** a proverbial saying.

ACT V

Scene 4   ⟨SIR POLITIC'*s house*⟩•

[*Enter* PEREGRINE *disguised, and three* MERCHANTS.]

PEREGRINE   Am I enough disguised?
FIRST MERCHANT   I warrant you.
PEREGRINE   All my ambition is to fright him only.
SECOND MERCHANT   If you could ship him away, 'twere excellent.
THIRD MERCHANT   To Zant, or to Aleppo?
PEREGRINE   Yes, and ha' his
     Adventures put i' th' book of voyages,   5
     And his gulled story registered for truth?
     Well, gentlemen, when I am in a while,
     And that you think us warm in our discourse,
     Know your approaches.
FIRST MERCHANT   Trust it to our care. [*Exeunt* MERCHANTS.]

[*Enter* WOMAN.]

PEREGRINE   Save you, fair lady. Is Sir Pol within?   10
WOMAN   I do not know, sir.
PEREGRINE   Pray you say unto him,
     Here is a merchant, upon earnest business,
     Desires to speak with him.
WOMAN   I will see, sir.
PEREGRINE   Pray you.
                                              [*Exit* WOMAN.]
     I see the family is all female here.

[*Re-enter* WOMAN.]

WOMAN   He says, sir, he has weighty affairs of state   15
     That now require him whole; some other time
     You may possess him.
PEREGRINE   Pray you, say again,
     If those require him whole, these will exact him,
     Whereof I bring him tidings. [*Exit* WOMAN.] What might be
     His grave affair of state now? How to make   20

🏃 ACT V, Scene 4.   **1** *warrant* assure.   **4** *Zant* one of the Ionian islands.   **5** *book
of voyages* popular collections of foreign voyages such as Hakluyt's.   **9** *Know . . .
approaches* Come in at the right time.   **16** *require him whole* occupy his entire
attention.   **17** *possess* Sir Pol's elaborate way of saying "see."   **18** *exact* force.

Bolognian sausages here in Venice, sparing
One o' th'ingredients? [*Re-enter* WOMAN.]
WOMAN   Sir, he says he knows
By your word "tidings" that you are no statesman,
And therefore wills you stay.
PEREGRINE   Sweet, pray you return him:
I have not read so many proclamations   25
And studied them for words, as he has done,
But—Here he deigns to come. [*Enter* SIR POLITIC.]
SIR POLITIC   Sir, I must crave
Your courteous pardon. There hath chanced today
Unkind disaster 'twixt my lady and me,
And I was penning my apology   30
To give her satisfaction, as you came now.
PEREGRINE   Sir, I am grieved I bring you worse disaster:
The gentleman you met at th' port today,
That told you he was newly arrived—
SIR POLITIC   Ay, was
A fugitive punk?
PEREGRINE   No, sir, a spy set on you,   35
And he has made relation to the Senate
That you professed to him to have a plot
To sell the state of Venice to the Turk.
SIR POLITIC   O me!
PEREGRINE   For which warrants are signed by this time
To apprehend you and to search your study   ✦ 40
For papers—
SIR POLITIC   Alas, sir, I have none but notes
Drawn out of play-books—
PEREGRINE   All the better, sir.
SIR POLITIC   And some essays. What shall I do?
PEREGRINE   Sir, best
Convey yourself into a sugar-chest,
Or, if you could lie round, a frail were rare,   45
And I could send you aboard.
SIR POLITIC   Sir, I but talked so
For discourse' sake merely. *They knock without.*
PEREGRINE   Hark, they are there.

---

21 *sparing* leaving out. **23** *tidings* "intelligences" would be the statesman's word.
24 *return him* say to him in return. **35** *punk* prostitute. **42** *play-books* printed
plays. **45** *frail* rush basket used for packing figs. **47** *discourse'* conversation's.

SIR POLITIC   I am a wretch, a wretch!

PEREGRINE   What will you do, sir?
   Ha' you ne'er a currant-butt to leap into?
   They'll put you to the rack, you must be sudden.   50

SIR POLITIC   Sir, I have an engine—

THIRD MERCHANT   [*Calling from off-stage.*] Sir Politic Wouldbe!

SECOND MERCHANT   Where is he?

SIR POLITIC   That I have thought upon beforetime.

PEREGRINE   What is it?

SIR POLITIC   I shall ne'er endure the torture!
   Marry, it is, sir, of a tortoise-shell,
   Fitted for these extremities. Pray you, sir, help me.   55

[*He gets into a large tortoise shell.*]

   Here I've a place, sir, to put back my legs;
   Please you to lay it on, sir. With this cap
   And my black gloves, I'll lie, sir, like a tortoise,
   Till they are gone.

PEREGRINE   And call you this an engine?

SIR POLITIC   Mine own device—Good sir, bid my wife's women   60
   To burn my papers. *They* [*the three* MERCHANTS] *rush in.*

FIRST MERCHANT   Where's he hid?

THIRD MERCHANT   We must,
   And will, sure, find him.

SECOND MERCHANT   Which is his study?

FIRST MERCHANT   What
   Are you, sir?

PEREGRINE   I'm a merchant that came here
   To look upon this tortoise.

THIRD MERCHANT   How!

FIRST MERCHANT   St. Mark!
   What beast is this?

PEREGRINE   It is a fish.

SECOND MERCHANT   [*Striking the tortoise.*] Come out here!   65

PEREGRINE   Nay, you may strike him, sir, and tread upon him.
   He'll bear a cart.

FIRST MERCHANT   What, to run over him?

PEREGRINE   Yes.

THIRD MERCHANT   Let's jump upon him.

---

49 currant-butt cask for currants. **51** *engine* device. **55** *Fitted* The quarto reads
"apted," i.e. suited. **57** *it* the shell.

SECOND MERCHANT   Can he not go?
PEREGRINE   He creeps, sir.
FIRST MERCHANT   Let's see him creep. [*Prodding him.*]
PEREGRINE   No, good sir, you will hurt him.
SECOND MERCHANT   Heart, I'll see him creep, or prick his guts.   70
THIRD MERCHANT   Come out here!
PEREGRINE   [*Aside to* SIR POLITIC.] Pray you, sir, creep a little.
FIRST MERCHANT   Forth!
SECOND MERCHANT   Yet further.
PEREGRINE   [*Aside to* SIR POLITIC.] Good sir, creep.
SECOND MERCHANT   We'll see his legs.

   They pull off the shell and discover him.

THIRD MERCHANT   Godso, he has garters!
FIRST MERCHANT   Ay, and gloves!
SECOND MERCHANT   Is this
   Your fearful tortoise?
PEREGRINE   Now, Sir Pol, we are even;

   [*Throwing off his disguise.*]

   For your next project I shall be prepared.   75
   I am sorry for the funeral of your notes, sir.
FIRST MERCHANT   'Twere a rare motion to be seen in Fleet Street.
SECOND MERCHANT   Ay, i' the term.
FIRST MERCHANT   Or Smithfield, in the fair.
THIRD MERCHANT   Methinks 'tis but a melancholic sight.
PEREGRINE   Farewell, most politic tortoise!

                 [*Exeunt* PEREGRINE *and* MERCHANTS.]
SIR POLITIC   Where's my lady?   80
   Knows she of this?
WOMAN   I know not, sir.
SIR POLITIC   Inquire.   [*Exit* WOMAN.]
   O, I shall be the fable of all feasts,
   The freight of the *gazetti,* ship-boys' tale,
   And, which is worst, even talk for ordinaries.

   [*Re-enter* WOMAN.]

---

68 go walk. **70 Heart** a mild oath. **SD discover** disclose. **76 funeral** burning.
The ironic comparison is to a funeral pyre. **77 motion** puppet show. **78 term** the
period when the courts were in session and London filled with people. **Smithfield . . .
fair** Bartholomew Fair, with many sideshows, was held in Smithfield. **83 freight**
topic. **gazetti** newspapers. **84 ordinaries** taverns.

WOMAN   My lady's come most melancholic home,   85
         And says, sir, she will straight to sea, for physic.
SIR POLITIC   And I, to shun this place and clime forever,
         Creeping with house on back, and think it well
         To shrink my poor head in my politic shell.   [*Exeunt.*]

ACT V

Scene 5   ᒛVOLPONE'*s house*᙮

[*Enter* VOLPONE *in the habit of a commendatore,* MOSCA *of a clarissimo.*]

VOLPONE   Am I then like him?
MOSCA   O sir, you are he;
         No man can sever you.
VOLPONE   Good.
MOSCA   But what am I?
VOLPONE   'Fore heav'n, a brave *clarissimo,* thou becomst it!
         Pity thou wert not born one.
MOSCA   If I hold
         My made one, 'twill be well.
VOLPONE   I'll go and see   5
         What news, first, at the court.
MOSCA   Do so. My fox
         Is out on his hole, and ere he shall re-enter,
         I'll make him languish in his borrowed case,
         Except he come to composition with me.
         Androgyno, Castrone, Nano!

[*Enter* ANDROGYNO, CASTRONE, *and* NANO.]

ALL   Here.   10
MOSCA   Go recreate yourselves abroad, go sport.   [*Exeunt the three.*]
         So, now I have the keys and am possessed.

---

86 *straight . . . sea* sail at once. *for physic* for health.
𝕩 ACT V, Scene 5.   1 *him* the commendatore.   2 *sever* separate, distinguish.   4 *hold*
retain.   5 *made one* assumed status (of *clarissimo*).   6–7 *fox . . . hole* Fox-in-the-hole
was a game played by English boys. They hopped about on one leg and beat one another
with gloves and pieces of leather tied on a string.   7 *on* of.   8 *case* disguise.   9 *Except*
unless.   *composition* agreement.   11 *recreate* enjoy.   12 *possessed* in possession.

Since he will needs be dead afore his time,
I'll bury him, or gain by him. I'm his heir,
And so will keep me, till he share at least.   15
To cozen him of all were but a cheat
Well placed; no man would cònstrue it a sin.
Let his sport pay for't. This is called the fox-trap.   [*Exit.*]

ACT V
Scene 6   ⟩{*A Venetian street*}⟨

[*Enter* CORBACCIO *and* CORVINO.]

CORBACCIO   They say the court is set.
CORVINO   We must maintain
  Our first tale good, for both our reputations.
CORBACCIO   Why, mine's no tale! My son would, there, have killed
      me.
CORVINO   That's true, I had forgot. Mine is, I am sure.
  But for your will, sir.
CORBACCIO   Ay, I'll come upon him   5
  For that hereafter, now his patron's dead.

  [*Enter* VOLPONE *in disguise.*]

VOLPONE   Signior Corvino! And Corbaccio! Sir,
  Much joy unto you.
CORVINO   Of what?
VOLPONE   The sudden good
  Dropped down upon you—
CORBACCIO   Where?
VOLPONE   And none knows how,
  From old Volpone, sir.
CORBACCIO   Out, arrant knave!   10
VOLPONE   Let not your too much wealth, sir, make you furious.

---

13 *will needs be*   insists on being.   **15** *keep me*   remain.   **18** *Let . . . for't*   Let the
pleasure he is getting from all this pay him for what it is going to cost.
🦊 **ACT V, Scene 6.**   **1–2** *maintain . . . good*   continuing to insist on the truth of the
tales told first in court.   **5** *him*   Mosca.

CORBACCIO   Away, thou varlet.

VOLPONE   Why, sir?

CORBACCIO   Dost thou mock me?

VOLPONE   You mock the world, sir; did you not change wills?

CORBACCIO   Out, harlot!

VOLPONE   O! Belike you are the man,
 Signior Corvino? Faith, you carry it well;   15
 You grow not mad withal. I love your spirit.
 You are not over-leavened with your fortune.
 You should ha' some would swell now like a wine-fat
 With such an autumn—Did he gi' you all, sir?

CORVINO   Avoid, you rascal.

VOLPONE   Troth, your wife has shown   20
 Herself a very woman! But you are well,
 You need not care, you have a good estate
 To bear it out, sir, better by this chance.
 Except Corbaccio have a share?

CORBACCIO   Hence, varlet.

VOLPONE   You will not be a'known, sir? Why, 'tis wise.   25
 Thus do all gamesters, at all games, dissemble.
 No man will seem to win. [*Exeunt* CORVINO *and* CORBACCIO.]
        Here comes my vulture,
 Heaving his beak up i' the air, and snuffing.

ACT V Scene 7

[*Enter* VOLTORE *to* VOLPONE.]

VOLTORE   Outstripped thus, by a parasite! A slave,
 Would run on errands, and make legs for crumbs?
 Well, what I'll do—

VOLPONE   The court stays for your worship.
 I e'en rejoice, sir, at your worship's happiness,

---

12 *varlet*   low fellow; also the title for a sergeant of the court.   **13** *change*   exchange.
17 *over-leavened*   puffed up.   **18** *fat*   vat.   **19** *autumn*   i.e. rich harvest.   **20** *Avoid*
get out!   **21** *very*   true.   **23** *bear it out*   carry it off.   **24** *Except*   unless.   **25** *a'known*
acknowledged (the heir).
� ACT V, Scene 7.   **1** *Outstripped*   outrun, beaten.   **2** *Would*   who used to.   *legs*
bows.

And that it fell into so learned hands,   5
That understand the fingering—

VOLTORE   What do you mean?

VOLPONE   I mean to be a suitor to your worship
For the small tenement, out of reparations,
That at the end of your long row of houses,
By the *Pescheria;* it was, in Volpone's time,   10
Your predecessor, ere he grew diseased,
A handsome, pretty, customed bawdy-house
As any was in Venice—none dispraised—
But fell with him. His body and that house
Decayed together.

VOLTORE   Come, sir, leave your prating.   15

VOLPONE   Why, if your worship give me but your hand,
That I may ha' the refusal, I have done.
'Tis a mere toy to you, sir, candle-rents.
As your learned worship knows—

VOLTORE   What do I know?

VOLPONE   Marry, no end of your wealth, sir, God decrease it.   20

VOLTORE   Mistaking knave! What, mock'st thou my misfortune?

VOLPONE   His blessing on your heart, sir; would 'twere more!

[*Exit* VOLTORE.]

Now, to my first again, at the next corner.

ACT V   Scene 8

[VOLPONE *remains on stage to one side.* CORBACCIO *and* CORVINO *enter.*
MOSCA *passes slowly across stage.*]

CORBACCIO   See, in our habit! See the impudent varlet!

CORVINO   That I could shoot mine eyes at him, like gunstones!

[*Exit* MOSCA.]

VOLPONE   But is this true, sir, of the parasite?

---

8 *reparations* repairs.   10 *Pescheria* fish-market.   12 *customed* well-patronized.
13 *none dispraised* not to say anything bad of the others.   17 *refusal* option. *have
done* am finished (asking favors).   18 *toy* trifle. *candle-rents* rents from slums.
20 *decrease* an intentional malapropism—he pretends to mean "increase."
🙎 ACT V, Scene 8.   1 *our habit* the dress of a *clarissimo.*   2 *gunstones* stone
cannonballs.

CORBACCIO   Again t'afflict us? Monster!

VOLPONE   In good faith, sir,
I'm heartily grieved a beard of your grave length   5
Should be so over-reached. I never brooked
That parasite's hair; methought his nose should cozen.
There still was somewhat in his look did promise
The bane of a *clarissimo*.

CORBACCIO   Knave—

VOLPONE   Methinks
Yet you, that are so traded i' the world,   10
A witty merchant, the fine bird Corvino,
That have such moral emblems on your name,
Should not have sung your shame, and dropped your cheese,
To let the fox laugh at your emptiness.

CORVINO   Sirrah, you think the privilege of the place,   15
And your red, saucy cap, that seems to me
Nailed to your jolt-head with those two chequins,
Can warrant your abuses. Come you hither:
You shall perceive, sir, I dare beat you. Approach.

VOLPONE   No haste, sir. I do know your valor well,   20
Since you durst publish what you are, sir.

CORVINO   Tarry,
I'd speak with you.

VOLPONE   Sir, sir, another time—

[*Backing away.*]

CORVINO   Nay, now.

VOLPONE   O God, sir! I were a wise man
Would stand the fury of a distracted cuckold.

MOSCA *walks by 'em.*

CORBACCIO   What, come again!

VOLPONE   [*Aside.*] Upon 'em, Mosca; save me.   25

---

5 beard . . . length man as old and wise as you. **6 over-reached** outsmarted. **brooked** could endure. **8 still** always. **somewhat** something. **10 traded** experienced. **12–14 moral . . . emptiness** In the emblem books popular at this time drawings of various animals were used to symbolize human vices, which were then explained in verses. Volpone has in mind here a picture of a crow dropping a piece of cheese while the fox laughs at him. The moral would point out that the bird, or man, who opens his mouth too freely loses his prize. **15 privilege . . . place** the immunity conferred by your rank. **16–17 cap . . . chequins** A commendatore wore a red hat with two gilt buttons on the front. **17 jolt-head** blockhead. **18 warrant** sanction. **21 what you are** i.e. a cuckold. **24 Would** if I would. **stand** oppose.

CORBACCIO   The air's infected where he breathes.
CORVINO   Let's fly him.
                        [*Exeunt* CORVINO *and* CORBACCIO.]
VOLPONE   Excellent basilisk! Turn upon the vulture.

ACT V   Scene 9

[*Enter* VOLTORE.]

VOLTORE   Well, flesh-fly, it is summer with you now;
      Your winter will come on.
MOSCA   Good advocate,
      Pray thee not rail, nor threaten out of place thus;
      Thou'lt make a solecism, as Madam says.
      Get you a biggen more; your brain breaks loose.   [*Exit.*]   5
VOLTORE   Well, sir.
VOLPONE   Would you ha' me beat the insolent slave?
      Throw dirt upon his first good clothes?
VOLTORE   This same
      Is doubtless some familiar!
VOLPONE   Sir, the court,
      In troth, stays for you. I am mad; a mule
      That never read Justinian, should get up   10
      And ride an advocate! Had you no quirk
      To avoid gullage, sir, by such a creature?
      I hope you do but jest; he has not done't;
      This's but confederacy to blind the rest.
      You are the heir?
VOLTORE   A strange, officious,   15
      Troublesome knave! Thou dost torment me.
VOLPONE   [*Aside.*] —I know—
      It cannot be, sir, that you should be cozened;

---

27 basilisk a serpent believed to be able to kill with its glance.
🦟 **ACT V, Scene 9.** **1 *flesh-fly*** the meaning of "Mosca."   **4 *Madam*** Lady
Wouldbe. See IV.2.43.   **5 *biggen*** lawyer's cap.   ***more*** to add to the one you have.
7 *This same* Volpone.   **8 *familiar*** evil spirit.   **9 *I am mad*** it is madness (to believe
that this has happened).   **10 *Justinian*** Roman legal code assembled at the order of the
Emperor Justinian.   **11 *quirk*** device.   **12 *gullage*** being gulled, fooled.   **14 *confederacy***
an agreement (between Voltore and Mosca).

'Tis not within the wit of man to do it.
You are so wise, so prudent, and 'tis fit
That wealth and wisdom still should go together.   [*Exeunt.*]   20

ACT V

Scene 10   ⟨*The Scrutineo*⟩

[*Enter four* AVOCATORI, NOTARIO, COMMENDATORI, BONARIO, CELIA,
CORBACCIO, CORVINO.]

FIRST AVOCATORE   Are all the parties here?

NOTARIO   All but the advocate.

SECOND AVOCATORE   And here he comes.

   [*Enter* VOLTORE, VOLPONE *following him.*]

AVOCATORI   Then bring 'em forth to sentence.

VOLTORE   O my most honored fathers, let your mercy
   Once win upon your justice, to forgive—
   I am distracted—

VOLPONE   [*Aside.*] What will he do now?

VOLTORE   O,   5
   I know not what t'address myself to first,
   Whether your fatherhoods, or these innocents—

CORVINO   [*Aside.*] Will he betray himself?

VOLTORE   Whom equally
   I have abused, out of most covetous ends—

CORVINO   The man is mad!

CORBACCIO   What's that?

CORVINO   He is possessed.   10

VOLTORE   For which, now struck in conscience, here I prostrate
   Myself at your offended feet, for pardon.

   [*He kneels.*]

🐾 ACT V, Scene 10.   2 *avocatori* The speech ascription here and in line 20 below
reads in Quarto and Folio 1, "*Avo.*" The usual practice of editors has been to assign this
line to a particular *avocatore.* Here and at line 20 it seems equally reasonable to have all the
judges speak.   '*em* Celia and Bonario.   4 *win upon* overcome.   9 *out . . . ends*
because of covetous desires.   10 *possessed* in the possession of the devil.

FIRST, SECOND AVOCATORI   Arise.

CELIA   O heav'n, how just thou art!

VOLPONE   [*Aside.*] I'm caught
  I' mine own noose.

CORVINO   [*Aside to* CORBACCIO.] Be constant, sir, nought now
  Can help but impudence.

FIRST AVOCATORE   Speak forward.

COMMENDATORE   [*To the courtroom.*]   Silence!   15

VOLTORE   It is not passion in me, reverend fathers,
  But only conscience, conscience, my good sires,
  That makes me now tell truth. That parasite,
  That knave, hath been the instrument of all.

AVOCATORI   Where is that knave? Fetch him.

VOLPONE   I go. [*Exit.*]

CORVINO   Grave fathers,   20
  This man's distracted, he confessed it now,
  For, hoping to be old Volpone's heir,
  Who now is dead—

THIRD AVOCATORE   How!

SECOND AVOCATORE   Is Volpone dead?

CORVINO   Dead since, grave fathers—

BONARIO   O sure vengeance!

FIRST AVOCATORE   Stay.
  Then he was no deceiver.

VOLTORE   O, no, none;   25
  The parasite, grave fathers.

CORVINO   He does speak
  Out of mere envy, 'cause the servant's made
  The thing he gaped for. Please your fatherhoods,
  This is the truth; though I'll not justify
  The other, but he may be some-deal faulty.   30

VOLTORE   Ay, to your hopes, as well as mine, Corvino.
  But I'll use modesty. Pleaseth your wisdoms
  To view these certain notes, and but confer them;

  [*Gives them notes.*]

  As I hope favor, they shall speak clear truth.

---

14 constant continue firm (in your story). **15 impudence** Latin *impudens*, shameless.
forward on. **19 instrument of all** arranger of everything. **21 distracted** out of
his wits—see line 5 above. **30 some-deal** somewhat. Quarto reads "somewhere."
32 modesty restraint. **33 certain** particular. *confer* compare.

CORVINO   The devil has entered him!

BONARIO   Or bides in you.   35

FOURTH AVOCATORE   We have done ill, by a public officer
    To send for him, if he be heir.

SECOND AVOCATORE   For whom?

FOURTH AVOCATORE   Him that they call the parasite.

THIRD AVOCATORE   'Tis true,
    He is a man of great estate now left.

FOURTH AVOCATORE   Go you, and learn his name, and say the court   40
    Entreats his presence here, but to the clearing
    Of some few doubts.   [*Exit* NOTARIO.]

SECOND AVOCATORE   This same's a labyrinth!

FIRST AVOCATORE   Stand you unto your first report?

CORVINO   My state,
    My life, my fame—

BONARIO   Where is't?

CORVINO   Are at the stake.

FIRST AVOCATORE   Is yours so too?

CORBACCIO   The advocate's a knave,   45
    And has a forkèd tongue—

SECOND AVOCATORE   Speak to the point.

CORBACCIO   So is the parasite too.

FIRST AVOCATORE   This is confusion.

VOLTORE   I do beseech your fatherhoods, read but those.

CORVINO   And credit nothing the false spirit hath writ.
    It cannot be but he is possessed, grave fathers.   50

ACT V

Scene 11   ⟩{*A street*}⟨

[VOLPONE *alone*.]

VOLPONE   To make a snare for mine own neck! And run
    My head into it wilfully, with laughter!
    When I had newly 'scaped, was free and clear!

---

35 *devil . . . him*   the "possession" referred to by Corvino in V.10.10 above. Technically, possession was the entry into the body by the evil spirit, while "obsession" was an attack by the devil from without. *bides* abides, dwells. 36–37 *We . . . heir* Mosca's new dignity entitles him to a ceremonious invitation, not a rude summons. 41 *but to* only for. 42 *doubts* questions. 48 *those* i.e. the notes he has given them. 49 *credit* believe.

Out of mere wantonness! O, the dull devil
Was in this brain of mine when I devised it,   5
And Mosca gave it second; he must now
Help to sear up this vein, or we bleed dead.

[*Enter* NANO, ANDROGYNO, *and* CASTRONE.]

How now! Who let you loose? Whither go you now?
What, to buy gingerbread, or to drown kitlings?

NANO   Sir, Master Mosca called us out of doors,   10
And bid us all go play, and took the keys.

ANDROGYNO   Yes.

VOLPONE   Did Master Mosca take the keys? Why, so!
I am farther in. These are my fine conceits!
I must be merry, with a mischief to me!
What a vile wretch was I, that could not bear   15
My fortune soberly; I must ha' my crotchets
And my conundrums! Well, go you and seek him.
His meaning may be truer than my fear.
Bid him, he straight come to me to the court;
Thither will I, and if 't be possible,   20
Unscrew my advocate, upon new hopes.
When I provoked him, then I lost myself.   [*Exeunt.*]

ACT V

Scene 12   ⟨ *The Scrutineo* ⟩

[*Four* AVOCATORI, NOTARIO, VOLTORE, BONARIO, CELIA, CORBACCIO,
CORVINO.]

FIRST AVOCATORE   [*Looking over* VOLTORE'*s notes.*] These things can ne'er
be reconciled. He here
Professeth that the gentleman was wronged,

🐝 ACT V, Scene 11.   4 *wantonness* playfulness. 6 *gave it second* seconded the idea.
7 *sear* treat with a hot iron—one method for closing cut veins. 9 *kitlings* kittens.
13 *farther in* deeper in (trouble). *conceits* ideas, plans. 16 *crotchets* fancies, whims.
17 *conundrums* puzzles—perhaps a reference to the puzzling of the three disappointed
heirs in scenes 6–9. 18 *His . . . fear* His intentions may be more honest than I fear they
are. 21 *Unscrew* get him to change his position again—Voltore is pictured as being as
crooked and as retentive as a screw, or perhaps some variety of boring insect.

And that the gentlewoman was brought thither,
Forced by her husband, and there left.

VOLTORE   Most true.

CELIA   How ready is heav'n to those that pray!

FIRST AVOCATORE   But that   5
Volpone would have ravished her, he holds
Utterly false, knowing his impotence.

CORVINO   Grave fathers, he is possessed; again, I say,
Possessed. Nay, if there be possession
And obsession, he has both.

THIRD AVOCATORE   Here comes our officer.   10

[*Enter* VOLPONE, *still disguised.*]

VOLPONE   The parasite will straight be here, grave fathers.

FOURTH AVOCATORE   You might invent some other name, sir varlet.

THIRD AVOCATORE   Did not the notary meet him?

VOLPONE   Not that I know.

FOURTH AVOCATORE   His coming will clear all.

SECOND AVOCATORE   Yet, it is misty.

VOLTORE   May't please your fatherhoods—

VOLPONE   Sir, the parasite   15

VOLPONE *whispers* [*to*] *the* ADVOCATE.

Willed me to tell you that his master lives;
That you are still the man; your hopes the same;
And this was only a jest—

VOLTORE   How?

VOLPONE   Sir, to try
If you were firm, and how you stood affected.

VOLTORE   Art sure he lives?

VOLPONE   Do I live, sir?

VOLTORE   O me!   20
I was too violent.

VOLPONE   Sir, you may redeem it:
They said you were possessed: fall down, and seem so.
I'll help to make it good. God bless the man!

VOLTORE *falls.*

🐾 ACT V, Scene 12.   5 *ready*   available (to help).   9–10 *possession . . . obsession*
See note to V.10.35.   12 *invent*   find—because Mosca is now wealthy the term parasite
is no longer suitable.   14 *clear*   clear up.   *misty*   confused.   19 *stood affected*   truly
felt (?).   20 *Do . . . sir?*   Considering the speed with which Voltore changes at this
point, it seems likely that Volpone manages to make Voltore pierce his disguise.

[*Aside to* VOLTORE.] —Stop your wind hard, and swell—See, see,
    see, see!
He vomits crooked pins! His eyes are set   25
Like a dead hare's hung in a poulter's shop!
His mouth's running away! Do you see, signior?
Now, 'tis in his belly.
CORVINO   Ay, the devil!
VOLPONE   Now, in his throat.
CORVINO   Ay, I perceive it plain.
VOLPONE   'Twill out, 'twill out! Stand clear. See where it flies!   30
In shape of a blue toad, with a bat's wings!

[*Pointing.*]

Do you not see it, sir?
CORBACCIO   What? I think I do.
CORVINO   'Tis too manifest.
VOLPONE   Look! He comes t' himself.
VOLTORE   Where am I?
VOLPONE   Take good heart, the worst is past, sir.
You are dispossessed.
FIRST AVOCATORE   What accident is this?   35
SECOND AVOCATORE Sudden, and full of wonder!
THIRD AVOCATORE   If he were
Possessed, as it appears, all this is nothing.

[*Waving notes.*]

CORVINO   He has been often subject to these fits.
FIRST AVOCATORE Show him that writing.—Do you know it, sir?
VOLPONE   [*Aside.*] Deny it sir, forswear it, know it not.   40
VOLTORE   Yes, I do know it well, it is my hand;

---

24 Stop . . . wind Hold your breath. **24–31 Stop . . . wings** All of these details:
swelling, vomiting crooked pins, eyes strangely set, the appearance of something running
in the body from place to place, and the expulsion of some strange animal from the mouth
were all taken as signs of possession by the devil. Herford and Simpson point out (9,
731–32) that a number of these symptoms had appeared in a recent sensational case of
witchcraft and exorcism. John Darrell, a minister, in the late 1590's had remarkable effectiveness as an exorciser; he was thought to have freed from demonic possession some of
the most stubborn cases in England. But in 1599 his activities were shown to have been
faked—though he never admitted it—and some of his patients swore that he had coached
them. The details of the fraud were published by Samuel Harsnett, future Archbishop of
York, in a book titled *Discovery of the Fraudulent Practices of John Darrell* (1599).
26 poulter's poultry seller's. **27 running away** awry and moving wildly. **33 comes t'
himself** revives.

But all that it contains is false.

BONARIO   O practice!

SECOND AVOCATORE What maze is this!

FIRST AVOCATORE   Is he not guilty then,
    Whom you, there, name the parasite?

VOLTORE   Grave fathers,
    No more than his good patron, old Volpone.   45

FOURTH AVOCATORE Why, he is dead.

VOLTORE   O, no, my honored fathers.
    He lives—

FIRST AVOCATORE How! Lives?

VOLTORE   Lives.

SECOND AVOCATORE   This is subtler yet!

THIRD AVOCATORE You said he was dead.

VOLTORE   Never.

THIRD AVOCATORE   You said so!

CORVINO   I heard so.

FOURTH AVOCATORE Here comes the gentleman, make him way.

    [*Enter* MOSCA.]

THIRD AVOCATORE   A stool!

FOURTH AVOCATORE A proper man and, were Volpone dead,   50
    A fit match for my daughter.

THIRD AVOCATORE   Give him way.

VOLPONE [*Aside to* MOSCA.] Mosca, I was almost lost; the advocate
    Had betrayed all; but now it is recovered.
    All's o' the hinge again. Say I am living.

MOSCA What busy knave is this? Most reverend fathers,   55
    I sooner had attended your grave pleasures,
    But that my order for the funeral
    Of my dear patron did require me—

VOLPONE   [*Aside.*] Mosca!

MOSCA Whom I intend to bury like a gentleman.

VOLPONE [*Aside.*] Ay, quick, and cozen me of all.

SECOND AVOCATORE   Still stranger!   60

---

42 *practice* intrigue. **47** *subtler* more intricate. **49** *make him way* Open a path
for him. **50** *proper* handsome. **53** *recovered* Volpone uses this word several times
to mean "the problem is solved"; but in a play where disguise and obliterating the truth
with falsehood appear so consistently, we must take the word in its literal sense as well:
covering reality over once more with pretense. **54** *o'* on. **55** *busy* meddling.
60 *quick* alive.

More intricate!
FIRST AVOCATORE   And come about again!
FOURTH AVOCATORE   [*Aside.*] It is a match, my daughter is bestowed.
MOSCA   [*Aside to* VOLPONE.] Will you gi' me half?
VOLPONE   [*Half aloud.*] First I'll be hanged.
MOSCA   [*Aside.*] I know
Your voice is good, cry not so loud.
FIRST AVOCATORE   Demand
The advocate. Sir, did not you affirm   65
Volpone was alive?
VOLPONE   Yes, and he is;
This gent'man told me so. [*Aside to* MOSCA.] Thou shalt have half.
MOSCA   Whose drunkard is this same? Speak, some that know him.
I never saw his face. [*Aside to* VOLPONE.] I cannot now
Afford it you so cheap.
VOLPONE   [*Aside.*] No?
FIRST AVOCATORE   [*To* VOLTORE.]
                          What say you?   70
VOLTORE   The officer told me.
VOLPONE   I did, grave fathers,
And will maintain he lives with mine own life,
And that this creature told me. [*Aside.*] I was born
With all good stars my enemies!
MOSCA   Most grave fathers,
If such an insolence as this must pass   75
Upon me, I am silent; 'twas not this
For which you sent, I hope.
SECOND AVOCATORE   Take him away.
VOLPONE   [*Aside.*] Mosca!
THIRD AVOCATORE   Let him be whipped.
VOLPONE   [*Aside.*] Wilt thou betray me?
Cozen me?
THIRD AVOCATORE   And taught to bear himself
Toward a person of his rank.

[*The* OFFICERS *seize* VOLPONE.]

FOURTH AVOCATORE   Away.   80

---

61 *come . . . again* reversed once more—i.e. having been declared dead, then living,
Volpone is once more dead. **62** *bestowed* i.e. in marriage. **64** *Demand* question.
80 *his* Mosca's.

MOSCA I humbly thank your fatherhoods.

VOLPONE   [*Aside.*] Soft, soft. Whipped?
    And lose all that I have? If I confess,
    It cannot be much more.

FOURTH AVOCATORE [*To* MOSCA.] Sir, are you married?

VOLPONE [*Aside.*] They'll be allied anon; I must be resolute:
    The fox shall here uncase. *He puts off his disguise.*

MOSCA   Patron!

VOLPONE   Nay, now   85
    My ruins shall not come alone; your match
    I'll hinder sure. My substance shall not glue you,
    Nor screw you, into a family.

MOSCA   Why, patron!

VOLPONE I am Volpone, and this is my knave;
    This, his own knave; this, avarice's fool;   90
    This, a chimera of wittol, fool, and knave.
    And, reverend fathers, since we all can hope
    Nought but a sentence, let's not now despair it.
    You hear me brief.

CORVINO   May it please your fatherhoods—

COMMENDATORE   Silence.

FIRST AVOCATORE The knot is now undone by miracle!   95

SECOND AVOCATORE Nothing can be more clear.

THIRD AVOCATORE   Or can more prove
    These innocent.

FIRST AVOCATORE Give 'em their liberty.

BONARIO Heaven could not long let such gross crimes be hid.

SECOND AVOCATORE If this be held the highway to get riches,
    May I be poor!

THIRD AVOCATORE This's not the gain, but torment.   100

FIRST AVOCATORE These possess wealth as sick men possess fevers,
    Which trulier may be said to possess them.

SECOND AVOCATORE Disrobe that parasite.

CORVINO, MOSCA   Most honored fathers—

FIRST AVOCATORE Can you plead aught to stay the course of justice?
    If you can, speak.

CORVINO, VOLTORE We beg favor.

CELIA   And mercy.   105

---

81 *Soft, soft* Easy, easy. **84** *anon* soon. **85** *uncase* take off disguise. **87** *substance* fortune. **89–91** *this . . . This* He points in turn to Mosca, Voltore, Corbaccio, and Corvino. **89** *knave* servant. **91** *chimera* mythical beast, part lion, goat, and serpent. **93** *let's . . . it* Don't disappoint us by delay. **94** *brief* (speak) briefly.

FIRST AVOCATORE   You hurt your innocence, suing for the guilty.
    Stand forth; and first the parasite. You appear
    T'have been the chiefest minister, if not plotter,
    In all these lewd impostures; and now, lastly,
    Have with your impudence abused the court,   110
    And habit of a gentleman of Venice,
    Being a fellow of no birth or blood.
    For which our sentence is, first thou be whipped;
    Then live perpetual prisoner in our galleys.
VOLPONE   I thank you for him.
MOSCA   Bane to thy wolfish nature.   115
FIRST AVOCATORE   Deliver him to the *Saffi*. [MOSCA *is taken out*.] Thou
    Volpone,
    By blood and rank a gentleman, canst not fall
    Under like censure; but our judgment on thee
    Is that thy substance all be straight confiscate
    To the hospital of the *Incurabili*.   120
    And since the most was gotten by imposture,
    By feigning lame, gout, palsy, and such diseases,
    Thou art to lie in prison, cramped with irons,
    Till thou be'st sick and lame indeed. Remove him.
VOLPONE   This is called mortifying of a fox.   125
FIRST AVOCATORE   Thou, Voltore, to take away the scandal
    Thou hast giv'n all worthy men of thy profession,
    Art banished from their fellowship, and our state.
    Corbaccio, bring him near! We here possess
    Thy son of all thy state, and confine thee   130
    To the monastery of *San' Spirito;*
    Where, since thou knewst not how to live well here,
    Thou shalt be learned to die well.
CORBACCIO   [*Cupping his ear.*]   Ha! What said he?
COMMENDATORE   You shall know anon, sir.
FIRST AVOCATORE   Thou, Corvino, shalt

---

108 *minister* agent. **109** *lewd impostures* base pretenses. **115** *Bane to* a curse on. **116** *Saffi* bailiffs. **119** *straight confiscate* instantly confiscated. **120** *Incurabili* incurables. **125** *mortifying* The literal meaning here is "humiliation," but two other senses apply. A cooking term: to mortify an animal was to allow it to hang after it had been killed until the meat became tender. But, as in our term "mortification of the flesh," the word also means subjecting the body and the passions to ascetic discipline and rigorous austerities. **130** *state* property. **131** *San' Spirito* the Monastery of the Holy Spirit, where Corbaccio, who has heretofore been completely without soul or spirit, will be painfully instructed to forget the things of this world and prepare his soul for the next. **133** *learned* taught.

Be straight embarked from thine own house, and rowed   135
Round about Venice, through the Grand Canal,
Wearing a cap with fair long ass's ears
Instead of horns; and so to mount, a paper
Pinned on thy breast, to the *Berlina*—

CORVINO   Yes,
And have mine eyes beat out with stinking fish,   140
Bruised fruit, and rotten eggs—'Tis well, I'm glad
I shall not see my shame yet.

FIRST AVOCATORE   And to expiate
Thy wrongs done to thy wife, thou art to send her
Home to her father, with her dowry trebled.
And these are all your judgments.

ALL   Honored fathers!   145

FIRST AVOCATORE   Which may not be revoked. Now you begin,
When crimes are done and past, and to be punished,
To think what your crimes are. Away with them!
Let all that see these vices thus rewarded,
Take heart, and love to study 'em. Mischiefs feed   150
Like beasts, till they be fat, and then they bleed.   [*Exeunt.*]

[VOLPONE *comes forward.*]

VOLPONE   The seasoning of a play is the applause.
Now, though the fox be punished by the laws,
He yet doth hope there is no suff'ring due
For any fact which he hath done 'gainst you.   155
If there be, censure him; here he doubtful stands.
If not, fare jovially, and clap your hands.

---

135 *embarked* put on a boat. **139** *Berlina* the stage on which malefactors were exposed, the pillory. **140** *eyes beat out* The crowd threw refuse at those in pillory. **143–44** *Thy . . . trebled* The return of Celia to her father's house is worth comment. It is usual in comedy for the young lovers to be united in some fashion, often quite an unrealistic one, by the end of the play; and thus the marriage or feast—or even seduction— with which comedy usually ends signals the triumph of vitality, beauty, and cleverness over foolishness and those idiocies which obstruct life rather than furthering it. So general is this pattern in comedy that we anticipate, I believe, in *Volpone* that a way will be found to void the marriage of Corvino and Celia and bring about her union with Bonario. Her return to her single state—celibacy is never a matter for celebration in comedy—is therefore a disruption of the normal comic pattern and a grim reminder that in the world Jonson has here constructed greed and foolishness are not always completely overcome. Even though they may destroy themselves in the end, they nevertheless leave permanent scars on the world. **155** *fact* crime.

THE
REVENGER'S
TRAGEDY
(1607)

Cyril Tourneur

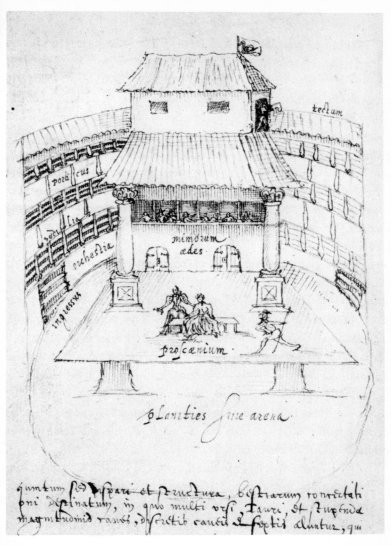

This interior view of the Swan, the only interior view of an Elizabethan theater extant, is from a copy of a sketch made about 1596 by a Dutch traveler, Johannes De Witt, who was greatly impressed by the size and magnificence of the large London public theaters. The Globe, in which The Revenger's Tragedy *was first presented, presumably looked much the same. Not an exact diagram, this sketch can provide only a general idea of what the theaters were like. Bibliotheek Der Rijksuniversiteit Te Utrecht, Nederland.*

FOR THE MODERN READER, WHO TAKES FOR granted the greatness of the Elizabethan theater, one of the most difficult points to understand is that in the sixteenth and early seventeenth centuries plays were considered a form of entertainment rather than art. Despite the serious intentions of many playwrights, the theater was essentially what would now be known as "an entertainment industry," and the scripts of plays were treated about as seriously as movie scenarios are today. The great playing companies of London were repertory companies in keen competition with one another and with other more spectacular forms of entertainment such as bearbaiting and fencing matches. To keep going, they required an enormous number of plays: it has been estimated that one company alone might produce between forty and fifty new plays a year as well as a great many old favorites. Supplying this heavy demand was a big business, and numerous free-lance writers were engaged in turning out plays. The names of most of the plays that were the staple of the Elizabethan theaters have vanished along with their authors. Those that have survived are for the most part the work of playwrights of real genius or of such voluminous productivity that no historical accident could entirely obliterate their work. But here and there the name of one of these passing writers who worked for a brief time supplying plays is remembered—though almost no vital facts are connected with the name—because one or two plays of unmistakable genius associated with him have survived.

Cyril Tourneur belongs in this category. We know little about him for certain except that he was a soldier and that he died in Ireland in 1626. Beyond this we are sure only that he was a writer, that he was the author of a satirical poem, The Transformed Metamorphosis, published in 1600, and that he probably wrote for the stage during the years 1607 to 1611. The title page of The Atheist's Tragedy, published in 1611, bears his name, and it has been assumed that he was also the author of The Revenger's Tragedy. The first edition of the latter play, which is the basis of the text printed here, appeared in 1607. No author's name, *however, appeared on the title page, and it was not until nearly a half-century later that the play was attributed to him. Recently, it has been argued that* The Revenger's Tragedy *was written by either John Webster or Thomas Middleton, but majority opinion still assigns it to Cyril Tourneur.*

⟪DRAMATIS PERSONAE⟫

⟪THE DUKE
LUSSURIOSO, *the Duke's son and heir by earlier marriage*
SPURIO, *his bastard son*
AMBITIOSO, *the Duchess' eldest son*
SUPERVACUO, *the Duchess' second son*
THE YOUNGEST SON *of the Duchess*
ANTONIO ⟩ *lords of the*
PIERO ⟩ *Duke's court*
VINDICE, *the revenger, sometimes disguised as* PIATO

HIPPOLITO, *his brother, also called* CARLO
DONDOLO, *Castiza's servant*
NENCIO ⟩ *servants of*
SORDIDO ⟩ *Lussurioso*
JUDGES, NOBLES, GENTLEMEN, OFFICERS, *a* PRISON-KEEPER, GUARDS, *and* SERVANTS
THE DUCHESS
CASTIZA, *sister of Vindice and Hippolito*
GRATIANA, *a widow, and mother of Vindice, Hippolito, and Castiza* ⟩

⟪The Scene : *An unidentified court, somewhere in Italy*⟫

Dramatis Personae 2–16 *Lussurioso . . . Gratiana* In this play, as in *Volpone,* the Italian names are often emblematic of character. Lussurioso means lustful or lecherous; Spurio, bastard or counterfeit; Ambitioso, ambitious; Supervacuo, useless; Dondolo, fool; Nencio, idiot; Sordido, corrupt or beastly; Castiza, chaste; and Gratiana, grace.
Scene 17 *Italy* To the Elizabethans, Italy was notorious for its violence, intrigue, and corruption—in short, for its Machiavellianism.

ACT I   Scene I

Enter VINDICE *[holding a skull]. The* DUKE; DUCHESS; LUSSURIOSO, *his son;* SPURIO, *the bastard; with a train, pass over the stage with torchlight.*

VINDICE   Duke, royal lecher! Go, gray-haired adultery,
And thou his son, as impious steeped as he,
And thou his bastard true-begot in evil,
And thou his duchess that will do with devil:
Four exc'lent characters. —O, that marrowless age   5
Would stuff the hollow bones with damned desires,
And 'stead of heat kindle infernal fires
Within the spendthrift veins of a dry duke,
A parched and juiceless luxur! O God! one
That has scarce blood enough to live upon,   10
And he to riot it like a son and heir?
O, the thought of that
Turns my abusèd heartstrings into fret.—
[*To the skull.*] Thou sallow picture of my poisoned love,
My studies' ornament, thou shell of death,   15

🐉 **ACT I, Scene 1.** SD *holding a skull*   The skull is that of Vindice's dead lover, Gloriana, murdered by the Duke because she would not submit to his lustful embraces. As many modern critics have pointed out, this skull has crucial thematic significance. From the opening moment of the play, we are presented with a dramatic image of man's limitation and corruption: beneath all human beauty, countermanding all human aspirations, is the undeniable, unaccommodated fact of death; symbolically embodied in the hollow, grinning skull, it leers continually at man, maligning his achievements and mocking his hopes. It is, of course, only a very short, logical step from such a vision to the despairing conclusion that man is *no more* than this—a skull that, however painted and regally adorned, is nevertheless merely a skull: ugly, corrupt, and decaying. Such a conclusion is the one that Hamlet considers and rejects during the graveyard scene (*Hamlet*, V.1) and that Vindice in this play ultimately embraces. In this distinction between Hamlet's world view and Vindice's is one of the crucial differences in tone between the two "revenge" tragedies.   **2** *his*   The quarto reads "her."   **4** *do*   copulate.   **5** *characters*   portraits reflecting moral qualities.   **6** *Would*   should.   **9** *luxur*   voluptuary.   **13** *fret*   both "anger" and "a ridge of metal fixed across the fingerboard of a stringed instrument to help control the fingering."   **15** *studies*   because the skull is usually kept in his study and because as a *momento mori* it reminds him of the vanity of human endeavor and of his studies.   *shell of death*   another pun, since later in the play the skull, marked with poison, will become a murder weapon.

Once the bright face of my betrothèd lady,
When life and beauty naturally filled out
These ragged imperfections,
When two heaven-pointed diamonds were set
In those unsightly rings—then 'twas a face   20
So far beyond the artificial shine
Of any woman's bought complexion
That the uprightest man (if such there be,
That sin but seven times a day) broke custom
And made up eight with looking after her.   25
O she was able to ha' made a usurer's son
Melt all his patrimony in a kiss,
And what his father fifty years told
To have consumed, and yet his suit been cold.
But O, accursèd palace!   30
Thee, when thou wert appareled in thy flesh,
The old duke poisoned,
Because thy purer part would not consent
Unto his palsy-lust; for old men lustful
Do show like young men angry, eager-violent,   35
Outbid like their limited performances.
O 'ware an old man hot and vicious.
"Age, as in gold, in lust is covetous."—
Vengeance, thou murder's quit-rent, and whereby

---

19 *diamonds* her eyes. **28** *years* pronounced as a disyllable. *told* saved. **34–36** *for
. . . performances* for old men who are lustful resemble young men who are angry: both
are violently eager and yet promise more than they can perform (presumably because the
young man is rash, the old man no longer sexually capable). **38** *Age . . . covetous*
In the quarto certain lines are periodically set off from the rest of the text by introductory
double commas (, ,Age . . .). In this way attention is drawn to sententious verses, which
seem to be important more because of what they overlook than because of what they
say. Often maxims provide characters with excuses for not thinking about problems, for
they are so neatly phrased that they either hide complexity or oversimplify it. In using
this particular maxim, for example, Vindice does not realize that he is indirectly providing a commentary on his own limitations as well as on the Duke's. First, it reflects his
tendency to think too much in terms of the superficial values honored by the court world
—values represented here by "gold" and earlier by his talk about the "patrimony" of the
usurer, the "diamonds" of Gloriana's eyes, and Gloriana's worth in general, which he
measures by her beauty and by the desire she aroused in other men. Second, the maxim
indirectly condemns the speaker because in warning against the Duke's monomania it
also draws attention to Vindice's single-mindedness, which drives him, in his very next
breath, to call for "Vengeance." We see that any strong emotion, pursued to the extreme,
becomes a vice. **39** *quit–rent* rent paid by a freeholder of land in place of services ordinarily required of him; but a pun on "quit," here meaning death, is also implied: Vengeance proves itself a servant ("tenant") of Tragedy by rendering murder its due payment.

Thou showst thyself tenant to Tragedy,   40
O keep thy day, hour, minute, I beseech,
For those thou hast determined. Hum! who e'er knew
Murder unpaid? Faith, give Revenge her due,
Sh' has kept touch hitherto. —Be merry, merry;
Advance thee, O thou terror to fat folks,   45
To have their costly three-piled flesh worn off
As bare as this—for banquets, ease, and laughter
Can make great men, as greatness goes by clay,
But wise men little are more great than they.

Enter his brother HIPPOLITO.

HIPPOLITO   Still sighing o'er death's vizard?
                              Brother, welcome.   50
VINDICE   What comfort bringst thou? how go things at court?
HIPPOLITO   In silk and silver, brother; never braver.
VINDICE   Puh,
Thou playst upon my meaning. Prithee say,
Has that bald madam, Opportunity,   55
Yet thought upon's? Speak, are we happy yet?
Thy wrongs and mine are for one scabbard fit.
HIPPOLITO   It may prove happiness.
VINDICE   What is't may prove?
Give me to taste.
HIPPOLITO   Give me your hearing then.
You know my place at court.
VINDICE   Ay, the Duke's chamber.   60
But 'tis a marvel thou'rt not turned out yet!
HIPPOLITO   Faith, I have been shoved at, but 'twas still my hap
To hold by th' Duchess' skirt—you guess at that:
Whom such a coat keeps up can ne'er fall flat.
But to the purpose.   65
Last evening, predecessor unto this,
The Duke's son warily inquired for me,
Whose pleasure I attended. He began

---

45 thee death through revenge. **46 three-piled** regally attired, as in three-piled velvet. **47 this** the skull. **48 as . . . clay** both "great in size" and "great according to the superficial values of society." **49 little** both "small in size" and "low in social station." **great** nobly virtuous. **SD his** The quarto reads "her." **50 vizard** mask. **52 braver** more splendidly. **55 Opportunity** In the Renaissance, Opportunity was often pictured as a woman, bald except for the forelock, by which it was thought she could be seized. **64 coat** skirt. **Whom . . . flat** Hippolito's meaning here is, in part, sexual.

By policy to open and unhusk me
About the time and common rumor;   70
But I had so much wit to keep my thoughts
Up in their built houses, yet afforded him
An idle satisfaction without danger.
But the whole aim and scope of his intent
Ended in this—conjuring me in private,   75
To seek some strange-digested fellow forth
Of ill-contented nature, either disgraced
In former times, or by new grooms displaced
Since his stepmother's nuptials; such a blood,
A man that were for evil only good—   80
To give you the true word, some based-coined pander.
VINDICE   I reach you; for I know his heat is such,
Were there as many concubines as ladies,
He would not be contained; he must fly out.
I wonder how ill-featured, vild-proportioned   85
That one should be, if she were made for woman,
Whom at the insurrection of his lust
He would refuse for once; heart, I think none,
Next to a skull, though more unsound than one:
Each face he meets he strongly dotes upon.   90
HIPPOLITO   Brother, y' have truly spoke him.
He knows not you, but I'll swear you know him.
VINDICE   And therefore I'll put on that knave for once,
And be a right man then, a man o' th' time;
For to be honest is not to be i' th' world.   95
Brother, I'll be that strange-composed fellow.
HIPPOLITO   And I'll prefer you, brother.
VINDICE   Go to, then.
The small'st advantage fattens wrongèd men.
It may point out Occasion; if I meet her,
I'll hold her by the foretop fast enough,   100
Or like the French mole heave up hair and all.

---

72 *Up . . . houses* hidden.   **76** *strange-digested* evilly dispositioned.   **79** *his* Lussurioso's.   **81** *base-coined* of base nature, depraved.   **85** *vild* vilely.   **89** *Next to* with the exception of.   **93** *put . . . knave* pretend to be such a knave (as you just spoke of).   **94** *right* cunning, with an ironic reference to the meaning "honest."   **97** *prefer* recommend.   **100** *foretop* again a reference to the forelock of Opportunity (cf. I.1.55).   **101** *French mole* syphilis, which in the second stage destroys the hair follicules and in the third stage raises gummas, tumorous swellings often located on the head.

I have a habit that will fit it quaintly.
Here comes our mother.
HIPPOLITO   And sister.
VINDICE   We must coin.
Women are apt, you know, to take false money,
But I dare stake my soul for these two creatures—   105
Only excuse excepted, that they'll swallow,
Because their sex is easy in belief.

[*Enter* GRATIANA *and* CASTIZA.]

GRATIANA   What news from court, son Carlo?
HIPPOLITO   Faith, mother,
'Tis whispered there the Duchess' youngest son
Has played a rape on Lord Antonio's wife.   110
GRATIANA   On that religious lady!
CASTIZA   Royal blood! Monster! he deserves to die,
If Italy had no more hopes but he.
VINDICE   Sister, y' have sentenced most direct and true;
The law's a woman, and would she were you.—   115
Mother, I must take leave of you.
GRATIANA   Leave for what?
VINDICE   I intend speedy travel.
HIPPOLITO   That he does, madam.
GRATIANA   Speedy indeed!
VINDICE   For since my worthy father's funeral,
My life's unnatural to me, e'en compelled,   120
As if I lived now when I should be dead.
GRATIANA   Indeed, he was a worthy gentleman,
Had his estate been fellow to his mind.
VINDICE   The Duke did much deject him.
GRATIANA   Much!
VINDICE   Too much.

---

102 habit outfit. **quaintly** both "cleverly" and "handsomely." **103 coin** counterfeit. **104 Women . . . money** "Women in general are susceptible to deception," but
also, "Women often take money they have earned falsely (by prostituting themselves)."
106 swallow believe (a good excuse). **112 Royal blood** a sarcastic exclamation, like
Vindice's in the opening line of the play. **115 The . . . woman** Justice was often personified as a woman holding a set of balance scales. **117 travel** with a pun on "travail,"
which is etymologically the same word; the quarto spelling is "trauaile." **120 unnatural**
The quarto reads "unnaturally." **compelled** forced upon me against my will.
123 Had . . . mind if his social station had equaled his virtue.

And through disgrace, oft smothered in his spirit,   125
When it would mount, surely I think he died
Of discontent, the nobleman's consumption.
GRATIANA   Most sure he did.
VINDICE   Did he? 'lack. You know all;
   You were his midnight secretary.
GRATIANA   No.
   He was too wise to trust me with his thoughts.   130
VINDICE   I'faith then, father, thou wast wise indeed:
   "Wives are but made to go to bed and feed."
   Come mother, sister. —You'll bring me onward, brother?
HIPPOLITO   I will.
VINDICE   [*Aside.*] I'll quickly turn into another.   *Exeunt.*   135

⦃ACT I   Scene 2⦄

Enter the old DUKE; LUSSURIOSO, *his son; the* DUCHESS; [SPURIO,] *the
bastard; the Duchess' two sons,* AMBITIOSO *and* SUPERVACUO; *the
third, her* YOUNGEST, *brought out with* OFFICERS *for the rape;* [*and*] *two*
JUDGES.

DUKE   Duchess, it is your youngest son, we're sorry.
   His violent act has e'en drawn blood of honor
   And stained our honors;
   Thrown ink upon the forehead of our state
   Which envious spirits will dip their pens into   5
   After our death, and blot us in our tombs.
   For that which would seem treason in our lives
   Is laughter when we're dead: who dares now whisper
   That dares not then speak out, and e'en proclaim
   With loud words and broad pens our closest shame.   10
FIRST JUDGE   Your grace hath spoke like to your silver years,
   Full of confirmèd gravity; for what is it to have
   A flattering false insculption on a tomb,

125–127 *And . . . discontent* And because he continually had to suppress his sense of
mounting disgrace (at the Duke's ill conduct), he eventually died from the psychic dis-
ruptions of this discontent.   **129** *midnight secretary* intimate confidante.   **133** *bring
me onward* see to my preferment.
🐾 **ACT I, Scene 2.**   **7** *in . . . lives* while we live.   **13** *insculption* inscription.

And in men's hearts reproach? The boweled corpse
May be cered in, but—with free tongue I speak—   15
"The faults of great men through their cerecloths break."
DUKE   They do, we're sorry for't. It is our fate
To live in fear and die to live in hate.
I leave him to your sentence; doom him, lords—
The fact is great—whilst I sit by and sigh.   20
DUCHESS   [*Kneeling.*] My gracious lord, I pray be merciful.
Although his trespass far exceed his years,
Think him to be your own as I am yours;
Call him not son-in-law: the law I fear
Will fall too soon upon his name and him   25
Temper his fault with pity!
LUSSURIOSO   Good my lord,
Then 'twill not taste so bitter and unpleasant
Upon the judges' palate; for offenses
Gilt o'er with mercy show like fairest women,
Good only for their beauties, which washed off,   30
No sin is uglier.
AMBITIOSO   I beseech your grace,
Be soft and mild; let not relentless law
Look with an iron forehead on our brother.
SPURIO   [*Aside.*] He yields small comfort yet; hope he shall die.
And if a bastard's wish might stand in force,   35
Would all the court were turned into a corse.
DUCHESS   No pity yet? Must I rise fruitless then?
A wonder in a woman! Are my knees
Of such low metal, that without respect—
FIRST JUDGE   Let the offender stand forth: 40
'Tis the Duke's pleasure that impartial doom
Shall take fast hold of his unclean attempt.
A rape! why, 'tis the very core of lust,

---

14 *boweled* Corpses were often disemboweled in being prepared for burial (cf.
1 Henry IV, V.4.109). 15 *cered in* sealed up in a coffin. 16 *cerecloths* wax-covered
cloth used for wrapping corpses. The quarto reads "searce clothes." 20 *fact* crime.
24 *Call . . . son-in-law* Treat him as if he were your own son, instead of showing him
the coldness often offered a stepson. 33 *iron forehead* countenance unmoved by
sympathy. 34 *He . . . yet* So far the Duke offers little comfort (to the accused). *hope*
(I) hope. 36 *corse* corpse. 38–39 *Are . . . metal* Are my supplications, then, worth
so little. 41 *doom* judgment. 42 *fast* The quarto reads "first." *unclean attempt*
lascivious assault.

Double adultery.

YOUNGEST SON   So, sir.

SECOND JUDGE   And which was worse,
Committed on the Lord Antonio's wife,   45
That general-honest lady. Confess, my lord,
What moved you to't?

YOUNGEST SON   Why, flesh and blood, my lord.
What should move men unto a woman else?

LUSSURIOSO   O do not jest thy doom; trust not an ax
Or sword too far: the law is a wise serpent   50
And quickly can beguile thee of thy life.
Though marriage only has made thee my brother,
I love thee so far: play not with thy death.

YOUNGEST SON   I thank you, troth; good admonitions, faith.
If I'd the grace now to make use of them.   55

FIRST JUDGE   That lady's name has spread such a fair wing
Over all Italy, that if our tongues
Were sparing toward the fact, judgment itself
Would be condemned and suffer in men's thoughts.

YOUNGEST SON   Well then, 'tis done, and it would please me well   60
Were it to do again: sure she's a goddess,
For I'd no power to see her, and to live.
It falls out true in this, for I must die;
Her beauty was ordained to be my scaffold.
And yet, methinks, I might be easier ceased: 65
My fault being sport, let me but die in jest.

FIRST JUDGE   This be the sentence—

DUCHESS   O keep't upon your tongue; let it not slip:
Death too soon steals out of a lawyer's lip.
Be not so cruel-wise!

FIRST JUDGE   Your grace must pardon us;   70
'Tis but the justice of the law.

DUCHESS   The law.
Is grown more subtle than a woman should be.

SPURIO   [*Aside.*] Now, now he dies; rid 'em away.

---

44 Double adultery "double" because it violates the marriage bed of both partners.
46 general-honest undeniably chaste. **49–50 trust . . . far** Be careful how you treat
a potentially destructive instrument. **50 wise** cunning. **53 so far** as if you were actually
my brother. **58 fact** crime. **63 die** The common Renaissance meaning, "experience
sexual orgasm," is also implied here and in line 66. **65 methinks** The quarto reads "my
thinks." **66 sport** both "fun" and "sexual play." **73 away** immediately.

DUCHESS   [*Aside.*] O what it is to have an old-cool duke,
   To be as slack in tongue as in performance!   75
FIRST JUDGE   Confirmed, this be the doom irrevocable.
DUCHESS   O!
FIRST JUDGE   Tomorrow early—
DUCHESS   Pray be abed, my lord.
FIRST JUDGE   Your grace much wrongs yourself.
AMBITIOSO   [*Aside.*] No, 'tis that tongue:
   Your too much right does do us too much wrong.
FIRST JUDGE   Let that offender—
DUCHESS   Live, and be in health.   80
FIRST JUDGE   —Be on a scaffold—
DUKE   Hold, hold, my lord!
SPURIO   [*Aside.*] Pox on't,
   What makes my dad speak now?
DUKE   We will defer the judgment till next sitting;
   In the meantime, let him be kept close prisoner.—
   Guard, bear him hence.   85
AMBITIOSO   [*To* YOUNGEST SON.] Brother, this makes for thee;
   Fear not, we'll have a trick to set thee free.
YOUNGEST SON   [*Apart.*] Brother, I will expect it from you both;
   And in that hope I rest.
SUPERVACUO   Farewell, be merry.
                        Exit [YOUNGEST SON] *with a* GUARD.
SPURIO   [*Aside.*] Delayed, deferred! Nay then, if judgment have   90
   Cold blood, flattery and bribes will kill it.
DUKE   About it then, my lords, with your best powers;
   More serious business calls upon our hours.
                        Exeunt; manet DUCHESS.
DUCHESS   Was't ever known step-duchess was so mild
   And calm as I? Some now would plot his death   95
   With easy doctors, those loose-living men,
   And make his withered grace fall to his grave,

---

75 *performance* sexually.   **76** *confirmed* either "once confirmed by the Duke" or "once confirmed in the judgment of this court."   **78** *that* your.   **79** *Your . . . right* your undisciplined use of your right, as a judge, to speak.   **81** *Pox* The quarto reads "pax."   **82** *dad* a sarcastic use of the word, which in the early seventeenth century occurred principally in the speech of children and rustics.   **86** *makes . . . thee* works to your advantage.   **90–91** *if . . . it* If judgment acts cold-bloodedly (and metes out punishments commensurate with offenses), bribery and flattery soon put an end to such verdicts.   **96** *easy* easily corrupted.

And keep church better.
Some second wife would do this, and dispatch
Her double-loathèd lord at meat, and sleep.   100
Indeed 'tis true an old man's twice a child;
Mine cannot speak: one of his single words
Would quite have freed my youngest, dearest son
From death or durance, and have made him walk
With a bold foot upon the thorny law,   105
Whose prickles should bow under him. But 'tis not,
And therefore wedlock faith shall be forgot:
I'll kill him in his forehead; hate, there feed;
That wound is deepest though it never bleed.

[*Enter* SPURIO.]

And here comes he whom my heart points unto,   110
His bastard son, but my love's true-begot;
Many a wealthy letter have I sent him,
Swelled up with jewels, and the timorous man
Is yet but coldly kind.
That jewel's mine that quivers in his ear,   115
Mocking his master's chillness and vain fear.
H' has spied me now.
SPURIO   Madam, your grace so private?
My duty on your hand.
DUCHESS   Upon my hand, sir. Troth, I think you'd fear
To kiss my hand too if my lip stood there.   120
SPURIO   Witness I would not, madam. [*He kisses her.*]
DUCHESS   'Tis a wonder,
For ceremony has made many fools.
It is as easy way unto a duchess
As to a hatted dame—if her love answer—
But that by timorous honors, pale respects,   125
Idle degrees of fear, men make their ways
Hard of themselves—What have you thought of me?

---

98 keep . . . better attend church more regularly (by being placed in its graveyard).
99–100 and . . . sleep and twice poison her doubly hated lord, both at dinner and before
going to bed; but there is also an obscene innuendo.   **101 twice** for a second time.
108 in . . . forehead by making a cuckold of him (cuckolded husbands were traditionally
thought to grow horns as a sign of their disgrace).   **111 but . . . true-begot** but a true,
not false ("bastard") object of my love.   **114 kind** polite.   **124 hatted dame** a woman
of the lower classes; gentlewomen wore headdresses, not hats.

SPURIO Madam, I ever think of you in duty,
        Regard, and—
DUCHESS   Puh! Upon my love, I mean.
SPURIO I would 'twere love, but 'tis a fouler name   130
        Than lust: you are my father's wife,
        Your grace may guess now what I could call it.
DUCHESS Why, thou'rt his son but falsely;
        'Tis a hard question whether he begot thee.
SPURIO I'faith, 'tis true too; I'm an uncertain man of more uncertain   135
        woman. Maybe his groom o' th' stable begot me; you know I
        know not. He could ride a horse well—a shrewd suspicion, marry!
        He was wondrous tall; he had his length, i'faith, for peeping over
        half-shut holiday windows: men would desire him light. When
        he was afoot he made a goodly show under a penthouse; and when   140
        he rid, his hat would check the signs, and clatter barbers' basins.
DUCHESS Nay, set you a-horseback once, you'll ne'er light off.
SPURIO Indeed, I am a beggar.
DUCHESS That's more the sign thou'rt great. —But to our love.
        Let it stand firm, both in thought and mind.   145

---

130 *'tis* The quarto reads "'tus." **135–43** *I'faith . . . beggar* In some editions of
The Revenger's Tragedy these lines are printed as poetry; but because Tourneur's irregular
verse almost never achieves the kind of steady cadence which, for example, is characteristic of Marlowe's "mighty line," it is sometimes impossible to determine conclusively
whether or not a passage in this play really is poetry. In addition, complications are also
produced by the nature of Tourneur's prose, which sometimes falls into metrical patterns
closely resembling iambic pentameter. Thus—as the reader may already have noticed—
there is little difference between Tourneur's prose and his poetry; and the original edition
of the play provides only a very unreliable measure of this difference because, in the quarto,
poetry is sometimes set as prose and prose as poetry. In order to untangle this perplexing
textual problem, every editor of *The Revenger's Tragedy* has had to develop his own
theory about how to correct the lineation in the quarto. In this particular edition we have
"corrected" it as little as possible: lineation changes have been made only where the
language seemed to demand them; elsewhere the text of the quarto has been honored,
even where prose appears suddenly in the midst of poetry. Tourneur's strength as a
dramatist does not reside in his skill as a poet, and it seems unreasonable to emphasize his
weakness by labeling as poetry passages that may never have been intended to be anything
but prose. **137** *He . . . well,* **138** *he . . . length* Both statements have sexual, as
well as literal, meanings. **138–39** *He . . . light* So tall was he that on horseback he
could see over the "holiday windows" (whose bottom halves only were shut) and
observe, in private situations, men who wished that he would dismount. **140** *penthouse*
sloping, overhanging roof. **141** *rid* rode. *check* bump. *barbers' basins* commonly hung out to advertise a barbershop. **142** *set . . . off,* **144** *that's . . . great* The
Duchess' meaning here is, in part, sexual. **143** *Indeed . . . beggar* Spurio develops the
Duchess' oblique reference to the proverb "Set a beggar upon horseback, and he will
ride at a gallop."

That the Duke was thy father, as no doubt then
He bid fair for't, thy injury is the more:
For had he cut thee a right diamond,
Thou hadst been next set in the dukedom's ring,
When his worn self, like age's easy slave,   150
Had dropped out of the collet into th' grave.
What wrong can equal this? Canst thou be tame
And think upon't?
SPURIO   No, mad and think upon't.
DUCHESS Who would not be revenged of such a father,
E'en in the worst way? I would thank that sin   155
That could most injury him, and be in league with it.
O what a grief 'tis, that a man should live
But once i' th' world, and then to live a bastard,
The curse o' the womb, the thief of nature,
Begot against the seventh commandement,   160
Half damned in the conception by the justice
Of that unbribèd, everlasting law.
SPURIO O, I'd a hot-backed devil to my father.
DUCHESS Would not this mad e'en patience, make blood rough?
Who but an eunuch would not sin, his bed   165
By one false minute disinherited?
SPURIO Ay, there's the vengeance that my birth was wrapped in!
I'll be revenged for all. Now, hate, begin;
I'll call foul incest but a venial sin.
DUCHESS Cold still? In vain then must a duchess woo?   170
SPURIO Madam, I blush to say what I will do.
DUCHESS Thence flew sweet comfort. [*Kisses him.*] Earnest and fare-
well.
SPURIO O, one incestuous kiss picks open hell.
DUCHESS Faith, now, old Duke, my vengeance shall reach high:
I'll arm thy brow with woman's heraldry.   *Exit* [DUCHESS].   175
SPURIO Duke, thou didst do me wrong, and by thy act
Adultery is my nature.
Faith, if the truth were known, I was begot

---

147 *He . . . for't* he was licentious enough to have been. **148** *had . . . diamond* had
he made you his legitimate son instead of his bastard. **151** *collet* setting in a ring where
the stone is placed. **156** *injury* injure—an obsolete form of the verb. **163** *to* for.
164 *rough* unsettled. **167** *that . . . in* that was predetermined by the very nature of
my birth. **172** *Thence . . . comfort* Those words conveyed sweet comfort to me.
Earnest Her kiss is a pledge of love to come. **175** *heraldry* cuckold's horns.

After some gluttonous dinner; some stirring dish
Was my first father. When deep healths went round,   180
And ladies' cheeks were painted red with wine,
Their tongues, as short and nimble as their heels,
Uttering words sweet and thick; and when they rose,
Were merrily disposed to fall again.
In such a whisp'ring and withdrawing hour,   185
When base male-bawds kept sentinel at stair-head,
Was I stol'n softly. O, damnation met
The sin of feasts, drunken adultery.
I feel it swell me; my revenge is just:
I was begot in impudent wine and lust.   190
Stepmother, I consent to thy desires;
I love thy mischief well, but I hate thee,
And those three cubs, thy sons—wishing confusion,
Death, and disgrace may be their epitaphs.
As for my brother, the Duke's only son,   195
Whose birth is more beholding to report
Than mine, and yet perhaps as falsely sown
(Women must not be trusted with their own),
I'll loose my days upon him, hate-all I.
Duke, on thy brow I'll draw my bastardy.   200
For indeed a bastard by nature should make cuckolds,
Because he is the son of a cuckold-maker.   *Exit.*

⊰ACT I   Scene 3⊱

Enter VINDICE *and* HIPPOLITO, VINDICE *in disguise to attend* L[ord]
LUSSURIOSO, *the Duke's son.*

VINDICE   What, brother, am I far enough from my self?
HIPPOLITO   As if another man had been sent whole
    Into the world, and none wist how he came.
VINDICE   It will confirm me bold—the child o' th' court.

---

179 *stirring dish* stimulant.   **182 *as . . . heels*** a reference to the easy virtue of court
women, who—in the modern vernacular—seemed to have hinges on their heels.   **183 *rose***
The quarto reads "rise."   **187 *stol'n softly*** illicitly conceived.   **189 *swell*** both "give
me courage" and "arouse me sexually."   **199 *I'll . . . him*** I will spend my days
maligning him.

Let blushes dwell i' th' country. Impudence,   5
Thou goddess of the palace, mistress of mistresses,
To whom the costly-perfumed people pray,
Strike thou my forehead into dauntless marble,
Mine eyes to steady sapphires; turn my visage,
And if I must needs glow, let me blush inward,   10
That this immodest season may not spy
That scholar in my cheeks, fool bashfulness,
That maid in the old time, whose flush of grace
Would never suffer her to get good clothes.
Our maids are wiser, and are less ashamed;   15
Save Grace the bawd, I seldom hear grace named!

HIPPOLITO   Nay, brother, you reach out o' th' verge now—'sfoot, the
Duke's son; settle your looks.

[*Enter* LUSSURIOSO, *attended.*]

VINDICE   Pray let me not be doubted.   [*He steps back.*]
HIPPOLITO   My lord—
LUSSURIOSO   Hippolito?— [*To* SERVANTS.] Be absent, leave us.   20
                                    [*Exit* SERVANTS.]

HIPPOLITO   My lord, after long search, wary inquiries,
And politic siftings, I made choice of yon fellow,
Whom I guess rare for many deep employments.
This our age swims within him; and if Time
Had so much hair, I should take him for Time,   25
He is so near kin to this present minute.

LUSSURIOSO   'Tis enough;
We thank thee; yet words are but great men's blanks.
Gold, though it be dumb, does utter the best thanks.

[*Gives* HIPPOLITO *money.*]

🎰 ACT I, Scene 3.   14 *to . . . clothes*   to put on regal dress and, with it, the perverse
values of the corrupted court world.   17 *out . . . verge*   beyond the limit, but also—
because of the suggestion by sound—outside of the realm of virginity.   *'sfoot*   an
exclamation, contracted from "by God's foot."   19 *doubted*   suspected.   23 *rare . . .
employments*   unusually well-suited for affairs that demand cunning and craft.   24 *This
. . . him*   This line vividly presents two notable characteristics of the Renaissance
imagination, first, in its claim that the age is truly distinct, and second, in its implication
that the distinctness has been defined by the men of the time—it is "our age." This idea
is further developed by the suggestiveness of the word "swims." Vast in desires and hopes,
allusive in definition, and teeming with activity, the age is still thought to be bounded
and defined by the individual psyche: it is an age that, however much it may "swim,"
can still be thought to swim *within* one man.   *Time*   another reference to Opportunity.
28 *blanks*   checks or coins worthless until they are stamped with value.

HIPPOLITO   Your plenteous honor.   An exc'lent fellow, my lord.   30
LUSSURIOSO   So, give us leave. [*Exit* HIPPOLITO.] [*To* VINDICE.] Wel-
come, be not far off; we must be better acquainted. Push, be bold
with us: thy hand.
VINDICE   With all my heart, i'faith.   How dost, sweet muskcat?
When shall we lie together? [*Embraces* LUSSURIOSO.]   35
LUSSURIOSO   [*Aside.*] Wondrous knave!
Gather him into boldness? 'Sfoot, the slave's
Already as familiar as an ague,
And shakes me at his pleasure. [*To* VINDICE.] Friend, I can
Forget myself in private, but elsewhere   40
I pray do you remember me.
VINDICE   O very well, sir.—I conster myself saucy.
LUSSURIOSO   What hast been? Of what profession?
VINDICE   A bone-setter.
LUSSURIOSO   A bone-setter?   45
VINDICE   A bawd, my lord, one that sets bones together.
LUSSURIOSO   Notable bluntness!
[*Aside.*] Fit, fit for me, e'en trained up to my hand.—
Thou hast been scrivener to much knavery, then.
VINDICE   Fool to abundance, sir; I have been witness to the surrenders   50
of a thousand virgins, and not so little. I have seen patrimonies
washed a-pieces, fruit fields turned into bastards, and in a world of
acres, not so much dust due to the heir 'twas left to as would well
gravel a petition.
LUSSURIOSO   [*Aside.*] Fine villain! troth, I like him wonderously.   55
He's e'en shaped for my purpose. [*To* VINDICE.] Then thou knowst
I' th' world strange lust.
VINDICE   O Dutch lust! fulsome lust!
Drunken procreation, which begets so many drunkards.
Some father dreads not (gone to bed in wine)

---

32 *far off* coolly distant.   **34** *muskcat* a source of perfume and, metaphorically, a fop (who wore it).   **35** *When . . . together* When shall we prove our familiarity by sleeping together (as lovers)?   **37** *Gather . . . boldness* What need had I to encourage his familiarity with me?   **39** *shakes* The ague afflicted its victims with fever and the shakes.   **41** *remember me* remember who I am (and act accordingly).   **42** *conster* understand.   **46** *sets . . . together* brings bodies together, with an obscene pun implicit in "bone."   **49** *scrivener* agent.   **50** *Fool* accessory—as differentiated from knaves, who execute the corrupt deeds.   **52** *bastards* unproductive shoots on a fruit tree.   **54** *gravel a petition* Legal documents were lightly sprinkled with sand to dry the ink on them.   **57** *Dutch lust* The Dutch, or more properly the Germans (*Deutsch*), were traditionally considered heavy drinkers.   **59** *Some . . . wine* In the quarto this line is extended through "mother."

To slide from the mother and cling the daughter-in-law;   60
Some uncles are adulterous with their nieces,
Brothers with brothers' wives. O hour of incest!
Any kin now, next to the rim o' th' sister,
Is man's meat in these days; and in the morning,
When they are up and dressed, and their mask on,   65
Who can perceive this, save that eternal eye
That sees through flesh and all? Well, if any thing
Be damned, it will be twelve o'clock at night;
That twelve will never 'scape:
It is the Judas of the hours, wherein   70
Honest salvation is betrayed to sin.

LUSSURIOSO   In troth, it is, too. But let this talk glide.
It is our blood to err, though hell gaped loud:
Ladies know Lucifer fell, yet still are proud.
Now, sir, wert thou as secret as thou'rt subtle   75
And deeply fathomed into all estates,
I would embrace thee for a near employment,
And thou shouldst swell in money, and be able
To make lame beggars crouch to thee.

VINDICE   My lord!
Secret? I ne'er had that disease o' th' mother,   80
I praise my father. Why are men made close
But to keep thoughts in best? I grant you this,
Tell but some woman a secret over night,
Your doctor may find it in the urinal i' th' morning.
But, my lord—

LUSSURIOSO   So, thou'rt confirmed in me,   85
And thus I enter thee. [*Gives him money.*]

VINDICE   This Indian devil
Will quickly enter any man, but a usurer;
He prevents that, by ent'ring the devil first.

LUSSURIOSO   Attend me. I am past my depth in lust,

---

60 cling embrace. **63 next to** with the exception of. **rim** rim (of the womb).
75 secret (able to keep) a secret. **76 deeply . . . estates** knowing well all kinds of
people. **77 near** secretly intimate. **80 disease . . . mother** overtalkativeness, but
there is also implicit a pun on "mother," a particular kind of hysteria. **81 men . . . close,
84 Your . . . morning** an obscene reference to the difference between the male and
female anatomies. **85 confirmed in me** taken into my trust. **86 enter** admit.
Indian devil the coin, whose gold source was the Indies. **87 enter** win over. **88 by
. . . first** by possessing the Indian devil before it is used to bribe and possess ("enter") him.

And I must swim or drown. All my desires   90
Are leveled at a virgin not far from court,
To whom I have conveyed by messenger
Many waxed lines, full of my neatest spirit,
And jewels that were able to ravish her
Without the help of man; all of which and more   95
She, foolish-chaste, sent back, the messengers
Receiving frowns for answers.
VINDICE   Possible?
'Tis a rare Phoenix, whoe'er she be.
If your desires be such, she so repugnant,
In troth, my lord, I'd be revenged and marry her.   100
LUSSURIOSO   Push! the dowry of her blood and of her fortunes
Are both too mean—good enough to be bad withal.
I'm one of that number can defend
Marriage is good, yet rather keep a friend.
Give me my bed by stealth—there's true delight;   105
What breeds a loathing in't, but night by night?
VINDICE   A very fine religion!
LUSSURIOSO   Therefore, thus:
I'll trust thee in the business of my heart
Because I see thee well experienced
In this luxurious day wherein we breathe.   110
Go thou, and with a smooth enchanting tongue
Bewitch her ears, and cozen her of all grace;
Enter upon the portion of her soul,
Her honor, which she calls her chastity,
And bring it into expense; for honesty   115
Is like a stock of money laid to sleep,
Which ne'er so little broke, does never keep.
VINDICE   You have gi'en't the tang, i'faith, my lord.
Make known the lady to me, and my brain
Shall swell with strange invention; I will move it   120
Till I expire with speaking, and drop down
Without a word to save me; but I'll work—

---

93 waxed lines letters sealed with wax.   **98 rare Phoenix** a person so unusual that we might even doubt her existence (the Phoenix was a unique mythical bird).   **99 repugnant** determined in resistance.   **102 good ... bad** only good enough to make her a prostitute. **104 friend** mistress.   **110 luxurious** lust-filled.   **113 portion** both "what has been allotted to her by providence" and "her dowry or marriage-portion."   **115 expense** expenditure.   **117 ne'er ... broke** once it has been broken into.   **118 gi'en ... tang** described it appropriately.   **120 move it** serve your cause.

LUSSURIOSO   We thank thee, and will raise thee. Receive her name: it
    is the only daughter to Madame Gratiana, the late widow.

VINDICE   [*Aside.*] O, my sister, my sister!

LUSSURIOSO   Why dost walk aside?   125

VINDICE   My lord, I was thinking how I might begin,
    As thus, "O lady"—or twenty hundred devices;
    Her very bodkin will put a man in.

LUSSURIOSO   Ay, or the wagging of her hair.

VINDICE   No, that shall put you in, my lord.   130

LUSSURIOSO   Shall't? why, content. Dost know the daughter then?

VINDICE   O exc'lent well by sight.

LUSSURIOSO   That was her brother
    That did prefer thee to us.

VINDICE   My lord, I think so;
    I knew I had seen him somewhere—

LUSSURIOSO   And therefore, prithee, let thy heart to him   135
    Be as a virgin, close.

VINDICE   O me, good lord.

LUSSURIOSO   We may laugh at that simple age within him—

VINDICE   Ha, ha, ha.

LUSSURIOSO   Himself being made the subtle instrument,
    To wind up a good fellow—

VINDICE   That's I, my lord.   140

LUSSURIOSO   That's thou—
    To entice and work his sister.

VINDICE   A pure novice!

LUSSURIOSO   'Twas finely managed.

VINDICE   Gallantly carried;
    A pretty, perfumed villain.

LUSSURIOSO   I've bethought me,
    If she prove chaste still and immovable,   145
    Venture upon the mother, and with gifts
    As I will furnish thee, begin with her.

VINDICE   O fie, fie! that's the wrong end, my lord. 'Tis mere impossible
    that a mother by any gifts should become a bawd to her own
    daughter!   150

---

128 bodkin   a pin-shaped ornament used to hold a woman's hair in place.   ***put . . . in***
serve as an excuse to begin a conversation.   **130 *No . . . in***   Vindice puns on the obscene
meanings of both "put in" and "wagging of her hair."   **136 *me***   either a printer's
error for "my" or a contraction for "trust me."   **140 *wind up***   set in readiness for
action.   **142 *work***   plot against.

LUSSURIOSO   Nay, then, I see thou'rt but a puny in the subtle mystery
    of a woman. Why, 'tis held now no dainty dish: the name
    Is so in league with age, that nowadays
    It does eclipse three quarters of a mother.
VINDICE   Does't so, my lord?   155
    Let me alone then to eclipse the fourth.
LUSSURIOSO   Why, well said; come, I'll furnish thee; but first
    Swear to be true in all.
VINDICE   True!
LUSSURIOSO   Nay, but swear!
VINDICE   Swear?—I hope your honor little doubts my faith.
LUSSURIOSO   Yet for my humor's sake, 'cause I love swearing.   160
VINDICE   'Cause you love swearing, 'slud, I will.
LUSSURIOSO   Why, enough.
    Ere long look to be made of better stuff.
VINDICE   That will do well indeed, my lord.
LUSSURIOSO   Attend me!
                              [*Exit* LUSSURIOSO.]
VINDICE   O,
    Now let me burst, I've eaten noble poison;   165
    We are made strange fellows, brother: innocent villains.
    Wilt not be angry when thou hear'st on't, thinkst thou?
    I'faith, thou shalt. Swear me to foul my sister!
    Sword, I durst make a promise of him to thee:
    Thou shalt disheir him; it shall be thine honor.   170
    And yet, now angry froth is down in me,
    It would not prove the meanest policy
    In this disguise to try the faith of both.
    Another might have had the selfsame office,
    Some slave, that would have wrought effectually,   175
    Ay, and perhaps o'erwrought 'em; therefore I,
    Being thought traveled, will apply myself
    Unto the selfsame form, forget my nature,

---

151 *puny* beginner. **152** *name* that of bawd. **153** *age* old age. **154** *It . . . mother*
Old women are three parts bawd for every one part mother. **156** *to . . . fourth* and
make her completely a bawd. **161** *'slud* a contraction from "by God's blood."
163 *Attend me* serve me attentively. **170** *disheir* make him no longer an heir (to the
Duke)—by killing him. **171** *now . . . me* now that my anger is under control.
176 *o'erwrought* manipulated them so as to win them over. **177** *traveled* away on
travels.

As if no part about me were kin to 'em;
So touch 'em—though I durst, almost for good,   180
Venture my lands in heaven upon their blood.   *Exit.*

{ACT I   Scene 4}

Enter the discontented LORD ANTONIO, *whose wife the Duchess' young-*
est son ravished; he discovering the body of her dead to certain lords[,
PIERO,] *and* HIPPOLITO.

ANTONIO   Draw nearer, lords, and be sad witnesses
   Of a fair, comely building newly fallen,
   Being falsely undermined: violent rape
   Has played a glorious act. Behold, my lords,
   A sight that strikes man out of me.   5
PIERO   That virtuous lady!
ANTONIO   Precedent for wives!
HIPPOLITO   The blush of many women, whose chaste presence
   Would e'en call shame up to their cheeks,
   And make pale wanton sinners have good colors.
ANTONIO   Dead!
   Her honor first drunk poison, and her life,   10
   Being fellows in one house, did pledge her honor.
PIERO   O grief of many!
ANTONIO   I marked not this before—
   A prayer book the pillow to her cheek.
   This was her rich confection; and another
   Placed in her right hand, with a leaf tucked up,   15
   Pointing to these words:
   Melius virtute mori, quam per dedecus vivere.
   True and effectual it is indeed.

---

180 *touch* test.   180–81 *though ... blood* although I almost certainly wager my place
in heaven on their nobility.   181 *blood* The quarto reads "good," borrowed by mistake
from the end of the preceding line.
  ACT I, Scene 4.   SD *discovering* displaying.   5 *strikes ... me* makes me weep.
7–8 *The ... cheeks* By her chaste presence she would cause many women, less pure
than she, to blush with shame.   10 *drunk poison* by being raped.   11 *pledge* drink
as a faithful pledge to.   14 *confection* medicine.   15 *Placed* The quarto reads "Plastc'd."
17 *Melius ... vivere* "Better to die in virtue, than to live through dishonor."

HIPPOLITO   My lord, since you invite us to your sorrows,
    Let's truly taste 'em, that with equal comfort,   20
    As to ourselves, we may relieve your wrongs.
    We have grief too, that yet walks without tongue:
    Curae leves loquuntur, majores stupent.
ANTONIO   You deal with truth, my lord.
    Lend me but your attentions, and I'll cut   25
    Long grief into short words. Last reveling night,
    When torchlight made an artificial noon
    About the court, some courtiers in the masque,
    Putting on better faces than their own
    (Being full of fraud and flattery), amongst whom   30
    The Duchess' youngest son—that moth to honor—
    Filled up a room; and with long lust to eat
    Into my wearing, amongst all the ladies
    Singled out that dear form, who ever lived
    As cold in lust as she is now in death   35
    (Which that step-duchess' monster knew too well);
    And, therefore, in the height of all the revels,
    When music was heard loudest, courtiers busiest,
    And ladies great with laughter—O vicious minute,
    Unfit but for relation to be spoke of!—   40
    Then with a face more impudent than his vizard
    He harried her amidst a throng of panders
    That live upon damnation of both kinds,
    And fed the ravenous vulture of his lust.
    O death to think on't! She, her honor forced,   45
    Deemed it a nobler dowry for her name
    To die with poison than to live with shame.
HIPPOLITO   A wondrous lady, of rare fire compact;
    Sh' has made her name an empress by that act.
PIERO   My lord, what judgment follows the offender?   50
ANTONIO   Faith, none, my lord; it cools and is deferred.
PIERO   Delay the doom for rape?

---

23 Curae . . . stupent "Light cares speak out; greater ones remain silent." **31 moth to honor** because he feeds upon it. (The metaphor is continued in the next line.) **32 Filled . . . room** had a place (in the group). **40 but . . . relation** except for its essential part in my narration. **42 harried** raped. **43 of . . . kinds** both those who prostitute themselves and those who visit prostitutes; or, perhaps, those who sin and those who encourage others to become sinners. **46 dowry** offering to her husband. **52 doom** judgment.

ANTONIO   O, you must note who 'tis should die—
　　　The Duchess' son; she'll look to be a saver:
　　　"Judgment in this age is near kin to favor."   55
HIPPOLITO   Nay then, step forth thou bribeless officer.

　　　[*He draws his sword.*]

　　　I bind you all in steel to bind you surely;
　　　Here let your oaths meet, to be kept and paid,
　　　Which else will stick like rust, and shame the blade.
　　　Strengthen my vow, that if at the next sitting   60
　　　Judgment speak all in gold, and spare the blood
　　　Of such a serpent, e'en before their seats
　　　To let his soul out, which long since was found
　　　Guilty in heaven.
ALL   We swear it and will act it.
ANTONIO   Kind gentlemen, I thank you in mine ire.   65
HIPPOLITO   'Twere pity
　　　The ruins of so fair a monument
　　　Should not be dipped in the defacer's blood.
PIERO   Her funeral shall be wealthy, for her name
　　　Merits a tomb of pearl. My Lord Antonio,   70
　　　For this time wipe your lady from your eyes;
　　　No doubt our grief and yours may one day court it,
　　　When we are more familiar with revenge.
ANTONIO   That is my comfort, gentlemen; and I joy
　　　In this one happiness above the rest,   75
　　　Which will be called a miracle at last—
　　　That, being an old man, I'd a wife so chaste.   *Exeunt.*

ACT II   Scene 1

Enter CASTIZA, *the sister.*

CASTIZA   How hardly shall that maiden be beset
　　　Whose only fortunes are her constant thoughts,

---

54 she'll . . . saver She'll plan to save him. **61 speak . . . gold** is successfully bribed.
62–63 e'en . . . out Right in the court itself (we swear) to let his soul out of his body (by
murdering him). **72 court it** make itself known openly.
🐾 **ACT II, Scene 1.   1 hardly** with hardship. **2 constant thoughts** thoughts of
constancy (to virtue).

That has no other child's-part but her honor,
That keeps her low and empty in estate.
Maids and their honors are like poor beginners;   5
Were not sin rich, there would be fewer sinners.
Why had not virtue a revenue? Well,
I know the cause: 'twould have impoverished hell.

[*Enter* DONDOLO.]

How now, Dondolo?

DONDOLO   Madonna, there is one, as they say, a thing of flesh and   10
blood, a man I take him by his beard, that would very desirously
mouth to mouth with you.

CASTIZA   What's that?

DONDOLO   Show his teeth in your company.

CASTIZA   I understand thee not.   15

DONDOLO   Why, speak with you, madonna!

CASTIZA   Why, say so, madman, and cut off a great deal of dirty way;
had it not been better spoke in ordinary words, that one would
speak with me?

DONDOLO   Ha, ha, that's as ordinary as two shillings. I would strive a   20
little to show myself in my place; a gentleman-usher scorns to
use the phrase and fancy of a servingman.

CASTIZA   Yours be your own, sir; go, direct him hither.

[*Exit* DONDOLO.]

I hope some happy tidings from my brother,
That lately traveled, whom my soul affects.   25
Here he comes.

Enter VINDICE, *her brother, disguised.*

VINDICE   Lady, the best of wishes to your sex:
Fair skins and new gowns. [*Gives her a letter.*]

CASTIZA   O, they shall thank you, sir.
Whence this?

VINDICE   O, from a dear and worthy friend,

---

3 *child's-part* inheritance left to a child. 10-16 *Madonna . . . madonna* This foolish
gentleman-usher employs circumlocutions similar to those practiced by Osric in *Hamlet,*
(cf. V.2); and, like Osric, he says more than he knows. His metaphors for "speak"—"would
. . . mouth to mouth" and "show his teeth"—draw attention to the lustful and rapacious
activities that consume the energies and lives of the people caught up in the revenger's
tragedy. Similarly, his definition of man as "a thing of flesh and blood" suggests that
spiritual values, once an important focus of man's interest, have been abandoned: in the
world of this play, man considers himself only a creature of passions, of "flesh and blood."
17 *dirty way* tediousness (nasty traveling). 23 *own* The quarto reads "one."

    Mighty!
CASTIZA   From whom?
VINDICE   The Duke's son!
CASTIZA   Receive that!   30

    A box o' th'ear to her brother.

    I swore I'd put anger in my hand,
    And pass the virgin limits of my self
    To him that next appeared in that base office,
    To be his sin's attorney. Bear to him
    That figure of my hate upon thy cheek   35
    Whilst 'tis yet hot, and I'll reward thee for't;
    Tell him my honor shall have a rich name
    When several harlots shall share his with shame.
    Farewell; commend me to him in my hate!   *Exit.*
VINDICE   It is the sweetest box that e'er my nose came nigh,   40
    The finest drawn-work cuff that e'er was worn;
    I'll love this blow forever, and this cheek
    Shall still henceforward take the wall of this.
    O, I'm above my tongue: most constant sister,
    In this thou hast right honorable shown;   45
    Many are called by their honor that have none.
    Thou art approved forever in my thoughts.
    It is not in the power of words to taint thee.
    And yet for the salvation of my oath,
    As my resolve in that point, I will lay   50
    Hard siege unto my mother, though I know
    A siren's tongue could not bewitch her so.
    [*Enter* GRATIANA.]
    Mass, fitly here she comes!—Thanks, my disguise.—

---

35 *figure* sign. **40 *box*** a pun, since the word was often used to describe a container for fragrant ointment. There is, though, the possibility that Vindice, unable to put away entirely his role as a pander, is punning obscenely. **41 *drawn-work cuff*** a cuff ornamented with needlework, but here also the mark made by the cuff she has given him across the face. **43 *take the wall*** occupy the privileged place (on seventeenth-century streets the person who walked nearest the walls of the buildings was least subject to splashing and danger from passing carriages). **44 *I'm . . . tongue*** I cannot find words to express my feelings adequately. **45 *right honorable*** Here and in the next line, Vindice puns on the phrase used to address persons of noble rank. **49 *salvation*** fulfillment. **50 *As . . . point*** as I resolved to do (when I formulated the oath). **52 *siren*** mythical creature whose song was so beautiful that it lured sailors to steer their ships to destruction upon the shoreline rocks. **53 *Mass*** contracted from the exclamation "by the mass."

Madame, good afternoon.

GRATIANA   Y'are welcome, sir.

VINDICE   The next of Italy commends him to you,   55
Our mighty expectation, the Duke's son.

GRATIANA   I think myself much honored that he pleases
To rank me in his thoughts.

VINDICE   So may you, lady:
One that is like to be our sudden duke;
The crown gapes for him every tide, and then   60
Commander o'er us all. Do but think on him;
How blessed were they now that could pleasure him,
E'en with anything almost.

GRATIANA   Ay, save their honor.

VINDICE   Tut, one would let a little of that go, too,
And ne'er be seen in't: ne'er be seen in't, mark you.   65
I'd wink and let it go—

GRATIANA   Marry, but I would not.

VINDICE   Marry, but I would, I hope; I know you would too,
If you'd that blood now which you gave your daughter:
To her indeed 'tis, this wheel comes about;
That man that must be all this, perhaps ere morning   70
(For his white father does but mold away),
Has long desired your daughter.

GRATIANA   Desired?

VINDICE   Nay, but hear me:
He desires now that will command hereafter;
Therefore be wise. I speak as more a friend   75
To you than him. Madam, I know y'are poor,
And, 'lack the day, there are too many poor ladies already.
Why should you vex the number? 'tis despised.
Live wealthy, rightly understand the world;
And chide away that foolish country girl   80
Keeps company with your daughter, Chastity.

GRATIANA   O fie, fie! the riches of the world cannot hire a mother to
such a most unnatural task.

---

59 to . . . duke to become our duke at any moment.   60 tide occasion (cf. *Julius Caesar*, IV.3.218).   65 And . . . in't and its loss would never be noticed.   68 If . . . daughter if you had again your former youth, now mirrored in your daughter.   69 wheel the wheel of fortune (which is raising her to prosperity).   78 vex the number afflict the number of poor ladies (by adding to their ranks, and thus making it even more difficult for them to survive).

VINDICE   No, but a thousand angels can;
   Men have no power, angels must work you to't.   85
   The world descends into such base-born evils
   That forty angels can make fourscore devils.
   There will be fools still, I perceive, still fools.
   Would I be poor, dejected, scorned of greatness,
   Swept from the palace, and see other daughters   90
   Spring with the dew o' th' court, having mine own
   So much desired and loved—by the Duke's son?
   No, I would raise my state upon her breast,
   And call her eyes my tenants; I would count
   My yearly maintenance upon her cheeks,   95
   Take coach upon her lip; and all her parts
   Should keep men after men, and I would ride
   In pleasure upon pleasure.
   You took great pains for her, once when it was;
   Let her requite it now, though it be but some.   100
   You brought her forth; she may well bring you home.
GRATIANA   O heavens! this overcomes me!
VINDICE   *[Aside.]* Not, I hope, already?
GRATIANA   *[Aside.]* It is too strong for me; men know that know us,
   We are so weak their words can overthrow us.   105
   He touched me nearly, made my virtues bate,
   When his tongue struck upon my poor estate.
VINDICE   *[Aside.]* I e'en quake to proceed, my spirit turns edge.
   I fear me she's unmothered; yet I'll venture.
   "That woman is all male, whom none can enter."—   110
   What think you now, lady? Speak, are you wiser?
   What said advancement to you? Thus it said:
   The daughter's fall lifts up the mother's head.
   Did it not, madam? But I'll swear it does
   In many places; tut, this age fears no man.   115
   " 'Tis no shame to be bad, because 'tis common."

---

84 *thousand angels* a pun, since an "angel" was also a gold coin. **88** *still fools* The quarto reads "still foole." **91** *dew* refreshing essence (i.e. wealth). **93** *state* social standing. **95** *maintenance* livelihood. **100** *but some* only somewhat. **101** *bring . . . home* A pun on the figurative meaning, "make you wealthy," is implied. **104** *men . . . us* Men who truly understand us know that. **106** *He . . . nearly* He touched intimately ("nearly") on my problem; but the phrase is also an ironic echo of Vindice's earlier claim that he will "touch" his mother and sister (I.3.180). *bate* abate. **109** *she's unmothered* She has abandoned her responsibilities as a mother. **110** *That . . . enter* an obscene version of the maxim "Every woman has her price."

GRATIANA   Ay, that's the comfort on't.
VINDICE   The comfort on't!
   I keep the best for last; can these persuade you
   To forget heaven, and— [*Gives her money.*]
GRATIANA   Ay, these are they—
VINDICE   [*Aside.*] O!
GRATIANA   —that enchant our sex; these are the means   120
   That govern our affections. That woman
   Will not be troubled with the mother long,
   That sees the comfortable shine of you:
   I blush to think what for your sakes I'll do!
VINDICE   [*Aside.*] O suff'ring heaven, with thy invisible finger   125
   E'en at this instant turn the precious side
   Of both mine eyeballs inward, not to see myself.
GRATIANA   Look you, sir.
VINDICE   Holla.
GRATIANA   Let us thank your pains.
   [*She tips him.*]
VINDICE   O, you're a kind madam.
GRATIANA   I'll see how I can move.
VINDICE   [*Aside.*] Your words will sting.   130
GRATIANA   If she be still chaste, I'll ne'er call her mine.
VINDICE   [*Aside.*] Spoke truer than you meant it.
GRATIANA   Daughter Castiza!
   [*Re-enter* CASTIZA *at the other side of the stage.*]
CASTIZA   Madam.
VINDICE   O, she's yonder;
   Meet her.—
   [*Aside.*] Troops of celestial soldiers guard her heart.   135
   Yon dam has devils enough to take her part.
CASTIZA   Madam, what makes yon evil-officed man
   In presence of you?
GRATIANA   Why?
CASTIZA   He lately brought
   Immodest writing sent from the Duke's son
   To tempt me to dishonorable act.   140
GRATIANA   Dishonorable act!—Good honorable fool,

---

122 mother a pun, meaning both "the feelings of a mother" and "hysteria." **129 kind** a pun, meaning both "natural" and "generous." **madam** "bawd" as well as "woman." The quarto reads "Mad-man." **130 move** convince (her).

That wouldst be honest 'cause thou wouldst be so,
Producing no one reason but thy will.
And 't has a good report, prettily commended,
But pray, by whom?—mean people, ignorant people;   145
The better sort, I'm sure, cannot abide it.
And by what rule should we square out our lives,
But by our betters' actions? O, if thou knewst
What 'twere to lose it, thou would never keep it.
But there's a cold curse laid upon all maids,   150
Whilst others clip the sun, they clasp the shades.
Virginity is paradise locked up.
You cannot come by your selves without fee,
And 'twas decreed that man should keep the key!
Deny advancement, treasure, the Duke's son!   155

CASTIZA   I cry you mercy, lady, I mistook you.
Pray, did you see my mother? Which way went you?
Pray God I have not lost her.

VINDICE   [*Aside.*] Prettily put by.

GRATIANA   Are you as proud to me as coy to him?
Do you not know me now?

CASTIZA   Why, are you she?   160
The world's so changed one shape into another,
It is a wise child now that knows her mother.

VINDICE   [*Aside.*] Most right, i'faith.

GRATIANA   I owe your cheek my hand
For that presumption now, but I'll forget it.
Come, you shall leave those childish 'haviors,   165
And understand your time. Fortunes flow to you;
What, will you be a girl?
If all feared drowning that spy waves ashore,
Gold would grow rich, and all the merchants poor.

CASTIZA   It is a pretty saying of a wicked one;   170
But methinks now
It does not show so well out of your mouth;
Better in his.

VINDICE   [*Aside.*] Faith, bad enough in both,

---

142 *honest* chaste. **145** *mean* of low social standing. **147** *square out* model.
151 *Whilst . . . shades* While others choose to embrace life (and the "son" of the ruler),
they choose darkness (and death). **159** *coy* coldly distant. **167** *a girl* a child (instead
of a woman). **169** *Gold . . . rich* The interest rate on borrowed gold would go up.

Were I in earnest, as I'll seem no less.—
I wonder, lady, your own mother's words   175
Cannot be taken, nor stand in full force.
'Tis honesty you urge; what's honesty?
'Tis but heaven's beggar;
And what woman is so foolish to keep honesty,
And be not able to keep herself? No,   180
Times are grown wiser and will keep less charge.
A maid that has small portion now intends
To break up house, and live upon her friends.
How blessed are you! You have happiness alone;
Others must fall to thousands, you to one,   185
Sufficient in himself to make your forehead
Dazzle the world with jewels, and petitionary people
Start at your presence.

GRATIANA   O, if I were young,
I should be ravished.

CASTIZA   Ay, to lose your honor.

VINDICE   'Slid, how can you lose your honor   190
To deal with my lord's grace?
He'll add more honor to it by his title;
Your mother will tell you how.

GRATIANA   That I will.

VINDICE   O, think upon the pleasure of the palace!
Securèd ease and state; the stirring meats   195
Ready to move out of the dishes,
That e'en now quicken when they're eaten;
Banquets abroad by torchlight, musics, sports;
Bareheaded vassals, that had ne'er the fortune
To keep on their own hats, but let horns wear 'em;   200
Nine coaches waiting—hurry, hurry, hurry!

CASTIZA   Ay, to the devil.

VINDICE   [Aside.] Ay, to the devil.—[Aloud.] To th' Duke, by my faith.

---

181 keep ... charge both "concern themselves less with virtue" and "run up fewer expenses." **182 small portion** both "small inheritance" and "virginity." **183 break up house** sell what she has (with, of course, sexual implications). **186–88 Sufficient ... presence** because you will be mistress to the ruler of Italy. **189 ravished** Gratiana means "exquisitely delighted," but Vindice picks up the sexual implications of the word. **195 stirring** aphrodisiac in effect. **197 quicken** stimulate, but an obscene pun is also intended, since quicken also means "to become pregnant." **198 abroad** outside. **200 horns** the sign of the cuckold.

GRATIANA   Ay, to the Duke; daughter, you'd scorn to think o' th'
          devil and you were there once.   205
VINDICE   [*Aside.*] True, for most there are as proud as he for his heart,
          i'faith.—
          Who'd sit at home in a neglected room,
          Dealing her short-lived beauty to the pictures,
          That are as useless as old men, when those   210
          Poorer in face and fortune than herself
          Walk with a hundred acres on their backs,
          Fair meadows cut into green foreparts?—O,
          It was the greatest blessing ever happened to woman,
          When farmers' sons agreed and met again   215
          To wash their hands, and come up gentlemen.
          That commonwealth has flourished ever since:
          Lands that were mete by the rod—that labor's spared—
          Tailors ride down, and measure 'em by the yard.
          Fair trees, those comely foretops of the field,   220
          Are cut to maintain head-tires—much untold.
          All thrives but Chastity—she lies a-cold.
          Nay, shall I come nearer to you? Mark but this:
          why are there so few honest women, but because 'tis the poorer
          profession? That's accounted best that's best followed—least in   225
          trade, least in fashion—and that's not honesty, believe it. And do
          but note the low and dejected price of it:
          "Lose but a pearl, we search, and cannot brook it;
          But that once gone, who is so mad to look it?"
GRATIANA   Troth, he says true.
CASTIZA   False! I defy you both.   230
          I have endured you with an ear of fire;
          Your tongues have struck hot irons on my face.—
          Mother, come from that poisonous woman there!
GRATIANA   Where?
CASTIZA   Do you not see her? She's too inward then.

---

205 *and* if.   **206** *as proud . . . heart* as proud as the devil even at the cost of life ("for
his heart").   **209** *to . . . pictures* to the pictures (on the walls).   **212** *with . . . backs*
Lords often sold land to buy rich clothes for their mistresses.   **213** *foreparts* ornamental
coverings for women's breasts.   **216** *and . . . gentlemen* and become gentlemen (by
selling their lands and following the practices of the court world).   **218** *mete* measured.
The quarto reads "meat."   **221** *head-tires* costly headpieces worn by court ladies
(differentiated from the "hats" of common people, I.2.123).   **225–26** *least . . . fashion*
(What's accounted of) least worth in trade is also least in fashion.   **227** *low* The quarto
reads "love."   **228** *brook it* bear its loss.   **229** *that* the "pearl," i.e. virginity.

[*To* VINDICE.] Slave, perish in thy office!—You heavens, please   235
　　Henceforth to make the mother a disease,
　　Which first begins with me—yet I've outgone you.   *Exit.*
VINDICE　[*Aside.*] O angels, clap your wings upon the skies,
　　And give this virgin crystal plaudities!
GRATIANA　Peevish, coy, foolish!—but return this answer: 240
　　My lord shall be most welcome, when his pleasure
　　Conducts him this way. I will sway mine own.
　　Women with women can work best alone.   *Exit.*
VINDICE　Indeed, I'll tell him so.—
　　O, more uncivil, more unnatural,   245
　　Than those base-titled creatures that look downward!
　　Why does not heaven turn black, or with a frown
　　Undo the world? Why does not earth start up
　　And strike the sins that tread upon't? O,
　　Were't not for gold and women, there would be no damnation;   250
　　Hell would look like a lord's great kitchen without fire in't.
　　But 'twas decreed before the world began,
　　That they should be the hooks to catch at man.   *Exit.*

{ACT II　　Scene 2}

Enter LUSSURIOSO *with* HIPPOLITO, *Vindice's brother.*

LUSSURIOSO　I much applaud thy judgment;
　　Thou art well read in a fellow,
　　And 'tis the deepest art to study man.
　　I know this, which I never learnt in schools:
　　The world's divided into knaves and fools.   5
HIPPOLITO　[*Aside.*] Knave in your face, my lord—behind your back.
LUSSURIOSO　And I much thank thee that thou hast preferred
　　A fellow of discourse—well mingled;

236–37 *Henceforth . . . me*　Henceforth the mother shall be a disease (with a pun on mother as "hysteria"), and I am the first victim (because my mother, like a disease, has afflicted me). **237** *outgone* overcome (by standing fast against). **239** *crystal plaudities* clear-sounding praise. **246** *those . . . downward* animals, whose four-legged stance makes them "look downward." **251** *without . . . in't* deserted.
🦌 **ACT II, Scene 2. 6** *Knave . . . back*　Then you are right now looking into the face of a knave (for I am no fool), who is carrying out his activity unbeknown to you ("behind your back"). **8** *of discourse* skillful in conversation.

    And whose brain time hath seasoned.

HIPPOLITO   True, my lord.

    [*Aside.*] We shall find season once, I hope. O villain!   10

    To make such an unnatural slave of me; but—

    [*Enter* VINDICE, *disguised.*]

LUSSURIOSO   Mass, here he comes.

HIPPOLITO   [*Aside.*] And now shall I have free leave to depart.

LUSSURIOSO   Your absence, leave us.

HIPPOLITO   [*Aside.*] Are not my thoughts true?—

    [*Apart to* VINDICE.] I must remove, but brother, you may stay.   15

    Heart, we are both made bawds a new-found way!

LUSSURIOSO   Now we're an even number; a third man's dangerous,

    Especially her brother; say, be free,

    Have I a pleasure toward?

VINDICE   O my lord!

LUSSURIOSO   Ravish me in thine answer; art thou rare?   20

    Hast thou beguiled her of salvation,

    And rubbed hell o'er with honey? Is she a woman?

VINDICE   In all but in desire.

LUSSURIOSO   Then she's in nothing—

    I bate in courage now.

VINDICE   The words I brought

    Might well have made indifferent-honest naught.   25

    A right good woman in these days is changed

    Into white money with less labor far.

    Many a maid has turned to Mahomet

    With easier working; I durst undertake,

    Upon the pawn and forfeit of my life,   30

    With half those words to flat a Puritan's wife.

    But she is close and good—yet 'tis a doubt

    By this time: O, the mother, the mother!

LUSSURIOSO   I never thought their sex had been a wonder

    Until this minute. What fruit from the mother?   35

VINDICE   [*Aside.*] Now must I blister my soul: be forsworn,

    Or shame the woman that received me first.

---

10 *find season* find opportunity (to avenge ourselves on you). 19 *toward* imminent, about to come. 24 *bate in courage* decline in vigor (with sexual implications). 25 *made . . . naught* corrupted ordinary virtue. 26–27 *changed . . . money* coined into silver (i.e. made into a prostitute). 28 *turned to Mahomet* abandoned her religion (perhaps, again, with the implicit meaning "prostituted herself"). 31 *flat* lay flat (i.e. seduce). 37 *received me first* first welcomed me (when I was born).

I will be true, thou liv'st not to proclaim:
Spoke to a dying man, shame has no shame.—
My lord.

LUSSURIOSO   Who's that?

VINDICE   Here's none but I, my lord.   40

LUSSURIOSO   What would thy haste utter?

VINDICE   Comfort.

LUSSURIOSO   Welcome.

VINDICE   The maid being dull, having no mind to travel
Into unknown lands, what did me I straight,
But set spurs to the mother? Golden spurs
Will put her to a false gallop in a trice.   45

LUSSURIOSO   Is't possible that in this
The mother should be damned before the daughter?

VINDICE   O, that's good manners, my lord; the mother, for her age,
must go foremost, you know.

LUSSURIOSO   Thou'st spoke that true; but where comes in this comfort?   50

VINDICE   In a fine place, my lord. —The unnatural mother
Did with her tongue so hard beset her honor,
That the poor fool was struck to silent wonder.
Yet still the maid, like an unlighted taper,
Was cold and chaste, save that her mother's breath   55
Did blow fire on her cheeks. The girl departed,
But the good ancient madam, half mad, threw me
These promising words, which I took deeply note of:
"My lord shall be most welcome—"

LUSSURIOSO   Faith, I thank her.

VINDICE   —"When his pleasure conducts him this way—"   60

LUSSURIOSO   That shall be soon, i'faith.

VINDICE   —"I will sway mine own—"

LUSSURIOSO   She does the wiser; I commend her for't.

VINDICE   —"Women with women can work best alone."

LUSSURIOSO   By this light, and so they can, give 'em their due; men are
not comparable to 'em.   65

VINDICE   No, that's true; for you shall have one woman knit more in
a hour than any man can ravel again in seven and twenty year.

---

38 be true speak the truth. **thou** Lussurioso. **proclaim** talk about my mother's
corruption. **44 Golden spurs** the spur provided by gold coins. **45 false gallop** a
pun, technically meaning "canter" but here also implying "a headlong run into false
dealings." **56 Did . . . cheeks** angered her. **66 knit** successfully compact. **67 ravel**
unravel.

LUSSURIOSO   Now my desires are happy; I'll make 'em freemen now.—
    Thou art a precious fellow; faith, I love thee;
    Be wise and make it thy revenue: beg, leg!   70
    What office couldst thou be ambitious for?
VINDICE   Office, my lord? Marry, if I might have my wish, I would
    have one that was never begged yet.
LUSSURIOSO   Nay, then thou canst have none.
VINDICE   Yes, my lord, I could pick out another office yet; nay, and   75
    keep a horse and drab upon't.
LUSSURIOSO   Prithee, good bluntness, tell me.
VINDICE   Why, I would desire but this, my lord: to have all the fees
    behind the arras, and all the farthingales that fall plump about
    twelve o'clock at night upon the rushes.   80
LUSSURIOSO   Thou'rt a mad, apprehensive knave. Dost think to make
    any great purchase of that?
VINDICE   O, 'tis an unknown thing, my lord; I wonder 't has been
    missed so long.
LUSSURIOSO   Well, this night I'll visit her, and 'tis till then   85
    A year in my desires. Farewell.—Attend:
    Trust me with thy preferment. *Exit.*
VINDICE   My loved lord.—
    O, shall I kill him o' th' wrong side now? No!
    Sword, thou wast never a backbiter yet.
    I'll pierce him to his face; he shall die looking upon me.   90
    Thy veins are swelled with lust; this shall unfill 'em:
    Great men were gods, if beggars could not kill 'em.
    Forgive me, heaven, to call my mother wicked.
    O, lessen not my days upon the earth;
    I cannot honor her. By this, I fear me,   95
    Her tongue has turned my sister into use.
    I was a villain not to be forsworn
    To this our lecherous hope, the Duke's son;
    For lawyers, merchants, some divines, and all

---

68 *make 'em freemen* give them free rein.   **70 *beg, leg*** ask a favor of me (by bowing
formally).   **76 *drab*** prostitute.   **78–79 *fees . . . arras*** money paid servants for arrang-
ing secret meetings of lovers behind wall draperies.   **79 *farthingales*** petticoats.   ***plump***
in a heap.   **80 *rushes*** Castle floors were often strewn with rushes, as insulation from
the cold.   **81 *apprehensive*** keen-witted.   **82 *purchase*** profit.   **88 *o' . . . side*** by
stabbing him in the back.   **94–95 *O . . . her*** a reference to Exodus 20:12: "Honor thy
father and thy mother: that thy days may be long upon the land . . . ."   **96 *use*** (sexual)
use.

    Count beneficial perjury a sin small.   100
    It shall go hard yet, but I'll guard her honor,
    And keep the ports sure.

    Enter HIPPOLITO.

HIPPOLITO   Brother, how goes the world? I would know news of you,
    but I have news to tell you.
VINDICE   What, in the name of knavery?
HIPPOLITO   Knavery, faith: 105
    This vicious old Duke's worthily abused:
    The pen of his bastard writes him cuckold!
VINDICE   His bastard?
HIPPOLITO   Pray, believe it; he and the Duchess
    By night meet in their linen; they have been seen
    By stair-foot panders.
VINDICE   O sin foul and deep!   110
    Great faults are winked at when the Duke's asleep.

    [*Enter* SPURIO *with two* SERVANTS.]

    See, see, here comes the Spurio.
HIPPOLITO   Monstrous luxur!
VINDICE   Unbraced, two of his valiant bawds with him.
    O, there's a wicked whisper; hell is in his ear.
    Stay, let's observe his passage—   [*They withdraw.*]   115
SPURIO   O, but are you sure on't?
SERVANT   My lord, most sure on't, for 'twas spoke by one
    That is most inward with the Duke's son's lust:
    That he intends within this hour to steal
    Unto Hippolito's sister, whose chaste life   120
    The mother has corrupted for his use.
SPURIO   Sweet word, sweet occasion! Faith then, brother,
    I'll disinherit you in as short time
    As I was when I was begot in haste;
    I'll damn you at your pleasure: precious deed!   125
    After your lust, O, 'twill be fine to bleed.
    Come, let our passing out be soft and wary.
                    Exeunt [SPURIO *and* SERVANTS.]

---

101 *go hard,* 102 *keep the ports* double-entendres. 107 *pen* again, a double-entendre.
112 *luxur* lecher. 113 *Unbraced* in unfastened clothes. 127 *soft* quiet.

VINDICE   Mark! there, there, that step, now to the Duchess.
   This is their second meeting writes the Duke cuckold
   With new additions, his horns newly revived.   130
   Night! thou that lookst like funeral herald's fees
   Torn down betimes i' th' morning, thou hangst fitly
   To grace those sins that have no grace at all.
   Now 'tis full sea abed over the world:
   There's juggling of all sides; some that were maids   135
   E'en at sunset are now perhaps i' th' toll-book.
   This woman in immodest thin apparel
   Lets in her friend by water; here a dame,
   Cunning, nails leather hinges to a door
   To avoid proclamation. Now cuckolds are   140
   A-coining, apace, apace, apace, apace!
   And careful sisters spin that thread i' th' night
   That does maintain them and their bawds i' th' day!
HIPPOLITO   You flow well, brother.
VINDICE   Puh, I'm shallow yet,
   Too sparing and too modest. Shall I tell thee?   145
   If every trick were told that's dealt by night,
   There are few here that would not blush outright.
HIPPOLITO   I am of that belief, too.
VINDICE   Who's this comes?

   [*Enter* LUSSURIOSO.]

   The Duke's son up so late?—Brother, fall back

---

128 now . . . Duchess It is difficult to tell whether or not Hippolito and Vindice have
heard Spurio's conversation. They have, of course, resolved to "observe" him in his passage, but the observation has probably been only visual. At any rate, they seem to misun-
derstand Spurio's immediate intentions, perhaps as a result of their excitement about
uncovering his affair, for Spurio is not now going to the Duchess' chamber; he is more
probably, as his "unbraced" appearance suggests, coming from there, and his concern as
he leaves the stage is with taking Lussurioso in Castiza's bed. This misunderstanding
initiates the precipitous error in the next scene.   **131–32 funeral . . . morning** Here the
mourning curtains draped about palace walls at a Renaissance funeral are associated with
an accompanying expense—the fees paid to a herald for attending and displaying heraldic
signs of the dead man's noble lineage. The basis of association seems to be that both are
part of the over-all cost and ceremony of a funeral.   **132 betimes** early.   **134 full sea**
high tide (in sexual activities).   **136 i' th' toll-book** enlisted as prostitutes (the toll-book
was a register of animals sold in the marketplace).   **138 friend** lover.   ***by water***
through back entrances opening onto the canals of Venice or, since the setting of the play
is more English than Italian, the Thames River.   **142 sisters** prostitutes.   ***spin . . .***
thread a metaphor for "copulate" (cf. *Twelfth Night,* I.3.109–10).

And you shall learn some mischief. [HIPPOLITO *retires.*]
                                        —My good lord.   150
LUSSURIOSO   Piato! why, the man I wished for! Come,
    I do embrace this season for the fittest
    To taste of that young lady.
VINDICE   [*Aside.*] Heart and hell!
HIPPOLITO   [*Aside.*] Damned villain.
VINDICE   [*Aside.*] I ha' no way to cross it but to kill him.   155
LUSSURIOSO   Come, only thou and I.
VINDICE   My lord, my lord!
LUSSURIOSO   Why dost thou start us?
VINDICE   I'd almost forgot—the bastard!
LUSSURIOSO   What of him?
VINDICE   This night, this hour—this minute, now—
LUSSURIOSO   What, what?
VINDICE   Shadows the Duchess—   160
LUSSURIOSO   Horrible word!
VINDICE   And, like strong poison, eats
    Into the Duke your father's forehead.
LUSSURIOSO   O!
VINDICE   He makes horn royal.
LUSSURIOSO   Most ignoble slave!
VINDICE   This is the fruit of two beds.
LUSSURIOSO   I am mad.
VINDICE   That passage he trod warily—
LUSSURIOSO   He did!   165
VINDICE   —And hushed his villains every step he took.
LUSSURIOSO   His villains? I'll confound them.
VINDICE   Take 'em finely, finely now.
LUSSURIOSO   The Duchess' chamber door shall not control me.
                                Exeunt [LUSSURIOSO *and* VINDICE].
HIPPOLITO   Good, happy, swift! There's gunpowder i' th' court,   170
    Wildfire at midnight. In this heedless fury
    He may show violence to cross himself.
    I'll follow the event.   *Exit.*

---

150 *mischief* evil. **152** *this season* right now. **156** *only . . . I* just the two of
us. **157** *start* startle. **us** Lussurioso uses the formal "we" in speaking of himself.
160 *Shadows* enfolds, covers, but also "casts a shadow across her reputation." **164** *the
. . . beds* the result of begetting a bastard. **166** *his villains* his bawds. **168** *finely*
craftily. **172** *to . . . himself* which will work to interfere with his plans.

ᚎ{ACT II   Scene 3}ᚎ

Enter again [LUSSURIOSO *and* VINDICE, *upon the* DUKE *and the* DUCHESS *in a curtained bed*].

LUSSURIOSO   Where is that villain?

VINDICE   Softly, my lord, and you may take 'em twisted.

LUSSURIOSO   I care not how!

VINDICE   O, 'twill be glorious
To kill 'em doubled, when they're heaped. Be soft, my lord.

LUSSURIOSO   Away, my spleen is not so lazy; thus and thus   5
I'll shake their eyelids ope, and with my sword
Shut 'em again forever.
                              —Villain! strumpet!

[*Pulls back the bed curtains.*]

DUKE   You upper guard, defend us!

DUCHESS   Treason, treason!

DUKE   O, take me not in sleep; I have great sins!   10
I must have days—
Nay, months, dear son, with penitential heaves,
To lift 'em out, and not to die unclear.
O, thou wilt kill me both in heaven and here.

LUSSURIOSO   I am amazed to death.

DUKE   Nay, villain, traitor,
Worse than the foulest epithet, now I'll gripe thee   15
E'en with the nerves of wrath, and throw thy head
Amongst the lawyers!—Guard!

Enter NOBLES *and sons* [AMBITIOSO *and* SUPERVACUO, *followed by* HIPPOLITO].

FIRST NOBLE   How comes the quiet of your grace disturbed?

DUKE   This boy, that should be myself after me,
Would be my self before me, and in heat   20
Of that ambition bloodily rushed in,
Intending to depose me in my bed!

SECOND NOBLE   Duty and natural loyalty forfend!

ᚎ **ACT II, Scene 3.   2** *twisted*   in the sexual act.   **5** *spleen*   thought to be the source of anger.   **11** *heaves*   sighs.   **12** *unclear*   marked with sins.   **15** *gripe*   grip. **16** *nerves*   sinews.   **17** *lawyers!—Guard*   The quarto reads "lawyers gard."   **19** *should be myself*   should become duke.

DUCHESS   He called his father villain; and me strumpet,
    A word that I abhor to file my lips with.   25
AMBITIOSO   That was not so well done, brother.
LUSSURIOSO   [*Aside.*] I am abused—
    I know there's no excuse can do me good.
VINDICE   [*Apart to* HIPPOLITO.] 'Tis now good policy to be from sight.
    His vicious purpose to our sister's honor
    Is crossed, beyond our thought.
HIPPOLITO   [*Apart to* VINDICE.]   You little dreamt   30
    His father slept here.
VINDICE   [*Apart to* HIPPOLITO.] O, 'twas far beyond me.
    But since it fell so—without frightful word,
    Would he had killed him; 'twould have eased our swords.
                      [VINDICE *and* HIPPOLITO *exit stealthily.*]
DUKE   Be comforted, our Duchess, he shall die.   [*Exit the* DUCHESS.]
LUSSURIOSO   [*Aside.*] Where's this slave-pander now? out of mine eye,   35
    Guilty of this abuse.

Enter SPURIO *with his* VILLAINS.

SPURIO   Y'are villains, fablers!
    You have knaves' chins and harlots' tongues; you lie,
    And I will damn you with one meal a day.
FIRST SERVANT   O good my lord!
SPURIO   'Sblood, you shall never sup.
SECOND SERVANT   O, I beseech you, sir!
SPURIO   To let my sword   40
    Catch cold so long, and miss him.
FIRST SERVANT   Troth, my lord,
    'Twas his intent to meet there.
SPURIO   Heart, he's yonder.
    Ha, what news here? Is the day out o' th' socket,
    That it is noon at midnight? the court up?
    How comes the guard so saucy with his elbows?   45
LUSSURIOSO   [*Aside.*] The bastard here?
    Nay, then the truth of my intent shall out.—
    My lord and father, hear me.
DUKE   Bear him hence.
LUSSURIOSO   I can with loyalty excuse—

---

25 *file* defile. **SD** *Vindice . . . stealthily* The quarto stage direction reads "dissemble
a flight" beside lines 33–34. **36** *fablers* liars. **45** *How . . . elbows* The guard is
apparently holding Lussurioso by pinioning his arms behind his back.

DUKE   Excuse?—To prison with the villain!   50
    Death shall not long lag after him.

SPURIO   [*Aside.*] Good, i'faith; then 'tis not much amiss.

LUSSURIOSO   Brothers, my best release lies on your tongues;
    I pray, persuade for me.

AMBITIOSO   It is our duties; make yourself sure of us.   55

SUPERVACUO   We'll sweat in pleading.

LUSSURIOSO   And I may live to thank you.
                     Exeunt [LUSSURIOSO *and* GUARDS].

AMBITIOSO   [*Aside.*] No, thy death shall thank me better.

SPURIO   [*Aside.*] He's gone; I'll after him,
    And know his trespass, seem to bear a part
    In all his ills, but with a Puritan heart.   *Exit.*   60

AMBITIOSO   [*To* SUPERVACUO.] Now, brother, let our hate and love be
      woven
    So subtly together, that in speaking one word for his life,
    We may make three for his death.
    The craftiest pleader gets most gold for breath.

SUPERVACUO   [*To* AMBITIOSO.] Set on, I'll not be far behind you,
      brother.   65

DUKE   Is't possible a son should be disobedient as far as the sword?
    It is the highest; he can go no farther.

AMBITIOSO   My gracious lord, take pity—

DUKE   Pity, boys?

AMBITIOSO   Nay, we'd be loath to move your grace too much;
    We know the trespass is unpardonable,   70
    Black, wicked, and unnatural.

SUPERVACUO   In a son, O monstrous!

AMBITIOSO   Yet, my lord,
    A duke's soft hand strokes the rough head of law,
    And makes it lie smooth.

DUKE   But my hand shall ne'er do't.

AMBITIOSO   That as you please, my lord.

SUPERVACUO   We must needs confess,   75
    Some father would have entered into hate
    So deadly pointed, that before his eyes
    He would ha' seen the execution sound,
    Without corrupted favor.

AMBITIOSO   But, my lord,

---

60 Puritan one who only affects concern.   **78 sound** immediately carried out.
79 corrupted favor mercy.

Your grace may live the wonder of all times,   80
In pard'ning that offense which never yet
Had face to beg a pardon.
DUKE   Honey, how's this?
AMBITIOSO   Forgive him, good my lord; he's your own son,
And I must needs say 'twas the vildlier done.
SUPERVACUO   He's the next heir; yet this true reason gathers: 85
None can possess that dispossess their fathers.
Be merciful—
DUKE   [*Aside.*] Here's no stepmother's wit;
I'll try 'em both upon their love and hate.
AMBITIOSO   Be merciful, although—
DUKE   You have prevailed.
My wrath, like flaming wax, hath spent itself.   90
I know 'twas but some peevish moon in him;
Go, let him be released.
SUPERVACUO   [*To* AMBITIOSO.] 'Sfoot, how now, brother?
AMBITIOSO   Your grace doth please to speak beside your spleen;
I would it were so happy.
DUKE   Why, go, release him.
SUPERVACUO   O, my good lord, I know the fault's too weighty   95
And full of general loathing, too inhumane,
Rather by all men's voices worthy death.
DUKE   'Tis true too.
Here, then, receive this signet: doom shall pass.
Direct it to the judges; he shall die   100
Ere many days. Make haste.
AMBITIOSO   All speed that may be.
We could have wished his burden not so sore;
We knew your grace did but delay before.
                              Exeunt [AMBITIOSO *and* SUPERVACUO].
DUKE   Here's envy with a poor thin cover o'er't,
Like scarlet hid in lawn, easily spied through.   105
This their ambition by the mother's side.

---

84 *vildlier* more vilely. **85 *gathers*** knows. **87 *Here's . . . wit*** "Here there is no
genuine concern." Nominally, the Duchess' two sons, in asking mercy of the Duke, have
taken over the role that would have belonged to Lussurioso's mother if she were still alive
(cf. *Richard II,* V.3.88ff.); they are thus appearing to act as a "stepmother" to him in the
absence of his real mother. But the Duke realizes that their role as pleading stepmother
is fraudulent, for they have too much to gain by Lussurioso's death. **91 *peevish moon***
fit of madness (effected by the moon). **93 *beside . . . spleen*** putting aside your anger.
99 *signet* a small seal of authority, here probably a ring. **104 *envy*** malice. **105 *lawn***
a fine, light linen.

Is dangerous, and for safety must be purged.
I will prevent their envies; sure it was
But some mistaken fury in our son,
Which these aspiring boys would climb upon.   110
He shall be released suddenly.

Enter NOBLES.

FIRST NOBLE   Good morning to your grace.
DUKE   Welcome, my lords.
SECOND NOBLE   Our knees shall take away
    The office of our feet forever,
    Unless your grace bestow a father's eye   115
    Upon the clouded fortunes of your son,
    And in compassionate virtue grant him that
    Which makes e'en mean men happy—liberty.
DUKE   How seriously their loves and honors woo
    For that which I am about to pray them do: 120
    Which—rise, my lords; your knees sign his release.
    We freely pardon him.
FIRST NOBLE   We owe your grace much thanks, and he much duty.
                                    Exeunt [NOBLES].
DUKE   It well becomes that judge to nod at crimes,
    That does commit greater himself, and lives.   125
    I may forgive a disobedient error,
    That expect pardon for adultery
    And in my old days am a youth in lust.
    Many a beauty have I turned to poison
    In the denial, covetous of all.   130
    Age hot, is like a monster to be seen:
    My hairs are white, and yet my sins are green.   [*Exit.*]

ACT III   ❴Scene 1❵

Enter AMBITIOSO *and* SUPERVACUO.

SUPERVACUO   Brother, let my opinion sway you once;
    I speak it for the best, to have him die

---

111 *suddenly* immediately. **113–14** *Our . . . forever* We shall forever remain on
bended knees. **129–30** *have . . . denial* have I had poisoned because she denied my
advances.

Surest and soonest. If the signet come
Unto the judges' hands, why then his doom
Will be deferred till sittings and court days,   5
Juries and further. Faiths are bought and sold;
Oaths in these days are but the skin of gold.

AMBITIOSO   In troth, 'tis true too.

SUPERVACUO   Then let's set by the judges
And fall to the officers. 'Tis but mistaking
The duke our father's meaning, and where he named   10
"Ere many days"—'tis but forgetting that,
And have him die i' th' morning.

AMBITIOSO   Excellent!
Then am I heir—duke in a minute.

SUPERVACUO   [*Aside.*] Nay,
And he were once puffed out, here is a pin
Should quickly prick your bladder.

AMBITIOSO   Blessed occasion!   15
He being packed, we'll have some trick and wile
To wind our younger brother out of prison,
That lies in for the rape: the lady's dead,
And people's thoughts will soon be buried.

SUPERVACUO   We may with safety do't, and live and feed;   20
The Duchess' sons are too proud to bleed.

AMBITIOSO   We are, i'faith, to say true. —Come, let's not linger.
I'll to the officers; go you before,
And set an edge upon the executioner.

SUPERVACUO   Let me alone to grind him. *Exit.*

AMBITIOSO   Meet; farewell.—   25
I am next now; I rise just in that place
Where thou'rt cut off, upon thy neck, kind brother.
The falling of one heads lifts up another.   *Exit.*

⁅ACT III   Scene 2⁆

Enter, with the NOBLES, LUSSURIOSO *from prison.*

LUSSURIOSO   My lords, I am so much indebted to your loves

🦋 **ACT III, Scene 1.   7 *but . . . gold***   merely cover what has actually been secured with gold.   **8 *set by***   circumvent.   **14 *And . . . out***   "Once Lussurioso has been snuffed out" (though also implicit is the meaning "Once you are puffed out with self-importance").   ***pin***   his sword.   **15 *Blessed***   The quarto reads "Blast."   **25 *Meet***   (It is) fitting.

For this, O, this delivery—
FIRST NOBLE   But our duties,
My lord, unto the hopes that grow in you.
LUSSURIOSO   If e'er I live to be my self, I'll thank you.
O liberty, thou sweet and heavenly dame!   5
But hell for prison is too mild a name.   *Exeunt.*

⟨ACT III   Scene 3⟩

Enter AMBITIOSO *and* SUPERVACUO *with* OFFICERS.

AMBITIOSO   Officers, here's the Duke's signet, your firm warrant,
Brings the command of present death along with it
Unto our brother, the Duke's son; we are sorry
That we are so unnaturally employed
In such an unkind office, fitter far   5
For enemies than brothers.
SUPERVACUO   But, you know,
The Duke's command must be obeyed.
FIRST OFFICER   It must and shall, my lord—this morning then,
So suddenly?
AMBITIOSO   Ay, alas! poor, good soul,
He must breakfast betimes; the executioner   10
Stands ready to put forth his cowardly valor.
SECOND OFFICER   Already?
SUPERVACUO   Already, i'faith, O sir, destruction hies,
And that is least imprudent, soonest dies.
FIRST OFFICER   Troth, you say true. My lord, we take our leaves.   15
Our office shall be sound; we'll not delay
The third part of a minute.
AMBITIOSO   Therein you show
Yourselves good men and upright officers.
Pray, let him die as private as he may;
Do him that favor, for the gaping people   20
Will but trouble him at his prayers

🐾 ACT III, Scene 2.   **2** *but* merely.   **4** *my self* duke.
🐾 ACT III, Scene 3.   **10** *betimes* early.   **13** *hies* hastens.   **14** *that is* he who is.
16 *sound* infallibly carried out.

And make him curse and swear, and so die black.
Will you be so far kind?
FIRST OFFICER   It shall be done, my lord.
AMBITIOSO   Why, we do thank you; if we live to be,
You shall have a better office.
SECOND OFFICER   Your good lordship.   25
SUPERVACUO   Commend us to the scaffold in our tears.
FIRST OFFICER   We'll weep, and do your commendations.
                                              Exeunt [OFFICERS].
AMBITIOSO   Fine fools in office!
SUPERVACUO   Things fall out so fit!
AMBITIOSO   So happily! Come, brother, ere next clock
His head will be made serve a bigger block.   *Exeunt.*   30

⟨ACT III   Scene 4⟩

Enter in prison [*the Duchess'* YOUNGEST SON].

YOUNGEST SON   Keeper! [*Enter* KEEPER.]
KEEPER   My lord.
YOUNGEST SON   No news lately from our brothers?
Are they unmindful of us?
KEEPER   My lord, a messenger came newly in
And brought this from 'em. [*He gives him a letter.*]
YOUNGEST SON   Nothing but paper comforts?
I looked for my delivery before this,   5
Had they been worth their oaths. —Prithee, be from us.
                                              [*Exit* KEEPER.]
Now, what say you, forsooth? Speak out, I pray.
[*Reading the*] *letter:* "Brother, be of good cheer."—'Slud, it begins
like a whore, with good cheer. "Thou shalt not be long a prisoner."
—Not five and thirty year, like a bankrout, I think so. "We have   10
thought upon a device to get thee out by a trick."—By a trick?
Pox o' your trick and it be so long a-playing. "And so rest comforted, be merry and expect it suddenly."—Be merry! Hang
merry! Draw and quarter merry! I'll be mad. Is't not strange that

---

22 **black** tainted with fresh sin (therefore, eternally damned).   24 **to be** to be duke.
30 *a . . . block* a bigger block (than the one used to hold a hat).
❧ ACT III, Scene 4.   10 **bankrout** bankrupt.   12 **and it** if it.

a man should lie in a whole month for a woman? Well, we shall   15
see how sudden our brothers will be in their promise. I must expect
still a trick; I shall not be long a prisoner. [*He tears up the letter.*]

[*Re-enter* KEEPER.]

—How now, what news?

KEEPER   Bad news, my lord, I am discharged of you.

YOUNGEST SON   Slave, callst thou that bad news?—I thank you,
    brothers.   20

KEEPER   My lord, 'twill prove so: here come the officers
    Into whose hands I must commit you.

[*Enter* OFFICERS.]

YOUNGEST SON   Ha? Officers! what? why?

FIRST OFFICER   You must pardon us, my lord,
    Our office must be sound. Here is our warrant,
    The signet from the Duke: you must straight suffer.   25

YOUNGEST SON   Suffer? I'll suffer you to be gone; I'll suffer you
    To come no more. What would you have me suffer?

SECOND OFFICER   My lord, those words were better changed to prayers;
    The time's but brief with you: prepare to die.

YOUNGEST SON   Sure 'tis not so.

THIRD OFFICER   It is too true, my lord.   30

YOUNGEST SON   I tell you 'tis not, for the Duke my father
    Deferred me till next sitting, and I look
    E'en every minute threescore times an hour
    For a release, a trick wrought by my brothers.

FIRST OFFICER   A trick, my lord? If you expect such comfort,   35
    Your hope's as fruitless as a barren woman;
    Your brothers were the unhappy messengers
    That brought this powerful token for your death.

YOUNGEST SON   My brothers?—No, no!

SECOND OFFICER   'Tis most true, my lord.

YOUNGEST SON   My brothers to bring a warrant for my death?   40
    How strange this shows!

THIRD OFFICER   There's no delaying time.

YOUNGEST SON   Desire 'em hither, call 'em up!—my brothers?
    They shall deny it to your faces.

FIRST OFFICER   My lord,
    They're far enough by this, at least at court;

44 *by this*   by now.

And this most strict command they left behind 'em.   45
When grief swum in their eyes, they showed like brothers,
Brimful of heavy sorrow; but the Duke
Must have his pleasure.
YOUNGEST SON   His pleasure!
FIRST OFFICER   These were their last words, which my memory bears:
"Commend us to the scaffold in our tears."   50
YOUNGEST SON   Pox dry their tears! What should I do with tears?
I hate 'em worse than any citizen's son
Can hate salt water. Here came a letter now,
New-bleeding from their pens, scarce stinted yet—
Would I'd been torn in pieces when I tore it.   55

[*He picks up the pieces.*]

Look you officious whoresons, words of comfort:
"Not long a prisoner."
FIRST OFFICER   It says true in that, sir, for you must suffer presently.
YOUNGEST SON   A villainous Duns upon the letter, knavish exposition.
Look you then here, sir: "We'll get thee out by a trick," says he.   60
SECOND OFFICER   That may hold too, sir, for you know a trick is
commonly four cards, which was meant by us four officers.
YOUNGEST SON   Worse and worse dealing.
FIRST OFFICER   The hour beckons us;
The headman waits: lift up your eyes to heaven.
YOUNGEST SON   I thank you, faith; good, pretty-wholesome counsel!   65
I should look up to heaven, as you said,
Whilst he behind me cozens me of my head.
Ay, that's the trick.
THIRD OFFICER   You delay too long, my lord.
YOUNGEST SON   Stay, good Authority's bastards; since I must
Through brothers' perjury die, O let me venom   70
Their souls with curses.
FIRST OFFICER   Come, 'tis no time to curse.
YOUNGEST SON   Must I bleed then, without respect of sign? Well—
My fault was sweet sport, which the world approves;
I die for that which every woman loves.   *Exeunt.*

---

52 *citizen's son* one raised in the city (and, figuratively, a landlubber). **54 *stinted***
stopped. **59 *Duns . . . letter*** pun upon the literal meaning (the allusion is to Duns
Scotus, a medieval theologian, famous for his ability to make use of logic). **61 *trick***
hand of cards. **72 *I . . . sign*** Seventeenth-century surgeons often looked for favorable
astrological signs before they proceeded with bloodletting for curative purposes.

{ACT III　　Scene 5}

Enter VINDICE [*disguised*] *with* HIPPOLITO *his brother.*

VINDICE　O sweet, delectable, rare, happy, ravishing!

HIPPOLITO　Why, what's the matter, brother?

VINDICE　　　　　　　　　　　　　　O, 'tis able
To make a man spring up, and knock his forehead
Against yon silver ceiling.

HIPPOLITO　　　　　　　　Prithee, tell me;
Why may not I partake with you? You vowed once　　　　　　　5
To give me share to every tragic thought.

VINDICE　By th' mass, I think I did too;
Then I'll divide it to thee: the old duke,
Thinking my outward shape and inward heart
Are cut out of one piece (for he that prates his secrets,　　　10
His heart stands o' th' outside), hires me by price
To greet him with a lady
In some fit place veiled from the eyes o' th' court,
Some darkened, blushless angle, that is guilty
Of his forefathers' lusts and great folks' riots;　　　　　　15
To which I easily (to maintain my shape)
Consented, and did wish his impudent grace
To meet her here in this unsunnèd lodge,
Wherein 'tis night at noon; and here the rather
Because, unto the torturing of his soul,　　　　　　　　　20
The bastard and the Duchess have appointed
Their meeting too in this luxurious circle—
Which most afflicting sight will kill his eyes
Before we kill the rest of him.

HIPPOLITO　'Twill, i'faith! Most dreadfully digested!　　　25
I see not how you could have missed me, brother.

VINDICE　True, but the violence of my joy forgot it.

HIPPOLITO　Ay, but where's that lady now?

VINDICE　　　　　　　　　　　　O, at that word
I'm lost again: you cannot find me yet,

🦌 ACT III, Scene 5.　**4** *yon . . . ceiling*　both the moon and the roof of the Elizabethan playhouse, which was probably painted to represent the sky.　**14** *angle*　an out-of-the-way place.　**15** *riots*　revels of debauchery.　**22** *luxurious*　lecherous.　**25** *digested* thought out.　**26** *missed me*　excluded me from this plan.　**29** *lost*　lost (in my excitement).

I'm in a throng of happy apprehensions.   30
He's suited for a lady; I have took care
For a delicious lip, a sparkling eye—
You shall be witness, brother.
Be ready; stand with your hat off.   *Exit.*

HIPPOLITO   Troth, I wonder what lady it should be?   35
Yet 'tis no wonder, now I think again,
To have a lady stoop to a duke, that stoops unto his men.
'Tis common to be common through the world:
And there's more private, common shadowing vices
Than those who are known both by their names and prices.   40
'Tis part of my allegiance to stand bare
To the Duke's concubine; and here she comes.

Enter VINDICE, *with the skull of his love dressed up in tires.*

VINDICE   [*Addressing the skull.*] Madam, his grace will not be absent
      long.—
Secret? ne'er doubt us, madame. 'Twill be worth
Three velvet gowns to your ladyship. —Known?   45
Few ladies respect that! Disgrace?—a poor thin shell!
'Tis the best grace you have to do it well.
I'll save your hand that labor; I'll unmask you!

HIPPOLITO   Why brother, brother!

VINDICE   Art thou beguiled now? Tut, a lady can,   50
At such all hid, beguile a wiser man.
Have I not fitted the old surfeiter
With a quaint piece of beauty? Age and bare bone
Are e'er allied in action. Here's an eye,
Able to tempt a great man—to serve God;   55
A pretty hanging lip, that has forgot now to dissemble;
Methinks this mouth should make a swearer tremble,
A drunkard clasp his teeth and not undo 'em

---

31 suited for provided with a suitable.   **34 with . . . off** in deference to this "lady."
37 lady stoop submit herself sexually.   **that stoops** who degrades himself (by showing
such uncontrollable lust).   **38 to be common** to be a prostitute.   **39 private . . . vices**
dark and secret vices (principally sexual because of the implication of "private") that are
commonly pursued.   **SD tires** adorned headdresses.   **46 a . . . shell** The phrase refers
figuratively to disgrace—something the world considers of little substance. However, it
also anticipates the unveiling of the skull, which is only a "poor thin shell" of a lady, but
which—as the following line suggests—is enough to do its job of beguiling the Duke.
51 At . . . hid in such matters of deceitful appearance.   **53 quaint piece** cunningly
appropriate, but the phrase also has sexual implications.

To suffer wet damnation to run through 'em.
Here's a cheek keeps her color, let the wind go whistle.   60
Spout rain, we fear thee not; be hot or cold,
All's one with us. And is not he absurd,
Whose fortunes are upon their faces set,
That fear no other god but wind and wet?
HIPPOLITO   Brother, y' have spoke that right.   65
Is this the form that, living, shone so bright?
VINDICE   The very same.
And now methinks I could e'en chide myself
For doting on her beauty, though her death
Shall be revenged after no common action.—   70
Does the silkworm expend her yellow labors
For thee? for thee does she undo herself?
Are lordships sold to maintain ladyships
For the poor benefit of a bewitching minute?
Why does yon fellow falsify highways,   75
And put his life between the judge's lips,
To refine such a thing, keeps horse and men
To beat their valors for her?
Surely we're all mad people, and they
Whom we think are, are not. We mistake those: 80
'Tis we are mad in sense, they but in clothes.
HIPPOLITO   Faith, and in clothes too we; give us our due.
VINDICE   Does every proud and self-affecting dame
Camphire her face for this? and grieve her Maker
In sinful baths of milk, when many an infant starves,   85
For her superfluous outside—all for this?—
Who now bids twenty pounds a night, prepares

60 *keeps . . . color* that does not, like women's faces, have to be painted to retain its color. 62 *he* the Duke specifically and any lustful man in general. 63 *their* beautiful women's. 64 *That . . . wet* feared both because they disturb women's make-up and because, as natural elements, they work to wear down human life. 68 *could* The quarto reads "cold." 70 *after . . . action* in no common way. 71 *yellow labors* The silk-worm's cocoon, from which silk is made, is ordinarily yellow. 72 *undo* both "open herself up" (in the process of spinning silk out of her body) and "expend all her energies." 73 *lordships* the lands of lords, but also, the honor associated with lords. 75 *falsify* corrupt (by robbing travelers). 76 *put . . . lips* subject his life to the sentence of a judge. 77 *To refine* to clothe such a thing (as a "ladyship") in finery. 78 *To . . . valors* exhaust their energies (with a sexual pun implicit). 81 *we . . . clothes* We are mad in actuality; they but in superficial appearance. 84 *Camphire* Camphor was used as a perfume in soaps. 87 *bids . . . night* will pay twenty pounds a night (for your services as a prostitute)?

Music, perfumes, and sweetmeats?—All are hushed;
Thou mayst lie chaste now! It were fine, methinks,
To have thee seen at revels, forgetful feasts, 90
And unclean brothels; sure, 'twould fright the sinner
And make him a good coward, put a reveler
Out of his antic amble,
And cloy an epicure with empty dishes.
Here might a scornful and ambitious woman 95
Look through and through herself. —See, ladies, with false forms
You deceive men, but cannot deceive worms.—
—Now to my tragic business. Look you, brother,
I have not fashioned this only for show
And useless property; no, it shall bear a part 100
E'en in its own revenge. This very skull,
Whose mistress the Duke poisoned, with this drug,
The mortal curse of the earth, shall be revenged
In the like strain, and kiss his lips to death.
As much as the dumb thing can, he shall feel; 105
What fails in poison, we'll supply in steel.

HIPPOLITO Brother, I do applaud thy constant vengeance,
The quaintness of thy malice, above thought.

VINDICE [Putting poison on the mouth of the skull.] So, 'tis laid on: now
come and welcome, Duke;
I have her for thee.—I protest it, brother, 110
Methinks she makes almost as fair a fine
As some old gentlewoman in a periwig.—
[To the skull.] Hide thy face now for shame; thou hadst need have
a mask now.

[Puts mask on skull.]

'Tis vain when beauty flows, but when it fleets,
This would become graves better than the streets. 115

HIPPOLITO You have my voice in that. [Voices within.]
Hark, the Duke's come.

---

88 *All . . . hushed* No one now solicits you. 90 *forgetful feasts* feasts where one's
duties and obligations are forgotten. 93 *antic amble* grotesque dances. 97 *worms*
which eventually will feed on the body. 100 *property* stage effect. 101 *its* The
quarto prints "it," a relatively common Elizabethan form of the possessive case. 104 *In
. . . strain* in a similar manner. 105 *can* can accomplish (in the way of murder).
108 *quaintness* cunning inventiveness. 111 *fine* an end (of life). 112 *periwig* a
wig used to conceal grey hairs or baldness. 114 *'Tis . . . flows* It is vain to wear a mask
when beauty abounds. 115 *This* this masked skull.

VINDICE   Peace, let's observe what company he brings,
    And how he does absent 'em; for you know
    He'll wish all private. —Brother, fall you back a little
    With the bony lady.
HIPPOLITO   That I will. [*They retire.*]
VINDICE   So, so—   120
    Now nine years' vengeance crowd into a minute!

[*Enter the* DUKE *and* GENTLEMEN.]

DUKE   You shall have leave to leave us, with this charge,
    Upon your lives: if we be missed by th' Duchess
    Or any of the nobles, to give out
    We're privately rid forth.
VINDICE   [*Aside.*] O happiness!   125
DUKE   With some few honorable gentlemen, you may say;
    You may name those that are away from court.
FIRST GENTLEMAN   Your will and pleasure shall be done, my lord.
                              [*Exeunt* GENTLEMEN.]
VINDICE   [*Aside.*] "Privately rid forth!"
    He strives to make sure work on't. [*He advances.*]
                  —Your good grace.   130
DUKE   Piato, well done. Hast brought her? What lady is't?
VINDICE   Faith, my lord, a country lady, a little bashful at first, as
    most of them are, but after the first kiss, my lord, the worst is past
    with them. Your grace knows now what you have to do. Sh' has
    somewhat a grave look with her, but—   135
DUKE   I love that best. Conduct her.
VINDICE   [*Aside.*] Have at all!
DUKE   In gravest looks the greatest faults seem less;
    Give me that sin that's robed in holiness.
VINDICE   [*Apart.*] Back with the torch, brother; raise the perfumes.
DUKE   How sweet can a duke breathe! Age has no fault;   140
    Pleasure should meet in a perfumed mist.—
    Lady, sweetly encountered. I came from court,
    I must be bold with you. [*Kisses the skull.*]
                O, what's this! O!

---

125 O happiness Vindice's exclamation is prompted by the sexual innuendo implicit
in the Duke's statement that he has chosen to go riding, and also by the knowledge that
there is an important pun in the speech that escapes even the speaker: to be "rid forth"
also can mean to be "violently disposed of." **132 country** an obscene pun is implicit
(cf. *Hamlet,* III.2.123). **136 Have at all** Go to it! **140 How . . . breathe** The Duke
is here speaking of both his own scented breath and the "lady's" perfume he is breathing
in. **Age . . . fault** Age has no defects (that perfume will not cover over).

VINDICE   Royal villain! white devil!
DUKE   O!
VINDICE   Brother,
    Place the torch here, that his affrighted eyeballs   145
    May start into those hollows. Duke, dost know
    Yon dreadful vizard? View it well; 'tis the skull
    Of Gloriana, whom thou poisonedst last.
DUKE   O, 't has poisoned me.
VINDICE   Didst not know that till now?
DUKE   What are you two?   150
VINDICE   Villains, all three!—The very ragged bone
    Has been sufficiently revenged.
DUKE   O, Hippolito, call treason!
HIPPOLITO   Yes, my good lord: treason! treason! treason!

    Stamping on him.

DUKE   Then I'm betrayed.   155
VINDICE   Alas, poor lecher, in the hands of knaves,
    A slavish duke is baser than his slaves.
DUKE   My teeth are eaten out.
VINDICE   Hadst any left?
HIPPOLITO   I think but few.
VINDICE   Then those that did eat are eaten.
DUKE   O, my tongue!   160
VINDICE   Your tongue? 'twill teach you to kiss closer,
    Not like a slobbering Dutchman. You have eyes still:
    Look monster, what a lady hast thou made me
    My once-betrothed wife.
DUKE   Is it thou, villain?
    Nay, then—
VINDICE   'Tis I, 'tis Vindice, 'tis I!   165
HIPPOLITO   And let this comfort thee: our lord and father
    Fell sick upon the infection of thy frowns,
    And died in sadness; be that thy hope of life.
DUKE   O!
VINDICE   He had his tongue, yet grief made him die speechless.
    Puh, 'tis but early yet; now I'll begin   170

---

144 *white devil* both "hypocrite" and "white-haired devil." **161** *closer* more carefully. **162** *slobbering* The quarto reads "Flobbering." **Dutchman** traditionally
thought of by the English as a sot. **163** *made me* provided for me of. **167** *upon . . .
frowns* as a result of your disfavor. **170** *'tis . . . yet* You have heard only the beginning
of your ruin.

To stick thy soul with ulcers. I will make
Thy spirit grievous sore: it shall not rest,
But like some pestilent man toss in thy breast.
Mark me, Duke:
Thou'rt a renownèd, high, and mighty cuckold.

DUKE   O!   175

VINDICE   Thy bastard, thy bastard rides a-hunting in thy brow.

DUKE   Millions of deaths!

VINDICE   Nay, to afflict thee more,
Here in this lodge they meet for damnèd clips;
Those eyes shall see the incest of their lips.

DUKE   Is there a hell besides this, villains?

VINDICE   Villain?   180
Nay, heaven is just: scorns are the hires of scorns;
I ne'er knew yet adulterer without horns.

HIPPOLITO   Once ere they die 'tis quitted. [*Music within.*]

VINDICE   Hark, the music;
Their banquet is prepared, they're coming—

DUKE   Kill me not with that sight.   185

VINDICE   Thou shalt not lose that sight for all thy dukedom.

DUKE   Traitors, murderers!

VINDICE   What! Is not thy tongue eaten out yet?
Then we'll invent a silence.—Brother, stifle the torch.

DUKE   Treason, murder!   190

VINDICE   Nay, faith, we'll have you hushed.—Now with thy dagger
Nail down his tongue, and mine shall keep possession
About his heart; if he but gasp, he dies.
We dread not death to quittance injuries. Brother,
If he but wink, not brooking the foul object,   195
Let our two other hands tear up his lids
And make his eyes like comets shine through blood:
When the bad bleeds, then is the tragedy good.

HIPPOLITO   Whist, brother! Music's at our ear; they come.

Enter [SPURIO] *the bastard meeting the* DUCHESS [*and* ATTENDANTS].
[*They kiss.*]

---

173 pestilent diseased. **176 rides** again, with the sexual implications earlier present in
line 125. **in thy brow** where the Duke figuratively wears the horns of a cuckold.
178 clips sexual embraces. **183 'tis quitted** Adultery is repaid (by cuckolding).
194 quittance repay. **195 not . . . object** not watching the foul sight (of the adultery).
197 like . . . blood Comets were thought to be signs of impending disasters (cf. V.3.15),
so "blood" here is a reference to both the torn eyelids and destruction in general.

SPURIO Had not that kiss a taste of sin, 'twere sweet.   200
DUCHESS Why, there's no pleasure sweet, but it is sinful.
SPURIO True, such a bitter sweetness fate hath given,
    Best side to us is the worst side to heaven.
DUCHESS Push, come: 'tis the old duke, thy doubtful father,
    The thought of him rubs heaven in thy way.   205
    But I protest, by yonder waxen fire,
    Forget him, or I'll poison him.
SPURIO Madam, you urge a thought which ne'er had life:
    So deadly do I loathe him for my birth,
    That if he took me hasped within his bed,   210
    I would add murder to adultery,
    And with my sword give up his years to death.
DUCHESS Why, now thou'rt sociable; let's in and feast:—
    Loud'st music sound! Pleasure is banquet's guest.
          Exeunt [SPURIO *and* DUCHESS, *with* ATTENDANTS].
DUKE I cannot brook— [VINDICE *stabs him.*]
VINDICE   The brook is turned to blood.   215
HIPPOLITO Thanks to loud music.
VINDICE   'Twas our friend indeed.
    'Tis state in music for a duke to bleed.
    The dukedom wants a head, though yet unknown:
    As fast as they peep up, let's cut 'em down.   *Exeunt.*

⟨ACT III Scene 6⟩

Enter the Duchess' two sons, AMBITIOSO *and* SUPERVACUO.

AMBITIOSO Was not his execution rarely plotted?
    We are the Duke's sons now.
SUPERVACUO Ay, you may thank my policy for that.
AMBITIOSO Your policy? For what?
SUPERVACUO Why, was't not my invention, brother,   5
    To slip the judges? And in lesser compass

---

205 *rubs* stirs up a reminder of. **208** *a . . . life* an argument (in saying that I feel guilty about offending my father) that I never even dreamed of. **210** *hasped* locked in an embrace (with the Duchess). **217** *'Tis . . . bleed* 'Tis stately for a duke to die to the sound of music.
✤ ACT III, Scene 6. **6** *slip* bypass the authority of.

Did not I draw the model of his death,
Advising you to sudden officers,
And e'en extemporal execution?

AMBITIOSO   Heart, 'twas a thing I thought on too.   10

SUPERVACUO   You thought on't too. 'Sfoot, slander not your thoughts
With glorious untruth; I know 'twas from you.

AMBITIOSO   Sir, I say, 'twas in my head.

SUPERVACUO   Ay, like your brains then:
Ne'er to come out as long as you lived.

AMBITIOSO   You'd have the honor on't, forsooth, that your wit   15
Led him to the scaffold.

SUPERVACUO   Since it is my due,
I'll publish't, but I'll ha't in spite of you.

AMBITIOSO   Methinks y'are much too bold; you should a little
Remember us, brother, next to be honest duke.

SUPERVACUO   [*Aside.*] Ay, it shall be as easy for you to be duke   20
As to be honest, and that's never, i'faith.

AMBITIOSO   Well, cold he is by this time; and because
We're both ambitious, be it our amity,
And let the glory be shared equally.

SUPERVACUO   I am content to that.   25

AMBITIOSO   This night our younger brother shall out of prison;
I have a trick.

SUPERVACUO   A trick, prithee, what is't?

AMBITIOSO   We'll get him out by a wile.

SUPERVACUO   Prithee, what wile?

AMBITIOSO   No sir, you shall not know it till't be done;
For then you'd swear 'twere yours.   30

[*Enter an* OFFICER, *with a head, covered.*]

SUPERVACUO   How now? what's he?

AMBITIOSO   One of the officers.

SUPERVACUO   Desired news.

AMBITIOSO   How now, my friend?

OFFICER   My lords, under your pardon, I am allotted
To that desertless office, to present you
With the yet bleeding head.

SUPERVACUO   [*Aside.*] Ha, ha, excellent.   35

---

7 model plan. **8 sudden** swift-acting. **9 extemporal** immediate. **12 from you**
far from your thoughts. **13–14 Ay . . . lived** The quarto, confusing "Sup." with
"Spu.," assigns this speech to Spurio.

AMBITIOSO   [*Apart to* SUPERVACUO.] All's sure our own. Brother, canst
    weep, thinkst thou?
   'Twould grace our flattery much. Think of some dame;
   'Twill teach thee to dissemble.
SUPERVACUO   [*Apart to* AMBITIOSO.] I have thought;
   Now for yourself.
AMBITIOSO   Our sorrows are so fluent,
   Our eyes o'erflow our tongues; words spoke in tears   40
   Are like the murmurs of the waters: the sound
   Is loudly heard, but cannot be distinguished.
SUPERVACUO   How died he, pray?
OFFICER   O, full of rage and spleen.
SUPERVACUO   He died most valiantly, then; we're glad
   To hear it.
OFFICER   We could not woo him once to pray.   45
AMBITIOSO   He showed himself a gentleman in that,
   Give him his due.
OFFICER   But in the stead of prayer,
   He drew forth oaths.
SUPERVACUO   Then did he pray, dear heart,
   Although you understood him not.
OFFICER   My lords,
   E'en at his last, with pardon be it spoke,   50
   He cursed you both.
SUPERVACUO   He cursed us? 'las, good soul.
AMBITIOSO   It was not in our powers, but the Duke's pleasure.—
   [*Aside.*] Finely dissembled o' both sides, sweet fate;
   O happy opportunity!
   Enter LUSSURIOSO.

LUSSURIOSO   Now, my lords—
BOTH   O!
LUSSURIOSO   Why do you shun me, brothers?   55
   You may come nearer now;
   The savor of the prison has forsook me.
   I thank such kind lords as yourselves, I'm free.
AMBITIOSO   Alive!
SUPERVACUO   In health!
AMBITIOSO   Released?
   We were both e'en amazed with joy to see it.   60

45 *woo*   The quarto reads "woe."

LUSSURIOSO   I am much to thank you.

SUPERVACUO   Faith, we spared no tongue unto my lord the Duke.

AMBITIOSO   I know your delivery, brother,
    Had not been half so sudden but for us.

SUPERVACUO   O how we pleaded!

LUSSURIOSO   Most deserving brothers,   65
    In my best studies I will think of it.   *Exit* LUSSURIOSO.

AMBITIOSO   O death and vengeance!

SUPERVACUO   Hell and torments!

AMBITIOSO   Slave, cam'st thou to delude us?

OFFICER   Delude you, my lords?

SUPERVACUO   Ay, villain; where's this head now?

OFFICER   Why, here, my lord.
    Just after his delivery, you both came   70
    With warrant from the Duke to behead your brother.

AMBITIOSO   Ay, our brother, the Duke's son.

OFFICER   The Duke's son,
    My lord, had his release before you came.

AMBITIOSO   Whose head's that then?

OFFICER   His whom you left command for,
    Your own brother's.

AMBITIOSO   Our brother's? O furies!   75

SUPERVACUO   Plagues!

AMBITIOSO   Confusions!

SUPERVACUO   Darkness!

AMBITIOSO   Devils!

SUPERVACUO   Fell it out so accursedly?

AMBITIOSO   So damnedly?

SUPERVACUO   Villain, I'll brain thee with it.

OFFICER   O my good lord!

SUPERVACUO   The devil overtake thee! [*Exit* OFFICER.]

AMBITIOSO   O, fatal!

SUPERVACUO   O prodigious to our bloods.

AMBITIOSO   Did we dissemble?   80

SUPERVACUO   Did we make our tears women for thee?

AMBITIOSO   Laugh and rejoice for thee?

SUPERVACUO   Bring warrant for thy death?

AMBITIOSO   Mock off thy head?

---

80 prodigious monstrous.   **81 women** The quarto spelling, "woemen," makes the pun
in this word explicit.

SUPERVACUO   You had a trick, you had a wile, forsooth.

AMBITIOSO   A murrain meet 'em! There's none of these wiles that ever   85
    come to good. I see now, there is nothing sure in mortality, but
    mortality.
    Well, no more words; shalt be revenged, i'faith.
    Come, throw off clouds now, brother; think of vengeance
    And deeper-settled hate. —Sirrah, sit fast,   90
    We'll pull down all, but thou shalt down at last.   *Exeunt.*

ACT IV   Scene 1

Enter LUSSURIOSO *with* HIPPOLITO.

LUSSURIOSO   Hippolito.

HIPPOLITO   My lord, has your good lordship
    Aught to command me in?

LUSSURIOSO   I prithee, leave us.

HIPPOLITO   [*Aside.*] How's this? come and leave us?

LUSSURIOSO   Hippolito.

HIPPOLITO   Your honor, I stand ready for any duteous employment.

LUSSURIOSO   Heart, what mak'st thou here?

HIPPOLITO   [*Aside.*] A pretty lordly humor: 5
    He bids me to be present to depart; something
    Has stung his honor.

LUSSURIOSO   Be nearer, draw nearer.
    Y'are not so good, methinks; I'm angry with you.

HIPPOLITO   With me, my lord? I'm angry with myself for't.

LUSSURIOSO   You did prefer a goodly fellow to me;   10
    'Twas wittily elected, 'twas. I thought
    H' had been a villain, and he proves a knave—
    To me a knave.

HIPPOLITO   I chose him for the best, my lord.
    'Tis much my sorrow, if neglect in him

---

85 *murrain* plague.   **90** *Sirrah* a contemptuous term of address, directed at the absent
Lussurioso.
🔅 **ACT IV, Scene 1.**   **10** *prefer* recommend.   **11** *'Twas . . . elected* He was cun-
ningly chosen.

      Breed discontent in you.

LUSSURIOSO   Neglect! 'twas will.   15
      Judge of it:
      Firmly to tell of an incredible act,
      Not to be thought, less to be spoken of,
      'Twixt my stepmother and the bastard, O,
      Incestuous sweets between 'em.

HIPPOLITO   Fie, my lord!   20

LUSSURIOSO   I in kind loyalty to my father's forehead
      Made this a desperate arm, and in that fury
      Committed treason on the lawful bed,
      And with my sword e'en rased my father's bosom,
      For which I was within a stroke of death.   25

HIPPOLITO   Alack, I'm sorry.— *Enter* VINDICE.
               [*Aside.*] 'Sfoot, just upon the stroke
      Jars in my brother; 'twill be villainous music.

VINDICE   My honored lord.

LUSSURIOSO   Away! Prithee forsake us; hereafter we'll not know thee.

VINDICE   Not know me, my lord! Your lordship cannot choose.   30

LUSSURIOSO   Begone, I say; thou art a false knave.

VINDICE   Why, the easier to be known, my lord.

LUSSURIOSO   Push, I shall prove too bitter with a word,
      Make thee a perpetual prisoner,
      And lay this iron age upon thee.   35

VINDICE   [*Aside.*] Mum, for there's a doom would make a woman
      dumb.
      Missing the bastard, next him; the wind's come about;
      Now 'tis my brother's turn to stay, mine to go out.

                                    Exit VINDICE.

LUSSURIOSO   H' has greatly moved me.

HIPPOLITO   Much to blame, i'faith.

---

15 *will* malicious intent. **21 *forehead*** where he would wear the cuckold's horns.
24 *rased* cut. **SD *Enter Vindice*** This stage direction appears at line 29 in the quarto.
27 *Jars in* joins in, jarringly. **35 *iron age*** According to classical mythology, the Iron
Age was the last and worst age of the world, and it was to be characterized by the rule
of evil and cruelty. Here the reference to "iron age" is meant to suggest both a time of
detention in prison, under irons, and a time of evil and oppression for Vindice, whose
corruption is representative of "this our age" (I.3.24). **36 *would . . . dumb*** would
make even a woman keep quiet. **37 *Missing . . . about*** First I missed getting Spurio
killed (because he was not in bed with the Duchess), and afterwards Lussurioso escaped
my revenge (by being pardoned of the death penalty); now I have fallen out of favor
("the wind's come about").

LUSSURIOSO   But I'll recover, to his ruin. 'Twas told me lately,   40
    I know not whether falsely, that you'd a brother.
HIPPOLITO   Who, I? Yes, my good lord, I have a brother.
LUSSURIOSO   How chance the court ne'er saw him? Of what nature?
    How does he apply his hours?
HIPPOLITO   Faith, to curse fates,
    Who, as he thinks, ordained him to be poor: 45
    Keeps at home, full of want and discontent.
LUSSURIOSO   [Aside.] There's hope in him, for discontent and want
    Is the best clay to mold a villain of.
    —Hippolito, wish him repair to us.
    If there be aught in him to please our blood,   50
    For thy sake we'll advance him, and build fair
    His meanest fortunes; for it is in us
    To rear up towers from cottages.
HIPPOLITO   It is so, my lord. He will attend your honor;
    But he's a man in whom much melancholy dwells.   55
LUSSURIOSO   Why, the better; bring him to court.
HIPPOLITO   With willingness and speed.
    [Aside.] Whom he cast off e'en now, must now succeed.
    Brother, disguise must off;
    In thine own shape now I'll prefer thee to him: 60
    How strangely does himself work to undo him.   *Exit.*
LUSSURIOSO   This fellow will come fitly; he shall kill
    That other slave, that did abuse my spleen
    And made it swell to treason. I have put
    Much of my heart into him; he must die.   65
    He that knows great men's secrets and proves slight,
    That man ne'er lives to see his beard turn white.
    Ay, he shall speed him. I'll employ thee, brother:
    Slaves are but nails to drive out one another.
    He being of black condition, suitable   70
    To want and ill content, hope of preferment
    Will grind him to an edge.
    The NOBLES *enter.*
FIRST NOBLE   Good days unto your honor.

64–65 *I . . . him* I have confided much in him.   **66 slight** untrustworthy.   **70 black
condition** melancholy (supposed to result from an excess of black bile in the system).
SD *The . . . enter* In the quarto, this entrance is printed as if it were part of Lussurioso's
speech.

LUSSURIOSO   My kind lords, I do return the like.
SECOND NOBLE   Saw you my lord the Duke?
LUSSURIOSO   My lord and father—   75
   Is he from court?
FIRST NOBLE   He's sure from court,
   But where, which way, his pleasure took we know not,
   Nor can we hear on't. [*Enter the Duke's* GENTLEMEN.]
LUSSURIOSO   Here come those should tell.
   Saw you my lord and father?
THIRD GENTLEMAN   Not since two hours before noon, my lord.   80
   And then he privately rid forth.
LUSSURIOSO   O, he's rode forth.
FIRST NOBLE   'Twas wondrous privately.
SECOND NOBLE   There's none i' th' court had any knowledge on't.
LUSSURIOSO   His grace is old and sudden; 'tis no treason
   To say, the Duke my father has a humor,   85
   Or such a toy about him; what in us
   Would appear light, in him seems virtuous.
THIRD GENTLEMAN   'Tis oracle, my lord.   *Exeunt.*

⟨ACT IV   Scene 2⟩

Enter VINDICE *and* HIPPOLITO, VINDICE *out of his disguise.*

HIPPOLITO   So, so, all's as it should be; y'are yourself.
VINDICE   How that great-villain puts me to my shifts.
HIPPOLITO   He that did lately in disguise reject thee
   Shall, now thou art thyself, as much respect thee.
VINDICE   'Twill be the quainter fallacy. But brother,   5
   'Sfoot, what use will he put me to now, thinkst thou?
HIPPOLITO   Nay, you must pardon me in that, I know not.
   H' has some employment for you, but what 'tis
   He and his secretary, the Devil, knows best.
VINDICE   Well, I must suit my tongue to his desires,   10

---

84 *sudden* whimsical. 85 *humor* whim. 86 *toy* trifling fancy. 87 *light* frivolous.
🦌ACT IV, Scene 2.   2 *shifts* both "changes of clothes" and "sly tricks."   5 *quainter fallacy* cunning deception.   9 *secretary* confidant.

What color soe'er they be, hoping at last
To pile up all my wishes on his breast.
HIPPOLITO   Faith, brother, he himself shows the way.
VINDICE   Now the Duke is dead, the realm is clad in clay.
His death being not yet known, under his name   15
The people still are governed. Well, thou his son
Art not long-lived; thou shalt not joy his death.
To kill thee, then, I should most honor thee:
For 'twould stand firm in every man's belief,
Thou'st a kind child, and only died'st with grief.   20
HIPPOLITO   You fetch about well, but let's talk in present.
How will you appear in fashion different,
As well as in apparel, to make all things possible?
If you be but once tripped, we fall forever.
It is not the least policy to be doubtful;   25
You must change tongue—familiar was your first.
VINDICE   Why, I'll bear me in some strain of melancholy,
And string myself with heavy-sounding wire,
Like such an instrument that speaks merry things sadly.
HIPPOLITO   Then 'tis as I meant;   30
I gave you out at first in discontent.
VINDICE   I'll turn myself, and then— [Enter LUSSURIOSO.]
HIPPOLITO   'Sfoot, here he comes;
HIPPOLITO   Hast thought upon't?
VINDICE   Salute him, fear not me.
LUSSURIOSO   Hippolito.
HIPPOLITO   Your lordship.
LUSSURIOSO   What's he yonder?
HIPPOLITO   'Tis Vindice, my discontented brother,   35
Whom, 'cording to your will, I 'ave brought to court.
LUSSURIOSO   Is that thy brother? Beshrew me, a good presence.
I wonder h' has been from the court so long.—
Come nearer.
HIPPOLITO   Brother, Lord Lussurioso, the Duke's son.   40

---

12 *To . . . breast* and so press him to death with the weight of my hatred.   14 *clad in clay* either "subject to decay, like human flesh" or "buried."   17 *joy* enjoy (by becoming duke).   21 *You . . . present* You theorize well, but let's talk about our present plans.   22 *fashion* manner.   25 *It . . . doubtful* It is good policy to be cautious.   26 *familiar* not self-restrained.   28 *heavy-sounding* sorrowful sounding.   31 *I . . . discontent* I described you as melancholy.   32 *turn* change.

LUSSURIOSO   Be more near to us. Welcome; nearer yet.

[VINDICE] *snatches off his hat and makes legs to him.*

VINDICE   How don you? God you good den.

LUSSURIOSO   We thank thee.
How strangely such a coarse, homely salute
Shows in the palace, where we greet in fire:
Nimble and desperate tongues, should we name   45
God in a salutation, 'twould ne'er be stood on't—heaven!
Tell me, what has made thee so melancholy?

VINDICE   Why, going to law.

LUSSURIOSO   Why, will that make a man melancholy?

VINDICE   Yes, to look long upon ink and black buckram. I went me to   50
law in *Anno quadragesimo secundo,* and I waded out of it in *Anno
sextagesimo tertio.*

LUSSURIOSO   What, three and twenty years in law?

VINDICE   I have known those that have been five and fifty, and all
about pullen and pigs.   55

LUSSURIOSO   May it be possible such men should breathe,
To vex the terms so much?

VINDICE   'Tis food to some, my lord.
There are old men at the present, that are so poisoned with the
affectation of law words (having had many suits canvassed), that
their common talk is nothing but Barbary Latin. They cannot so   60
much as pray but in law, that their sins may be removed with a
writ of error, and their souls fetched up to heaven with a sasarara.

LUSSURIOSO   It seems most strange to me;
Yet all the world meets round in the same bent:
Where the heart's set, there goes the tongue's consent.   65
How dost apply thy studies, fellow?

VINDICE   Study? Why, to think how a great rich man lies a-dying,
and a poor cobbler tolls the bell for him. How he cannot depart

---

42 How . . . den   Vindice, pretending to be a rustic, says, essentially, "How do you do?
God give you good evening."   **43 coarse, homely**   The quarto reads "course-homely."
44 in fire   with ardor.   **46 stood on't**   accepted as believable.   **50 black buckram**   The
bags carried by lawyers were made from black buckram.   **51 Anno . . . secundo**   the
forty-second year (of the sovereign's reign).   **51–52 Anno . . . tertio**   the sixty-third year.
55 pullen   poultry.   **57 terms**   court sessions.   **59 canvassed**   debated.   **60 Barbary**
barbarous.   **62 writ of error**   a writ arguing for the reversal of a judgment, on the
grounds of error.   **sasarara**   a writ of certiorari, issued by a superior court at the
complaint of one who claims he has not received justice in a lower court.   **64 bent**   way.
65 Where . . . consent   What the heart desires, the tongue speaks for.   **68 cobbler**   any
poor workman, who might also serve as the town bell-ringer.

the world and see the great chest stand before him; when he lies
speechless, how he will point you readily to all the boxes; and   70
when he is past all memory, as the gossips guess, then thinks he of
forfeitures and obligations. Nay, when to all men's hearings he
whurls and rottles in the throat, he's busy threat'ning his poor
tenants. And this would last me now some seven years' thinking
or thereabouts. But, I have a conceit a-coming in picture upon   75
this: I draw it myself, which i'faith, la, I'll present to your honor.
You shall not choose but like it, for your lordship shall give me
nothing for it.

LUSSURIOSO Nay, you mistake me then,
For I am published bountiful enough.   80
Let's taste of your conceit.

VINDICE In picture, my lord?

LUSSURIOSO Ay, in picture.

VINDICE Marry, this it is—*A usuring father, to be boiling in hell, and his
son and heir with a whore dancing over him.*   85

HIPPOLITO [*Aside.*] H' has pared him to the quick.

LUSSURIOSO The conceit's pretty, i'faith, but take't upon my life,
'twill ne'er be liked.

VINDICE No? why I'm sure the whore will be liked well enough.

HIPPOLITO [*Aside.*] Ay, if she were out o' th' picture, he'd like her then   90
himself.

VINDICE And as for the son and heir, he shall be an eyesore to no
young revelers, for he shall be drawn in cloth of gold breeches.

LUSSURIOSO And thou hast put my meaning in the pockets,
And canst not draw that out? My thought was this: 95
To see the picture of a usuring father
Boiling in hell, our rich men would ne'er like it.

---

69 great chest The great chest is where his wealth is kept, and the dying miser wants it
closed because he desperately wants to hold onto his treasure, even though it has become
useless to him. There may also be here an oblique reference to the chest as a coffin.
70 boxes money-boxes. **72 forfeitures and obligations** These two legal terms are used
principally for their ironic value here. Instead of thinking about moral and spiritual
concerns, about his sins (moral "forfeitures") and his spiritual "obligations" to heaven, the
rich man concerns himself with new sources of revenue from his tenants—forfeitures (loss
of an estate or goods through breach of contract) and obligations (legal bonds compelling
payment of money). **73 whurls** rumbles. **75 conceit** witty artistic creation. **in
picture** in the form of a painted picture. **80 published** known to be. **93 gold
breeches** undoubtedly a description of the breeches Lussurioso wears in this scene.
94–95 And . . . out The gist of what Lussurioso says here is: "You have understood my
words but not their meaning"; but in the process the young duke is punning on Vindice's
earlier reference, "in picture": his meaning, like a miniature portrait, has been put "in the
pockets," not "drawn" out.

VINDICE   O true, I cry you heartily mercy. I know the reason, for some
    of 'em had rather be damned indeed than damned in colors.
LUSSURIOSO   [*Aside.*] A parlous melancholy! H' has wit enough   100
    To murder any man, and I'll give him means.—
    I think thou art ill-monied?
VINDICE   Money! ho, ho.
    'Tas been my want so long, 'tis now my scoff;
    I've e'en forgot what color silver's of.
LUSSURIOSO   [*Aside.*] It hits as I could wish.
VINDICE   I get good clothes   105
    Of those that dread my humor, and for table-room
    I feed on those that cannot be rid of me.
LUSSURIOSO   Somewhat to set thee up withal. [*He gives him gold.*]
VINDICE   O, mine eyes!
LUSSURIOSO   How now, man?
VINDICE   Almost struck blind:
    This bright unusual shine to me seems proud;   110
    I dare not look till the sun be in a cloud.
LUSSURIOSO   [*Aside.*] I think I shall affect his melancholy.—
    How are they now?
VINDICE   The better for your asking.
LUSSURIOSO   You shall be better yet if you but fasten
    Truly on my intent. Now y'are both present,   115
    I will unbrace such a close, private villain
    Unto your vengeful swords, the like ne'er heard of,
    Who hath disgraced you much and injured us.
HIPPOLITO   Disgraced us, my lord?
LUSSURIOSO   Ay, Hippolito.
    I kept it here till now, that both your angers   120
    Might meet him at once.
VINDICE   I'm covetous
    To know the villain.
LUSSURIOSO   [*To* HIPPOLITO.] You know him—that slave pander
    Piato, whom we threatened last
    With irons in perpetual 'prisonment.
VINDICE   [*Aside.*] All this is I.

---

99 *in colors* in a painting.   **100 *parlous*** keen-edged.   **112 *affect*** feel affection for.
116 *close* secret.   **120 *here*** closed within his breast.

HIPPOLITO   Is't he, my lord?
LUSSURIOSO   I'll tell you;   125
　　You first preferred him to me.
VINDICE   Did you, brother?
HIPPOLITO   I did indeed.
LUSSURIOSO   And the ingrateful villain,
　　To quit that kindness, strongly wrought with me,
　　Being as you see a likely man for pleasure,
　　With jewels to corrupt your virgin sister.   130
HIPPOLITO   O villain!
VINDICE   He shall surely die that did it.
LUSSURIOSO   I, far from thinking any virgin harm,
　　Especially knowing her to be as chaste
　　As that part which scarce suffers to be touched,
　　Th'eye, would not endure him.
VINDICE   Would you not, my lord?   135
　　'Twas wondrous honorably done.
LUSSURIOSO   But with some fine frowns kept him out.
VINDICE   Out, slave!
LUSSURIOSO   What did me he but, in revenge of that,
　　Went of his own free will to make infirm
　　Your sister's honor, whom I honor with my soul   140
　　For chaste respect; and not prevailing there
　　(As 'twas but desperate folly to attempt it),
　　In mere spleen, by the way, waylays your mother,
　　Whose honor being a coward, as it seems,
　　Yielded by little force.
VINDICE   Coward indeed.   145
LUSSURIOSO   He, proud of their advantage (as he thought),
　　Brought me these news for happy; but I, heaven
　　Forgive me for't—
VINDICE   What did your honor?
LUSSURIOSO   —In rage pushed him from me,
　　Trampled beneath his throat, spurned him, and bruised.   150
　　Indeed I was too cruel, to say troth.

---

128 *quit* requite. *wrought with* worked to convince me. 135 *eye* an obscene pun. 141 *For . . . respect* out of respect to her chasteness. 146 *their advantage* the advantage they seemed to have over Castiza (by being doubly allied against her). 147 *for happy* as indicative of good fortune (good "hap").

HIPPOLITO   Most nobly managed!

VINDICE   [*Aside.*] Has not heaven an ear? Is all the lightning wasted?

LUSSURIOSO   If I now were so impatient in a modest cause,
    What should you be?

VINDICE   Full mad; he shall not live   155
    To see the moon change.

LUSSURIOSO   He's about the palace.
    Hippolito, entice him this way, that thy brother
    May take full mark of him.

HIPPOLITO   Heart! that shall not need, my lord;
    I can direct him so far.

LUSSURIOSO   Yet for my hate's sake,   160
    Go, wind him this way; I'll see him bleed myself.

HIPPOLITO   [*Apart to* VINDICE.] What now, brother?

VINDICE   [*Apart to* HIPPOLITO.] Nay, e'en what you will; y'are put to it,
    brother!

HIPPOLITO   [*Aside.*] An impossible task, I'll swear,
    To bring him hither that's already here.   *Exit* HIPPOLITO.   165

LUSSURIOSO   Thy name? I have forgot it.

VINDICE   Vindice, my lord.

LUSSURIOSO   'Tis a good name that.

VINDICE   Ay, a revenger.

LUSSURIOSO   It does betoken courage; thou shouldst be valiant,
    And kill thine enemies.

VINDICE   That's my hope, my lord.

LUSSURIOSO   This slave is one.

VINDICE   I'll doom him.

LUSSURIOSO   Then I'll praise thee!   170
    Do thou observe me best, and I'll best raise thee.

    Enter HIPPOLITO.

VINDICE   Indeed, I thank you.

LUSSURIOSO   Now, Hippolito, where's the slave pander?

HIPPOLITO   Your good lordship
    Would have a loathsome sight of him, much offensive.   175
    He's not in case now to be seen, my lord;
    The worst of all the deadly sins is in him—
    That beggarly damnation, drunkenness.

---

161 wind lure.   **171 observe** satisfy my wishes.   **176 in case** in any kind of position.

LUSSURIOSO   Then he's a double slave.
VINDICE   [*Aside.*] 'Twas well conveyed,
    Upon a sudden wit.
LUSSURIOSO   What, are you both   180
    Firmly resolved? I'll see him dead myself.
VINDICE   Or else, let not us live.
LUSSURIOSO   You may direct
    Your brother to take note of him.
HIPPOLITO   I shall.
LUSSURIOSO   Rise but in this, and you shall never fall.
VINDICE   Your honor's vassals.
LUSSURIOSO   [*Aside.*] This was wisely carried.   185
    Deep policy in us makes fools of such:
    Then must a slave die when he knows too much.
                                        Exit LUSSURIOSO.
VINDICE   O, thou almighty patience! 'Tis my wonder
    That such a fellow, impudent and wicked,
    Should not be cloven as he stood,   190
    Or with a secret wind burst open!
    Is there no thunder left, or is't kept up
    In stock for heavier vengeance? [*Thunder.*] There it goes!
HIPPOLITO   Brother, we lose ourselves.
VINDICE   But I have found it.
    'Twill hold, 'tis sure; thanks, thanks to any spirit   195
    That mingled it 'mongst my inventions.
HIPPOLITO   What is't?
VINDICE   'Tis sound, and good; thou shalt partake it.
    I'm hired to kill myself.
HIPPOLITO   True.
VINDICE   Prithee, mark it.
    And the old duke being dead, but not conveyed;

---

179 conveyed carried out. **SD Thunder** The thunder is a dramatic testimony that
there is an ordering force behind the apparent chaos of the violent world presented in this
play. A modern equivalent is the sound of thunder at the end of T. S. Eliot's *The Wasteland*.
194 we . . . ourselves "We have lost our sense of proportion (by promising to show the
Duke your dead body)." But because the statement comes immediately after the thunder,
another meaning, unknown to the speaker, is implied as well: the two brothers have lost
themselves because their single-minded concern for revenge has made them ignore almost
all the values represented by the voice behind the thunder. **it** the way to success in
this venture. **196 inventions** ideas. **199 conveyed** disposed of.

For he's already missed too, and you know   200
Murder will peep out of the closest husk—

HIPPOLITO   Most true.

VINDICE   What say you then to this device?
If we dressed up the body of the Duke—

HIPPOLITO   In that disguise of yours.

VINDICE   Y'are quick, y' have reached it.

HIPPOLITO   I like it wonderously.   205

VINDICE   And being in drink, as you have published him,
To lean him on his elbow, as if sleep had caught him,
Which claims most interest in such sluggy men.

HIPPOLITO   Good yet, but here's a doubt:
We—thought by th' Duke's son to kill that pander—   210
Shall, when he is known, be thought to kill the Duke.

VINDICE   Neither—O thanks—it is substantial:
For that disguise being on him which I wore, it will be thought I,
which he calls the pander, did kill the Duke and fled away in his
apparel, leaving him so disguised to avoid swift pursuit.   215

HIPPOLITO   Firmer and firmer.

VINDICE   Nay, doubt not 'tis in grain;
I warrant it hold color.

HIPPOLITO   Let's about it.

VINDICE   But by the way too, now I think on't, brother,
Let's conjure that base devil out of our mother.   *Exeunt.*

⦃ACT IV   Scene 3⦄

Enter the DUCHESS *arm in arm with* [SPURIO] *the bastard; he seemeth
lasciviously to her. After them, enter* SUPERVACUO, *running with a
rapier; his brother* [AMBITIOSO] *stops him.*

SPURIO   Madam, unlock yourself; should it be seen,
Your arm would be suspected.

DUCHESS   Who is't that dares suspect or this or these?
May not we deal our favors where we please?

---

201 *husk* covering.   202 *device* plan.   206 *published* i.e. in line 178.   208 *sluggy*
sluggish.   210 *We* The quarto reads "Me."   212 *substantial* flawlessly thought out.
216 *'tis in grain* (The dye) is well set.   219 *conjure* exorcise.
⦃ ACT IV, Scene 3.   SD *he . . . her* He embraces her lasciviously.   1 *unlock
yourself* Disengage yourself (from me).   2 *Your . . . suspected* The embrace would
be incriminating.   3 *or . . . these* probably "either this embrace or these kisses."

SPURIO   I'm confident you may. *Exeunt* [SPURIO *and* DUCHESS].
AMBITIOSO   'Sfoot, brother, hold.   5
SUPERVACUO   Wouldst let the bastard shame us?
AMBITIOSO   Hold, hold, brother!
There's fitter time than now.
SUPERVACUO   Now, when I see it.
AMBITIOSO   'Tis too much seen already.
SUPERVACUO   Seen and known.
The nobler she's, the baser is she grown.
AMBITIOSO   If she were bent lasciviously, the fault   10
Of mighty women that sleep soft—O death!
Must she needs choose such an unequal sinner,
To make all worse?
SUPERVACUO   A bastard, the Duke's bastard!
Shame heaped on shame!
AMBITIOSO   O our disgrace!
Most women have small waist the world throughout;   15
But their desires are thousand miles about.
SUPERVACUO   Come, stay not here; let's after and prevent;
Or else they'll sin faster than we'll repent.   *Exeunt.*

{ACT IV   Scene 4}

Enter VINDICE *and* HIPPOLITO *bringing out* [GRATIANA,] *their mother,*
one by one shoulder, and the other by the other, with daggers in their
hands.

VINDICE   O thou, for whom no name is bad enough!
GRATIANA   What means my sons? What, will you murder me?
VINDICE   Wicked, unnatural parent!
HIPPOLITO   Fiend of women!
GRATIANA   O! are sons turned monsters? Help!
VINDICE   In vain.
GRATIANA   Are you so barbarous to set iron nipples   5

---

6 *Wouldst* The quarto reads "Woult." 10 *bent lasciviously* determined to be lascivious. 12 *unequal* socially unequal. 15 *waist* The quarto reads "waste." 18 *than . . . repent* than we can force them to repent. SD *Exeunt* This stage direction appears after line 16 in the quarto.
🦅 ACT IV, Scene 4. 3 *parent* The quarto reads "parents." 5 *iron nipples* the daggers.

Upon the breast that gave you suck?

VINDICE   That breast
Is turned to quarled poison.

GRATIANA   Cut not your days fort; am not I your mother?

VINDICE   Thou dost usurp that title now by fraud,
For in that shell of mother breeds a bawd.   10

GRATIANA   A bawd? O name far loathsomer than hell!

HIPPOLITO   It should be so, knewst thou thy office well.

GRATIANA   I hate it.

VINDICE   Ah, is't possible, thou only, you powers on high,
That women should dissemble when they die?   15

GRATIANA   Dissemble?

VINDICE   Did not the Duke's son direct
A fellow of the world's condition hither,
That did corrupt all that was good in thee?
Made thee uncivilly forget thyself,
And work our sister to his lust?

GRATIANA   Who, I?   20
That had been monstrous! I defy that man
For any such intent. None lives so pure,
But shall be soiled with slander.
Good son, believe it not.

VINDICE   [*Aside.*] O I'm in doubt
Whether I'm myself or no!—   25
Stay, let me look again upon this face.
Who shall be saved when mothers have no grace?

HIPPOLITO   'Twould make one half despair.

VINDICE   I was the man.
Defy me now! Let's see, do't modestly.

---

7 quarled soured, curdled.   **8 Cut . . . fort** Do not cut short your days by refusing to honor your mother. As in II.2.94–95, there is a reference here to Exodus 20:12.   **12 office** duty (as a mother).   **13 it** the name "bawd."   **14 thou only** Printed in the quarto in italics with the "thou" capitalized, this phrase has an ambiguous reference: it seems to refer either elliptically to Gratiana or proleptically to "you powers." With each of these references, however, there is some difficulty of interpretation, for it is hard to say how "thou only" can be applied to Gratiana or how "thou" could refer to the plural substantive "powers." Perhaps "powers," like "parents" in line 3, is a printer's error for what was intended to be a singular noun; or possibly the movement from "thou" to "powers" is merely another example of the mixture of pagan and Christian imagery so common in the literature of the Renaissance. At any rate, the phrase has been punctuated here as if it referred to "powers."   **17 of . . . condition** corrupt, worldly.   **19 uncivilly** in an uncivilized manner, barbarously.

GRATIANA   O hell unto my soul!   30
VINDICE   In that disguise, I, sent from the Duke's son,
    Tried you, and found you base metal—
    As any villain might have done.
GRATIANA   O no,
    No tongue but yours could have bewitched me so.
VINDICE   O nimble in damnation, quick in tune.   35
    There is no devil could strike fire so soon:
    I am confuted in a word.
GRATIANA   O sons, forgive me! To myself I'll prove more true;
    You that should honor me, I kneel to you.

    [*She kneels, weeping.*]

VINDICE   A mother to give aim to her own daughter!   40
HIPPOLITO   True, brother; how far beyond nature 'tis,
    Though many mothers do't.
VINDICE   Nay, and you draw tears once, go you to bed.

    [*He sheaths his dagger.*]

    Wet will make you blush and change to red.
    Brother, it rains; 'twill spoil your dagger; house it.   45
HIPPOLITO   [*Puts away his dagger.*] 'Tis done.
VINDICE   I'faith, 'tis a sweet shower; it does much good:
    The fruitful grounds and meadows of her soul
    Has been long dry. Pour down, thou blessed dew.—
    Rise, mother. Troth, this shower has made you higher.   50
GRATIANA   O you heavens!
    Take this infectious spot out of my soul.
    I'll rinse it in seven waters of mine eyes!
    Make my tears salt enough to taste of grace:

---

35 O . . . tune O nimble (at winning) damnation, quick in (keeping) tune (with evil).
37 confuted confounded. **38 To myself** as mother. **40 aim** either "direct" (Castiza)
or "to direct Lussurioso's aim toward Castiza" (with an obvious sexual innuendo). **43 and**
if. **you** his dagger. **44 Wet** The quarto reads "Wee." **Wet . . . red** The wet (of
Gratiana's tears) will make the dagger blush (with embarrassment at its shameless boldness—by rusting). **47 shower** of tears. **49 Has** The verb is singular because of the
proximity of "soul"; such constructions are common in Elizabethan English. **53 I'll . . .
eyes** "I will fully purify myself by the contrition of these tears." The tears are "seven
waters" because that number is often associated with purification in biblical tradition:
Naaman the leper, for example, was cured, and "his flesh came again like unto the flesh
of a little child" when he dipped himself seven times in the river Jordan (II Kings 5:14).
54 salt enough Salt is used in holy water as a sign of the efficacy of the church, a practice
which no doubt owes its origins to the characteristics of salt as a healing agent (cf. II Kings
2:20–22 and Matthew 5:13).

To weep is to our sex naturally given;   55
But to weep truly, that's a gift from heaven.
VINDICE   Nay, I'll kiss you now. —Kiss her, brother.
Let's marry her to our souls, wherein's no lust,
And honorably love her.
HIPPOLITO   Let it be.
VINDICE   For honest women are so seld and rare,   60
'Tis good to cherish those poor few that are.—
O you of easy wax, do but imagine,
Now the disease has left you, how leprously
That office would have clinged unto your forehead.
All mothers that had any graceful hue   65
Would have worn masks to hide their face at you.
It would have grown to this: at your foul name,
Green-colored maids would have turned red with shame.
HIPPOLITO   And then our sister, full of hire, and baseness.
VINDICE   There had been boiling lead again.   70
The Duke's son's great concubine!
A drab of state, a cloth-o'-silver slut,
To have her train borne up, and her soul trail i' th' dirt.
Great—
HIPPOLITO   To be miserably great, rich, to be
Eternally wretched.
VINDICE   O common madness!   75
Ask but the thriving'st harlot in cold blood:
She'd give the world to make her honor good.
Perhaps you'll say, "But only to th' Duke's son,
In private." Why, she first begins with one,
Who afterward to thousand proves a whore: 80
"Break ice in one place, it will crack in more."
GRATIANA   Most certainly applied.
HIPPOLITO   O brother, you forget our business.
VINDICE   And well remembered. Joy's a subtle elf;
I think man's happiest when he forgets himself.   85

---

60 seld seldom found.   **62 of . . . wax** easily moulded or manipulated.   **63–64 how
. . . forehead** based on the neo-Platonic theory that corruption within would be reflected
without—in one's appearance—as well.   **68 Green-colored maids** both "inexperienced
maids" and maids afflicted with green-sickness, or chlorosis, an anemia common in adol-
escent girls (cf. *'Tis Pity She's a Whore,* III.2.82–83).   **69 hire** an ironic echo of "higher"
in line 50, here meaning "pay earned as a prostitute."   **70 boiling lead** thought to be
one of the characteristics of hell.   **72 drab** prostitute.   **83 business** their business of
taking revenge on Lussurioso.   **84 elf** spirit.

—Farewell, once dried, now holy-watered mead;
Our hearts wear feathers that before wore lead.
GRATIANA   I'll give you this: that one I never knew
Plead better for, and 'gainst the devil, than you.
VINDICE   You make me proud on't.   90
HIPPOLITO   Commend us in all virtue to our sister.
VINDICE   Ay, for the love of heaven, to that true maid.
GRATIANA   With my best words.
VINDICE   Why, that was motherly said.
                        Exeunt [VINDICE *and* HIPPOLITO].
GRATIANA   I wonder now what fury did transport me?
I feel good thoughts begin to settle in me.   95
O, with what forehead can I look on her,
Whose honor I've so impiously beset?

[*Enter* CASTIZA.]

And here she comes.
CASTIZA   Now, mother, you have wrought with me so strongly.
That what for my advancement, as to calm   100
The trouble of your tongue, I am content.
GRATIANA   Content to what?
CASTIZA   To do as you have wished me:
To prostitute my breast to the Duke's son,
And put myself to common usury.
GRATIANA   I hope you will not so.
CASTIZA   Hope you I will not?   105
That's not the hope you look to be saved in.
GRATIANA   Truth, but it is.
CASTIZA   Do not deceive yourself;
I am as you e'en out of marble wrought.
What would you now? Are ye not pleased yet with me?
You shall not wish me to be more lascivious   110
Than I intend to be.
GRATIANA   Strike not me cold.
CASTIZA   How often have you charged me on your blessing

---

86 holy-watered mead "reward won by contrition"; but the phrase picks up two images
used earlier in the scene: in its root meaning of meadow, "mead" recalls the reference to
the dried-up fields of Gratiana's soul, while "holy-watered" refers to the previous identification between her tears and salt-treated holy water.   **104 common usury** public use
or hire (sexually).   **106 That's . . . in** Your salvation will not come through such an
idle hope as that (but rather in the hope that you have shown in encouraging me to sell
myself to the Duke).   **108 I . . . wrought** I am as you earlier made me when, although
I seemed as cold as marble, you wrought me to your will.

To be a cursèd woman? When you knew
Your blessing had no force to make me lewd,
You laid your curse upon me; that did more.   115
The mother's curse is heavy: where that fights,
Sons set in storm, and daughters lose their lights.

GRATIANA   Good child, dear maid, if there be any spark
Of heavenly intellectual fire within thee,
O let my breath revive it to a flame;   120
Put not all out with woman's wilful follies.
I am recovered of that foul disease
That haunts too many mothers; kind, forgive me,
Make me not sick in health. If then
My words prevailed when they were wickedness,   125
How much more now when they are just and good!

CASTIZA   I wonder what you mean? Are not you she
For whose infect persuasions I could scarce
Kneel out my prayers, and had much ado,
In three hours' reading, to untwist so much   130
Of the black serpent as you wound about me?

GRATIANA   'Tis unfruitful, held tedious, to repeat what's past.
I'm now your present mother.

CASTIZA   Push, now 'tis too late.

GRATIANA   Bethink again, thou knowst not what thou sayst.

CASTIZA   No?—"Deny advancement, treasure, the Duke's son?"   135

GRATIANA   O see, I spoke those words, and now they poison me.
What will the deed do then?
Advancement?—true: as high as shame can pitch.
For treasure—who e'er knew a harlot rich?
Or could build by the purchase of her sin   140
An hospital to keep their bastards in?
The Duke's son?—O, when women are young courtiers,
They are sure to be old beggars.
To know the miseries most harlots taste,
Thou'dst wish thyself unborn, when thou art unchaste.   145

CASTIZA   O mother, let me twine about your neck,
And kiss you till my soul melt on your lips.

---

119 *heavenly intellectual* spiritual. **123 *kind*** forgiving child (with an indirect emphasis on the meaning "natural," which accents Gratiana's attempt to act again as a true mother). **128 *For*** on account of. **130 *reading*** (of prayers). **133 *I'm . . . mother*** Now I'm truly a mother to you.

I did but this to try you.
GRATIANA   O speak truth!
CASTIZA   Indeed, I did not;
    For no tongue has force to alter me from honest.   150
    If maidens would, men's words could have no power;
    A virgin honor is a crystal tower,
    Which, being weak, is guarded with good spirits.
    Until she basely yields, no ill inherits.
GRATIANA   O happy child! Faith and thy birth hath saved me.   155
    'Mongst thousand daughters, happiest of all others,
    Be thou a glass for maids, and I for mothers.   *Exeunt.*

⟨ACT V   Scene 1⟩

Enter VINDICE *and* HIPPOLITO [*with the Duke's corpse dressed in
Vindice's disguise; they arrange it to look like a sleeping man*].

VINDICE   So, so, he leans well; take heed you wake him not, brother.
HIPPOLITO   I warrant you, my life for yours.
VINDICE   That's a good lay, for I must kill myself. Brother, that's I;
    that sits for me; do you mark it? And I must stand ready here to
    make away my self yonder. I must sit to be killed, and stand to   5
    kill myself. I could vary it not so little as thrice over again; 't has
    some eight returns, like Michaelmas Term.
HIPPOLITO   That's enow, o' conscience.
VINDICE   But, sirrah, does the Duke's son come single?
HIPPOLITO   No, there's the hell on't. His faith's too feeble to go alone;   10

---

149 *I . . . not* I did not (speak truth when I talked licentiously).   **151 *would*** would
(truly resolve to remain honest).   **155 *happy*** bringing happiness.   **157 *Be*** The quarto
reads "Buy."   *a . . . maids* a looking glass for maids to see their ideal form in (cf. *2 Henry
IV*, II.3.21–22).

⚜ ACT V, Scene 1.   3 *lay* bet.   **7 *returns*** "different ways of being expressed";
"returns" are technically the reports issued by a sheriff on writs delivered to him by a court
of law, and during the Michaelmas Term (November 2 to 25, when the superior courts
of England were in session) there were eight days on which such returns were required.
The reference here seems relevant more to the number than to the nature of the returns,
though the fact that law required such returns may also relate them to Vindice's belief
(I.1.39–44) that he is compelled to action by implacable laws of revenge.

he brings flesh-flies after him that will buzz against supper-time,
and hum for his coming out.

VINDICE   Ah, the fly-flop of vengeance beat 'em to pieces! Here was
the sweetest occasion, the fittest hour, to have made my revenge
familiar with him: show him the body of the Duke his father, and   15
how quaintly he died like a politician, in hugger-mugger, made
no man acquainted with it; and in catastrophe, slain him over his
father's breast, and—O, I'm mad to lose such a sweet opportunity.

HIPPOLITO   Nay, push, prithee be content. There's no remedy present.
May not hereafter times open in as fair faces as this?   20

VINDICE   They may, if they can paint so well.

HIPPOLITO   Come, now to avoid all suspicion, let's forsake this room,
and be going to meet the Duke's son.

VINDICE   Content, I'm for any weather. Heart, step close; here he
comes.   25

   Enter LUSSURIOSO.

HIPPOLITO   My honored lord.

LUSSURIOSO   O me! you both present?

VINDICE   E'en newly, my lord, just as your lordship entered now.
About this place we had notice given he should be, but in some
loathsome plight or other.

HIPPOLITO   Came your honor private?   30

LUSSURIOSO   Private enough for this; only a few
Attend my coming out.

VINDICE   [*Aside*.] Death rot those few.

LUSSURIOSO   Stay, yonder's the slave.

VINDICE   Mass, there's the slave indeed, my lord.
   [*Aside*.] 'Tis a good child; he calls his father slave.   35

LUSSURIOSO   Ay, that's the villain, the damned villain. Softly,
Tread easy.

VINDICE   Puh, I warrant you, my lord,
We'll stifle in our breaths.

LUSSURIOSO   That will do well.—
Base rogue, thou sleepest thy last.— [*Aside*.] 'Tis policy
To have him killed in's sleep, for if he waked,   40
He would betray all to them.

VINDICE   But, my lord—

---

11 *flesh-flies* the sycophants who are Lussurioso's followers.   *against* when it is.
13 *fly-flop* fly swatter. 15 *familiar with* known to. 16 *quaintly* cunningly.
politician evil schemer. *in hugger-mugger* secretly. 17 *in catastrophe* in the
conclusion of the tragedy. 24 *step close* Watch your step.

LUSSURIOSO   Ha, what sayst?

VINDICE   Shall we kill him now he's drunk?

LUSSURIOSO   Ay, best of all.

VINDICE   Why then he will ne'er live to be sober.

LUSSURIOSO   No matter, let him reel to hell.   45

VINDICE   But being so full of liquor, I fear he will put out all the fire.

LUSSURIOSO   Thou art a mad beast.

VINDICE   [*Aside.*] —And leave none to warm your lordship's golls
    withal,—for he that dies drunk falls into hellfire like a bucket,
    qush, qush.   50

LUSSURIOSO   Come, be ready; nake your swords; think of your
    wrongs. This slave has injured you.

VINDICE   Troth, so he has. [*Aside.*] And he has paid well for't.

LUSSURIOSO   Meet with him now.

VINDICE   You'll bear us out, my lord?

LUSSURIOSO   Puh, am I a lord for nothing, think you?   55
    Quickly now.

VINDICE   Sa, sa, sa, thump. [*He stabs the corpse.*]
                        There he lies.

LUSSURIOSO   Nimbly done. —Ha! O, villains, murderers,
    'Tis the old duke my father!

VINDICE   That's a jest.

LUSSURIOSO   What! stiff and cold already?
    O pardon me to call you from your names;   60
    'Tis none of your deed. That villain Piato,
    Whom you thought now to kill, has murdered him
    And left him thus disguised.

HIPPOLITO   And not unlikely.

VINDICE   O rascal! Was he not ashamed
    To put the Duke into a greasy doublet?   65

LUSSURIOSO   He has been cold and stiff, who knows how long?

VINDICE   [*Aside.*] Marry, that do I.

LUSSURIOSO   No words, I pray, of anything intended.

VINDICE   O my lord.

HIPPOLITO   I would fain have your lordship think that we have small   70
    reason to prate.

LUSSURIOSO   Faith, thou sayst true. I'll forthwith send to court,
    For all the nobles, bastard, Duchess, all;

---

48 golls hands.   **51 nake** draw.   **54 Meet with** both "encounter" and "punish."
bear us out give us your support (if we are accused of murder).   **60 to . . . names** to
call you names far from your true nature.   **68 No . . . intended** Say nothing about what
our intentions in this action were.

How here by miracle we found him dead,
And in his raiment that foul villain fled.   75
VINDICE   That will be the best way, my lord, to clear us all; let's cast
about to be clear.
LUSSURIOSO   Ho, Nencio, Sordido, and the rest!

Enter all [his FOLLOWERS*].*

FIRST SERVANT   My lord.
SECOND SERVANT   My lord.   80
LUSSURIOSO   Be witnesses of a strange spectacle.
Choosing for private conference that sad room,
We found the Duke my father gealed in blood.
FIRST SERVANT   My lord the Duke!—Run, hie thee, Nencio,
Startle the court by signifying so much.   [*Exit* NENCIO.]   85
VINDICE   [*Aside.*] Thus much by wit a deep revenger can:
When murder's known, to be the clearest man.
We're farthest off, and with as bold an eye
Survey his body as the standers-by.
LUSSURIOSO   My royal father, too basely let blood   90
By a malevolent slave.
HIPPOLITO   [*Apart to* VINDICE.] Hark,
He calls thee slave again.
VINDICE   [*Apart to* HIPPOLITO.] H' has lost; he may.
LUSSURIOSO   O sight! Look hither, see, his lips are gnawn
With poison.
VINDICE   How!—his lips? By th' mass, they be.
O villain! O rogue! O slave! O rascal!   95
HIPPOLITO   [*Aside.*] O good deceit: he quits him with like terms.

[*Enter* NOBLES, *before* AMBITIOSO *and* SUPERVACUO.]

FIRST NOBLE   Where?
SECOND NOBLE   Which way?
AMBITIOSO   Over what roof hangs this prodigious comet
In deadly fire?
LUSSURIOSO   Behold, behold, my lords:

76–77 *cast about* devise plans (to clear ourselves of suspicion). **SD** *all* When they
speak in this scene, servants and nobles are identified by the quarto merely as "Nobl.,"
"1.," or "2." **86** *can* can accomplish. **87** *clearest* clearest from suspicion. **90** *let
blood* a pun on the seventeenth-century practice of blood-letting as a treatment for
illness. **92** *H' has lost* He is as good as dead already. **96** *he . . . terms* He pays
back Lussurioso in appropriate terms (by indirectly addressing the insults at him).
98–99 *Over . . . fire* Ambitioso's figurative description of the murder anticipates the
comet's actual appearance in V.3.

The Duke my father's murdered by a vassal,   100
That owes this habit, and here left disguised.

[*Enter* DUCHESS *and* SPURIO.]

DUCHESS   My lord and husband!
SECOND NOBLE   Reverend majesty!
FIRST NOBLE   I have seen these clothes often attending on him.
VINDICE   [*Aside.*] That nobleman has been i' th' country, for he does
     not lie!
SUPERVACUO   [*Apart to* AMBITIOSO.] Learn of our mother. Let's dis-
     semble too.   105
     I am glad he's vanished; so I hope are you.
AMBITIOSO   [*Apart to* SUPERVACUO.]
     Ay, you make take my word for't.
SPURIO   Old dad, dead?—
     [*Aside.*] I, one of his cast sins, will send the Fates
     Most hearty commendations by his own son.
     I'll tug in the new stream till strength be done.   110
LUSSURIOSO   Where be those two, that did affirm to us
     My lord the Duke was privately rid forth?
FIRST GENTLEMAN   O, pardon us, my lords; he gave that charge
     Upon our lives, if he were missed at court,
     To answer so; he rode not anywhere.   115
     We left him private with that fellow here.
VINDICE   [*Aside.*] Confirmed.
LUSSURIOSO   O heavens, that false charge was his death.
     Impudent beggars! durst you to our face
     Maintain such a false answer?—Bear him straight
     To execution.
FIRST GENTLEMAN   My lord!
LUSSURIOSO   Urge me no more.   120
     In this, the excuse may be called half the murder!
VINDICE   [*Aside.*] You've sentenced well.
LUSSURIOSO   Away, see it be done.
                              [*Exeunt* GENTLEMEN, *guarded.*]

---

101 *owes . . . habit* owns this outfit. 104 *That . . . lie* Because he is telling the truth,
that nobleman seems to come from the country (where people are honest, rather than from
the court, where they practice deceit). 105 *Learn . . . mother* Follow the example of
our mother (who feigns sorrow at her husband's death). 108 *cast* scattered. 109 *by
. . . son* by way of his son (who will soon be joining him in death). 110 *I'll . . . done*
I'll contend in the rushing stream of events until supremacy is decided. 116 *that . . . here*
The gentleman presumes that the corpse is Piato, since it is dressed in his clothes.
117 *charge* report.

VINDICE [*Aside.*] Could you not stick? See what confession doth?
Who would not lie when men are hanged for truth?

HIPPOLITO [*Apart to* VINDICE.]
Brother, how happy is our vengeance.

VINDICE [*Apart to* HIPPOLITO.]   Why, it hits   125
Past the apprehension of indifferent wits.

LUSSURIOSO My lord, let post horse be sent
Into all places to entrap the villain.

VINDICE [*Aside.*] Post horse! ha, ha.

FIRST NOBLE My lord, we're something bold to know our duty.   130
Your father's accidentally departed;
The titles that were due to him meet you.

LUSSURIOSO Meet me? I'm not at leisure, my good lord:
I've many griefs to dispatch out o' th' way.—
[*Aside.*] Welcome, sweet titles!—Talk to me, my lords,   135
Of sepulchers and mighty emperors' bones;
That's thought for me.

VINDICE   [*Aside.*] So one may see by this
How foreign markets go:
Courtiers have feet o' th' nines, and tongues o' th' twelves;
They flatter dukes, and dukes flatter themselves.   140

SECOND NOBLE My lord, it is your shine must comfort us.

LUSSURIOSO Alas, I shine in tears, like the sun in April.

FIRST NOBLE You're now my lord's grace.

LUSSURIOSO   My lord's grace!
I perceive you'll have it so.

FIRST NOBLE   'Tis but your own.

LUSSURIOSO Then, heavens, give me grace to be so!   145

VINDICE [*Aside.*] He prays well for himself.

SECOND NOBLE [*To the* DUCHESS.]   Madam, all sorrows
Must run their circles into joys. No doubt but time
Will make the murderer bring forth himself.

VINDICE [*Aside.*] He were an ass then, i'faith.

FIRST NOBLE   In the mean season,

---

123 *stick* remain silent. **125** *happy* blessed with good fortune. **127** *let . . . horse*
With haste, let men be sent upon swift horses. **138** *foreign markets* Since Vindice
ostensibly comes from the country, the court would be a place "foreign" to him; it is a
"market" because everything in it is for sale, at one price or another. **139** *Courtiers . . .
twelves* Courtiers have size-nine feet but size-twelve tongues (tongues in shoes being
equated by a pun with tongues in mouths) because they are so quick to use flattery.
141 *your shine* your newly gained luster as duke.

Let us bethink the latest funeral honors   150
Due to the Duke's cold body—and, withal,
Calling to memory our new happiness,
Spread in his royal son. Lords, gentlemen,
Prepare for revels.
VINDICE   [*Aside.*] Revels!
SECOND NOBLE   Time hath several falls;
Griefs lift up joys, feasts put down funerals.   155
LUSSURIOSO   Come then, my lords, my favors to you all.—
[*Aside.*] The Duchess is suspected foully bent;
I'll begin dukedom with her banishment.
                    Exeunt DUKE [LUSSURIOSO], NOBLES, *and* DUCHESS.
HIPPOLITO   [*Apart to* VINDICE.] Revels!
VINDICE   [*Apart to* HIPPOLITO.]   Ay, that's the word; we are firm
     yet;
Strike one strain more, and then we crown our wit.   160
                    Exeunt Brothers [VINDICE *and* HIPPOLITO].
SPURIO   [*Aside.*] Well, have at the fairest mark—
So said the Duke when he begot me;
And if I miss his heart or near about,
Then have at any; a bastard scorns to be out.   [*Exit* SPURIO.]
SUPERVACUO   Note'st thou that Spurio, brother?   165
AMBITIOSO   Yes, I note him to our shame.
SUPERVACUO   He shall not live, his hair shall not grow much longer.
In this time of revels, tricks may be set afoot. Seest thou yon new
moon? It shall outlive the new duke by much: this hand shall
dispossess him; then we're mighty.   170
A mask is treason's license: that build upon;
'Tis murder's best face when a vizard's on.   *Exit* SUPERVACUO.
AMBITIOSO   Is't so? 't's very good;
And do you think to be duke then, kind brother?
I'll see fair play: drop one, and there lies t'other. *Exit* AMBITIOSO.   175

---

153 *Spread* blossoming forth. **154** *Time . . . falls* Time periodically falls away from
joy. **159** *firm* secure in success. **163** *his* Lussurioso's. **171** *A mask* part of a
reveler's costume.

⟨ACT V   Scene 2⟩

Enter VINDICE *and* HIPPOLITO, *with* PIERO *and other* LORDS.

VINDICE   My lords, be all of music;
  Strike old griefs into other countries
  That flow in too much milk and have faint livers,
  Not daring to stab home their discontents.
  Let our hid flames break out, as fire, as lightning,   5
  To blast this villainous dukedom vexed with sin;
  Wind up your souls to their full height again.

PIERO   How?

FIRST LORD   Which way?

THIRD LORD   Any way; our wrongs are such,
  We cannot justly be revenged too much.

VINDICE   You shall have all enough. Revels are toward,   10
  And those few nobles that have long suppressed you
  Are busied to the furnishing of a masque,
  And do affect to make a pleasant tale on't.
  The masquing suits are fashioning—now comes in
  That which must glad us all: we to take pattern   15
  Of all those suits, the color, trimming, fashion,
  E'en to an undistinguished hair almost.
  Then, ent'ring first, observing the true form,
  Within a strain or two we shall find leisure
  To steal our swords out handsomely,   20
  And when they think their pleasure sweet and good,
  In midst of all their joys, they shall sigh blood.

PIERO   Weightily, effectually!

THIRD LORD   Before the t'other masquers come—

VINDICE   We're gone, all done and past.   25

PIERO   But how for the Duke's guard?

VINDICE   Let that alone;
  By one and one their strengths shall be drunk down.

🦅 ACT V, Scene 2.   **3** *milk*   of human kindness and gentleness.   *have . . . livers*
lack courage (the liver was thought to be the seat of man's passions).   **7** *Wind . . . height*
Ready yourselves for courageous action.   **10** *toward*   imminent.   **13** *affect*   intend.
18 *observing . . . form*   dancing to the music as if we were the masquers.   **27** *their
. . . down*   Their strength will be dissipated in drunkenness.

HIPPOLITO   There are five hundred gentlemen in the action,
    That will apply themselves, and not stand idle.
PIERO   O, let us hug your bosoms!
VINDICE   Come, my lords,   30
    Prepare for deeds; let other times have words.   *Exeunt.*

⸦ACT V   Scene 3⸧

*In a dumb show, the possessing of the young duke, with all his nobles;
then sounding music. A furnished table is brought forth; then enters
[again] the* DUKE *and his* NOBLES *to the banquet. A blazing star
appeareth.*

FIRST NOBLE   Many harmonious hours and choicest pleasures
    Fill up the royal numbers of your years.
LUSSURIOSO   My lords, we're pleased to thank you, though we know
    'Tis but your duty now to wish it so.
SECOND NOBLE   That shine makes us all happy.
THIRD NOBLE   [*Aside.*] His grace frowns.   5
SECOND NOBLE   [*Aside.*] Yet we must say he smiles.
FIRST NOBLE   [*Aside.*] I think we must.
LUSSURIOSO   [*Aside.*] That foul-incontinent Duchess we have banished;
    The bastard shall not live. After these revels,
    I'll begin strange ones; he and the stepsons
    Shall pay their lives for the first subsidies.   10
    We must not frown so soon, else 't had been now.
FIRST NOBLE   My gracious lord, please you prepare for pleasure;
    The masque is not far off.
LUSSURIOSO   We are for pleasure—
    [*To the star.*] Beshrew thee! what art thou mad'st me start?
    Thou hast committed treason. —A blazing star!   15
FIRST NOBLE   A blazing star? O where, my lord?
LUSSURIOSO   Spy out.

---

28 in . . . action   of joining with them in heavy drinking; or, perhaps, "those watching
the masque will rise as a mass to support us against this debauched duke."
⸙ **ACT V, Scene 3.**   SD *possessing*   formal crowning.   **10 subsidies**   payment (to
reinforce the power of the ruler).   **11 else . . . now**   or else I will have to sentence them
now (to keep them from fleeing).   **15 Thou**   the star (by frightening the young duke;
cf. 18–24).

SECOND NOBLE   See, see, my lords, a wondrous-dreadful one!
LUSSURIOSO   I am not pleased at that ill-knotted fire,
    That bushing-flaring star. Am not I duke?
    It should not quake me now; had it appeared   20
    Before it, I might then have justly feared.
    But yet they say, whom art and learning weds,
    When stars wear locks, they threaten great men's heads.
    Is it so? You are read, my lords.
FIRST NOBLE   May it please your grace,
    It shows great anger.
LUSSURIOSO   That does not please our grace.   25
SECOND NOBLE   Yet here's the comfort, my lord: many times,
    When it seems most, it threatens farthest off.
LUSSURIOSO   Faith, and I think so too.
FIRST NOBLE   Beside, my lord,
    You're gracefully established with the loves
    Of all your subjects; and for natural death,   30
    I hope it will be threescore years a-coming.
LUSSURIOSO   True.—No more but threescore years?
FIRST NOBLE   Fourscore, I hope, my lord.
SECOND NOBLE   And fivescore, I.
THIRD NOBLE   But 'tis my hope, my lord, you shall ne'er die.
LUSSURIOSO   Give me thy hand, these others I rebuke;   35
    He that hopes so is fittest for a duke.
    Thou shalt sit next me. —Take your places, lords;
    We're ready now for sports; let 'em set on.—
    You thing, we shall forget you quite anon!
THIRD NOBLE   I hear 'em coming, my lord.

Enter the masque of revengers: the two brothers [VINDICE *and* HIPPOLITO],
and two LORDS *more.*

LUSSURIOSO   Ah, 'tis well.—   40
    [*Aside.*] Brothers, and bastard, you dance next in hell.

*The revengers dance; at the end, steal out their swords, and these four
kill the four at the table, in their chairs. It thunders.*

VINDICE   Mark, thunder!

---

20 *quake* frighten.   **21** *it* the Duke's "possessing."   *feared* feared (for my life at the
hands of a jealous usurper).   **22** *whom . . . weds* those in whom astrological skill and
learning are fruitfully combined.   **23** *wear locks* leave a trail that looks like hair. (The
quarto reads "were locks.")   **27** *most* nearest.   **39** *thing* the comet.

Dost know thy cue, thou big-voiced crier?
Dukes' groans are thunder's watchwords.
HIPPOLITO   So, my lords, you have enough.   45
VINDICE   Come, let's away, no ling'ring.
HIPPOLITO   Follow! Go!
                              Exeunt [revengers except VINDICE].
VINDICE   No power is angry when the lustful die;
    When thunder claps, heaven likes the tragedy.   *Exit* VINDICE.
LUSSURIOSO   O, O.

    Enter the other masque of intended murderers: stepsons [AMBITIOSO *and*
    SUPERVACUO], *bastard* [SPURIO], *and a* FOURTH MAN, *coming in*
    dancing. The Duke [LUSSURIOSO] *recovers a little in voice, and groans—*
    calls "A guard, treason." At which they all start out of their measure,
    and turning towards the table, they find them all to be murdered.

SPURIO   Whose groan was that?
LUSSURIOSO   Treason, a guard.
AMBITIOSO   How now? All murdered!
SUPERVACUO   Murdered!   50
FOURTH MAN   And those his nobles!
AMBITIOSO   Here's a labor saved;
    I thought to have sped him. 'Sblood, how came this?
SUPERVACUO   Then I proclaim myself; now I am duke.
AMBITIOSO   Thou duke! brother, thou liest. [*Stabs* SUPERVACUO.]
SPURIO   Slave, so dost thou.
    [*Stabs* AMBITIOSO.]
FOURTH MAN   Base villain, hast thou slain my lord and master?   55
    [*Stabs* SPURIO.]
    Enter the first men [VINDICE, HIPPOLITO, *and the two* LORDS].
VINDICE   Pistols! treason! murder! help! Guard my lord
    The Duke! [*Enter* ANTONIO *and the* GUARD.]

---

44 watchwords signals to begin sounding. **SD Exeunt** The quarto prints after
"ling'ring." **53 Then ... duke** Here, as in III.6.13, the quarto confuses "Sup." with
"Spu." and assigns this speech to Spurio, who could hardly consider himself the immediate
heir to the throne. There is, though, a problem raised by reassigning the speech to
Supervacuo, for Ambitioso has twice announced (III.1.13 and III.6.19) that he is next-in-line
to the dukedom. But since Supervacuo has long been planning to displace his brother once
Lussurioso has been dispatched, it is not unreasonable to assume that he is making his move
here. He considers Ambitioso his inferior as a political schemer (cf. III.6.3–14) and very
probably hopes to surprise him and overcome him in the confusion.

HIPPOLITO   Lay hold upon this traitor! [*They seize* FOURTH MAN.]

LUSSURIOSO   O.

VINDICE   Alas, the Duke is murdered!

HIPPOLITO   And the nobles!

VINDICE   Surgeons, surgeons!— [*Aside.*] Heart! does he breathe so
    long?

ANTONIO   A piteous tragedy! able to wake   60
    An old man's eyes bloodshot.

LUSSURIOSO   O.

VINDICE   Look to my lord the Duke. [*Aside.*] A vengeance throttle
    him.
    [*To* FOURTH MAN.] Confess, thou murd'rous and unhallowed man!
    Didst thou kill all these?

FOURTH MAN   None but the bastard, I.

VINDICE   How came the Duke slain, then?

FOURTH MAN   We found him so.   65

LUSSURIOSO   O villain!

VINDICE   Hark.

LUSSURIOSO   Those in the masque did murder us.

VINDICE   Law you now, sir.
    O marble impudence! will you confess now?

FOURTH MAN   'Slud, 'tis all false!

ANTONIO   Away with that foul monster,
    Dipped in a prince's blood.

FOURTH MAN   Heart, 'tis a lie!   70

ANTONIO   Let him have bitter execution.

                  [*Exit* FOURTH MAN, *guarded.*]

VINDICE   [*Aside.*]   New marrow! No, I cannot be expressed.—
    How fares my lord, the Duke?

LUSSURIOSO   Farewell to all;
    He that climbs highest has the greatest fall.
    My tongue is out of office.

VINDICE   Air, gentlemen, air!—   75

                  [*The others step back.*]

    [*Whispers to* LUSSURIOSO.] Now thou'lt not prate on't, 'twas
    Vindice murdered thee—

LUSSURIOSO   O.

---

57 *traitor* The quarto prints "Traytors." **67** *Law you* an exclamation, meaning
roughly "There is your evidence!" **68** *marble* unfeeling. **72** *New marrow* new
depth to my revenge! *I . . . expressed* "I must be still," or "I cannot find words for
my feelings."

VINDICE   [*Whispers.*] Murdered thy father—
LUSSURIOSO   O.
VINDICE   [*Whispers.*]   —And I am he.
                                                    [LUSSURIOSO *dies.*]
   Tell nobody. —[*Aloud.*] So, so, the Duke's departed.
ANTONIO   It was a deadly hand that wounded him;   80
   The rest, ambitious who should rule and sway
   After his death, were so made all away.
VINDICE   My lord was unlikely.
HIPPOLITO   [*To* ANTONIO.]   Now the hope
   Of Italy lies in your reverend years.
VINDICE   Your hair will make the silver age again,   85
   When there was fewer but more honest men.
ANTONIO   The burden's weighty and will press age down.
   May I so rule that heaven may keep the crown.
VINDICE   The rape of your good lady has been 'quited,
   With death on death.
ANTONIO   Just is the law above.   90
   But of all things it puts me most to wonder
   How the old duke came murdered.
VINDICE   O, my lord.
ANTONIO   It was the strangeliest carried; I've not heard of the like.
HIPPOLITO   'Twas all done for the best, my lord.
VINDICE   All for your grace's good. We may be bold to speak it now.   95
   'Twas somewhat witty carried though we say it: 'twas we two
   murder'd him.
ANTONIO   You two?
VINDICE   None else, i'faith, my lord; nay, 'twas well managed.
ANTONIO   Lay hands upon those villains. [GUARDS *seize them.*]
VINDICE   How! on us?   100
ANTONIO   Bear 'em to speedy execution.
VINDICE   Heart! was't not for your good, my lord?
ANTONIO   My good?—Away with 'em. —Such an old man as he!
   You, that would murder him, would murder me!
VINDICE   Is't come about?
HIPPOLITO   'Sfoot, brother, you begun.   105
VINDICE   May not we set as well as the Duke's son?

---

83 *unlikely* unsuited to be a ruler.   **88 *may keep*** The quarto reads "nay keepe."
103 *he* the old duke.   **105 *Is't . . . about*** probably a reference to the wheel of fortune.
you begun (not I) but you were responsible for all these murders.   **106 *set*** go down, die.

Thou hast no conscience: are we not revenged?
Is there one enemy left alive amongst those?
'Tis time to die, when we are ourselves our foes.
When murd'rers shut deeds close, this curse does seal 'em: 110
If none disclose 'em, they themselves reveal 'em!
This murder might have slept in tongueless brass,
But for ourselves, and the world died an ass.
Now I remember too, here was Piato
Brought forth a knavish sentence once: 115
No doubt, said he, but time
Will make the murderer bring forth himself.
'Tis well he died; he was a witch.—
And now, my lord, since we are in forever:
This work was ours, which else might have been slipped;   120
And if we list, we could have nobles clipped
And go for less than beggars; but we hate
To bleed so cowardly. We have enough,
I'faith, we're well: our mother turned, our sister true,
We die after a nest of dukes—adieu.   125
                    Exeunt [VINDICE *and* HIPPOLITO, *guarded*].
ANTONIO   How subtly was that murder closed! Bear up
        Those tragic bodies; 'tis a heavy season.
        Pray heaven their blood may wash away all treason.   [*Exeunt.*]

---

107 *conscience* "memory of misdeeds (done us)," though the word has obviously ironic implications because of Vindice's crimes. **109** *when . . . foes* when we quarrel with one another. **110** *murd'rers* The quarto reads "murders." **112** *tongueless brass* church plaques made of brass that would be the memorials to the murdered men. **113** *and . . . ass* and the world would never have known. **118** *witch* because he had the power of prophecy. **120** *slipped* forgotten. **121–22** *And . . . beggars* "And if we chose, we could betray the nobles in the masque who joined with us in the murder; then they would, like us, have to undergo execution (being 'clipped') and as a consequence, they would be worse off than beggars." The whole metaphor is built out of a pun on "nobles," coins that were sometimes "clipped" about the edges by cheats pilfering gold. **124** *turned* redeemed. **126** *closed* probably a triple pun, meaning "kept secret," "ended," and "disclosed."

THE
DUCHESS
OF MALFI

(1613)

John Webster

This detail from Hollar's Long View of London (1647) provides an outside view of two public theaters on the south bank of the Thames. The names of the theaters are interchanged; the "Bearbaiting House" is the Globe, Shakespeare's theater, built in 1599, destroyed by fire in 1613, and rebuilt immediately, where The Duchess of Malfi was first performed publicly in 1613–14. It was razed in 1644, shortly after the closing of the theaters, so Hollar is drawing either from memory or from an earlier map, although the theaters in some earlier maps are polygonal. The two peaked roofs are the upper part of the "shadow," which projected out over the stage and housed the machinery. The Guildhall Library, London.

J OHN WEBSTER WAS PROBABLY BORN ABOUT 1580 and died in an undetermined year in the 1630's. It is no exaggeration to say that not one definite fact about Webster's life is known except that he wrote plays. He began to work in the theater early in the 1600's and most of his work was done in collaboration with other playwrights. Only four plays solely from his hand survive, and of these, only two, The White Devil and The Duchess of Malfi, are generally read and played. But the power of these two is so great that they alone have been sufficient to establish John Webster as one of the greatest writers for the English theater.

By 1613, when The Duchess of Malfi was written, the corner between the Elizabethan and the Jacobean ages had been turned. The bright hopes of the earlier drama had darkened, and the scene of the drama had shifted from the great open world of Tamburlaine to the shadowy, enclosed world of the Italian palace. The grandeur of imagination and belief in the greatness of man are still discernible, though weakened, in Webster's Duchess, but the voice that is heard most distinctly in this somber play is that of the cynical satirist Bosola. He was once a scholar and still knows of a better world and more spacious dreams, but now he sees only corruption, hypocrisy, and emptiness. Although his voice and his point of view do not dominate The Duchess of Malfi (nor the remainder of Jacobean drama), they do provide the background, the whisper of fear sounding through the palace, against which these later dramatic heroes must operate. Whatever victories the Jacobean hero wins must be achieved in the face of Bosola's forcefully presented arguments that the world is no more than dung and the best of men no more than a walking appetite.

The Duchess of Malfi was not printed until 1623; that edition is the basis of the text offered here.

To the

Right Honorable George Harding,

Baron Berkeley,

of Berkeley Castle

and Knight of the Order of the Bath   5

To the

Illustrious Prince Charles

MY NOBLE LORD,

    That I may present my excuse why (being a stranger to your
Lordship) I offer this poem to your patronage, I plead this warrant; men   10
who never saw the sea yet desire to behold that regiment of waters,
choose some eminent river to guide them thither, and make that, as it
were, their conduct or postilion. By the like ingenious means has your
fame arrived at my knowledge, receiving it from some of worth, who
both in contemplation and practice owe to your Honor their clearest   15
service. I do not altogether look up at your title: The ancientest nobility
being but a relic of time past, and the truest honor indeed being for a
man to confer honor on himself, which your learning strives to
propagate, and shall make you arrive at the dignity of a great example.
I am confident this work is not unworthy your Honor's perusal, for by   20
such poems as this, poets have kissed the hands of great princes and
drawn their gentle eyes to look down upon their sheets of paper when
the poets themselves were bound up in their winding sheets. The like
courtesy from your Lordship shall make you live in your grave, and
laurel spring out of it, when the ignorant scorners of the Muses (that,   25
like worms in libraries, seem to live only to destroy learning) shall
wither, neglected and forgotten. This work and myself I humbly

Dedication 2–3 *George Harding, Baron Berkeley* a patron of the King's Men,
Shakespeare's theater company. **13** *conduct* means of conduct.

present to your approved censure. It being the utmost of my wishes, to have your honorable self my weighty and perspicuous comment, which grace so done me, shall ever be acknowledged 30

By your Lordship's
in all duty and
observance,
JOHN WEBSTER.

---

28 *approved censure* proven judgment. 29 *perspicuous* easily seen.

In the just worth

of that well deserver,

MR. JOHN WEBSTER,

and upon this

masterpiece of tragedy   5

In this thou imitat'st one rich and wise,

That sees his good deeds done before he dies;

As he by works, thou by this work of fame,

Hast well provided for thy living name;

To trust to others' honorings, is worth's crime,   10

Thy monument is raised in thy lifetime;

And 'tis most just; for every worthy man

Is his own marble; and his merit can

Cut him to any figure, and express

More art, than death's cathedral palaces,   15

Where royal ashes keep their court: thy note

Be ever plainness, 'tis the richest coat:

Thy epitaph only the title be,

Write, *Duchess,* that will fetch a tear for thee,

For who e'er saw this *Duchess* live, and die,   20

That could get off under a bleeding eye?

In Tragaediam.

Ut lux ex tenebris ictu percussa tonantis;

Illa, (ruina malis) claris sit vita poetis.

Thomas Middletonus,   25

Poëta & Chron:

Londinensis

Poems of Praise: Middleton's Poem   15 *death's . . . palaces*   splendid tombs.
21 *That . . . eye*   that could avoid weeping.   **22–24** *In . . . poetis*   To Tragedy. As
light is struck from darkness by the blow of the thunderer (bringing ruin to the evil),
may it be life to great poets.   **25–27** *Thomas . . . Londinensis*   Thomas Middleton held
the office of Chronologer of London.

To his friend
MR. JOHN WEBSTER
upon his
Duchess of Malfi

I never saw thy Duchess, till the day,   5
That she was lively bodied in thy play;
Howe'er she answered her low-rated love,
Her brothers' anger did so fatal prove,
Yet my opinion is, she might speak more;
But never (in her life) so well before.   10

WIL: ROWLEY

To the reader of the author,
and his
Duchess of Malfi

Crown him a poet, whom nor Rome nor Greece
Transcend in all theirs for a masterpiece: 5
In which—whiles words and matter change, and men
Act one another—he, from whose clear pen
They all took life, to memory hath lent
A lasting fame, to raise his monument.

JOHN FORD   10

Rowley's Poem 6 *she . . . bodied* both "given living form by an actor" and "given
the life of artistic form by Webster."
Ford's Poem 6 *whiles . . . change* while the action on the stage ("words and matter")
progresses.

⟨DRAMATIS PERSONAE⟩

BOSOLA, *gentleman of the Duchess' horse*

FERDINAND, *Duke of Calabria*

CARDINAL, *his brother*

ANTONIO, *steward of the Duchess' household*

DELIO, *his friend*

FOROBOSCO

MALATESTE, *a count*

The Marquis of PESCARA

SILVIO, *a lord*

CASTRUCHIO, *an old lord*

RODERIGO ⎱ *lords*
GRISOLAN ⎰

THE DUCHESS, *sister of Ferdinand and the Cardinal*

CARIOLA, *her woman*

JULIA, *wife to Castruchio and mistress to the Cardinal*

The DOCTOR

COURT OFFICERS

The several madmen, including: ASTROLOGER, TAILOR, PRIEST, DOCTOR

OLD LADY

THREE YOUNG CHILDREN

TWO PILGRIMS

ATTENDANTS, LADIES, EXECUTIONERS

456

ACT I

Scene I   ⟨*The* DUCHESS' *palace in Amalfi*⟩

[*Enter* ANTONIO *and* DELIO.]

DELIO   You are welcome to your country, dear Antonio,
　　　You have been long in France, and you return
　　　A very formal Frenchman, in your habit.
　　　How do you like the French court?

ANTONIO 　　　　　　　　　　　I admire it;
　　　In seeking to reduce both State and people   5
　　　To a fixed order, their judicious king
　　　Begins at home. Quits first his royal palace
　　　Of flatt'ring sycophants, of dissolute,
　　　And infamous persons, which he sweetly terms
　　　His Master's masterpiece, the work of Heaven,   10
　　　Consid'ring duly, that a prince's court
　　　Is like a common fountain, whence should flow
　　　Pure silver-drops in general. But if 't chance
　　　Some cursed example poison 't near the head,
　　　Death and diseases through the whole land spread.   15
　　　And what is 't makes this blessèd government,
　　　But a most provident council, who dare freely
　　　Inform him the corruption of the times?
　　　Though some o' th' court hold it presumption
　　　To instruct princes what they ought to do,   20
　　　It is a noble duty to inform them
　　　What they ought to foresee. Here comes Bosola,
　　　The only court-gall: yet I observe his railing
　　　Is not for simple love of piety:
　　　Indeed he rails at those things which he wants,   25
　　　Would be as lecherous, covetous, or proud,
　　　Bloody, or envious, as any man,
　　　If he had means to be so.—Here's the Cardinal.

🦁 **ACT I, Scene I.**   **3** *habit* dress.   **7** *Quits* empties.   **9** *which* modifies either the "royal palace" or the process of ridding.   **14** *head* both the source of the fountain and the chief of state.   **18** *Inform him* inform him about.   **23** *court-gall* both a sore spot in the court and a bitter railer against the court.

[*Enter* BOSOLA *and the* CARDINAL.]

BOSOLA I do haunt you still.

CARDINAL So.   30

BOSOLA I have done you better service than to be slighted thus.
Miserable age, where only the reward of doing well, is the doing of it!

CARDINAL You enforce your merit too much.

BOSOLA I fell into the galleys in your service, where, for two years
together, I wore two towels instead of a shirt, with a knot on the   35
shoulder, after the fashion of a Roman mantle. Slighted thus, I
will thrive some way: blackbirds fatten best in hard weather, why
not I, in these dog days?

CARDINAL Would you could become honest,—

BOSOLA With all your divinity, do but direct me the way to it.   40
I have known many travel far for it, and yet return as arrant
knaves, as they went forth; because they carried themselves
always along with them. [*Exit* CARDINAL.] Are you gone? Some
fellows, they say, are possessed with the devil, but this great
fellow were able to possess the greatest devil, and make him   45
worse.

ANTONIO He hath denied thee some suit?

BOSOLA He and his brother are like plum trees, that grow crooked
over standing pools, they are rich, and o'erladen with fruit, but
none but crows, pies, and caterpillars feed on them. Could I be   50
one of their flatt'ring panders, I would hang on their ears like a
horseleech, till I were full, and then drop off. I pray, leave me.
Who would rely upon these miserable dependences, in expectation
to be advanced tomorrow? What creature ever fed worse, than
hoping Tantalus; nor ever died any man more fearfully, than he   55
that hoped for a pardon? There are rewards for hawks, and dogs,
when they have done us service; but for a soldier, that hazards his
limbs in a battle, nothing but a kind of geometry is his last sup-
portation.

DELIO Geometry?   60

---

32 only the the only. **33 enforce** emphasize. **37 blackbirds . . . weather** It was
commonly thought that blackbirds grew fat in cold weather—perhaps because their
ruffled feathers made them seem heavier then. **38 dog days** corrupt times. **42–43 because . . . them** because they could not get away from the evil within themselves.
49 standing stagnant. **50 pies** magpies. **53 dependence** social inferiority that
makes one dependent upon the favors of another. **55 Tantalus** a wrongdoer who was
punished in Hades by being set, thirsty and hungry, in a pool of water that receded
whenever he tried to drink from it and under a tree whose fruit he could never reach.
58 kind of geometry hanging in a stiff, angular position.

BOSOLA   Ay, to hang in a fair pair of slings, take his latter swing in
the world, upon an honorable pair of crutches, from hospital to
hospital. Fare ye well sir, and yet do not you scorn us; for places
in the court are but like beds in the hospital, where this man's
head lies at that man's foot, and so lower and lower. [*Exit* BOSOLA.]   65
DELIO   I knew this fellow seven years in the galleys,
For a notorious murther, and 'twas thought
The Cardinal suborned it: he was released
By the French general, Gaston de Foix
When he recovered Naples.
ANTONIO   'Tis great pity   70
He should be thus neglected: I have heard
He's very valiant. This foul melancholy
Will poison all his goodness; for, I'll tell you,
If too immoderate sleep be truly said
To be an inward rust unto the soul,   75
It then doth follow want of action
Breeds all black malcontents, and their close rearing,
Like moths in cloth, do hurt for want of wearing.

⟨ACT I⟩   Scene 2

[DELIO *and* ANTONIO *pass into the inner stage, where* CASTRUCHIO,
SILVIO, RODERIGO, *and* GRISOLAN *are entering.*]

DELIO   The presence 'gins to fill. You promised me
To make me the partaker of the natures
Of some of your great courtiers.
ANTONIO   The Lord Cardinal's

---

66 seven . . . galleys This statement only appears to contradict Bosola's complaint in
lines 34–35. His claim there that for two years—an arbitrary identification of an indefinite
period of time—he has gone without a change of clothes is presented as an illustration of
the wretched conditions imposed upon galley slaves. **68 suborned it** secretly induced
him to do it. **69 Gaston de Foix** Webster is confused here, for although Gaston de
Foix was a French general who won an important victory over the Spanish and papal
armies at Ravenna in 1512, he had nothing to do with the conquest of Naples in 1501:
at that time he was only thirteen years old. **77 their . . . rearing** their self-centered,
invidious brooding. **78 do hurt** hurts (the verb governs "close rearing," but it is given
a plural form because of its proximity to "moths in cloth"). **wearing** exposure to the
air (of action).
ACT I, Scene 2. SD Castruchio The name is meant to suggest impotence.
1 presence presence chamber, where nobility received official visitors. **2–3 To . . . Of**
to tell me about the characters of.

And other strangers', that are now in court?

I shall. Here comes the great Calabrian duke.   5

[*Enter* FERDINAND *and* ATTENDANTS.]

FERDINAND   Who took the ring oft'nest?

SILVIO   Antonio Bologna, my lord.

FERDINAND   Our sister Duchess' great master of her household? Give
   him the jewel.—When shall we leave this sportive action, and fall
   to action indeed?   10

CASTRUCHIO   Methinks, my lord, you should not desire to go to war
   in person.

FERDINAND   [*Aside*.] Now for some gravity:—why, my lord?

CASTRUCHIO   It is fitting a soldier arise to be a prince, but not necessary
   a prince descend to be a captain!   15

FERDINAND   No?

CASTRUCHIO   No, my lord, he were far better do it by a deputy.

FERDINAND   Why should he not as well sleep, or eat, by a deputy?
   This might take idle, offensive, and base office from him, whereas
   the other deprives him of honor.   20

CASTRUCHIO   Believe my experience: that realm is never long in
   quiet where the ruler is a soldier.

FERDINAND   Thou toldst me thy wife could not endure fighting.

CASTRUCHIO   True, my lord.

FERDINAND   And of a jest she broke of a captain she met full of wounds: 25
   I have forgot it.

CASTRUCHIO   She told him, my lord, he was a pitiful fellow, to lie,
   like the children of Ismael, all in tents.

FERDINAND   Why, there's a wit were able to undo all the chirurgeons
   o' the city, for although gallants should quarrel, and had drawn   30
   their weapons, and were ready to go to it; yet her persuasions
   would make them put up.

CASTRUCHIO   That she would, my lord.

   How do you like my Spanish jennet?

---

6 took the ring won at jousting (by carrying off a ring with one's lance).   **8 great
master** steward.   **25 broke of** told about.   **28 children of Ismael** Arabs.   **tents** a
pun, meaning both "tents" in the modern sense and also rolls of lint used for dressing
wounds.   **29–32 there's . . . up** The sexual innuendoes in this speech—obvious in
"drawn their weapons," "go to it," and "put up" and probable in "undo" and "persuasions"—suggest both Julia's promiscuity and Ferdinand's licentiousness. The lewdness
prevalent in Ferdinand's idiom suggests powerful incestuous desires, not fully suppressed.
29 chirurgeons surgeons.   **34 jennet** a small Spanish horse.

RODERIGO He is all fire.   35

FERDINAND I am of Pliny's opinion. I think he was begot by the
wind; he runs as if he were ballassed with quicksilver.

SILVIO True, my lord, he reels from the tilt often.

RODERIGO *and* GRISOLAN Ha, ha, ha!

FERDINAND Why do you laugh? Methinks you that are courtiers   40
should be my touchwood: take fire when I give fire; that is,
laugh when I laugh, were the subject never so witty—

CASTRUCHIO True, my lord, I myself have heard a very good jest,
and have scorned to seem to have so silly a wit, as to understand it.

FERDINAND But I can laugh at your fool, my lord.   45

CASTRUCHIO He cannot speak, you know, but he makes faces; my
lady cannot abide him.

FERDINAND No?

CASTRUCHIO Nor endure to be in merry company: for she says too
much laughing, and too much company, fills her too full of the   50
wrinkle.

FERDINAND I would then have a mathematical instrument made for
her face, that she might not laugh out of compass. I shall shortly
visit you at Milan, Lord Silvio.

SILVIO Your grace shall arrive most welcome.   55

FERDINAND You are a good horseman, Antonio; you have excellent
riders in France, what do you think of good horsemanship?

ANTONIO Nobly, my lord: as out of the Grecian horse issued many
famous princes: so out of brave horsemanship, arise the first
sparks of growing resolution, that raise the mind to noble   60
action.

FERDINAND You have bespoke it worthily.

[*Enter* DUCHESS, CARDINAL, CARIOLA, JULIA, *and* ATTENDANTS.]

---

36 Pliny's opinion In his *Natural History,* Pliny wrote that some Portuguese mares
were impregnated by the West Wind. **37 ballassed** ballasted. **quicksilver** the element mercury, noted for its mobility. **38 reels . . . tilt** shies away from the ring that
is the target in tilting (cf. I.2.6). **41 touchwood** tinder. **44 silly** simple. **50–51 fills
. . . wrinkle** There is in this speech a sexual pun, which Castruchio, who is stupidly
innocent of his wife's unfaithfulness, does not recognize. **wrinkle** both a physical and
a moral blemish and, here, pudendum as well. **52 mathematical instrument** some
compasslike device for confining movement. **53 out of compass** to excess. **58 Grecian
horse** The huge wooden horse which the Greeks secretly filled with their best and
noblest soldiers and which the Trojans foolishly transported within the walls of their city.
SD Cariola Cariola's name, like Castruchio's, is thematically appropriate. A "carriolo"
was, among other things, a trundle bed, which servants like Cariola used to sleep in so
that they might remain accessible to their mistresses.

SILVIO   Your brother, the Lord Cardinal, and sister Duchess.

CARDINAL   Are the galleys come about?

GRISOLAN   They are, my lord.   65

FERDINAND   Here's the Lord Silvio, is come to take his leave.

DELIO   [*Aside to* ANTONIO.] Now sir, your promise: what's that
    Cardinal? I mean his temper? They say he's a brave fellow, will
    play his five thousand crowns at tennis, dance, court ladies, and
    one that hath fought single combats.   70

ANTONIO   Some such flashes superficially hang on him, for form;
    but observe his inward character: he is a melancholy churchman.
    The spring in his face is nothing but the engend'ring of toads:
    where he is jealous of any man, he lays worse plots for them, than
    ever was imposed on Hercules, for he strews in his way flatterers,   75
    panders, intelligencers, atheists, and a thousand such political
    monsters. He should have been Pope, but instead of coming to it
    by the primitive decency of the Church, he did bestow bribes, so
    largely and so impudently as if he would have carried it away
    without Heaven's knowledge. Some good he hath done—   80

DELIO   You have given too much of him. What's his brother?

ANTONIO   The Duke there? a most perverse and turbulent nature:
    What appears in him mirth, is merely outside;
    If he laugh heartily, it is to laugh
    All honesty out of fashion.

DELIO   Twins?

ANTONIO   In quality: 85
    He speaks with others' tongues, and hears men's suits
    With others' ears, will seem to sleep o' th' bench
    Only to entrap offenders in their answers;
    Dooms men to death by information,
    Rewards, by hearsay.

DELIO   Then the law to him   90
    Is like a foul black cobweb to a spider:

---

64 come about returned to port. **71 flashes** examples of showy behavior. **73 spring
. . . toads** countenance of nobility hides a vicious, scheming temperament.
75 Hercules a mythical hero, considered the strongest mortal, who performed twelve
superhuman "labors." **76 political** plotting. **78 primitive decency** simple and
straightforward honesty. **85 Twins** Are these two brothers twins, then? **86 He**
Ferdinand. **89 information** the testimony of informers. **89–90 Dooms . . . hearsay**
Antonio implies that Ferdinand's judgments are arbitrary and cruel, for the testimony of
informers, who are paid for what they say, is hardly more reliable evidence than hearsay.
When Ferdinand is their judge, men are doomed to death or rewarded indiscriminately
as he chooses.

He makes it his dwelling, and a prison
To entangle those shall feed him.

ANTONIO   Most true:
He ne'er pays debts, unless they be shrewd turns,
And those he will confess that he doth owe.   95
Last, for his brother there, the Cardinal:
They that do flatter him most say oracles
Hang at his lips, and verily I believe them:
For the devil speaks in them.
But for their sister, the right noble Duchess,   100
You never fixed your eye on three fair medals,
Cast in one figure, of so different temper.
For her discourse, it is so full of rapture,
You only will begin, then to be sorry
When she doth end her speech; and wish, in wonder,   105
She held it less vainglory to talk much
Than your penance, to hear her. Whilst she speaks,
She throws upon a man so sweet a look,
That it were able to raise one to a galliard
That lay in a dead palsy; and to dote   110
On that sweet countenance. But in that look
There speaketh so divine a continence,
As cuts off all lascivious and vain hope.
Her days are practiced in such noble virtue,
That sure her nights, nay more, her very sleeps,   115
Are more in heaven, than other ladies' shrifts.
Let all sweet ladies break their flatt'ring glasses,
And dress themselves in her.

DELIO   Fie, Antonio,
You play the wire-drawer with her commendations.

---

93 those . . . him those that he feeds upon.   **94 shrewd turns** evil doings.
97 oracles words of great wisdom.   **101–02 You . . . temper** You have never seen
three medals depicting the same figure which are made of such different kinds of metal
as these three people.   **104–07 You . . . her** a deceptively difficult statement, which
may be paraphrased: Just when you have begun (to feel this rapture), you will become
sorry that she has ended her speech. And then, under the wonder of her spell, you will
wish that she thought it more noble ("less vainglory") to talk a great deal than she
thought it discomforting to you ("your penance") to hear her talk.   **109 galliard** a
lively dance.   **110 and to** and (it is also able to make one).   **114 practiced** habitually
spent.   **116 shrifts** confessions to a priest.   **117 glasses** mirrors.   **118 And . . . her**
and follow her example.   **119 wire-drawer** one who draws out wire from metal and,
metaphorically, one who overextends the limits of truth.

ANTONIO   I'll case the picture up. Only thus much—   120
   All her particular worth grows to this sum:
   She stains the time past, lights the time to come.
CARIOLA   You must attend my lady, in the gallery,
   Some half an hour hence.
ANTONIO   I shall.   [*Exeunt* ANTONIO *and* DELIO.]
FERDINAND   Sister, I have a suit to you.
DUCHESS   To me, sir?   125
FERDINAND   A gentleman here: Daniel de Bosola,
   One that was in the galleys.
DUCHESS   Yes, I know him.
FERDINAND   A worthy fellow h'is. Pray let me entreat for
   The provisorship of your horse.
DUCHESS   Your knowledge of him
   Commends him, and prefers him.
FERDINAND   Call him hither.   130
                  [*Exit* ATTENDANT.]
   We are now upon parting. Good Lord Silvio
   Do us commend to all our noble friends
   At the leaguer.
SILVIO   Sir, I shall.
DUCHESS   You are for Milan?
SILVIO   I am.
DUCHESS   Bring the caroches. We'll bring you down to the haven.   135
   [*Exeunt* DUCHESS, CARIOLA, SILVIO, CASTRUCHIO, RODERIGO, GRISO-
                LAN, JULIA, *and* ATTENDANTS.]
CARDINAL   Be sure you entertain that Bosola
   For your intelligence. I would not be seen in't.
   And therefore many times I have slighted him
   When he did court our furtherance, as this morning.
FERDINAND   Antonio, the great master of her household   140
   Had been far fitter.
CARDINAL   You are deceived in him,
   His nature is too honest for such business.—

---

120 *I'll . . . up*   I'll put this picture of her (that I have presented) away.   *Only . . .*
much   Only this will I say in summary.   122 *stains*   deprives of luster.   125 *a . . .*
you   one who has a request to make of you.   128–29 *let . . . horse*   Let me entreat you
to let him serve as your groom.   131 *upon parting*   preparing to leave.   133 *leaguer*
camp.   135 *caroches*   coaches.   136–37 *entertain . . . intelligence*   use Bosola to gather
information secretly.

He comes: I'll leave you.

[*Enter* BOSOLA.]

BOSOLA   I was lured to you.   [*Exit* CARDINAL.]

FERDINAND   My brother here, the Cardinal, could never
Abide you.

BOSOLA   Never since he was in my debt.   145

FERDINAND   May be some oblique character in your face
Made him suspect you?

BOSOLA   Doth he study physiognomy?
There's no more credit to be given to th' face,
Than to a sick man's urine, which some call
The physician's whore, because she cozens him.   150
He did suspect me wrongfully.

FERDINAND   For that
You must give great men leave to take their times:
Distrust doth cause us seldom be deceived;
You see, the oft shaking of the cedar tree
Fastens it more at root.

BOSOLA   Yet take heed: 155
For to suspect a friend unworthily,
Instructs him the next way to suspect you,
And prompts him to deceive you.

FERDINAND   There's gold.

BOSOLA   So:
What follows? Never rained such showers as these
Without thunderbolts i' th' tail of them.   160
Whose throat must I cut?

FERDINAND   Your inclination to shed blood rides post
Before my occasion to use you. I give you that
To live i' th' court, here, and observe the Duchess,
To note all the particulars of her havior: 165
What suitors do solicit her for marriage

---

143 lured called, with the implicit idea of "enticed into a trap."   **148–50 There's . . .
him** Most kinds of sickness would not be recognizable in a urinary analysis.   **153 seldom
be** to be seldom.   **157 the . . . way** in the quickest way.   **159–60 Never . . . them**
Bosola here refers to the mythical story in which Zeus transforms himself into a shower
of gold in order to possess Danae, who is imprisoned in a brass tower. The obscene use
of the word "tail" in this speech provides almost as good an example of Bosola's cyni-
cism as his bold conclusion: "Whose throat must I cut?"   **162 rides post** rides swiftly,
upon horseback, changing mounts often.   **163 I . . . that** I command you.

And whom she best affects. She's a young widow;
I would not have her marry again.

BOSOLA   No, sir?

FERDINAND   Do not you ask the reason, but be satisfied
I say I would not.

BOSOLA   It seems you would create me   170
One of your familiars.

FERDINAND   Familiar? what's that?

BOSOLA   Why, a very quaint invisible devil in flesh,
An intelligencer.

FERDINAND   Such a kind of thriving thing
I would wish thee; and ere long, thou mayst arrive
At a higher place by't.

BOSOLA   [*Trying to give the money back.*] Take your devils,   175
Which hell calls angels: these cursed gifts would make
You a corrupter, me an impudent traitor,
And should I take these they'd take me to hell.

FERDINAND   Sir, I'll take nothing from you that I have given.
There is a place that I procured for you   180
This morning, the provisorship o' th' horse,
Have you heard on't?

BOSOLA   No.

FERDINAND   'Tis yours; is't not worth thanks?

BOSOLA   I would have you curse yourself now, that your bounty,
Which makes men truly noble, e'er should make
Me a villain: oh, that to avoid ingratitude   185
For the good deed you have done me, I must do
All the ill man can invent. Thus the devil
Candies all sins o'er, and what Heaven terms vild,
That names he complimental.

FERDINAND   Be yourself.
Keep your old garb of melancholy: 'twill express   190
You envy those that stand above your reach,
Yet strive not to come near 'em. This will gain
Access to private lodgings, where yourself

---

175 *higher place* the kind of ambiguous statement that is characteristic of villains in
Renaissance drama. Ferdinand may mean either a better social position or a scaffold (from
which to be hanged). **176** *angels* gold coins, which derived their name from the image
of the archangel Michael on them. **184** *Which . . . noble* because money gives man
a position of nobility in society. **188** *Candies . . . o'er* makes sins seem tempting.
vild vile. **189** *complimental* worthy of compliment, good.

            May, like a politic dormouse,—
BOSOLA   As I have seen some,
    Feed in a lord's dish, half asleep, not seeming   195
    To listen to any talk, and yet these rogues
    Have cut his throat in a dream. What's my place?
    The provisorship o' th' horse? say then my corruption
    Grew out of horse dung. I am your creature.
FERDINAND   Away!   200
BOSOLA   Let good men, for good deeds, covet good fame,
    Since place and riches oft are bribes of shame;
    Sometimes the devil doth preach.   *Exit* BOSOLA.

    [*Enter* CARDINAL, DUCHESS, *and* CARIOLA.]

CARDINAL   We are to part from you: and your own discretion
    Must now be your director.
FERDINAND   You are a widow: 205
    You know already what man is; and therefore
    Let not youth, high promotion, eloquence,—
CARDINAL   No, nor any thing without the addition, honor,
    Sway your high blood.
FERDINAND   Marry? they are most luxurious,
    Will wed twice.
CARDINAL   O fie!
FERDINAND   Their livers are more spotted   210
    Than Laban's sheep.
DUCHESS   Diamonds are of most value,
    They say, that have passed through most jewelers' hands.
FERDINAND   Whores, by that rule, are precious.
DUCHESS   Will you hear me?
    I'll never marry—
CARDINAL   So most widows say,
    But commonly that motion lasts no longer   215
    Than the turning of an hourglass; the funeral sermon
    And it, end both together.
FERDINAND   Now hear me:
    You live in a rank pasture; here, i' th' court,
    There is a kind of honeydew that's deadly:

---

197 in a dream while he slept.   **209 luxurious** incontinent.   **210 Will** who will.
livers The liver was believed to be the source of passion.   **211 Laban's sheep** In
Laban's flock were many spotted sheep (Genesis 30:29–43).   **215 motion** resolution.
219 honeydew a sweet, sticky substance secreted by some plants.

'Twill poison your fame; look to't; be not cunning,   220
For they whose faces do belie their hearts
Are witches, ere they arrive at twenty years,
Ay, and give the devil suck.
DUCHESS   This is terrible good counsel.
FERDINAND   Hypocrisy is woven of a fine small thread,
Subtler than Vulcan's engine: yet, believe't,   225
Your darkest actions, nay, your privat'st thoughts,
Will come to light.
CARDINAL   You may flatter yourself,
And take your own choice, privately be married
Under the eaves of night—
FERDINAND   Think't the best voyage
That e'er you made; like the irregular crab,   230
Which, though't goes backward, thinks that it goes right,
Because it goes its own way; but observe,
Such weddings may more properly be said
To be executed, than celebrated.
CARDINAL   The marriage night
Is the entrance into some prison.
FERDINAND   And those joys,   235
Those lustful pleasures, are like heavy sleeps
Which do forerun man's mischief.
CARDINAL   Fare you well.
Wisdom begins at the end: remember it.   [*Exit* CARDINAL.]
DUCHESS   I think this speech between you both was studied,
It came so roundly off.
FERDINAND   You are my sister,   240
This was my father's poniard: do you see,
I'd be loath to see't look rusty, 'cause 'twas his.
I would have you to give o'er these chargeable revels;
A visor and a mask are whispering-rooms
That were ne'er built for goodness: fare ye well.   245
And women like that part, which, like the lamprey,

---

220 *fame* reputation. **225** *Vulcan's engine* the net that Vulcan used to catch his wife,
Venus, and her paramour, Mars. **237** *mischief* misfortune. **238** *Wisdom . . . end*
considers the end before beginning an action. **241** *poniard* dagger. **242** *I'd . . . rusty*
I would not like to see it covered with your blood ("rusty"). **243** *chargeable* expen-
sive. **244** *visor . . . mask* part of the costume used by lords and ladies participating in
the revelry of a masque. *whispering-rooms* small rooms where secret, often amorous,
interviews were held. **246** *lamprey* eel-like fish.

Hath ne'er a bone in't.
DUCHESS   Fie sir!
FERDINAND   Nay,
I mean the tongue—variety of courtship—
What cannot a neat knave with a smooth tale
Make a woman believe? Farewell, lusty widow.   250

                    [Exit FERDINAND.*]*

DUCHESS   Shall this move me? If all my royal kindred
Lay in my way unto this marriage,
I'd make them my low footsteps. And even now,
Even in this hate, as men in some great battles,
By apprehending danger, have achiev'd   255
Almost impossible actions (I have heard soldiers say so),
So I, through frights and threat'nings, will assay
This dangerous venture. Let old wives report
I winked, and chose a husband. Cariola,
To thy known secrecy I have given up   260
More than my life, my fame.
CARIOLA   Both shall be safe:
For I'll conceal this secret from the world
As warily as those that trade in poison
Keep poison from their children.
DUCHESS   Thy protestation
Is ingenious and hearty: I believe it.   265
Is Antonio come?
CARIOLA   He attends you.
DUCHESS   Good, dear soul,
Leave me; but place thyself behind the arras,
Where thou mayst overhear us. Wish me good speed,
For I am going into a wilderness,
Where I shall find nor path, nor friendly clew   270
To be my guide.

*[*CARIOLA *goes behind the curtain, and the* DUCHESS *draws the traverse
to reveal* ANTONIO.*]*

          I sent for you. Sit down:

---

248 *variety of courtship* (the source of) variety in courtship (because it can express
love in so many different ways). (?) **253 *footsteps*** steppingstones. **261 *fame*** reputation. **265 *ingenious*** straightforward. **270 *clew*** something that helps one out of a
labyrinth.

Take pen and ink, and write. Are you ready?

ANTONIO   Yes.

DUCHESS What did I say?

ANTONIO   That I should write somewhat.

DUCHESS Oh, I remember:

    After these triumphs and this large expense   275
    It's fit, like thrifty husbands, we inquire
    What's laid up for tomorrow.

ANTONIO So please your beauteous excellence.

DUCHESS   Beauteous?

    Indeed I thank you. I look young for your sake:
    You have ta'en my cares upon you.

ANTONIO   I'll fetch your grace   280
    The particulars of your revenue and expense.

DUCHESS Oh, you are an upright treasurer, but you mistook,

    For when I said I meant to make inquiry
    What's laid up for tomorrow, I did mean
    What's laid up yonder for me.

ANTONIO   Where?

DUCHESS   In heaven.   285

    I am making my will, as 'tis fit princes should,
    In perfect memory, and I pray, sir, tell me
    Were not one better make it smiling, thus,
    Than in deep groans and terrible ghastly looks,
    As if the gifts we parted with procured   290
    That violent distraction?

ANTONIO   Oh, much better.

DUCHESS If I had a husband now, this care were quit;

    But I intend to make you overseer.
    What good deed shall we first remember? Say.

ANTONIO Begin with that first good deed, began i' th' world,   295

    After man's creation, the sacrament of marriage.
    I'd have you first provide for a good husband;
    Give him all.

DUCHESS   All?

ANTONIO   Yes, your excellent self.

DUCHESS In a winding sheet?

ANTONIO   In a couple.

---

276 husbands a pun, meaning both "stewards" and "married men." **282 *mistook***
misunderstood (me).

DUCHESS St. Winifred! that were a strange will.

ANTONIO   'Twere strange   300
 If there were no will in you to marry again.

DUCHESS What do you think of marriage?

ANTONIO I take't, as those that deny purgatory:
 It locally contains or heaven, or hell;
 There's no third place in't.

DUCHESS   How do you affect it?   305

ANTONIO My banishment, feeding my melancholy,
 Would often reason thus:—

DUCHESS   Pray, let's hear it.

ANTONIO Say a man never marry, nor have children,
 What takes that from him? only the bare name
 Of being a father, or the weak delight   310
 To see the little wanton ride a-cock-horse
 Upon a painted stick, or hear him chatter
 Like a taught starling.

DUCHESS   Fie, fie, what's all this?
 One of your eyes is bloodshot, use my ring to't.
 They say 'tis very sovereign: 'twas my wedding ring,   315
 And I did vow never to part with it,
 But to my second husband.

ANTONIO You have parted with it now.

DUCHESS   Yes, to help your eyesight.

ANTONIO You have made me stark blind.

DUCHESS   How?

ANTONIO There is a saucy and ambitious devil   320
 Is dancing in this circle.

DUCHESS   Remove him.

ANTONIO   How?

DUCHESS There needs small conjuration, when your finger
 May do it: thus, is it fit?

[She puts the ring on his finger and] he kneels.

ANTONIO   What said you?

DUCHESS   Sir,

---

300 St. Winifred a Welsh saint of the seventh century who was beheaded by Caradoc ap Alauc when she rejected his amorous advances. **304 locally** in itself. **305 affect** feel about. **311 wanton** fellow. **315 sovereign** effective. **321 circle** the ring. **322 small conjuration** little magic. **323 is it fit** Does it fit?

This goodly roof of yours is too low built;
I cannot stand upright in't, nor discourse   325
Without I raise it higher: raise yourself,
Or if you please, my hand to help you: so.

[*Raises him.*]

ANTONIO   Ambition, madam, is a great man's madness
That is not kept in chains and close-pent rooms,
But in fair lightsome lodgings, and is girt   330
With the wild noise of prattling visitants,
Which makes it lunatic, beyond all cure.
Conceive not I am so stupid, but I aim
Whereto your favors tend. But he's a fool
That, being a-cold, would thrust his hand i' th' fire   335
To warm them.

DUCHESS   So, now the ground's broke,
You may discover what a wealthy mine
I make you lord of.

ANTONIO   O my unworthiness!

DUCHESS   You were ill to sell yourself.
This dark'ning of your worth is not like that   340
Which tradesmen use i' th' city; their false lights
Are to rid bad wares off. And I must tell you
If you will know where breathes a complete man,
(I speak it without flattery), turn your eyes
And progress through yourself.

ANTONIO   Were there nor heaven, nor hell, 345
I should be honest: I have long served virtue,
And ne'er ta'en wages of her.

DUCHESS   Now she pays it.
The misery of us that are born great:
We are forced to woo, because none dare woo us.
And as a tyrant doubles with his words,   350
And fearfully equivocates, so we

---

324 *This . . . built* Your humble attitude makes me uncomfortable. **326** *Without* unless. **327** *my hand* (here is) my hand. **331** *visitants* visitors. **333** *so stupid* so lunatic (as to be ambitious). **339** *ill* ill-advised. **341** *tradesmen use* Food shops were kept dark so that buyers could not closely examine a tradesman's wares. **342** *rid* pass. **345** *progress through* look carefully at. **350** *doubles . . . words* employs phrases with ambiguous, double meanings. **351** *fearfully* causing fear (in others).

Are forced to express our violent passions
In riddles and in dreams, and leave the path
Of simple virtue, which was never made
To seem the thing it is not. Go, go brag   355
You have left me heartless; mine is in your bosom:
I hope 'twill multiply love there. You do tremble:
Make not your heart so dead a piece of flesh
To fear more than to love me. Sir, be confident.
What is't distracts you? This is flesh and blood, sir,   360
'Tis not the figure cut in alabaster
Kneels at my husband's tomb. Awake, awake, man!
I do here put off all vain ceremony,
And only do appear to you, a young widow
That claims you for her husband, and like a widow,   365
I use but half a blush in't.
ANTONIO   Truth speak for me,
I will remain the constant sanctuary
Of your good name.
DUCHESS   I thank you, gentle love,
And 'cause you shall not come to me in debt,
Being now my steward, here upon your lips   370
I sign your *Quietus est*. This you should have begged now:
I have seen children oft eat sweetmeats thus,
As fearful to devour them too soon.
ANTONIO   But for your brothers?
DUCHESS   Do not think of them:
All discord without this circumference   375
Is only to be pitied, and not feared.

361–62 'Tis . . . tomb   The whiteness of alabaster made it, like marble, suitable for use
in funeral monuments. The Duchess' reference here is, no doubt, to a statue that marks
her first husband's tomb. But like much of the language in this scene—with its talk of
wills, winding sheets, and wildly jabbering lunatics—the imagery looks forward to the
Duchess' future as well as backward to her past. By the careful repetition of images
such as these, Webster skillfully outlines the hostile, constricting world that circumscribes
the lovers and threatens their happiness.   **366 I . . . in't**   I have been made bold by my
experience.   **369 'cause**   so that.   **371 Quietus est**   This phrase, which was often
used in account books, literally means "It is finished," and in this instance the reference
is to Antonio's obligations as steward. But the word "quietus" is also associated with
death (cf. *Hamlet* III.1.75), since man makes his acquittance with nature at death. Here,
although the Duchess is conscious of only the first meaning, both are implicit because the
marriage hastens Antonio's death.   **375 without**   outside.

Yet, should they know it, time will easily
Scatter the tempest.

ANTONIO   These words should be mine,
And all the parts you have spoke, if some part of it
Would not have savored flattery.

DUCHESS   Kneel.

[*Enter* CARIOLA.]

ANTONIO   Ha?   380

DUCHESS   Be not amazed; this woman's of my counsel.
I have heard lawyers say, a contract in a chamber,
Per verba [de] presenti, is absolute marriage.
Bless, Heaven, this sacred gordian, which let violence
Never untwine.   385

ANTONIO   And may our sweet affections, like the spheres,
Be still in motion.

DUCHESS   Quick'ning, and make
The like soft music.

ANTONIO   That we may imitate the loving palms,
Best emblem of a peaceful marriage,   390
That ne'er bore fruit divided.

DUCHESS   What can the Church force more?

ANTONIO   That Fortune may not know an accident
Either of joy or sorrow, to divide
Our fixèd wishes.

DUCHESS   How can the Church build faster?   395
We now are man and wife, and 'tis the Church
That must but echo this. Maid, stand apart,
I now am blind.

ANTONIO   What's your conceit in this?

DUCHESS   I would have you lead your fortune by the hand,
Unto your marriage bed: 400
(You speak in me this, for we now are one)

---

380 *savored* resembled. **383** *Per . . . presenti* "through words of the present (tense)":
the lovers henceforth accept each other as husband and wife, in a contract that is legally
valid. **384** *gordian* a knot that cannot be untied. **386–87** *like . . . motion* Planets
were thought to revolve around the earth in concentric, transparent, spherical shells.
387 *still* always. *Quick'ning* stirring to life. **388** *music* The harmonious motion
of the planets in the spheres was supposed to make sweet music. **389–91** *That . . .
divided* Fruit-bearing palm trees were thought to depend for their productivity upon
a male palm tree. **397** *Maid* Cariola. **398** *I . . . blind* I have been made blind by
love (because I have eyes only for Antonio). *conceit* meaning.

We'll only lie, and talk together, and plot
T'appease my humorous kindred; and if you please,
Like the old tale, in *Alexander and Lodowick,*
Lay a naked sword between us, keep us chaste.   405
Oh, let me shroud my blushes in your bosom,
Since 'tis the treasury of all my secrets.

                    [ANTONIO *and the* DUCHESS *begin to exit slowly.*]
CARIOLA   Whether the spirit of greatness, or of woman
         Reign most in her, I know not, but it shows
         A fearful madness: I owe her much of pity.   *Exeunt.*   410

ACT II

Scene I   ⟨*The* DUCHESS' *palace about a year later*⟩.

[*Enter* BOSOLA *and* CASTRUCHIO.]

BOSOLA   You say you would fain be taken for an eminent courtier?
CASTRUCHIO   'Tis the very main of my ambition.
BOSOLA   Let me see, you have a reasonable good face for't already,
   and your nightcap expresses your ears sufficient largely. I would
   have you learn to twirl the strings of your band with a good   5
   grace; and in a set speech, at th'end of every sentence, to hum
   three or four times, or blow your nose till it smart again, to
   recover your memory. When you come to be a president in
   criminal causes, if you smile upon a prisoner, hang him, but if
   you frown upon him and threaten him, let him be sure to scape   10
   the gallows.
CASTRUCHIO   I would be a very merry president,—
BOSOLA   Do not sup a-nights; 'twill beget you an admirable wit.

---

403 *humorous*   volatile, subject to many humors.   **404** *Alexander and Lodowick*   two
legendary friends so alike no one could tell them apart; so true was Lodowick to their
friendship that he married the Princess of Hungaria in Alexander's name and then every
night placed a naked sword in the bed between himself and the Princess in order to keep
from wronging Alexander.   **406** *shroud*   bury.
❀ ACT II, Scene I.   **2** *main*   goal.   **4** *nightcap*   the coif, a white cap worn by
lawyers.   *expresses . . . largely*   makes your ears stick out far enough.   **5** *band*   white
tabs that were also part of the lawyer's official costume.   **8** *president*   presiding judge.

CASTRUCHIO Rather it would make me have a good stomach to
quarrel, for they say your roaring boys eat meat seldom, and   15
that makes them so valiant. But how shall I know whether the
people take me for an eminent fellow?

BOSOLA I will teach a trick to know it: give out you lie a–dying, and
if you hear the common people curse you, be sure you are taken
for one of the prime nightcaps.   20

[*Enter* OLD LADY.]

You come from painting now?

OLD LADY From what?

BOSOLA Why, from your scurvy face-physic. To behold thee not
painted inclines somewhat near a miracle. These, in thy face here,
were deep ruts and foul sloughs the last progress. There was a   25
lady in France that, having had the smallpox, flayed the skin off
her face, to make it more level; and whereas before she looked like
a nutmeg grater, after she resembled an abortive hedgehog.

OLD LADY Do you call this painting?

BOSOLA No, no, but you call it careening of an old morphewed lady,   30
to make her disembogue again. There's rough-cast phrase to your
plastic.

OLD LADY It seems you are well acquainted with my closet?

BOSOLA One would suspect it for a shop of witchcraft, to find in it
the fat of serpents, spawn of snakes, Jews' spittle, and their young   35
children's ordure, and all these for the face. I would sooner eat a
dead pigeon, taken from the soles of the feet of one sick of the
plague, than kiss one of you fasting. Here are two of you, whose
sin of your youth is the very patrimony of the physician, makes

---

14 *good stomach* predisposition. **15** *roaring boys* bullies, quarrelsome young men.
20 *nightcaps* lawyers. **23** *face-physic* a preparation that purges the face of unwanted
layers of skin. **25** *sloughs* both "ditches" and "layers of dead skin." *the . . . progress*
the last time a journey was made by our ruler (and by the coach of time across your
face). **28** *nutmeg grater* because her face was so pock-marked. *hedgehog* In
flaying, the skin would be removed in strips that would roll up and stick out like spines
on a hedgehog. **30** *careening* scraping. *morphewed* covered with scaly skin.
31 *disembogue* set out on a journey. *rough-cast* cast in a kind of rough plaster.
31–32 *There's . . . plastic* There's language as ugly as your appearance. **32** *plastic*
molding. **33** *closet* most private room. **37** *dead pigeon* Pigeons were sometimes
pressed against plague sores in the hope that the poison would be drawn to the birds and
out of the sores. **38** *fasting* when your stomach is empty (and your breath foul).
38–39 *whose . . . physician* whose sins of lust in your youth have infected you with
syphilis, and have thus guaranteed the physician an income for life.

him renew his footcloth with the spring, and change his high-   40
prized courtesan with the fall of the leaf: I do wonder you do not
loathe yourselves. Observe my meditation now:
What thing is in this outward form of man
To be beloved? We account it ominous,
If nature do produce a colt, or lamb,   45
A fawn, or goat, in any limb resembling
A man; and fly from't as a prodigy.
Man stands amazed to see his deformity,
In any other creature but himself.
But in our own flesh, though we bear diseases   50
Which have their true names only ta'en from beasts,
As the most ulcerous wolf, and swinish measle;
Though we are eaten up of lice and worms,
And though continually we bear about us
A rotten and dead body, we delight   55
To hide it in rich tissue: all our fear,
Nay, all our terror, is lest our physician
Should put us in the ground, to be made sweet.
Your wife's gone to Rome. You two couple, and get you
To the wells at Lucca, to recover your aches.   60

                    [*Exeunt* CASTRUCHIO *and* OLD LADY.]

I have other work on foot: I observe our Duchess
Is sick a-days, she pukes, her stomach seethes,
The fins of her eyelids look most teeming blue,
She wanes i' th' cheek, and waxes fat i' th' flank;
And, contrary to our Italian fashion,   65
Wears a loose-bodied gown. There's somewhat in't.
I have a trick may chance discover it,
A pretty one; I have bought some apricocks,
The first our spring yields. [*Enter* ANTONIO *and* DELIO.]

DELIO   [*Aside.*] And so long since married?

---

40 footcloth decorative accouterments for a horse, which advertised the eminence of the owner. **40–41 high-prized** both highly prized and high-priced. **47 prodigy** unnatural monster. **52 wolf** ulcer. **swinish measle** leprosy. **56 rich tissue** elaborate clothing. **59 couple** join, both as traveling and as sleeping companions. **60 wells at Lucca** warm springs near Pisa. **recover** heal. **62 seethes** is violently agitated. **63 fins** edges. **teeming blue** the blue color characteristic of the eyelids of pregnant women. **67–69 I . . . yields** Bosola intends to find out if the Duchess is pregnant by offering her apricots and thus appealing to the strong craving for fruit that is often demonstrated by pregnant women. **68 apricocks** apricots.

You amaze me.

ANTONIO   [*Aside.*] Let me seal your lips for ever,   70
    For did I think that anything but th' air
    Could carry these words from you, I should wish
    You had no breath at all. [*To* BOSOLA.] Now sir, in your contem-
      plation?
    You are studying to become a great wise fellow?

BOSOLA   Oh sir, the opinion of wisdom is a foul tetter, that runs all   75
over a man's body: if simplicity direct us to have no evil, it
directs us to a happy being. For the subtlest folly proceeds from
the subtlest wisdom. Let me be simply honest.

ANTONIO   I do understand your inside.

BOSOLA   Do you so?   80

ANTONIO   Because you would not seem to appear to th' world
    Puffed up with your preferment, you continue
    This out-of-fashion melancholy; leave it, leave it.

BOSOLA   Give me leave to be honest in any phrase, in any compliment
whatsoever. Shall I confess myself to you? I look no higher than   85
I can reach: they are the gods, that must ride on winged horses;
a lawyer's mule of a slow pace will both suit my disposition and
business. For, mark me, when a man's mind rides faster than his
horse can gallop they quickly both tire.

ANTONIO   You would look up to heaven, but I think   90
    The devil, that rules i' th' air, stands in your lights.

BOSOLA   Oh, sir, you are lord of the ascendant, chief man with the
Duchess: a duke was your cousin-german, removed. Say you
were lineally descended from King Pippin, or he himself, what
of this? Search the heads of the greatest rivers in the world, you 95
shall find them but bubbles of water. Some would think the souls
of princes were brought forth by some more weighty cause than
those of meaner persons; they are deceived; there's the same
hand to them: the like passions sway them; the same reason that
makes a vicar go to law for a tithe pig and undo his neighbors,   100
makes them spoil a whole province, and batter down goodly
cities with the cannon.

---

73 *in your contemplation* (Have we interrupted you while you were rapt) in contemplation? **75** *opinion* teachings. *tetter* skin disease, eczema. **76** *have no* have
nothing to do with. **79** *inside* the true nature that you are covering up. **92** *lord . . .
ascendant* ruling power. **93** *cousin-german* first ("germane") cousin. **94** *King
Pippin* father of Charlemagne. **100** *tithe pig* a pig owed to the vicar as a tithe.
101 *them* princes.

[*Enter* DUCHESS *and* LADIES.]

DUCHESS   Your arm, Antonio; do I not grow fat?
I am exceeding short-winded. Bosola,
I would have you, sir, provide for me a litter,   105
Such a one, as the Duchess of Florence rode in.

BOSOLA   The Duchess used one, when she was great with child.

DUCHESS   I think she did. [*To one of her ladies.*] Come hither, mend my
ruff,
Here. When? Thou art such a tedious lady; and
Thy breath smells of lemon peels; would thou hadst done;   110
Shall I sound under thy fingers? I am
So troubled with the mother.

BOSOLA   [*Aside.*] I fear too much.

DUCHESS   [*To* ANTONIO.] I have heard you say that the French courtiers
Wear their hats on 'fore the King.

ANTONIO   I have seen it.

DUCHESS   In the presence?

ANTONIO   Yes.   115

DUCHESS   Why should not we bring up that fashion?
'Tis ceremony more than duty that consists
In the removing of a piece of felt:
Be you the example to the rest o' th' court;
Put on your hat first.

ANTONIO   You must pardon me: 120
I have seen, in colder countries than in France,
Nobles stand bare to th' prince; and the distinction
Methought showed reverently.

BOSOLA   I have a present for your grace.

DUCHESS   For me, sir?

---

108 *ruff* a lace collar. **109 *When*** an expression of impatience. **110 *peels*** In the
first three editions of the play, the word is spelled "pils" and "pills," which could mean
either pills or peels. Though the spelling becomes "peels" in the fourth edition, we cannot know for certain whether this waiting-woman sweetened her breath with lemon peels
or with little lemon pills. The exact particulars of this reference, though, are not important; what matters is its general effect: the Duchess' complaint again draws attention to
one of the corruptions of the flesh that Bosola has just railed against. ***would . . . done***
I wish you were finished. **111 *sound*** swoon. **112 *mother*** the name Elizabethans
gave to a kind of hysteria that was accompanied by swelling in the throat and choking.
The pun on the obvious meaning of "mother" is also intended, and it is this meaning of
the word that Bosola refers to in his subsequent aside. **115 *presence*** presence chamber.
121 *in . . . France* i.e. in England. **122 *bare*** bare-headed.

BOSOLA Apricocks, madam.

DUCHESS   O sir, where are they?   125
    I have heard of none to-year.

BOSOLA   [*Aside.*] Good, her color rises.

DUCHESS Indeed, I thank you: they are wondrous fair ones.
    What an unskillful fellow is our gardener!
    We shall have none this month.

BOSOLA Will not your grace pare them?   130

DUCHESS No, they taste of musk, methinks; indeed they do.

BOSOLA I know not: yet I wish your grace had pared 'em.

DUCHESS Why?

BOSOLA   I forgot to tell you the knave gard'ner,
    Only to raise his profit by them the sooner,
    Did ripen them in horse dung.

DUCHESS   Oh, you jest.   135
    [*To* ANTONIO.] You shall judge: pray taste one.

ANTONIO   Indeed, madam,
    I do not love the fruit.

DUCHESS   Sir, you are loath
    To rob us of our dainties: 'tis a delicate fruit,
    They say they are restorative?

BOSOLA   'Tis a pretty art,
    This grafting.

DUCHESS   'Tis so: a bett'ring of nature.   140

BOSOLA To make a pippin grow upon a crab,
    A damson on a blackthorn. [*Aside.*] How greedily she eats them!
    A whirlwind strike off these bawd farthingales,
    For, but for that, and the loose-bodied gown,
    I should have discovered apparently   145
    The young springal cutting a caper in her belly.

DUCHESS I thank you, Bosola: they were right good ones,
    If they do not make me sick.

ANTONIO   How now, madam?

---

126 to-year this year. **131 musk** an animal secretion used in making perfume.
135 Oh, you jest The Duchess' unruffled reaction to Bosola's vile suggestion attests to
the intensity of her desire for fruit. **139 restorative** healthful. **140 grafting** a double-
entendre, referring to propagation both in fruit trees and in human beings (because the
physical union in sexual intercourse can be considered another form of grafting).
141 pippin, crab different kinds of apples. **142 damson, blackthorn** different kinds of
plums. **143 farthingales** hooped petticoats. **145 apparently** openly manifesting
itself. **146 springal** youth.

DUCHESS   This green fruit and my stomach are not friends.
   How they swell me!   150
BOSOLA   [*Aside.*] Nay, you are too much swelled already.
DUCHESS   Oh, I am in an extreme cold sweat.
BOSOLA   I am very sorry. [*Exit.*]
DUCHESS   Lights to my chamber! O, good Antonio,
   I fear I am undone.   *Exit* DUCHESS.
DELIO   Lights there, lights!
ANTONIO   O my most trusty Delio, we are lost: 155
   I fear she's fall'n in labor, and there's left
   No time for her remove.
DELIO   Have you prepared
   Those ladies to attend her? and procured
   That politic safe conveyance for the midwife
   Your Duchess plotted?
ANTONIO   I have.   160
DELIO   Make use then of this forced occasion:
   Give out that Bosola hath poisoned her,
   With these apricocks. That will give some color
   For her keeping close.
ANTONIO   Fie, fie, the physicians
   Will then flock to her.
DELIO   For that you may pretend   165
   She'll use some prepared antidote of her own,
   Lest the physicians should repoison her.
ANTONIO   I am lost in amazement. I know not what to think on't.
                                 Ex[eunt].

{ACT II}

Scene 2 {*A hall in the* DUCHESS' *palace*}

[*Enter* BOSOLA *and* OLD LADY.]

BOSOLA   So, so: there's no question but her tetchiness and most
   vulturous eating of the apricocks are apparent signs of breeding—
   [*To the* OLD LADY.] Now?

---

159 *politic* secret. **160** *plotted* planned. **161** *forced occasion* circumstances forced
upon us. **163** *color* reason. **164** *close* privately shut away.
❧ **ACT II, Scene 2.** **1** *tetchiness* touchiness. **2** *apparent* obvious.

OLD LADY   I am in haste, sir.

BOSOLA   There was a young waiting-woman, had a monstrous desire   5
to see the glasshouse—

OLD LADY   Nay, pray let me go!

BOSOLA   And it was only to know what strange instrument it was,
should swell up a glass to the fashion of a woman's belly.

OLD LADY   I will hear no more of the glasshouse; you are still abusing   10
women!

BOSOLA   Who, I? no, only, by the way now and then, mention your
frailties. The orange tree bears ripe and green fruit and blossoms
altogether. And some of you give entertainment for pure love,
but more, for more precious reward. The lusty spring smells   15
well, but drooping autumn tastes well. If we have the same golden
showers that rained in the time of Jupiter the Thunderer, you
have the same Danaes still, to hold up their laps to receive them.
Didst thou never study the mathematics?

OLD LADY   What's that, sir?   20

BOSOLA   Why, to know the trick how to make a many lines meet in
one center. Go, go; give your foster daughters good counsel:
tell them, that the devil takes delight to hang at a woman's girdle,
like a false rusty watch, that she cannot discern how the time
passes.   [*Exit* OLD LADY.]   25

[*Enter* ANTONIO, DELIO, RODERIGO, GRISOLAN.]

ANTONIO   Shut up the court gates.

RODERIGO   Why sir? What's the danger?

ANTONIO   Shut up the posterns presently, and call
All the officers o' th' court.

GRISOLAN   I shall instantly.   [*Exit.*]

ANTONIO   Who keeps the key o' th' park gate?

RODERIGO   Forobosco.

ANTONIO   Let him bring't presently.   [*Exit* RODERIGO.]   30

6 *glasshouse* glass factory. 8 *instrument* a double-entendre. 15–16 *The . . . well*
The lusty young woman and the aging whore both find something rewarding in love—
one, the act itself; the other, the money she receives for it. 16–18 *If . . . them* See
note to I.2.159–60. Bosola's argument here is simply that where there are men who are
willing to pay for love, there are women to sell it. 21–22 *Why . . . center* another
obscene reference to the lap of a whore. 22 *foster daughters* women for whom she
serves as a midwife. 23–25 *the . . . passes* Because the devil impassions men with
desires even for women who are old, women are deluded into thinking that they have
not lost the beauty of their youth (and have, consequently, not grown old). 27 *posterns*
back gates. *presently* now, at this present moment.

[*Enter* SERVANTS, GRISOLAN, RODERIGO.]

FIRST SERVANT   Oh, gentlemen o' th' court, the foulest treason!
BOSOLA   [*Aside.*] If that these apricocks should be poisoned now,
    Without my knowledge!
FIRST SERVANT   There was taken even now
    A Switzer in the Duchess' bedchamber.
SECOND SERVANT   A Switzer?
FIRST SERVANT   With a pistol in his great codpiece.
BOSOLA   Ha, ha, ha.   35
FIRST SERVANT   The codpiece was the case for't.
SECOND SERVANT   There was a cunning traitor.
    Who would have searched his codpiece?
FIRST SERVANT   True, if he had kept out of the ladies' chambers.
    And all the moulds of his buttons were leaden bullets.
SECOND SERVANT   Oh wicked cannibal: a firelock in's codpiece?   40
FIRST SERVANT   'Twas a French plot, upon my life.
SECOND SERVANT   To see what the devil can do.
ANTONIO   All the officers here?
SERVANTS   We are.
ANTONIO   Gentlemen,
    We have lost much plate you know; and but this evening
    Jewels, to the value of four thousand ducats
    Are missing in the Duchess' cabinet.   45
    Are the gates shut?
FIRST SERVANT   Yes.
ANTONIO   'Tis the Duchess' pleasure
    Each officer be locked into his chamber
    Till the sun-rising; and to send the keys
    Of all their chests, and of their outward doors
    Into her bedchamber. She is very sick.   50
RODERIGO   At her pleasure.
ANTONIO   She entreats you take't not ill. The innocent
    Shall be the more approved by it.

---

34 *Switzer* a Swiss mercenary. **35 *With . . . codpiece*** The codpiece was a baglike
flap formerly worn in the front of men's breeches and since replaced by the fly. Bosola's
laughter upon hearing that the pistol has been hidden in the Switzer's codpiece results
from his recognition of the obvious double-entendre in "pistol"—a double-entendre that
is developed by the servants in the succeeding speeches. **43 *plate*** money. **45 *in . . .
cabinet*** from the Duchess' chamber. **51 *At . . . pleasure*** perhaps an unintentional pun.
53 *approved* proven good.

BOSOLA   Gentlemen o' th' wood yard, where's your Switzer now?

FIRST SERVANT   By this hand, 'twas credibly reported by one o' th'   55
 black guard.   [*Exeunt* BOSOLA, RODERIGO, *and* SERVANTS.]

DELIO   How fares it with the Duchess?

ANTONIO   She's exposed
 Unto the worst of torture, pain, and fear.

DELIO   Speak to her all happy comfort.

ANTONIO   How I do play the fool with mine own danger!   60
 You are this night, dear friend, to post to Rome;
 My life lies in your service.

DELIO   Do not doubt me.

ANTONIO   Oh, 'tis far from me: and yet fear presents me
 Somewhat that looks like danger.

DELIO   Believe it,
 'Tis but the shadow of your fear, no more: 65
 How superstitiously we mind our evils!
 The throwing down salt, or crossing of a hare;
 Bleeding at nose, the stumbling of a horse:
 Or singing of a cricket, are of power
 To daunt whole man in us. Sir, fare you well: 70
 I wish you all the joys of a blessèd father;
 And, for my faith, lay this unto your breast,
 Old friends, like old swords, still are trusted best. [*Exit* DELIO.]

[*Enter* CARIOLA *with a child.*]

CARIOLA   Sir, you are the happy father of a son:
 Your wife commends him to you.

ANTONIO   Blessèd comfort!   75
 For heaven's sake tend her well: I'll presently
 Go set a figure for's nativity.   *Exeunt.*

---

54 *wood yard* place where firewood was cut. **56 *black guard*** kitchen servants.
60 *How . . . danger* What a fool I am to increase the possibility of revealing our secret
marriage (by having a child). **61 *Rome*** where the Duchess' brothers are. **64 *Somewhat*** something. **66 *mind*** notice. **70 *To . . . us*** to rob us of all our bravery.
72 *this* my faith. **77 *set a figure*** check the horoscope for.

{ACT II}

Scene 3 {*A hall in the* DUCHESS' *palace*}

[*Enter* BOSOLA *with a dark lanthorn.*]

BOSOLA Sure I did hear a woman shriek: list, ha?
And the sound came, if I received it right,
From the Duchess' lodgings; there's some stratagem
In the confining all our courtiers
To their several wards. I must have part of it,   5
My intelligence will freeze else. List again,
It may be 'twas the melancholy bird,
Best friend of silence, and of solitariness,
The owl, that screamed so—ha!—Antonio?

[*Enter* ANTONIO *with a candle, his sword drawn.*]

ANTONIO I heard some noise: who's there? What art thou? Speak.   10
BOSOLA Antonio! Put not your face nor body
To such a forced expression of fear—
I am Bosola, your friend.
ANTONIO   Bosola!
[*Aside.*] This mole does undermine me—heard you not
A noise even now?
BOSOLA   From whence?
ANTONIO   From the Duchess' lodging.   15
BOSOLA Not I. Did you?
ANTONIO   I did, or else I dreamed.
BOSOLA Let's walk towards it.
ANTONIO   No. It may be 'twas
But the rising of the wind.
BOSOLA   Very likely.
Methinks 'tis very cold, and yet you sweat.
You look wildly.
ANTONIO   I have been setting a figure   20
For the Duchess' jewels.
BOSOLA   Ah, and how falls your question?

ॐ ACT II, Scene 3. SD *dark lanthorn* a lantern with only one opening, which could be closed to shut off the light (often used by someone who wanted to move stealthily at night). **5 *have . . . of*** find out about. **6 *intelligence*** information gathered as a spy. **20–21 *I . . . jewels*** I have been checking a horoscope (to see if I can trace) the Duchess' jewels.

Do you find it radical?
ANTONIO   What's that to you?
'Tis rather to be questioned what design,
When all men were commanded to their lodgings,
Makes you a nightwalker.
BOSOLA   In sooth I'll tell you: 25
Now all the court's asleep, I thought the devil
Had least to do here; I came to say my prayers,
And if it do offend you I do so,
You are a fine courtier.
ANTONIO   [*Aside.*] This fellow will undo me.
You gave the Duchess apricocks today;   30
Pray heaven they were not poisoned.
BOSOLA   Poisoned! a Spanish fig
For the imputation!
ANTONIO   Traitors are ever confident,
Till they are discovered. There were jewels stol'n too,
In my conceit, none are to be suspected   35
More than yourself.
BOSOLA   You are a false steward.
ANTONIO   Saucy slave! I'll pull thee up by the roots.
BOSOLA   May be the ruin will crush you to pieces.
ANTONIO   You are an impudent snake indeed, sir,
Are you scarce warm, and do you show your sting?   40
[BOSOLA   . . .
ANTONIO]   You libel well, sir.
BOSOLA   No sir, copy it out,
And I will set my hand to't.
ANTONIO   My nose bleeds.
One that were superstitious would count
This ominous—when it merely comes by chance.

---

22 radical resolvable by astrology.   **28 *I*** that I.   **32 *Spanish fig*** an expression of
contempt, accompanied by the obscene gesture of thrusting the thumb between the fore-
finger and the middle finger.   **35 *conceit*** opinion.   **40 *Are . . . sting*** The reference
is to the fiftieth fable of Aesop, "The Countryman and the Snake." A villager finds a
snake almost frozen and takes it home to warm it by the fire, but as soon as it is revived
by the heat, the serpent tries to attack the countryman's wife and children. The reference
to Bosola as "scarce warm" here is motivated by the fact that he has only recently been
appointed to the provisorship of the Duchess' horses.   **40–41 *Bosola*** A speech seems
to be missing here.   **41–42 *copy . . . to't*** Make your charges formally, and I will set
my hand to the task of answering them. (Otherwise, be quiet.) (?)   **44 *merely comes***
in actuality comes merely.

Two letters, that are wrought here for my name   45
Are drowned in blood!
Mere accident. For you, sir, I'll take order:
I' th' morn you shall be safe. [*Aside.*] 'Tis that must color
Her lying-in. [*To* BOSOLA.] Sir, this door you pass not.
I do not hold it fit that you come near   50
The Duchess' lodgings till you have quit yourself;
[*Aside.*] The great are like the base; nay, they are the same,
When they seek shameful ways to avoid shame.   *Ex*[*it*].
BOSOLA   Antonio hereabout did drop a paper,
Some of your help, false friend: oh, here it is.   55
What's here?—a child's nativity calculated?
[*Reads.*] The Duchess was delivered of a son, 'tween the hours
twelve and one, in the night: Anno Dom: 1504.—That's this
year—*decimo nono Decembris,*—That's this night—taken according
to the Meridian of Malfi—That's our Duchess: happy discovery!—   60
The Lord of the first house, being combust in the ascendant,
signifies short life, and Mars being in a human sign, joined to the
tail of the Dragon, in the eighth house, doth threaten a violent
death; *Caetera non scrutantur.*
Why now 'tis most apparent. This precise fellow   65
Is the Duchess' bawd: I have it to my wish.
This is a parcel of intelligency
Our courtiers were cased up for! It needs must follow,
That I must be committed, on pretense
Of poisoning her, which I'll endure and laugh at.   70
If one could find the father now—but that
Time will discover. Old Castruchio
I' th' morning posts to Rome; by him I'll send

45–46 *Two . . . blood* Exactly what Antonio is referring to here is a mystery. He may
be holding two handkerchiefs, embroidered with his initials, that he has used to absorb
the blood from his nosebleed; or he may hold two official letters that required his signature as steward and have become spotted with blood.   47 *I'll . . . order* I'll issue an
order for your arrest.   48 *safe* in custody.   51 *quit* acquitted yourself (of any blame
for her sickness).   55 *false friend* the dark lantern (associated with secret, underhanded
dealings proceeding under the cover of night).   61 *Lord . . . house* the planet that
controls the boy's nativity.   *combust* burned up by being too near the sun (and, therefore, having lost its power).   64 *Caetera non scrutantur* The rest (of the horoscope)
remains unexamined.   65 *precise* (seemingly) strait-laced.   66 *bawd* pander.   *I . . .
wish* I have succeeded in getting what I wanted (i.e. important secret information).
67 *parcel of intelligency* a piece of really significant information.   68 *cased up*
ordered to keep to their quarters.

A letter, that shall make her brothers' galls
O'erflow their livers. This was a thrifty way.   75
Though lust do mask in ne'er so strange disguise
She's oft found witty, but is never wise.   [*Exit.*]

⟨ACT II⟩

Scene 4   ⟨*The* CARDINAL'*s palace in Rome*⟩

[*Enter* CARDINAL *and* JULIA.]

CARDINAL   Sit: thou art my best of wishes. Prithee, tell me
  What trick didst thou invent to come to Rome
  Without thy husband?

JULIA   Why, my lord, I told him
  I came to visit an old anchorite
  Here, for devotion.

CARDINAL   Thou art a witty false one: 5
  I mean to him.

JULIA   You have prevailèd with me
  Beyond my strongest thoughts: I would not now
  Find you inconstant.

CARDINAL   Do not put thyself
  To such a voluntary torture, which proceeds
  Out of your own guilt.

JULIA   How, my lord?

CARDINAL   You fear   10
  My constancy, because you have approved
  Those giddy and wild turnings in yourself.

JULIA   Did you e'er find them?

CARDINAL   Sooth, generally for women:
  A man might strive to make glass malleable,
  Ere he should make them fixed.

JULIA   So, my lord!—   15

---

75 thrifty way shrewd scheme.
❧ **ACT II, Scene 4. 4 anchorite** hermit. **5 witty** an ironic echo of the same word
from the closing line of the preceding scene. **7 I . . . not** I could not bear to.
11 approved given vent to.

CARDINAL   We had need go borrow that fantastic glass
      Invented by Galileo the Florentine,
      To view another spacious world i' th' moon,
      And look to find a constant woman there.
JULIA   This is very well, my lord.
CARDINAL   Why do you weep?   20
      Are tears your justification? The selfsame tears
      Will fall into your husband's bosom, lady,
      With a loud protestation that you love him
      Above the world. Come, I'll love you wisely,
      That's jealously, since I am very certain   25
      You cannot me make cuckold.
JULIA   I'll go home
      To my husband.
CARDINAL   You may thank me, lady,
      I have taken you off your melancholy perch,
      Bore you upon my fist, and showed you game,
      And let you fly at it. I pray thee, kiss me.   30
      When thou wast with thy husband, thou wast watched
      Like a tame elephant: (still you are to thank me)
      Thou hadst only kisses from him, and high feeding,
      But what delight was that? 'Twas just like one
      That hath a little fing'ring on the lute,   35
      Yet cannot tune it: (still you are to thank me)
JULIA   You told me of a piteous wound i' th' heart,
      And a sick liver, when you wooed me first,
      And spake like one in physic.
CARDINAL   Who's that?

      [*Enter* SERVANT.]

      Rest firm, for my affection to thee,   40
      Lightning moves slow to't.
SERVANT   Madam, a gentleman

---

16 *fantastic glass*   telescope.   **25–26** *I . . . cuckold*   You cannot make me a cuckold (because I am not married to you).   **28–30** *I . . . me*   The Cardinal's imagery here is derived from the sport of falconry, but there are double-entendres in what he says—a habit of speech that links him psychologically with his brother.   **32** *tame elephant* Elephants were tamed by being kept awake for so long that they would do anything in order to sleep.   **33** *high feeding*   Obscene jokes are directed at Castruchio's impotence, which makes him capable only of kissing Julia.   **36** *tune it*   make it play a tune.   **39** *in physic*   under the care of a physician.

That's come post from Malfi desires to see you.

CARDINAL   Let him enter; I'll withdraw.   *Exit.*

SERVANT   He says
Your husband, old Castruchio, is come to Rome,
Most pitifully tired with riding post.   [*Exit* SERVANT.]   45

[*Enter* DELIO.]

JULIA   Signior Delio! [*Aside.*] 'Tis one of my old suitors.

DELIO   I was bold to come and see you.

JULIA   Sir, you are welcome.

DELIO   Do you lie here?

JULIA   Sure your own experience
Will satisfy you no; our Roman prelates
Do not keep lodging for ladies.

DELIO   Very well.   50
I have brought you no commendations from your husband,
For I know none by him.

JULIA   I hear he's come to Rome?

DELIO   I never knew man and beast, of a horse and a knight,
So weary of each other. If he had had a good back,
He would have undertook to have borne his horse,   55
His breach was so pitifully sore.

JULIA   Your laughter
Is my pity.

DELIO   Lady, I know not whether
You want money, but I have brought you some.

JULIA   From my husband?

DELIO   No, from mine own allowance.

JULIA   I must hear the condition, ere I be bound to take it.   60

DELIO   Look on't, 'tis gold. Hath it not a fine color?

JULIA   I have a bird more beautiful.

DELIO   Try the sound on't.

JULIA   A lute string far exceeds it;
It hath no smell, like cassia or civet;

---

48 *lie* stay. *Sure* surely. **56** *breach* behind. **56–57** *Your . . . pity* Julia's answer
here is purposely ambiguous. She may be saying either "What you laugh at, I pity," or
"What you laugh at makes my position (as Castruchio's wife) pitiful." **59** *allowance*
income. **61–63** *Look . . . it* As Delio proposes a liaison with her, Julia thinks about the
Cardinal, her present lover, and she unconsciously replies to Delio's proposition by
employing the same kind of imagery (from falconry and lute-playing) that the Cardinal
has just finished using. **64** *cassia* cinnamon. *civet* an animal secretion used in
making perfume.

Nor is it physical, though some fond doctors   65
Persuade us, seethe't in cullises. I'll tell you,
This is a creature bred by— [*Enter* SERVANT.]
SERVANT   Your husband's come,
Hath delivered a letter to the Duke of Calabria,
That, to my thinking, hath put him out of his wits.

                                        [*Exit* SERVANT.]

JULIA   Sir, you hear.   70
Pray let me know your business and your suit,
As briefly as can be.
DELIO   With good speed. I would wish you,
At such time, as you are nonresident
With your husband, my mistress.
JULIA   Sir, I'll go ask my husband if I shall,   75
And straight return your answer.   *Exit.*
DELIO   Very fine,
Is this her wit or honesty that speaks thus?
I heard one say the Duke was highly moved
With a letter sent from Malfi. I do fear
Antonio is betrayed. How fearfully   80
Shows his ambition now; unfortunate Fortune!
They pass through whirlpools, and deep woes do shun,
Who the event weigh, ere the action's done.   *Exit.*

⊰{ACT II}⊱
Scene 5   ⊰{ *The same* }⊱

[*Enter*] CARDINAL, *and* FERDINAND, *furious, with a letter.*

FERDINAND   I have this night digged up a mandrake.
CARDINAL   Say you?
FERDINAND   And I am grown mad with't.
CARDINAL   What's the prodigy?

---

65 *physical* health-restoring. *fond* foolish. 65–66 *Nor . . . cullises* Nor is it
health-restoring—though some foolish doctors argue to the contrary—when it is boiled in
a broth. 66 *cullises* broths. 77 *honesty* chastity.
⊰ ACT II, Scene 5. 1 *mandrake* a root that was thought to induce madness if
plucked. 2 *prodigy* unnatural event.

FERDINAND   Read there, a sister damned; she's loose, i' th' hilts:
  Grown a notorious strumpet.
CARDINAL   Speak lower.
FERDINAND   Lower?
  Rogues do not whisper't now, but seek to publish't—   5
  As servants do the bounty of their lords—
  Aloud; and with a covetous, searching eye,
  To mark who note them. Oh, confusion seize her:
  She hath had most cunning bawds to serve her turn,
  And more secure conveyances for lust,   10
  Than towns of garrison, for service.
CARDINAL   Is't possible?
  Can this be certain?
FERDINAND   Rhubarb, oh for rhubarb
  To purge this choler; here's the cursèd day
  To prompt my memory, and here't shall stick
  Till of her bleeding heart I make a sponge   15
  To wipe it out.
CARDINAL   Why do you make yourself
  So wild a tempest?
FERDINAND   Would I could be one,
  That I might toss her palace 'bout her ears,
  Root up her goodly forests, blast her meads,
  And lay her general territory as waste,   20
  As she hath done her honor's.
CARDINAL   Shall our blood,
  The royal blood of Aragon and Castile,
  Be thus attainted?
FERDINAND   Apply desperate physic,
  We must not now use balsamum, but fire,
  The smarting cupping-glass, for that's the mean   25
  To purge infected blood, such blood as hers.
  There is a kind of pity in mine eye;
  I'll give it to my handkercher, and now 'tis here:
  I'll bequeath this to her bastard.

---

3 *loose . . . hilts* unchaste. 10 *secure conveyances* secret arrangements. 11 *towns
of* towns (have) of. 12 *Rhubarb* thought to cure men of excessive anger by purging
them of it. 13 *here's . . . day* Ferdinand refers here to the horoscope that Bosola has
enclosed. 14 *To prompt* to keep in. 19 *meads* meadows. 24 *balsamum* healing
ointment. 25 *cupping-glass* a small vacuum glass used for drawing blood. 29 *this*
the handkerchief.

CARDINAL   What to do?

FERDINAND   Why, to make soft lint for his mother's wounds,   30
When I have hewèd her to pieces.

CARDINAL   Cursed creature!
Unequal nature, to place women's hearts
So far upon the left side.

FERDINAND   Foolish men,
That e'er will trust their honor in a bark,
Made of so slight, weak bulrush as is woman,   35
Apt every minute to sink it!

CARDINAL   Thus ignorance, when it hath purchased honor
It cannot wield it.

FERDINAND   Methinks I see her laughing,
Excellent hyena! Talk to me somewhat, quickly,
Or my imagination will carry me   40
To see her in the shameful act of sin.

CARDINAL   With whom?

FERDINAND   Happily, with some strong-thighed bargeman;
Or one o' th' wood yard, that can quoit the sledge
Or toss the bar, or else some lovely squire   45
That carries coals up to her privy lodgings.

CARDINAL   You fly beyond your reason.

FERDINAND   Go to, mistress!
'Tis not your whore's milk, that shall quench my wildfire,
But your whore's blood.

CARDINAL   How idly shows this rage! which carries you,   50
As men conveyed by witches, through the air
On violent whirlwinds. This intemperate noise
Fitly resembles deaf men's shrill discourse,
Who talk aloud, thinking all other men
To have their imperfection.

FERDINAND   Have not you   55
My palsy?

32–33 *to . . . side*   It was thought that only the hearts of deceitful persons were located on the left ("sinister") side.   **39** *hyena*   Its lechery, as well as its laughter, makes it an appropriate image for Ferdinand to use here.   **43** *Happily*   probably, by hap.   **43–45** *Happily . . . squire*   The violence of the Duke's rage and the nature of his visions about the Duchess' lovers—as powerful, physically active men—suggest an intense sexual jealousy.   **44** *quoit the sledge*   throw the hammer.   **47** *mistress*   Ferdinand jealously rails against the Duchess—as if she were a mistress who had deserted him for another lover.

CARDINAL   Yes, I can be angry
Without this rupture; there is not in nature
A thing, that makes man so deformed, so beastly,
As doth intemperate anger. Chide yourself.
You have diverse men, who never yet expressed   60
Their strong desire of rest but by unrest,
By vexing of themselves. Come, put yourself
In tune.
FERDINAND   So, I will only study to seem
The thing I am not. I could kill her now,
In you, or in myself, for I do think   65
It is some sin in us, heaven doth revenge
By her.
CARDINAL   Are you stark mad?
FERDINAND   I would have their bodies
Burnt in a coal-pit, with the ventage stopped
That their cursed smoke might not ascend to heaven;
Or dip the sheets they lie in, in pitch or sulphur,   70
Wrap them in't, and then light them like a match;
Or else to boil their bastard to a cullis,
And give't his lecherous father, to renew
The sin of his back.
CARDINAL   I'll leave you.
FERDINAND   Nay, I have done;
I am confident, had I been damned in hell,   75
And should have heard of this, it would have put me
Into a cold sweat. In, in, I'll go sleep:
Till I know who leaps my sister, I'll not stir.
That known, I'll find scorpions to string my whips,
And fix her in a general eclipse.   *Exeunt.*   80

---

57 *rupture*   complete lack of control.   63 *study*   work.   64–65 *I could . . . myself*
I could kill you, and even myself, now.   68 *ventage*   chimney.   73–74 *to . . . back*   to
make him, literally, take his son back.   80 *And . . . eclipse*   and cast her forever into
darkness.

ACT III

Scene I   { *The* DUCHESS' *palace at Amalfi,* *a few years later* }

[*Enter* ANTONIO *and* DELIO.]

ANTONIO   Our noble friend, my most beloved Delio,
   Oh, you have been a stranger long at court,
   Came you along with the Lord Ferdinand?
DELIO   I did, sir, and how fares your noble Duchess?
ANTONIO   Right fortunately well. She's an excellent   5
   Feeder of pedigrees: since you last saw her,
   She hath had two children more, a son and daughter.
DELIO   Methinks 'twas yesterday. Let me but wink,
   And not behold your face, which to mine eye
   Is somewhat leaner: verily I should dream   10
   It were within this half hour.
ANTONIO   You have not been in law, friend Delio,
   Nor in prison, nor a suitor at the court,
   Nor begged the reversion of some great man's place,
   Nor troublèd with an old wife, which doth make   15
   Your time so insensibly hasten.
DELIO   Pray sir tell me,
   Hath not this news arrived yet to the ear
   Of the Lord Cardinal?
ANTONIO   I fear it hath;
   The Lord Ferdinand, that's newly come to court,
   Doth bear himself right dangerously.
DELIO   Pray why?   20
ANTONIO   He is so quiet, that he seems to sleep
   The tempest out, as dormice do in winter;
   Those houses that are haunted are most still,
   Till the devil be up.
DELIO   What say the common people?
ANTONIO   The common rabble do directly say   25
   She is a strumpet.

🦁 **ACT III, Scene I.**   **8–9** *Let . . . face*   It seems hardly more than a wink's time since I last saw your face.   **12** *in law*   involved in a legal case.   **14** *reversion*   right of succession to.   **15** *which*   because you are not involved in any of these tedious undertakings.   **16** *insensibly*   exceeding the powers of the senses to record.

DELIO   And your graver heads,
    Which would be politic, what censure they?
ANTONIO   They do observe I grow to infinite purchase
    The left-hand way, and all suppose the Duchess
    Would amend it, if she could. For, say they,   30
    Great princes, though they grudge their officers
    Should have such large and unconfinèd means
    To get wealth under them, will not complain
    Lest thereby they should make them odious
    Unto the people. For other obligation   35
    Of love, or marriage, between her and me,
    They never dream of.

    [*Enter* FERDINAND, DUCHESS, *and* BOSOLA.]

DELIO   The Lord Ferdinand
    Is going to bed.
FERDINAND   I'll instantly to bed,
    For I am weary: I am to bespeak
    A husband for you.
DUCHESS   For me, sir! pray who is't?   40
FERDINAND   The great Count Malateste.
DUCHESS   Fie upon him,
    A count? He's a mere stick of sugar candy,
    You may look quite thorough him: when I choose
    A husband, I will marry for your honor.
FERDINAND   You shall do well in't. How is't, worthy Antonio?   45
DUCHESS   But, sir, I am to have private conference with you,
    About a scandalous report is spread
    Touching mine honor.
FERDINAND   Let me be ever deaf to't:
    One of Pasquil's paper bullets, court calumny,
    A pestilent air, which princes' palaces   50
    Are seldom purged of. Yet, say that it were true,
    I pour it in your bosom, my fixed love
    Would strongly excuse, extenuate, nay, deny

---

27 *politic*   more prudent.   28 *purchase*   wealth.   29 *left-hand*   underhanded.
39–40 *I am . . . you*   I am to speak in favor of a prospective husband for you.
41 *Count Malateste*   a name Webster chose probably for the effect of the obscene pun.
42 *He's . . . candy*   He is of little worth.   43 *thorough*   through.   45 *How is't*   How
is business?   49 *Pasquil's . . . bullets*   satirical attacks. (Pasquil, or Pasquin, was the
name given a statue to which Italian writers commonly affixed satires.)   52 *pour . . .
bosom*   I confess to you that.

Faults were they apparent in you. Go, be safe
In your own innocency.

DUCHESS   Oh blessed comfort: 55
This deadly air is purged.   *Exeunt* [DUCHESS, ANTONIO, DELIO].

FERDINAND   Her guilt treads on
Hot burning cultures. Now, Bosola,
How thrives our intelligence?

BOSOLA   Sir, uncertainly:
'Tis rumored she hath had three bastards, but
By whom we may go read i' th' stars.

FERDINAND   Why some   60
Hold opinion all things are written there.

BOSOLA   Yes, if we could find spectacles to read them;
I do suspect, there hath been some sorcery
Used on the Duchess.

FERDINAND   Sorcery? To what purpose?

BOSOLA   To make her dote on some desertless fellow,   65
She shames to acknowledge.

FERDINAND   Can your faith give way
To think there's power in potions or in charms
To make us love, whether we will or no?

BOSOLA   Most certainly.

FERDINAND   Away, these are mere gulleries, horrid things   70
Invented by some cheating mountebanks
To abuse us. Do you think that herbs or charms
Can force the will? Some trials have been made
In the foolish practice. But the ingredients
Were lenative poisons, such as are of force   75
To make the patient mad; and straight the witch
Swears, by equivocation, they are in love.
The witchcraft lies in her rank blood: this night
I will force confession from her. You told me
You had got, within these two days, a false key   80

---

57 cultures the iron blade in the front of a plow. In medieval England, people could
demonstrate their innocence of a crime if they could walk unharmed on red-hot cultures.
58 intelligence system for spying. **60 we . . . stars** we cannot determine by any
factual evidence. **70 gulleries** tricks. **71 mountebanks** charlatans, pitchmen who
mounted benches and peddled their wares, which were usually elixirs and cure-alls.
75 lenative poisons powerful drugs. **77 by equivocation** by equating love with
madness. **78 her** the Duchess'. **80 false key** pass key.

Into her bedchamber.

BOSOLA   I have.

FERDINAND   As I would wish.

BOSOLA   What do you intend to do?

FERDINAND   Can you guess?

BOSOLA   No.

FERDINAND   Do not ask then.

He that can compass me, and know my drifts,

May say he hath put a girdle 'bout the world,   85

And sounded all her quicksands.

BOSOLA   I do not

Think so.

FERDINAND   What do you think then, pray?

BOSOLA   That you

Are your own chronicle too much, and grossly

Flatter yourself.

FERDINAND   Give me thy hand; I thank thee.

I never gave pension but to flatterers   90

Till I entertainèd thee: farewell,

That friend a great man's ruin strongly checks,

Who rails into his belief all his defects.   *Exeunt.*

⟬ACT III⟭

Scene 2   ⟬ *The* DUCHESS' *bedchamber* ⟭

[*Enter* DUCHESS, ANTONIO, *and* CARIOLA.]

DUCHESS   Bring me the casket hither, and the glass;

You get no lodging here tonight, my lord.

ANTONIO   Indeed, I must persuade one.

DUCHESS   Very good:

I hope in time 'twill grow into a custom,

That noblemen shall come with cap and knee,   5

---

81 *As . . . wish* I want it. **84** *compass* comprehend. *drifts* secret schemes.
85 *put . . . world* traveled around the world (i.e. has done everything). **88** *Are . . .*
much talk too much about the enormity of your deeds. **90** *pension* reward for
service. **93** *belief* awareness.
❧ **ACT III, Scene 2.** 1 *glass* mirror. **5** *with . . . knee* on bended knee, with cap
in hand.

To purchase a night's lodging of their wives.

ANTONIO   I must lie here.

DUCHESS   Must? you are a lord of misrule.

ANTONIO   Indeed, my rule is only in the night.

DUCHESS   To what use will you put me?

ANTONIO   We'll sleep together.

DUCHESS   Alas, what pleasure can two lovers find in sleep?   10

CARIOLA   My lord, I lie with her often, and I know
    She'll much disquiet you.

ANTONIO   See, you are complained of.

CARIOLA   For she's the sprawling'st bedfellow.

ANTONIO   I shall like her the better for that.

CARIOLA   Sir, shall I ask you a question?   15

ANTONIO   I pray thee Cariola.

CARIOLA   Wherefore still, when you lie with my lady
    Do you rise so early?

ANTONIO   Laboring men,
    Count the clock oft'nest, Cariola,
    Are glad when their task's ended.

DUCHESS   I'll stop your mouth.   20

    [*Kisses him.*]

ANTONIO   Nay, that's but one. Venus had two soft doves
    To draw her chariot: I must have another.

    [*Kisses her.*]

    When wilt thou marry, Cariola?

CARIOLA   Never, my lord.

ANTONIO   O fie upon this single life: forgo it.
    We read how Daphne, for her peevish slight   25
    Became a fruitless bay tree; Syrinx turned
    To the pale empty reed; Anaxarete
    Was frozen into marble: whereas those
    Which married, or proved kind unto their friends
    Were, by a gracious influence, transhaped   30

---

7 **lord of misrule** master of the court revels (which were held at night). **18 rise** a double-entendre. **25 Daphne** a nymph who, pursued by Pan, was transformed into a bay tree at her own entreaty. **peevish slight** foolish rejection of Pan. **26 Syrinx** a nymph who was changed into a reed in order to escape Pan's pursuit. **27 Anaxarete** a mythical Grecian queen who scorned the advances of Iphis and stood unmoved as he hanged himself, for which she was punished by being turned into marble. **29 friends** lovers.

Into the olive, pomegranate, mulberry;
Became flowers, precious stones, or eminent stars.
CARIOLA   This is vain poetry; but I pray you tell me,
If there were proposed me wisdom, riches, and beauty,
In three several young men, which should I choose?   35
ANTONIO   'Tis a hard question. This was Paris' case,
And he was blind in't, and there was great cause:
For how was't possible he could judge right,
Having three amorous goddesses in view,
And they stark naked? 'Twas a motion   40
Were able to benight the apprehension
Of the severest counselor of Europe.
Now I look on both your faces, so well formed,
It puts me in mind of a question I would ask.
CARIOLA   What is't?
ANTONIO   I do wonder why hard-favored ladies,   45
For the most part, keep worse-favored waiting-women
To attend them, and cannot endure fair ones.
DUCHESS   Oh, that's soon answered.
Did you ever in your life know an ill painter
Desire to have his dwelling next door to the shop   50
Of an excellent picture maker? 'Twould disgrace
His face-making, and undo him. I prithee
When were we so merry? My hair tangles.
ANTONIO   [*Aside to* CARIOLA.] Pray thee, Cariola, let's steal forth the
room,
And let her talk to herself: I have diverse times   55
Served her the like when she hath chafed extremely.
I love to see her angry—softly Cariola.
                            Exeunt [ANTONIO *and* CARIOLA].   ·
DUCHESS   Doth not the color of my hair 'gin to change?
When I wax grey, I shall have all the court

36 Paris' case Paris, the handsomest of men, was asked to judge who among the goddesses was the fairest—Hera, Athena, or Aphrodite. Because all three of the goddesses, who stood naked before him, were beautiful, he could not choose a winner; so each offered him a reward as a bribe. Hera promised greatness, Athena offered success in war, and Aphrodite told him that she would give him the most beautiful woman in the world for his wife. Finally, he judged Aphrodite the winner, and she subsequently helped him to carry off Helen, with disastrous consequences for himself and his city. **40 motion** spectacle. **41 benight the apprehension** obscure the judgment. **45 hard-favored** unattractive. **52 face-making** a pun, meaning both portrait-painting and make-up work. **54 forth** forth from.

Powder their hair with arras, to be like me: 60
You have cause to love me, I entered you into my heart

[*Enter* FERDINAND, *unseen.*]

Before you would vouchsafe to call for the keys.
We shall one day have my brothers take you napping.
Methinks his presence, being now in court,
Should make you keep your own bed, but you'll say   65
Love mixed with fear is sweetest. I'll assure you
You shall get no more children till my brothers
Consent to be your gossips. Have you lost your tongue?

[*In the mirror she sees* FERDINAND *holding a poniard.*]

'Tis welcome:
For know, whether I am doomed to live, or die,   70
I can do both like a prince. FERDINAND *gives her a poniard.*
FERDINAND   Die then, quickly.
Virtue, where art thou hid? What hideous thing
Is it, that doth eclipse thee?
DUCHESS   Pray, sir, hear me—
FERDINAND   Or is it true, thou art but a bare name,
And no essential thing?
DUCHESS   Sir—
FERDINAND   Do not speak.   75
DUCHESS   No sir:
I will plant my soul in mine ears, to hear you.
FERDINAND   Oh most imperfect light of human reason,
That mak'st us so unhappy, to foresee
What we can least prevent. Pursue thy wishes   80
And glory in them: there's in shame no comfort,
But to be past all bounds and sense of shame.
DUCHESS   I pray sir, hear me: I am married—
FERDINAND   So!
DUCHESS   Happily, not to your liking, but for that
Alas, your shears do come untimely now   85
To clip the bird's wings, that's already flown.
Will you see my husband?
FERDINAND   Yes, if I could change

---

60 *arras* a white powder. 61 *entered . . . into* offered you. 63 *take* discover.
68 *gossips* sponsors at a baptism. 77 *I will . . . you* I will listen to you with the
utmost attention. 84 *Happily* probably.

Eyes with a basilisk.
DUCHESS   Sure, you came hither
    By his confederacy.
FERDINAND   The howling of a wolf
    Is music to thee, screech owl; prithee, peace.   90
    Whate'er thou art that hast enjoyed my sister,
    (For I am sure thou hear'st me), for thine own sake
    Let me not know thee. I came hither prepared
    To work thy discovery, yet am now persuaded
    It would beget such violent effects   95
    As would damn us both. I would not for ten millions
    I had beheld thee; therefore, use all means
    I never may have knowledge of thy name;
    Enjoy thy lust still, and a wretched life,
    On that condition. And for thee, vild woman,   100
    If thou do wish thy lecher may grow old
    In thy embracements, I would have thee build
    Such a room for him, as our anchorites
    To holier use inhabit. Let not the sun
    Shine on him, till he's dead. Let dogs and monkeys   105
    Only converse with him, and such dumb things
    To whom nature denies use to sound his name.
    Do not keep a paraquito, lest she learn it;
    If thou do love him, cut out thine own tongue,
    Lest it bewray him.
DUCHESS   Why might not I marry?   110
    I have not gone about, in this, to create
    Any new world, or custom.
FERDINAND   Thou art undone:
    And thou hast ta'en that massy sheet of lead
    That hid thy husband's bones, and folded it
    About my heart.
DUCHESS   Mine bleeds for't.
FERDINAND   Thine? thy heart?   115

---

88 *basilisk* a legendary reptile that could kill with a look.   **89 *By his confederacy***
The Duchess remains hopeful, thinking that Ferdinand's appearance has been arranged
with Antonio. But she is, of course, mistaken, and the indefiniteness of her reference in
the phrase "By his confederacy" emphasizes the magnitude of her error. It is not a
"confederacy" with Antonio that has prompted Ferdinand's appearance; instead, it is his
emotional and psychological commitment to the forces of evil and destruction represented by the basilisk.   **96 *damn*** The first quarto edition reads "dampe."   **100 *vild***
vile.   **103 *anchorites*** hermits.   **107 *use*** skill.

What should I name't, unless a hollow bullet
Filled with unquenchable wildfire?

DUCHESS   You are in this
Too strict, and were you not my princely brother
I would say too willful. My reputation
Is safe.

FERDINAND   Dost thou know what reputation is?   120
I'll tell thee, to small purpose, since th'instruction
Comes now too late:
Upon a time Reputation, Love and Death
Would travel o'er the world: and it was concluded
That they should part, and take three several ways.   125
Death told them they should find him in great battles,
Or cities plagued with plagues. Love gives them counsel
To inquire for him 'mongst unambitious shepherds,
Where dow'ries were not talked of, and sometimes
'Mongst quiet kindred, that had nothing left   130
By their dead parents. "Stay," quoth Reputation,
"Do not forsake me: for it is my nature,
If once I part from any man I meet,
I am never found again." And so, for you:
You have shook hands with Reputation,   135
And made him invisible. So fare you well.
I will never see you more.

DUCHESS   Why should only I,
Of all the other princes of the world
Be cased up, like a holy relic? I have youth,
And a little beauty.

FERDINAND   So you have some virgins   140
That are witches. I will never see thee more.   *Exit.*

Enter [CARIOLA *and*] ANTONIO *with a pistol.*

DUCHESS   You saw this apparition?

ANTONIO   Yes: we are
Betrayed. How came he hither? I should turn
This, to thee, for that. [*Points the pistol at* CARIOLA.]

CARIOLA   Pray, sir, do; and when
That you have cleft my heart, you shall read there   145

---

116 *hollow bullet* cannon ball. **118** *strict* unyielding. **123** *Upon a time* once.
124 *would* wished to. **135** *shook . . . with* parted from. **140** *So . . . virgins* So,
you know, have some virgins. **142** *apparition* the sudden and unexpected appearance
of Ferdinand.

Mine innocence.

DUCHESS   That gallery gave him entrance.

ANTONIO   I would this terrible thing would come again,
That, standing on my guard, I might relate
My warrantable love. Ha! what means this?

DUCHESS   He left this with me. *She shows the poniard.*

ANTONIO   And, it seems, did wish   150
You would use it on yourself?

DUCHESS   His action seemed
To intend so much.

ANTONIO   This hath a handle to't
As well as a point: turn it towards him, and
So fasten the keen edge in his rank gall.

[*Knocking.*]

How now? Who knocks? More earthquakes?   155

DUCHESS   I stand
As if a mine, beneath my feet, were ready
To be blown up.

CARIOLA   'Tis Bosola.

DUCHESS   Away!
Oh misery, methinks unjust actions
Should wear these masks and curtains, and not we.
You must instantly part hence: I have fashioned it already.   160

Ex[*it*] ANT[ONIO].

[*Enter* BOSOLA.]

BOSOLA   The Duke your brother is ta'en up in a whirlwind;
Hath took horse, and's rid post to Rome.

DUCHESS   So late?

BOSOLA   He told me, as he mounted into th' saddle,
You were undone.

DUCHESS   Indeed, I am very near it.   165

BOSOLA   What's the matter?

DUCHESS   Antonio, the master of our household,
Hath dealt so falsely with me in's accounts:
My brother stood engaged with me for money
Ta'en up of certain Neapolitan Jews,

---

146 *gallery* upstairs corridor (in this case, the upper stage).   **148** *relate* demonstrate.
152 *intend so much* imply as much.   **155** *earthquakes* serious problems.   **160**
fashioned it contrived a plan.   **168** *engaged* committed.   **169** *Ta'en up of* borrowed from.

And Antonio lets the bonds be forfeit.   170
BOSOLA   Strange. [*Aside.*] This is cunning.
DUCHESS   And hereupon
   My brother's bills at Naples are protested
   Against. Call up our officers.
BOSOLA   I shall.   *Exit.*

   [*Enter* ANTONIO.]

DUCHESS   The place that you must fly to, is Ancona.
   Hire a house there. I'll send after you   175
   My treasure, and my jewels. Our weak safety
   Runs upon enginous wheels: short syllables
   Must stand for periods. I must now accuse you
   Of such a feignèd crime, as Tasso calls
   Magnanima mensogna: a noble lie,   180
   'Cause it must shield our honors—Hark, they are coming.

   [*Enter* BOSOLA *and* OFFICERS. *The* DUCHESS *and* ANTONIO *begin their feigned dispute.*]

ANTONIO   Will your grace hear me?
DUCHESS   I have got well by you: you have yielded me
   A million of loss; I am like to inherit
   The people's curses for your stewardship.   185
   You had the trick, in audit time, to be sick
   Till I had signed your *Quietus;* and that cured you
   Without help of a doctor. Gentlemen,
   I would have this man be an example to you all:
   So shall you hold my favor. I pray let him;   190
   For h'as done that, alas, you would not think of;
   And, because I intend to be rid of him,
   I mean not to publish. Use your fortune elsewhere.
ANTONIO   I am strongly armed to brook my overthrow,
   As commonly men bear with a hard year: 195
   I will not blame the cause on't; but do think
   The necessity of my malevolent star
   Procures this, not her humor. O, the inconstant

172–73 *protested Against* called in for payment. **177** *Runs . . . wheels* depends upon speed and ingenuity. **178** *periods* well-proportioned sentences. **183** *got . . . by* had enough of. **190** *let him* let him go. **193** *publish* publicly announce (what he has done). **196–98** *but . . . humor* This overthrow has been brought about by evil Fortune's unalterable decree, not by the capriciousness of the Duchess.

And rotten ground of service, you may see;
'Tis ev'n like him that, in a winter night,   200
Takes a long slumber o'er a dying fire,
As loth to part from't, yet parts thence as cold
As when he first sat down.
DUCHESS   We do confiscate,
Towards the satisfying of your accounts,
All that you have.
ANTONIO   I am all yours; and 'tis very fit   205
All mine should be so.
DUCHESS   So, sir, you have your pass.
ANTONIO   You may see, gentlemen, what 'tis to serve
A prince with body and soul.   *Exit.*
BOSOLA   Here's an example for extortion: what moisture is drawn
out of the sea, when foul weather comes, pours down, and runs   210
into the sea again.
DUCHESS   I would know what are your opinions
Of this Antonio.
SECOND OFFICER   He could not abide to see a pig's head gaping.
I thought your grace would find him a Jew.   215
THIRD OFFICER   I would you had been his officer, for your own sake.
FOURTH OFFICER   You would have had more money.
FIRST OFFICER   He stopped his ears with black wool, and to those came
to him for money said he was thick of hearing.
SECOND OFFICER   Some said he was an hermaphrodite, for he could   220
not abide a woman.
FOURTH OFFICER   How scurvy proud he would look, when the treasury
was full. Well, let him go.
FIRST OFFICER   Yes, and the chippings of the butt'ry fly after him, to
scour his gold chain.   225
DUCHESS   Leave us. What do you think of these?   *Exeunt* [OFFICERS].
BOSOLA   That these are rogues, that in's prosperity,
But to have waited on his fortune, could have wished

---

206 *pass* leave to go.   **214** *He . . . gaping* He could not stand to see people feasting
on pork (because he hated feasting in general and the eating of pork in particular).
215 *Jew* an unusually clever miser.   **220** *hermaphrodite* an individual having both
male and female sexual characteristics.   **224** *chippings . . . butt'ry* bread crumbs, used
for polishing gold.   **225** *gold chain* steward's badge of office.   **226** *these* these
officers.   **227-72** *That . . . virtue* Bosola's praise of Antonio is primarily a clever trick:
he thinks that the steward has been acting as the Duchess' bawd, and he hopes that his
praise of him will win for himself the Duchess' confidence. It is not, however, beyond
Bosola's power to recognize worth, even though he sees very little of it around him, so
there is just enough honesty in his speech to make it a consummate work of deception.

His dirty stirrup riveted through their noses:
And followed after's mule, like a bear in a ring.   230
Would have prostituted their daughters to his lust;
Made their first-born intelligencers; thought none happy
But such as were born under his blessed planet;
And wore his livery. And do these lice drop off now?
Well, never look to have the like again;   235
He hath left a sort of flatt'ring rogues behind him;
Their doom must follow. Princes pay flatterers,
In their own money. Flatterers dissemble their vices,
And they dissemble their lies: that's justice.
Alas, poor gentleman,—   240

DUCHESS   Poor! he hath amply filled his coffers.

BOSOLA   Sure he was too honest. Pluto the god of riches,
When he's sent by Jupiter to any man,
He goes limping, to signify that wealth
That comes on God's name, comes slowly; but when he's sent   245
On the devil's errand, he rides post and comes in by scuttles.
Let me show you what a most unvalued jewel
You have, in a wanton humor, thrown away
To bless the man shall find him. He was an excellent
Courtier, and most faithful; a soldier that thought it   250
As beastly to know his own value too little,
As devilish to acknowledge it too much:
Both his virtue and form deserved a far better fortune.
His discourse rather delighted to judge itself, than show itself.
His breast was filled with all perfection,   255
And yet it seemed a private whisp'ring room:
It made so little noise of't.

DUCHESS   But he was basely descended.

BOSOLA   Will you make yourself a mercenary herald,
Rather to examine men's pedigrees, than virtues?
You shall want him: 260

---

230 *after's* after Antonio's. *like . . . ring* Rings were thrust through the noses of bears so that they could be marched in procession before bearbaiting events. **232** *intelligencers* spies. **235** *the like* one as good as Antonio. **238–39** *Flatterers . . . lies* Flatterers pretend that princes do not have vices, and princes pretend that flatterers do not lie. **242** *Pluto* actually King of the Underworld; the god of riches was Plutus. Webster's error in this case may, however, be intentional, for he may want to emphasize the extent to which Bosola's thinking is dominated by the powers of blackness. **243** *Jupiter* king of the gods. **246** *by scuttles* runs quickly. **247** *unvalued* invaluable. **249** *man shall* man who shall. **254** *to . . . itself* to be sound, rather than showy. **260** *want* miss.

For know an honest statesman to a prince,
Is like a cedar, planted by a spring:
The spring bathes the tree's root; the grateful tree
Rewards it with his shadow. You have not done so;
I would sooner swim to the Bermoothas on   265
Two politicians' rotten bladders, tied
Together with an intelligencer's heartstring,
Than depend on so changeable a prince's favor.
Fare thee well, Antonio, since the malice of the world
Would needs down with thee, it cannot be said yet   270
That any ill happened unto thee,
Considering thy fall was accompanied with virtue.
DUCHESS   Oh, you render me excellent music.
BOSOLA   Say you?
DUCHESS   This good one that you speak of—is my husband.
BOSOLA   Do I not dream? Can this ambitious age   275
Have so much goodness in't as to prefer
A man merely for worth, without these shadows
Of wealth, and painted honors? possible?
DUCHESS   I have had three children by him.
BOSOLA   Fortunate lady,
For you have made your private nuptial bed   280
The humble and fair seminary of peace.
No question but many an unbeneficed scholar
Shall pray for you for this deed, and rejoice
That some preferment in the world can yet
Arise from merit. The virgins of your land   285
That have no dowries shall hope your example
Will raise them to rich husbands. Should you want
Soldiers, 'twould make the very Turks and Moors
Turn Christians, and serve you for this act.
Last, the neglected poets of your time,   290
In honor of this trophy of a man,
Raised by that curious engine, your white hand,
Shall thank you in your grave for't; and make that
More reverend than all the cabinets

---

265 Bermoothas Bermuda, which was thought of as a distant and primitive island.
266 politicians self-interested schemers.   **278 possible** (Is it) possible?   **281 seminary**
seed bed.   **282 unbeneficed** not supported by a lord.   **291 trophy** prize.   **292 engine**
source of power.   **294 cabinets** advisors.

                                                                    295
Of living princes. For Antonio,
His fame shall likewise flow from many a pen,
When heralds shall want coats, to sell to men.
DUCHESS   As I taste comfort, in this friendly speech,
So would I find concealment—
BOSOLA   Oh the secret of my prince,
Which I will wear on th'inside of my heart.   300
DUCHESS   You shall take charge of all my coin and jewels
And follow him, for he retires himself
To Ancona.
BOSOLA   So.
DUCHESS   Whither, within few days,
I mean to follow thee.
BOSOLA   Let me think:
I would wish your grace to feign a pilgrimage   305
To Our Lady of Loretto, scarce seven leagues
From fair Ancona, so may you depart
Your country with more honor, and your flight
Will seem a princely progress, retaining
Your usual train about you.
DUCHESS   Sir, your direction   310
Shall lead me, by the hand.
CARIOLA   In my opinion,
She were better progress to the baths at Lucca,
Or go visit the Spa
In Germany: for, if you will believe me,
I do not like this jesting with religion,   315
This feigned pilgrimage.
DUCHESS   Thou art a superstitious fool!
Prepare us instantly for our departure.
Past sorrows, let us moderately lament them;
For those to come, seek wisely to prevent them.
                          Exit [DUCHESS *with* CARIOLA].
BOSOLA   A politician is the devil's quilted anvil: 320
He fashions all sins on him, and the blows

---

297 When . . . men   when heralds no longer shall deal in the corrupt practice of selling coats of arms to men (i.e. when men are rewarded for virtue rather than for bribery). **299 concealment** secrecy.   **309 progress** official journey.   **312 Lucca** a resort near Pisa.   **313 Spa** a town in Belgium famous for its mineral waters.   **320 quilted** covered with a sound-absorbing material.

Are never heard; he may work in a lady's chamber,
As here for proof. What rests, but I reveal
All to my lord? Oh, this base quality
Of intelligencer! Why, every quality i' th' world   325
Prefers but gain, or commendation.
Now for this act, I am certain to be raised:
And men that paint weeds to the life are praised.   *Exit.*

⁅ACT III⁆

Scene 3   ⁅*The* CARDINAL's *palace in Rome*⁆

[*Enter*] CARDINAL, FERDINAND, MALATESTE, PESCARA, SILVIO, DELIO.

CARDINAL   Must we turn soldier then?
MALATESTE   The Emperor,
   Hearing your worth that way, ere you attained
   This reverend garment, joins you in commission
   With the right fortunate soldier, the Marquis of Pescara
   And the famous Lannoy.
CARDINAL   He that had the honor   5
   Of taking the French king prisoner?
MALATESTE   The same.
   Here's a plot drawn for a new fortification
   At Naples.
FERDINAND   This great Count Malateste, I perceive
   Hath got employment.
DELIO   No employment, my lord,
   A marginal note in the muster book, that he is   10

---

323 *rests* remains.   **325–26** *Why . . . commendation* Every quality of character leads
to some reward: (if the quality is evil), the reward is gain; (if it is good), the prize is only
commendation.   **328** *to the life* so that they seem lifelike.
⁋ **ACT III, Scene 3.** **1** *Emperor* Charles V, the greatest of all Hapsburg emperors,
who ruled from 1519 to 1558.   **4** *Marquis of Pescara* the soldier who commanded the
Italian army in its victory over Francis I of France at Pavia in 1525.   **5** *Lannoy* Viceroy of Naples, one of the Italian commanders at Pavia and a favorite of Charles V.
6 *French king* Francis I, who would surrender his sword at Pavia only to Lannoy.
7 *plot* diagram.   **8** *Malateste* the ruling family in Rimini, Italy, during the sixteenth
century.   **10** *muster book* a register of the officers and men in a military unit.

A voluntary lord.
FERDINAND   He's no soldier?
DELIO   He has worn gunpowder, in's hollow tooth,
    For the toothache.
SILVIO   He comes to the leaguer with a full intent
    To eat fresh beef, and garlic; means to stay   15
    Till the scent be gone, and straight return to court.
DELIO   He hath read all the late service,
    As the city chronicle relates it,
    And keeps two pewterers going, only to express
    Battles in model.
SILVIO   Then he'll fight by the book.   20
DELIO   By the almanac, I think,
    To choose good days and shun the critical.
    That's his mistress' scarf.
SILVIO   Yes, he protests
    He would do much for that taffeta,—
DELIO   I think he would run away from a battle   25
    To save it from taking prisoner.
SILVIO   He is horribly afraid
    Gunpowder will spoil the perfume on't,—
DELIO   I saw a Dutchman break his pate once
    For calling him pot-gun; he made his head
    Have a bore in't, like a musket.   30
SILVIO   I would he had made a touchhole to't.
    He is indeed a guarded sumpter-cloth
    Only for the remove of the court.

    [*Enter* BOSOLA.]

PESCARA   Bosola arrived? What should be the business?
    Some falling out amongst the cardinals?   35
    These factions amongst great men, they are like

---

11 *voluntary lord*   a lord who volunteers for military service.   **14** *leaguer*   alliance.
16 *Till . . . gone*   until the good food is eaten.   **17** *all . . . service*   all about the recent
military maneuvers.   **18** *city chronicle*   official reports about the affairs of a city.
20 *model*   miniature reproductions (with pewter soldiers).   *by the book*   according to
some generally accepted treatise on military strategy.   **22** *critical*   days of crisis.
26 *taking*   being taken.   **28** *break his pate*   strike him across the head.   **29** *pot-gun*
popgun, a braggart.   **31** *touchhole*   the vent in firearms through which the charge was
ignited.   *I . . . to't*   I wish he had burst his false pride completely.   **32** *guarded sumpter-
cloth*   ornamental blanket.   **33** *remove*   location.

Foxes when their heads are divided:
They carry fire in their tails, and all the country
About them goes to wrack for't.

SILVIO   What's that Bosola?

DELIO   I knew him in Padua—a fantastical scholar, like such who   40
study to know how many knots was in Hercules' club; of what
color Achilles' beard was, or whether Hector were not troubled
with the toothache. He hath studied himself half blear-eyed to
know the true symmetry of Caesar's nose by a shoeing horn.
And this he did to gain the name of a speculative man.   45

PESCARA   Mark Prince Ferdinand,
A very salamander lives in's eye,
To mock the eager violence of fire.

SILVIO   That cardinal hath made more bad faces with his oppression
than ever Michael Angelo made good ones: he lifts up's nose, like   50
a foul porpoise before a storm,—

PESCARA   The Lord Ferdinand laughs.

DELIO   Like a deadly cannon, that lightens ere it smokes.

PESCARA   These are your true pangs of death,
The pangs of life, that struggle with great statesmen,—   55

DELIO   In such a deformèd silence, witches whisper their charms.

CARDINAL   [*On the other side of the stage.*] Doth she make religion her
riding hood

---

37 *heads are divided* when they are tied tail to tail (cf. Judges 15:4).   **40 *fantastical***
pursuing foolish fantasies.   **42 *Achilles*** the greatest Greek warrior in the Trojan War.
Hector the greatest Trojan warrior.   **43–44 *to . . . horn*** to learn that Caesar's nose
was as symmetrical and well-tapered as a shoehorn.   **47 *salamander*** thought capable
of living in fire.   **50 *lifts up's nose*** He sniffs around for trouble.   **51 *foul porpoise*** The
appearance of porpoises around a ship was believed to be a warning of foul weather to
come.   **53 *lightens*** gives off light (of fire).   **54–55 *These . . . statesmen*** This passage
is confusing enough to be textually corrupt: it is difficult to see how "The pangs of life,
that struggle with great statesmen" can be an accurate description of "true pangs of
death." The general meaning of the statement is, however, clear. The whispered secrets
between statesmen are pangs of death because they soon result in destructive actions; the
pangs of life are either the life of suffering that comes to those who struggle against great
statesmen or, more likely, the pains that accompany the formulation of the statesmen's
ideas—in actuality pangs of death because of the nature of their results. This interpretation of Pescara's speech, however, demands an emendation of the second line so that it
reads: "The pangs of life, that struggles within great statesmen." But whether there is a
textual corruption in this passage or not, its implication is that the whispered secrets
between the Cardinal and Ferdinand are directed toward evil ends.   **56 *In . . . silence***
in such unnatural whispers.

To keep her from the sun and tempest?
FERDINAND   That!
    That damns her. Methinks her fault and beauty
    Blended together show like leprosy: 60
    The whiter, the fouler. I make it a question
    Whether her beggarly brats were ever christened.
CARDINAL   I will instantly solicit the state of Ancona
    To have them banished.
FERDINAND   [*To the* CARDINAL.]   You are for Loretto?
    I shall not be at your ceremony; fare you well.   65
    [*To* BOSOLA.] Write to the Duke of Malfi, my young nephew
    She had by her first husband, and acquaint him
    With's mother's honesty.
BOSOLA   I will.
FERDINAND   Antonio!
    A slave, that only smelled of ink and counters
    And ne'er in's life looked like a gentleman   70
    But in the audit time. Go, go presently;
    Draw me out an hundred and fifty of our horse,
    And meet me at the fort bridge.   *Exeunt.*

⟨ACT III⟩
Scene 4   ⟨*Loretto*⟩

[*Enter*] TWO PILGRIMS *to the Shrine of Our Lady of Loretto.*

FIRST PILGRIM   I have not seen a goodlier shrine than this;
    Yet I have visited many.
SECOND PILGRIM   The Cardinal of Aragon
    Is this day to resign his cardinal's hat;
    His sister Duchess likewise is arrived

---

58 *sun . . . tempest*   the Cardinal, who theoretically represents the light of God, and Ferdinand, whose anger is violent, like a tempest. ***That***   That is correct! **64** *for* headed for. **65** *ceremony*   his official installation as a soldier. **69** *counters*   pieces of wood or bone used in keeping accounts. **71** *But . . . time*   In audit time, the Duke implies, Antonio made enough money to qualify as a gentleman. **73** *fort bridge*   draw-bridge.
❧ **ACT III, Scene 4.**   **3** *to . . . hat*   resigning his church position (to become a soldier).

To pay her vow of pilgrimage. I expect   5
A noble ceremony.
FIRST PILGRIM   No question.—They come.

Here the ceremony of the Cardinal's installment in the habit of a soldier:
performed in delivering up his cross, hat, robes, and ring at the shrine,
and investing him with sword, helmet, shield, and spurs. Then ANTONIO,
the DUCHESS, *and their children, having presented themselves at the*
shrine, are (by a form of banishment in dumb show expressed towards
them by the CARDINAL *and the state of* ANCONA) *banished. During all*
which ceremony this ditty is sung to very solemn music, by diverse
churchmen; and then exeunt.

The author disclaims this ditty to be his.

Arms and honors deck thy story
To thy fame's eternal glory.
Adverse fortune ever fly thee;
No disastrous fate come nigh thee.   10

I alone will sing thy praises,
Whom to honor virtue raises;
And thy study that divine is,
Bent to martial discipline is.
Lay aside all those robes lie by thee,   15
Crown thy arts with arms; they'll beautify thee.

O worthy of worthiest name, adorned in this manner,
Lead bravely thy forces on, under war's warlike banner.
O mayst thou prove fortunate in all martial courses,
Guide thou still by skill, in arts and forces: 20
Victory attend thee nigh, whilst fame sings loud thy powers;
Triumphant conquest crown thy head, and blessings pour
    down showers.

FIRST PILGRIM Here's a strange turn of state: who would have thought
    So great a lady would have matched herself
    Unto so mean a person? Yet the Cardinal   25
    Bears himself much too cruel.
SECOND PILGRIM   They are banished.

25 *mean* of a low social class.

FIRST PILGRIM   But I would ask what power hath this state
    Of Ancona, to determine of a free prince?
SECOND PILGRIM   They are a free state, sir, and her brother showed
    How that the Pope, forehearing of her looseness,   30
    Hath seized into th' protection of the Church
    The dukedom which she held as dowager.
FIRST PILGRIM   But by what justice?
SECOND PILGRIM   Sure I think by none,
    Only her brother's instigation.
FIRST PILGRIM   What was it, with such violence he took   35
    Off from her finger?
SECOND PILGRIM   'Twas her wedding ring,
    Which he vowed shortly he would sacrifice
    To his revenge.
FIRST PILGRIM   Alas Antonio!
    If that a man be thrust into a well,
    No matter who sets hand to't, his own weight   40
    Will bring him sooner to th' bottom. Come, let's hence.
    Fortune makes this conclusion general:
    All things do help th'unhappy man to fall.   *Exeunt.*

·{ACT III}·

Scene 5   ·{*Somewhere near Loretto*}·

[*Enter*] ANTONIO, DUCHESS, CHILDREN, CARIOLA, SERVANTS.

DUCHESS   Banished Ancona?
ANTONIO   Yes, you see what power
    Lightens in great men's breath.
DUCHESS   Is all our train
    Shrunk to this poor remainder?
ANTONIO   These poor men,
    Which have got little in your service, vow
    To take your fortune. But your wiser buntings,   5

---

28 determine of pass judgment against.   **32 dowager** property received by a widow
upon the death of her husband.   **40 sets. . . to't** gives him the initial push.
🦗 **ACT III, Scene 5. 2 Lightens** explodes.   **5 take . . . fortune** endure your misfortune with you.   **buntings** little birds.

Now they are fledged, are gone.

DUCHESS   They have done wisely.
This puts me in mind of death: physicians thus,
With their hands full of money, use to give o'er
Their patients.

ANTONIO   Right the fashion of the world:
From decayed fortunes every flatterer shrinks;   10
Men cease to build where the foundation sinks.

DUCHESS   I had a very strange dream tonight.

ANTONIO   What was't?

DUCHESS   Methought I wore my coronet of state,
And on a sudden all the diamonds
Were changed to pearls.

ANTONIO   My interpretation   15
Is, you'll weep shortly; for to me, the pearls
Do signify your tears.

DUCHESS   The birds that live i' th' field
On the wild benefit of nature live
Happier than we; for they may choose their mates,
And carol their sweet pleasures to the spring.   20

[*Enter* BOSOLA *with a letter, which he gives to the* DUCHESS.]

BOSOLA   You are happily o'erta'en.

DUCHESS   From my brother?

BOSOLA   Yes, from the Lord Ferdinand, your brother,
All love, and safety—

DUCHESS   Thou dost blanch mischief;
Wouldst make it white. See, see, like to calm weather
At sea before a tempest, false hearts speak fair   25
To those they intend most mischief. [*She reads*] *a letter:*
"Send Antonio to me; I want his head in a business."
A politic equivocation—
He doth not want your counsel, but your head:
That is, he cannot sleep till you be dead.   30
And here's another pitfall, that's strewed o'er
With roses. Mark it, 'tis a cunning one:
"I stand engaged for your husband for several debts at Naples. Let

---

6 are fledged have acquired enough feathers to fly. **8 o'er** up. **9 Right** such is.
23–24 Thou . . . white You try to cover the blackness of your evil intentions with the
whiteness (of feigned friendliness).

not that trouble him: I had rather have his heart than his mon-
          ey."
And I believe so too.   35
BOSOLA   What do you believe?
DUCHESS   That he so much distrusts my husband's love,
          He will by no means believe his heart is with him
          Until he see it. The devil is not cunning enough
          To circumvent us in riddles.   40
BOSOLA   Will you reject that noble and free league
          Of amity and love which I present you?
DUCHESS   Their league is like that of some politic kings
          Only to make themselves of strength and power
          To be our after-ruin. Tell them so.   45
BOSOLA   And what from you?
ANTONIO   Thus tell him: I will not come.
BOSOLA   And what of this?
ANTONIO   My brothers have dispersed
          Bloodhounds abroad, which till I hear are muzzled
          No truce—though hatched with ne'er such politic skill—
          Is safe that hangs upon our enemies' will.   50
          I'll not come at them.
BOSOLA   This proclaims your breeding.
          Every small thing draws a base mind to fear,
          As the adamant draws iron. Fare you well, sir;
          You shall shortly hear from's.   *Exit.*
DUCHESS   I suspect some ambush:
          Therefore, by all my love, I do conjure you   55
          To take your eldest son and fly towards Milan.
          Let us not venture all this poor remainder
          In one unlucky bottom.
ANTONIO   You counsel safely.
          Best of my life, farewell. Since we must part,
          Heaven hath a hand in't: but no otherwise   60
          Than as some curious artist takes in sunder
          A clock or watch, when it is out of frame,
          To bring't in better order.
DUCHESS   I know not which is best,

---

43 *politic* conniving. **47 *brothers*** brothers-in-law. **48–50 *which . . . will*** Until
those bloodhounds are tied up, no truce that depends on our enemies' good will is safe
for us—no matter how skillfully couched in ambiguous language it may be. **53 *adamant***
magnet. **58 *bottom*** the hold of a ship (i.e. in one precarious place). **62 *frame*** order.

To see you dead, or part with you. Farewell, boy,
Thou art happy, that thou hast not understanding   65
To know thy misery. For all our wit
And reading brings us to a truer sense
Of sorrow. In the eternal Church, sir,
I do hope we shall not part thus.

ANTONIO   O be of comfort,
Make patience a noble fortitude: 70
And think not how unkindly we are used.
Man, like to cassia, is proved best being bruised.

DUCHESS   Must I, like to a slave-born Russian,
Account it praise to suffer tyranny?
And yet, O Heaven, thy heavy hand is in't.   75
I have seen my little boy oft scourge his top,
And compared myself to't: nought made me e'er go right,
But Heaven's scourge stick.

ANTONIO   Do not weep:
Heaven fashioned us of nothing; and we strive
To bring ourselves to nothing. Farewell, Cariola,   80
And thy sweet armful. [*To the* DUCHESS.] If I do never see thee
    more,
Be a good mother to your little ones,
And save them from the tiger: fare you well.

DUCHESS   Let me look upon you once more, for that speech
Came from a dying father: your kiss is colder   85
Than I have seen an holy anchorite
Give to a dead man's skull.

ANTONIO   My heart is turned to a heavy lump of lead,
With which I sound my danger: fare you well.
                                    Exit [*with elder* SON].

DUCHESS   My laurel is all witherèd.   90

CARIOLA   Look, madam, what a troop of armèd men
Make toward us.

    Enter BOSOLA *with a guard*[, *all wearing armored masks*].

DUCHESS   O, they are very welcome:

---

71 unkindly both evilly and unnaturally.   **72 cassia** bark that, when pounded, is a
source of cinnamon.   **76 scourge his top** spin his toy top.   **81 sweet armful** the
babies she holds.   **88 lump of lead** Sailors took depth readings by dropping heavy
lumps of lead overboard.   **92 Make** The verb is plural because of its proximity to
"men."

When Fortune's wheel is overcharged with princes,
The weight makes it move swift. I would have my ruin
Be sudden. I am your adventure, am I not?   95
BOSOLA   You are. You must see your husband no more,—
DUCHESS   What devil art thou, that counterfeits Heaven's thunder?
BOSOLA   Is that terrible? I would have you tell me whether
   Is that note worse that frights the silly birds
   Out of the corn, or that which doth allure them   100
   To the nets? You have harkened to the last too much.
DUCHESS   O misery! like to a rusty o'erchargèd cannon,
   Shall I never fly in pieces? Come: to what prison?
BOSOLA   To none.
DUCHESS   Whither then?
BOSOLA   To your palace.
DUCHESS   I have heard that Charon's boat serves to convey   105
   All o'er the dismal lake, but brings none back again.
BOSOLA   Your brothers mean you safety and pity.
DUCHESS   Pity!
   With such a pity men preserve alive
   Pheasants and quails, when they are not fat enough   110
   To be eaten.
BOSOLA   These are your children?
DUCHESS   Yes.
BOSOLA   Can they prattle?
DUCHESS   No.
   But I intend, since they were born accursed,
   Curses shall be their first language.
BOSOLA   Fie, madam!   115
   Forget this base, low fellow.
DUCHESS   Were I a man,
   I'd beat that counterfeit face into thy other—
BOSOLA   One of no birth.
DUCHESS   Say that he was born mean:
   Man is most happy, when's own actions
   Be arguments and examples of his virtue.   120
BOSOLA   A barren, beggarly virtue.
DUCHESS   I prithee, who is greatest? Can you tell?

---

93 *overcharged with* turned over by (the weight of the princes tied to it). **95** *adventure*
what you venture after. **98–99** *whether . . . worse that* which note is worse, that
which. **105** *Charon* the old boatman who ferried the souls of the dead across the river
Styx to Hades. **112** *prattle* talk. **117** *counterfeit face* the armored visor.

Sad tales befit my woe: I'll tell you one.
A salmon, as she swam unto the sea,
Met with a dogfish, who encounters her   125
With this rough language: "Why art thou so bold
To mix thyself with our high state of floods
Being no eminent courtier, but one
That for the calmest and fresh time o' th' year
Dost live in shallow rivers, rankst thyself   130
With silly smelts and shrimps? And darest thou
Pass by our dogship without reverence?"
"O," quoth the salmon, "sister, be at peace:
Thank Jupiter, we both have passed the net.
Our value never can be truly known,   135
Till in the fisher's basket we be shown;
I' th' market then my price may be the higher,
Even when I am nearest to the cook, and fire."
So, to great men, the moral may be stretched:
Men oft are valued high, when th'are most wretched.   140
But, come, whither you please. I am armed 'gainst misery,
Bent to all sways of the oppressor's will.
There's no deep valley, but near some great hill.   *Ex[eunt]*.

ACT IV

Scene 1   {*In a prison somewhere near Loretto*}

[*Enter* FERDINAND *and* BOSOLA.]

FERDINAND   How doth our sister Duchess bear herself
    In her imprisonment?
BOSOLA   Nobly. I'll describe her:
    She's sad, as one long used to't, and she seems
    Rather to welcome the end of misery

---

127 high . . . floods the deep sea (of the court's high intrigue).   **132 our** The plural
was used in any address to royal persons.   **dogship** a term of abuse, satirizing such types
of formal address as "your lordship."   **140 valued high** judged worthy (by God).
143 There's . . . hill Even in despair man finds cause for hope—in the power of God.

Than shun it—a behavior so noble,   5
As gives a majesty to adversity.
You may discern the shape of loveliness
More perfect in her tears, than in her smiles.
She will muse four hours together, and her silence,
Methinks, expresseth more than if she spake.   10
FERDINAND   Her melancholy seems to be fortified
With a strange disdain.
BOSOLA   'Tis so, and this restraint
(Like English mastives, that grow fierce with tying)
Makes her too passionately apprehend
Those pleasures she's kept from.
FERDINAND   Curse upon her!   15
I will no longer study in the book
Of another's heart: inform her what I told you.   *Exit.*

[BOSOLA *enters the* DUCHESS' *inner-stage prison.*]

BOSOLA   All comfort to, your grace;—
DUCHESS   I will have none.
'Pray thee, why dost thou wrap thy poisoned pills
In gold and sugar?   20
BOSOLA   Your elder brother, the Lord Ferdinand,
Is come to visit you, and sends you word,
'Cause once he rashly made a solemn vow
Never to see you more. He comes i' th' night,
And prays you, gently, neither torch nor taper   25
Shine in your chamber. He will kiss your hand;
And reconcile himself, but, for his vow,
He dares not see you.
DUCHESS   At his pleasure.
Take hence the lights: he's come.   [*Exeunt* SERVANTS *with lights.*]

[*Enter* FERDINAND.]

FERDINAND   Where are you?
DUCHESS   Here sir.
FERDINAND   This darkness suits you well.
DUCHESS   I would ask your pardon.   30

🦌 **ACT IV, Scene 1.   16–17** *I . . . heart*   I will no longer waste my time trying to
figure out what is in her heart.   **19–20** *why . . . sugar*   Why do you cover up your
hatred and evil designs with feigned courtesy?

FERDINAND   You have it;
    For I account it the honorabl'st revenge
    Where I may kill, to pardon. Where are your cubs?
DUCHESS   Whom?
FERDINAND   Call them your children;   35
    For though our national law distinguish bastards
    From true legitimate issue, compassionate nature
    Makes them all equal.
DUCHESS   Do you visit me for this?
    You violate a sacrament o' th' Church
    Shall make you howl in hell for't.
FERDINAND   It had been well,   40
    Could you have lived thus always, for indeed
    You were too much i' th' light. But no more;
    I come to seal my peace with you: here's a hand,

    Gives her a dead man's hand.

    To which you have vowed much love; the ring upon't
    You gave.
DUCHESS   I affectionately kiss it.   45
FERDINAND   Pray do, and bury the print of it in your heart.
    I will leave this ring with you, for a love-token,
    And the hand, as sure as the ring. And do not doubt
    But you shall have the heart too. When you need a friend
    Send it to him that owed it: you shall see   50
    Whether he can aid you.
DUCHESS   You are very cold.
    I fear you are not well after your travel.
    Ha, lights!—Oh, horrible!
FERDINAND   Let her have lights enough.   [*Exit.*]

    [*Enter* SERVANTS *with lights.*]

DUCHESS   What witchcraft doth he practice, that he hath left
    A dead man's hand here?—   55

    Here is discovered, behind a traverse, the artificial figures of ANTONIO
    and his children, appearing as if they were dead.

32–33 For . . . pardon For I consider it most honorable to pardon, when I could kill.
39 sacrament . . . Church her marriage to Antonio, which she believes is recognized
by the eternal Church (cf. III.5.68). **41 thus** in darkness. **42 too . . . light** too conspicuous. **44 ring** her wedding ring, which was earlier seized by the Cardinal.
50 owed owned. **54 What . . . practice** A dead man's hand was one of the charms
used in attempts to cure madness by witchcraft.

BOSOLA Look you, here's the piece from which 'twas ta'en.
    He doth present you this sad spectacle
    That, now you know directly they are dead,
    Hereafter you may wisely cease to grieve
    For that which cannot be recovered.   60
DUCHESS There is not between heaven and earth one wish
    I stay for after this. It wastes me more,
    Than were't my picture, fashioned out of wax,
    Stuck with a magical needle, and then buried
    In some foul dunghill. And yond's an excellent property   65
    For a tyrant, which I would account mercy,—
BOSOLA What's that?
DUCHESS If they would bind me to that lifeless trunk,
    And let me freeze to death.
BOSOLA   Come, you must live.
DUCHESS That's the greatest torture souls feel in hell: 70
    In hell that they must live, and cannot die.
    Portia, I'll new kindle thy coals again,
    And revive the rare and almost dead example
    Of a loving wife.
BOSOLA   O, fie! despair? remember
    You are a Christian.
DUCHESS   The Church enjoins fasting: 75
    I'll starve myself to death.
BOSOLA   Leave this vain sorrow;
    Things, being at the worst, begin to mend:
    The bee when he hath shot his sting into your hand
    May then play with your eyelid.
DUCHESS   Good comfortable fellow,
    Persuade a wretch that's broke upon the wheel   80

63–65 *my . . . dunghill* The reference here is to the black-magic practice of putting an evil spell on someone by sticking pins into a doll that looks like him. By then burying the doll in a dunghill, the magician calls upon supernatural spirits to curse even the corpse of the intended victim by denying it proper burial. **68** *lifeless trunk* (the statue of) dead Antonio. **72** *Portia* Brutus' wife, who committed suicide by swallowing red-hot coals after she heard of her husband's death. **75** *You . . . Christian* Suicide is forbidden by Christianity. **78–79** *The . . . eyelid* After it has used its stinger on your hand, the bee may sit even on your eyelid without being able to do any harm. **79** *comfortable* free from pain. **80** *broke . . . wheel* In Webster's time, men were tortured by being bound to a wheel and then stretched until their bones broke under the strain. Fortune, too, was often thought of as a great wheel of torture, to which all men were tied and upon which they were eventually broken if they trusted too much in material rewards (see the Duchess' reference to this belief at III.5.93).

To have all his bones new set: entreat him live,
To be executed again. Who must dispatch me?
I account this world a tedious theater,
For I do play a part in't 'gainst my will.

BOSOLA   Come, be of comfort, I will save your life.   85

DUCHESS   Indeed, I have not leisure to tend so small a business.

BOSOLA   Now, by my life, I pity you.

DUCHESS   Thou art a fool then,
To waste thy pity on a thing so wretched
As cannot pity itself. I am full of daggers.
Puff! let me blow these vipers from me.   90

[*She turns to a* SERVANT.]

What are you?

SERVANT   One that wishes you long life.

DUCHESS   I would thou wert hanged for the horrible curse
Thou hast given me: I shall shortly grow one
Of the miracles of pity. I'll go pray. No,
I'll go curse.

BOSOLA   Oh fie!

DUCHESS   I could curse the stars.   95

BOSOLA   Oh, fearful!

DUCHESS   And those three smiling seasons of the year
Into a Russian winter—nay, the world
To its first chaos.

BOSOLA   Look you, the stars shine still.

DUCHESS   Oh, but you must   100
Remember, my curse hath a great way to go:
Plagues, that make lanes through largest families,
Consume them.

BOSOLA   Fie lady!

DUCHESS   Let them like tyrants
Never be remembered, but for the ill they have done:
Let all the zealous prayers of mortifièd   105
Churchmen forget them,—

BOSOLA   O uncharitable!

DUCHESS   Let Heaven, a little while, cease crowning martyrs
To punish them.

---

93 *grow* become.   **97–99** *And . . . chaos* And (I could curse) spring, summer, and fall
so that they became one long winter; in fact, I could wish the world restored to its
original state of chaos.   **103** *them* her brothers.

Go, howl them this, and say I long to bleed.
It is some mercy when men kill with speed.   110

Exit [with SERVANTS].

[*Enter* FERDINAND.]

FERDINAND   Excellent, as I would wish: she plagued in art.
These presentations are but framed in wax
By the curious master in that quality,
Vincentio Lauriola, and she takes them
For true, substantial bodies.

BOSOLA   Why do you do this?   115

FERDINAND   To bring her to despair.

BOSOLA   'Faith, end here,
And go no farther in your cruelty.
Send her a penitential garment, to put on
Next to her delicate skin, and furnish her
With beads and prayerbooks.

FERDINAND   Damn her! that body of hers,   120
While that my blood ran pure in't, was more worth
Than that which thou wouldst comfort, called a soul.
I will send her masques of common courtesans,
Have her meat served up by bawds and ruffians,
And, 'cause she'll needs be mad, I am resolved   125
To remove forth the common hospital
All the mad folk, and place them near her lodging.
There let them practice together, sing, and dance,
And act their gambols to the full o' th' moon:
If she can sleep the better for it, let her.   130
Your work is almost ended.

BOSOLA   Must I see her again?

FERDINAND   Yes.

BOSOLA   Never.

FERDINAND   You must.

BOSOLA   Never in mine own shape;

III *she . . . art* She was tormented by these wax figures. **II3** *curious* ingenious.
II4 *Vincentio Lauriola* historically unidentifiable, but here he is clearly meant to be a
skillful wax-worker. **II6** *'Faith* an interjection, contracted from "in faith." **I20** *beads*
rosary beads. **I20–22** *that . . . soul* There is in this declaration—because the Duchess'
body is its focus—another unconscious suggestion of Ferdinand's sexual desires for his
sister. **I23** *masques* courtly entertainments. **I25** *needs be* willfully continues to be.
I26 *forth* from. **I28** *practice* carry on their activities. **I29** *full . . . moon* the time
when madmen were thought to be most mad. **I32** *in . . . shape* without being
disguised.

That's forfeited by my intelligence
And this last cruel lie. When you send me next,
The business shall be comfort.

FERDINAND   Very likely.   135
Thy pity is nothing of kin to thee. Antonio
Lurks about Milan; thou shalt shortly thither,
To feed a fire as great as my revenge,
Which ne'er will slack till it have spent his fuel;
Intemperate agues make physicians cruel.   *Exeunt.*   140

⟨ACT IV⟩
Scene 2   ⟨*The same place*⟩

[*Enter* DUCHESS *and* CARIOLA.]

DUCHESS   What hideous noise was that?

CARIOLA   'Tis the wild consort
Of madmen, lady, which your tyrant brother
Hath placed about your lodging. This tyranny,
I think, was never practiced till this hour.

DUCHESS   Indeed, I thank him: nothing but noise and folly   5
Can keep me in my right wits, whereas reason
And silence make me stark mad. Sit down.
Discourse to me some dismal tragedy.

CARIOLA   O 'twill increase your melancholy.

DUCHESS   Thou art deceived;
To hear of greater grief would lessen mine.   10
This is a prison?

CARIOLA   Yes, but you shall live
To shake this durance off.

DUCHESS   Thou art a fool:
The robin red-breast and the nightingale
Never live long in cages.

CARIOLA   Pray dry your eyes.
What think you of, madam?   15

---

133 *intelligence* work as a spy. **135** *Very likely* a cynical rejoinder, because Bosola
will then offer her the "comfort" of death.
🦌 **ACT IV, Scene 2.   12** *durance* hardship.

DUCHESS   Of nothing:
    When I muse thus, I sleep.
CARIOLA   Like a madman, with your eyes open?
DUCHESS   Dost thou think we shall know one another
    In th'other world?
CARIOLA   Yes, out of question.   20
DUCHESS   O, that it were possible we might
    But hold some two days' conference with the dead:
    From them I should learn somewhat I am sure
    I never shall know here. I'll tell thee a miracle;
    I am not mad yet, to my cause of sorrow.   25
    Th' heaven o'er my head seems made of molten brass,
    The earth of flaming sulphur, yet I am not mad.
    I am acquainted with sad misery,
    As the tanned galley slave is with his oar.
    Necessity makes me suffer constantly,   30
    And custom makes it easy. Who do I look like now?
CARIOLA   Like to your picture in the gallery,
    A deal of life in show, but none in practice:
    Or rather like some reverend monument
    Whose ruins are even pitied.
DUCHESS   Very proper: 35
    And Fortune seems only to have her eyesight,
    To behold my tragedy.
    How now! What noise is that? [*Enter* SERVANT.]
SERVANT   I am come to tell you,
    Your brother hath intended you some sport.
    A great physician when the Pope was sick   40
    Of a deep melancholy, presented him
    With several sorts of madmen, which wild object,
    Being full of change and sport, forced him to laugh,
    And so th'imposthume broke: the selfsame cure
    The Duke intends on you.
DUCHESS   Let them come in.   45
SERVANT   There's a mad lawyer, and a secular priest,

---

25 *to . . . sorrow*   which is why I feel sorrow.   **33** *show*   appearance   *practice*   action.
36 *Fortune . . . eyesight*   Traditionally, the goddess Fortune was pictured as blindfolded because she distributed her rewards so arbitrarily. Here the Duchess implies that momentarily Fortune's blindfold has been removed so that she can see the sad results of her handiwork.   **39** *sport*   entertainment.   **44** *imposthume*   ulcer (which caused the melancholy).

A doctor that hath forfeited his wits
By jealousy; an astrologian
That in his works said such a day o' th' month
Should be the day of doom, and, failing of 't,   50
Ran mad; an English tailor, crazed i' th' brain
With the study of new fashion; a gentleman usher
Quite beside himself with care to keep in mind
The number of his lady's salutations
Or "How do you?" she employed him in each morning;   55
A farmer too, an excellent knave in grain,
Mad, 'cause he was hindered transportation;
And let one broker, that's mad, loose to these,
You'd think the devil were among them.

DUCHESS   Sit Cariola. Let them loose when you please,   60
For I am chained to endure all your tyranny.

[*Enter* MADMEN.] *Here, by a* MADMAN, *this song is sung to a dismal
kind of music.*

O let us howl, some heavy note,
    Some deadly-doggèd howl,
Sounding, as from the threat'ning throat,
    Of beasts and fatal fowl.
As ravens, screech owls, bulls, and bears,   65
    We'll bell, and bawl our parts,
Till irksome noise have cloyed your ears,
    And corrosived your hearts.
At last when as our choir wants breath,   70
    Our bodies being blest,
We'll sing like swans, to welcome death,
    And die in love and rest.

MAD ASTROLOGER   Doomsday not come yet? I'll draw it nearer by a
perspective, or make a glass that shall set all the world on fire   75
upon an instant. I cannot sleep; my pillow is stuffed with a litter
of porcupines.

---

52 *usher*   an attendant who walks before a person of rank, greeting guests and intro-
ducing strangers.   55 *How . . . morning*   a double-entendre, meaning the usher was
made to serve her sexually as well as socially.   56 *in grain*   both "in the grain trade"
and "in essence (a knave)."   57 *hindered transportation*   denied export.   58 *let*   turn.
broker   pawnbroker.   67 *bell*   bellow.   69 *corrosived*   corroded.   75 *perspective*
telescope.

MAD LAWYER   Hell is a mere glasshouse, where the devils are continually blowing up women's souls on hollow irons, and the fire
never goes out.   80

MAD PRIEST   I will lie with every woman in my parish the tenth night:
I will tithe them over like haycocks.

MAD DOCTOR   Shall my pothecary outgo me, because I am a cuckold?
I have found out his roguery: he makes alum of his wife's urine
and sells it to Puritans, that have sore throats with over-straining.   85

MAD ASTROLOGER   I have skill in heraldry.

MAD LAWYER   Hast?

MAD ASTROLOGER   You do give for your crest a woodcock's head,
with the brains picked out on't. You are a very ancient gentleman.

MAD PRIEST   Greek is turned Turk; we are only to be saved by the   90
Helvetian translation.

MAD ASTROLOGER   [To LAWYER.] Come on sir, I will lay the law to you.

MAD LAWYER   Oh, rather lay a corrosive: the law will eat to the bone.

MAD PRIEST   He that drinks but to satisfy nature is damned.

MAD DOCTOR   If I had my glass here, I would show a sight should   95
make all the women here call me mad doctor.

MAD ASTROLOGER   [Pointing to PRIEST.] What's he, a ropemaker?

MAD LAWYER   No, no, no, a snuffling knave that, while he shows the
tombs, will have his hand in a wench's placket.

MAD PRIEST   Woe to the caroche that brought home my wife from   100
the masque at three o'clock in the morning; it had a large feather-
bed in it.

MAD DOCTOR   I have pared the devil's nails forty times, roasted them
in raven's eggs, and cured agues with them.

---

78 *glasshouse*   a factory where glass is made.   79 *blowing . . . irons*   A sexual meaning
is implicit in this statement, and in most of the lunatic raving that follows; these madmen, like Lear on the heath, are acutely conscious of the intensity of man's sexual desires.
82 *haycocks*   stacks of hay, but an obscene pun is intended as well.   83 *pothecary*
druggist.   *outgo*   get the best of.   84 *alum*   an astringent formerly used to treat in-
flamed tissue.   85 *over-straining*   singing too loudly and, also, straining too much of
the life out of religion.   88 *woodcock*   thought to be a stupid bird.   90 *Greek . . .
Turk*   The Greek text of the Bible has been made to serve nonbelievers (all non-
Puritans).   91 *Helvetian translation*   the translation of the Bible officially approved by
the Puritans.   92 *I . . . you*   I will explain the church law to you.   93 *Oh . . . lay*
You might just as well apply.   95 *glass*   some sort of magnifying glass.   97 *ropemaker*   i.e. one who is in league with the hangman.   98 *snuffling*   sanctimonious.
99 *placket*   both "pocket" and "pudendum."   100 *caroche*   a luxurious carriage.
103 *I . . . nails*   I have brought the devil under my control.

MAD PRIEST   Get me three hundred milch bats, to make possets to   105
  procure sleep.

MAD DOCTOR   All the college may throw their caps at me; I have made
  a soap-boiler costive: it was my masterpiece—

Here the dance consisting of eight MADMEN, *with music answerable
thereunto, after which* BOSOLA, *like an old man, enters.*

DUCHESS   Is he mad too?

SERVANT   Pray question him; I'll leave you.
                              [*Exeunt* SERVANT *and* MADMEN.]

BOSOLA   I am come to make thy tomb.

DUCHESS   Ha, my tomb?   110
  Thou speakst as if I lay upon my deathbed,
  Gasping for breath. Dost thou perceive me sick?

BOSOLA   Yes, and the more dangerously, since thy sickness is insensible.

DUCHESS   Thou art not mad, sure; dost know me?

BOSOLA   Yes.   115

DUCHESS   Who am I?

BOSOLA   Thou art a box of worm seed, at best but a salvatory of green
  mummy. What's this flesh? a little cruded milk, fantastical puff
  paste: our bodies are weaker than those paper prisons boys use
  to keep flies in, more contemptible—since ours is to preserve   120
  earthworms. Didst thou ever see a lark in a cage? such is the soul
  in the body: this world is like her little turf of grass and the
  heaven o'er our heads, like her looking glass, only gives us a
  miserable knowledge of the small compass of our prison.

DUCHESS   Am not I thy Duchess?   125

BOSOLA   Thou art some great woman, sure; for riot begins to sit
  on thy forehead (clad in grey hairs) twenty years sooner than on
  a merry milkmaid's. Thou sleepst worse, than if a mouse should

---

105 milch milk-bearing.   **possets** a hot drink made of sweetened, spiced milk
curdled with ale or wine.   **107 throw . . . caps** vainly seek to surpass me in skill.
107–08 I . . . costive I have made one who boils soap constipated (an unusual accom-
plishment because soap was an essential element used in manufacturing suppositories).
113 insensible not apparent to the senses.   **117 box . . . seed** a box of food for worms.
but only.   **117–18 salvatory . . . mummy** either a container for an unripened mummy
(because you are still alive) or an ointment box for fresh mummia, a drug derived from
embalmed bodies.   **118 cruded** curdled.   **118–19 puff paste** a light pastry.   **122 turf of
grass,** **123 looking glass** articles that were put into bird cages in an attempt to keep
the captured birds happy.   **126 riot** lines of sorrow that disturb the previous order of
beauty.

be forced to take up her lodging in a cat's ear. A little infant, that
breeds its teeth, should it lie with thee, would cry out, as if thou   130
wert the more unquiet bedfellow.

DUCHESS   I am Duchess of Malfi still.

BOSOLA   That makes thy sleeps so broken:
   Glories, like glowworms, afar off shine bright,
   But looked to near, have neither heat nor light.   135

DUCHESS   Thou art very plain.

BOSOLA   My trade is to flatter the dead, not the living: I am a tomb-
maker.

DUCHESS   And thou comst to make my tomb?

BOSOLA   Yes.   140

DUCHESS   Let me be a little merry;
   Of what stuff wilt thou make it?

BOSOLA   Nay, resolve me first. Of what fashion?

DUCHESS   Why, do we grow fantastical in our deathbed?
   Do we affect fashion in the grave?   145

BOSOLA   Most ambitiously. Princes' images on their tombs
   Do not lie as they were wont, seeming to pray
   Up to heaven, but with their hands under their cheeks,
   As if they died of the toothache. They are not carved
   With their eyes fixed upon the stars; but, as   150
   Their minds were wholly bent upon the world,
   The selfsame way they seem to turn their faces.

DUCHESS   Let me know fully therefore the effect
   Of this thy dismal preparation,
   This talk, fit for a charnel.

BOSOLA   Now I shall;   155

[*Enter* EXECUTIONERS *with*] *a coffin, cords, and a bell.*

   Here is a present from your princely brothers,
   And may it arrive welcome, for it brings
   Last benefit, last sorrow.

DUCHESS   Let me see it.
   I have so much obedience in my blood
   I wish it in their veins, to do them good.   160

129–31 *A . . . bedfellow*   You sleep more restlessly than a baby cutting teeth.
136 *plain* plain-spoken. **143** *resolve me* Answer my question. **144** *fantastical*
obsessed by fantasies. **148** *with . . . cheeks* in a semirecumbent position. **155** *charnel*
cemetery.

BOSOLA   This is your last presence chamber.

CARIOLA   O my sweet lady!

DUCHESS   Peace! it affrights not me.

BOSOLA   I am the common bellman,
      That usually is sent to condemned persons,
      The night before they suffer.

DUCHESS   Even now thou saidst   165
      Thou wast a tomb-maker?

BOSOLA   'Twas to bring you
      By degrees to mortification. Listen:

[*Rings the bell.*]

      Hark, now every thing is still,
      The screech owl and the whistler shrill
      Call upon our dame, aloud,   170
      And bid her quickly don her shroud.
      Much you had of land and rent,
      Your length in clay's now competent.
      A long war disturbed your mind;
      Here your perfect peace is signed.   175
      Of what is't fools make such vain keeping?
      Sin their conception, their birth, weeping:
      Their life, a general mist of error,
      Their death, a hideous storm of terror.
      Strew your hair with powders sweet: 180
      Don clean linen, bathe your feet,
      And, the foul fiend more to check,
      A crucifix let bless your neck.
      'Tis now full tide 'tween night and day,
      End your groan, and come away.   185

[EXECUTIONERS *approach.*]

CARIOLA   Hence, villains, tyrants, murderers. Alas!
      What will you do with my lady? Call for help.

DUCHESS   To whom? To our next neighbors? They are mad-folks.

---

163 *bellman*   one who was supposed to drive evil spirits away from the soul.
166–67 *'Twas . . . mortification* It was to get you accustomed to the idea of dying.
169 *whistler shrill* a bird whose song was supposed to be a foreboding of evil.
170 *our dame* the Duchess.   **177** *Sin* The word here assumes the meanings of both
"since" and "sin" (which attends man's conception).   **182** *foul fiend* the devil.

BOSOLA   Remove that noise.

[EXECUTIONERS *seize* CARIOLA, *who struggles*.]

DUCHESS   Farewell, Cariola,
   In my last will I have not much to give: 190
   A many hundred guests have fed upon me;
   Thine will be a poor reversion.
CARIOLA   I will die with her.
DUCHESS   I pray thee, look thou givst my little boy
   Some syrup for his cold, and let the girl
   Say her prayers, ere she sleep.   [CARIOLA *is forced off*.]
                  Now, what you please.   195
   What death?
BOSOLA   Strangling. Here are your executioners.
DUCHESS   I forgive them:
   The apoplexy, catarrh, or cough o' th' lungs
   Would do as much as they do.   200
BOSOLA   Doth not death fright you?
DUCHESS   Who would be afraid on't?
   Knowing to meet such excellent company
   In th'other world.
BOSOLA   Yet, methinks,
   The manner of your death should much afflict you;
   This cord should terrify you?
DUCHESS   Not a whit: 205
   What would it pleasure me, to have my throat cut
   With diamonds? or to be smotherèd
   With cassia? or to be shot to death with pearls?
   I know death hath ten thousand several doors
   For men to take their exits; and 'tis found   210
   They go on such strange geometrical hinges,
   You may open them both ways. Any way, for heaven sake,
   So I were out of your whispering. Tell my brothers
   That I perceive death, now I am well awake,
   Best gift is they can give, or I can take.   215
   I would fain put off my last woman's fault:
   I'll not be tedious to you.
EXECUTIONERS   We are ready.

---

192 *reversion* estate passed on to her. **199** *catarrh* hemorrhage. **212** *You . . . ways*
Death may come and get you, or you may go to it (by committing suicide).

DUCHESS   Dispose my breath how please you, but my body
    Bestow upon my women, will you?
EXECUTIONERS   Yes.
DUCHESS   Pull, and pull strongly, for your able strength   220
    Must pull down heaven upon me—
    Yet stay, heaven-gates are not so highly arched
    As princes' palaces: they that enter there
    Must go upon their knees. [*She kneels.*] Come violent death,
    Serve for mandragora to make me sleep.   225
    Go tell my brothers, when I am laid out,
    They then may feed in quiet. *They strangle her.*
BOSOLA   Where's the waiting woman?
    Fetch her. Some other strangle the children.
                        [*Exeunt* EXECUTIONERS.]

[*Enter one with* CARIOLA.]

    Look you, there sleeps your mistress.
CARIOLA   O you are damned
    Perpetually for this. My turn is next,   230
    Is't not so ordered?
BOSOLA   Yes, and I am glad
    You are so well prepared for't.
CARIOLA   You are deceived sir,
    I am not prepared for't. I will not die;
    I will first come to my answer, and know
    How I have offended.
BOSOLA   Come, dispatch her.   235
    You kept her counsel; now you shall keep ours.
CARIOLA   I will not die—I must not—I am contracted
    To a young gentleman.
EXECUTIONER   [*Showing the noose.*] Here's your wedding ring.
CARIOLA   Let me but speak with the Duke. I'll discover
    Treason to his person.
BOSOLA   Delays: throttle her.   240
EXECUTIONER   She bites and scratches.
CARIOLA   If you kill me now,
    I am damned. I have not been at confession

---

225 mandragora a plant formerly used as a narcotic. **236 her** the Duchess'.

  This two years.
BOSOLA   When!
CARIOLA   I am quick with child.
BOSOLA   Why then,
  Your credit's saved. Bear her into th' next room.
  Let this lie still.
      [EXECUTIONERS *strangle* CARIOLA *and exeunt with her body.*]
  [*Enter* FERDINAND.]
FERDINAND   Is she dead?
BOSOLA   She is what   245
  You'd have her. But here begin your pity.
  [BOSOLA *draws the traverse and*] *shows the children strangled.*
  Alas, how have these offended?
FERDINAND   The death
  Of young wolves is never to be pitied.
BOSOLA Fix your eye here.
FERDINAND   Constantly.
BOSOLA   Do you not weep?
  Other sins only speak; murther shrieks out: 250
  The element of water moistens the earth,
  But blood flies upwards and bedews the heavens.
FERDINAND Cover her face. Mine eyes dazzle: she died young.
BOSOLA I think not so: her infelicity
  Seemed to have years too many.
FERDINAND   She and I were twins: 255
  And should I die this instant I had lived
  Her time to a minute.
BOSOLA   It seems she was born first:
  You have bloodily approved the ancient truth,
  That kindred commonly do worse agree
  Than remote strangers.
FERDINAND   Let me see her face again— 260
  Why didst not thou pity her? What an excellent

---

243 *When* an exclamation of impatience. *quick . . . child* pregnant. (Criminals who were pregnant were sometimes granted a stay of execution until the birth of the child.) **244** *Your . . . saved* Your reputation is saved—because your death will prevent you from bearing a bastard child. **253** *dazzle* are dazzled. **258** *approved* proven. **259** *do . . . agree* differ more.

Honest man mightst thou have been
If thou hadst borne her to some sanctuary!
Or, bold in a good cause, opposed thyself
With thy advancèd sword above thy head,   265
Between her innocence and my revenge!
I bade thee, when I was distracted of my wits,
Go kill my dearest friend, and thou hast done't.
For let me but examine well the cause.
What was the meanness of her match to me?   270
Only, I must confess, I had a hope,
Had she continued widow, to have gained
An infinite mass of treasure by her death;
And that was the main cause—her marriage,
That drew a stream of gall quite through my heart.   275
For thee (as we observe in tragedies
That a good actor many times is cursed
For playing a villain's part), I hate thee for't.
And, for my sake, say thou hast done much ill, well.

BOSOLA   Let me quicken your memory, for I perceive   280
You are falling into ingratitude. I challenge
The reward due to my service.

FERDINAND   I'll tell thee,
What I'll give thee—

BOSOLA   Do.

FERDINAND   I'll give thee a pardon
For this murther.

BOSOLA   Ha?

FERDINAND   Yes: and 'tis
The largest bounty I can study to do thee.   285
By what authority didst thou execute
This bloody sentence?

BOSOLA   By yours.

FERDINAND   Mine? Was I her judge?
Did any ceremonial form of law
Doom her to not-being? Did a complete jury

271–73 *Only . . . death* The Duke, desperately searching for the reason why he found
his sister's marriage to Antonio so hateful, here presents an obvious rationalization: even
if the Duchess had died without remarrying, her estate would have gone to her first son,
the young Duke of Malfi (see III.3.66). The real explanation for Ferdinand's intense jealousy
of Antonio is, of course, too frightening for him to admit, or even to recognize consciously.
285 *study* consciously bring myself.

Deliver her conviction up i' th' court?   290
Where shalt thou find this judgment registered
Unless in hell? See, like a bloody fool
Th' hast forfeited thy life, and thou shalt die for't.

BOSOLA   The office of justice is perverted quite
When one thief hangs another. Who shall dare   295
To reveal this?

FERDINAND   Oh, I'll tell thee:
The wolf shall find her grave and scrape it up,
Not to devour the corpse, but to discover
The horrid murther.

BOSOLA   You, not I, shall quake for't.

FERDINAND   Leave me.

BOSOLA   I will first receive my pension.   300

FERDINAND   You are a villain.

BOSOLA   When your ingratitude
Is judge, I am so—

FERDINAND   O horror!
That not the fear of Him which binds the devils
Can prescribe man obedience.
Never look upon me more.

BOSOLA   Why fare thee well.   305
Your brother and yourself are worthy men;
You have a pair of hearts are hollow graves—
Rotten, and rotting others. And your vengeance,
Like two chained bullets, still goes arm in arm.
You may be brothers, for treason, like the plague,   310
Doth take much in a blood. I stand like one
That long hath ta'en a sweet and golden dream:
I am angry with myself, now that I wake.

FERDINAND   Get thee into some unknown part o' th' world,
That I may never see thee.

BOSOLA   Let me know   315
Wherefore I should be thus neglected? Sir,
I served your tyranny, and rather strove
To satisfy yourself, than all the world;
And though I loathed the evil, yet I loved

---

300 pension reward for services. **309 chained bullets** Cannon balls were sometimes chained together to increase the extent of their destructive force. **311 take . . . blood** runs in the blood of particular families.

You that did counsel it, and rather sought   320
To appear a true servant than an honest man.
FERDINAND   I'll go hunt the badger by owl-light:
'Tis a deed of darkness.   *Exit.*
BOSOLA   He's much distracted. Off my painted honor!
While with vain hopes our faculties we tire,   325
We seem to sweat in ice and freeze in fire.
What would I do, were this to do again?
I would not change my peace of conscience
For all the wealth of Europe. She stirs; here's life.
Return, fair soul, from darkness, and lead mine   330
Out of this sensible hell. She's warm; she breathes:
Upon thy pale lips I will melt my heart
To store them with fresh color. Who's there?
Some cordial drink! Alas! I dare not call:
So pity would destroy pity. Her eye opes,   335
And heaven in it seems to ope, that late was shut,
To take me up to mercy.
DUCHESS   Antonio!
BOSOLA   Yes, madam, he is living,
The dead bodies you saw were but feigned statues;
He's reconciled to your brothers: the Pope hath wrought   340
The atonement.
DUCHESS   Mercy.   *She dies.*
BOSOLA   Oh, she's gone again: there the cords of life broke.
Oh sacred innocence, that sweetly sleeps
On turtles' feathers, whilst a guilty conscience
Is a black register, wherein is writ   345
All our good deeds and bad, a perspective
That shows us hell. That we cannot be suffered
To do good when we have a mind to it!
This is manly sorrow:
These tears, I am very certain, never grew   350
In my mother's milk. My estate is sunk

---

322 *badger* an animal that avoided daylight. *owl-light* night. *I'll . . . owl-light*
I shall henceforth carry out my activities in darkness **324** *painted honor* false sense of
importance, as a spy for Ferdinand. **326** *We . . . fire* We are always uncomfortably
restless and unsatisfied. **331** *sensible* apparent to the senses. **334** *cordial drink* medicine to induce revival. **335** *So . . . pity* By pitying her and calling out for help, I would
only destroy her whom I pity because Ferdinand would return and kill her. **344** *turtles*
turtledoves (traditionally a symbol of love and peace). **351** *estate* condition.

Below the degree of fear: where were
These penitent fountains while she was living?
Oh, they were frozen up! Here is a sight
As direful to my soul as is the sword   355
Unto a wretch hath slain his father. Come,
I'll bear thee hence,
And execute thy last will—that's deliver
Thy body to the reverend dispose
Of some good women: that the cruel tyrant   360
Shall not deny me. Then I'll post to Milan,
Where somewhat I will speedily enact
Worth my dejection.   *Exit [carrying the body].*

ACT V

Scene 1   *{A public place in Milan}*

[*Enter* ANTONIO *and* DELIO.]

ANTONIO   What think you of my hope of reconcilement
    To the Aragonian brethren?
DELIO   I misdoubt it,
    For though they have sent their letters of safe conduct
    For your repair to Milan, they appear
    But nets to entrap you. The Marquis of Pescara,   5
    Under whom you hold certain land in cheat,
    Much 'gainst his noble nature, hath been moved
    To seize those lands, and some of his dependants
    Are at this instant making it their suit
    To be invested in your revenues.   10
    I cannot think they mean well to your life
    That do deprive you of your means of life,
    Your living.
ANTONIO   You are still an heretic.

---

363 ***Worth my dejection***   keeping with my abasement.
🦁 **ACT V, Scene 1.   4** *repair*   return.   **6** *in cheat*   subject to return to the lord only
if the tenant dies without an heir or if he commits a felony.   **13** *heretic*   skeptic.

To any safety I can shape myself.

DELIO Here comes the Marquis. I will make myself   15
    Petitioner for some part of your land,
    To know whether it is flying.

ANTONIO   I pray do.

    [*Enter* PESCARA.]

DELIO Sir, I have a suit to you.

PESCARA   To me?

DELIO   An easy one:
    There is the citadel of St. Bennet,
    With some demesnes, of late in the possession   20
    Of Antonio Bologna; please you bestow them on me?

PESCARA You are my friend. But this is such a suit
    Nor fit for me to give, nor you to take.

DELIO No sir?

PESCARA   I will give you ample reason for't
    Soon, in private. Here's the Cardinal's mistress.   25

    [*Enter* JULIA.]

JULIA My lord, I am grown your poor petitioner,
    And should be an ill beggar had I not
    A great man's letter here, the Cardinal's,
    To court you in my favor.

    [*She gives him a letter.*]

PESCARA   He entreats for you
    The citadel of St. Bennet, that belonged   30
    To the banished Bologna.

JULIA   Yes.

PESCARA I could not have thought of a friend I could
    Rather pleasure with it: 'tis yours.

JULIA   Sir, I thank you.
    And he shall know how doubly I am engaged,
    Both in your gift and speediness of giving,   35
    Which makes your grant the greater.   *Exit.*

ANTONIO   [*Aside.*] How they fortify
    Themselves with my ruin!

DELIO   Sir, I am

---

17 *whether* The second and third quarto editions read "whither." *it . . . flying* it is
wantonly being given away. **19** *St. Bennet* St. Benedict. **20** *demesnes* land attached
to the citadel.

Little bound to you.

PESCARA   Why?

DELIO   Because you denied this suit to me, and gave't
       To such a creature.

PESCARA   Do you know what it was?   40
       It was Antonio's land—not forfeited
       By course of law, but ravished from his throat
       By the Cardinal's entreaty. It were not fit
       I should bestow so main a piece of wrong
       Upon my friend: 'tis a gratification   45
       Only due to a strumpet; for it is injustice.
       Shall I sprinkle the pure blood of innocents
       To make those followers I call my friends
       Look ruddier upon me? I am glad
       This land, ta'en from the owner by such wrong,   50
       Returns again unto so foul an use,
       As salary for his lust. Learn, good Delio,
       To ask noble things of me, and you shall find
       I'll be a noble giver.

DELIO   You instruct me well.

ANTONIO   [Aside.] Why, here's a man, now, would fright impudence   55
       From sauciest beggars.

PESCARA   Prince Ferdinand's come to Milan
       Sick, as thy give out, of an apoplexy;
       But some say 'tis a frenzy. I am going
       To visit him.   Exit.

ANTONIO   'Tis a noble old fellow.

DELIO   What course do you mean to take, Antonio?   60

ANTONIO   This night I mean to venture all my fortune,
       Which is no more than a poor ling'ring life,
       To the Cardinal's worst of malice. I have got
       Private access to his chamber, and intend
       To visit him, about the mid of night,   65
       As once his brother did our noble Duchess.

---

49 ruddier more glowingly.   **55 fright** drive away.   **59 old fellow** The Marquis of
Pescara never actually lived to be an "old fellow"; he died when he was thirty-six. There
is, however, a good reason why Webster makes him old: that way he commands respect
as one who has lived long enough to become wise.   **63 To ... malice** against the worst
malice of the Cardinal.   **66 As ... Duchess** The reference is to the time that Ferdinand
came unexpectedly into the Duchess' bedchamber while she was combing her hair and
readying herself for bed. Antonio does not yet know about the murderous visit that
Ferdinand made while the Duchess was in prison.

It may be that the sudden apprehension
Of danger—for I'll go in mine own shape—,
When he shall see it fraight with love and duty,
May draw the poison out of him, and work   70
A friendly reconcilement. If it fail,
Yet it shall rid me of this infamous calling,
For better fall once, than be ever falling.
DELIO   I'll second you in all danger; and, howe'er,
My life keeps rank with yours.   75
ANTONIO   You are still my loved and best friend.   *Exeunt.*

⟨ACT V⟩

Scene 2   ⟨ *The palace of the Aragonian*
               brothers in Milan ⟩

[*Enter* PESCARA *and* DOCTOR.]

PESCARA   Now, doctor, may I visit your patient?
DOCTOR   If't please your lordship, but he's instantly
   To take the air here in the gallery,
   By my direction.
PESCARA   Pray thee, what's his disease?
DOCTOR   A very pestilent disease, my lord,   5
   They call lycanthropia.
PESCARA   What's that?
   I need a dictionary to't.
DOCTOR   I'll tell you:
   In those that are possessed with't there o'erflows
   Such melancholy humor, they imagine
   Themselves to be transformèd into wolves,   10
   Steal forth to churchyards in the dead of night,
   And dig dead bodies up: as two nights since
   One met the Duke, 'bout midnight in a lane
   Behind St. Mark's church, with the leg of a man

---

69 *fraight*   abounding with.   **72** *infamous calling*   life of disgrace.
🐾 **ACT V, Scene 2.   6** *lycanthropia*   a mania in which the victim imagines himself a
wolf.

Upon his shoulder; and he howled fearfully—   15
Said he was a wolf; only the difference
Was a wolf's skin was hairy on the outside,
His on the inside. Bade them take their swords,
Rip up his flesh, and try. Straight I was sent for,
And having ministered to him, found his grace   20
Very well recoverèd.

PESCARA   I am glad on't.

DOCTOR   Yet not without some fear
Of a relapse. If he grow to his fit again,
I'll go a nearer way to work with him
Than ever Paracelsus dreamed of. If   25
They'll give me leave, I'll buffet his madness out of him.
Stand aside: he comes.

[*Enter* CARDINAL, FERDINAND, MALATESTE, *and* BOSOLA, *who remains behind.*]

FERDINAND   Leave me.

MALATESTE   Why doth your lordship love this solitariness?

FERDINAND   Eagles commonly fly alone. They are crows, daws, and   30
starlings that flock together. Look, what's that follows me?

MALATESTE   Nothing, my lord.

FERDINAND   Yes.

MALATESTE   'Tis your shadow.

FERDINAND   Stay it; let it not haunt me.   35

MALATESTE   Impossible, if you move, and the sun shine.

FERDINAND   I will throttle it.

[*He attacks his shadow.*]

MALATESTE   Oh, my lord, you are angry with nothing.

FERDINAND   You are a fool. How is't possible I should catch my
shadow unless I fall upon't? When I go to hell, I mean to carry a   40
bribe: for, look you, good gifts evermore make way for the
worst persons.

PESCARA   Rise, good my lord.

FERDINAND   I am studying the art of patience.

PESCARA   'Tis a noble virtue—   45

FERDINAND   To drive six snails before me, from this town to Moscow;
neither use goad nor whip to them, but let them take their own

---

25 *Paracelsus* a German physician and alchemist noted for his radical ways of treating diseases. **30** *daws* crowlike birds.

time—the patient'st man i' th' world match me for an experiment!
And I'll crawl after like a sheep-biter.

CARDINAL   Force him up.   50

[*They make* FERDINAND *stand up.*]

FERDINAND   Use me well, you were best.
What I have done, I have done. I'll confess nothing.

DOCTOR   Now let me come to him. Are you mad, my lord?
Are you out of your princely wits?

FERDINAND   What's he?

PESCARA   Your doctor.

FERDINAND   Let me have his beard sawed off, and his eyebrows   55
Filed more civil.

DOCTOR   I must do mad tricks with him,
For that's the only way on't. I have brought
Your grace a salamander's skin, to keep you
From sun-burning.

FERDINAND   I have cruel sore eyes.

DOCTOR   The white of a cockatrice egg is present remedy.   60

FERDINAND   Let it be a new-laid one, you were best.
Hide me from him: physicians are like kings:
They brook no contradiction.

DOCTOR   Now he begins
To fear me; now let me alone with him.

[FERDINAND *tries to take off his gown;* CARDINAL *seizes him.*]

CARDINAL   How now, put off your gown?   65

DOCTOR   Let me have some forty urinals filled with rose-water: he
and I'll go pelt one another with them: now he begins to fear me.
Can you fetch a frisk, sir? [*Aside to* CARDINAL.] Let him go; let
him go upon my peril. I find by his eye, he stands in awe of me:
I'll make him as tame as a dormouse.   70

[CARDINAL *releases* FERDINAND.]

---

49 *sheep-biter* a sheep-stealing dog. **51 *you . . . best*** an interjectory phrase meaning
"you would be well-advised to." **55–56 *Let . . . civil*** I wish his appearance were not
so hostile. **58 *salamander*** thought capable of living in fire. **60 *cockatrice*** a legendary
monster with the head, wings, and legs of a cock and the tail of a serpent. Because most
of its power was thought to be vested in its eyes—its look was deadly—and because egg
whites were often used in treating sore eyes, the white of a cockatrice's egg would
theoretically be an ideal remedy for the affliction the Duke complains of. **68 *fetch a frisk***
dance a caper.

FERDINAND   Can you fetch your frisks, sir! I will stamp him into a
  cullis; flay off his skin, to cover one of the anatomies. This rogue
  hath set i' th' cold yonder, in Barber-Chirurgeons' Hall. Hence,
  hence! you are all of you like beasts for sacrifice: [*throws the*
  DOCTOR *down and beats him*] there's nothing left of you, but   75
  tongue and belly, flattery and lechery.   [*Exit.*]
PESCARA   Doctor, he did not fear you throughly.
DOCTOR   True, I was somewhat too forward.
BOSOLA   [*Aside.*] Mercy upon me! What a fatal judgment
  Hath fall'n upon this Ferdinand!
PESCARA   Knows your grace   80
  What accident hath brought unto the Prince
  This strange distraction?
CARDINAL   [*Aside.*] I must feign somewhat. Thus they say it grew:
  You have heard it rumored for these many years,
  None of our family dies but there is seen   85
  The shape of an old woman, which is given
  By tradition to us to have been murdered
  By her nephews, for her riches. Such a figure
  One night, as the Prince sat up late at's book,
  Appeared to him; when crying out for help,   90
  The gentlemen of's chamber found his grace
  All on a cold sweat, altered much in face
  And language. Since which apparition
  He hath grown worse and worse, and I much fear
  He cannot live.   95
BOSOLA   Sir, I would speak with you.
PESCARA   We'll leave your grace,
  Wishing to the sick Prince, our noble lord,
  All health of mind and body.
CARDINAL   You are most welcome.
     [*Exeunt* PESCARA, MALATESTE, *and* DOCTOR.]
  Are you come? [*Aside.*] So—this fellow must not know

---

72 cullis broth, made partly by pounding fowl. **anatomies** skeletons. **73 Barber-
Chirurgeons' Hall** the place where barber-surgeons went to pick up corpses of executed
felons, which they used for anatomical experiments. **76 tongue and belly** In ancient
religious ceremonies, the tongues and entrails of sacrificial animals were left for the gods.
But Ferdinand intends another meaning as well: in his despair he sees man as essentially
a deceiver and a creature of appetite; he is not a complex, integrated human being, but
only a tongue and a belly. **77 throughly** completely. **83 feign somewhat** make up
something.

By any means I had intelligence   100
In our Duchess' death. For, though I counseled it,
The full of all th'engagement seemed to grow
From Ferdinand. Now sir, how fares our sister?
I do not think but sorrow makes her look
Like to an oft-dyed garment. She shall now   105
Taste comfort from me—Why do you look so wildly?
Oh, the fortune of your master here, the Prince,
Dejects you, but be you of happy comfort:
If you'll do one thing for me I'll entreat,
Though he had a cold tombstone o'er his bones,   110
I'll make you what you would be.
BOSOLA   Anything?
Give it me in a breath, and let me fly to't:
They that think long, small expedition win,
For musing much o' th' end, cannot begin.

[*Enter* JULIA.]

JULIA   Sir, will you come in to supper?
CARDINAL   I am busy! Leave me!   115
JULIA   [*Aside.*] What an excellent shape hath that fellow!   *Exit.*
CARDINAL   'Tis thus: Antonio lurks here in Milan;
Inquire him out, and kill him. While he lives,
Our sister cannot marry, and I have thought
Of an excellent match for her. Do this, and style me   120
Thy advancement.
BOSOLA   But by what means shall I find him out?
CARDINAL   There is a gentleman called Delio
Here in the camp, that hath been long approved
His loyal friend. Set eye upon that fellow,
Follow him to mass; may be Antonio,   125
Although he do account religion
But a school-name, for fashion of the world
May accompany him. Or else go inquire out
Delio's confessor, and see if you can bribe
Him to reveal it. There are a thousand ways   130
A man might find to trace him—as, to know

100–1 *had . . . In* had a part in the planning of.   **102** *full . . . engagement* everything
to do with the deed.   **112** *in a breath* quickly.   **113** *small . . . win* accomplish little.
120 *style me* call me the means to.   **123** *hath . . . approved* has long proved to be.
127 *school-name* mere word.   **131** *know* find out.

What fellows haunt the Jews for taking up
Great sums of money, for sure he's in want;
Or else go to th' picture makers, and learn
Who brought her picture lately. Some of these   135
Happily may take—
BOSOLA   Well, I'll not freeze i' th' business,
I would see that wretched thing, Antonio,
Above all sights i' th' world.
CARDINAL   Do, and be happy.   *Exit.*
BOSOLA   This fellow doth breed basilisks in's eyes,
He's nothing else but murder: yet he seems   140
Not to have notice of the Duchess' death.
'Tis his cunning. I must follow his example:
There cannot be a surer way to trace,
Than that of an old fox. [*Enter* JULIA, *pointing a pistol at him.*]
JULIA   So, sir, you are well met.
BOSOLA   How now?
JULIA   Nay, the doors are fast enough.   145
Now sir, I will make you confess your treachery.
BOSOLA   Treachery?
JULIA   Yes, confess to me
Which of my women 'twas you hired to put
Love-powder into my drink?
BOSOLA   Love-powder?
JULIA   Yes, when I was at Malfi—   150
Why should I fall in love with such a face else?
I have already suffered for thee so much pain,
The only remedy to do me good
Is to kill my longing.
BOSOLA   Sure, your pistol holds

---

132 *for taking up*   to borrow.   **134–35** *Or . . . lately*   The exact meaning of this
passage is difficult to determine: "brought" may be a printer's misreading of "bought."
If the verb is "brought," the passage is an obvious development of the Cardinal's idea
that Antonio is "in want": needing cash, he has sold a miniature of the Duchess to a
dealer. If, however, the verb is "bought," the "Who" governing it is ambiguous. It may
refer either to "picture makers" or to Antonio, depending on whether he has sold his
wife's picture to get money or bought it as a keepsake. Most modern editions emend
to "bought," but because the first quarto reading seems to develop logically out of the
Cardinal's thought, "brought" is here retained.   **137** *wretched*   an equivocation, meaning
either despicable or pitiable.   **138** *be happy*   Be happy (in the advancement that will
follow as a result of your seeing him).   **139** *basilisk*   a mythical monster that could kill
with a look.

Nothing but perfumes or kissing comfits. Excellent lady,   155
You have a pretty way on't to discover
Your longing. Come, come, I'll disarm you
And arm you thus— [*embraces her*] yet this is wondrous strange.

JULIA   Compare thy form and my eyes together,
You'll find my love no such great miracle.   160
[*Kisses him.*] Now you'll say
I am a wanton. This nice modesty in ladies
Is but a troublesome familiar
That haunts them.

BOSOLA   Know you me, I am a blunt soldier.

JULIA   The better: 165
Sure, there wants fire where there are no lively sparks
Of roughness.

BOSOLA   And I want compliment.

JULIA   Why, ignorance
In courtship cannot make you do amiss,
If you have a heart to do well.

BOSOLA   You are very fair.

JULIA   Nay, if you lay beauty to my charge,   170
I must plead unguilty.

BOSOLA   Your bright eyes
Carry a quiver of darts in them, sharper
Than sunbeams.

JULIA   You will mar me with commendation.
Put yourself to the charge of courting me,
Whereas now I woo you.   175

BOSOLA   [*Aside.*] I have it, I will work upon this creature.
Let us grow most amorously familiar.
If the great Cardinal now should see me thus,
Would he not count me a villain?

JULIA   No, he might count me a wanton,   180
Not lay a scruple of offense on you:
For if I see and steal a diamond,
The fault is not i' th' stone, but in me, the thief

---

155 kissing comfits breath sweeteners. **156 discover** make known. **162 nice** foolish.
163 familiar family spirit (Webster's ironic echo of the Cardinal's prevarication, ll. 83–
95). **165 blunt soldier** a double-entendre, like most of the language in this interview.
167 compliment The homonym, "complement," is also implied. **171–72 Your . . .
them** Cupid was supposed to afflict people with love by shooting them with enchanted
darts, and it was through the eyes that love was most commonly thought to enter the body.

That purloins it. I am sudden with you:
We that are great women of pleasure, use to cut off   185
These uncertain wishes and unquiet longings,
And in an instant join the sweet delight
And the pretty excuse together; had you been i' th' street
Under my chamber window, even there
I should have courted you.

BOSOLA   Oh, you are an excellent lady.   190

JULIA   Bid me do somewhat for you presently
To express I love you.

BOSOLA   I will, and if you love me,
Fail not to effect it.
The Cardinal is grown wondrous melancholy;
Demand the cause, let him not put you off   195
With feigned excuse; discover the main ground on't.

JULIA   Why would you know this?

BOSOLA   I have depended on him,
And I hear that he is fallen in some disgrace
With the Emperor. If he be, like the mice
That forsake falling houses, I would shift   200
To other dependence.

JULIA   You shall not need follow the wars:
I'll be your maintenance.

BOSOLA   And I your loyal servant;
But I cannot leave my calling.

JULIA   Not leave an   205
Ungrateful general for the love of a sweet lady?
You are like some, cannot sleep in featherbeds,
But must have blocks for their pillows.

BOSOLA   Will you do this?

JULIA   Cunningly.

BOSOLA   Tomorrow I'll expect th'intelligence.

JULIA   Tomorrow! Get you into my cabinet;   210
You shall have it with you: do not delay me—
No more than I do you. I am like one
That is condemned: I have my pardon promised,

---

185 *use . . . off* are in the habit of dispensing with. **199–200** *like . . . houses* Mice were thought to desert old houses just before they fell down. **202** *follow the wars* follow after the Cardinal when he goes to war. **210** *Tomorrow* Not tomorrow, but now! *cabinet* closet. **211** *with you* at your appearance.

But I would see it sealed. Go, get you in;
You shall see me wind my tongue about his heart   215
Like a skein of silk.   [BOSOLA *withdraws behind the traverse.*]

[*Enter* CARDINAL.]

CARDINAL   Where are you? [*Enter* SERVANTS.]
SERVANTS   Here.
CARDINAL   Let none, upon your lives,
Have conference with the Prince Ferdinand,
Unless I know it. [*Aside.*] In this distraction
He may reveal the murther.   [*Exeunt* SERVANTS.]   220
Yond's my ling'ring consumption:
I am weary of her; and by any means
Would be quit of—
JULIA   How now, my lord?
What ails you?
CARDINAL   Nothing.
JULIA   Oh, you are much altered:
Come, I must be your secretary, and remove   225
This lead from off your bosom—What's the matter?
CARDINAL   I may not tell you.
JULIA   Are you so far in love with sorrow,
You cannot part with part of it? or think you
I cannot love your grace when you are sad,
As well as merry? or do you suspect   230
I, that have been a secret to your heart
These many winters, cannot be the same
Unto your tongue?
CARDINAL   Satisfy thy longing.
The only way to make thee keep my counsel
Is not to tell thee.
JULIA   Tell your echo this—   235
Or flatterers, that, like echoes, still report
What they hear, though most imperfect—and not me;
For, if that you be true unto yourself,
I'll know.
CARDINAL   Will you rack me?
JULIA   No, judgment shall

---

225 *secretary* one entrusted with secrets. **238–39 *For . . . know*** for you can be true
to yourself only by telling me. **239 *rack me*** put me upon the rack.

Draw it from you. It is an equal fault   240
To tell one's secrets unto all, or none.
CARDINAL   The first argues folly.
JULIA   But the last, tyranny.
CARDINAL   Very well. Why, imagine I have committed
Some secret deed which I desire the world
May never hear of!
JULIA   Therefore may not I know it?   245
You have concealed for me as great a sin
As adultery. Sir, never was occasion
For perfect trial of my constancy
Till now. Sir, I beseech you.
CARDINAL   You'll repent it.
JULIA   Never.
CARDINAL   It hurries thee to ruin: I'll not tell thee.   250
Be well advised, and think what danger 'tis
To receive a prince's secrets. They that do,
Had need have their breasts hooped with adamant
To contain them. I pray thee yet be satisfied.
Examine thine own frailty; 'tis more easy   255
To tie knots, than unloose them. 'Tis a secret
That, like a ling'ring poison, may chance lie
Spread in thy veins, and kill thee seven year hence.
JULIA   Now you dally with me.
CARDINAL   No more. Thou shalt know it.
By my appointment, the great Duchess of Malfi   260
And two of her young children, four nights since,
Were strangled.
JULIA   Oh heaven! Sir, what have you done?
CARDINAL   How now? How settles this? Think you your bosom
Will be a grave dark and obscure enough
For such a secret?
JULIA   You have undone yourself, sir.   265
CARDINAL   Why?
JULIA   It lies not in me to conceal it.
CARDINAL   No?
Come, I will swear you to't upon this book.

253 *adamant*   unyielding steel.   **259** *dally with*   make a fool of.   **260** *appointment*
order.

JULIA   Most religiously.

CARDINAL   Kiss it.

[*She kisses a Bible.*]

Now you shall never utter it. Thy curiosity
Hath undone thee: thou'rt poisoned with that book.   270
Because I knew thou couldst not keep my counsel,
I have bound thee to't by death.

[*Enter* BOSOLA.]

BOSOLA   For pity sake, hold.

CARDINAL   Ha, Bosola!

JULIA   [*To the* CARDINAL.]   I forgive you
This equal piece of justice you have done,
For I betrayed your counsel to that fellow: 275
He overheard it. That was the cause I said
It lay not in me to conceal it.

BOSOLA   Oh foolish woman,
Couldst not thou have poisoned him?

JULIA   'Tis weakness,
Too much to think what should have been done. I go,
I know not whither.   [*Dies.*]

CARDINAL   Wherefore comst thou hither?   280

BOSOLA   That I might find a great man, like yourself,
Not out of his wits, as the Lord Ferdinand,
To remember my service.

CARDINAL   I'll have thee hewed in pieces.

BOSOLA   Make not yourself such a promise of that life
Which is not yours to dispose of.

CARDINAL   Who placed thee here?   285

BOSOLA   Her lust, as she intended.

CARDINAL   Very well,
Now you know me for your fellow murderer.

BOSOLA   And wherefore should you lay fair marble colors
Upon your rotten purposes to me?
Unless you imitate some that do plot great treasons,   290
And when they have done, go hide themselves i' th' graves
Of those were actors in't.

CARDINAL   No more: there is a fortune attends thee.

BOSOLA   Shall I go sue to Fortune any longer?

---

288 *fair . . . colors*   paint to make wood look like marble.   **289** *to*   toward.

'Tis the fool's pilgrimage.

CARDINAL   I have honors in store for thee.   295

BOSOLA   There are a many ways that conduct to seeming
Honor, and some of them very dirty ones.

CARDINAL   Throw to the devil
Thy melancholy. The fire burns well,
What need we keep a stirring of 't, and make   300
A greater smother? Thou wilt kill Antonio?

BOSOLA   Yes.

CARDINAL   Take up that body.

BOSOLA   I think I shall
Shortly grow the common bier for churchyards!

CARDINAL   I will allow thee some dozen of attendants,
To aid thee in the murther.   305

BOSOLA   Oh, by no means: physicians that apply horseleeches to any
rank swelling use to cut off their tails, that the blood may run
through them the faster. Let me have no train when I go to shed
blood, lest it make me have a greater—when I ride to the gallows.

CARDINAL   Come to me after midnight, to help to remove that body   310
to her own lodging. I'll give out she died o' th' plague; 'twill
breed the less inquiry after her death.

BOSOLA   Where's Castruchio her husband?

CARDINAL   He's rode to Naples to take possession of Antonio's citadel.   315

BOSOLA   Believe me, you have done a very happy turn.

CARDINAL   Fail not to come. There is the master key
Of our lodgings, and by that you may conceive
What trust I plant in you.   *Exit.*

BOSOLA   You shall find me ready.
Oh poor Antonio, though nothing be so needful   320
To thy estate, as pity, yet I find
Nothing so dangerous. I must look to my footing;
In such slippery ice-pavements men had need
To be frost-nailed well: they may break their necks else.
The precedent's here afore me: how this man   325
Bears up in blood! seems fearless! Why, 'tis well:
Security some men call the suburbs of hell,

---

301 *smother* smoke. **308** *no train* no procession at my back (waiting to betray me).
324 *frost-nailed* equipped with hobnailed boots for gripping the ice. **326** *Bears . . .
blood* shows his courage. **327** *Security* lack of danger.

Only a dead wall between. Well, good Antonio,
I'll seek thee out; and all my care shall be
To put thee into safety from the reach   330
Of these most cruel biters, that have got
Some of thy blood already. It may be
I'll join with thee in a most just revenge.
The weakest arm is strong enough, that strikes
With the sword of justice. Still methinks the Duchess   335
Haunts me—there, there!—'tis nothing but my melancholy.
O penitence, let me truly taste thy cup,
That throws men down, only to raise them up.   *Exit.*

⊰[ACT V]⊱

Scene 3   ⊰*Somewhere near the* DUCHESS' *grave*⊱

[*Enter* ANTONIO *and* DELIO.] ECHO *from the* DUCHESS' *grave.*

DELIO   Yond's the Cardinal's window. This fortification
Grew from the ruins of an ancient abbey.
And to yond side o' th' river lies a wall,
Piece of a cloister, which in my opinion
Gives the best echo that you ever heard;   5
So hollow, and so dismal, and withal
So plain in the distinction of our words,
That many have supposed it is a spirit
That answers.

ANTONIO   I do love these ancient ruins:
We never tread upon them, but we set   10
Our foot upon some reverend history,
And, questionless, here in this open court,
Which now lies naked to the injuries
Of stormy weather, some men lie interred
Loved the Church so well and gave so largely to't   15
They thought it should have canopied their bones
Till doomsday. But all things have their end:
Churches and cities, which have diseases like to men,

𝕣ACT V, Scene 3. **7** *distinction* articulation. **12** *questionless* unquestionably.

    Must have like death that we have.
ECHO   *Like death that we have.*
DELIO   Now the echo hath caught you.
ANTONIO   It groaned, methought, and gave   20
    A very deadly accent!
ECHO   *Deadly accent.*
DELIO   I told you 'twas a pretty one. You may make it
    A huntsman, or a falconer, a musician,
    Or a thing of sorrow.
ECHO   *A thing of sorrow.*
ANTONIO   Ay sure, that suits it best.
ECHO   *That suits it best.*   25
ANTONIO 'Tis very like my wife's voice.
ECHO   *Ay, wife's voice.*
DELIO   Come, let's walk farther from't.
    I would not have you go to th' Cardinal's tonight.
    Do not.
ECHO   *Do not.*
DELIO   Wisdom doth not more moderate wasting sorrow   30
    Than time. Take time for't: be mindful of thy safety.
ECHO   *Be mindful of thy safety.*
ANTONIO   Necessity compels me:
    Make scrutiny throughout the passages
    Of your own life; you'll find it impossible
    To fly your fate.
ECHO   *O fly your fate.*   35
DELIO   Hark, the dead stones seem to have pity on you
    And give you good counsel.
ANTONIO   Echo, I will not talk with thee,
    For thou art a dead thing.
ECHO   *Thou art a dead thing.*
ANTONIO   My Duchess is asleep now,
    And her little ones—I hope sweetly. Oh, heaven   40
    Shall I never see her more?
ECHO   *Never see her more.*
ANTONIO   I marked not one repetition of the Echo
    But that: and, on the sudden, a clear light

30–31 *Wisdom . . . time*   Wisdom does not alleviate the pain of consuming sorrow any better than time (?).   **33 *passages***   events.   **42 *I . . . one***   I did not notice the significance of one.

Presented me a face folded in sorrow.

DELIO   Your fancy, merely.

ANTONIO   Come, I'll be out of this ague;   45
For to live thus, is not indeed to live:
It is a mockery, and abuse of life.
I will not henceforth save myself by halves.
Lose all, or nothing.

DELIO   Your own virtue save you!
I'll fetch your eldest son, and second you.   50
It may be that the sight of his own blood,
Spread in so sweet a figure, may beget
The more compassion.

ANTONIO   However, fare you well.
Though in our miseries Fortune hath a part
Yet in our noble sufferings she hath none.   55
Contempt of pain—that we may call our own.   *Exe*[*unt*].

⁌ACT V⁍

Scene 4   ⁅ *The palace of the Aragonian* ⁆
           brothers in Milan

[*Enter*] CARDINAL, PESCARA, MALATESTE, RODERIGO, GRISOLAN.

CARDINAL   You shall not watch tonight by the sick Prince;
His grace is very well recovered.

MALATESTE   Good my lord, suffer us.

CARDINAL   Oh, by no means:
The noise and change of object in his eye
Doth more distract him. I pray, all to bed;   5
And though you hear him in his violent fit,
Do not rise, I entreat you.

PESCARA   So sir, we shall not—

CARDINAL   Nay, I must have you promise

---

45 *ague* a sickness characterized by intermittent chills and fever.   **51** *his* the Cardinal's family's.
⁕ **ACT V, Scene 4.   3** *suffer us* Allow us then to watch over him.

Upon your honors, for I was enjoined to't
By himself; and he seemed to urge it sensibly.   10
PESCARA   Let our honors bind this trifle.
CARDINAL   Nor any of your followers.
PESCARA   Neither.
CARDINAL   It may be, to make trial of your promise,
   When he's asleep, myself will rise, and feign
   Some of his mad tricks, and cry out for help,   15
   And feign myself in danger.
MALATESTE   If your throat were cutting,
   I'd not come at you, now I have protested against it.
CARDINAL   Why, I thank you.   [*Withdraws.*]
GRISOLAN   'Twas a foul storm tonight.
RODERIGO   The Lord Ferdinand's chamber shook like an osier.
MALATESTE   'Twas nothing but pure kindness in the devil,   20
   To rock his own child.
                    Exeunt [RODERIGO, MALATESTE, PESCARA, GRISOLAN].
CARDINAL   The reason why I would not suffer these
   About my brother is because at midnight
   I may with better privacy convey
   Julia's body to her own lodging. O, my conscience!   25
   I would pray now, but the devil takes away my heart
   For having any confidence in prayer.
   About this hour I appointed Bosola
   To fetch the body: when he hath served my turn,
   He dies.   *Exit.*   30

   [*Enter* BOSOLA.]

BOSOLA   Ha! 'twas the Cardinal's voice. I heard him name
   Bosola, and my death—listen, I hear one's footing.

   [*Enter* FERDINAND.]

FERDINAND   Strangling is a very quiet death.
BOSOLA   Nay, then, I see I must stand upon my guard.
FERDINAND   What say' to that? Whisper, softly: do you agree to't?   35
   So it must be done i' th' dark: the Cardinal
   'Would not for a thousand pounds the doctor should see it. *Exit.*
BOSOLA   My death is plotted; here's the consequence of murther.
   We value not desert, nor Christian breath,

---

10 sensibly when he was in full possession of his senses.   **19 osier**   willow tree.
38 here's the plotting of my death.   ***murther*** (my doing) murder.

When we know black deeds must be cured with death.   40
                                              [*Withdraws.*]

[*Enter* ANTONIO *and a* SERVANT.]

SERVANT   Here stay, sir, and be confident, I pray:
   I'll fetch you a dark lanthorn. *Exit.*
ANTONIO   Could I take him
   At his prayers, there were hope of pardon.
BOSOLA   Fall right my sword:

[*Half-crazed by fears that he will be murdered,* BOSOLA *mistakes*
ANTONIO *for the Cardinal or one of the henchmen and runs him through,
from behind.*]

   I'll not give thee so much leisure as to pray.   45
ANTONIO   Oh, I am gone. Thou hast ended a long suit,
   In a minute.
BOSOLA   What art thou?
ANTONIO   A most wretched thing,
   That only have thy benefit in death,
   To appear myself. [*Enter* SERVANT *with a dark lanthorn.*]
SERVANT   Where are you sir?
ANTONIO   Very near my home. Bosola?
SERVANT   Oh misfortune!   50
BOSOLA   [*To* SERVANT.] Smother thy pity, thou art dead else—Antonio!
   The man I would have saved 'bove mine own life!
   We are merely the stars' tennis balls, struck and banded
   Which way please them. Oh, good Antonio,
   I'll whisper one thing in thy dying ear,   55
   Shall make thy heart break quickly. Thy fair Duchess
   And two sweet children—
ANTONIO   Their very names
   Kindle a little life in me.
BOSOLA   Are murdered!
ANTONIO   Some men have wished to die
   At the hearing of sad tidings: I am glad   60
   That I shall do't in sadness. I would not now
   Wish my wounds balmed, nor healed: for I have no use
   To put my life to. In all our quest of greatness,

48–49 *That . . . myself*   The only benefit that I get from you in death is to be again
myself (and no longer have to run and hide).   **50** *home*   final resting place.   **53** *banded*
bandied.

Like wanton boys whose pastime is their care,
We follow after bubbles, blown in th'air.   65
Pleasure of life, what is't? only the good hours
Of an ague; merely a preparative to rest,
To endure vexation. I do not ask
The process of my death. Only commend me
To Delio.
BOSOLA   Break, heart!   70
ANTONIO   And let my son fly the courts of princes.   [*Dies.*]
BOSOLA   Thou seemst to have loved Antonio?
SERVANT   I brought him hither,
To have reconciled him to the Cardinal.
BOSOLA   I do not ask thee that.
Take him up, if thou tender thine own life,   75
And bear him where the Lady Julia
Was wont to lodge. Oh, my fate moves swift.
I have this Cardinal in the forge already;
Now I'll bring him to th' hammer. (O direful misprision!)
I will not imitate things glorious,   80
No more than base: I'll be mine own example.
[*To the* SERVANT.] On, on! And look thou represent, for silence,
The thing thou bearst.   *Exeunt.*

⟨ACT V⟩

Scene 5   ⟨*The same*⟩

[*Enter*] CARDINAL *with a book.*

CARDINAL   I am puzzled in a question about hell:
He says in hell there's one material fire,
And yet it shall not burn all men alike.
Lay him by. How tedious is a guilty conscience!
When I look into the fishponds in my garden,   5
Methinks I see a thing armed with a rake

---

79 *misprision* mistake. **81 *No . . . base*** any more than I will seek to copy what is
base. **82 *represent*** imitate.
❧ ACT V, Scene 5. 2 *He* the author of the book. **6 *armed . . . rake*** The devil
was traditionally thought to carry a fork of some sort.

That seems to strike at me. Now? Art thou come?

[*Enter* BOSOLA *and* SERVANT, *with* ANTONIO'*s body.*]

Thou lookst ghastly:
There sits in thy face some great determination,
Mixed with some fear.

BOSOLA   Thus it lightens into action: 10
I am come to kill thee.

CARDINAL   Ha? Help! our guard!

BOSOLA   Thou art deceived:
They are out of thy howling.

CARDINAL   Hold, and I will faithfully divide
Revenues with thee.

BOSOLA   Thy prayers and proffers   15
Are both unseasonable.

CARDINAL   Raise the watch:
We are betrayed!

BOSOLA   I have confined your flight:
I'll suffer your retreat to Julia's chamber,
But no further.

CARDINAL   Help! We are betrayed!

[*Enter* PESCARA, MALATESTE, RODERIGO, *and* GRISOLAN, *above.*]

MALATESTE   Listen.

CARDINAL   My dukedom for rescue!

RODERIGO   Fie upon his counterfeiting.   20

MALATESTE   Why, 'tis not the Cardinal.

RODERIGO   Yes, yes, 'tis he:
But I'll see him hanged ere I'll go down to him.

CARDINAL   Here's a plot upon me! I am assaulted! I am lost,
Unless some rescue!

GRISOLAN   He doth this pretty well,
But it will not serve to laugh me out of mine honor.   25

CARDINAL   The sword's at my throat!

RODERIGO   You would not bawl so loud then.

MALATESTE   Come, come. Let's go to bed: he told us thus much afore-
         hand.

---

10 *lightens into* shows itself as it rises to.   **17 *We*** The Cardinal uses the royal "we"
here, perhaps in an unconscious attempt to establish his authority over Bosola, and certainly
in an effort to summon others to his help.   **25 *laugh me*** trick me.   ***mine honor*** my
vow to him not to interfere.

PESCARA   He wished you should not come at him, but believ't,
 The accent of the voice sounds not in jest.
 I'll down to him, howsoever, and with engines
 Force ope the doors. [*Exit.*]   30
RODERIGO   Let's follow him aloof,
 And note how the Cardinal will laugh at him.   [*Exeunt above.*]
BOSOLA   There's for you first:
 'Cause you shall not unbarricade the door
 To let in rescue.   35

 He kills the SERVANT.

CARDINAL   What cause hast thou to pursue my life?
BOSOLA   Look there.
CARDINAL   Antonio!
BOSOLA   Slain by my hand unwittingly.
 Pray, and be sudden: when thou killedst thy sister,
 Thou tookst from Justice her most equal balance,
 And left her naught but her sword.
CARDINAL   O mercy!   40
 [*He falls to his knees.*]

BOSOLA   Now it seems thy greatness was only outward:
 For thou fallst faster of thyself than calamity
 Can drive thee. I'll not waste longer time. There.
 [*Stabs the* CARDINAL.]

CARDINAL   Thou hast hurt me.
BOSOLA   Again. [*Stabs him again.*]
CARDINAL   Shall I die like a leveret,
 Without any resistance? Help! help! help!
 I am slain.   45

 [*Enter* FERDINAND.]

FERDINAND   Th'alarum? give me a fresh horse.
 Rally the vaunt-guard, or the day is lost.
 Yield, yield! I give you the honor of arms,
 Shake my sword over you. Will you yield?
CARDINAL   Help me! I am your brother.
FERDINAND   The devil!   50
 My brother fight upon the adverse party!

---

30 *engines*   tools.   **34** *'Cause*   so that.   **38** *sudden*   quick.   **44** *leveret*   small hare.
46 *alarum*   the trumpet call to arms.   **47** *vaunt-guard*   the foremost ranks of the army.

He wounds the CARDINAL *and, in the scuffle, gives* BOSOLA *his death wound.*

There flies your ransom.

CARDINAL   Oh justice,
  I suffer now for what hath former been:
  Sorrow is held the eldest child of sin.

FERDINAND   Now you're brave fellows. Caesar's fortune was harder   55
  than Pompey's: Caesar died in the arms of prosperity, Pompey
  at the feet of disgrace. You both died in the field; the pain's
  nothing. Pain many times is taken away with the apprehension of
  greater—as the toothache with the sight of a barber that comes to
  pull it out: there's philosophy for you.   60

BOSOLA   Now my revenge is perfect. Sink, thou main cause
  Of my undoing!—The last part of my life
  Hath done me best service.

He kills FERDINAND.

FERDINAND   Give me some wet hay: I am broken winded.
  I do account this world but a dog kennel: 65
  I will vault credit, and affect high pleasures
  Beyond death.

BOSOLA   He seems to come to himself,
  Now he's so near the bottom.

FERDINAND   My sister! oh, my sister! there's the cause on't.
  Whether we fall by ambition, blood, or lust,   70
  Like diamonds, we are cut with our own dust.   [*Dies.*]

CARDINAL   Thou hast thy payment too.

BOSOLA   Yes, I hold my weary soul in my teeth:
  'Tis ready to part from me. I do glory
  That thou, which stoodst like a huge pyramid   75
  Begun upon a large and ample base,
  Shalt end in a little point, a kind of nothing.

[*Enter* PESCARA, MALATESTE, RODERIGO, *and* GRISOLAN.]

PESCARA   How now, my lord?

MALATESTE   O sad disaster!

---

52 ransom (chance for) being ransomed.   **59 barber** Barbers served also as surgeons at this time.   **61 perfect** complete.   **64 wet hay** thought to be the best food for a broken-winded horse.   **66–67 I . . . death** I will leap over things credited to be of worth in this world, and I will strive after the true pleasures that lie beyond death.

RODERIGO   How comes this?

BOSOLA   Revenge!—for the Duchess of Malfi, murderèd
    By th'Aragonian brethren; for Antonio,   80
    Slain by this hand; for lustful Julia,
    Poisoned by this man; and lastly, for myself,
    That was an actor in the main of all,
    Much 'gainst mine own good nature, yet i' th' end
    Neglected.

PESCARA   How now, my lord?

CARDINAL   Look to my brother: 85
    He gave us these large wounds as we were struggling
    Here i' th' rushes. And now, I pray, let me
    Be laid by, and never thought of.   [*Dies.*]

PESCARA   How fatally, it seems, he did withstand
    His own rescue!

MALATESTE   Thou wretched thing of blood,   90
    How came Antonio by his death?

BOSOLA   In a mist—I know not how—
    Such a mistake as I have often seen
    In a play. Oh, I am gone—
    We are only like dead walls or vaulted graves   95
    That, ruined, yield no echo. Fare you well.
    It may be pain, but no harm, to me to die
    In so good a quarrel. Oh this gloomy world,
    In what a shadow or deep pit of darkness
    Doth, womanish and fearful, mankind live?   100
    Let worthy minds ne'er stagger in distrust
    To suffer death or shame for what is just:
    Mine is another voyage.   [*Dies.*]

PESCARA   The noble Delio, as I came to th' palace,
    Told me of Antonio's being here, and showed me   105
    A pretty gentleman, his son and heir.

[*Enter* DELIO *with* ANTONIO's *son.*]

MALATESTE   O, sir, you come too late.

84–85 *yet . . . Neglected* "which, ultimately, I neglected." There may be a hint here, too, of Bosola's feeling of alienation from society—his feeling that he, as well as his own "good nature," was neglected. **86** *He* Bosola. **87** *rushes* Greens and reeds were sometimes used to cover cold castle floors. **89** *withstand* offer opposition to (by counseling us against). **100** *womanish* timorous. *fearful* both frightened and frightening.

DELIO   I heard so, and
    Was armed for't ere I came. Let us make noble use
    Of this great ruin, and join all our force
    To establish this young hopeful gentleman   110
    In's mother's right. These wretched, eminent things
    Leave no more fame behind 'em, than should one
    Fall in a frost and leave his print in snow:
    As soon as the sun shines, it ever melts
    Both form and matter. I have ever thought   115
    Nature doth nothing so great for great men,
    As when she's pleased to make them lords of truth:
    Integrity of life is fame's best friend,
    Which nobly, beyond death, shall crown the end.   *Exeunt.*

108 *armed* prepared.   **111** *eminent* conspicuous.

THE CHANGE-LING

(1622)

Thomas Middleton
and
William Rowley

The Changeling.

ACTUS PRIMUS.

Enter Alsemero.

TWas in the Temple where I first beheld her,
And now agen the same , what *Omen* yet
Follows of that ? None but imaginary,
Why should my hopes or fate be timerous ?
The place is holy, so is my intent :
I love her beauties to the holy purpose,
And that(me thinks)admits comparison
With mans first creation, the place blest
And is his right home back (if he atchieve it.)
The Church hath first begun our interview
And that's the place must joyn us into one,
So there's beginning and perfection too.

Enter Jasperino.

Jasp. O Sir,are you here ? Come, the wind's fair with you,
Y'are like to have a swift and pleasant passage.
Als. Sure y'are deceived friend, 'tis contrary
In my best judgement.
Jas. What for *Malta* ?
If you could buy a gale amongst the Witches,
They could not serve you such a lucky penyworth

B   As

Written and played as early as 1623, The Changeling *was not printed until 1653. Such
a delay in printing was not unusual, and some plays were apparently never printed.
The first text page of the 1653 edition is typical of the cheap quarto editions, carelessly
printed to take advantage of a play's popularity. Unbound, they sold for about six pence.
Berg Collection, The New York Public Library, Astor, Lenox, and Tilden Foundations.*

B ASED PRIMARILY ON A STORY FROM A collection of moral tales entitled The Triumphs of God's Revenge Against the Crying and Execrable Sin of Murther, The Changeling is the product of a collaboration between Thomas Middleton (1570–1627) and William Rowley (1585?–1626?). Middleton was a professional playwright who spent the greater part of his career in the theater writing satiric comedies. About 1620 he shifted emphasis and wrote several tragedies, of which The Changeling is the most famous. William Rowley was an actor in the King's Men, Shakespeare's theater company. He managed, however, in addition to his acting to write a number of plays, chiefly in collaboration with more famous playwrights. He was primarily an actor of comic parts, and it has been suggested that he was responsible for the comic sections of most of his collaborations. In The Changeling the comic subplot as well as the opening and the close of the play are usually attributed to him.

The continuing popularity of The Changeling is largely a result of the cool precision with which it dramatizes complex psychological states: De Flores' almost amused acceptance of the fate his passion marks out for him, and Beatrice-Joanna's continued assumption that she remains an innocent lady who has scarcely heard named the bestial actions she has caused or performed. The subplot in the madhouse— which parallels in many ways the events at Charenton in Marat-Sade by the twentieth-century German writer Peter Weiss—is, with the Portuguese subplot in The Spanish Tragedy and the Politic-Wouldbe subplot in Volpone, one of the most perfect instances of that characteristic Elizabethan dramatic device, the double plot. The academic critics of the age, drawing their authority from the classics, believed that the action of a play should be single and that comedy and tragedy should never be mixed. They therefore judged the use of the double plots barbaric, but the Elizabethan playwrights were so extraordinarily fond of this device that we must conclude that it permitted them to dramatize some essential part of their world view. In general, it presented the Renaissance sense of a vast and diverse world, large enough to contain, in the case of The Changeling, *both palace and lunatic asylum. Each dramatist, however, played his own special meanings on the instrument of the double plot, and in* The Changeling *the world of the madhouse resembles in an antic fashion the world of the palace in so many ways that it forces the audience to consider the possibility that the "sane" world may indeed be mad in many ways and the "mad" world strangely sane.*

It was not unusual for publication of popular plays to be long delayed, and though The Changeling *was on stage by 1622, it was not printed until 1653, eleven years after the Puritans closed the theaters. The 1653 quarto was a good edition, as play texts of the period go, and is the basis of the text offered here.*

DRAMATIS PERSONAE

VERMANDERO, *father to Beatrice [and lord of the castle of Alicant]*

TOMAZO DE PIRACQUO, *a noble lord*

ALONZO DE PIRACQUO, *his brother, suitor to Beatrice*

ALSEMERO, *a nobleman, afterwards married to Beatrice*

JASPERINO, *his friend*

ALIBIUS, *a jealous doctor*

LOLLIO, *his man*

PEDRO, *friend to Antonio*

ANTONIO, *the changeling [and counterfeit fool]*

FRANCISCUS, *the counterfeit madman*

DE FLORES, *servant to Vermandero*

MADMEN [*and* FOOLS]

SERVANTS

BEATRICE [-JOANNA], *daughter to Vermandero*

DIAPHANTA, *her waiting-woman*

ISABELLA, *wife to Alibius*

The Scene *Alicant*

The Scene *Alicant* a Valencian seaport on the east coast of Spain.

570

ACT I

{Scene I   *Near the harbor of the city*}

Enter ALSEMERO.

ALSEMERO 'Twas in the temple where I first beheld her,
And now again the same; what omen yet
Follows of that? None but imaginary.
Why should my hopes or fate be timorous?
The place is holy, so is my intent: 5
I love her beauties to the holy purpose,
And that, methinks, admits comparison
With man's first creation, the place blest,
And is his right home back, if he achieve it.
The church hath first begun our interview,   10
And that's the place must join us into one;
So there's beginning and perfection too.

Enter JASPERINO.

JASPERINO Oh, sir, are you here? Come, the wind's fair with you;
Y'are like to have a swift and pleasant passage.

ALSEMERO Sure y'are deceived, friend; 'tis contrary   15
In my best judgment.

JASPERINO   What, for Malta?
If you could buy a gale amongst the witches,
They could not serve you such a lucky pennyworth

Title *Changeling* In Middleton and Rowley's time a "changeling" was most often an infant left by fairies in exchange for another infant. But the word had at least three other meanings as well: (1) a person who was a waverer or given to changing his mind; (2) an idiot or half-witted person; and (3) a person surreptitiously put in the place of another. In this play Antonio is identified as the changeling because he appears to be an idiot, but clearly the title has a wider application. During the course of the drama almost every character demonstrates that he is a changeling, in one of the senses of the word. Alsemero changes his mind twice during his opening speeches, though he claims to be unwavering in thought; Antonio, Francisco, Isabella, and Diaphanta all assume disguises, temporarily changing their identities; and Beatrice-Joanna three times alters the focus of her love—loving first Alonzo de Piracquo, then Alsemero, and at last De Flores.
❧ **ACT I, Scene I.** **1** *temple* The movement of the plot is significantly from the temple, where it begins, to hell, where it ends. **6** *holy purpose* marriage. **7** *that* marriage to Beatrice. **8** *With . . . blest* with the joy of man's creation in paradise. **9** *right . . . back* paradise regained.

As comes o' God's name.

ALSEMERO   Even now I observed
The temple's vane to turn full in my face;   20
I know 'tis against me.

JASPERINO   Against you?
Then you know not where you are.

ALSEMERO   Not well indeed.

JASPERINO   Are you not well, sir?

ALSEMERO   Yes, Jasperino,—
Unless there be some hidden malady
Within me that I understand not.

JASPERINO   And that   25
I begin to doubt, sir; I never knew
Your inclinations to travels at a pause
With any cause to hinder it, till now.
Ashore you were wont to call your servants up
And help to trap your horses for the speed;   30
At sea I have seen you weigh the anchor with 'em,
Hoist sails for fear to lose the foremost breath,
Be in continual prayers for fair winds.
And have you changed your orisons?

ALSEMERO   No, friend,
I keep the same church, same devotion.   35

JASPERINO   Lover I'm sure y'are none, the stoic
Was found in you long ago; your mother nor
Best friends who have set snares of beauty (ay,
And choice ones too) could never trap you that way.
What might be the cause?

ALSEMERO   Lord, how violent   40
Thou art. I was but meditating of
Somewhat I heard within the temple.

JASPERINO   Is this violence? 'Tis but idleness
Compared with your haste yesterday.

ALSEMERO   I'm all this while a-going, man.   45

    Enter SERVANTS.

JASPERINO   Backwards, I think, sir. Look, your servants.

---

19 o' God's name   free, by the grace of God, without any conjuration.   **20 vane**
weather vane.   **22 Then . . . are**   The meaning here is, of course, metaphorical as
well as literal.   **30 trap**   harness and prepare.   *for the speed*   to speed up preparation.
31 'em   the soldiers beside whom he worked in order to save time.   **34 changed**   a word
whose frequent repetition draws attention to its thematic importance.   **42 Somewhat**
something.   **43 this**   his haste to get under way.

FIRST SERVANT   The seamen call; shall we board your trunks?

ALSEMERO   No, not today.

JASPERINO   'Tis the critical day it seems, and the sign in Aquarius.

SECOND SERVANT   [*Aside.*] We must not to sea today; this smoke will
    bring forth fire.   50

ALSEMERO   Keep all on shore. I do not know the end—
    Which needs I must do—of an affair in hand
    Ere I can go to sea.

FIRST SERVANT   Well, your pleasure.

SECOND SERVANT   [*Aside.*] Let him e'en take his leisure too, we are
    safer on land.   *Exeunt* SERVANTS.   55

    Enter BEATRICE, DIAPHANTA, *and* SERVANTS. [ALSEMERO *greets and*
    kisses BEATRICE.]

JASPERINO   [*Aside.*] How now! The laws of the Medes are changed
    sure. Salute a woman? He kisses too; wonderful! Where learnt
    he this? And does it perfectly too; in my conscience he ne'er
    rehearsed it before. Nay, go on, this will be stranger and better
    news at Valencia than if he had ransomed half Greece from the   60
    Turk.

BEATRICE   You are a scholar, sir.

ALSEMERO   A weak one, lady.

BEATRICE   Which of the sciences is this love you speak of?

ALSEMERO   From your tongue I take it to be music.

BEATRICE   You are skillful in't, can sing at first sight.   65

ALSEMERO   And I have showed you all my skill at once.
    I want more words to express me further
    And must be forced to repetition:
    I love you dearly.

BEATRICE   Be better advised, sir.
    Our eyes are sentinels unto our judgments   70
    And should give certain judgment what they see,
    But they are rash sometimes and tell us wonders
    Of common things, which when our judgments find,
    They can then check the eyes and call them blind.

---

49 *Aquarius*   the eleventh sign of the zodiac, a water-carrier, whose ascendency was
thought to be propitious for sea travel.   **SD** In the quarto, "Joanna" enters separately
from "Beatrice" and after the servants. The printer obviously made an error: not knowing
that Beatrice and Joanna were the same person, the printer must have altered the copy
which probably read "Enter Beatrice Joanna etc."   **56** *laws . . . Medes*   unalterable laws
(see Daniel 6:8).   **60–61** *than . . . Turk*   At this time Greece was part of the Turkish
Empire.   **65** *can . . . sight*   can sight-read music.   **67** *want*   lack.

ALSEMERO   But I am further, lady; yesterday   75
    Was mine eyes' employment, and hither now
    They brought my judgment, where are both agreed.
    Both houses then consenting, 'tis agreed;
    Only there wants the confirmation
    By the hand royal, that's your part, lady.   80
BEATRICE   Oh, there's one above me, sir.— [*Aside.*] For five days past
    To be recalled! Sure, mine eyes were mistaken;
    This was the man was meant me. That he should come
    So near his time, and miss it!
JASPERINO   [*Aside.*] We might have come by the carriers from   85
Valencia, I see, and saved all our sea-provision; we are at farthest
sure. [*Eyeing* DIAPHANTA.] Methinks I should do something too;
I meant to be a venturer in this voyage. Yonder's another vessel,
I'll board her; if she be lawful prize, down goes her topsail.

[*Greets* DIAPHANTA *and talks with her, apart.*] *Enter* DE FLORES.

DE FLORES   Lady, your father—
BEATRICE   Is in health, I hope.   90
DE FLORES   Your eye shall instantly instruct you, lady;
    He's coming hitherward.
BEATRICE   What needed then
    Your duteous preface? I had rather
    He had come unexpected; you must stall
    A good presence with unnecessary blabbing,   95
    And how welcome for your part you are,
    I'm sure you know.
DE FLORES   [*Aside.*] Will't never mend, this scorn,

---

75 But . . . further But I have examined the question further than with my eyes only.
78–80 Both . . . royal Both houses of the legislature ("eyes" and "judgment") have
consented to the bill and now only the signature of the royal hand is needed to make it
law.   **81 For . . . past** for the events of five days ago (when she was betrothed to Alonzo
de Piracquo).   **82 Sure . . . mistaken** Surely, my eyes erred (in making me think that
I loved Alonzo).   **85 by the carriers** by land transport.   **86 farthest** at the farthest
point away from our intended plan.   **88 vessel, 89 board, down goes** The sexual innuendoes in this speech are the first of many in this play, and though they most obviously
appear in the language of the characters in the subplot, such innuendoes periodically
thrust their way into the conversation of every lover in *The Changeling*. The thematic
reason for their appearance seems principally to be that they emphasize the appetitive
instincts inherent in every human being, which must be recognized and controlled if man
is to escape consignment to hell, here symbolized by madness and idiocy.   **89 down . . .
topsail** a sign of surrender in naval battles.   **94 stall** forestall.   **95 good presence**
that of her father.

    One side nor other? Must I be enjoined
    To follow still whilst she flies from me? Well,
    Fates do your worst, I'll please myself with sight   100
    Of her at all opportunities
    If but to spite her anger. I know she had
    Rather see me dead than living, and yet
    She knows no cause for't but a peevish will.
ALSEMERO   You seemed displeased, lady, on the sudden.   105
BEATRICE   Your pardon, sir, 'tis my infirmity;
    Nor can I other reason render you
    Than his or hers, of some particular thing
    They must abandon as a deadly poison,
    Which to a thousand other tastes were wholesome.   110
    Such to mine eyes is that same fellow there,
    The same that report speaks of the basilisk.
ALSEMERO   This is a frequent frailty in our nature.
    There's scarce a man amongst a thousand sound
    But hath his imperfection: one distastes   115
    The scent of roses, which to infinites
    Most pleasing is and odoriferous;
    One oil, the enemy of poison;
    Another wine, the cheerer of the heart
    And lively refresher of the countenance.   120
    Indeed this fault, if so it be, is general;
    There's scarce a thing but is both loved and loathed.
    Myself, I must confess, have the same frailty.
BEATRICE   And what may be your poison, sir? I am bold with you.
ALSEMERO   What might be your desire perhaps—a cherry.   125
BEATRICE   I am no enemy to any creature
    My memory has but yon gentleman.
ALSEMERO   He does ill to tempt your sight, if he knew it.

102–4 *I . . . will* Beatrice's feeling of revulsion from De Flores is, at least in part, an unconscious defense mechanism: irrationally drawn to the evil associated with his ugliness, she protects herself from consciously acknowledging this attraction by meeting him with violent hatred. 112 *basilisk* a legendary reptile that could kill merely with a look. 114 *sound* Most editors emend to "found" but the emendation is unnecessary, for "sound" makes perfectly good sense. What Alsemero says is "There's hardly a man among a thousand of sound mind and body who does not have his own particular quirk of taste." 116 *infinites* innumerable people. 125 *What* The quarto reads "And what," but that beginning, which hardly makes sense here, was probably inadvertently picked up by the printer from the preceding line.

BEATRICE   He cannot be ignorant of that, sir;
  I have not spared to tell him so, and I want   130
  To help myself, since he's a gentleman
  In good respect with my father and follows him.
ALSEMERO   He's out of his place then now.

 [They talk apart.]

JASPERINO   I am a mad wag, wench.
DIAPHANTA   So methinks; but for your comfort I can tell you we have 135
 a doctor in the city that undertakes the cure of such.
JASPERINO   Tush, I know what physic is best for the state of mine
 own body.
DIAPHANTA   'Tis scarce a well-governed state, I believe.
JASPERINO   I could show thee such a thing with an ingredient that we 140
 two would compound together, and if it did not tame the maddest
 blood i' th' town for two hours after, I'll ne'er profess physic
 again.
DIAPHANTA   A little poppy, sir, were good to cause you sleep.
JASPERINO   Poppy! I'll give thee a pop i' th' lips for that first and 145
 begin there. *[Kisses her.]* Poppy is one simple, indeed, and cuckoo
 (what you call't) another. I'll discover no more now; another
 time I'll show thee all.
BEATRICE   My father, sir.

 Enter VERMANDERO *and* SERVANTS.

VERMANDERO   Oh, Joanna, I came to meet thee.
  Your devotion's ended?
BEATRICE   For this time, sir.—   150
  [Aside.] I shall change my saint, I fear me; I find
  A giddy turning in me. —Sir, this while
  I am beholding to this gentleman,
  Who left his own way to keep me company,

130–31 *want . . . myself* lack the means to help myself.   **132** *respect* reputation.
134 *wag* mischievous fellow.   **136** *doctor* Alibius, who is introduced in the next scene.
140 *such a thing* The reference is, of course, to the male sexual organ.   **142** *physic* the
art of healing.   **144** *poppy* an opiate.   **146** *simple* an herb or plant used for medicinal
purposes.   *cuckoo* any one of a number of species of herbs and wild flowers. There are,
though, sexual innuendoes implicit in this word because of the cuckoo's association with
lechery and cuckolding.   **147** *discover* reveal.   **151** *saint* object of devotion, here
meaning both the saint she prays to (from one who protected virgins to one who was a
patron of married women) and the man she loves (from Piracquo to Alsemero).

And in discourse I find him much desirous   155
To see your castle. He hath deserved it, sir,
If ye please to grant it.
VERMANDERO   With all my heart, sir.
Yet there's an article between: I must know
Your country. We use not to give survey
Of our chief strengths to strangers; our citadels   160
Are placed conspicuous to outward view
On promonts' tops, but within are secrets.
ALSEMERO   A Valencian, sir.
VERMANDERO   A Valencian?
That's native, sir; of what name, I beseech you?
ALSEMERO   Alsemero, sir.
VERMANDERO   Alsemero? Not the son   165
Of John de Alsemero?
ALSEMERO   The same, sir.
VERMANDERO   My best love bids you welcome.
BEATRICE   [Aside.] He was wont
To call me so, and then he speaks a most
Unfeignèd truth.
VERMANDERO   Oh, sir, I knew your father.
We two were in acquaintance long ago   170
Before our chins were worth iulan down
And so continued till the stamp of time
Had coined us into silver. Well, he's gone;
A good soldier went with him.
ALSEMERO   You went together in that, sir.   175
VERMANDERO   No, by Saint Jacques, I came behind him;
Yet I have done somewhat too. An unhappy day
Swallowed him at last at Gibraltar
In fight with those rebellious Hollanders,

155–56 *And . . . castle*   Alsemero has said no such thing, so what is presented here is an
example of the way Beatrice, like a spoiled child, willfully sets about getting exactly what
she wants while paying little attention either to truth or to the imaginativeness of her
method of circumventing it.   158 *an . . . between*   a condition that must first be met.
159 *use*   do.   162 *promonts*   promontories.   171 *Before . . . down*   before we had our
first growth of beard.   173 *Had . . . silver*   had made our hair grey ("silver").   176 *Saint
Jacques*   the patron saint of Spain.   177–79 *An . . . Hollanders*   Alsemero's father was
drowned in April, 1607, at the Battle of Gibraltar, where the Dutch fleet defeated the
Spanish.

Was it not so?

ALSEMERO   Whose death I had revenged   180
    Or followed him in fate, had not the late league
    Prevented me.

VERMANDERO   Ay, ay, 'twas time to breathe.
    Oh, Joanna, I should ha' told thee news—
    I saw Piracquo lately.

BEATRICE   [*Aside.*] That's ill news.

VERMANDERO   He's hot preparing for this day of triumph;   185
    Thou must be a bride within this sevennight.

ALSEMERO   [*Aside.*] Ha!

BEATRICE   Nay, good sir, be not so violent; with speed
    I cannot render satisfaction
    Unto the dear companion of my soul,   190
    Virginity, whom I thus long have lived with,
    And part with it so rude and suddenly.
    Can such friends divide, never to meet again,
    Without a solemn farewell?

VERMANDERO   Tush tush, there's a toy.

ALSEMERO   [*Aside.*] I must now part and never meet again   195
    With any joy on earth. —Sir, your pardon,
    My affairs call on me.

VERMANDERO   How, sir? By no means;
    Not changed so soon, I hope? You must see my castle
    And her best entertainment ere we part;
    I shall think myself unkindly used else.   200
    Come, come, let's on; I had good hope your stay
    Had been a while with us in Alicant;
    I might have bid you to my daughter's wedding.

ALSEMERO   [*Aside.*] He means to feast me and poisons me beforehand.—
    I should be dearly glad to be there, sir,   205
    Did my occasions suit as I could wish.

BEATRICE   I shall be sorry if you be not there
    When it is done, sir, but not so suddenly.

---

181 *late league* a Spanish treaty with Holland, signed in April, 1609, which provided for twelve years of truce between the two countries. **182** *time to breathe* the period of truce. **188** *violent* It is no accident that Beatrice echoes the very word that Alsemero earlier used in talking to Jasperino about his own preparations: her earlier plans, like his, have to be changed in order to include a new love in them. **194** *toy* a thing of little consequence. **195** *never . . . again* As if demonstrating his emotional involvement with Beatrice, Alsemero unconsciously echoes her language. **208** *suddenly* soon.

VERMANDERO   I tell you, sir, the gentleman's complete,
  A courtier and a gallant, enriched   210
  With many fair and noble ornaments;
  I would not change him for a son-in-law
  For any he in Spain, the proudest he.
  And we have great ones, that you know.
ALSEMERO   He's much
  Bound to you, sir.
VERMANDERO   He shall be bound to me   215
  As fast as this tie can hold him; I'll want
  My will else.
BEATRICE [*Aside.*] I shall want mine if you do it.
VERMANDERO   But come, by the way I'll tell you more of him.
ALSEMERO   [*Aside.*] How shall I dare to venture in his castle
  When he discharges murderers at the gate?   220
  But I must on, for back I cannot go.
BEATRICE   [*Aside.*] Not this serpent gone yet?
VERMANDERO   Look, girl, thy glove's
    fall'n;
  Stay, stay, De Flores, help a little.
DE FLORES   Here, lady.
BEATRICE   Mischief on your officious forwardness;
  Who bade you stoop? They touch my hand no more;   225
  There, for t'other's sake I part with this;

She throws down the other glove.

  Take 'em and draw thine own skin off with 'em.

                              Exeunt [all but DE FLORES].
DE FLORES   Here's a favor come with mischief. Now, I know
  She had rather wear my pelt tanned in a pair
  Of dancing pumps, than I should thrust my fingers   230
  Into her sockets here. I know she hates me,
  Yet cannot choose but love her.
  No matter, if but to vex her, I'll haunt her still;
  Though I get nothing else, I'll have my will.   *Exit.*

---

213 *he* man. **216** *fast* firmly. *want* lack. **220** *discharges murderers* fires small
cannon. **230–31** *thrust . . . sockets* Here again a sexual innuendo is intended (cf.
I.2.27–31).

ACT I

Scene 2   ALIBIUS' *madhouse*

Enter ALIBIUS *and* LOLLIO.

ALIBIUS   Lollio, I must trust thee with a secret,
    But thou must keep it.

LOLLIO   I was ever close to a secret, sir.

ALIBIUS   The diligence that I have found in thee,
    The care and industry already past,   5
    Assures me of thy good continuance.
    Lollio, I have a wife.

LOLLIO   Fie, sir, 'tis too late to keep her secret: she's known to be
    married all the town and country over.

ALIBIUS   Thou goest too fast, my Lollio, that knowledge,   10
    I allow, no man can be barred it;
    But there is a knowledge which is nearer,
    Deeper and sweeter, Lollio.

LOLLIO   Well, sir, let us handle that between you and I.

ALIBIUS   'Tis that I go about, man; Lollio,   15
    My wife is young.

LOLLIO   So much the worse to be kept secret, sir.

ALIBIUS   Why, now thou meet'st the substance of the point;
    I am old, Lollio.

LOLLIO   No, sir, 'tis I am old Lollio.   20

ALIBIUS   Yet why may not this concord and sympathize?
    Old trees and young plants often grow together,
    Well enough agreeing.

LOLLIO   Ay, sir, but the old trees raise themselves higher and broader
    than the young plants.   25

ALIBIUS   Shrewd application. There's the fear, man;
    I would wear my ring on my own finger;
    Whilst it is borrowed, it is none of mine,
    But his that useth it.

LOLLIO   You must keep it on still then; if it but lie by, one or other   30
    will be thrusting into't.

🔆 **ACT I, Scene 2.   3** *close to*   silent about.   **21** *sympathize*   to be in harmony with.
24–26 *old . . . fear*   What Lollio suggests and Alibius fears, is that the old husband will
be raised higher than his young wife by being given a set of cuckold's horns.   **27** *ring*
Pudendum as well as ring is implied here (cf. *All's Well That Ends Well*, IV.2.45–65).

ALIBIUS   Thou conceivst me, Lollio; here thy watchful eye
    Must have employment; I cannot always be
    At home.
LOLLIO   I dare swear you cannot. 35
ALIBIUS   I must look out.
LOLLIO   I know't; you must look out. 'Tis every man's case.
ALIBIUS   Here I do say must thy employment be
    To watch her treadings and in my absence
    Supply my place. 40
LOLLIO   I'll do my best, sir; yet surely I cannot see who you should
have cause to be jealous of.
ALIBIUS   Thy reason for that, Lollio? 'Tis a comfortable question.
LOLLIO   We have but two sorts of people in the house and both
under the whip, that's fools and madmen; the one has not wit 45
enough to be knaves and the other not knavery enough to be
fools.
ALIBIUS   Ay, those are all my patients, Lollio.
    I do profess the cure of either sort:
    My trade, my living 'tis, I thrive by it. 50
    But here's the care that mixes with my thrift:
    The daily visitants that come to see
    My brainsick patients I would not have
    To see my wife. Gallants I do observe
    Of quick, enticing eyes, rich in habits, 55
    Of stature and proportion very comely:
    These are most shrewd temptations, Lollio.
LOLLIO   They may be easily answered, sir. If they come to see the
fools and madmen, you and I may serve the turn, and let my
mistress alone; she's of neither sort. 60
ALIBIUS   'Tis a good ward. Indeed come they to see
    Our madmen or our fools, let 'em see no more
    Than what they come for. By that consequent
    They must not see her; I'm sure she's no fool.
LOLLIO   And I'm sure she's no madman. 65

---

37 case The word has the same double meaning as "ring" above (cf. *All's Well That Ends Well*, I.3.23–25). **39 treadings** paces. **43 comfortable** comforting. **45 fools** idiots. **51 mixes . . . thrift** comes along with my prosperity. **52 visitants** visitors, who came to the madhouse to be entertained by the antics of the inmates. **55 quick** bright. **habits** dress. **56 comely** attractive. **57 shrewd** dangerous. **59 serve the turn** show them around. **61 ward** protective measure. **63 By . . . consequent** as a logical result of that condition.

ALIBIUS   Hold that buckler fast, Lollio; my trust
    Is on thee, and I account it firm and strong.
    What hour is't, Lollio?

LOLLIO   Towards belly-hour, sir.

ALIBIUS   Dinner time? Thou meanst twelve o'clock.   70

LOLLIO   Yes, sir, for every part has his hour. We wake at six and look
    about us, that's eye-hour; at seven we should pray, that's knee-
    hour; at eight walk, that's leg-hour; at nine gather flowers and
    pluck a rose, that's nose-hour; at ten we drink, that's mouth-
    hour; at eleven lay about us for victuals, that's hand-hour; at   75
    twelve go to dinner, that's belly-hour.

ALIBIUS   Profoundly, Lollio; it will be long
    Ere all thy scholars learn this lesson, and
    I did look to have a new one entered. Stay,
    I think my expectation is come home.   80

    Enter PEDRO *and* ANTONIO [*dressed*] *like an idiot.*

PEDRO   Save you, sir, my business speaks itself;
    This sight takes off the labor of my tongue.

ALIBIUS   Ay, ay, sir.
    'Tis plain enough, you mean him for my patient.

PEDRO   And if your pains prove but commodious, to give but some   85
    little strength to his sick and weak part of nature in him, these
    are [*gives money*] but patterns to show you of the whole pieces
    that will follow to you, beside the charge of diet, washing, and
    other necessaries fully defrayed.

ALIBIUS   Believe it, sir, there shall no care be wanting.   90

LOLLIO   Sir, an officer in this place may deserve something; the
    trouble will pass through my hands.

PEDRO   'Tis fit something should come to your hands then, sir.

    [*Gives money.*]

LOLLIO   Yes, sir, 'tis I must keep him sweet and read to him. What
    is his name?   95

PEDRO   His name is Antonio; marry, we use but half to him, only
    Tony.

---

66 *buckler* shield.   74 *pluck a rose* also a euphemism for defecating.   77 *Profoundly*
wisely argued.   80 *come home* fulfilled.   81 *Save you* a greeting, contracted from
"God save you."   85 *commodious* profitable.   85–86 *to . . . him* There is again a
sexual innuendo implied.   91–92 *the . . . hands* The trouble of his keeping will be
entrusted to me.   94 *sweet* clean.

LOLLIO   Tony, Tony, 'tis enough, and a very good name for a fool.
  What's your name, Tony?

ANTONIO   He, he, he, well, I thank you, cousin, he, he, he.   100

LOLLIO   Good boy, hold up your head. He can laugh; I perceive by
  that he is no beast.

PEDRO   Well, sir,
  If you can raise him but to any height,
  Any degree of wit, might he attain,   105
  As I might say, to creep but on all four
  Towards the chair of wit, or walk on crutches,
  'Twould add an honor to your worthy pains,
  And a great family might pray for you—
  To which he should be heir had he discretion   110
  To claim and guide his own. Assure you, sir,
  He is a gentleman.

LOLLIO   Nay, there's nobody doubted that; at first sight I knew him
  for a gentleman. He looks no other yet.

PEDRO   Let him have good attendance and sweet lodging.   115

LOLLIO   As good as my mistress lies in, sir; and as you allow us time
  and means, we can raise him to the higher degree of discretion.

PEDRO   Nay, there shall no cost want, sir.

LOLLIO   He will hardly be stretched up to the wit of a magnifico.

PEDRO   Oh, no, that's not to be expected; far shorter will be enough.   120

LOLLIO   I warrant you I'll make him fit to bear office in five weeks;
  I'll undertake to wind him up to the wit of constable.

PEDRO   If it be lower than that, it might serve turn.

LOLLIO   No, fie, to level him with a headborough, beadle, or watchman, were but little better than he is; constable I'll able him. If   125
  he do come to be a justice afterwards, let him thank the keeper.
  Or I'll go further with you: say I do bring him up to my own
  pitch, say I make him as wise as myself.

PEDRO   Why, there I would have it.

LOLLIO   Well, go to, either I'll be as arrant a fool as he, or he shall be   130
  as wise as I, and then I think 'twill serve his turn.

---

98 good . . . fool   During the seventeenth century, "Tony" sometimes meant "fool."
101-2 I . . . beast   One of the characteristics that was thought to differentiate man from
beasts was man's capacity for laughter.   **105 might he attain**   even if it be only that he
manage.   **118 there . . . want**   No money shall be spared in paying you.   **119 magnifico**
a Venetian nobleman of great authority.   **122 constable**   traditionally thought of as a
stupid officer. For example, Dogberry in *Much Ado About Nothing* is a constable.
124-25 headborough . . . watchman   low-ranking judicial officials.   **125 able**   make.

PEDRO　Nay, I do like thy wit passing well.

LOLLIO　Yes, you may; yet if I had not been a fool, I had had more wit than I have too; remember what state you find me in.

PEDRO　I will, and so leave you; your best cares, I beseech you.　　135

ALIBIUS　Take you none with you; leave 'em all with us. *Exit* PEDRO.

ANTONIO　Oh, my cousin's gone, cousin, cousin, oh!

LOLLIO　Peace, peace, Tony, you must not cry, child; you must be whipped if you do; your cousin is here still: I am your cousin, Tony.　　140

ANTONIO　He, he, then I'll not cry, if thou be'st my cousin, he, he, he.

LOLLIO　I were best try his wit a little, that I may know what form to place him in.

ALIBIUS　Ay, do, Lollio, do.

LOLLIO　I must ask him easy questions at first. Tony, how many true　　145 fingers has a tailor on his right hand?

ANTONIO　As many as on his left, cousin.

LOLLIO　Good, and how many on both?

ANTONIO　Two less than a deuce, cousin.

LOLLIO　Very well answered. I come to you again, cousin Tony: how　　150 many fools goes to a wise man?

ANTONIO　Forty in a day sometimes, cousin.

LOLLIO　Forty in a day? How prove you that?

ANTONIO　All that fall out amongst themselves, and go to a lawyer to be made friends.　　155

LOLLIO　A parlous fool, he must sit in the fourth form at least; I perceive that. I come again, Tony: how many knaves make an honest man?

ANTONIO　I know not that, cousin.

LOLLIO　No, the question is too hard for you; I'll tell you, cousin.　　160 There's three knaves may make an honest man: a sergeant, a jailer, and a beadle: the sergeant catches him, the jailor holds him, and the beadle lashes him. And if he be not honest then, the hangman must cure him.

ANTONIO　Ha. ha, ha, that's fine sport, cousin.　　165

ALIBIUS　This was too deep a question for the fool, Lollio.

---

134 *state* i.e. as a keeper of fools and madmen.　**135** *your . . . cares* (Give him) your best care.　**142** *form* group of inmates in the madhouse.　**145-49** *how . . . deuce* Tailors were notorious for their dishonesty and, as a consequence, were traditionally thought to have no true fingers.　**151** *goes to* both "goes into the composition of" and "goes to call on."　**154-55** *and . . . friends* another example of the ubiquitous satire directed against lawyers in English literature.　**156** *parlous* clever.

LOLLIO Yes, this might have served yourself, though I say't. Once more and you shall go play, Tony.

ANTONIO Ay, play at push-pin, cousin, ha, he.

LOLLIO So thou shalt; say how many fools are here— 170

ANTONIO Two, cousin, thou and I.

LOLLIO Nay, y'are too forward there, Tony; mark my question: how many fools and knaves are here: a fool before a knave, a fool behind a knave, between every two fools a knave; how many fools, how many knaves? 175

ANTONIO I never learnt so far, cousin.

ALIBIUS Thou putt'st too hard questions to him, Lollio.

LOLLIO I'll make him understand it easily; cousin, stand there.

ANTONIO Ay, cousin.

LOLLIO Master, stand you next the fool. 180

ALIBIUS Well, Lollio?

LOLLIO Here's my place. Mark now, Tony; there a fool before a knave.

ANTONIO That's I, cousin.

LOLLIO Here's a fool behind a knave—that's I; and between us two 185
fools there is a knave—that's my master; 'tis but we three, that's all.

ANTONIO We three, we three, cousin.

FIRST [MADMAN] *Within.* Put's head i' th' pillory, the bread's too little. 190

SECOND [MADMAN] *Within.* Fly, fly, and he catches the swallow.

THIRD [MADMAN] *Within.* Give her more onion, or the devil put the rope about her crag.

---

167 served yourself "challenged your wit," but the sexual meaning associated with "serve" is also implicit because Tony intends to cuckold Alibius. **169 push-pin** a child's game in which one player tries to push his pin across the other player's pin, but Antonio's principal meaning here is sexual. **180 next** next to. **189-93 Put's . . . crag** Just exactly what the madmen are talking about here is a mystery, although an Elizabethan audience might have been able to understand particular meanings in these three speeches; perhaps they are echoes of children's games or of songs. One common characteristic is significant though: imprisonment is the obsessive concern of every speaker; however mad these men may be, they are yet sane enough to sense the horror of close confinement. One effect of such speeches is, obviously, to give detail to the atmosphere of Alibius' madhouse, but another more important thematic purpose is also served by the inclusion of this apparently mindless chatter. The madmen's talk of imprisonment draws attention to the constrictions, of one kind or another, that bind almost every character in this play. Lust, rashness, stupidity, and self-interestedness—such limitations make man a prisoner where there are no confining madhouse walls and a victim where there is no scourging wire whip. **193 crag** neck.

LOLLIO   You may hear what time of day it is, the chimes of Bedlam
    goes.   195
ALIBIUS   Peace, peace, or the wire comes!
THIRD [MADMAN]   *Within.* Cat whore, cat whore, her permasant, her
    permasant.
ALIBIUS   Peace, I say.—Their hour's come, they must be fed,
    Lollio.   200
LOLLIO   There's no hope of recovery of that Welsh madman; was
    undone by a mouse that spoiled him a parmesan; lost his wits
    for't.
ALIBIUS   Go to your charge, Lollio; I'll to mine.
LOLLIO   Go you to your madmen's ward; let me alone with your   205
    fools.
ALIBIUS   And remember my last charge, Lollio.
LOLLIO   Of which your patients do you think I am?   *Exit* [ALIBIUS].
    —Come, Tony, you must amongst your schoolfellows now;
    there's pretty scholars amongst 'em, I can tell you; there's some   210
    of 'em at *stultus, stulta, stultum.*
ANTONIO   I would see the madmen, cousin, if they would not bite me.
LOLLIO   No, they shall not bite thee, Tony.
ANTONIO   They bite when they are at dinner, do they not, coz?
LOLLIO   They bite at dinner, indeed, Tony. Well, I hope to get credit   215
    by thee; I like thee the best of all the scholars that ever I brought
    up, and thou shalt prove a wise man, or I'll prove a fool myself.
                                              Exeunt.

ACT II

{Scene I   VERMANDERO's *castle in Alicant*}

Enter BEATRICE *and* JASPERINO *severally.*

BEATRICE   Oh, sir, I'm ready now for that fair service
    Which makes the name of friend sit glorious on you.

---

194 Bedlam originally the Hospital of St. Mary of Bethlehem, used after 1547 as an
asylum for the insane and hence, afterwards, any madhouse.   **196 wire** whip.   **197 Cat
. . . permasant** The madman seems to be condemning his cat for not guarding his
Parmesan cheese.   **207 And . . . charge** And don't forget to watch carefully over my
wife.   **208 Of . . . am** Do you think me some fool or madman?   **211 at . . . stultum**
able to decline the Latin adjective for "foolish."   **215 credit** reputation.
🦟 **ACT II, Scene 1.   1 fair service** as a go-between for her and Alsemero.

Good angels and this conduct be your guide;

[*Gives a paper.*]

Fitness of time and place is there set down, sir.

JASPERINO   The joy I shall return rewards my service.   *Exit.*   5

BEATRICE   How wise is Alsemero in his friend!
It is a sign he makes his choice with judgment.
Then I appear in nothing more approved
Than making choice of him;
For 'tis a principle, he that can choose   10
That bosom well, who of his thoughts partakes,
Proves most discreet in every choice he makes.
Methinks I love now with the eyes of judgment
And see the way to merit, clearly see it.
A true deserver like a diamond sparkles: 15
In darkness you may see him—that's, in absence,
Which is the greatest darkness falls on love;
Yet is he best discerned then
With intellectual eyesight. What's Piracquo
My father spends his breath for? And his blessing   20
Is only mine as I regard his name;
Else it goes from me and turns head against me,
Transformed into a curse. Some speedy way
Must be remembered; he's so forward too,
So urgent that way, scarce allows me breath   25
To speak to my new comforts.

Enter DE FLORES.

DE FLORES   [*Aside.*] Yonder's she.
Whatever ails me? Now a-late especially
I can as well be hanged as refrain seeing her;
Some twenty times a day, nay, not so little,
Do I force errands, frame ways and excuses   30
To come into her sight, and I have small reason for't
And less encouragement; for she baits me still

---

5 return bring you.   **13 eyes of judgment**   Beatrice is here again echoing Alsemero's language (cf. I.1.75-80).   **15-16 like . . . darkness**   Diamonds were thought to be luminous.   **17 falls** that falls.   **20-21 And . . . name**   And my father's blessing is given to me in marriage only so long as I accept his choice of a husband.   **23-24 Some . . . remembered**   (And in the course of fulfilling his wishes) I must act without delay.   **32 baits** taunts.

Every time worse than other, does profess herself
The cruelest enemy to my face in town,
At no hand can abide the sight of me,   35
As if danger or ill-luck hung in my looks.
I must confess, my face is bad enough,
But I know far worse has better fortune,
And not endured alone, but doted on.
And yet, such pick-haired faces, chins like witches',   40
Here and there five hairs whispering in a corner
As if they grew in fear one of another,
Wrinkles like troughs where swine deformity swills
The tears of perjury that lie there like wash
Fallen from the slimy and dishonest eye,   45
Yet such a one plucked sweets without restraint
And has the grace of beauty to his sweet.
Though my hard fate has thrust me out to servitude,
I tumbled into th' world a gentleman.
She turns her blessed eye upon me now,   50
And I'll endure all storms before I part with't.

BEATRICE   Again!—
[*Aside.*] This ominous ill-faced fellow more disturbs me
Than all my other passions.
DE FLORES   [*Aside.*] Now't begins again;
I'll stand this storm of hail though the stones pelt me.   55
BEATRICE   Thy business? What's thy business?
DE FLORES   [*Aside.*] Soft and fair,
I cannot part so soon now.
BEATRICE   [*Aside.*] The villain's fixed.—
Thou standing toad-pool.
DE FLORES   [*Aside.*] The shower falls amain now.
BEATRICE   Who sent thee? What's thy errand? Leave my sight.
DE FLORES   My lord your father charged me to deliver   60
A message to you.
BEATRICE   What, another since?
Do't and be hanged then; let me be rid of thee.
DE FLORES   True service merits mercy.
BEATRICE   What's thy message?

---

35 *At no hand*   under no conditions.   **40** *pick-haired*   tufted with sharp, bristly hair.
43 *where . . . deformity*   where that swine, deformity.   **44** *wash*   eye medicine.
47 *And . . . sweet*   and is graced with a beautiful lover.   **56** *Soft and fair*   an interjection
meaning "I must be careful."   **58** *standing*   stagnant.

DE FLORES   Let beauty settle but in patience,
    You shall hear all.
BEATRICE   A dallying, trifling torment.   65
DE FLORES   Signor Alonzo de Piracquo, lady,
    Sole brother to Tomazo de Piracquo—
BEATRICE   Slave, when wilt make an end?
DE FLORES   Too soon I shall.
BEATRICE   What all this while of him?
DE FLORES   The said Alonzo
    With the foresaid Tomazo—
BEATRICE   Yet again?   70
DE FLORES   Is new alighted.
BEATRICE   Vengeance strike the news!
    Thou thing most loathed, what cause was there in this
    To bring thee to my sight?
DE FLORES   My lord your father
    Charged me to seek you out.
BEATRICE   Is there no other
    To send his errand by?
DE FLORES   It seems 'tis my luck   75
    To be i' th' way still.
BEATRICE   Get thee from me.
DE FLORES   So—
    [Aside.] Why, am not I an ass to devise ways
    Thus to be railed at? I must see her still!
    I shall have a mad qualm within this hour again,
    I know't, and like a common Garden bull
    I do but take breath to be lugged again.   80
    What this may bode I know not; I'll despair the less
    Because there's daily precedents of bad faces
    Beloved beyond all reason. These foul chops
    May come into favor one day 'mongst his fellows.   85
    Wrangling has proved the mistress of good pastime;
    As children cry themselves asleep, I ha' seen
    Women have chid themselves abed to men.   Exit DE FLORES.
BEATRICE   I never see this fellow but I think
    Of some harm towards me; danger's in my mind still: 90
    I scarce leave trembling of an hour after.

---

76 still as before.   **79 qualm** a sudden attack of faintness or illness.   **80 like . . . bull** the allusion is to bull baiting, carried on at Paris Garden in Southwark, England.   **81 lugged** baited.   **84 chops** sides of the face.   **85 his** their.   **91 of** for.

The next good mood I find my father in
I'll get him quite discarded.—Oh, I was
Lost in this small disturbance and forgot
Affliction's fiercer torrent that now comes   95
To bear down all my comforts.

Enter VERMANDERO, ALONZO, TOMAZO.

VERMANDERO   Y'are both welcome,
But an especial one belongs to you, sir,
To whose most noble name our love presents
The addition of a son, our son Alonzo.
ALONZO   The treasury of honor cannot bring forth   100
A title I should more rejoice in, sir.
VERMANDERO   You have improved it well. Daughter, prepare;
The day will steal upon thee suddenly.
BEATRICE   [*Aside.*] Howe'er, I will be sure to keep the night,
If it should come so near me.

[BEATRICE *and* VERMANDERO *talk apart.*]

TOMAZO   Alonzo.
ALONZO   Brother.   105
TOMAZO   In troth I see small welcome in her eye.
ALONZO   Fie, you are too severe a censurer;
Of love in all points, there's no bringing on you;
If lovers should mark everything a fault,
Affection would be like an ill-set book   110
Whose faults might prove as big as half the volume.
BEATRICE   [*To her father.*] That's all I do entreat.
VERMANDERO   It is but reasonable;
I'll see what my son says to't. —Son Alonzo,
Here's a motion made but to reprieve
A maidenhead three days longer; the request   115
Is not far out of reason, for indeed
The former time is pinching.
ALONZO   Though my joys
Be set back so much time as I could wish
They had been forward, yet since she desires it,

---

102 *improved* proved. **104** *keep the night* be on my guard or, perhaps, kill myself
(and so keep night eternally rather than see the day of my marriage to Piracquo).
108 *Of . . . you* There's no bringing you to see the true nature of love. **109** *If . . .
fault* if lovers should notice everything that could be considered a fault. **117–19** *Though
. . . forward* though I would rather have the wedding time advanced three days.

The time is set as pleasing as before,   120
I find no gladness wanting.
VERMANDERO   May I ever meet it in that point still.
Y'are nobly welcome, sirs.   *Exeunt* VERMANDERO *and* BEATRICE.
TOMAZO   So, did you mark the dullness of her parting now?
ALONZO   What dullness? Thou art so exceptious still.   125
TOMAZO   Why, let it go then; I am but a fool
To mark your harms so heedfully.
ALONZO   Where's the oversight?
TOMAZO   Come, your faith's cozened in her, strongly cozened.
Unsettle your affection with all speed
Wisdom can bring it to, your peace is ruined else.   130
Think what a torment 'tis to marry one
Whose heart is leaped into another's bosom:
If ever pleasure she receive from thee,
It comes not in thy name or of thy gift;
She lies but with another in thine arms,   135
He the half father unto all thy children.
In the conception, if he get 'em not in his passions,
She helps to get 'em for him; and how dangerous
And shameful her restraint may go in time to,
It is not to be thought on without sufferings.   140
ALONZO   You speak as if she loved some other then.
TOMAZO   Do you apprehend so slowly?
ALONZO   Nay, and that
Be your fear only, I am safe enough.
Preserve your friendship and your counsel, brother,
For times of more distress. I should depart   145
An enemy, a dangerous, deadly one

---

122 May . . . still May I know you never to lack gladness. **125 *exceptious*** fault-finding. **127 mark . . . harms** warn you. **128 *cozened*** belied. **133 *pleasure*** sexual pleasure. **137 *in his passions*** In the quarto this phrase, which is often entirely omitted from modern editions of the play, appears after "him" in the next line. There, however, it would be very confusing for an audience because it could only refer to the husband, while the other two masculine pronouns in these lines have the lover as their object. It is likely that the source of this problem is a transposition error by the printer, who may have omitted "in his passions" from the end of one line and then put it into the next. In that case, the original text appeared either as it does here, or else it contained a line that was partially omitted: "She helps to get 'em for him, in his passions, / . . . and how dangerous." Since it is impossible to know what Middleton wrote, if indeed part of a verse is actually missing, the first conjecture is honored in this edition. **138 *helps*** by copulating with him in her imagination. **139 *her . . . to*** restraining her may become.

To any but thyself that should but think
She knew the meaning of inconstancy,
Much less the use and practice; yet w'are friends.
Pray let no more be urged; I can endure   150
Much till I meet an injury to her,
Then I am not myself. Farewell, sweet brother,
How much w'are bound to heaven to depart lovingly.   *Exit.*

TOMAZO   Why here is love's tame madness; thus a man
    Quickly steals into his vexation.   *Exit.*   155

ACT II

Scene 2   *A cabinet in* VERMANDERO's *castle*

Enter DIAPHANTA *and* ALSEMERO.

DIAPHANTA   The place is my charge, you have kept your hour,
    And the reward of a just meeting bless you.
    I hear my lady coming; complete gentleman,
    I dare not be too busy with my praises,
    Th'are dangerous things to deal with.   *Exit.*

ALSEMERO   This goes well;   5
    These women are the ladies' cabinets:
    Things of most precious trust are locked into 'em.

Enter BEATRICE.

BEATRICE   I have within mine eye all my desires;
    Requests that holy prayers ascend heaven for
    And brings 'em down to furnish our defects   10
    Come not more sweet to our necessities
    Than thou unto my wishes.

ALSEMERO   W'are so like
    In our expressions, lady, that unless I borrow
    The same words, I shall never find their equals.

    [*Embraces her.*]

BEATRICE   How happy were this meeting, this embrace,   15

🏵 ACT II, Scene 2.   3 *complete* perfect.   10 *brings* The subject may be "heaven"
but, more probably, the singular verb is governed by the plural noun, "requests"—a
grammatical practice common during the Renaissance.

If it were free from envy? This poor kiss,
It has an enemy, a hateful one
That wishes poison to't: how well were I now
If there were none such name known as Piracquo,
Nor no such tie as the command of parents!   20
I should be but too much blessed.

ALSEMERO   One good service
Would strike off both your fears, and I'll go near it too
Since you are so distressed. Remove the cause,
The command ceases; so there's two fears blown out
With one and the same blast.

BEATRICE   Pray let me find you, sir;   25
What might that service be so strangely happy?

ALSEMERO   The honorablest piece 'bout man, valor.
I'll send a challenge to Piracquo instantly.

BEATRICE   How? Call you that extinguishing of fear
When 'tis the only way to keep it flaming?   30
Are not you ventured in the action,
That's all my joys and comforts? Pray, no more, sir.
Say you prevailed: you're danger's and not mine then.
The law would claim you from me, or obscurity
Be made the grave to bury you alive.   35
I'm glad these thoughts come forth; oh, keep not one
Of this condition, sir. Here was a course
Found to bring sorrow on her way to death;
The tears would ne'er 'a' dried till dust had choked 'em.
Blood-guiltiness becomes a fouler visage,   40
And now I think on one—[Aside.] I was too blame,
I ha' marred so good a market with my scorn;
'T had been done questionless. The ugliest creature
Creation framed for some use, yet to see
I could not mark so much where it should be.   45

ALSEMERO   Lady.

BEATRICE   [Aside.] Why, men of art make much of poison—
Keep one to expel another; where was my art?

ALSEMERO   Lady, you hear not me.

BEATRICE   I do especially, sir;

---

17 *enemy* i.e. Alonzo. 21 *service* i.e. murder. 25 *find* understand. 32 *That's . . . comforts* modifies "you," not "action." 37 *Of . . . condition* thought of this kind. 38 *to death* until death. 43 *questionless* without any delay.

The present times are not so sure of our side
As those hereafter may be; we must use 'em then   50
As thrifty folks their wealth, sparingly now
Till the time opens.

ALSEMERO   You teach wisdom, lady.

BEATRICE   Within there, Diaphanta!

Enter DIAPHANTA.

DIAPHANTA   Do you call, madam?

BEATRICE   Perfect your service and conduct this gentleman
The private way you brought him.

DIAPHANTA   I shall, madam.   55

ALSEMERO   My love's as firm as love e'er built upon.

Exeunt DIAPHANTA *and* ALSEMERO.

Enter DE FLORES.

DE FLORES   [*Aside.*] I have watched this meeting and do wonder much
What shall become of t'other; I'm sure both
Cannot be served unless she trangress. Happily
Then I'll put in for one; for if a woman   60
Fly from one point, from him she makes a husband,
She spreads and mounts then like arithmetic—
One, ten, one hundred, one thousand, ten thousand—
Proves in time sutler to any army royal.
Now do I look to be most richly railed at,   65
Yet I must see her.

BEATRICE   [*Aside.*] Why, put case I loathed him
As much as youth and beauty hates a sepulchre,
Must I needs show it? Cannot I keep that secret
And serve my turn upon him? See, he's here.—
De Flores.

DE FLORES   [*Aside.*] Ha, I shall run mad with joy;   70
She called me fairly by my name De Flores,
And neither rogue nor rascal!

BEATRICE   What ha' you done
To your face a-late? Y' have met with some good physician;
Y' have pruned yourself, methinks; you were not wont

---

49 *so . . . side* propitious.   **54** *Perfect* finish.   **62** *spreads and mounts* The metaphor
is of flying, but De Flores' sexual puns are consciously intended.   **64** *sutler* provider.
65 *richly* violently.   **66** *put case* consider hypothetically that.   **69** *serve . . . upon*
do as I wish.

To look so amorously.

DE FLORES   *[Aside.]* Not I,   75
'Tis the same physnomy, to a hair and pimple,
Which she called scurvy scarce an hour ago.
How is this?

BEATRICE   Come hither—nearer, man!

DE FLORES   *[Aside.]* I'm up to the chin in heaven.

BEATRICE   Turn, let me see;
Faugh, 'tis but the heat of the liver, I perceiv't.   80
I thought it had been worse.

DE FLORES   *[Aside.]* Her fingers touched me;
She smells all amber.

BEATRICE   I'll make a water for you shall cleanse this
Within a fortnight.

DE FLORES   With your own hands, lady?

BEATRICE   Yes, mine own, sir; in a work of cure,   85
I'll trust no other.

DE FLORES   *[Aside.]* 'Tis half an act of pleasure
To hear her talk thus to me.

BEATRICE   When w'are used
To a hard face, 'tis not so unpleasing.
It mends still in opinion, hourly mends,
I see it by experience.

DE FLORES   *[Aside.]* I was blest   90
To light upon this minute; I'll make use on't.

BEATRICE   Hardness becomes the visage of a man well;
It argues service, resolution, manhood,
If cause were of employment.

DE FLORES   'Twould be soon seen
If e'er your ladyship had cause to use it.   95
I would but wish the honor of a service
So happy as that mounts to.

BEATRICE   We shall try you.
Oh, my De Flores!

DE FLORES   *[Aside.]* How's that?
She calls me hers already, "my De Flores."—
You were about to sigh out somewhat, madam.   100

---

75 *amorously* like a lover. **80 *liver*** The liver was thought to be the source of the
passions. **83 *this*** your face. **94 *If . . . employment*** if it were needed in a cause.
100 *somewhat* something.

BEATRICE   No, was I? I forgot. Oh!

DE FLORES   There 'tis again,
   The very fellow on't.

BEATRICE   You are too quick, sir.

DE FLORES   There's no excuse for't now, I heard it twice, madam.
   That sigh would fain have utterance; take pity on't
   And lend it a free word; 'las, how it labors   105
   For liberty, I hear the murmur yet
   Beat at your bosom.

BEATRICE   Would creation—

DE FLORES   Ay, well said, that's it.

BEATRICE   Had formed me man.

DE FLORES   Nay, that's not it.

BEATRICE   Oh, 'tis the soul of freedom;
   I should not then be forced to marry one   110
   I hate beyond all depths; I should have power
   Then to oppose my loathings, nay, remove 'em
   Forever from my sight.

DE FLORES   Oh, blest occasion!
   Without change to your sex, you have your wishes.
   Claim so much man in me.

BEATRICE   In thee, De Flores?   115
   There's small cause for that.

DE FLORES   Put it not from me,
   It's a service that I kneel for to you.

   [*Kneels.*]

BEATRICE   You are too violent to mean faithfully;
   There's horror in my service, blood, and danger;
   Can those be things to sue for?

DE FLORES   If you knew   120
   How sweet it were to me to be employed
   In any act of yours, you would say then
   I failed and used not reverence enough
   When I receive the charge on't.

BEATRICE   [*Aside.*] This is much, methinks;
   Belike his wants are greedy, and to such   125
   Gold tastes like angels' food. —Rise.

---

102 *The . . . on't* the duplicate of the first sigh.   **125** *Belike* it seems that.   **125–26** *to
. . . food* To one so greedy as he, gold seems manna from heaven.

DE FLORES   I'll have the work first.

BEATRICE   [*Aside.*] Possible his need
Is strong upon him. —There's to encourage thee;

[*Gives money.*]

As thou art forward and thy service dangerous,
Thy reward shall be precious.

DE FLORES   That I have thought on;   130
I have assured myself of that beforehand
And know it will be precious; the thought ravishes.

BEATRICE   Then take him to thy fury.

DE FLORES   I thirst for him.

BEATRICE   Alonzo de Piracquo.

DE FLORES   His end's upon him; he shall be seen no more.   135

[*Rises.*]

BEATRICE   How lovely now dost thou appear to me!
Never was man dearlier rewarded.

DE FLORES   I do think of that.

BEATRICE   Be wondrous careful in the execution.

DE FLORES   Why, are not both our lives upon the cast?   140

BEATRICE   Then I throw all my fears upon thy service.

DE FLORES   They ne'er shall rise to hurt you.

BEATRICE   When the deed's done,
I'll furnish thee with all things for thy flight;
Thou mayst live bravely in another country.

DE FLORES   Ay, ay, we'll talk of that hereafter.

BEATRICE   [*Aside.*] I shall rid myself   145
Of two inveterate loathings at one time,
Piracquo and his dog-face. *Exit.*

DE FLORES   Oh my blood!
Methinks I feel her in mine arms already,
Her wanton fingers combing out this beard
And, being pleased, praising this bad face;   150
Hunger and pleasure, they'll commend sometimes
Slovenly dishes and feed heartily on 'em;
Nay, which is stranger, refuse daintier for 'em.

---

132 *ravishes* The sexual pun here is intentional, and it serves principally to emphasize the vast discrepancy between De Flores' idea of what his reward will be and Beatrice's misguided belief that she can buy his services with gold only.   **140 *upon the cast*** at stake in this venture.   **144 *bravely*** splendidly.

Some women are odd feeders. I'm too loud.
Here comes the man goes supperless to bed,   155
Yet shall not rise tomorrow to his dinner.

Enter ALONZO.

ALONZO   De Flores.
DE FLORES   My kind, honorable lord.
ALONZO   I am glad I ha' met with thee.
DE FLORES   Sir.
ALONZO   Thou canst show me the full strength of the castle?
DE FLORES   That I can, sir.
ALONZO   I much desire it.   160
DE FLORES   And if the ways and straits of some of the passages be not
    too tedious for you, I will assure you worth your time and sight,
    my lord.
ALONZO   Puh, that shall be no hindrance.
DE FLORES   I'm your servant, then. 'Tis now near dinner time; 'gainst 165
    your lordship's rising I'll have the keys about me.
ALONZO   Thanks, kind De Flores.
DE FLORES   [*Aside.*] He's safely thrust upon me beyond hopes.
                                                              Exeunt.

ACT III

◀[Scene I   *A narrow passage in* ALSEMERO's *castle*]▶

In the act-time, DE FLORES *hides a naked rapier.*

Enter ALONZO *and* DE FLORES.

DE FLORES   Yes, here are all the keys; I was afraid, my lord,
    I'd wanted for the postern: this is it.
    I've all, I've all, my lord; this for the sconce.

155 *goes . . . bed* by being killed before he has eaten, but a sexual meaning is also implicit
because of the preceding reference to women as "odd feeders": Alonzo will be put
permanently to sleep before he has bedded Beatrice.   165–66 *'gainst . . . rising* before
you have risen from dinner.
🍃 ACT III, Scene I.   SD *act-time* interval between the acts. In the quarto this stage
direction follows the entry of Alonzo and De Flores.   2 *postern* back gate.   3 *sconce*
small fort for defending a castle gate.

ALONZO   'Tis a most spacious and impregnable fort.
DE FLORES   You'll tell me more, my lord. This descent   5
   Is somewhat narrow; we shall never pass
   Well with our weapons; they'll but trouble us.
ALONZO   Thou sayst true.
DE FLORES   Pray let me help your lordship.
ALONZO   'Tis done. Thanks, kind De Flores.
DE FLORES   Here are hooks, my lord,
   To hang such things on purpose. [*He hangs the swords up.*]
ALONZO   Lead, I'll follow thee.   10
               Exeunt at one door and enter at the other.

ACT III
Scene 2   *A close chamber*

DE FLORES   All this is nothing, you shall see anon
   A place you little dream on.
ALONZO   I am glad
   I have this leisure; all your master's house
   Imagine I ha' taken a gondola.
DE FLORES   All but myself, sir—[*Aside.*] which makes up my safety.—   5
   My lord, I'll place you at a casement here
   Will show you the full strength of all the castle.
   Look, spend your eye awhile upon that object.
ALONZO   Here's rich variety, De Flores.
DE FLORES   Yes, sir.
ALONZO   Goodly munition.
DE FLORES   Ay, there's ordnance, sir,   10
   No bastard metal, will ring you a peal like bells
   At great men's funerals. Keep your eye straight, my lord;
   Take special notice of that sconce before you,
   There you may dwell awhile.
ALONZO   I am upon't.
DE FLORES   And so am I. [*Stabs him.*]
ALONZO   De Flores, oh, De Flores,   15

5 *You'll . . . more*   You'll be even more impressed when you have seen it all.
🎭 ACT III, Scene 2.   10 *ordnance*   artillery.

Whose malice hast thou put on?

DE FLORES   Do you question

A work of secrecy? I must silence you.

[*Stabs him.*]

ALONZO   Oh, oh, oh.

DE FLORES   I must silence you.   [*Stabs him; he dies.*]

So, here's an undertaking well accomplished.

This vault serves to good use now. Ha! what's that   20

Threw sparkles in my eye? Oh, 'tis a diamond

He wears upon his finger; it was well found:

This will approve the work. What, so fast on?

Not part in death? I'll take a speedy course then;

Finger and all shall off. [*Cuts off finger.*] So, now I'll clear   25

The passages from all suspect or fear.   *Exit with body.*

ACT III

{ Scene 3   ALIBIUS' *madhouse* }

Enter ISABELLA *and* LOLLIO.

ISABELLA   Why, sirrah? Whence have you commission

To fetter the doors against me? If you

Keep me in a cage, pray whistle to me,

Let me be doing something.

LOLLIO   You shall be doing, if it please you; I'll whistle to you if   5

you'll pipe after.

ISABELLA   Is it your master's pleasure or your own

To keep me in this pinfold?

LOLLIO   'Tis for my master's pleasure, lest being taken in another

man's corn, you might be pounded in another place.   10

ISABELLA   'Tis very well, and he'll prove very wise.

LOLLIO   He says you have company enough in the house, if you please

to be sociable, of all sorts of people.

---

23 approve prove.

✲ **ACT III, Scene 3.   3 pray . . . me** Then command me to do tricks.   **5–6 if . . .**
after if you'll do as I say.   **8 pinfold** pen for stray animals.   **10 pounded** both
"impounded" and "possessed sexually."

ISABELLA   Of all sorts? Why, here's none but fools and madmen.

LOLLIO   Very well; and where will you find any other, if you should   15
go abroad? There's my master and I to boot too.

ISABELLA   Of either sort one, a madman and a fool.

LOLLIO   I would ev'n participate of both then if I were as you. I know
y'are half mad already; be half foolish too.

ISABELLA   Y'are a brave saucy rascal! Come on, sir,   20
Afford me then the pleasure of your bedlam;
You were commending once today to me
Your last-come lunatic: what a proper
Body there was without brains to guide it,
And what a pitiful delight appeared   25
In that defect, as if your wisdom had found
A mirth in madness. Pray, sir, let me partake
If there be such a pleasure.

LOLLIO   If I do not show you the handsomest, discreetest madman,
one that I may call the understanding madman, then say I am a   30
fool.

ISABELLA   Well, a match, I will say so.

LOLLIO   When you have a taste of the madman, you shall, if you
please, see fools' college, o' th' side; I seldom lock there, 'tis
but shooting a bolt or two and you are amongst 'em.   *Exit.*   35

Enter presently LOLLIO [*with*] FRANCISCUS. Come on, sir, let me
see how handsomely you'll behave yourself now.

FRANCISCUS   How sweetly she looks! Oh, but there's a wrinkle in
her brow as deep as philosophy. Anacreon, drink to my mistress'
health, I'll pledge it. Stay, stay, there's a spider in the cup! No,   40
'tis but a grapestone; swallow it, fear nothing, poet; so, so, lift
higher.

17 *Of . . . fool* "One of you two is a madman, the other a fool." Isabella implies that
her husband is mad because he locks her up and that Lollio is a fool because he thinks he
can convince her to accept Alibius' decision.   18 *participate*   both "keep company with"
and "have sexual intercourse with."   18–19 *I know . . . too*   The words are a dare: Lollio
encourages Isabella to act promiscuously and to take him as her lover.   20 *brave*   fine.
21 *Afford*   show.   *pleasure . . . bedlam*   Isabella's sexual pun here is intentional.
23 *proper*   handsome.   32 *a match*   It is a deal.   34 *fools' . . . side*   a whole group of
idiots kept in another part of the house.   35 *shooting a bolt*   unbolting a lock—with an
obscene sexual innuendo intended.   36 SD   The quarto here reads only "Enter presently,"
and then, at the end of this speech, "Enter Loll:Franciscus."   39 *Anacreon*   a Greek lyric
poet of the sixth century B.C.   40 *spider*   The spider was thought to be poisonous.   41 *'tis
. . . nothing*   Franciscus' claim that the wine is harmless because it contains a grape pit and
not a poisoning spider is ironic: Anacreon died by choking on a grape seed in his wine.

ISABELLA   Alack, alack, 'tis too full of pity
    To be laughed at. How fell he mad? Canst thou tell?
LOLLIO   For love, mistress. He was a pretty poet too, and that set   45
    him forwards first; the muses then forsook him, he ran mad for
    a chambermaid, yet she was but a dwarf neither.
FRANCISCUS   Hail, bright Titania!
    Why standst thou idle on these flowery banks?
    Oberon is dancing with his dryades;   50
    I'll gather daisies, primrose, violets,
    And bind them in a verse of poesie.
LOLLIO   Not too near, you see your danger.

    [*Shows whip.*]

FRANCISCUS   Oh, hold thy hand, great Diomede;
    Thou feedst thy horses well, they shall obey thee.   55
    Get up; Bucephalus kneels.

    [*Kneels.*]

LOLLIO   You see how I awe my flock? A shepherd has not his dog at
    more obedience.
ISABELLA   His conscience is unquiet; sure that was
    The cause of this. A proper gentleman.   60
FRANCISCUS   Come hither, Aesculapius; hide the poison.
LOLLIO   Well, 'tis hid.

    [*Conceals whip.*]

FRANCISCUS   Didst thou never hear of one Tiresias,
    A famous poet?

    [*Rises.*]

LOLLIO   Yes, that kept tame wild-geese.   65

45–46 set . . . forwards made him prominent.   **47 but . . . neither** only a dwarf (?).
48 Titania, 50 Oberon the queen and king of fairies.   **dryades** wood nymphs.
Franciscus' implication is that since Oberon is cavorting with his wood nymphs, Titania
(i.e. Isabella) should live gaily too—by copulating with him.   **54 Diomede** In Greek
mythology, Diomede was a king who fed his horses human flesh.   **56 Bucephalus** the
wild horse that only Alexander the Great could tame and ride.   **61 Aesculapius** the
Greek god of medicine.   **63 Tiresias** a Greek prophet who was changed from a man
to a woman and, after seven years, changed back to a man again. He was later blinded by
Juno as a punishment for revealing that women derived more pleasure from love than
men did.   **65 that . . . wild-geese** Here Lollio seems to describe Tiresias as a neighbor
known for keeping "tame wild-geese." Just what the reference to those geese would have
meant to an Elizabethan audience is now a mystery, but it is safe to say that the birds,
which are neither entirely tame nor wild, may signify just another form of changeling.

FRANCISCUS   That's he; I am the man.

LOLLIO   No.

FRANCISCUS   Yes, but make no words on't; I was a man
  Seven years ago.

LOLLIO   A stripling, I think you might.   70

FRANCISCUS   Now I'm a woman, all feminine.

LOLLIO   I would I might see that.

FRANCISCUS   Juno struck me blind.

LOLLIO   I'll ne'er believe that; for a woman, they say, has an eye
  more than a man.   75

FRANCISCUS   I say she struck me blind.

LOLLIO   And Luna made you mad; you have two trades to beg with.

FRANCISCUS   Luna is now big-bellied, and there's room
  For both of us to ride with Hecate.
  I'll drag thee up into her silver sphere,   80
  And there we'll kick the dog, and beat the bush,
  That barks against the witches of the night;
  The swift lycanthropi that walks the round
  We'll tear their wolvish skins and save the sheep.

  [*Beats* LOLLIO.]

LOLLIO   Is't come to this? Nay then, my poison comes forth again;   85
  mad slave indeed, abuse your keeper!

  [*Shows whip.*]

ISABELLA   I prithee hence with him, now he grows dangerous.

FRANCISCUS   *Sings.* Sweet love, pity me;
  Give me leave to lie with thee.

LOLLIO   No, I'll see you wiser first. To your own kennel.   90

FRANCISCUS   No noise, she sleeps, draw all the curtains round;
  Let no soft sound molest the pretty soul
  But love, and love creeps in at a mouse-hole.

LOLLIO   I would you would get into your hole.   *Exit* FRANCISCUS.
  Now, mistress, I will bring you another sort; you shall be fooled   95
  another while. Tony, come hither, Tony. *Enter* ANTONIO. Look
  who's yonder, Tony.

ANTONIO   Cousin, is it not my aunt?

---

70 might might (have been).   **74 eye** Lollio's reference here is, of course, obscene.
77 Luna the moon.   **two trades** madness and blindness.   **78 big-bellied** full, but
throughout this speech there are conscious sexual innuendoes.   **79 Hecate** a Greek
goddess of witchcraft, associated with the moon.   **83 lycanthropi** madmen who think
they are wolves.   **98 aunt** mistress.

LOLLIO   Yes, 'tis one of 'em, Tony.

ANTONIO   He, he, how do you, uncle?   100

LOLLIO   Fear him not, mistress; 'tis a gentle nidget. You may play
with him, as safely with him as with his bauble.

ISABELLA   How long hast thou been a fool?

ANTONIO   Ever since I came hither, cousin.

ISABELLA   Cousin? I'm none of thy cousins, fool.   105

LOLLIO   Oh, mistress, fools have always so much wit as to claim
their kindred.

MADMAN   *Within.* Bounce, bounce, he falls, he falls.

ISABELLA   Hark you, your scholars in the upper room
Are out of order.   110

LOLLIO   Must I come amongst you there? Keep you the fool, mistress;
I'll go up and play left-handed Orlando amongst the madmen.

Exit.

ISABELLA   Well, sir.

ANTONIO   [*Abandoning the manner of an idiot.*] 'Tis opportuneful now,
sweet lady. Nay,
Cast no amazing eye upon this change.   115

ISABELLA   Ha!

ANTONIO   This shape of folly shrouds your dearest love,
The truest servant to your powerful beauties,
Whose magic had this force thus to transform me.

ISABELLA   You are a fine fool, indeed.

ANTONIO   Oh, 'tis not strange;   120
Love has an intellect that runs through all
The scrutinous sciences and, like
A cunning poet, catches a quantity
Of every knowledge; yet brings all home
Into one mystery, into one secret   125
That he proceeds in.

ISABELLA   Y'are a parlous fool.

ANTONIO   No danger in me; I bring nought but love
And his soft-wounding shafts to strike you with.
Try but one arrow; if it hurt you,

---

101 *nidget*   idiot.   **102** *bauble*   the baton of the fool or court jester, but a sexual pun is
also intended.   **105** *cousins*   Lovers sometimes carried on illicit affairs by pretending to
be cousins, and it is this implication of the word, as well as the obvious one, that Isabella
is denying.   **112** *play . . . Orlando*   do a rough imitation of Orlando scattering his
adversaries (in Ariosto's *Orlando Furioso*).   **115** *amazing*   amazed.   **124–26** *yet . . . in*
A sexual pun is again implicit.   **126** *parlous*   dangerously clever.

I'll stand you twenty back in recompense.   130
ISABELLA   A forward fool, too.
ANTONIO   This was love's teaching;
  A thousand ways she fashioned out my way,
  And this I found the safest and the nearest
  To tread the galaxia to my star.
ISABELLA   Profound, withal! Certain, you dreamed of this;   135
  Love never taught it waking.
ANTONIO   Take no acquaintance
  Of these outward follies; there is within
  A gentleman that loves you.
ISABELLA   When I see him,
  I'll speak with him; so in the meantime
  Keep your habit, it becomes you well enough.   140
  As you are a gentleman, I'll not discover you;
  That's all the favor that you must expect.
  When you are weary, you may leave the school,
  For all this while you have but played the fool.

  Enter LOLLIO.

ANTONIO   And must again. He, he, I thank you, cousin;   145
  I'll be your valentine tomorrow morning.
LOLLIO   How do you like the fool, mistress?
ISABELLA   Passing well, sir.
LOLLIO   Is he not witty, pretty well for a fool?
ISABELLA   If he holds on as he begins, he is like   150
  To come to something.
LOLLIO   Ay, thank a good tutor. You may put him to't; he begins to
  answer pretty hard questions. Tony, how many is five times
  six?
ANTONIO   Five times six is six times five.   155
LOLLIO   What arithmetician could have answered better? How many
  is one hundred and seven?
ANTONIO   One hundred and seven is seven hundred and one, cousin.
LOLLIO   This is no wit to speak on. Will you be rid of the fool now?
ISABELLA   By no means; let him stay a little.   160

---

132 *she* Most modern editors emend to "he," but the reference here could be to Venus, the goddess of love, as well as to Cupid.   **134** *galaxia* Milky Way.   **140** *habit* dress.   **141** *discover you* give you away.   **151** *To . . . something* Isabella's sexual pun is again intentional.

MADMEN   *Within.* Catch there, catch the last couple in hell!

LOLLIO   Again? Must I come amongst you? Would my master were
come home! I am not able to govern both these wards together.

                                                  Exit.

ANTONIO   Why should a minute of love's hour be lost?

ISABELLA   Fie, out again! I had rather you kept   165
   Your other posture; you become not your tongue
   When you speak from your clothes.

ANTONIO   How can he freeze
   Lives near so sweet a warmth? Shall I alone
   Walk through the orchard of the Hesperides
   And cowardly not dare to pull an apple?   170
   This with the red cheeks I must venture for.

   Enter LOLLIO *above* [*as* ANTONIO *kisses* ISABELLA].

ISABELLA   Take heed, there's giants keep 'em.

LOLLIO   [*Aside.*] How now, fool, are you good at that? Have you
read Lipsius? He's past *Ars Amandi;* I believe I must put harder
questions to him, I perceive that—   175

ISABELLA   You are bold without fear too.

ANTONIO   What should I fear,
   Having all joys about me? Do you smile
   And love shall play the wanton on your lip:
   Meet and retire, retire and meet again;
   Look you but cheerfully, and in your eyes   180
   I shall behold mine own deformity
   And dress myself up fairer. I know this shape
   Becomes me not, but in those bright mirrors
   I shall array me handsomely.

---

161 catch . . . hell The reference of the madmen is to the game of barley-break, which
they may be presumed to be playing within. In this game, usually played by three couples,
two players who occupied a center area called "hell" tried to catch the other couples as
they ran by them. The symbolic significance of this reference is that it draws attention to
the way characters driven by sexual desires to form unions opposing society's alliances are
soon imprisoned in the hell of solipsism, where they commit acts of madness or idiocy
merely to satisfy their self-interested desires. This theme receives its most obvious
statement at V.3.163–64. **166–67 you . . . clothes** Your appearance is out of keeping
with your speech when you talk seriously. **169 orchard . . . Hesperides** a mythological
garden of paradise where golden apples grew. **172 giants** The gardens of the Hesperides
were guarded by the dragon Ladon, who was sired by a giant. **174 Lipsius** a sixteenth-
century Flemish scholar, whose name is used here only because of the pun on the first
syllable. *Ars Amandi* a Latin poem about the art of loving, written by Ovid. Lollio
thus implies that Antonio is an accomplished lover. **177 Do you** you need only to.
183 bright mirrors her eyes.

LOLLIO   [*Aside.*] Cuckoo, cuckoo.   *Exit* [*above*].   185

    [*Enter*] MADMEN *above, some as birds, others as beasts.*

ANTONIO   What are these?

ISABELLA   Of fear enough to part us,
    Yet are they but our schools of lunatics,
    That act their fantasies in any shapes
    Suiting their present thoughts; if sad, they cry;
    If mirth by their conceit, they laugh again.   190
    Sometimes they imitate the beasts and birds,
    Singing or howling, braying, barking; all
    As their wild fancies prompt 'em. [*Exit* MADMEN.]

ANTONIO   These are no fears.

    Enter LOLLIO.

ISABELLA   But here's a large one, my man.

ANTONIO   Ha, he, that's fine sport indeed, cousin.   195

LOLLIO   I would my master were come home; 'tis too much for one
    shepherd to govern two of these flocks, nor can I believe that
    one churchman can instruct two benefices at once; there will
    be some incurable mad of the one side and very fools on the
    other. Come, Tony.   200

ANTONIO   Prithee cousin, let me stay here still.

LOLLIO   No, you must to your book now, you have played sufficiently.

ISABELLA   Your fool is grown wondrous witty.

LOLLIO   Well, I'll say nothing, but I do not think but he will put
    you down one of these days.   *Exeunt* LOLLIO *and* ANTONIO.   205

ISABELLA   Here the restrainèd current might make breach,
    Spite of the watchful bankers. Would a woman stray,
    She need not gad abroad to seek her sin;
    It would be brought home one ways or other:
    The needle's point will to the fixed north,   210
    Such drawing arctics women's beauties are.

    Enter LOLLIO.

LOLLIO   How dost thou, sweet rogue?

ISABELLA   How now?

LOLLIO   Come, there are degrees; one fool may be better than another.

---

185 *Cuckoo, cuckoo* Lollio implies that Alibius is being cuckolded. **186** *Of fear*
frightening. **190** *conceit* notion. **198** *instruct . . . once* minister to two churches at
one time. **202** *played,* **204–5** *put you down* again, double-entendres. **207** *bankers*
those who reinforce the banks of a flooding river.

ISABELLA What's the matter?   215

LOLLIO Nay, if thou givst thy mind to fool's-flesh, have at thee.

[*Tries to kiss her.*]

ISABELLA You bold slave, you.

LOLLIO I could follow now as t'other fool did:
  "What should I fear,
  Having all joys about me? Do you but smile   220
  And love shall play the wanton on your lip:
  Meet and retire, retire and meet again;
  Look you but cheerfully, and in your eyes
  I shall behold my own deformity
  And dress myself up fairer. I know this shape   225
  Becomes me not—"
  And so as it follows. But is not this the more foolish way?
  Come, sweet rogue, kiss me, my little Lacedaemonian; let me
  feel how thy pulses beat. Thou hast a thing about thee would do
  a man pleasure, I'll lay my hand on't.   230

ISABELLA Sirrah, no more; I see you have discovered
  This love's knight errant, who hath made adventure
  For purchase of my love; be silent, mute,
  Mute as a statue, or his injunction
  For me enjoying shall be to cut thy throat.   235
  I'll do it, though for no other purpose,
  And be sure he'll not refuse it.

LOLLIO My share, that's all; I'll have my fool's part with you.

ISABELLA No more, your master.

  Enter ALIBIUS.

ALIBIUS   Sweet, how dost thou?

ISABELLA Your bounden servant, sir.

ALIBIUS   Fie, fie, sweetheart,   240
  No more of that.

ISABELLA   You were best lock me up.

ALIBIUS In my arms and bosom, my sweet Isabella,
  I'll lock thee up most nearly. Lollio,
  We have employment, we have task in hand.
  At noble Vermandero's, our castle-captain,   245
  There is a nuptial to be solemnized,

---

228 *Lacedaemonian* one who does not waste words, but acts directly. **241** *You . . . up*
You might as well lock me up as keep me under such close surveillance here.

Beatrice-Joanna his fair daughter, bride,
For which the gentleman hath bespoke our pains:
A mixture of our madmen and our fools
To finish, as it were, and make the fag   250
Of all the revels the third night from the first.
Only an unexpected passage over
To make a frightful pleasure, that is all,
But not the all I aim at. Could we so act it,
To teach it in a wild, distracted measure—   255
Though out of form and figure, breaking time's head,
It were no matter; 'twould be healed again
In one age or other, if not in this—
This, this, Lollio, there's a good reward begun
And will beget a bounty, be it known.   260

LOLLIO   This is easy, sir, I'll warrant you. You have about you fools
    and madmen that can dance very well, and 'tis no wonder your
    best dancers are not the wisest men; the reason is, with often
    jumping they jolt their brains down into their feet, that their
    wits lie more in their heels than in their heads.   265

ALIBIUS   Honest Lollio, thou givst me a good reason
    And a comfort in it.

ISABELLA   Y' have a fine trade on't:
    Madmen and fools are a staple commodity.

ALIBIUS   Oh, wife, we must eat, wear clothes, and live.
    Just at the lawyers' haven we arrive: 270
    By madmen and by fools we both do thrive.   *Exeunt.*

ACT III

Scene 4   VERMANDERO's *castle*

Enter VERMANDERO, ALSEMERO, JASPERINO, *and* BEATRICE.

VERMANDERO   Valencia speaks so nobly of you, sir,
    I wish I had a daughter now for you.

---

250 *fag* end.   **252** *Only . . . over* The madmen are to rush suddenly across the main
castle hall.   **254–60** *Could . . . known* Though the particulars of Alibius' statement here
are somewhat confusing, the general sense is clear: if he can get his patients to dance
energetically—even if they do not keep time properly—they may set a style for succeeding
marriage celebrations and, as a consequence, win him a generous monetary reward.

ALSEMERO The fellow of this creature were a partner
 For a king's love.
VERMANDERO   I had her fellow once, sir,
 But heaven has married her to joys eternal;   5
 'Twere sin to wish her in this vale again.
 Come, sir, your friend and you shall see the pleasures
 Which my health chiefly joys in.
ALSEMERO I hear the beauty of this seat largely.
VERMANDERO It falls much short of that. *Exeunt. Manet* BEATRICE.
BEATRICE   So, here's one step 10
 Into my father's favor; time will fix him.
 I have got him now the liberty of the house;
 So wisdom by degrees works out her freedom.
 And if that eye be darkened that offends me
 (I wait but that eclipse), this gentleman   15
 Shall soon shine glorious in my father's liking
 Through the refulgent virtue of my love.

 Enter DE FLORES.

DE FLORES [*Aside.*] My thoughts are at a banquet for the deed;
 I feel no weight in't, 'tis but light and cheap
 For the sweet recompense that I set down for't.   20
BEATRICE De Flores.
DE FLORES   Lady.
BEATRICE   Thy looks promise cheerfully.
DE FLORES All things are answerable: time, circumstance,
 Your wishes, and my service.
BEATRICE   Is it done then?
DE FLORES Piracquo is no more.
BEATRICE My joys start at mine eyes; our sweet'st delights 25
 Are evermore born weeping.
DE FLORES   I've a token for you.
BEATRICE For me?
DE FLORES But it was sent somewhat unwillingly;
 I could not get the ring without the finger.

 [*Shows the finger.*]

🎜 **ACT III, Scene 4.** **3** *fellow* equal. *this creature* Beatrice. **6** *vale* world of sorrows. **7–8** *pleasures . . . in* the castle and its grounds. **9** *I . . . largely* Reports of your castle's impressiveness are widespread. **14** *if . . . me* if Piracquo has been killed. **18** *My . . . deed* My imagination dwells on the rich satisfactions I shall receive in return for the deed. **22** *answerable* in correspondence.

BEATRICE   Bless me! What hast thou done?

DE FLORES   Why, is that more   30
  Than killing the whole man? I cut his heart-strings.
  A greedy hand thrust in a dish at court
  In a mistake hath had as much as this.

BEATRICE   'Tis the first token my father made me send him.

DE FLORES   And I made him send it back again   35
  For his last token; I was loath to leave it,
  And I'm sure dead men have no use of jewels.
  He was as loath to part with't, for it stuck
  As if the flesh and it were both one substance.

BEATRICE   At the stag's fall the keeper has his fees;   40
  'Tis soon applied: all dead men's fees are yours, sir.
  I pray bury the finger, but the stone
  You may make use on shortly; the true value,
  Take't of my truth, is near three hundred ducats.

DE FLORES   'Twill hardly buy a capcase for one's conscience, though,   45
  To keep it from the worm, as fine as 'tis.
  Well, being my fees, I'll take it;
  Great men have taught me that, or else my merit
  Would scorn the way on't.

BEATRICE   It might justly, sir.
  Why, thou mistak'st, De Flores; 'tis not given   50
  In state of recompense.

DE FLORES   No, I hope so, lady;
  You should soon witness my contempt to't then.

BEATRICE   Prithee, thou lookst as if thou wert offended.

DE FLORES   That were strange, lady; 'tis not possible
  My service should draw such a cause from you.   55
  Offended? Could you think so? That were much
  For one of my performance and so warm
  Yet in my service.

BEATRICE   'Twere misery in me to give you cause, sir.

DE FLORES   I know so much; it were so; misery   60
  In her most sharp condition.

BEATRICE   'Tis resolved then.

---

33 *hath . . . this* has had a finger cut off.   **40** *At . . . fees* When a stag was killed, the
warden was usually given some part of it in return for allowing the hunt. But here again,
as often in the play and particularly in this scene, a sexual innuendo is implicit.   **45** *capcase*
container.   **46** *worm* the gnawing worm of conscience.   **55** *such a cause* reason to be
offended.   **57–58** *so . . . service* so newly returned from my deed.

Look you, sir, here's three thousand golden florins;
I have not meanly thought upon thy merit.

DE FLORES   What, salary? Now you move me.

BEATRICE   How, De Flores?

DE FLORES   Do you place me in the rank of verminous fellows   65
To destroy things for wages? Offer gold?
The lifeblood of man! Is anything
Valued too precious for my recompense?

BEATRICE   I understand thee not.

DE FLORES   I could ha' hired
A journeyman in murder at this rate   70
And mine own conscience might have slept at ease
And have had the work brought home.

BEATRICE   [*Aside.*] I'm in a labyrinth.
What will content him? I would fain be rid of him.—
I'll double the sum, sir.

DE FLORES   You take a course
To double my vexation, that's the good you do.   75

BEATRICE   [*Aside.*] Bless me! I am now in worse plight than I was;
I know not what will please him. —For my fear's sake,
I prithee make away with all speed possible;
And if thou be'st so modest not to name
The sum that will content thee, paper blushes not: 80
Send thy demand in writing; it shall follow thee.
But prithee take thy flight.

DE FLORES   You must fly too, then.

BEATRICE   I?

DE FLORES   I'll not stir a foot else.

BEATRICE   What's your meaning?

DE FLORES   Why, are not you as guilty? In, I'm sure,
As deep as I? And we should stick together.   85
Come, your fears counsel you but ill; my absence
Would draw suspect upon you instantly.
There were no rescue for you.

BEATRICE   [*Aside.*] He speaks home.

DE FLORES   Nor is it fit we two engaged so jointly

---

70 journeyman hireling.   **71 slept at ease** an addition of modern editors; in the quarto
the line ends, unfinished, at "have."   **72 labyrinth** a maze; the original labyrinth built
by Daedalus imprisoned its creator.

Should part and live asunder. [*Tries to kiss her.*]
BEATRICE   How now, sir?   90
  This shows not well.
DE FLORES   What makes your lip so strange?
  This must not be 'twixt us.
BEATRICE   [*Aside.*] The man talks wildly.
DE FLORES   Come, kiss me with a zeal, now.
BEATRICE   [*Aside.*] Heaven, I doubt him.
DE FLORES   I will not stand so long to beg 'em shortly.
BEATRICE   Take heed, De Flores, of forgetfulness;   95
  'Twill soon betray us.
DE FLORES   Take you heed first;
  Faith, y'are grown much forgetful; y'are too blame in't.
BEATRICE   [*Aside.*] He's bold, and I am blamed for't.
DE FLORES   I have eased
  You of your trouble, think on't; I'm in pain
  And must be eased of you; 'tis a charity.   100
  Justice invites your blood to understand me.
BEATRICE   I dare not.
DE FLORES   Quickly!
BEATRICE   Oh, I never shall!
  Speak it yet further off, that I may lose
  What has been spoken and no sound remain on't.
  I would not hear so much offense again   105
  For such another deed.
DE FLORES   Soft, lady, soft;
  That last is not yet paid for. Oh, this act
  Has put me into spirit; I was as greedy on't
  As the parched earth of moisture when the clouds weep.
  Did you not mark I wrought myself into't?   110
  Nay, sued and kneeled for't? Why was all that pains took?
  You see I have thrown contempt upon your gold;
  Not that I want it not, for I do piteously;
  In order I will come unto't and make use on't.
  But 'twas not held so precious to begin with,   115
  For I place wealth after the heels of pleasure;
  And were I not resolved in my belief
  That thy virginity were perfect in thee,

***

91 *strange* distant. **92** *This* this coldness. **100** *of* by. **101** *your . . . me* you to
feel my passion. **114** *In order* in due time.

I should but take my recompense with grudging,
As if I had but half my hopes I agreed for.   120
BEATRICE   Why, 'tis impossible thou canst be so wicked
Or shelter such a cunning cruelty,
To make his death the murderer of my honor.
Thy language is so bold and vicious
I cannot see which way I can forgive it   125
With any modesty.
DE FLORES   Push! you forget yourself;
A woman dipped in blood and talk of modesty!
BEATRICE   Oh, misery of sin! Would I had been bound
Perpetually unto my living hate
In that Piracquo, than to hear these words.   130
Think but upon the distance that creation
Set 'twixt thy blood and mine, and keep thee there.
DE FLORES   Look but into your conscience, read me there:
'Tis a true book; you'll find me there your equal.
Push, fly not to your birth, but settle you   135
In what the act has made you; y'are no more now.
You must forget your parentage to me;
Y'are the deed's creature; by that name
You lost your first condition, and I challenge you,
As peace and innocency has turned you out   140
And made you one with me.
BEATRICE   With thee, foul villain?
DE FLORES   Yes, my fair murd'ress. Do you urge me?
Though thou writ'st maid, thou whore in thy affection,
'Twas changed from thy first love, and that's a kind
Of whoredom in thy heart. And he's changed now   145
To bring thy second on, thy Alsemero,
Whom (by all sweets that ever darkness tasted),
If I enjoy thee not, thou ne'er enjoyst.
I'll blast the hopes and joys of marriage;
I'll confess all. My life I rate at nothing.   150
BEATRICE   De Flores.
DE FLORES   I shall rest from all lovers' plagues then;
I live in pain now. That shooting eye

---

126 *Push* an exclamation of disdain.   137 *to* in your relation to.   138 *by . . . name*
because of the deed.   142 *urge* order.   144 *'Twas* which was.   145 *changed* dead.
151 *I . . . then* Death will free me from the pain of loving where I am despised.

Will burn my heart to cinders.
BEATRICE   Oh, sir, hear me.
DE FLORES   She that in life and love refuses me,
    In death and shame my partner she shall be.   155
BEATRICE   Stay, hear me once for all; [*Kneels.*] I make thee master
    Of all the wealth I have in gold and jewels;
    Let me go poor unto my bed with honor,
    And I am rich in all things.
DE FLORES   Let this silence thee:
    The wealth of all Valencia shall not buy   160
    My pleasure from me.
    Can you weep fate from its determined purpose?
    So soon may you weep me.
BEATRICE   Vengeance begins:
    Murder, I see, is followed by more sins.
    Was my creation in the womb so cursed   165
    It must engender with a viper first?
DE FLORES   Come, rise and shroud your blushes in my bosom;

    [*Raises her.*]

    Silence is one of pleasure's best receipts.
    Thy peace is wrought forever in this yielding.
    'Las, how the turtle pants! Thou'lt love anon   170
    What thou so fear'st and faint'st to venture on.   *Exeunt.*

ACT IV
{*Dumb Show*}

Enter GENTLEMEN, VERMANDERO *meeting them with action of wonder-
ment at the flight of* PIRACQUO. *Enter* ALSEMERO *with* JASPERINO *and*
GALLANTS; VERMANDERO *points to him, the* GENTLEMEN *seeming to
applaud the choice.* [*Exeunt in procession* VERMANDERO,] ALSEMERO,
JASPERINO, *and* GENTLEMEN. [*Then enter*] BEATRICE, *the bride, following in great state, accompanied with* DIAPHANTA, ISABELLA, *and other*

---

168 *Silence . . . receipts* Pleasure is often secured by silence. **170** *turtle* turtledove.

GENTLEWOMEN. [*Enter*] DE FLORES, *after all, smiling at the accident.*
ALONZO'S GHOST *appears to* DE FLORES *in the midst of his smile,*
startles him, showing him the hand whose finger he had cut off. They
pass over in great solemnity.

ACT IV

Scene I   *Outside a cabinet in* VERMANDERO'*s castle*

Enter BEATRICE.

BEATRICE   This fellow has undone me endlessly;
    Never was bride so fearfully distressed.
    The more I think upon th'ensuing night
    And whom I am to cope with in embraces—
    One that's ennobled both in blood and mind,   5
    So clear in understanding (that's my plague now),
    Before whose judgment will my fault appear
    Like malefactors' crimes before tribunals,
    There is no hiding on't—the more I dive
    Into my own distress. How a wise man   10
    Stands for a great calamity! There's no venturing
    Into his bed, what course soe'er I light upon,
    Without my shame, which may grow up to danger.
    He cannot but in justice strangle me
    As I lie by him, as a cheater use me.   15
    'Tis a precious craft to play with a false die
    Before a cunning gamester. Here's his closet,
    The key left in't, and he abroad i' th' park;
    Sure, 'twas forgot; I'll be so bold as look in't.
    Bless me! A right physician's closet 'tis,   20
    Set round with vials; every one her mark, too.
    Sure, he does practice physic for his own use,

SD *accident* occurrence.
ACT IV, Scene I. **1** *endlessly* for all time. **11** *Stands for* either "stands open
to" (because he will not be deceived into overlooking the truth) or "for me promises"
(because "'Tis a precious craft to play with a false die / Before a cunning gamester.").
16 *precious* hazardous.

Which may be safely called your great man's wisdom.
What manuscript lies here? "The Book of Experiment,
Called Secrets in Nature." So 'tis, 'tis so: 25
"How to know whether a woman be with child or no."
I hope I am not yet. If he should try, though—
Let me see, folio forty-five. Here 'tis,
The leaf tucked down upon't, the place suspicious.
"If you would know whether a woman be with child or not,   30
give her two spoonfuls of the white water in glass C—"
Where's that glass C? Oh, yonder I see't now—
"and if she be with child, she sleeps full twelve hours after; if
not, not."
None of that water comes into my belly;   35
I'll know you from a hundred. I could break you now
Or turn you into milk and so beguile
The master of the mystery, but I'll look to you.
Ha! That which is next is ten times worse:
"How to know whether a woman be a maid or not."   40
If that should be applied, what would become of me?
Belike he has a strong faith of my purity
That never yet made proof, but this he calls
"A merry sleight but true experiment, the author, Antonius
Mizaldus: Give the party you suspect the quantity of a spoonful 45
of the water in the glass M, which upon her that is a maid makes
three several effects: 'twill make her incontinently gape, then fall
into a sudden sneezing, last into a violent laughing; else dull,
heavy, and lumpish."
Where had I been?   50
I fear it: yet 'tis seven hours to bedtime.

Enter DIAPHANTA.

DIAPHANTA   Cuds, madam, are you here?
BEATRICE   [*Aside.*] Seeing that wench now,

---

23 Which ... wisdom because such practice protects him from being poisoned to death.
36 you glass C. **38 look to** look out for. **42 Belike** probably. **44–45 Antonius**
Mizaldus a French scholar (1520–78) who composed several scientific and quasiscientific
treatises, among which was a book like the one Beatrice finds here. It was entitled *De
Arcanis Naturae* (*Concerning the Secrets of Nature*) and though it did not contain explanations
of ways for detecting pregnancy or maidenhood, such tests were actually included in one
of Mizaldus' other books, *Centuriae IX Memorabilium.* **50 Where ... been?** Where
could I have been (if I had not discovered this)? **52 Cuds** an interjection of surprise—
a corruption of "God's."

A trick comes in my mind; 'tis a nice piece
Gold cannot purchase. —I come hither, wench,
To look my lord.

DIAPHANTA   [*Aside.*] Would I had such a cause   55
To look him too.—Why, he's i' th' park, madam.

BEATRICE   There let him be.

DIAPHANTA   Ay, madam, let him compass
Whole parks and forests as great rangers do;
At roosting time a little lodge can hold 'em.
Earth-conquering Alexander, that thought the world   60
Too narrow for him, in the end had but his pit-hole.

BEATRICE   I fear thou art not modest, Diaphanta.

DIAPHANTA   Your thoughts are so unwilling to be known, madam;
'Tis ever the bride's fashion towards bedtime
To set light by her joys as if she owned 'em not.   65

BEATRICE   Her joys? Her fears, thou wouldst say.

DIAPHANTA   Fear of what?

BEATRICE   Art thou a maid and talkst so to a maid?
You leave a blushing business behind,
Beshrew your heart for't.

DIAPHANTA   Do you mean good sooth, madam?

BEATRICE   Well, if I'd thought upon the fear at first,   70
Man should have been unknown.

DIAPHANTA   Is't possible?

BEATRICE   I will give a thousand ducats to that woman
Would try what my fear were and tell me true
Tomorrow when she gets from't: as she likes,
I might perhaps be drawn to't.

DIAPHANTA   Are you in earnest?   75

BEATRICE   Do you get the woman, then challenge me,
And see if I'll fly from't; but I must tell you
This by the way, she must be a true maid
Else there's no trial; my fears are not hers else.

DIAPHANTA   Nay, she that I would put into your hands, madam,   80
Shall be a maid.

BEATRICE   You know I should be shamed else,

53–54 *'tis . . . purchase* It is an unusual girl who cannot be bought with gold.
58 *rangers* wanderers. **59** *roosting time, little lodge,* **61** *pit-hole* Again, obscene
puns are implicit. **65** *owned* The quarto reads "ow'd." **70** *at first* before I made
this marriage. **71** *Is't possible?* Is it possible (that you are afraid of the love act)?
76 *Do you get* just get. **78** *true maid* honest virgin.

Because she lies for me.

DIAPHANTA   'Tis a strange humor;
But are you serious still? Would you resign
Your first night's pleasure and give money too?

BEATRICE   As willingly as live.—[*Aside.*] Alas, the gold   85
Is but a by-bet to wedge in the honor.

DIAPHANTA   I do not know how the world goes abroad
For faith or honesty; there's both required in this.
Madam, what say you to me, and stray no further?
I've a good mind, in troth, to earn your money.   90

BEATRICE   Y'are too quick, I fear, to be a maid.

DIAPHANTA   How? Not a maid? Nay then, you urge me, madam,
Your honorable self is not a truer
With all your fears upon you—

BEATRICE   [*Aside.*] Bad enough then.

DIAPHANTA   Than I with all my lightsome joys about me.   95

BEATRICE   I'm glad to hear't; then you dare put your honesty
Upon an easy trial?

DIAPHANTA   Easy? Anything.

BEATRICE   I'll come to you straight. [*Goes to the closet.*]

DIAPHANTA   [*Aside.*] She will not search me, will she?
Like the forewoman of a female jury?

BEATRICE   Glass M, ay, this is it. —Look, Diaphanta,   100
You take no worse than I do. [*Drinks.*]

DIAPHANTA   And in so doing
I will not question what 'tis, but take it.

[*Drinks.*]

BEATRICE   [*Aside.*] Now if the experiment be true, 'twill praise itself
And give me noble ease. Begins already.

[DIAPHANTA *gapes.*]

There's the first symptom; and what haste it makes   105
To fall into the second, there by this time.

[DIAPHANTA *sneezes.*]

Most admirable secret! On the contrary,

85–86 *the . . . honor* The gold is but a minor issue (a side bet) added to secure the protection of my honor. **89 *what . . . further*** Why not use me and seek no further? **91 *quick*** willing. **92 *urge*** pass judgment too quickly upon. **98–99 *She . . . jury*** This is probably an allusion to the divorce trial in 1613 of the Countess of Essex, whose claim that her marriage had never been consummated was put to the test of a physical examination by a jury of women. **103 *praise itself*** show itself praiseworthy.

It stirs not me a whit, which most concerns it.

DIAPHANTA   Ha, ha, ha.

BEATRICE   [*Aside.*] Just in all things, and in order   110
   As if 'twere circumscribed, one accident
   Gives way unto another.

DIAPHANTA   Ha, ha, ha!

BEATRICE   How now, wench?

DIAPHANTA   Ha, ha, ha! I am so, so light
   At heart—ha, ha, ha!—so pleasurable.
   But one swig more, sweet madam.

BEATRICE   Ay, tomorrow;   115
   We shall have time to sit by't.

DIAPHANTA   Now I'm sad again.

BEATRICE   [*Aside.*] It lays itself so gently, too. —Come, wench,
   Most honest Diaphanta I dare call thee now.

DIAPHANTA   Pray tell me, madam, what trick call you this?

BEATRICE   I'll tell thee all hereafter; we must study   120
   The carriage of this business.

DIAPHANTA   I shall carry't well
   Because I love the burden.

BEATRICE   About midnight
   You must not fail to steal forth gently
   That I may use the place.

DIAPHANTA   Oh, fear not, madam;
   I shall be cool by that time.—The bride's place   125
   And with a thousand ducats! I'm for a justice now,
   I bring a portion with me, I scorn small fools.   *Exeunt.*

ACT IV

Scene 2   *Another room in the castle*

Enter VERMANDERO *and* SERVANT.

VERMANDERO   I tell thee, knave, mine honor is in question,
   A thing till now free from suspicion,

---

108 *which . . . it*   who is to be its most immediate concern.   **111** *circumscribed*
inalterably bound.   **117** *It . . . itself*   Its effects come on and recede.   **121–22** *I . . .*
burden   an intentional double-entendre.   **126–27** *I'm . . . fools*   I'm ready to marry
well now because I shall bring a dowry with me; I shall have no petty fool for a husband.

Nor ever was there cause. Who of my gentlemen
Are absent?
Tell me and truly, how many and who.   5
SERVANT   Antonio, sir, and Franciscus.
VERMANDERO   When did they leave the castle?
SERVANT   Some ten days since, sir; the one intending to Briamata,
   th'other for Valencia.
VERMANDERO   The time accuses 'em. A charge of murder   10
   Is brought within my castle gate—Piracquo's murder;
   I dare not answer faithfully their absence.
   A strict command of apprehension
   Shall pursue 'em suddenly and either wipe
   The stain off clear or openly discover it.   15
   Provide me wingèd warrants for the purpose.
   See, I am set on again.   *Exit* SERVANT.

   Enter TOMAZO.

TOMAZO   I claim a brother of you.
VERMANDERO   Y'are too hot,
   Seek him not here.
TOMAZO   Yes, 'mongst your dearest bloods,
   If my peace find no fairer satisfaction;   20
   This is the place must yield account for him,
   For here I left him, and the hasty tie
   Of this snatched marriage gives strong testimony
   Of his most certain ruin.
VERMANDERO   Certain falsehood!
   This is the place indeed; his breach of faith   25
   Has too much marred both my abusèd love,
   The honorable love I reserved for him,
   And mocked my daughter's joy; the prepared morning
   Blushed at his infidelity; he left
   Contempt and scorn to throw upon those friends   30
   Whose belief hurt 'em. Oh, 'twas most ignoble
   To take his flight so unexpectedly
   And throw such public wrongs on those that loved him.
TOMAZO   Then this is all your answer?
VERMANDERO   'Tis too fair

🝊 **ACT IV, Scene 2.   8 *Briamata*** Vermandero's country estate, located about twenty
miles from his castle.   **18 *I . . . you*** You are responsible for the death of my brother.

For one of his alliance, and I warn you   35
That this place no more see you.   *Exit.*
TOMAZO   The best is
There is more ground to meet a man's revenge on.

Enter DE FLORES.

Honest De Flores.
DE FLORES   That's my name indeed.
Saw you the bride? Good sweet sir, which way took she?
TOMAZO   I have blessed mine eyes from seeing such a false one.   40
DE FLORES   [*Aside.*] I'd fain get off; this man's not for my company;
I smell his brother's blood when I come near him.
TOMAZO   Come hither, kind and true one, I remember
My brother loved thee well.
DE FLORES   Oh, purely, dear sir.—
[*Aside.*] Methinks I am now again a-killing on him,   45
He brings it so fresh to me.
TOMAZO   Thou canst guess, sirrah,
One honest friend has an instinct of jealousy
At some foul guilty person.
DE FLORES   'La sir, I am so charitable, I think none
Worse than myself.—You did not see the bride, then?   50
TOMAZO   I prithee name her not. Is she not wicked?
DE FLORES   No, no; a pretty, easy, round-packed sinner
As your most ladies are, else you might think
I flattered her; but, sir, at no hand wicked
Till th'are so old their sins and vices meet   55
And they salute witches. I am called, I think sir.—
[*Aside.*] His company ev'n o'erlays my conscience.   *Exit.*
TOMAZO   That De Flores has a wondrous honest heart;
He'll bring it out in time, I'm assured on't.
Oh, here's the glorious master of the day's joy;   60

---

52 round-packed plump. **55 sins and vices** Most modern editors, arguing that the
compositor misread his copy text, emend this phrase to "chins and noses," but the original
reading makes perfectly good sense once the difference between a sin and a vice is
recognized. A vice is a defect in moral conduct, the kind of frailty to which all human
beings are subject; a sin, on the other hand, is a transgression against divine law, a grievous
moral offense. De Flores' argument is thus that women become more and more corrupt
as they grow older. So long do they satisfy the demands of their vices that these vices
eventually ripen into sins. When a woman grows old the desperation born of age combines
itself with the corruption born of habit to produce depravity: then sins and vices meet.
60 glorious . . . joy the bridegroom.

'Twill not be long till he and I do reckon.

Enter ALSEMERO.

Sir.

ALSEMERO   You are most welcome.

TOMAZO   You may call that word back;
    I do not think I am, nor wish to be.

ALSEMERO   'Tis strange you found the way to this house then.

TOMAZO   Would I'd ne'er known the cause! I'm none of those, sir,   65
    That come to give you joy and swill your wine;
    'Tis a more precious liquor that must lay
    The fiery thirst I bring.

ALSEMERO   Your words and you
    Appear to me great strangers.

TOMAZO   Time and our swords
    May make us more acquainted. This the business: 70
    I should have a brother in your place;
    How treachery and malice have disposed of him
    I'm bound to inquire of him which holds his right,
    Which never could come fairly.

ALSEMERO   You must look
    To answer for that word, sir.

TOMAZO   Fear you not;   75
    I'll have it ready drawn at our next meeting.
    Keep your day solemn; farewell, I disturb it not.
    I'll bear the smart with patience for a time.   *Exit.*

ALSEMERO   'Tis somewhat ominous, this: a quarrel entered
    Upon this day; my innocence relieves me,   80

Enter JASPERINO.

    I should be wondrous sad else.—Jasperino,
    I have news to tell thee, strange news.

JASPERINO   I ha' some too,
    I think as strange as yours; would I might keep
    Mine, so my faith and friendship might be kept in't.
    Faith, sir, dispense a little with my zeal   85
    And let it cool in this.

ALSEMERO   This puts me on

---

76 *it* his sword. **85–86** *dispense . . . this* Let me be a little less zealous in your service, that I may hold back this information. **86** *This . . . on* Your hesitancy has only intensified my interest.

And blames thee for thy slowness.

JASPERINO   All may prove nothing,
Only a friendly fear that leaped from me, sir.

ALSEMERO   No question it may prove nothing; let's partake it, though.

JASPERINO   'Twas Diaphanta's chance (for to that wench   90
I pretend honest love, and she deserves it)
To leave me in a back part of the house,
A place we chose for private conference;
She was no sooner gone, but instantly
I heard your bride's voice in the next room to me   95
And, lending more attention, found De Flores
Louder than she.

ALSEMERO   De Flores? Thou art out now.

JASPERINO   You'll tell me more anon.

ALSEMERO   Still I'll prevent thee:
The very sight of him is poison to her.

JASPERINO   That made me stagger too, but Diaphanta   100
At her return confirmed it.

ALSEMERO   Diaphanta!

JASPERINO   Then fell we both to listen, and words passed
Like those that challenge interest in a woman.

ALSEMERO   Peace, quench thy zeal; 'tis dangerous to thy bosom.

JASPERINO   Then truth is full of peril.

ALSEMERO   Such truths are;   105
Oh, were she the sole glory of the earth,
Had eyes that could shoot fire into kings' breasts,
And touched, she sleeps not here; yet I have time,
Though night be near, to be resolved hereof,
And prithee do not weigh me by my passions.   110

JASPERINO   I never weighed friend so.

ALSEMERO   Done charitably.
That key will lead thee to a pretty secret

[*Gives key.*]

By a Chaldean taught me, and I've made
My study upon some. Bring from my closet
A glass inscribed there with the letter M,   115

---

89 though The quarto reads "thou." **91 pretend** present. **97 out** mistaken. **103 Like
. . . woman** as if he were claiming her. **108 touched** thus tainted. **109 to . . .
hereof** to find out for certain about this. **113 Chaldean** a term loosely used to
describe an astrologer or magician because of the extensive astronomical knowledge of the
ancient Chaldeans.

And question not my purpose.
JASPERINO   It shall be done, sir.   *Exit.*
ALSEMERO   How can this hang together? Not an hour since
   Her woman came pleading her lady's fears,
   Delivered her for the most timorous virgin
   That ever shrunk at man's name, and so modest   120
   She charged her weep out her request to me
   That she might come obscurely to my bosom.

Enter BEATRICE.

BEATRICE   [*Aside.*] All things go well. My woman's preparing yonder
   For her sweet voyage which grieves me to lose;
   Necessity compels it, I lose all else.   125
ALSEMERO   [*Aside.*] Push, modesty's shrine is set in yonder forehead;
   I cannot be too sure, though. —My Joanna.
BEATRICE   Sir, I was bold to weep a message to you;
   Pardon my modest fears.
ALSEMERO   [*Aside.*] The dove's not meeker;
   She's abused questionless.— *Enter* JASPERINO [*with glass*].
                 Oh, are you come, sir?   130
BEATRICE   [*Aside.*] The glass, upon my life. I see the letter.
JASPERINO   Sir, this is M.
ALSEMERO   'Tis it.
BEATRICE   [*Aside.*] I am suspected.
ALSEMERO   How fitly our bride comes to partake with us.
BEATRICE   What is't, my lord?
ALSEMERO   No hurt.
BEATRICE   Sir, pardon me,
   I seldom taste of any composition.   135
ALSEMERO   But this upon my warrant you shall venture on.
BEATRICE   I fear 'twill make me ill. [*Drinks.*]
ALSEMERO   Heaven forbid that.
BEATRICE   [*Aside.*] I'm put now to my cunning; th'effects I know,
   If I can now but feign 'em handsomely.
ALSEMERO   [*To* JASPERINO.] It has that secret virtue it ne'er missed, sir,   140
   Upon a virgin.
JASPERINO   Treble qualited?

   [BEATRICE *gapes, then sneezes.*]

ALSEMERO   [*Aside.*] By all that's virtuous! It takes there, proceeds.

---

119 *Delivered her for*   described her as.   **122** *obscurely*   in darkness.   **125** *else*   otherwise.   **141** *Treble qualited*   completely reliable.

JASPERINO   [*Aside.*] This is the strangest trick to know a maid by.
BEATRICE   Ha, ha, ha,
    You have given me joy of heart to drink, my lord.   145
ALSEMERO   No, thou hast given me such joy of heart
    That never can be blasted.
BEATRICE   What's the matter, sir?
ALSEMERO   [*Aside.*] See now, 'tis settled in a melancholy
    Keeps both the time and method.—My Joanna,
    Chaste as the breath of heaven or morning's womb   150
    That brings the day forth, thus my love encloses thee.
                    [*He embraces her.*] *Exeunt.*

ACT IV
Scene 3   ALIBIUS' *madhouse*

Enter ISABELLA *and* LOLLIO.

ISABELLA   Oh heaven! Is this the waiting moon?
    Does love turn fool, run mad, and all at once?
    Sirrah, here's a madman, akin to the fool, too,
    A lunatic lover.
LOLLIO   No, no, not he I brought the letter from?   5
ISABELLA   Compare his inside with his out and tell me.
LOLLIO   The out's mad, I'm sure of that, I had a taste on't. [*Reads
    letter.*] "To the bright Andromeda, chief chambermaid to the
    knight of the sun, at the sign of Scorpio in the middle region,
    sent by the bellows-mender of Aeolus. Pay the post." This is   10
    stark madness.

---

149 *Keeps* The quarto reads "keep." ***Keeps . . . method*** That is the natural con-
cluding effect of the drink.
⚸ ACT IV, Scene 3.   1 *waiting* full—when the moon waits momentarily between
waxing and waning and when madmen were thought to be most crazy. **4 *lunatic
lover*** Franciscus. **7 *I . . . on't*** when Franciscus beat Lollio (III.3.84). **8 *Andromeda***
In classical mythology, Andromeda, daughter of Cepheus, King of the Ethiopians, was
rescued from imprisonment by Perseus. Franciscus' implication here is that he similarly
has come to rescue Isabella from her captivity. **9 *the sign . . . region*** Because
Scorpio was the sign of the zodiac thought to govern the private parts of the body,
"middle region" here is an obscene pun. **10 *Aeolus*** the god of the winds. ***post*** letter-
bearer, but another double-entendre is implicit.

ISABELLA   Now mark the inside. [*Takes letter and reads.*] "Sweet lady,
    having now cast off this counterfeit cover of a madman, I appear
    to your best judgment a true and faithful lover of your beauty."
LOLLIO   He is mad still.   15
ISABELLA   [*Reads.*] "If any fault you find, chide those perfections in
    you which have made me imperfect; 'tis the same sun that
    causeth to grow and enforceth to wither—"
LOLLIO   Oh, rogue!
ISABELLA   [*Reads.*] "Shapes and transshapes, destroys and builds   20
    again. I come in winter to you dismantled of my proper orna-
    ments; by the sweet splendor of your cheerful smiles, I spring
    and live a lover."
LOLLIO   Mad rascal still.
ISABELLA   [*Reads.*] "Tread him not underfoot, that shall appear an   25
    honor to your bounties. I remain, mad till I speak with you
    from whom I expect my cure, yours all, or one beside himself,
    Franciscus."
LOLLIO   You are like to have a fine time on't; my master and I may
    give over our professions: I do not think but you can cure fools   30
    and madmen faster than we, with little pains too.
ISABELLA   Very likely.
LOLLIO   One thing I must tell you, mistress: you perceive that I am
    privy to your skill; if I find you minister once and set up the
    trade, I put in for my thirds, I shall be mad or fool else.   35
ISABELLA   The first place is thine, believe it, Lollio,
    If I do fall—
LOLLIO   I fall upon you.
ISABELLA   So.
LOLLIO   Well, I stand to my venture.   40
ISABELLA   But thy counsel now. How shall I deal with 'em?
LOLLIO   Why, do you mean to deal with 'em?
ISABELLA   Nay, the fair understanding, how to use 'em.
LOLLIO   Abuse 'em! That's the way to mad the fool and make a fool
    of the madman, and then you use 'em kindly.   45
ISABELLA   'Tis easy, I'll practice; do thou observe it.
    The key of thy wardrobe.

---

29 *on't* with him; but there is again a sexual innuendo.   **34–35** *minister . . . trade*
cure these madmen and fools by committing adultery with them.   **35** *my thirds* Her
lover and her husband receive the other two-thirds.   **43** *Nay . . . understanding* Nay,
understand my speeches fairly as they are spoken.

LOLLIO   There; fit yourself for 'em, and I'll fit 'em both for you.
        [*Gives her the key.*]

ISABELLA   Take thou no further notice than the outside.   *Exit.*
LOLLIO   Not an inch; I'll put you to the inside.   50

        Enter ALIBIUS.

ALIBIUS   Lollio, art there? Will all be perfect, thinkst thou?
        Tomorrow night, as if to close up the solemnity,
        Vermandero expects us.
LOLLIO   I mistrust the madmen most; the fools will do well enough,
        I have taken pains with them.   55
ALIBIUS   Tush, they cannot miss; the more absurdity,
        The more commends it,—so no rough behaviors
        Affright the ladies; they are nice things, thou knowst.
LOLLIO   You need not fear, sir; so long as we are there with our
        commanding pizzles, they'll be as tame as the ladies themselves.   60
ALIBIUS   I will see them once more rehearse before they go.
LOLLIO   I was about it, sir; look you to the madmen's morris, and
        let me alone with the other. There is one or two that I mistrust
        their fooling; I'll instruct them, and then they shall rehearse the
        whole measure.   65
ALIBIUS   Do so; I'll see the music prepared. But, Lollio,
        By the way, how does my wife brook her restraint?
        Does she not grudge at it?
LOLLIO   So, so; she takes some pleasure in the house; she would
        abroad, else. You must allow her a little more length; she's kept   70
        too short.
ALIBIUS   She shall along to Vermandero's with us;
        That will serve her for a month's liberty.
LOLLIO   What's that on your face, sir?
ALIBIUS   Where, Lollio? I see nothing.   75
LOLLIO   Cry you mercy, sir, 'tis your nose; it showed like the trunk
        of a young elephant.
ALIBIUS   Away, rascal; I'll prepare the music, Lollio.   *Exit* ALIBIUS.
LOLLIO   Do, sir, and I'll dance the whilst. —Tony, where art thou,
        Tony?   80

---

48 *fit yourself* make yourself ready.   **50 *I'll . . . inside*** I'll leave taking care of the
inside to you.   **58 *nice*** modest.   **60 *pizzle*** the penis of an animal, often a bull, dried
and used as a whip.   **62 *morris*** a country dance in which the participants usually dressed
as characters from the Robin Hood legend.   **65 *measure*** dance.   **76–77 *it . . . elephant***
A long nose, like a set of horns, was traditionally thought to identify a cuckold.

Enter ANTONIO.

ANTONIO   Here, cousin: where art thou?

LOLLIO   Come, Tony, the footmanship I taught you.

ANTONIO   I had rather ride, cousin.

LOLLIO   Ay, a whip take you, but I'll keep you out. Vault in; look
you, Tony, fa, la la la la.   85

[*Dances.*]

ANTONIO   Fa, la la la la.

[*Dances.*]

LOLLIO   There, an honor.

ANTONIO   Is this an honor, coz?

[*Bows.*]

LOLLIO   Yes, and it please your worship.

ANTONIO   Does honor bend in the hams, coz?   90

LOLLIO   Marry does it, as low as worship, squireship, nay, yeomanry
itself sometimes, from whence it first stiffened. There rise a
caper.

ANTONIO   Caper after an honor, coz?

LOLLIO   Very proper, for honor is but a caper, rises as fast and high,   95
has a knee or two, and falls to th' ground again. You can remember
your figure, Tony?   *Exit.*

ANTONIO   Yes, cousin; when I see thy figure, I can remember mine.

[*Dances.*] *Enter* ISABELLA [*dressed as a madwoman*].

ISABELLA   Hey, how he treads the air! Shoo, shoo, t'other way! He
burns his wings else; here's wax enough below, Icarus, more   100
than will be canceled these eighteen moons.

[ANTONIO *falls.*]

He's down, he's down. What a terrible fall he had!
Stand up, thou son of Cretan Daedalus,

90–96 Does...again   Sexual innuendoes are, again, implicit in these speeches.   **99 how
he**   The quarto reads "how she."   **99–101 He...moons**   In her pretended raving, Isabella
confuses the wax used in Icarus' wings with the wax in the seals of legal documents and,
specifically, with the seal on her marriage contract signed eighteen months before.
103 thou...Daedalus   Icarus was the son of a legendary Athenian craftsman who, when
he was in Crete, constructed the labyrinth for Minos. Later imprisoned in the maze with
his son Icarus, he made wings out of wax and feathers so that they both could fly away.
But in the course of the escape, the young boy, delighted with his new-found power of
flight, flew so near to the sun that the wax wings melted, and he hurtled into the Icarian
Sea where he drowned.

And let us tread the lower labyrinth;
I'll bring thee to the clue.   105

[ANTONIO *rises.*]

ANTONIO   Prithee, coz, let me alone.
ISABELLA   Art thou not drowned?
    About thy head I saw a heap of clouds,
    Wrapped like a Turkish turban; on thy back
    A crooked, chameleon-colored rainbow hung   110
    Like a tiara down unto thy hams.
    Let me suck out those billows in thy belly;
    Hark how they roar and rumble in the straits.
    Bless thee from the pirates.
ANTONIO   Pox upon you; let me alone.   115
ISABELLA   Why shouldst thou mount so high as Mercury
    Unless thou hadst reversion of his place?
    Stay in the moon with me, Endymion,
    And we will rule these wild rebellious waves
    That would have drowned my love.   120
ANTONIO   I'll kick thee if again thou touch me,
    Thou wild, unshapen antic; I am no fool,
    You bedlam.
ISABELLA   But you are as sure as I am, mad.
    Have I put on this habit of a frantic
    With love as full of fury to beguile   125
    The nimble eye of watchful jealousy,
    And am I thus rewarded?
ANTONIO   Ha! Dearest beauty!
ISABELLA   No, I have no beauty now,
    Nor never had, but what was in my garments.
    You a quick-sighted lover? Come not near me.   130
    Keep your caparisons, y'are aptly clad;
    I came a feigner to return stark mad.   *Exit.*

Enter LOLLIO.

ANTONIO   Stay, or I shall change condition

---

105 *clue*   thread to guide one out of the labyrinth.   **113** *straits*   The quarto reads
"streets."   **116** *Mercury*   the winged messenger of the gods.   **117** *Unless . . . place*
unless you were to inherit his position.   **118** *Endymion*   a beautiful young man loved
by Selene, the moon goddess, who put him into a perpetual sleep so that she could descend
every night and embrace him. Here, and in the succeeding lines, Isabella likens herself to
Selene.   **122** *unshapen*   disordered.   **130** *quick-sighted*   sharp-seeing.   **131** *caparisons*
garments.

And become as you are.

LOLLIO   Why, Tony, whither now? Why, fool—   135

ANTONIO   Whose fool, usher of idiots? You coxcomb,
    I have fooled too much.

LOLLIO   You were best be mad another while then.

ANTONIO   So I am, stark mad, I have cause enough;
    And I could throw the full effects on thee   140
    And beat thee like a fury.

LOLLIO   Do not, do not; I shall not forbear the gentleman under the
fool, if you do. Alas, I saw through your fox-skin before now.
Come, I can give you comfort: my mistress loves you, and
there is as arrant a madman i' th' house as you are a fool, your   145
rival, whom she loves not. If after the masque we can rid her
of him, you earn her love, she says, and the fool shall ride her.

ANTONIO   May I believe thee?

LOLLIO   Yes, or you may choose whether you will or no.

ANTONIO   She's eased of him; I have a good quarrel on't.   150

LOLLIO   Well, keep your old station yet, and be quiet.

ANTONIO   Tell her I will deserve her love.   [*Exit.*]

LOLLIO   And you are like to have your desire.

Enter FRANCISCUS.

FRANCISCUS   [*Sings.*] Down, down, down a-down a-down, and then
with a horse-trick   155
    To kick Latona's forehead and break her bowstring.

LOLLIO   This is t'other counterfeit; I'll put him out of his humor.
[*Reads.*] "Sweet lady, having now cast off this counterfeit cover
of a madman, I appear to your best judgment a true and faithful
lover of your beauty."—This is pretty well for a madman.   160

FRANCISCUS   Ha! What's that?

LOLLIO   [*Reads.*] "Chide those perfections in you which have made me
imperfect."

FRANCISCUS   I am discovered to the fool.

LOLLIO   I hope to discover the fool in you ere I have done with   165
you.—[*Reads.*] "Yours all, or one beside himself, Franciscus."—
This madman will mend sure.

---

136 usher both "attendant" and "leader."   **138 another while** for a while.   **142 forbear** pay attention to.   **143 fox-skin** covering for sly pursuits.   **150 eased of** both
"freed of his presence" and "eased of the burden of bearing his weight (in sexual intercourse)."   **155 horse-trick** caper.   **156 Latona** probably Diana, the moon goddess,
who being a huntress carried a bow.   **157 his humor** his customary way of acting.
164 discovered unmasked.

FRANCISCUS   What do you read, sirrah?

LOLLIO   Your destiny, sir; you'll be hanged for this trick and another
that I know.   170

FRANCISCUS   Art thou of counsel with thy mistress?

LOLLIO   Next her apron strings.

FRANCISCUS   Give me thy hand.

LOLLIO   Stay, let me put yours in my pocket first. [*Puts up letter.*]
Your hand is true, is it not? It will not pick? I partly fear it,   175
because I think it does lie.

FRANCISCUS   Not in a syllable.

LOLLIO   So, if you love my mistress so well as you have handled the
matter here, you are like to be cured of your madness.

FRANCISCUS   And none but she can cure it.   180

LOLLIO   Well, I'll give you over then, and she shall cast your water
next.

FRANCISCUS   Take for thy pains past.

[*Gives money.*]

LOLLIO   I shall deserve more, sir, I hope. My mistress loves you, but
must have some proof of your love to her.   185

FRANCISCUS   There I meet my wishes.

LOLLIO   That will not serve: you must meet her enemy and yours.

FRANCISCUS   He's dead already!

LOLLIO   Will you tell me that, and I parted but now with him?

FRANCISCUS   Show me the man.   190

LOLLIO   Ay, that's a right course now: see him before you kill him
in any case; and yet it needs not go so far neither; 'tis but a fool
that haunts the house and my mistress in the shape of an idiot.
Bang but his fool's coat well-favoredly, and 'tis well.

FRANCISCUS   Soundly, soundly.   195

LOLLIO   Only reserve him till the masque be past, and if you find
him not now in the dance yourself, I'll show you. In, in! My
master!

FRANCISCUS   He handles him like a feather. Hey!   [*Exit.*]

Enter ALIBIUS.

ALIBIUS   Well said; in a readiness, Lollio?   200

LOLLIO   Yes, sir.

ALIBIUS   Away then, and guide them in, Lollio;

---

174 *yours* your hand (i.e. his letter). **181** *cast . . . water* examine your urine.
188 *He's . . . already* His doom is sealed. **194** *Bang . . . coat* beat him. **200** *Well
. . . readiness* Well done. Is all in readiness (for the dance)?

Entreat your mistress to see this sight.
Hark, is there not one incurable fool
That might be begged? I have friends.   205
LOLLIO   I have him for you, one that shall deserve it too.
ALIBIUS   Good boy, Lollio.   [*Exit* LOLLIO.]

[*Enter* ISABELLA; *then* LOLLIO *with* MADMEN *and* FOOLS.] *The* MADMEN
and FOOLS *dance.*

'Tis perfect; well, fit but once these strains,
We shall have coin and credit for our pains.   *Exeunt.*

ACT V

⟨Scene I   VERMANDERO'*s castle*⟩.

Enter BEATRICE. *A clock strikes one.*

BEATRICE   One struck, and yet she lies by't. Oh, my fears!
This strumpet serves her own ends, 'tis apparent now,
Devours the pleasure with a greedy appetite
And never minds my honor or my peace,
Makes havoc of my right; but she pays dearly for't: 5
No trusting of her life with such a secret,
That cannot rule her blood to keep her promise.
Beside, I have some suspicion of her faith to me
Because I was suspected of my lord,
And it must come from her. Hark, by my horrors,   10
Another clock strikes two.

Strikes two. Enter DE FLORES.

DE FLORES   Pist, where are you?
BEATRICE   De Flores?
DE FLORES   Ay; is she not come from him yet?
BEATRICE   As I am a living soul, not.
DE FLORES   Sure the devil
Hath sowed his itch within her; who'd trust
A waiting-woman?
BEATRICE   I must trust somebody.   15

---

205 *That . . . begged* to whom I might become the guardian (and mulct).   **209** *fit*
move in harmony with.

DE FLORES   Push, they are termagants.
     Especially when they fall upon their masters
     And have their ladies' first-fruits; th'are mad whelps;
     You cannot stave 'em off from game royal then.
     You are so harsh and hardy, ask no counsel;   20
     And I could have helped you to an apothecary's daughter
     Would have fall'n off before eleven and thanked you too.
BEATRICE   Oh me, not yet? This whore forgets herself.
DE FLORES   The rascal fares so well; look, y'are undone,
     The day-star, by this hand. See Phosphorus plain yonder.   25
BEATRICE   Advise me now to fall upon some ruin;
     There is no counsel safe else.
DE FLORES   Peace; I ha't now;
     For we must force a rising; there's no remedy.
BEATRICE   How? Take heed of that.
DE FLORES   Tush, be you quiet
     Or else give over all.
BEATRICE   Prithee, I ha' done then.   30
DE FLORES   This is my reach: I'll set some part afire
     Of Diaphanta's chamber.
BEATRICE   How? Fire, sir?
     That may endanger the whole house.
DE FLORES   You talk of danger when your fame's on fire?
BEATRICE   That's true; do what thou wilt now.
DE FLORES   Push, I aim   35
     At a most rich success, strikes all dead sure.
     The chimney being afire and some light parcels
     Of the least danger in her chamber only,
     If Diaphanta should be met by chance then
     Far from her lodging, which is now suspicious,   40
     It would be thought her fears and affrights then
     Drove her to seek for succor; if not seen
     Or met at all, as that's the likeliest,
     For her own shame she'll hasten towards her lodging.
     I will be ready with a piece high-charged   45
     As 'twere to cleanse the chimney. There, 'tis proper now;

🦋 **ACT V, Scene 1.**   **16** *termagants* shrews.   **19** *game royal* game reserved for the royal hunt.   **20** *You . . . counsel* You are rash and foolhardy, acting without advice. **25** *Phosphorus* the morning star. The quarto reads "Bosphorus."   **31** *reach* plan. **34** *fame* reputation.   **45** *piece* gun.

But she shall be the mark.

BEATRICE   I'm forced to love thee now,
    'Cause thou provid'st so carefully for my honor.

DE FLORES 'Slid, it concerns the safety of us both,
    Our pleasure and continuance.

BEATRICE   One word now, prithee;   50
    How for the servants?

DE FLORES   I'll dispatch them:
    Some one way, some another, in the hurry,
    For buckets, hooks, ladders. Fear not you.
    The deed shall find its time,—and I've thought since
    Upon a safe conveyance for the body too.   55
    How this fire purifies wit! Watch you your minute.

BEATRICE Fear keeps my soul upon't; I cannot stray from't.

    Enter ALONZO'*s* GHOST.

DE FLORES Ha! What art thou that tak'st away the light
    'Twixt that star and me? I dread thee not.
    'Twas but a mist of conscience; all's clear again.   *Exit.*   60

BEATRICE Who's that, De Flores? Bless me! It slides by;
                                   [*Exit* GHOST.]
    Some ill thing haunts the house; 't has left behind it
    A shivering sweat upon me. I'm afraid now.
    This night hath been so tedious. Oh, this strumpet!
    Had she a thousand lives, he should not leave her   65
    Till he had destroyed the last! List, oh my terrors,
    Three struck by St. Sebastian's.

    Strikes three.

[DE FLORES] *Within.*   Fire, fire, fire!

BEATRICE Already! How rare is that man's speed!
    How heartily he serves me! His face loathes one,
    But look upon his care, who would not love him?   70
    The east is not more beauteous than his service.

[DE FLORES] *Within.* Fire, fire, fire.

    Enter DE FLORES. SERVANTS *pass over, ring a bell.*

DE FLORES Away, dispatch! hooks, buckets, ladders! that's well said.
    The fire bell rings, the chimney works; my charge;

---

49 'Slid an interjection, contracted from "By God's eyelid!" **56 *How . . . wit*** How
the fire of lust purifies the imagination! **SD *Strikes three*** The quarto reads "Struck
three o'clock." **69 *loathes one*** one looks at with loathing. **70 *care*** service.

The piece is ready. *Exit.*

BEATRICE   Here's a man worth loving.   75

Enter DIAPHANTA.

Oh, y'are a jewel.

DIAPHANTA   Pardon frailty, madam;
In troth I was so well, I e'en forgot myself.

BEATRICE   Y' have made trim work.

DIAPHANTA   What?

BEATRICE   Hie quickly to your chamber,
Your reward follows you.

DIAPHANTA   I never made
So sweet a bargain. *Exit.*

Enter ALSEMERO.

ALSEMERO   Oh, my dear Joanna;   80
Alas, art thou risen too? I was coming,
My absolute treasure—

BEATRICE   When I missed you,
I could not choose but follow.

ALSEMERO   Th'art all sweetness.
The fire is not so dangerous.

BEATRICE   Think you so, sir?

ALSEMERO   I prithee, tremble not; believe me, 'tis not.   85

Enter VERMANDERO, JASPERINO.

VERMANDERO   Oh, bless my house and me!

ALSEMERO   My lord your father.

Enter DE FLORES *with a piece.*

VERMANDERO   Knave, whither goes that piece?

DE FLORES   To scour the chimney.
                                                                Exit.

VERMANDERO   Oh, well said, well said;
That fellow's good on all occasions.

BEATRICE   A wondrous necessary man, my lord.   90

VERMANDERO   He hath a ready wit; he's worth 'em all, sir.
Dog at a house of fire; I ha' seen him singed ere now.

The piece goes off.

Ha, there he goes.

BEATRICE   'Tis done.

ALSEMERO   Come, sweet, to bed now;

88 *well said*   good idea.   **92** *Dog at*   He is quick (like a dog in the chase) at.

Alas, thou wilt get cold.

BEATRICE   Alas, the fear keeps that out;
My heart will find no quiet till I hear   95
How Diaphanta, my poor woman, fares;
It is her chamber, sir, her lodging chamber.

VERMANDERO   How should the fire come there?

BEATRICE   As good a soul as ever lady countenanced,
But in her chamber negligent and heavy.   100
She 'scap'd a mine twice.

VERMANDERO   Twice?

BEATRICE   Strangely twice, sir.

VERMANDERO   Those sleepy sluts are dangerous in a house,
And they be ne'er so good.

Enter DE FLORES.

DE FLORES   Oh, poor virginity!
Thou hast paid dearly for't.

VERMANDERO   Bless us! What's that?

DE FLORES   A thing you all knew once; Diaphanta's burnt.   105

BEATRICE   My woman, oh, my woman!

DE FLORES   Now the flames are
Greedy of her; burnt, burnt, burnt to death, sir.

BEATRICE   Oh, my presaging soul!

ALSEMERO   Not a tear more,
I charge you by the last embrace I gave you
In bed before this raised us.

BEATRICE   Now you tie me;   110
Were it my sister now, she gets no more.

Enter SERVANT.

VERMANDERO   How now?

SERVANT   All danger's past; you may now take
Your rests, my lords; the fire is throughly quenched.
Ah, poor gentlewoman, how soon was she stifled!

BEATRICE   De Flores, what is left of her inter,   115

---

101 *She . . . twice* Twice she narrowly escaped an accident.   **103** *And . . . good* even
if they are valuable in other respects.   **105** *A . . . once* "It is what you feared." It is
possible, though, to find in De Flores' words a cynical comment on the corruption of the
times. He may interpret Vermandero's question as a reference to the closest substantive
noun, "virginity," and then his answer would imply that sexual innocence was something
lost long ago, a thing known once but not any longer.   **108** *presaging* prophetic.
111 *no more* no more tears.   **113** *throughly* completely.

And we as mourners all will follow her.
I will entreat that honor to my servant
E'en of my lord himself.

ALSEMERO   Command it, sweetness.

BEATRICE   Which of you spied the fire first?

DE FLORES   'Twas I, madam.

BEATRICE   And took such pains in't too? A double goodness!   120
'Twere well he were rewarded.

VERMANDERO   He shall be;
De Flores, call upon me.

ALSEMERO   And upon me, sir.

                              Exeunt [*all but* DE FLORES].

DE FLORES   Rewarded? Precious, here's a trick beyond me;
I see in all bouts both of sport and wit
Always a woman strives for the last hit.   *Exit.*   125

ACT V

Scene 2   VERMANDERO's *castle*

Enter TOMAZO.

TOMAZO   I cannot taste the benefits of life
With the same relish I was wont to do.
Man I grow weary of, and hold his fellowship
A treacherous bloody friendship; and because
I am ignorant in whom my wrath should settle,   5
I must think all men villains, and the next
I meet, whoe'er he be, the murderer
Of my most worthy brother. Ha! What's he?

Enter DE FLORES, *passes over the stage.*

Oh, the fellow that some call honest De Flores.
But methinks honesty was hard bested   10
To come there for a lodging—as if a queen
Should make her palace of a pest-house.

117–18 *I . . . himself*   I will entreat even my husband to offer this honor to my dead
servant.
 ⚑ ACT V, Scene 2.   10 *bested*   pressed.

I find a contrariety in nature
Betwixt that face and me: the least occasion
Would give me game upon him; yet he's so foul,   15
One would scarce touch him with a sword he loved
And made account of. So most deadly venemous,
He would go near to poison any weapon
That should draw blood on him; one must resolve
Never to use that sword again in fight   20
In way of honest manhood that strikes him.
Some river must devour't, 'twere not fit
That any man should find it.—What, again?

Enter DE FLORES.

He walks o' purpose by, sure, to choke me up,
To infect my blood.
DE FLORES   My worthy noble lord.   25
TOMAZO   Dost offer to come near and breathe upon me?

[*Strikes him.*]

DE FLORES   A blow. [*Draws his sword.*]
TOMAZO   Yea; are you so prepared?
I'll rather like a soldier die by th' sword
Than like a politician by thy poison.
DE FLORES   Hold, my lord, as you are honorable.   30
TOMAZO   All slaves that kill by poison are still cowards.
DE FLORES   [*Aside.*] I cannot strike: I see his brother's wounds
Fresh bleeding in his eye as in a crystal.—
I will not question this, I know y'are noble;
I take my injury with thanks given, sir,   35
Like a wise lawyer; and as a favor,
Will wear it for the worthy hand that gave it.—
[*Aside.*] Why this from him that yesterday appeared
So strangely loving to me?
Oh, but instinct is of a subtler strain.   40
Guilt must not walk so near his lodge again;
He came near me now.   *Exit.*
TOMAZO   All league with mankind I renounce forever,
Till I find this murderer. Not so much

---

15 *give . . . upon* arouse me to challenge. **21** *In . . . manhood* against any honest man. **29** *politician* schemer. **33** *crystal* crystal ball. **36** *a . . . lawyer* because such a lawyer never does anything rash. **42** *came . . . me* nearly struck through my false front.

As common courtesy but I'll lock up,   45
For in the state of ignorance I live in
A brother may salute his brother's murderer
And wish good speed to th' villain in a greeting.

Enter VERMANDERO, ALIBIUS, *and* ISABELLA.

VERMANDERO   Noble Piracquo.
TOMAZO   Pray keep on your way, sir;
   I've nothing to say to you.
VERMANDERO   Comforts bless you, sir.   50
TOMAZO   I have forsworn compliment; in troth I have, sir;
   As you are merely man, I have not left
   A good wish for you, nor any here.
VERMANDERO   Unless you be so far in love with grief
   You will not part from't upon any terms,   55
   We bring that news will make a welcome for us.
TOMAZO   What news can that be?
VERMANDERO   Throw no scornful smile
   Upon the zeal I bring you; 'tis worth more, sir.
   Two of the chiefest men I kept about me
   I hide not from the law or your just vengeance.   60
TOMAZO   Ha!
VERMANDERO   To give your peace more ample satisfaction,
   Thank these discoverers.
TOMAZO   If you bring that calm,
   Name but the manner I shall ask forgiveness in
   For that contemptuous smile upon you: 65
   I'll perfect it with reverence that belongs
   Unto a sacred altar. [*Kneels.*]
VERMANDERO   Good sir, rise,
   [*Raises him.*]
   Why, now you overdo as much o' this hand
   As you fell short o' t'other. Speak, Alibius.
ALIBIUS   'Twas my wife's fortune, as she is most lucky   70
   At a discovery, to find out lately
   Within our hospital of fools and madmen
   Two counterfeits slipped into these disguises;
   Their names, Franciscus and Antonio.

---

45 *lock up* forswear. **63** *these discoverers* Alibius and Isabella. *calm* satisfaction
that will calm me. **64-65** *Name . . . you* Tell me how I may rectify the error of con-
temptuously insulting you earlier. **69** *fell short* fell short (of proper courtesy).

VERMANDERO   Both mine, sir, and I ask no favor for 'em.   75
ALIBIUS   Now that which draws suspicion to their habits:
      The time of their disguisings agrees justly
      With the day of the murder.
TOMAZO   Oh, blest revelation!
VERMANDERO   Nay more, nay more, sir, I'll not spare mine own
      In way of justice; they both feigned a journey   80
      To Briamata, and so wrought out their leaves;
      My love was so abused in't.
TOMAZO   Time's too precious
      To run in waste now. You have brought a peace
      The riches of five kingdoms could not purchase.
      Be my most happy conduct; I thirst for 'em.   85
      Like subtle lightning will I wind about 'em
      And melt their marrow in 'em.   *Exeunt.*

ACT V

Scene 3   *Another part of the castle*

Enter ALSEMERO *and* JASPERINO.

JASPERINO   Your confidence, I'm sure, is now of proof;
      The prospect from the garden has showed
      Enough for deep suspicion.
ALSEMERO   The black mask
      That so continually was worn upon't,
      Condemns the face for ugly ere't be seen—   5
      Her despite to him and so seeming bottomless—
JASPERINO   Touch it home then; 'tis not a shallow probe
      Can search this ulcer soundly. I fear you'll find it
      Full of corruption. 'Tis fit I leave you.
      She meets you opportunely from that walk;   10
      She took the back door at his parting with her.   *Exit* JASPERINO.

---

81 and . . . leaves and thus managed to take leave of their duties here. **85 Be . . . conduct** Lead me to them.
ACT V, Scene 3. 1 Your . . . proof Your confidential suspicions are now validated.
3 black mask Beatrice's hostile attitude toward De Flores. **7 Touch it home** Strike through to the base of it.

ALSEMERO   Did my fate wait for this unhappy stroke
At my first sight of woman? She's here.

Enter BEATRICE.

BEATRICE   Alsemero!
ALSEMERO   How do you?
BEATRICE   How do I?
Alas! How do you? You look not well.   15
ALSEMERO   You read me well enough; I am not well.
BEATRICE   Not well, sir? Is't in my power to better you?
ALSEMERO   Yes.
BEATRICE   Nay then, y'are cured again.
ALSEMERO   Pray resolve me one question, lady.
BEATRICE   If I can.
ALSEMERO   None can so sure. Are you honest?   20
BEATRICE   Ha, ha, ha, that's a broad question, my lord.
ALSEMERO   But that's not a modest answer, my lady.
Do you laugh? My doubts are strong upon me.
BEATRICE   'Tis innocence that smiles, and no rough brow
Can take away the dimple in her cheek.   25
Say I should strain a tear to fill the vault,
Which would you give the better faith to?
ALSEMERO   'Twere but hypocrisy of a sadder color,
But the same stuff; neither your smiles nor tears
Shall move or flatter me from my belief: 30
You are a whore.
BEATRICE   What a horrid sound it hath!
It blasts a beauty to deformity;
Upon what face soever that breath falls,
It strikes it ugly. Oh, you have ruined
What you can ne'er repair again.   35
ALSEMERO   I'll all demolish and seek out truth within you,
If there be any left. Let your sweet tongue
Prevent your heart's rifling; there I'll ransack
And tear out my suspicion.
BEATRICE   You may, sir;
'Tis an easy passage. Yet if you please,   40

---

21 *broad* "obvious," but the word also means "chaste."   **26** *vault*   vault (of heaven).
37–38 *Let . . . rifling*   Let your sweet-talking tongue (do its best to) prevent me from
examining the secrets of your heart.

Show me the ground whereon you lost your love;
My spotless virtue may but tread on that
Before I perish.
ALSEMERO   Unanswerable!
A ground you cannot stand on: you fall down
Beneath all grace and goodness when you set   45
Your ticklish heel on't. There was a visor
O'er that cunning face, and that became you;
Now impudence, in triumph, rides upon't.
How comes this tender reconcilement else
'Twixt you and your despite, your rancorous loathing,   50
De Flores? He that your eye was sore at sight of,
He's now become your arms' supporter, your lips' saint.
BEATRICE   Is there the cause?
ALSEMERO   Worse—your lust's devil, your adultery!
BEATRICE   Would any but yourself say that   55
'Twould turn him to a villain.
ALSEMERO   'Twas witnessed
By the counsel of your bosom, Diaphanta.
BEATRICE   Is your witness dead, then?
ALSEMERO   'Tis to be feared
It was the wages of her knowledge, poor soul:
She lived not long after the discovery.   60
BEATRICE   Then hear a story of not much less horror
Than this your false suspicion is beguiled with.
To your bed's scandal I stand up innocence,
Which even the guilt of one black other deed
Will stand for proof of: your love has made me   65
A cruel murd'ress.
ALSEMERO   Ha!
BEATRICE   A bloody one.
I have kissed poison for't, stroked a serpent,
That thing of hate, worthy in my esteem
Of no better employment; and him most worthy
To be so employed, I caused to murder   70
That innocent Piracquo, having no
Better means than that worst, to assure

---

46 ticklish   easily upset, and therefore, lecherous.   **visor**   mask (of modesty toward
Alsemero and loathing for De Flores).   **52 your . . . supporter**   both "one who bears
arms in support of you" and "one who holds you in his arms."

Yourself to me.

ALSEMERO   Oh, the place itself e'er since
Has crying been for vengeance, the temple
Where blood and beauty first unlawfully   75
Fired their devotion and quenched the right one.
'Twas in my fears at first, 'twill have it now;
Oh, thou art all deformed!

BEATRICE   Forget not, sir,
It for your sake was done; shall greater dangers
Make the less welcome?

ALSEMERO   Oh, thou shouldst have gone   80
A thousand leagues about to have avoided
This dangerous bridge of blood; here we are lost.

BEATRICE   Remember, I am true unto your bed.

ALSEMERO   The bed itself's a charnel, the sheets shrouds
For murdered carcasses. It must ask pause   85
What I must do in this; meantime you shall
Be my prisoner only: enter my closet;   *Exit* BEATRICE.
I'll be your keeper yet. Oh, in what part
Of this sad story shall I first begin?

Enter DE FLORES.

                              —Ha!
This same fellow has put me in.—De Flores.   90

DE FLORES   Noble Alsemero.

ALSEMERO   I can tell you
News, sir; my wife has her commended to you.

DE FLORES   That's news indeed, my lord; I think she would
Commend me to the gallows if she could,
She ever loved me so well; I thank her.   95

ALSEMERO   What's this blood upon your band, De Flores?

DE FLORES   Blood? No, sure 'twas washed since.

ALSEMERO   Since when, man?

DE FLORES   Since t'other day I got a knock
In a sword and dagger school; I think 'tis out.

ALSEMERO   Yes, 'tis almost out, but 'tis perceived, though.   100

---

73 *place*   temple where he first saw Beatrice.   **76** *the . . . one*   religious devotion, appropriate in a temple.   **77** *'twill . . . now*   The temple will have its vengeance now.   **79–80** *shall . . . welcome*   Shall you now welcome me less because it is dangerous to love me? (?)   **82** *bridge*   way (to your desires).   **84** *charnel*   a chamber for the deposit of dead bodies.   **85** *It . . . pause*   I need time to consider.   **90** *put me in*   given me a place to start at.   **97** *sure . . . since*   a slip of the tongue, prompted by guilt.

I had forgot my message; this it is:
What price goes murder?
DE FLORES   How, sir?
ALSEMERO   I ask you, sir.
My wife's behindhand with you, she tells me,
For a brave, bloody blow you gave for her sake
Upon Piracquo.
DE FLORES   Upon? 'Twas quite through him, sure.   105
Has she confessed it?
ALSEMERO   As sure as death to both of you,
And much more than that.
DE FLORES   It could not be much more;
'Twas but one thing, and that—she's a whore.
ALSEMERO   It could not choose but follow; oh, cunning devils!
How should blind men know you from fair-faced saints?   110
BEATRICE   *Within.* He lies! The villain does belie me!
DE FLORES   Let me go to her, sir.
ALSEMERO   Nay, you shall to her.
Peace, crying crocodile, your sounds are heard!
Take your prey to you. Get you in to her, sir.   *Exit* DE FLORES.
I'll be your pander now; rehearse again   115
Your scene of lust, that you may be perfect
When you shall come to act it to the black audience,
Where howls and gnashings shall be music to you.
Clip your adult'ress freely; 'tis the pilot
Will guide you to the *Mare Mortuum,*   120
Where you shall sink to fathoms bottomless.

Enter VERMANDERO, ALIBIUS, ISABELLA, TOMAZO, [*with*] FRANCISCUS
and ANTONIO [*captive*].

VERMANDERO   Oh, Alsemero, I have a wonder for you.
ALSEMERO   No, sir, 'tis I, I have a wonder for you.
VERMANDERO   I have suspicion near as proof itself
For Piracquo's murder.
ALSEMERO   Sir, I have proof   125
Beyond suspicion for Piracquo's murder.

---

103 *behindhand with* both "in debt to" and "having backhanded dealings with." **109 *It*** The quarto reads "I." **110 *blind men*** men not graced with godlike powers of perception. **113 *crying crocodile*** The crocodile was thought to deceive its victims into thinking it was compassionate by shedding tears. **117 *black audience*** audience in hell. **119 *Clip*** embrace. **120 *Mare Mortuum*** the Dead Sea, which, because it was thought to be bottomless, was associated with the bottomless pit of hell.

VERMANDERO   Beseech you, hear me; these two have been disguised
    E'er since the deed was done.
ALSEMERO   I have two other
    That were more close disguised than your two could be
    E'er since the deed was done.   130
VERMANDERO   You'll hear me. These mine own servants—
ALSEMERO   Hear me. Those nearer than your servants
    That shall acquit them and prove them guiltless.
FRANCISCUS   That may be done with easy truth, sir.
TOMAZO   How is my cause bandied through your delays!   135
    'Tis urgent in blood and calls for haste;
    Give me a brother alive or dead:
    Alive, a wife with him; if dead, for both
    A recompense, for murder and adultery.
BEATRICE   *Within.* Oh, oh, oh!
ALSEMERO   Hark, 'tis coming to you.   140
DE FLORES   *Within.* Nay, I'll along for company.
BEATRICE   *Within.*   Oh, oh!
VERMANDERO   What horrid sounds are these?
ALSEMERO   Come forth, you twins of mischief!

    Enter DE FLORES *bringing in* BEATRICE [*wounded*].

DE FLORES   Here we are. If you have any more
    To say to us, speak quickly; I shall not   145
    Give you the hearing else. I am so stout yet
    And so I think that broken rib of mankind.
VERMANDERO   An host of enemies entered my citadel
    Could not amaze like this. Joanna! Beatrice-Joanna!
BEATRICE   Oh, come not near me, sir; I shall defile you.   150
    I am that of your blood was taken from you
    For your better health; look no more upon't,
    But cast it to the ground regardlessly.
    Let the common sewer take it from distinction.

---

129 *close* secretly. **135** *bandied* tossed back and forth. **140** *'tis* your recompense is. **141** *I'll . . . company* I'll accompany you in death. **146** *stout* undaunted. **147** *broken . . . mankind* Beatrice. The allusion is, of course, to Genesis 2:21–23. De Flores implies that, like Adam, he has been led by woman into a fall. **151–52** *I . . . health* Beatrice here derives her metaphor from the medical practice, common in the seventeenth century, of blood-letting: a person taken ill was intermittently bled in the belief that the disease might thus pass out of his body with the blood. But not to be overlooked in these lines is the suggestion that Beatrice is also a kind of changeling, taken from her father for his own good. **153** *regardlessly* unregarded. **154** *distinction* condition of being distinct.

Beneath the stars, upon yon meteor   155
Ever hung my fate 'mongst things corruptible;
I ne'er could pluck it from him. My loathing
Was prophet to the rest but ne'er believed;
Mine honor fell with him, and now my life.
Alsemero, I am a stranger to your bed;   160
Your bed was cozened on the nuptial night
For which your false bride died.
ALSEMERO   Diaphanta!
DE FLORES   Yes, and the while I coupled with your mate
  At barley-break; now we are left in hell.
VERMANDERO   We are all there: it circumscribes here.   165
DE FLORES   I loved this woman in spite of her heart;
  Her love I earned out of Piracquo's murder.
TOMAZO   Ha, my brother's murderer!
DE FLORES   Yes, and her honor's prize
  Was my reward. I thank life for nothing
  But that pleasure; it was so sweet to me   170
  That I have drunk up all, left none behind
  For any man to pledge me.
VERMANDERO   Horrid villain!
  Keep life in him for further tortures.
DE FLORES   No!
  I can prevent you; here's my penknife still.
  It is but one thread more, [*Stabs himself.*] and now 'tis cut.   175
  Make haste, Joanna, by that token to thee
  Canst not forget so lately put in mind!
  I would not go to leave thee far behind.   *Dies.*
BEATRICE   Forgive me, Alsemero, all forgive;
  'Tis time to die, when 'tis a shame to live.   *Dies.*   180
VERMANDERO   Oh, my name is entered now in that record
  Where till this fatal hour 'twas never read.
ALSEMERO   Let it be blotted out; let your heart lose it,
  And it can never look you in the face
  Nor tell a tale behind the back of life   185
  To your dishonor. Justice hath so right
  The guilty hit, that innocence is quit

---

155 *Beneath . . . meteor* According to the doctrines of astrology, the stars were fixed and pure; meteors, sublunary and transitory. **156 *hung*** The quarto reads "hang." **157 *him*** De Flores. **176 *token to thee*** his self-inflicted wound. **177 *so . . . mind*** so recently reminded by my wound of my love (?). **187 *quit*** acquitted.

By proclamation and may joy again.
—Sir, you are sensible of what truth hath done;
'Tis the best comfort that your grief can find.   190

TOMAZO   Sir, I am satisfied; my injuries
Lie dead before me. I can exact no more,
Unless my soul were loose and could o'ertake
Those black fugitives that are fled from thence,
To take a second vengeance; but there are wraths   195
Deeper than mine, 'tis to be feared, about 'em.

ALSEMERO   What an opacous body had that moon
That last changed on us! Here's beauty changed
To ugly whoredom; here servant obedience
To a master sin, imperious murder.   200
I, a supposed husband, changed embraces
With wantonness, but that was paid before;
Your change is come, too, from an ignorant wrath
To knowing friendship. Are there any more on's?

ANTONIO   Yes, sir, I was changed too from a little ass as I was, to a   205
great fool as I am, and had like to ha' been changed to the gallows
but that you know my innocence always excuses me.

FRANCISCUS   I was changed from a little wit to be stark mad, almost
for the same purpose.

ISABELLA   [*To* ALIBIUS.] Your change is still behind,   210
But deserve best your transformation:
You are a jealous coxcomb, keep schools of folly,
And teach your scholars how to break your own head.

ALIBIUS   I see all apparent, wife, and will change now
Into a better husband, and never keep   215
Scholars that shall be wiser than myself.

ALSEMERO   Sir, you have yet a son's duty living.
Please you accept it; let that your sorrow,
As it goes from your eye, go from your heart;
Man and his sorrow at the grave must part.   220

---

194 *black fugitives* souls of Beatrice and De Flores, black with sin.   **196 *about*** after.
197 *opacous* darkened and, therefore, foreboding.   **202 *wantonness*** Diaphanta's lust-
fulness.   ***before*** earlier than this discovery (by Diaphanta's death).   **207 *innocence*** both
"freedom from guilt" and "idiocy."   **213 *break . . . head*** with a cuckold's horns.

EPILOGUE

ALSEMERO   All we can do to comfort one another,
    To stay a brother's sorrow for a brother,
    To dry a child from the kind father's eyes,
    Is to no purpose; it rather multiplies.
    Your only smiles have power to cause relive   5
    The dead again or, in their rooms, to give
    Brother a new brother, father a child:
    If these appear, all griefs are reconciled.   *Exeunt omnes.*

Epilogue **4** *multiplies* increases the sorrow.   **5** *Your only* only your.   *cause relive* revive.   **6** *rooms* places.

'TIS PITY
SHE'S
A WHORE

(1626–33)

John Ford

This frontispiece, to a 1662 collection of skits titled The Wits, *shows the interior of a private theater like the Phoenix, where* 'Tis Pity She's a Whore *was played. Indoor, private theaters gradually replaced the outdoor, public theaters during the period 1600–1640. Though they retained many features of the public theaters, such as the projecting stage and the small inner stage on the back wall (behind the curtain), they were rather small and being indoors required artificial lighting. Performances here were intimate, and the players catered to a more intellectual and fashionable audience. The figure marked "Changeling" suggests Middleton and Rowley's play, but the clerical dress does not seem to fit any particular character. The Folger Shakespeare Library, Washington, D. C.*

Changling

Simpleton

French Dancing M[aster]

S.^r I Falstafe

Hostes

Clause

J OHN FORD (1586–1639) *WAS THE LAST OF THE great Renaissance dramatists, but we know almost nothing of his career except that he was destined for the law but chose the theater instead. His major works, played in the ten or fifteen years before the closing of the theaters in 1642, continued to explore, in a specialized way, the great antagonism between the human imagination and the world in which it must work—between hero and theater—introduced a half-century earlier by Christopher Marlowe in* Tamburlaine. *Giovanni and Annabella, the heroes of* 'Tis Pity, *follow their own wills to the satisfaction of their love, despite society's prohibition of incest, just as Tamburlaine followed his will to absolute conquest of the world with obvious disregard for principles of morality and traditional values.*

But if the subject matter remains in some ways the same, the method of exploration is greatly changed. Where Marlowe offers mythic representations of human impulses and traces the destiny of his characters in heroic terms, John Ford—despite the sensationalism of his subject matter—presents the nature and the fate of his heroes in the most delicate and precise psychological terms. Where Marlowe offers the great dream of Renaissance man seen through a telescope, Ford examines it through a microscope. Underneath all the usual sensational trappings of Renaissance drama—incest, bloody murders, overt moralizing—Ford's plays follow with fascination the subtle, scarcely perceptible changes that take place in the human mind as man comes to know through his own suffering the meaning of his impulsive choices. Ford's plays look backward to Marlowe, but they also look forward to the next age, for their obsessive concern with the conflicts between love and honor anticipates the chief subject matter of Restoration drama.

'Tis Pity was written between 1626 and 1633. A fairly good quarto edition was published in 1633 and is the basis of the text printed here.

To the
Truly Noble, John,
Earl of Peterborough,
Lord Mordaunt
Baron of Turvey   5

MY LORD,

Where a truth of merit hath a general warrant, there love is but a
debt, acknowledgment a justice. Greatness cannot often claim virtue by
inheritance; yet, in this, yours appears most eminent, for that you are
not more rightly heir to your fortunes, than glory shall be to your   10
memory. Sweetness of disposition ennobles a freedom of birth; in both,
your lawful interest adds honor to your own name and mercy to my
presumption. Your noble allowance of these first fruits of my leisure in
the action emboldens my confidence of your as noble construction in
this presentment: especially since my service must ever owe particular   15
duty to your favors by a particular engagement. The gravity of the
subject may easily excuse the lightness of the title: otherwise I had been
a severe judge against mine own guilt. Princes have vouchsafed grace to
trifles offered from a purity of devotion; your lordship may likewise
please to admit into your good opinion, with these weak endeavors, the   20
constancy of affection from the sincere lover of your deserts in honor,

JOHN FORD.

Dedication   **2–4 *John Mordaunt***   (1599–1642), first Earl of Peterborough.   **13 *allow-***
ance   praise.   **13–14 *in the action***   when acted.   **14–15 *of . . . presentment***   of your
approval again, now it is printed.   **18 *against***   of.

THE ACTORS' NAMES

BONAVENTURA, *a friar*
A CARDINAL, *nuncio to the Pope*
SORANZO, *a nobleman*
FLORIO, *a citizen of Parma*
DONADO, *another citizen*
GRIMALDI, *a Roman gentleman*
GIOVANNI, *son to Florio*
BERGETTO, *nephew to Donado*
RICHARDETTO, *a supposed physician*
VASQUES, *servant to Soranzo*

POGGIO, *servant to Bergetto*
BANDITTI
[ATTENDANTS]

WOMEN

ANNABELLA, *daughter to Florio*
HIPPOLITA, *wife to Richardetto*
PHILOTIS, *his niece*
PUTANA, *tutoress to Annabella*
[LADIES]

The Scene   *Parma*

The Actors' Names *nuncio* a permanent official representative of the Holy See at a
foreign court.
The Scene *Parma* The duchy of Parma, situated on a tributary of the Po River, was,
in 1545, bestowed by Pope Paul III upon his son Pierluigi Farnese, whose descendants
ruled it until 1731.

ACT I

The cell of FRIAR BONAVENTURA}.

Enter FRIAR *and* GIOVANNI.

FRIAR Dispute no more in this, for know, young man,
    These are no school-points; nice philosophy
    May tolerate unlikely arguments,
    But Heaven admits no jest: wits that presumed
    On wit too much, by striving how to prove   5
    There was no God, with foolish grounds of art,
    Discovered first the nearest way to hell,
    And filled the world with devilish atheism.
    Such questions, youth, are fond; for better 'tis
    To bless the sun than reason why it shines,   10
    Yet He thou talkst of is above the sun.
    No more; I may not hear it.
GIOVANNI   Gentle father,
    To you I have unclasped my burdened soul,
    Emptied the storehouse of my thoughts and heart,
    Made myself poor of secrets; have not left   15
    Another word untold, which hath not spoke
    All what I ever durst or think or know;
    And yet is here the comfort I shall have:
    Must I not do what all men else may—love?
FRIAR Yes, you may love, fair son.
GIOVANNI   Must I not praise   20
    That beauty which, if framed anew, the gods
    Would make a god of, if they had it there,
    And kneel to it, as I do kneel to them?
FRIAR Why, foolish madman—
GIOVANNI   Shall a peevish sound,
    A customary form, from man to man,   25
    Of brother and of sister, be a bar
    'Twixt my perpetual happiness and me?
    Say that we had one father; say one womb
    (Curse to my joys) gave both us life, and birth.

ACT I, Scene 1. **2 nice** foolish. **6 art** academic learning. **9 fond** foolish.
25 customary form convention. ***from . . . man*** among men.

Are we not therefore each to other bound   30
So much the more by nature, by the links
Of blood, of reason—nay, if you will have't,
Even of religion—to be ever one,
One soul, one flesh, one love, one heart, one all?
FRIAR   Have done, unhappy youth, for thou art lost.   35
GIOVANNI   Shall then—for that I am her brother born—
My joys be ever banished from her bed?
No, father; in your eyes I see the change
Of pity and compassion; from your age,
As from a sacred oracle, distills   40
The life of counsel: tell me, holy man,
What cure shall give me ease in these extremes.
FRIAR   Repentance, son, and sorrow for this sin:
For thou hast moved a Majesty above
With thy unrangèd-almost blasphemy.   45
GIOVANNI   O do not speak of that, dear confessor!
FRIAR   Art thou, my son, that miracle of wit
Who once, within these three months, wert esteemed
A wonder of thine age, throughout Bononia?
How did the university applaud   50
Thy government, behavior, learning, speech,
Sweetness, and all that could make up a man!
I was proud of my tutelage, and chose
Rather to leave my books than part with thee.
I did so, but the fruits of all my hopes   55
Are lost in thee, as thou art in thyself.
O, Giovanni, hast thou left the schools
Of knowledge to converse with lust and death?
For death waits on thy lust. Look through the world,
And thou shalt see a thousand faces shine   60
More glorious than this idol thou adorst.
Leave her, and take thy choice; 'tis much less sin,
Though in such games as those, they lose that win.
GIOVANNI   It were more ease to stop the ocean
From floats and ebbs than to dissuade my vows.   65
FRIAR   Then I have done, and in thy willful flames

---

36 *for that* because. **45** *unrangèd-almost* almost unbounded. **49** *Bononia* Bologna,
where a famous Italian university was located. **51** *government* good bearing. **63** *those*
games of seduction. **65** *floats* flows.

Already see thy ruin; Heaven is just.
Yet hear my counsel.
GIOVANNI   As a voice of life.
FRIAR   Hie to thy father's house, there lock thee fast
Alone within thy chamber, then fall down   70
On both thy knees, and grovel on the ground.
Cry to thy heart, wash every word thou utterst
In tears, and, if't be possible, of blood.
Beg Heaven to cleanse the leprosy of lust
That rots thy soul, acknowledge what thou art—   75
A wretch, a worm, a nothing. Weep, sigh, pray
Three times a day, and three times every night.
For seven days' space do this; then if thou find'st
No change in thy desires, return to me:
I'll think on remedy. Pray for thyself   80
At home, whilst I pray for thee here.—Away!
My blessing with thee, we have need to pray.
GIOVANNI   All this I'll do, to free me from the rod
Of vengeance; else I'll swear my fate's my god.   *Exeunt.*

ACT I

Scene 2   *Before* FLORIO's *house*

Enter GRIMALDI *and* VASQUES *ready to fight.*

VASQUES   Come, sir, stand to your tackling; if you prove craven,
I'll make you run quickly.
GRIMALDI   Thou art no equal match for me.
VASQUES   Indeed I never went to the wars to bring home news, nor   5
cannot play the mountebank for a meal's meat, and swear I got
my wounds in the field. See you these grey hairs? They'll not
flinch for a bloody nose. Wilt thou to this gear?

---

73 *of*   in.   **84** *my . . . god*   that I am the victim of fate.
❧ **ACT I, Scene 2.   1** *stand . . . tackling*   Hold your ground.   **3** *equal . . . for*
socially fit to fight.   **4** *to bring . . . news*   to hear about the details of battles in order to
pretend to have fought in them (cf. Gower's speech in *Henry V*, III.6.70–85).   **5** *mounte-*
bank   impudent fraud.   **7** *gear*   affair (of fighting).

GRIMALDI   Why, slave, thinkst thou I'll balance my reputation with
a cast-suit? Call thy master, he shall know that I dare—

VASQUES   Scold like a cot-quean, that's your profession. Thou poor   10
shadow of a soldier, I will make thee know my master keeps
servants thy betters in quality and performance. Comst thou to
fight or prate?

GRIMALDI   Neither, with thee. I am a Roman and a gentleman, one
that have got mine honor with expense of blood.   15

VASQUES   You are a lying coward and a fool. Fight, or by these hilts
I'll kill thee!—Brave my lord!—You'll fight.

GRIMALDI   Provoke me not, for if thou dost—

VASQUES   Have at you!

> *They fight.* GRIMALDI *hath the worst. Enter* FLORIO, DONADO,
> SORANZO.

FLORIO   What mean these sudden broils so near my doors?   20
Have you not other places but my house
To vent the spleen of your disordered bloods?
Must I be haunted still with such unrest
As not to eat or sleep in peace at home?
Is this your love, Grimaldi? Fie, 'tis naught.   25

DONADO   And Vasques, I may tell thee, 'tis not well
To broach these quarrels; you are ever forward
In seconding contentions.

> *Enter above* ANNABELLA *and* PUTANA.

FLORIO   What's the ground?

SORANZO   That with your patience, signors, I'll resolve:
This gentleman, whom fame reports a soldier,   30
(For else I know not) rivals me in love
To Signor Florio's daughter, to whose ears
He still prefers his suit, to my disgrace,
Thinking the way to recommend himself
Is to disparage me in his report.   35
But know, Grimaldi, though may be thou art
My equal in thy blood, yet this bewrays
A lowness in thy mind which, wert thou noble,

---

9 cast-suit one who wears the cast-away clothes of his master. **10 cot-quean** vulgar
shrew. **12 thy** (that are) thy. **17 Brave my lord** How dare you think to challenge
my master! **20 sudden broils** violent quarreling. **30 fame** rumor. **31 For . . . not**
for otherwise I know not (why there should be a quarrel). **33 prefers** offers. **36 may
be** (it) may be (that). **37 this** this act of disparaging me. **bewrays** shows.

Thou wouldst as much disdain as I do thee
For this unworthiness; and on this ground   40
I willed my servant to correct his tongue,
Holding a man so base no match for me.

VASQUES   And had not your sudden coming prevented us, I had let
my gentleman blood under the gills; I should have wormed you,
sir, for running mad.   45

GRIMALDI   I'll be revenged, Soranzo.

VASQUES   On a dish of warm broth to stay your stomach—do, honest
innocence, do; spoon-meat is a wholesomer diet than a Spanish
blade.

GRIMALDI   Remember this!   50

SORANZO   I fear thee not, Grimaldi.   *Exit* GRIMALDI.

FLORIO   My Lord Soranzo, this is strange to me,
Why you should storm, having my word engaged:
Owing her heart, what need you doubt her ear?
Losers may talk by law of any game.   55

VASQUES   Yet the villainy of words, Signor Florio, may be such as
would make any unspleened dove choleric. Blame not my lord
in this.

FLORIO   Be you more silent.
I would not for my wealth my daughter's love   60
Should cause the spilling of one drop of blood.
Vasques, put up; let's end this fray in wine.

                    Exeunt [FLORIO, DONADO, SORANZO, *and* VASQUES].

PUTANA   How like you this, child? Here's threat'ning, challenging,
quarreling, and fighting on every side, and all is for your sake;
you had need look to yourself, charge, you'll be stolen away   65
sleeping else shortly.

---

41 *his* The quarto reads "this." **43** *had not* The quarto reads "had." **43–45** *I . . .*
mad Vasques cannot resist the chance to show off his wit as well as his courage, so his
challenge to Grimaldi here is marked by puns that mix medical and martial images. The
reference to bloodletting, for instance, ironically refers to the practice of draining some
of the blood from a sick man in the hope that the disease would drain from the body
with the blood. Like a physician, Vasques would cut open Grimaldi and "let" his blood,
but his intentions would not be medical in nature. Similarly, he would "worm" Grimaldi
if they fought—not by purging him of worms (which were thought to cause madness in
dogs), but by killing him and thus converting him into food for worms. (Cf. *I Henry IV*,
V.4.84–87.) **47** *On . . . stomach* You'll more likely have to swallow warm broth to
steady your queasy stomach. **48** *innocence* fool. *spoon-meat* soft or liquid food fed
to infants or invalids. **50** *Remember this* (I shall make you) remember this! **54** *Owing*
possessing. **57** *would . . . choleric* would anger even the mild-tempered dove.
62 *put up* Put your weapon away. **65** *charge* As Putana's tutoree, Annabella is her
"charge." **66** *sleeping* while you sleep.

ANNABELLA   But tut'ress, such a life gives no content
 To me; my thoughts are fixed on other ends.
 Would you would leave me.

PUTANA   Leave you? No marvel else. Leave me no leaving, charge;   70
 this is love outright. Indeed I blame you not, you have choice
 fit for the best lady in Italy.

ANNABELLA   Pray do not talk so much.

PUTANA   Take the worst with the best, there's Grimaldi the soldier,
 a very well-timbered fellow: they say he is a Roman, nephew   75
 to the Duke Montferrato; they say he did good service in the
 wars against the Milanese, but 'faith, charge, I do not like him,
 and be for nothing but for being a soldier; not one amongst
 twenty of your skirmishing captains but have some privy maim
 or other that mars their standing upright. I like him the worse,   80
 he crinkles so much in the hams; though he might serve if there
 were no more men, yet he's not the man I would choose.

ANNABELLA   Fie, how thou prat'st.

PUTANA   As I am a very woman, I like Signor Soranzo well; he is
 wise, and what is more, rich; and what is more than that, kind,   85
 and what is more than all this, a nobleman; such a one, were I
 the fair Annabella myself, I would wish and pray for. Then he is
 bountiful; besides, he is handsome, and by my troth, I think
 wholesome, and that's news in a gallant of three and twenty;
 liberal, that I know; loving, that you know; and a man sure,   90
 else he could never ha' purchased such a good name with Hippolita, the lusty widow, in her husband's lifetime: and 'twere
 but for that report, sweetheart, would 'a were thine. Commend
 a man for his qualities, but take a husband as he is a plain-sufficient,
 naked man: such a one is for your bed, and such a one is Signor   95
 Soranzo, my life for't.

ANNABELLA   Sure the woman took her morning's draught too soon.

 Enter BERGETTO *and* POGGIO.

PUTANA   But look, sweetheart, look what thing comes now: here's

---

70 *No . . . leaving* Nothing could be more surprising. Leave off this talk of leaving
(for a similar construction see *Romeo and Juliet,* III.5.153).   **75 *well-timbered*** well-
constructed.   **78 *and*** and (it).   *not one* The quarto reads "one."   **80 *standing
upright*** Putana's primary meaning here is sexual.   **81 *he . . . hams*** He bends so obsequiously; he cringes.   **89 *wholesome*** not infected (with venereal disease).   **90 *liberal***
generous (in his bribes of Putana).   **93 *report*** rumor.

another of your ciphers to fill up the number. O brave old ape in a silken coat. Observe. 100

BERGETTO Didst thou think, Poggio, that I would spoil my new clothes and leave my dinner to fight?

POGGIO No, sir, I did not take you for so arrant a baby.

BERGETTO I am wiser than so: for I hope, Poggio, thou never heardst of an elder brother that was a coxcomb. Didst, Poggio? 105

POGGIO Never indeed, sir, as long as they had either land or money left them to inherit.

BERGETTO Is it possible, Poggio? O monstrous! Why, I'll undertake with a handful of silver to buy a headful of wit at any time; but sirrah, I have another purchase in hand: I shall have the 110 wench, mine uncle says. I will but wash my face, and shift socks, and then have at her i'faith!—Mark my pace, Poggio.

[*Struts foolishly.*]

POGGIO Sir—[*Aside.*] I have seen an ass and a mule trot the Spanish pavin with a better grace, I know not how often.

Exeunt [BERGETTO *and* POGGIO].

ANNABELLA This idiot haunts me too. 115

PUTANA Ay, ay, he needs no description; the rich magnifico that is below with your father, charge, Signor Donado his uncle, for that he means to make this his cousin a golden calf, thinks that you will be a right Israelite and fall down to him presently: but I hope I have tutored you better. They say a fool's bauble 120 is a lady's playfellow; yet you having wealth enough, you need not cast upon the dearth of flesh at any rate: hang him, innocent!

Enter GIOVANNI [*below*].

ANNABELLA But see, Putana, see: what blessed shape
Of some celestial creature now appears?

---

99 another . . . number another nonentity who merely adds to the number of your suitors. **99–100 ape . . . coat** fool in rich dress. **104–5 thou . . . coxcomb** Because Bergetto believes that money makes a nobleman, he thinks the oldest brother in a family can never be a fool, since the laws of primogeniture dictate that he will become wealthy. **110 sirrah** a term of address expressing the speaker's authority. **113–14 Spanish pavin** a grave and stately dance. **116 magnifico** Italian nobleman of great importance. **118 golden calf** After they had been led out of bondage in Egypt, the people of Israel temporarily lost faith in Jehovah when Moses was delayed on Mt. Sinai. Gathering together, they convinced Aaron to fashion a golden calf, which they all worshipped. (See Exodus 32:1–6.) **120 bauble** the baton or stick of a court jester, but also, in this context, the male sexual organ. **121–22 you . . . flesh** You need not take a chance ("cast") on such an insubstantial man ("dearth of flesh").

What man is he, that with such sad aspect   125
Walks careless of himself?
PUTANA   Where?
ANNABELLA   Look below.
PUTANA   O, 'tis your brother sweet—
ANNABELLA   Ha!
PUTANA   'Tis your brother.
ANNABELLA   Sure 'tis not he; this is some woeful thing
Wrapped up in grief, some shadow of a man.
Alas, he beats his breast, and wipes his eyes   130
Drowned all in tears: methinks I hear him sigh.
Let's down, Putana, and partake the cause;
I know my brother, in the love he bears me,
Will not deny me partage in his sadness.
[*Aside.*] My soul is full of heaviness and fear. *Exit [with* PUTANA].   135
GIOVANNI   Lost, I am lost: my fates have doomed my death.
The more I strive, I love; the more I love,
The less I hope: I see my ruin, certain.
What judgment or endeavors could apply
To my incurable and restless wounds   140
I throughly have examined, but in vain:
O, that it were not in religion sin
To make our love a god and worship it!
I have even wearied Heaven with prayers, dried up
The spring of my continual tears, even starved   145
My veins with daily fasts: what wit or art
Could counsel, I have practiced; but alas,
I find all these but dreams and old men's tales
To fright unsteady youth; I'm still the same.
Or I must speak, or burst; 'tis not, I know,   150
My lust, but 'tis my fate that leads me on.
Keep fear and low, fainthearted shame with slaves;
I'll tell her that I love her, though my heart
Were rated at the price of that attempt.
O me! She comes.
Enter ANNABELLA *and* PUTANA.

ANNABELLA   Brother.

---

134 *partage* a share. 141 *throughly* completely. 146 *wit* learning. 150 *Or . . .
or* either . . . or. 152 *Keep* stay. 154 *rated* valued.

GIOVANNI   [*Aside.*] If such a thing   155
 As courage dwell in men, ye heavenly powers,
 Now double all that virtue in my tongue.
ANNABELLA   Why, brother, will you not speak to me?
GIOVANNI   Yes. How d'ee, sister?
ANNABELLA   Howsoever I am, methinks you are not well.   160
PUTANA   Bless us, why are you so sad, sir?
GIOVANNI   Let me entreat you, leave us awhile, Putana.
 Sister, I would be private with you.
ANNABELLA   Withdraw, Putana.
PUTANA   I will. [*Aside.*] If this were any other company for her, I   165
 should think my absence an office of some credit; but I will
 leave them together.   *Exit* PUTANA.
GIOVANNI   Come, sister, lend your hand, let's walk together.
 I hope you need not blush to walk with me:
 Here's none but you and I.   170
ANNABELLA   How's this?
GIOVANNI   Faith, I mean no harm.
ANNABELLA   Harm?
GIOVANNI   No, good faith; how is't with 'ee?
ANNABELLA   [*Aside.*] I trust he be not frantic. [*To him.*] I am very well,
 brother.   175
GIOVANNI   Trust me, but I am sick, I fear so sick
 'Twill cost my life.
ANNABELLA   Mercy forbid it! 'Tis not so, I hope.
GIOVANNI   I think you love me, sister.
ANNABELLA   Yes, you know I do.   180
GIOVANNI   I know't indeed.—Y'are very fair.
ANNABELLA   Nay then, I see you have a merry sickness.
GIOVANNI   That's as it proves. They poets feign, I read,
 That Juno for her forehead did exceed
 All other goddesses; but I durst swear   185
 Your forehead exceeds hers, as hers did theirs.
ANNABELLA   Troth, this is pretty.
GIOVANNI   Such a pair of stars

---

163 I . . . you The double meaning in this phrase is probably intended as an unconscious
expression of Giovanni's sexual infatuation with Annabella. **165–66 If . . . credit** If
this were any other man but her brother, I would be paid to leave him alone with her.
175 frantic mad. **183 They poets** they (who are) poets. **feign** relate. **184 Juno**
queen of the gods. **187 pretty** pleasingly artful.

As are thine eyes would, like Promethean fire,
If gently glanced, give life to senseless stones.
ANNABELLA   Fie upon 'ee!   190
GIOVANNI   The lily and the rose, most sweetly strange,
Upon your dimpled cheeks do strive for change.
Such lips would tempt a saint; such hands as those
Would make an anchorite lascivious.
ANNABELLA   D'ee mock me, or flatter me?   195
GIOVANNI   If you would see a beauty more exact
Than art can counterfeit or nature frame,
Look in your glass, and there behold your own.
ANNABELLA   O you are a trim youth!
GIOVANNI   Here.   200

Offers his dagger to her.

ANNABELLA   What to do?
GIOVANNI   And here's my breast; strike home.
Rip up my bosom, there thou shalt behold
A heart in which is writ the truth I speak.
Why stand 'ee?
ANNABELLA   Are you earnest?
GIOVANNI   Yes, most earnest.   205
You cannot love?
ANNABELLA   Whom?
GIOVANNI   Me. My tortured soul
Hath felt affliction in the heat of death.
O Annabella, I am quite undone:
The love of thee, my sister, and the view
Of thy immortal beauty hath untuned   210
All harmony both of my rest and life.
Why d'ee not strike?
ANNABELLA   Forbid it, my just fears!
If this be true, 'twere fitter I were dead.
GIOVANNI   True, Annabella; 'tis no time to jest.
I have too long suppressed the hidden flames   215
That almost have consumed me; I have spent
Many a silent night in sighs and groans,

---

188 *Promethean fire*   According to Greek mythology, Prometheus made mankind out
of clay and then stole fire from heaven for man's use. Giovanni's reference here combines
the concepts of Prometheus as fire-giver and as life-giver.   **194** *anchorite*   recluse.
199 *trim*   excellent.

Run over all my thoughts, despised my fate,
Reasoned against the reasons of my love,
Done all that smooth-cheeked virtue could advise,   220
But found all bootless; 'tis my destiny
That you must either love, or I must die.
ANNABELLA   Comes this in sadness from you?
GIOVANNI   Let some mischief
Befall me soon, if I dissemble aught.
ANNABELLA   You are my brother, Giovanni.
GIOVANNI   You   225
My sister, Annabella; I know this,
And could afford you instance why to love
So much the more for this; to which intent
Wise nature first in your creation meant
To make you mine: else't had been sin and foul   230
To share one beauty to a double soul.
Nearness in birth or blood doth but persuade
A nearer nearness in affection.
I have asked counsel of the holy church,
Who tells me I may love you, and 'tis just   235
That since I may, I should; and will, yes, will!
Must I now live, or die?
ANNABELLA   Live: thou hast won
The field, and never fought; what thou hast urged,
My captive heart had long ago resolved.
I blush to tell thee—but I'll tell thee now—   240
For every sigh that thou hast spent for me,
I have sighed ten; for every tear, shed twenty:
And not so much for that I loved, as that
I durst not say I loved, nor scarcely think it.
GIOVANNI   Let not this music be a dream, ye gods,   245
For pity's sake, I beg 'ee!
ANNABELLA   On my knees,

She kneels.

Brother, even by our mother's dust, I charge you,

---

218 *Run* The quarto reads "ran." **221 *bootless*** useless. **223 *Comes . . . you*** Are
you sincere in what you say? **227 *instance why to*** reason to. **231 *To share . . . soul***
to split our original union by making us two people. (Giovanni here seems to refer to a
time when he and Annabella were one complete soul, perhaps in the manner of the
whole beings that Aristophanes describes in Plato's *Symposium,* 189c–193e.)

Do not betray me to your mirth or hate:
Love me or kill me, brother.

GIOVANNI　　　　　　　　　　　　　　On my knees.

He kneels.

Sister, even by my mother's dust, I charge you,　　　　　　　250
Do not betray me to your mirth or hate:
Love me or kill me, sister.

ANNABELLA　You mean good sooth then?

GIOVANNI　　　　　　　　　　　　　In good troth, I do,
And so do you, I hope: say, "I'm in earnest."

ANNABELLA　I'll swear't, I.

GIOVANNI　　　　　　　　And I, and by this kiss,　　　　　　　255

Kisses her.

Once more, yet once more; now let's rise by this,

[*They rise.*]

I would not change this minute for Elysium.
What must we now do?

ANNABELLA　　　　　　　　　What you will.

GIOVANNI　　　　　　　　　　　　　Come then;
After so many tears as we have wept,
Let's learn to court in smiles, to kiss, and sleep.　　　*Exeunt.*　260

ACT I

Scene 3　　DONADO's *house*

Enter FLORIO *and* DONADO.

FLORIO　Signor Donado, you have said enough,
I understand you, but would have you know
I will not force my daughter 'gainst her will.
You see I have but two, a son and her;
And he is so devoted to his book,　　　　　　　　　　　5

---

253 *mean . . . sooth* speak truthfully. **255** *swear't, I* The quarto reads "swear't and
I." **256** *rise* At the very moment when Giovanni and Annabella resolve to ignore
traditional social restraints and to follow instead the dictates of appetite, sexual puns
appear in their language. **257** *Elysium* in Greek mythology, the dwelling place of
happy souls after death.

As I must tell you true, I doubt his health.
Should he miscarry, all my hopes rely
Upon my girl. As for worldly fortune,
I am, I thank my stars, blest with enough.
My care is how to match her to her liking: 10
I would not have her marry wealth, but love,
And if she like your nephew, let him have her,
Here's all that I can say.
DONADO   Sir, you say well,
Like a true father, and for my part, I,
If the young folks can like ('twixt you and me),   15
Will promise to assure my nephew presently
Three thousand florins yearly during life,
And after I am dead, my whole estate.
FLORIO   'Tis a fair proffer, sir; meantime your nephew
Shall have free passage to commence his suit: 20
If he can thrive, he shall have my consent.
So for this time I'll leave you, signor.   *Exit.*
DONADO   Well,
Here's hope yet, if my nephew would have wit;
But he is such another dunce, I fear
He'll never win the wench. When I was young   25
I could have done't, i'faith, and so shall he
If he will learn of me—and in good time
He comes himself.

Enter BERGETTO *and* POGGIO.

How now, Bergetto, whither away so fast?
BERGETTO   O uncle, I have heard the strangest news that ever came   30
   out of the mint, have I not, Poggio?
POGGIO   Yes indeed, sir.
DONADO   What news, Bergetto?
BERGETTO   Why, look ye, uncle, my barber told me just now that
   there is a fellow come to town who undertakes to make a mill   35
   go without the mortal help of any water or wind, only with
   sandbags. And this fellow hath a strange horse, a most excellent
   beast, I'll assure you, uncle,—my barber says—whose head, to
   the wonder of all Christian people, stands just behind where his
   tail is; is't not true, Poggio?   40

ACT I, Scene 3.   **6** ***doubt*** fear for.   **15** ***can like*** have a liking for one another
(echoes Florio's "liking" in line 10 above).   **19** ***proffer*** proposal.   **27** ***in . . . time*** at
an opportune moment.   **29** ***How . . . fast*** The quarto assigns this speech to Poggio.

POGGIO   So the barber swore, forsooth.

DONADO   And you are running thither?

BERGETTO   Ay forsooth, uncle.

DONADO   Wilt thou be a fool still? Come, sir, you shall not go:
you have more mind of a puppet play than on the business I   45
told ye. Why, thou great baby, wilt never have wit; wilt make
thyself a may-game to all the world?

POGGIO   Answer for yourself, master.

BERGETTO   Why, uncle, should I sit at home still, and not go abroad
to see fashions like other gallants?   50

DONADO   To see hobbyhorses! What wise talk, I pray, had you with
Annabella, when you were at Signor Florio's house?

BERGETTO   O, the wench: uds sa' me, uncle, I tickled her with a rare
speech, that I made her almost burst her belly with laughing.

DONADO   Nay, I think so, and what speech was't?   55

BERGETTO   What did I say, Poggio?

POGGIO   Forsooth, my master said that he loved her almost as well
as he loved parmasent, and swore (I'll be sworn for him) that
she wanted but such a nose as his was to be as pretty a young
woman as any was in Parma.   60

DONADO   O gross!

BERGETTO   Nay, uncle, then she asked me whether my father had
any more children than myself: and I said, "No, 'twere better
he should have had his brains knocked out first."

DONADO   This is intolerable.   65

BERGETTO   Then said she, "Will Signor Donado your uncle leave you
all his wealth?"

DONADO   Ha! that was good. Did she harp upon that string?

BERGETTO   Did she harp upon that string? Ay, that she did. I answered,
"Leave me all his wealth? Why, woman, he hath no other wit;   70
if he had, he should hear on't to his everlasting glory and confusion. I know," quoth I, "I am his white boy, and will not be
gulled." And with that she fell into a great smile and went away.
Nay, I did fit her.

DONADO   Ah, sirrah, then I see there is no changing of nature: well   75
Bergetto, I fear thou wilt be a very ass still.

BERGETTO   I should be sorry for that, uncle.

---

42 *thither*   The quarto reads "hither."   **45** *of*   to (watch).   **47** *may-game*   an object of
ridicule.   **51** *hobbyhorses*   frivolous fools.   **53** *uds sa' me*   an interjection, contracted
from "God save me."   **55** *I think so*   I (hardly) think so.   **58** *parmasent*   a cheese made
in Parma.   **70** *wit*   idea.   **71** *glory*   a malapropism: Bergetto means "dismay."
72 *white boy*   favorite.   **74** *fit*   satisfy.

DONADO Come, come you home with me; since you are no better
    a speaker, I'll have you write to her after some courtly manner,
    and enclose some rich jewel in the letter.   80
BERGETTO Ay marry, that will be excellent.
DONADO Peace, innocent.
    Once in my time I'll set my wits to school;
    If all fail, 'tis but the fortune of a fool.
BERGETTO Poggio, 'twill do, Poggio.   *Exeunt.*   85

ACT II

{Scene 1   FLORIO'*s house*}

Enter GIOVANNI *and* ANNABELLA, *as from their chamber.*

GIOVANNI Come, Annabella. No more sister now,
    But love, a name more gracious; do not blush,
    Beauty's sweet wonder, but be proud to know
    That yielding thou hast conquered and inflamed
    A heart whose tribute is thy brother's life.   5
ANNABELLA And mine is his. O, how these stolen contènts
    Would print a modest crimson on my cheeks,
    Had any but my heart's delight prevailed!
GIOVANNI I marvel why the chaster of your sex
    Should think this pretty toy called maidenhead   10
    So strange a loss, when, being lost, 'tis nothing,
    And you are still the same.
ANNABELLA   'Tis well for you;
    Now, you can talk.
GIOVANNI   Music as well consists
    In th'ear, as in the playing.
ANNABELLA   O, y'are wanton;
    Tell on't, y'are best: do.
GIOVANNI   Thou wilt chide me then.   15

---

81 *marry* an interjection, originally derived from "Virgin Mary." **82** *innocent* fool.
83 *Once . . . school* Once I have some time to myself, I'll think of a plan.
🦎 ACT II, Scene 1. **6** *stolen contènts* secret joys. **10** *pretty toy* insignificant
trifle. **13** *you . . . talk* You are hardly the one to talk (since you never had a maidenhead). **13–14** *Music . . . playing* The implication of Giovanni's statement is that men,
who take maidenheads, are as well qualified to judge their worth as women, who lose them.

Kiss me, so.—Thus hung Jove on Leda's neck,
And sucked divine ambrosia from her lips.
I envy not the mightiest man alive,
But hold myself in being king of thee
More great than were I king of all the world.   20
But I shall lose you, sweetheart.

ANNABELLA   But you shall not.

GIOVANNI   You must be married, mistress.

ANNABELLA   Yes? To whom?

GIOVANNI   Someone must have you.

ANNABELLA   You must.

GIOVANNI   Nay, some other.

ANNABELLA   Now prithee do not speak so without jesting.
You'll make me weep in earnest.

GIOVANNI   What, you will not!   25
But tell me, sweet, canst thou be dared to swear
That thou wilt live to me, and to no other?

ANNABELLA   By both our loves I dare, for didst thou know,
My Giovanni, how all suitors seem
To my eyes hateful, thou wouldst trust me then.   30

GIOVANNI   Enough, I take thy word. Sweet, we must part.
Remember what thou vowst: keep well my heart.

ANNABELLA   Will you be gone?

GIOVANNI   I must.

ANNABELLA   When to return?   35

GIOVANNI   Soon.

ANNABELLA   Look you do.

GIOVANNI   Farewell.   *Exit.*

ANNABELLA   Go where thou wilt, in mind I'll keep thee here,
And where thou art, I know I shall be there.   40
Guardian!

Enter PUTANA.

PUTANA   Child, how is't, child? Well, thank heaven.—Ha!

ANNABELLA   O guardian, what a paradise of joy
Have I passed over!

PUTANA   Nay, what a paradise of joy have you passed under! Why,   45
now I commend thee, charge. Fear nothing, sweetheart; what

---

16 *Jove, Leda* In classical mythology, Leda, the wife of a Spartan king, was loved by
Jove, who appeared to her as a swan.   **27 *live to me*** make your love for me the object
and purpose of your life.   **37 *Look*** make certain.

though he be your brother? Your brother's a man, I hope, and
I say still, if a young wench feel the fit upon her, let her take
anybody—father or brother, all is one.

ANNABELLA   I would not have it known for all the world.   50

PUTANA   Nor I, indeed, for the speech of the people; else 'twere
nothing.

FLORIO   *Within.* Daughter Annabella!

ANNABELLA   O me, my father!—Here, sir!—Reach my work.

FLORIO   *Within.* What are you doing?

ANNABELLA   So, let him come now.   55

Enter FLORIO, RICHARDETTO *like a doctor of physic, and* PHILOTIS *with
a lute in her hand.*

FLORIO   So hard at work? That's well, you lose no time.
    Look, I have brought you company: here's one,
    A learnèd doctor lately come from Padua,
    Much skilled in physic; and for that I see
    You have of late been sickly, I entreated   60
    This reverend man to visit you some time.

ANNABELLA   Y'are very welcome, sir.

RICHARDETTO   I thank you, mistress.
    Loud fame in large report hath spoke your praise
    As well for virtue as perfection:
    For which I have been bold to bring with me   65
    A kinswoman of mine, a maid for song
    And music, one perhaps will give content.
    Please you to know her.

ANNABELLA   They are parts I love,
    And she for them most welcome.

PHILOTIS   Thank you, lady.

FLORIO   Sir, now you know my house, pray make not strange,   70
    And if you find my daughter need your art,
    I'll be your paymaster.

RICHARDETTO   Sir, what I am
    She shall command.

FLORIO   You shall bind me to you.

---

54 Reach . . . work Hand me my needlework. **56–61 So . . . time** In the quarto
these lines are printed as prose. **56 lose** waste. **61 reverend** learned. **63 large** unrestrained. **64 perfection** flawless beauty. **67 will** (who) will. **68 parts** skills.
70 make . . . strange visit often. **72–73 Sir . . . command** The quarto prints as one
line. **73 You . . . you** I will be obliged to you.

Daughter, I must have conference with you
About some matters that concern us both.   75
Good master doctor, please you but walk in,
We'll crave a little of your cousin's cunning.
I think my girl hath not quite forgot
To touch an instrument: she could have done't;
We'll hear them both.   80
RICHARDETTO   I'll wait upon you, sir.   *Exeunt.*

ACT II
Scene 2   SORANZO's *house*

Enter SORANZO *in his study reading a book.*

SORANZO   "Love's measure is extreme, the comfort, pain,
The life unrest, and the reward disdain."
What's here? Look't o'er again: 'tis so, so writes
This smooth, licentious poet in his rhymes.
But Sannazar, thou liest, for had thy bosom   5
Felt such oppression as is laid on mine,
Thou wouldst have kissed the rod that made thee smart.
To work then, happy muse, and contradict
What Sannazar hath in his envy writ:
"Love's measure is the mean, sweet his annoys,   10
His pleasure's life, and his reward all joys."
Had Annabella lived when Sannazar
Did in his brief encomium celebrate
Venice, that queen of cities, he had left
That verse which gained him such a sum of gold,   15
And for one only look from Annabel
Had writ of her and her diviner cheeks.
O how my thoughts are—

---

77 *cunning*   skill (in playing the lute).
❧ **ACT II, Scene 2.   5 *Sannazar***   Jacopo Sannazaro (1458–1530), an Italian poet who
was richly rewarded by Venice for his praise of the city. He was the author of many Latin
poems, a number of Italian sonnets, and the first modern pastoral romance, *Arcadia* (1504).
7 *thee*   The quarto reads "the."   **16 *one only***   only one.

VASQUES   *Within.* Pray, forbear. In rules of civility, let me give notice
    on't: I shall be taxed of my neglect of duty and service.   20
SORANZO   What rude intrusion interrupts my peace?
    Can I be nowhere private?
VASQUES   *Within.* Troth you wrong your modesty.
SORANZO   What's the matter, Vasques? Who is't?

    Enter HIPPOLITA *and* VASQUES.

HIPPOLITA   'Tis I:
    Do you know me now? Look, perjured man, on her   25
    Whom thou and thy distracted lust have wronged.
    Thy sensual rage of blood hath made my youth
    A scorn to men and angels, and shall I
    Be now a foil to thy unsated change?
    Thou knowst, false wanton, when my modest fame   30
    Stood free from strain or scandal: all the charms
    Of hell or sorcery could not prevail
    Against the honor of my chaster bosom.
    Thine eyes did plead in tears, thy tongue in oaths
    Such and so many, that a heart of steel   35
    Would have been wrought to pity, as was mine:
    And shall the conquest of my lawful bed,
    My husband's death urged on by his disgrace,
    My loss of womanhood, be ill rewarded
    With hatred and contempt? No, know, Soranzo,   40
    I have a spirit doth as much distaste
    The slavery of fearing thee, as thou
    Dost loathe the memory of what hath passed.
SORANZO   Nay, dear Hippolita—
HIPPOLITA   Call me not dear,
    Nor think with supple words to smooth the grossness   45
    Of my abuses. 'Tis not your new mistress,
    Your goodly madam-merchant, shall triumph
    On my dejection: tell her thus from me,
    My birth was nobler and by much more free.

---

20 taxed of punished for. **28–29 and . . . change** And shall I act as a mere basis of
comparison in your next love affair? **30 modest fame** good reputation. **37 lawful**
belonging, by the law of marriage, to another. **47 madam-merchant** Hippolita judges
Annabella her inferior because Annabella's family was not always aristocratic like hers;
instead they bought their way into social prominence after becoming wealthy. They
are, Hippolita thus suggests, not noble but *nouveau riche.*

SORANZO   You are too violent.

HIPPOLITA   You are too double   50
    In your dissimulation. Seest thou this,
    This habit—these black mourning-weeds of care?
    'Tis thou art cause of this, and hast divorced
    My husband from his life and me from him,
    And made me widow in my widowhood.   55

SORANZO   Will you yet hear?

HIPPOLITA   More of thy perjuries?
    Thy soul is drowned too deeply in those sins;
    Thou needst not add to th' number.

SORANZO   Then I'll leave you;
    You are past all rules of sense.

HIPPOLITA   And thou, of grace.

VASQUES   Fie, mistress, you are not near the limits of reason: if my   60
    lord had a resolution as noble as virtue itself, you take the course
    to unedge it all. Sir, I beseech you, do not perplex her; griefs,
    alas, will have a vent. I dare undertake Madam Hippolita will
    now freely hear you.

SORANZO   Talk to a woman frantic! Are these the fruits of your love?   65

HIPPOLITA   They are the fruits of thy untruth, false man!
    Didst thou not swear, whilst yet my husband lived,
    That thou wouldst wish no happiness on earth
    More than to call me wife? Didst thou not vow,
    When he should die, to marry me? For which   70
    The devil in my blood and thy protests
    Caused me to counsel him to undertake
    A voyage to Ligorn, for that we heard
    His brother there was dead, and left a daughter
    Young and unfriended, who, with much ado,   75
    I wished him to bring hither. He did so,
    And went; and as thou knowst died on the way.
    Unhappy man, to buy his death so dear
    With my advice! Yet thou for whom I did it
    Forgetst thy vows, and leavst me to my shame.   80

---

52 *mourning-weeds* widow's clothes.   **55** *And . . . widowhood* Hippolita argues
that she is doubly widowed because she has lost both her husband and her lover.
60 *you . . . reason* You are being utterly unreasonable.   **63** *dare undertake* think.
71 *The . . . blood* her passion.   **73** *Ligorn* the seaport of Leghorn, situated on the
west coast of Italy, near Pisa.

SORANZO   Who could help this?

HIPPOLITA   Who? Perjured man, thou couldst,
　　　If thou hadst faith or love.

SORANZO   You are deceived.
　　　The vows I made, if you remember well,
　　　Were wicked and unlawful: 'twere more sin
　　　To keep them than to break them. As for me,   85
　　　I cannot mask my penitence. Think, thou,
　　　How much thou hast digressed from honest shame
　　　In bringing of a gentleman to death
　　　Who was thy husband, such a one as he,
　　　So noble in his quality, condition,   90
　　　Learning, behavior, entertainment, love,
　　　As Parma could not show a braver man.

VASQUES   You do not well; this was not your promise.

SORANZO   I care not; let her know her monstrous life.
　　　Ere I'll be servile to so black a sin,   95
　　　I'll be a curse. Woman, come here no more.
　　　Learn to repent and die, for by my honor
　　　I hate thee and thy lust: you have been too foul.   [*Exit.*]

VASQUES   [*Aside.*] This part has been scurvily played.

HIPPOLITA   How foolishly this beast contemns his fate,   100
　　　And shuns the use of that which I more scorn
　　　Than I once loved—his love; but let him go.
　　　My vengeance shall give comfort to his woe.

　　　She offers to go away.

VASQUES   Mistress, mistress, Madam Hippolita, pray, a word or two.

HIPPOLITA   With me, sir?   105

VASQUES   With you, if you please.

HIPPOLITA   What is't?

VASQUES   I know you are infinitely moved now, and you think you
　　　have cause. Some I confess you have, but sure not so much as
　　　you imagine.   110

HIPPOLITA   Indeed?

VASQUES   O, you were miserably bitter, which you followed even

---

96 *a curse* an object of execration. **99 *This . . . played*** He has acted like a knave.
103 *his woe* the pretenses of woe stemming from the sanctimoniousness that Soranzo
has demonstrated in lines 83–98. Perhaps, though, as one modern editor suggests, "his"
is a printer's error for "this." In that case, "this woe" would refer to Hippolita's sorrow.

to the last syllable. Faith, you were somewhat too shrewd; by
my life you could not have took my lord in a worse time, since
I first knew him: tomorrow you shall find him a new man.   115

HIPPOLITA   Well, I shall wait his leisure.

VASQUES   Fie, this is not a hearty patience; it comes sourly from
you. Troth, let me persuade you for once.

HIPPOLITA   [*Aside.*] I have it, and it shall be so. Thanks, opportunity!
[*To him.*] Persuade me to what?   120

VASQUES   Visit him in some milder temper. O if you could but
master a little your female spleen, how might you win him!

HIPPOLITA   He will never love me. Vasques, thou hast been a too
trusty servant to such a master, and I believe thy reward in the
end will fall out like mine.   125

VASQUES   So perhaps too.

HIPPOLITA   Resolve thyself it will. Had I one so true, so truly honest,
so secret to my counsels, as thou has been to him and his, I should
think it a slight acquittance not only to make him master of all
I have, but even of myself.   130

VASQUES   O you are a noble gentlewoman!

HIPPOLITA   Wilt thou feed always upon hopes? Well, I know thou
art wise, and seest the reward of an old servant daily, what it is.

VASQUES   Beggary and neglect.

HIPPOLITA   True. But Vasques, wert thou mine, and wouldst be   135
private to me and my designs, I here protest myself, and all
what I can else call mine, should be at thy dispose.

VASQUES   [*Aside.*] Work you that way, old mole? Then I have the
wind of you. [*To her.*] I were not worthy of it by any desert
that could lie within my compass; if I could—   140

HIPPOLITA   What then?

VASQUES   I should then hope to live in these my old years with rest
and security.

HIPPOLITA   Give me thy hand. Now promise but thy silence,
And help to bring to pass a plot I have;   145
And here in sight of Heaven, that being done,
I make thee lord of me and mine estate.

VASQUES   Come, you are merry. This is such a happiness that I can
neither think or believe.

---

113 *shrewd* shrewish. **138** *mole* one who moves in the darkness underground, or
is figuratively blind (cf. *Hamlet,* I.5.161). **138–39** *have . . . you* understand you.
139 *desert* act deserving reward.

HIPPOLITA   Promise thy secrecy, and 'tis confirmed.   150
VASQUES   Then here I call our good genii for witnesses, whatsoever
   your designs are, or against whomsoever, I will not only be a
   special actor therein, but never disclose it till it be effected.
HIPPOLITA   I take thy word, and with that, thee for mine.
   Come then, let's more confer of this anon.   155
   On this delicious bane my thoughts shall banquet:
   Revenge shall sweeten what my griefs have tasted.   *Exeunt.*

ACT II

Scene 3   RICHARDETTO's *house*

Enter RICHARDETTO *and* PHILOTIS.

RICHARDETTO   Thou seest, my lovely niece, these strange mishaps:
   How all my fortunes turn to my disgrace,
   Wherein I am but as a looker-on,
   Whiles others act my shame, and I am silent.
PHILOTIS   But uncle, wherein can this borrowed shape   5
   Give you content?
RICHARDETTO   I'll tell thee, gentle niece.
   Thy wanton aunt in her lascivious riots
   Lives now secure, thinks I am surely dead
   In my late journey to Ligorn for you,
   As I have caused it to be rumored out.   10
   Now would I see with what an impudence
   She gives scope to her loose adultery,
   And how the common voice allows hereof:
   Thus far I have prevailed.
PHILOTIS   Alas, I fear

---

151 *for witnesses*   The quarto reads "foe-witnesses."   **156** *On . . . banquet*   an example
of the kind of dramatic irony that is a favorite technique of Jacobean dramatists. Hippolita
means that she will think with self-satisfaction about her plan to poison Soranzo, but the
imagery that she uses alerts the audience to a problem that she herself does not recognize:
banqueting on delicious poison, even if one does so only metaphorically, is indeed a
dangerous activity. It is one that Hippolita will soon regret, for in her case the metaphorical becomes the literal, and she is fatally poisoned.
ACT II, Scene 3.   5 *borrowed shape*   his disguise.   **13** *And . . . hereof*   and how
her adultery is the subject of widespread gossip.

You mean some strange revenge.

RICHARDETTO   O, be not troubled;   15
  Your ignorance shall plead for you in all.
  But to our business: what, you learned for certain
  How Signor Florio means to give his daughter
  In marriage to Soranzo?

PHILOTIS   Yes, for certain.

RICHARDETTO   But how find you young Annabella's love   20
  Inclined to him?

PHILOTIS   For aught I could perceive,
  She neither fancies him, or any else.

RICHARDETTO   There's mystery in that which time must show.
  She used you kindly?

PHILOTIS   Yes.

RICHARDETTO   And craved your company?

PHILOTIS   Often.   25

RICHARDETTO   'Tis well. It goes as I could wish.
  I am the doctor now, and as for you,
  None knows you; if all fail not, we shall thrive.
  But who comes here? *Enter* GRIMALDI.
                            I know him; 'tis Grimaldi,
  A Roman and a soldier, near allied   30
  Unto the Duke of Montferrato, one
  Attending on the nuncio of the Pope
  That now resides in Parma, by which means
  He hopes to get the love of Annabella.

GRIMALDI   Save you, sir.

RICHARDETTO   And you, sir.

GRIMALDI   I have heard   35
  Of your approved skill, which through the city
  Is freely talked of, and would crave your aid.

RICHARDETTO   For what, sir?

GRIMALDI   Marry, sir, for this—
  But I would speak in private.

RICHARDETTO   Leave us, cousin.   *Exit* PHILOTIS.

GRIMALDI   I love fair Annabella, and would know   40

---

16 shall . . . all   shall insure your innocence in all I do.   **17 what**   a sign of interroga-
tion, used merely to introduce a question (cf. *Hamlet,* I.1.19).   **31 Montferrato**   a duchy
in northwest Italy, united to Mantua in 1536.   **32 nuncio . . . Pope**   the Cardinal.

Whether in art there may not be receipts
To move affection.
RICHARDETTO   Sir, perhaps there may,
But these will nothing profit you.
GRIMALDI   Not me?
RICHARDETTO   Unless I be mistook, you are a man
Greatly in favor with the Cardinal.   45
GRIMALDI   What of that?
RICHARDETTO   In duty to his grace,
I will be bold to tell you, if you seek
To marry Florio's daughter, you must first
Remove a bar 'twixt you and her.
GRIMALDI   Who's that?
RICHARDETTO   Soranzo is the man that hath her heart,   50
And while he lives, be sure you cannot speed.
GRIMALDI   Soranzo! What, mine enemy! Is't he?
RICHARDETTO   Is he your enemy?
GRIMALDI   The man I hate
Worse than confusion—
I'll kill him straight.
RICHARDETTO   Nay then, take mine advice,   55
Even for his grace's sake, the Cardinal:
I'll find a time when he and she do meet,
Of which I'll give you notice, and to be sure
He shall not 'scape you, I'll provide a poison
To dip your rapier's point in; if he had   60
As many heads as Hydra had, he dies.
GRIMALDI   But shall I trust thee, doctor?
RICHARDETTO   As yourself;
Doubt not in aught. [*Aside.*] Thus shall the fates decree:
By me Soranzo falls, that mined me.   *Exeunt.*

---

41 receipts drugs. **51 speed** prosper. **55 kill** The quarto reads "tell." **57 he**
Soranzo. **61 Hydra** in Greek mythology, a many-headed monster that grew new heads
whenever any were cut off. **64 mined** The corrected edition of the quarto emends to
"ruined," but the change is unnecessary because one of the seventeenth-century meanings
of "mine" is "to ruin" (cf. *Volpone*, III.2.28).

ACT II

Scene 4   DONADO's *house*

Enter DONADO, BERGETTO, *and* POGGIO.

DONADO   Well, sir, I must be content to be both your secretary and
your messenger myself. I cannot tell what this letter may work,
but as sure as I am alive, if thou come once to talk with her,
I fear thou wilt mar whatsoever I make.

BERGETTO   You make, uncle? Why, am not I big enough to carry   5
mine own letter, I pray?

DONADO   Ay, ay, carry a fool's head o' thy own! Why, thou dunce,
wouldst thou write a letter and carry it thyself?

BERGETTO   Yes, that I would, and read it to her with my own mouth;
for you must think, if she will not believe me myself when she   10
hears me speak, she will not believe another's handwriting.
O, you think I am a blockhead, uncle! No, sir, Poggio knows I
have indited a letter myself, so I have.

POGGIO   Yes, truly, sir; I have it in my pocket.

DONADO   A sweet one, no doubt. Pray, let's see't.   15

BERGETTO   I cannot read my own hand very well, Poggio; read it,
Poggio.

DONADO   Begin.

POGGIO   *Reads.* "Most dainty and honey-sweet mistress, I could call
you fair, and lie as fast as any that loves you, but my uncle being   20
the elder man, I leave it to him, as more fit for his age and the
color of his beard. I am wise enough to tell you I can board where
I see occasion: or if you like my uncle's wit better than mine,
you shall marry me; if you like mine better than his, I will marry
you in spite of your teeth. So commending my best parts to you,   25
I rest—Yours upwards and downwards, or you may choose,
Bergetto."

BERGETTO   Aha, here's stuff, uncle.

🏃 **ACT II, Scene 4.   2** *what* whether.   **4** *wilt* The quarto reads "wu't."   **10** *think*
realize.   **19–27** *Most . . . Bergetto* In this letter Bergetto is trying to be impressively
boastful, but he succeeds instead merely in publicly demonstrating his stupidity. In trying
to speak the blunt language that characterizes a man of action, he produces gibberish
because, as usual, he cannot avoid absurd non sequiturs, foolishly incongruous phrases,
and gauche sexual puns.   **20** *fast* zealously.   **22** *board* This word may be the printer's
misreading of "bourd," meaning "jest," or else it develops the double-entendre implicit
in "lie" in the preceding sentence.   **25** *in . . . teeth* in spite of your opposition.

DONADO   Here's stuff indeed to shame us all. Pray whose advice
 did you take in this learned letter?   30
POGGIO   None, upon my word, but mine own.
BERGETTO   And mine, uncle, believe it, nobody's else. 'Twas mine
 own brain; I thank a good wit for't.
DONADO   Get you home, sir, and look you keep within doors till I
 return.   35
BERGETTO   How? That were a jest indeed; I scorn it i'faith.
DONADO   What? You do not!
BERGETTO   Judge me, but I do now.
POGGIO   Indeed, sir, 'tis very unhealthy.
DONADO   Well, sir, if I hear any of your apish running to motions   40
 and fopperies, till I come back, you were as good not; look to't.
Exit DONADO.
BERGETTO   Poggio, shall's steal to see this horse with the head in's tail?
POGGIO   Ay, but you must take heed of whipping.
BERGETTO   Dost take me for a child, Poggio? Come, honest Poggio.
Exeunt.

ACT II

Scene 5 *The* FRIAR'*s cell*

Enter FRIAR *and* GIOVANNI.

FRIAR   Peace! Thou hast told a tale whose every word
 Threatens eternal slaughter to the soul.
 I'm sorry I have heard it; would mine ears
 Had been one minute deaf, before the hour
 That thou cam'st to me. O young man castaway,   5
 By the religious number of mine order,
 I day and night have waked my agèd eyes,
 Above my strength, to weep on thy behalf:
 But Heaven is angry, and be thou resolved,

---

40 apish foolish. **motions** puppet shows (cf. *Winter's Tale*, IV.3.103). **41 you . . .
not** You will be sorry. **not** The quarto reads "no." **42 shall's** shall we.
❧ **ACT II, Scene 5. 5 castaway** reprobate. **6 By . . . order** (I swear) by all those
who number themselves in my religious order that.

Thou art a man remarked to taste a mischief: 10
Look for't; though it come late, it will come sure.

GIOVANNI   Father, in this you are uncharitable;
What I have done, I'll prove both fit and good.
It is a principle, which you have taught
When I was yet your scholar, that the frame   15
And composition of the mind doth follow
The frame and composition of the body.
So where the body's furniture is beauty,
The mind's must needs be virtue; which allowed,
Virtue itself is reason but refined,   20
And love the quintessence of that. This proves
My sister's beauty being rarely fair
Is rarely virtuous—chiefly in her love,
And chiefly in that love, her love to me.
If hers to me, then so is mine to her,   25
Since in like causes are effects alike.

FRIAR   O ignorance in knowledge! Long ago,
How often have I warned thee this before?
Indeed, if we were sure there were no deity,
Nor heaven nor hell, then to be led alone   30
By nature's light, as were philosophers
Of elder times, might instance some defense.
But 'tis not so. Then, madman, thou wilt find
That Nature is in Heaven's positions blind.

GIOVANNI   Your age o'errules you; had you youth like mine,   35
You'd make her love, your heaven, and her, divine.

FRIAR   Nay then, I see thou'rt too far sold to hell,
It lies not in the compass of my prayers
To call thee back. Yet let me counsel thee:
Persuade thy sister to some marriage.   40

GIOVANNI   Marriage? Why, that's to damn her! That's to prove
Her greedy of variety of lust.

FRIAR   O fearful! If thou wilt not, give me leave
To shrive her, lest she should die unabsolved.

GIOVANNI   At your best leisure, father. Then she'll tell you   45

---

10 *remarked* destined. *mischief* misfortune. **15** *scholar* pupil. *frame* The quarto
reads "fame." **17** *the body* The quarto reads "body." **22** *rarely* unusually.
32 *elder* pre-Christian. *instance . . . defense* be defensible. **34** *Nature . . . blind*
Nature (ruled by appetite) is blind to the teachings of Christian doctrine. **44** *shrive her*
hear her confession.

How dearly she doth prize my matchless love.
Then you will know what pity 'twere we two
Should have been sundered from each other's arms.
View well her face, and in that little round
You may observe a world of variety—   50
For color, lips; for sweet perfumes, her breath;
For jewels, eyes; for threads of purest gold,
Hair; for delicious choice of flowers, cheeks;
Wonder in every portion of that throne.
Hear her but speak, and you will swear the spheres   55
Make music to the citizens in heaven.
But, father, what is else for pleasure framed,
Lest I offend your ears, shall go unnamed.
FRIAR   The more I hear, I pity thee the more,
That one so excellent should give those parts   60
All to a second death. What I can do
Is but to pray; and yet I could advise thee,
Wouldst thou be ruled.
GIOVANNI   In what?
FRIAR   Why, leave her yet.
The throne of mercy is above your trespass,
Yet time is left you both—
GIOVANNI   To embrace each other,   65
Else let all time be struck quite out of number.
She is like me, and I like her, resolved.
FRIAR   No more! I'll visit her; this grieves me most:
Things being thus, a pair of souls are lost.   *Exeunt.*

ACT II
Scene 6   FLORIO's *house*

Enter FLORIO, DONADO, ANNABELLA, PUTANA.

FLORIO   Where's Giovanni?
ANNABELLA   Newly walked abroad,
And, as I heard him say, gone to the friar,

---

54 *throne* her face (where such beauty is enthroned). **55–56** *Hear ... heaven* Her
speech is like celestial harmony. **61** *second death* damnation. **63** *yet* now, while
there is still time.

His reverend tutor.

FLORIO   That's a blessed man,
    A man made up of holiness; I hope
    He'll teach him how to gain another world.   5

DONADO   Fair gentlewoman, here's a letter sent
    To you from my young cousin. I dare swear
    He loves you in his soul: would you could hear
    Sometimes what I see daily, sighs and tears,
    As if his breast were prison to his heart.   10

FLORIO   Receive it, Annabella.

ANNABELLA   Alas, good man.

DONADO   What's that she said?

PUTANA   And please you, sir, she said, "Alas, good man." Truly I
    do commend him to her every night before her first sleep, because   15
    I would have her dream of him; and she hearkens to that most
    religiously.

DONADO   Sayst so? God a-mercy, Putana, there's something for thee
    [*gives her money*], and prithee, do what thou canst on his behalf;
    sha' not be lost labor, take my word for't.   20

PUTANA   Thank you most heartily, sir. Now I have a feeling of
    your mind, let me alone to work.

ANNABELLA   Guardian!

PUTANA   Did you call?

ANNABELLA   Keep this letter.   25

DONADO   Signor Florio, in any case bid her read it instantly.

FLORIO   Keep it for what? Pray read it me here-right.

ANNABELLA   I shall, sir.

    She reads.

DONADO   How d'ee find her inclined, signor?

FLORIO   Troth, sir, I know not how. Not all so well   30
    As I could wish.

ANNABELLA   Sir, I am bound to rest your cousin's debtor.
    The jewel I'll return; for if he love,
    I'll count that love a jewel.

DONADO   Mark you that?
    Nay, keep them both, sweet maid.

ANNABELLA   You must excuse me,   35

🐾 **ACT II, Scene 6.** **14** *And* and (may it). **16** *that* her commendation of Bergetto.
27 *here-right* right now.

Indeed, I will not keep it.

FLORIO   Where's the ring,
  That which your mother in her will bequeathed,
  And charged you on her blessing not to give't
  To any but your husband? Send back that.

ANNABELLA   I have it not.

FLORIO   Ha! Have it not? Where is't?   40

ANNABELLA   My brother in the morning took it from me,
  Said he would wear't today.

FLORIO   Well, what do you say
  To young Bergetto's love? Are you content
  To match with him? Speak.

DONADO   There's the point indeed.

ANNABELLA   [*Aside.*] What shall I do? I must say something now.   45

FLORIO   What say? Why d'ee not speak?

ANNABELLA   Sir, with your leave,
  Please you to give me freedom.

FLORIO   Yes, you have it.

ANNABELLA   Signor Donado, if your nephew mean
  To raise his better fortunes in his match,
  The hope of me will hinder such a hope.   50
  Sir, if you love him, as I know you do,
  Find one more worthy of his choice than me.
  In short, I'm sure I sha' not be his wife.

DONADO   Why, here's plain dealing. I commend thee for't,
  And all the worst I wish thee is: Heaven bless thee!   55
  Your father yet and I will still be friends,
  Shall we not, Signor Florio?

FLORIO   Yes, why not?
  Look, here your cousin comes.

  Enter BERGETTO *and* POGGIO.

DONADO   [*Aside.*] O coxcomb, what doth he make here?

BERGETTO   Where's my uncle, sirs?   60

DONADO   What's the news now?

BERGETTO   Save you, uncle, save you! You must not think I come
  for nothing, masters. And how, and how is't? What, you have
  read my letter? Ah, there I—tickled you i'faith!

POGGIO   But 'twere better you had tickled her in another place.   65

---

44 *match with* marry. **49** *To . . . better* to better his. **50** *of me* of winning my
love. **59** *make* do. **63** *and . . . is't* And what is it you are doing?

BERGETTO   Sirrah, sweetheart, I'll tell thee a good jest, and riddle
what 'tis.

ANNABELLA   You say you'd tell me.

BERGETTO   As I was walking just now in the street, I met a swaggering
fellow would needs take the wall of me, and because he did   70
thrust me, I very valiantly called him rogue. He hereupon bade
me draw: I told him I had more wit than so, but when he saw
that I would not, he did so maul me with the hilts of his rapier
that my head sung whilst my feet capered in the kennel.

DONADO   [*Aside.*] Was ever the like ass seen?   75

ANNABELLA   And what did you all this while?

BERGETTO   Laugh at him for a gull, till I see the blood run about
mine ears, and then I could not choose but find in my heart to
cry; till a fellow with a broad beard—they say he is a new-come
doctor—called me into his house, and gave me a plaster—look   80
you, here 'tis—and, sir, there was a young wench washed my
face and hands most excellently, i'faith, I shall love her as long
as I live for't. Did she not, Poggio?

POGGIO   Yes, and kissed him too.

BERGETTO   Why, la now, you think I tell a lie, uncle, I warrant.   85

DONADO   Would he that beat thy blood out of thy head had beaten
some wit into it; for I fear thou never wilt have any.

BERGETTO   O, uncle, but there was a wench, would have done a
man's heart good to have looked on her. By this light she had a
face methinks worth twenty of you, Mistress Annabella.   90

DONADO   Was ever such a fool born?

ANNABELLA   I am glad she liked you, sir.

BERGETTO   Are you so? By my troth I thank you, forsooth.

FLORIO   Sure 'twas the doctor's niece, that was last day with us here.

BERGETTO   'Twas she, 'twas she.   95

DONADO   How do you know that, simplicity?

BERGETTO   Why, does not he say so? If I should have said no, I should
have given him the lie, uncle, and so have deserved a dry-beating
again; I'll none of that.

---

70 *take . . . me* force me into the gutter.   **71** *thrust* push.   **74** *kennel* gutter.
80 *his* The quarto reads "this."   **92** *liked* pleased.   **96** *simplicity* simpleton.
98 *dry-beating* sound thrashing.

FLORIO   A very modest well-behaved young maid, as I have seen.   100
DONADO   Is she indeed?
FLORIO   Indeed she is, if I have any judgment.
DONADO   Well, sir, now you are free, you need not care for sending
    letters. Now you are dismissed, your mistress here will none of
    you.   105
BERGETTO   No. Why, what care I for that? I can have wenches
    enough in Parma for half-a-crown apiece; cannot I, Poggio?
POGGIO   I'll warrant you, sir.
DONADO   Signor Florio, I thank you for your free recourse you gave
    for my admittance; and to you, fair maid, that jewel I will give   110
    you 'gainst your marriage. Come, will you go, sir?
BERGETTO   Ay, marry, will I. Mistress, farewell, mistress. I'll come
    again tomorrow. Farewell, mistress.
                         Exit DONADO, BERGETTO, *and* POGGIO.

    Enter GIOVANNI.

FLORIO   Son, where have you been? What, alone, alone still?
    I would not have it so; you must forsake   115
    This over-bookish humor. Well, your sister
    Hath shook the fool off.
GIOVANNI   'Twas no match for her.
FLORIO   'Twas not, indeed. I meant it nothing less;
    Soranzo is the man I only like:
    Look on him, Annabella. Come, 'tis suppertime,   120
    And it grows late. *Exit* FLORIO.
GIOVANNI   Whose jewel's that?
ANNABELLA   Some sweetheart's.
GIOVANNI   So I think.
ANNABELLA   A lusty youth,
    Signor Donado, gave it me to wear
    Against my marriage.
GIOVANNI   But you shall not wear it:
    Send it him back again.
ANNABELLA   What, you are jealous?   125
GIOVANNI   That you shall know anon, at better leisure.
    Welcome, sweet night! The evening crowns the day.   *Exeunt.*

---

111 *'gainst . . . marriage* as part of your dowry. 114 *still* The quarto reads "still,
still?" 119 *only* chiefly.

ACT III

{Scene 1   *Outside* FLORIO's *house*}

Enter BERGETTO *and* POGGIO.

BERGETTO   Does my uncle think to make me a baby still? No, Poggio, he shall know I have a sconce now.

POGGIO   Ay, let him not bob you off like an ape with an apple.

BERGETTO   'Sfoot, I will have the wench if he were ten uncles, in despite of his nose, Poggio.   5

POGGIO   Hold him to the grindstone and give not a jot of ground. She hath in a manner promised you already.

BERGETTO   True, Poggio, and her uncle the doctor swore I should marry her.

POGGIO   He swore, I remember.   10

BERGETTO   And I will have her, that's more; didst see the codpiece-point she gave me, and the box of marmalade?

POGGIO   Very well—and kissed you, that my chops watered at the sight on't. There's no way but to clap up a marriage in hugger-mugger.   15

BERGETTO   I will do't, for I tell thee, Poggio, I begin to grow valiant methinks, and my courage begins to rise.

POGGIO   Should you be afraid of your uncle?

BERGETTO   Hang him, old doting rascal! No, I say I will have her.

POGGIO   Lose no time then.   20

BERGETTO   I will beget a race of wise men and constables, that shall cart whores at their own charges, and break the duke's peace ere I have done myself.—Come away.   *Exeunt.*

🎜 ACT III, Scene 1.   **2** *sconce*   head.   **3** *bob ... off*   make a fool of you.   *like ... apple*   like an ape (put through his tricks) for the reward of an apple.   **4** *'Sfoot*   an oath, contracted from "By God's foot."   **4–5** *in ... nose*   in spite of his opposition. **11–12** *codpiece-point*   an ornamented cord used to attach a codpiece.   **14–15** *in hugger-mugger*   clandestinely.   **21** *constables*   low-ranking law enforcement officers, traditionally depicted as stupid (e.g. Dogberry in *Much Ado about Nothing*).   **22** *cart whores* traditional punishment for whores, to put them on a cart and haul them about town.

ACT III

{ Scene 2   FLORIO's *house* }

Enter FLORIO, GIOVANNI, SORANZO, ANNABELLA, PUTANA, *and*
VASQUES.

FLORIO   My Lord Soranzo, though I must confess
 The proffers that are made me have been great
 In marriage of my daughter, yet the hope
 Of your still-rising honors have prevailed
 Above all other jointures; here she is.   5
 She knows my mind, speak for yourself to her,
 And hear you, daughter, see you use him nobly;
 For any private speech I'll give you time.
 Come, son, and you the rest, let them alone.
 Agree they as they may.
SORANZO   I thank you, sir.   10
GIOVANNI   [*Aside to* ANNABELLA.] Sister, be not all woman: think on
 me.
SORANZO   Vasques.
VASQUES   My lord?
SORANZO   Attend me without.
        Exeunt omnes, manet SORANZO *and* ANNABELLA.
ANNABELLA   Sir, what's your will with me?
SORANZO   Do you not know   15
 What I should tell you?
ANNABELLA   Yes, you'll say you love me.
SORANZO   And I'll swear it too; will you believe it?
ANNABELLA   'Tis not point of faith. *Enter* GIOVANNI *above.*
SORANZO   Have you not will to love?
ANNABELLA   Not you.
SORANZO   Whom then?
ANNABELLA   That's as the fates infer.
GIOVANNI   [*Aside.*] Of those I'm regent now.
SORANZO   What mean you, sweet? 20
ANNABELLA   To live and die a maid.
SORANZO   O, that's unfit.

🐾 ACT III, Scene 2.   11 *be ... woman*   Do not show a woman's weakness for having
lovers.   14 *Attend . . . without*   Wait for me outside.   18 *not point*   not a question.
19 *infer*   occasion, bring about.

GIOVANNI   [*Aside.*] Here's one can say that's but a woman's note.
SORANZO   Did you but see my heart, then would you swear—
ANNABELLA   That you were dead.
GIOVANNI   [*Aside.*] That's true, or somewhat near it.
SORANZO   See you these true love's tears?
ANNABELLA   No.
GIOVANNI   [*Aside.*] Now she winks.   25
SORANZO   They plead to you for grace.
ANNABELLA   Yet nothing speak.
SORANZO   O grant my suit!
ANNABELLA   What is't?
SORANZO   To let me live—
ANNABELLA   Take it.
SORANZO   —Still yours.
ANNABELLA   That is not mine to give.
GIOVANNI   [*Aside.*] One such another word would kill his hopes.
SORANZO   Mistress, to leave those fruitless strifes of wit,   30
    Know I have loved you long and loved you truly:
    Not hope of what you have, but what you are,
    Has drawn me on. Then let me not in vain
    Still feel the rigor of your chaste disdain.
    I'm sick, and sick to th' heart.
ANNABELLA   Help, aqua vitae!   35
SORANZO   What mean you?
ANNABELLA   Why, I thought you had been sick.
SORANZO   Do you mock my love?
GIOVANNI   [*Aside.*] There, sir, she was too nimble.
SORANZO   [*Aside.*] 'Tis plain, she laughs at me. [*To her.*] These scornful
    taunts
    Neither become your modesty or years.
ANNABELLA   You are no looking glass; or if you were,   40
    I'd dress my language by you.
GIOVANNI   [*Aside.*] I'm confirmed.
ANNABELLA   To put you out of doubt, my lord, methinks
    Your common sense should make you understand
    That if I loved you, or desired your love,
    Some way I should have given you better taste.   45

---

22 *that's . . . note* that she is lying. **26 *Yet . . . speak*** But yet say nothing.
31 *Know* The quarto reads "I know." **35 *aqua vitae*** liquor, used for medicinal
purposes. **40–41 *You . . . you*** You are not a looking glass (so I do not expect to be
reminded of my modesty and youth by you); if you were, I would dress up my
language—making it match my years—for you.

But since you are a nobleman, and one
I would not wish should spend his youth in hopes,
Let me advise you here to forbear your suit,
And think I wish you well: I tell you this.
SORANZO   Is't you speak this?
ANNABELLA   Yes, I myself. Yet know—   50
Thus far I give you comfort—if mine eyes
Could have picked out a man amongst all those
That sued to me, to make a husband of,
You should have been that man. Let this suffice;
Be noble in your secrecy and wise.   55
GIOVANNI   [*Aside.*] Why, now I see she loves me.
ANNABELLA   One word more:
As ever virtue lived within your mind,
As ever noble courses were your guide,
As ever you would have me know you loved me,
Let not my father know hereof by you: 60
If I hereafter find that I must marry,
It shall be you or none.
SORANZO   I take that promise.
ANNABELLA   O, O, my head!
SORANZO   What's the matter? Not well?
ANNABELLA   O, I begin to sicken.   65
GIOVANNI   [*Aside.*] Heaven forbid!   *Exit from above.*
SORANZO   Help, help within there, ho!
Look to your daughter, Signor Florio.

Enter FLORIO, GIOVANNI, PUTANA.

FLORIO   Hold her up, she swoons.
GIOVANNI   Sister, how d'ee?   70
ANNABELLA   Sick—brother, are you there?
FLORIO   Convey her to her bed instantly, whilst I send for a physician.
Quickly, I say!
PUTANA   Alas, poor child!   *Exeunt, manet* SORANZO.

Enter VASQUES.

VASQUES   My lord?   75
SORANZO   O Vasques, now I doubly am undone
Both in my present and my future hopes:
She plainly told me that she could not love,

---

47 spend . . . hopes   waste his youth in vain hopes.   **65 sicken**   with morning sickness.
68 Look . . . Florio   The quarto assigns this speech to Giovanni.

And thereupon soon sickened, and I fear
Her life's in danger.   80
VASQUES [*Aside.*] By'r lady, sir, and so is yours, if you knew all. [*To
him.*] 'Las, sir, I am sorry for that; may be 'tis but the maid's-
sickness, an over-flux of youth, and then, sir, there is no such
present remedy as present marriage. But hath she given you an
absolute denial?   85
SORANZO She hath and she hath not; I'm full of grief,
But what she said, I'll tell thee as we go.   *Exeunt.*

ACT III

Scene 3   *A chamber in* FLORIO's *house*

Enter GIOVANNI *and* PUTANA.

PUTANA O sir, we are all undone, quite undone, utterly undone,
and shamed forever: your sister, O your sister!
GIOVANNI What of her? For Heaven's sake, speak, how does she?
PUTANA O that ever I was born to see this day!
GIOVANNI She is not dead, ha? Is she?   5
PUTANA Dead? No, she is quick; 'tis worse, she is with child. You
know what you have done; Heaven forgive 'ee! 'Tis too late
to repent now, Heaven help us.
GIOVANNI With child? How dost thou know't?
PUTANA How do I know't? Am I at these years ignorant what the   10
meanings of qualms and water-pangs be? Of changing of colors,
queasiness of stomachs, pukings, and another thing that I could
name? Do not, for her and your credit's sake, spend the time in
asking how, and which way: 'tis so. She is quick, upon my word:
if you let a physician see her water, y'are undone.   15
GIOVANNI But in what case is she?
PUTANA Prettily amended; 'twas but a fit which I soon espied, and
she must look for often henceforward.

82–83 *maid's-sickness* chlorosis, an anemia to which young girls are particularly
susceptible.
❧ ACT III, Scene 3.   6 *quick* both "alive" and "pregnant."   11 *qualms* sudden
faintness. *water-pangs* cystitis.   15 *water* urine.   16 *in . . . she* How does she
feel now?

GIOVANNI   Commend me to her, bid her take no care.
    Let not the doctor visit her, I charge you;   20
    Make some excuse, till I return. —O me!
    I have a world of business in my head.
    Do not discomfort her.
    —How does this news perplex me! —If my father
    Come to her, tell him she's recovered well,   25
    Say 'twas but some ill diet. D'ee hear, woman?
    Look you to't.
PUTANA   I will, sir.   *Exeunt.*

ACT III

Scene 4   *Another chamber in the house*

Enter FLORIO *and* RICHARDETTO.

FLORIO   And how d'ee find her, sir?
RICHARDETTO   Indifferent well;
    I see no danger, scarce perceive she's sick,
    But that she told me, she had lately eaten
    Melons, and, as she thought, those disagreed
    With her young stomach.
FLORIO   Did you give her aught?   5
RICHARDETTO   An easy surfeit-water, nothing else.
    You need not doubt her health; I rather think
    Her sickness is a fullness of her blood—
    You understand me?
FLORIO   I do; you counsel well,
    And once, within these few days, will so order't   10
    She shall be married ere she know the time.
RICHARDETTO   Yet let not haste, sir, make unworthy choice;
    That were dishonor.
FLORIO   Master Doctor, no.
    I will not do so neither; in plain words,
    My Lord Soranzo is the man I mean.   15

---

19 *take . . . care*   not to worry.
🔖 **ACT III, Scene 4.   6** *easy surfeit-water*   mild antacid solution.   **8** *fullness . . .*
blood   restless, unexercised sexuality.

RICHARDETTO   A noble and a virtuous gentleman.
FLORIO   As any is in Parma. Not far hence
 Dwells Father Bonaventure, a grave friar,
 Once tutor to my son. Now at his cell
 I'll have 'em married.
RICHARDETTO   You have plotted wisely.   20
FLORIO   I'll send one straight to speak with him tonight.
RICHARDETTO   Soranzo's wise, he will delay no time.
FLORIO   It shall be so. *Enter* FRIAR *and* GIOVANNI.
FRIAR   Good peace be here and love.
FLORIO   Welcome, religious friar; you are one
 That still brings blessing to the place you come to. 25
GIOVANNI   Sir, with what speed I could, I did my best
 To draw this holy man from forth his cell
 To visit my sick sister, that with words
 Of ghostly comfort in this time of need,
 He might absolve her, whether she live or die. 30
FLORIO   'Twas well done, Giovanni. Thou herein
 Hast showed a Christian's care, a brother's love.
 Come, father, I'll conduct you to her chamber,
 And one thing would entreat you.
FRIAR   Say on, sir.
FLORIO   I have a father's dear impression, 35
 And wish, before I fall into my grave,
 That I might see her married, as 'tis fit;
 A word from you, grave man, will win her more
 Than all our best persuasions.
FRIAR   Gentle sir,
 All this I'll say, that Heaven may prosper her. *Exeunt.* 40

ACT III

Scene 5 RICHARDETTO's *house*

Enter GRIMALDI.

GRIMALDI   Now if the doctor keep his word, Soranzo,
 Twenty-to-one you miss your bride; I know

29 *ghostly* spiritual.   35 *impression* desire.

'Tis an unnoble act, and not becomes
A soldier's valor, but in terms of love,
Where merit cannot sway, policy must.   5
I am resolved: if this physician
Play not on both hands, then Soranzo falls.

Enter RICHARDETTO.

RICHARDETTO   You are come as I could wish. This very night
Soranzo, 'tis ordained, must be affied
To Annabella; and, for aught I know,   10
Married.
GRIMALDI   How!
RICHARDETTO   Yet your patience.
The place 'tis Friar Bonaventure's cell.
Now I would wish you to bestow this night
In watching thereabouts; 'tis but a night.
If you miss now, tomorrow I'll know all.   15
GRIMALDI   Have you the poison?
RICHARDETTO   Here 'tis in this box.
Doubt nothing, this will do't; in any case,
As you respect your life, be quick and sure.
GRIMALDI   I'll speed him.
RICHARDETTO   Do. Away! for 'tis not safe
You should be seen much here.—Ever my love!   20
GRIMALDI   And mine to you.   *Exit* GRIMALDI.
RICHARDETTO   So, if this hit, I'll laugh and hug revenge,
And they that now dream of a wedding feast
May chance to mourn the lusty bridegroom's ruin.
But to my other business.—Niece Philotis!   25

Enter PHILOTIS.

PHILOTIS   Uncle?
RICHARDETTO   My lovely niece, you have bethought 'ee?
PHILOTIS   Yes, and, as you counseled,
Fashioned my heart to love him; but he swears
He will tonight be married, for he fears   30
His uncle else, if he should know the drift,

❧ ACT III, Scene 5.   4 *terms* matters.   **5 *policy*** craft.   **7 *Play . . . hands*** does
not double-cross me by betraying me to Soranzo.   **9 *affied*** betrothed.   **13 *bestow***
spend.   **15 *I'll . . . all*** i.e. because the wedding will take place as planned.   **27 *bethought***
'ee thought (about marrying Bergetto).

Will hinder all, and call his coz to shrift.

RICHARDETTO   Tonight? Why, best of all!—but let me see,
I—ha—yes. So it shall be. In disguise
We'll early to the friar's; I have thought on't.   35

Enter BERGETTO *and* POGGIO.

PHILOTIS   Uncle, he comes.

RICHARDETTO   Welcome, my worthy coz.

BERGETTO   Lass, pretty lass, come buss, lass! [*Kisses her.*] —Aha,
Poggio!

PHILOTIS   There's hope of this yet.

RICHARDETTO   You shall have time enough; withdraw a little.
We must confer at large.   40

BERGETTO   Have you not sweetmeats or dainty devices for me?

PHILOTIS   You shall enough, sweetheart.

BERGETTO   Sweetheart! Mark that, Poggio! By my troth, I cannot
choose but kiss thee once more for that word "sweetheart."—
Poggio, I have a monstrous swelling about my stomach, what-   45
soever the matter be.

POGGIO   You shall have physic for't, sir.

RICHARDETTO   Time runs apace.

BERGETTO   Time's a blockhead.

RICHARDETTO   Be ruled. When we have done what's fit to do,   50
Then you may kiss your fill, and bed her too.   *Exeunt.*

---

32 *call . . . shrift*   force his nephew to repent.   **36** *coz*   friend.   **37** *buss*   kiss.
38 *There's . . . yet*   The meaning of this line is uncertain, and in an attempt to give it
clarity, editors sometimes assign it to other characters, to Richardetto or Poggio. Then it
can be interpreted as a comment on the possible success of the proposed, but apparently
absurd, marriage of the pretty young girl to the "ape in a silken coat." Both Richardetto
and Poggio, of course, have reason to desire such an alliance—Richardetto, because of
money; Poggio, because of Philotis' beauty. But since the quarto does assign this speech
to Philotis, an emendation seems necessary only as a last resort, and some sense can be made
out of the speech as it stands. If "yet" here means "in the immediate future," as it sometimes
does, Philotis may just be promising Bergetto more of "this" (i.e. lovemaking) shortly.
40 *at large*   at length (about the wedding).   **42** *shall enough*   shall (have) enough.
45 *monstrous swelling*   an erection.   **47** *physic*   sexual intercourse.

ACT III

{ Scene 6   ANNABELLA's *bedroom* }

Enter the FRIAR *sitting in a chair,* ANNABELLA *kneeling and whispering to him. A table before them and wax-lights. She weeps and wrings her hands.*

FRIAR   I am glad to see this penance; for, believe me,
    You have unripped a soul so foul and guilty
    As I must tell you true, I marvel how
    The earth hath borne you up. But weep, weep on,
    These tears may do you good; weep faster yet,   5
    Whiles I do read a lecture.
ANNABELLA   Wretched creature!
FRIAR   Ay, you are wretched, miserably wretched,
    Almost condemned alive. There is a place—
    List, daughter—in a black and hollow vault,
    Where day is never seen; there shines no sun,   10
    But flaming horror of consuming fires,
    A lightless sulphur, choked with smoky fogs
    Of an infected darkness. In this place
    Dwell many thousand thousand sundry sorts
    Of never-dying deaths: there damnèd souls   15
    Roar without pity; there are gluttons fed
    With toads and adders; there is burning oil
    Poured down the drunkard's throat; the usurer
    Is forced to sup whole draughts of molten gold;
    There is the murderer forever stabbed,   20
    Yet can he never die; there lies the wanton
    On racks of burning steel, whiles in his soul
    He feels the torment of his raging lust.
ANNABELLA   Mercy, O mercy!
FRIAR   There stand these wretched things
    Who have dreamed out whole years in lawless sheets   25
    And secret incests, cursing one another:
    Then you will wish each kiss your brother gave

🐾 **ACT III, Scene 6.   SD** *Annabella's bedroom*   The quarto stage direction says that the Friar is "in his study," but this statement contradicts both the fact that the Friar was on his way to Annabella's bedroom when he last appeared and that the scene seems clearly to take place inside Florio's house.   **6 read**   deliver.   **16 *without***   without (finding).

Had been a dagger's point; then you shall hear
How he will cry, "O would my wicked sister
Had first been damned, when she did yield to lust!"— 30
But, soft, methinks I see repentance work
New motions in your heart. Say, how is't with you?

ANNABELLA   Is there no way left to redeem my miseries?

FRIAR   There is, despair not: Heaven is merciful,
And offers grace even now. 'Tis thus agreed: 35
First, for your honor's safety, that you marry
The Lord Soranzo; next, to save your soul,
Leave off this life, and henceforth live to him.

ANNABELLA   Ay me!

FRIAR   Sigh not. I know the baits of sin
Are hard to leave—O, 'tis a death to do't. 40
Remember what must come. Are you content?

ANNABELLA   I am.

FRIAR   I like it well; we'll take the time.
Who's near us there?

Enter FLORIO *and* GIOVANNI.

FLORIO   Did you call, father?

FRIAR   Is Lord Soranzo come?

FLORIO   He stays below. 45

FRIAR   Have you acquainted him at full?

FLORIO   I have,
And he is overjoyed.

FRIAR   And so are we;
Bid him come near.

GIOVANNI   [*Aside.*] My sister weeping, ha?
I fear this friar's falsehood. [*To him.*] I will call him.   *Exit.*

FLORIO   Daughter, are you resolved?

ANNABELLA   Father, I am. 50

Enter GIOVANNI, SORANZO, *and* VASQUES.

FLORIO   My Lord Soranzo, here
Give me your hand; for that I give you this.

SORANZO   Lady, say you so too?

ANNABELLA   I do, and vow

---

38 *to* (faithful) to.   **42** *we'll . . . time* We'll take advantage of the occasion (offered
by Soranzo's proposal).   **52** *this* Annabella's hand.

To live with you and yours.

FRIAR   Timely resolved:
My blessing rest on both; more to be done,   55
You may perform it on the morning sun.   *Exeunt.*

ACT III

Scene 7   *Near the* FRIAR's *cell*

Enter GRIMALDI *with his rapier, drawn, and a dark lantern.*

GRIMALDI   'Tis early night as yet, and yet too soon
To finish such a work; here I will lie
To listen who comes next.

He lies down. Enter BERGETTO *and* PHILOTIS *disguised, and after*
RICHARDETTO *and* POGGIO.

BERGETTO   We are almost at the place, I hope, sweetheart.

GRIMALDI   [*Aside.*] I hear them near, and heard one say "sweetheart."   5
'Tis he! Now guide my hand, some angry justice,
Home to his bosom. [*Aloud.*] Now have at you, sir!
                              Strikes BERGETTO *and exit.*

BERGETTO   O help, help! Here's a stitch fallen in my guts! O for a
flesh-tailor quickly!—Poggio!

PHILOTIS   What ails my love?   10

BERGETTO   I am sure I cannot piss forward and backward, and yet I
am wet before and behind.—Lights, lights! Ho, lights!

PHILOTIS   Alas, some villain here has slain my love!

RICHARDETTO   O Heaven forbid it!—Raise up the next neighbors
Instantly, Poggio, and bring lights.   *Exit* POGGIO.   15
How is't, Bergetto? Slain? It cannot be!
Are you sure y'are hurt?

BERGETTO   O my belly seethes like a porridge-pot. Some cold water,
I shall boil over else! My whole body is in a sweat, that you
may wring my shirt: feel here—Why, Poggio!   20

🐾 **ACT III, Scene 7.**   SD *dark lantern*   a lantern with a slide to conceal the light.
SD *disguised*   in order to escape recognition by Donado, if he should see them.   **8** *stitch*
fallen   stab thrust.   **9** *flesh-tailor*   doctor—though in imitation of Mercutio (see *Romeo*
and Juliet, III. 1.96 ff.), Bergetto puns about his death, as he develops the tailoring imagery
of the previous line.

Enter POGGIO *with* OFFICERS *and lights and halberts.*

POGGIO   Here! Alas, how do you?

RICHARDETTO   Give me a light. What's here? All blood! O sirs,
Signor Donado's nephew now is slain.
Follow the murderer with all the haste
Up to the city: he cannot be far hence;   25
Follow, I beseech you.

OFFICERS   Follow, follow, follow!   *Exeunt* OFFICERS.

RICHARDETTO   Tear off thy linen, coz, to stop his wounds.
[*To* BERGETTO.] Be of good comfort, man.

BERGETTO   Is all this mine own blood? Nay, then, good night with   30
me. Poggio, commend me to my uncle, dost hear? Bid him for
my sake make much of this wench. O!—I am going the wrong
way sure, my belly aches so.—O, farewell, Poggio!—O!—O!—
Dies.

PHILOTIS   O, he is dead!

POGGIO   How! Dead!

RICHARDETTO   He's dead indeed.
'Tis now too late to weep; let's have him home,   35
And with what speed we may, find out the murderer.

POGGIO   O my master, my master, my master!   *Exeunt.*

ACT III

Scene 8   *Near* SORANZO'*s house*

Enter VASQUES *and* HIPPOLITA.

HIPPOLITA   Betrothed?

VASQUES   I saw it.

HIPPOLITA   And when's the marriage day?

VASQUES   Some two days hence.

HIPPOLITA   Two days! Why, man, I would but wish two hours   5
To send him to his last and lasting sleep.
And, Vasques, thou shalt see I'll do it bravely.

VASQUES   I do not doubt your wisdom, nor, I trust, you my secrecy;
I am infinitely yours.

SD *halberts* halberdiers, spear-bearing guards.   **32–33** *the . . . way* i.e. toward hell.
ACT III, Scene 8.   7 *bravely* splendidly.

HIPPOLITA   I will be thine in spite of my disgrace.   10
   —So soon? O, wicked man! I durst be sworn,
   He'd laugh to see me weep.
VASQUES   And that's a villainous fault in him.
HIPPOLITA   No, let him laugh. I'm armed in my resolves.
   Be thou still true.   15
VASQUES   I should get little by treachery against so hopeful a prefer-
   ment as I am like to climb to.
HIPPOLITA   Even to my bosom, Vasques. Let my youth
   Revel in these new pleasures; if we thrive,
   He now hath but a pair of days to live.   *Exeunt.*   20

ACT III

Scene 9   *Before the* CARDINAL'*s palace*

Enter FLORIO, DONADO, RICHARDETTO, POGGIO, *and* OFFICERS.

FLORIO   'Tis bootless now to show yourself a child,
   Signor Donado; what is done, is done.
   Spend not the time in tears, but seek for justice.
RICHARDETTO   I must confess, somewhat I was in fault
   That had not first acquainted you what love   5
   Passed 'twixt him and my niece; but, as I live,
   His fortune grieves me as it were mine own.
DONADO   Alas, poor creature, he meant no man harm;
   That I am sure of.
FLORIO   I believe that too.
   But stay, my masters, are you sure you saw   10
   The murderer pass here?
OFFICER   And it please you, sir, we are sure we saw a ruffian, with a
   naked weapon in his hand all bloody, get into my Lord Cardinal's
   grace's gate: that we are sure of. But for fear of his grace, bless
   us, we durst go no further.   15
DONADO   Know you what manner of man he was?
OFFICER   Yes, sure, I know the man, they say 'a is a soldier—he that
   loved your daughter, sir, an't please ye; 'twas he for certain.

18 *Even . . . bosom* I shall deny you nothing. **my youth** Soranzo.
❦ ACT III, Scene 9.   1 *to . . . child* to weep.

FLORIO   Grimaldi, on my life!
OFFICER   Ay, ay, the same.
RICHARDETTO   The Cardinal is noble; he no doubt   20
      Will give true justice.
DONADO   Knock, someone, at the gate.
POGGIO   I'll knock, sir.

      POGGIO knocks.

SERVANT   *Within.* What would 'ee?
FLORIO   We require speech with the Lord Cardinal   25
      About some present business; pray inform
      His grace that we are here.

      Enter CARDINAL *and* GRIMALDI.

CARDINAL   Why, how now, friends! What saucy mates are you,
      That know nor duty nor civility?
      Are we a person fit to be your host,   30
      Or is our house become your common inn,
      To beat our doors at pleasure? What such haste
      Is yours as that it cannot wait fit times?
      Are you the masters of this commonwealth,
      And know no more discretion? O, your news   35
      Is here before you: you have lost a nephew,
      Donado, last night by Grimaldi slain.
      Is that your business? Well, sir, we have knowledge on't.
      Let that suffice.
GRIMALDI   In presence of your grace,
      In thought I never meant Bergetto harm.   40
      But Florio, you can tell, with how much scorn
      Soranzo, backed with his confederates,
      Hath often wronged me; I to be revenged,
      —For that I could not win him else to fight—
      Had thought by way of ambush to have killed him,   45
      But was unluckily therein mistook,
      Else he had felt what late Bergetto did.
      And though my fault to him were merely chance,
      Yet humbly I submit me to your grace,
      To do with me as you please. [*Kneels.*]
CARDINAL   Rise up, Grimaldi.   50
      You citizens of Parma, if you seek

30 *host* tavernkeeper.   **44** *win* get.

For justice, know, as nuncio from the Pope,
For this offense I here receive Grimaldi
Into his holiness' protection.
He is no common man, but nobly born;   55
Of princes' blood, though you, Sir Florio,
Thought him too mean a husband for your daughter.
If more you seek for, you must go to Rome,
For he shall thither. Learn more wit, for shame.
Bury your dead.—Away, Grimaldi—leave 'em.   60

Exeunt CARDINAL *and* GRIMALDI.

DONADO   Is this a churchman's voice? Dwells justice here?
FLORIO   Justice is fled to heaven and comes no nearer.
Soranzo! Was't for him? O impudence!
Had he the face to speak it, and not blush?
Come, come, Donado, there's no help in this,   65
When cardinals think murder's not amiss.
Great men may do their wills; we must obey.
But Heaven will judge them for't another day.   *Exeunt.*

ACT IV

⁍Scene 1   FLORIO's *house*⁌

A banquet. Hautboys. Enter the FRIAR, GIOVANNI, ANNABELLA,
PHILOTIS, SORANZO, DONADO, FLORIO, RICHARDETTO, PUTANA,
and VASQUES.

FRIAR   These holy rites performed, now take your times
To spend the remnant of the day in feast;
Such fit repasts are pleasing to the saints,
Who are your guests, though not with mortal eyes
To be beheld. Long prosper in this day,   5
You happy couple, to each other's joy!
SORANZO   Father, your prayer is heard; the hand of goodness
Hath been a shield for me against my death,

---

59 *wit*   self-control.
⁂ ACT IV, Scene 1.   SD *Hautboys*   high-pitched wind instruments.

And, more to bless me, hath enriched my life
With this most precious jewel; such a prize   10
As earth hath not another like to this.
Cheer up, my love, and gentlemen, my friends,
Rejoice with me in mirth. This day we'll crown
With lusty cups to Annabella's health.

GIOVANNI   [*Aside.*] O torture! Were the marriage yet undone.   15
Ere I'd endure this sight, to see my love
Clipped by another, I would dare confusion,
And stand the horror of ten thousand deaths.

VASQUES   Are you not well, sir?

GIOVANNI   Prithee, fellow, wait;
I need not thy officious diligence.   20

FLORIO   Signor Donado, come, you must forget
Your late mishaps, and drown your cares in wine.

SORANZO   Vasques!

VASQUES   My lord?

SORANZO   Reach me that weighty bowl.
Here, brother Giovanni, here's to you:
Your turn comes next, though now a bachelor.   25
Here's to your sister's happiness and mine!

GIOVANNI   I cannot drink.

SORANZO   What!

GIOVANNI   'Twill indeed offend me.

ANNABELLA   Pray do not urge him if he be not willing.

[*Off-stage noise.*]

FLORIO   How now, what noise is this?

VASQUES   O, sir, I had forgot to tell you; certain young maidens   30
of Parma, in honor to Madam Annabella's marriage, have sent
their loves to her in a masque, for which they humbly crave your
patience and silence.

SORANZO   We are much bound to them, so much the more
As it comes unexpected; guide them in.   35

Hautboys. Enter [masked] HIPPOLITA *and* LADIES *in white robes, with
garlands of willows. Music and a dance.*

Thanks, lovely virgins; now might we but know

---

17 Clipped embraced.   **32 masque**   a courtly entertainment consisting chiefly of music
and dancing in which the participants wore masks of mythical or allegorical figures.
SD willows   traditionally associated with sorrow in love (cf. *Othello,* IV.3.41 ff.).

To whom we have been beholding for thy love,
We shall acknowledge it.

HIPPOLITA   Yes, you shall know;

[*Unmasks.*]

What think you now?

OMNES   Hippolita!

HIPPOLITA   'Tis she,
Be not amazed, nor blush, young lovely bride.   40
I come not to defraud you of your man.
'Tis now no time to reckon up the talk
What Parma long hath rumored of us both:
Let rash report run on; the breath that vents it
Will, like a bubble, break itself at last.   45
But now to you, sweet creature. Lend's your hand;
Perhaps it hath been said that I would claim
Some interest in Soranzo, now your lord.
What I have right to do, his soul knows best.
But in my duty to your noble worth,   50
Sweet Annabella, and my care of you,
Here take, Soranzo, take this hand from me:
I'll once more join what by the holy church
Is finished and allowed; have I done well?

SORANZO   You have too much engaged us.

HIPPOLITA   One thing more.   55
That you may know my single charity.
Freely I here remit all interest
I e'er could claim, and give you back your vows;
And to confirm't—reach me a cup of wine—
My Lord Soranzo, in this draught I drink   60
Long rest t'ee!—Look to it, Vasques.

VASQUES   Fear nothing.

He gives her a poisoned cup: she drinks.

SORANZO   Hippolita, I thank you, and will pledge
This happy union as another life;
Wine, there!   65

VASQUES   You shall have none, neither shall you pledge her.

HIPPOLITA   How!

---

46 Lend's lend us. **55 engaged us** put us in your debt. **56 single** honest. **64 another** a new.

VASQUES Know now, Mistress She-Devil, your own mischievous
    treachery hath killed you; I must not marry you.

HIPPOLITA Villain!   70

OMNES What's the matter?

VASQUES Foolish woman, thou art now like a firebrand that hath
    kindled others and burnt thyself; *troppo sperar, inganna:* thy vain
    hope hath deceived thee, thou art but dead; if thou hast any grace,
    pray.   75

HIPPOLITA Monster!

VASQUES Die in charity, for shame! This thing of malice, this woman,
    had privately corrupted me with promise of marriage, under
    this politic reconciliation, to poison my lord, whiles she might
    laugh at his confusion on his marriage day. I promised her fair,   80
    but I knew what my reward should have been; and would
    willingly have spared her life, but that I was acquainted with the
    danger of her disposition, and now have fitted her a just payment
    in her own coin. There she is, she hath yet—and end thy days in
    peace, vile woman; as for life there's no hope. Think not on't.   85

OMNES Wonderful justice!

RICHARDETTO   Heaven, thou art righteous.

HIPPOLITA O, 'tis true:
    I feel my minute coming. Had that slave
    Kept promise—O, my torment!—thou this hour
    Hadst died, Soranzo—heat above hell fire!—   90
    Yet ere I pass away—cruel, cruel flames!—
    Take here my curse amongst you: may thy bed
    Of marriage be a rack unto thy heart,
    Burn blood and boil in vengeance—O my heart,
    My flame's intolerable!—Mayst thou live   95
    To father bastards. May her womb bring forth
    Monsters, and die together in your sins,
    Hated, scorned, and unpitied!—O!—O!—   *Dies.*

FLORIO Was e'er so vile a creature?

RICHARDETTO   Here's the end
    Of lust and pride.

ANNABELLA   It is a fearful sight.   100

---

73 *troppo . . . inganna* Too much hope deceives. **78** *marriage* The quarto reads
"malice." **79** *politic* scheming. **80** *fair* encouragingly. **84** *she . . . yet—* Vasques
interrupts himself, perhaps as he is about to say, "She hath yet a few moments left to pray
in." **93** *rack* an instrument of torture.

SORANZO   Vasques, I know thee now a trusty servant,
    And never will forget thee.—Come, my love,
    We'll home, and thank the heavens for this escape.
    Father and friends, we must break up this mirth:
    It is too sad a feast.
DONADO   Bear hence the body.   105
FRIAR   Here's an ominous change;
    Mark this, my Giovanni, and take heed.
    I fear the event; that marriage seldom's good,
    Where the bride-banquet so begins in blood.   *Exeunt.*

ACT IV

Scene 2   RICHARDETTO's *house*

Enter RICHARDETTO *and* PHILOTIS.

RICHARDETTO   My wretched wife, more wretched in her shame
    Than in her wrongs to me, hath paid too soon
    The forfeit of her modesty and life;
    And I am sure, my niece, though vengeance hover,
    Keeping aloof yet from Soranzo's fall,   5
    Yet he will fall, and sink with his own weight.
    I need not now—my heart persuades me so—
    To further his confusion; there is One
    Above begins to work; for, as I hear,
    Debates already 'twixt his wife and him   10
    Thicken and run to head; she, as 'tis said,
    Slightens his love, and he abandons hers.
    Much talk I hear. Since things go thus, my niece,
    In tender love and pity of your youth,
    My counsel is, that you should free your years   15
    From hazard of these woes by flying hence
    To fair Cremona, there to vow your soul
    In holiness, a holy votaress:

---

108 *the event* what is to come.
❧ ACT IV, Scene 2. SD *Enter . . . Philotis* An unspecified interval of time, perhaps a week, has passed since the preceding scene. 17 *Cremona* a province in northwest Italy. 18 *votaress* nun.

Leave me to see the end of these extremes.
All human worldly courses are uneven;   20
No life is blessed but the way to heaven.

PHILOTIS   Uncle, shall I resolve to be a nun?

RICHARDETTO   Ay, gentle niece, and in your hourly prayers
Remember me, your poor unhappy uncle.
Hie to Cremona now, as fortune leads: 25
Your home, your cloister; your best friends, your beads.
Your chaste and single life shall crown your birth;
Who dies a virgin lives a saint on earth.

PHILOTIS   Then farewell, world, and worldly thoughts, adieu!
Welcome, chaste vows; myself I yield to you.   *Exeunt.*   30

ACT IV

Scene 3   SORANZO's *house*

Enter SORANZO *unbraced, and* ANNABELLA *dragged in.*

SORANZO   Come, strumpet, famous whore! Were every drop
Of blood that runs in thy adulterous veins
A life, this sword—dost see't?—should in one blow
Confound them all. Harlot! Rare, notable harlot,
That with thy brazen face maintainst thy sin,   5
Was there no man in Parma to be bawd
To your loose cunning whoredom else but I?
Must your hot itch and pleurisy of lust,
The heyday of your luxury, be fed
Up to a surfeit, and could none but I   10
Be picked out to be cloak to your close tricks,
Your belly-sports? Now I must be the dad
To all that gallimaufry that's stuffed
In thy corrupted, bastard-bearing womb.
Say, must I?

ANNABELLA   Beastly man! Why, 'tis thy fate.   15
I sued not to thee; for, but that I thought

🦋 **ACT IV, Scene 3. SD** *unbraced* with clothes loosened and askew (cf. *Hamlet,* II.1.78).   **9** *luxury* lasciviousness.   **11** *cloak* false front, pretext.   *close* secret. **13** *gallimaufry* hodgepodge.   **15** *Say* The quarto reads "Shey."

Your over-loving lordship would have run
Mad on denial, had ye lent me time,
I would have told 'ee in what case I was.
But you would needs be doing.

SORANZO   Whore of whores!   20
Darst thou tell me this?

ANNABELLA   O yes, why not?
You were deceived in me; 'twas not for love
I chose you, but for honor. Yet know this,
Would you be patient yet, and hide your shame,
I'd see whether I could love you.

SORANZO   Excellent quean!   25
Why, art thou not with child?

ANNABELLA   What needs all this
When 'tis superfluous? I confess I am.

SORANZO   Tell me by whom.

ANNABELLA   Soft, sir, 'twas not in my bargain.
Yet somewhat, sir, to stay your longing stomach,
I'm content t'acquaint you with; the man,   30
The more than man, that got this sprightly boy—
For 'tis a boy: that for glory, sir,
Your heir shall be a son—

SORANZO   Damnable monster!

ANNABELLA   Nay, and you will not hear, I'll speak no more.

SORANZO   Yes, speak; and speak thy last.

ANNABELLA   A match, a match!   35
This noble creature was in every part
So angel-like, so glorious, that a woman
Who had not been but human, as was I,
Would have kneeled to him, and have begged for love.
You! Why, you are not worthy once to name   40
His name without true worship, or, indeed,
Unless you kneeled, to hear another name him.

SORANZO   What was he called?

ANNABELLA   We are not come to that.
Let it suffice that you shall have the glory

---

18 *on denial* if I denied your confession of love to me. **20** *you . . . doing* You were
in a hurry. **25** *quean* whore. **26** *needs* matters. **32** *for glory* gloriously (for
you). The idea is more fully suggested in lines 44–45. **34** *and* since. **35** *A match*
agreed.

To father what so brave a father got.   45
In brief, had not this chance fall'n out as't doth,
I never had been troubled with a thought
That you had been a creature; but for marriage,
I scarce dream yet of that.
SORANZO   Tell me his name.
ANNABELLA   Alas, alas, there's all!   50
Will you believe?
SORANZO   What?
ANNABELLA   You shall never know.
SORANZO   How!
ANNABELLA   Never; if you do, let me be cursed.
SORANZO   Not know it, strumpet! I'll rip up thy heart,
And find it there.
ANNABELLA   Do, do!
SORANZO   And with my teeth   55
Tear the prodigious lecher joint by joint.
ANNABELLA   Ha, ha, ha! The man's merry!
SORANZO   Dost thou laugh?
Come, whore, tell me your lover, or, by truth,
I'll hew thy flesh to shreds! Who is't?
ANNABELLA   *Sings. Che morte piu dolce che morire per amore?*   60
SORANZO   Thus will I pull thy hair, and thus I'll drag
Thy lust-be-lepered body through the dust.
Yet tell his name!
ANNABELLA   *Sings. Morendo in gratia Dei, morire senza dolore.*
SORANZO   Dost thou triumph? The treasure of the earth   65
Shall not redeem thee. Were there kneeling kings
Did beg thy life, or angels did come down
To plead in tears, yet should not all prevail
Against my rage! Dost thou not tremble yet?
ANNABELLA   At what? To die? No, be a gallant hangman.   70
I dare thee to the worst: strike, and strike home!
I leave revenge behind, and thou shalt feel't.

---

45 brave splendid.   **46–49 had . . . that**   If I had not by chance become pregnant, I
would never even have noticed that you were alive; and even now I find it almost
impossible to imagine that I am married to you.   **60 Che . . . amore**   Can there be any
sweeter death than to die for love?   **62 lust-be-lepered**   infected with leprosy because
of lust.   **64 Morendo . . . dolore**   a combination of Latin and Italian: "Dying in the
grace of God, (is) to die free from pain."   ***Dei***   The quarto reads "Lei."   **65 The treasure**
all the wealth.

SORANZO   Yet tell me ere thou diest, and tell me truly,
    Knows thy old father this?
ANNABELLA   No, by my life.
SORANZO   Wilt thou confess, and I will spare thy life?   75
ANNABELLA   My life! I will not buy my life so dear.
SORANZO   I will not slack my vengeance.

    Enter VASQUES.

VASQUES   What d'ee mean, sir?
SORANZO   Forbear, Vasques: such a damnèd whore
    Deserves no pity.   80
VASQUES   Now the gods forfend! And would you be her executioner,
    and kill her in your rage too? O, 'twere most unmanlike. She is
    your wife. What faults hath been done by her before she married
    you, were not against you; alas, poor lady, what hath she com-
    mitted which any lady in Italy in the like case would not? Sir,   85
    you must be ruled by your reason and not by your fury: that
    were unhuman and beastly.
SORANZO   She shall not live.
VASQUES   Come, she must. You would have her confess the author
    of her present misfortunes, I warrant'ee. 'Tis an unconscionable   90
    demand, and she should lose the estimation that I, for my part,
    hold of her worth, if she had done it. Why, sir, you ought not
    of all men living to know it. Good sir, be reconciled; alas, good
    gentlewoman.
ANNABELLA   Pish, do not beg for me: I prize my life   95
    As nothing; if the man will needs be mad,
    Why, let him take it.
SORANZO   Vasques, hear'st thou this?
VASQUES   Yes, and commend her for it: in this she shows the noble-
    ness of a gallant spirit, and beshrew my heart, but it becomes
    her rarely. [*Aside to* SORANZO.] Sir, in any case smother your   100
    revenge; leave the scenting-out your wrongs to me. Be ruled,
    as you respect your honor, or you mar all. [*Aloud.*] Sir, if ever
    my service were of any credit with you, be not so violent in your
    distractions. You are married now; what a triumph might the
    report of this give to other neglected suitors! 'Tis as manlike to   105
    bear extremities as godlike to forgive.
SORANZO   O Vasques, Vasques, in this piece of flesh,

---

78 *What . . . sir* What are you doing, sir? **85** *in . . . case* i.e. pregnant and unmarried.

This faithless face of hers, had I laid up
The treasure of my heart!—Hadst thou been virtuous,
Fair, wicked woman, not the matchless joys   110
Of life itself had made me wish to live
With any saint but thee; deceitful creature,
How hast thou mocked my hopes, and in the shame
Of thy lewd womb even buried me alive!
I did too dearly love thee.

VASQUES   *Aside.* This is well: 115
Follow this temper with some passion.
Be brief and moving; 'tis for the purpose.

SORANZO   Be witness to my words thy soul and thoughts,
And tell me, didst not think that in my heart
I did too superstitiously adore thee?   120

ANNABELLA   I must confess I know you loved me well.

SORANZO   And wouldst thou use me thus? O, Annabella,
Be thus assured whatsoe'er the villain was
That thus hath tempted thee to this disgrace,
Well he might lust, but never loved like me.   125
He doted on the picture that hung out
Upon thy cheeks, to please his humorous eye;
Not on the part I loved, which was thy heart,
And, as I thought, thy virtues.

ANNABELLA   O my lord!
These words wound deeper than your sword could do.   130

VASQUES   Let me not ever take comfort, but I begin to weep myself,
so much I pity him; why, madam, I knew when his rage was
over-past, what it would come to.

SORANZO   Forgive me, Annabella. Though thy youth
Hath tempted thee above thy strength to folly,   135
Yet will not I forget what I should be,
And what I am, a husband; in that name
Is hid divinity. If I do find
That thou wilt yet be true, here I remit
All former faults, and take thee to my bosom.   140

VASQUES   By my troth, and that's a point of noble charity.

ANNABELLA   Sir, on my knees— [*Kneels.*]

SORANZO   Rise up, you shall not kneel.
Get you to your chamber, see you make no show

---

115 *too dearly* at too great cost to me.   **116 *passion*** declaration of your love for her.
120 *too superstitiously* with extravagant devotion.   **127 *humorous*** fickle.

Of alteration; I'll be with you straight.
My reason tells me now that 'tis as common   145
To err in frailty as to be a woman.
Go to your chamber.   *Exit* ANNABELLA.

VASQUES   So, this was somewhat to the matter; what do you think
of your heaven of happiness now, sir?

SORANZO   I carry hell about me; all my blood   150
Is fired in swift revenge.

VASQUES   That may be, but know you how, or on whom? Alas, to
marry a great woman, being made great in the stock to your
hand, is a usual sport in these days; but to know what ferret it
was that haunted your cony-berry, there's the cunning.   155

SORANZO   I'll make her tell herself, or—

VASQUES   Or what? You must not do so. Let me yet persuade your
sufferance a little while. Go to her, use her mildly, win her if it
be possible to a voluntary, to a weeping tune; for the rest, if all
hit, I will not miss my mark. Pray, sir, go in; the next news I   160
tell you shall be wonders.

SORANZO   Delay in vengeance gives a heavier blow.   *Exit.*

VASQUES   Ah, sirrah, here's work for the nonce! I had a suspicion
of a bad matter in my head a pretty whiles ago; but after my
madam's scurvy looks here at home, her waspish perverseness   165
and loud faultfinding, then I remembered the proverb that,
"Where hens crow and cocks hold their peace, there are sorry
houses." 'Sfoot, if the lower parts of a she-tailor's cunning can
cover such a swelling in the stomach, I'll never blame a false
stitch in a shoe whiles I live again! Up and up so quick? And so 170
quickly too? 'Twere a fine policy to learn by whom this must
be known; and I have thought on't—

Enter PUTANA.

[*Aside.*] Here's the way, or none.—What, crying, old mistress!
Alas, alas, I cannot blame 'ee; we have a lord, Heaven help us,
is so mad as the devil himself, the more shame for him.   175

---

148 *this . . . matter* You effectively adapted yourself to the situation.   **153** *great*
pregnant.   **153–54** *being . . . hand* being made pregnant before she is delivered into your
hands.   **155** *cony-berry* rabbit hole.   **159** *voluntary* both a "voluntary" (confession)
and a "musical piece sung spontaneously."   **159–60** *if . . . hit* succeed (a hunting term
meaning "to strike the scent").   **168–70** *if . . . again* The gist of this exclamation is that
no dressmaker will be skilled enough to hide the signs of Annabella's pregnancy.   **170** *Up
and up* (She is swelling) up and up.   **171–72** *by . . . known* who knows about the
pregnancy.   **SD** *Enter Putana* The quarto delays the entrance until line 175.

PUTANA   O Vasques, that ever I was born to see this day! Doth he
use thee so too, sometimes, Vasques?

VASQUES   Me? Why, he makes a dog of me. But if some were of
my mind, I know what we would do; as sure as I am an honest
man, he will go near to kill my lady with unkindness. Say she   180
be with child, is that such a matter for a young woman of her
years to be blamed for?

PUTANA   Alas, good heart, it is against her will full sore.

VASQUES   I durst be sworn, all his madness is for that she will not
confess whose 'tis, which he will know, and when he doth know   185
it, I am so well acquainted with his humor, that he will forget
all straight. Well, I could wish she would in plain terms tell all,
for that's the way indeed.

PUTANA   Do you think so?

VASQUES   Foh, I know't—provided that he did not win her to't by   190
force. He was once in a mind that you could tell, and meant to
have wrung it out of you, but I somewhat pacified him for that;
yet sure you know a great deal.

PUTANA   Heaven forgive us all! I know a little, Vasques.

VASQUES   Why should you not? Who else should? Upon my con-   195
science, she loves you dearly, and you would not betray her to
any affliction for the world.

PUTANA   Not for all the world, by my faith and troth, Vasques.

VASQUES   'Twere pity of your life if you should, but in this you
should both relieve her present discomforts, pacify my lord, and   200
gain yourself everlasting love and preferment.

PUTANA   Dost think so, Vasques?

VASQUES   Nay, I know't; sure 'twas some near and entire friend.

PUTANA   'Twas a dear friend indeed; but—

VASQUES   But what? Fear not to name him: my life between you   205
and danger. Faith, I think 'twas no base fellow.

PUTANA   Thou wilt stand between me and harm?

VASQUES   'Ud's pity, what else? You shall be rewarded too, trust me.

PUTANA   'Twas even no worse than her own brother.

VASQUES   Her brother Giovanni, I warrant 'ee!   210

PUTANA   Even he, Vasques—as brave a gentleman as ever kissed fair
lady. O, they love most perpetually!

VASQUES   A brave gentleman indeed; why, therein I commend her
choice. [*Aside.*] Better and better!—You are sure 'twas he?

203 *entire* beloved.   **208** *'Ud's* God's.   **213** *brave* noble.

PUTANA   Sure. And you shall see he will not be long from her too.   215

VASQUES   He were to blame if he would—But may I believe thee?

PUTANA   Believe me! Why, dost think I am a Turk or a Jew? No, Vasques, I have known their dealings too long to belie them now.

VASQUES   Where are you there? Within, sirs!   220

Enter BANDITTI.

PUTANA   How now, what are these?

VASQUES   You shall know presently. Come, sirs, take me this old damnable hag, gag her instantly, and put out her eyes. Quickly, quickly!

PUTANA   Vasques, Vasques!   225

VASQUES   Gag her, I say! 'Sfoot, d'ee suffer her to prate? What d'ee fumble about? Let me come to her; I'll help your old gums, you toad-bellied bitch. Sirs, carry her closely into the coalhouse, and put out her eyes instantly; if she roars, slit her nose: d'ee hear, be speedy and sure. Why, this is excellent and above   230
expectation.   *Exeunt* [BANDITTI] *with* PUTANA.
Her own brother? O horrible! To what a height of liberty in damnation hath the devil trained our age? Her brother! Well, there's yet but a beginning: I must to my lord, and tutor him better in his points of vengeance. Now I see how a smooth tale   235
goes beyond a smooth tail. But soft—What thing comes next?

Enter GIOVANNI.

Giovanni! As I would wish; my belief is strengthened: 'tis as firm as winter and summer.

GIOVANNI   Where's my sister?

VASQUES   Troubled with a new sickness, my lord; she's somewhat ill.   240

GIOVANNI   Took too much of the flesh, I believe.

VASQUES   Troth, sir, and you I think have e'en hit it. But my virtuous lady—

GIOVANNI   Where's she?

VASQUES   In her chamber; please you visit her; she is alone. [GIOVANNI   245
gives him gold.] Your liberality hath doubly made me your servant, and ever shall, ever.   *Exit* GIOVANNI.

---

233 *damnation* damnable acts.   *trained* led astray.   **235–36** *a . . . tail* an obscene pun, meaning clever words can uncover the deceptions of a lascivious woman.   **238** *firm . . . summer* certain as the change of seasons.   **241** *Took . . . flesh* both "ate too much meat" and "engaged too much in sexual intercourse."

Enter sᴏʀᴀɴᴢᴏ.

Sir, I am made a man: I have plied my cue with cunning and
success. I beseech you let's be private.

sᴏʀᴀɴᴢᴏ My lady's brother's come; now he'll know all.   250

ᴠᴀsǫᴜᴇs Let him know't: I have made some of them fast enough.
How have you dealt with my lady?

sᴏʀᴀɴᴢᴏ Gently, as thou hast counseled. O, my soul
Runs circular in sorrow for revenge!
But, Vasques, thou shalt know—   255

ᴠᴀsǫᴜᴇs Nay, I will know no more, for now comes your turn to
know; I would not talk so openly with you. Let my young
master take time enough, and go at pleasure; he is sold to death,
and the devil shall not ransom him. Sir, I beseech you, your
privacy.   260

sᴏʀᴀɴᴢᴏ No conquest can gain glory of my fear.   *Exeunt.*

ACT V

⟨Scene 1   *A chamber in* sᴏʀᴀɴᴢᴏ's *house*⟩·

Enter ᴀɴɴᴀʙᴇʟʟᴀ *above.*

ᴀɴɴᴀʙᴇʟʟᴀ Pleasures, farewell, and all ye thriftless minutes
Wherein false joys have spun a weary life.
To these my fortunes now I take my leave.
Thou, precious Time, that swiftly rid'st in post
Over the world, to finish up the race   5
Of my last fate, here stay thy restless course,
And bear to ages that are yet unborn
A wretched, woeful woman's tragedy.
My conscience now stands up against my lust
With depositions charactered in guilt,   10

---

248 *I . . . man* I am assured of success. 251 *made . . . fast* I have bound (and en-
trapped) some of them so that they cannot escape. 261 *No . . . fear* I will not be
prevented from triumphing because of fear.

⚜ ᴀᴄᴛ V, Sᴄᴇɴᴇ 1. 4 *in post* at great speed. 9 *stands . . . against* condemns.
10 *charactered in guilt* a pun, meaning both "written in gold (gilt)" and "characterized
by guilt."

Enter FRIAR [*below*].

And tells me I am lost. Now I confess
Beauty that clothes the outside of the face
Is cursèd if it be not clothed with grace.
Here like a turtle mewed up in a cage,
Unmated, I converse with air and walls,   15
And descant on my vile unhappiness.
O Giovanni, that hast had the spoil
Of thine own virtues and my modest fame,
Would thou hadst been less subject to those stars
That luckless reigned at my nativity: 20
O would the scourge due to my black offense
Might pass from thee, that I alone might feel
The torment of an uncontrollèd flame!

FRIAR   [*Aside.*] What's this I hear?

ANNABELLA   That man, that blessèd friar,
Who joined in ceremonial knot my hand   25
To him whose wife I now am, told me oft
I trod the path to death, and showed me how.
But they who sleep in lethargies of lust
Hug their confusion, making Heaven unjust,
And so did I.

FRIAR   [*Aside.*] Here's music to the soul.   30

ANNABELLA   Forgive me, my good genius, and this once
Be helpful to my ends; let some good man
Pass this way, to whose trust I may commit
This paper double-lined with tears and blood:
Which being granted, here I sadly vow   35
Repentance, and a leaving of that life
I long have died in.

FRIAR   Lady, Heaven hath heard you,
And hath by providence ordained that I
Should be his minister for your behoof.

ANNABELLA   Ha, what are you?

FRIAR   Your brother's friend, the friar;   40
Glad in my soul that I have lived to hear

---

14 *turtle* turtledove. *mewed* cooped. **17** *hast ... spoil* have experienced the ruin.
29 *making Heaven* accusing Heaven of being. **31** *good genius* attendant spirit of
goodness—thought to be opposed in every being by an evil genius (cf. *The Tempest*,
IV.1.27).

This free confession 'twixt your peace and you.
What would you, or to whom? Fear not to speak.
ANNABELLA   Is Heaven so bountiful? Then I have found
More favor than I hoped. Here, holy man—   45

Throws a letter.

Commend me to my brother. Give him that,
That letter; bid him read it and repent.
Tell him that I, imprisoned in my chamber,
Barred of all company, even of my guardian,
Who gives me cause of much suspect, have time   50
To blush at what hath passed. Bid him be wise,
And not believe the friendship of my lord.
I fear much more than I can speak: good father,
The place is dangerous, and spies are busy;
I must break off—you'll do't?
FRIAR   Be sure I will;   55
And fly with speed—my blessing ever rest
With thee, my daughter. Live to die more blessed!   *Exit* FRIAR.
ANNABELLA   Thanks to the heavens, who have prolonged my breath
To this good use: now I can welcome death.   *Exit.*

ACT V
Scene 2   *Another part of the house*

Enter SORANZO *and* VASQUES.

VASQUES   Am I to be believed now? First marry a strumpet that cast
herself away upon you but to laugh at your horns, to feast on
your disgrace, riot in your vexations, cuckold you in your bride-
bed, waste your estate upon panders and bawds!
SORANZO   No more, I say, no more!   5
VASQUES   A cuckold is a goodly tame beast, my lord.
SORANZO   I am resolved; urge not another word.
My thoughts are great, and all as resolute

---

50 *of . . . suspect*   to suspect her (or Soranzo) of betrayal.
※ ACT V, Scene 2.   2 *horns*   traditionally considered the mark of a cuckold.
6 *is . . . beast*   docilely submits (like a trained animal) to his wife's control.

As thunder; in mean time I'll cause our lady
To deck herself in all her bridal robes,   10
Kiss her, and fold her gently in my arms.
Begone!—Yet hear you, are the banditti ready
To wait in ambush?

VASQUES Good sir, trouble not yourself about other business than
your own resolution; remember that time lost cannot be recalled.   15

SORANZO With all the cunning words thou canst, invite
The states of Parma to my birthday's feast.
Haste to my brother-rival and his father:
Entreat them gently, bid them not to fail.
Be speedy, and return.   20

VASQUES Let not your pity betray you till my coming back; think
upon incest and cuckoldry.

SORANZO Revenge is all the ambition I aspire:
To that I'll climb or fall; my blood's on fire.   *Exeunt.*

ACT V
Scene 3   FLORIO's *house*

Enter GIOVANNI.

GIOVANNI Busy opinion is an idle fool,
That as a school rod keeps a child in awe,
Frights the unexperienced temper of the mind.
So did it me; who, ere my precious sister
Was married, thought all taste of love would die   5
In such a contract; but I find no change
Of pleasure in this formal law of sports.
She is still one to me, and every kiss
As sweet and as delicious as the first
I reaped, when yet the privilege of youth   10
Entitled her a virgin. O the glory
Of two united hearts like hers and mine!

---

17 *states* important noblemen.
🦌 **ACT V, Scene 3.** **1** *Busy opinion* meddlesome preconceptions. **5** *taste of*
desire for. **7** *formal . . . sports* her marriage contract, which legalizes the sport (of
sexual intercourse with Soranzo).

Let poring bookmen dream of other worlds;
My world, and all of happiness, is here,
And I'd not change it for the best to come: 15
A life of pleasure is Elysium.

Enter FRIAR.

Father, you enter on the jubilee
Of my retired delights; now I can tell you,
The hell you oft have prompted is nought else
But slavish and fond superstitious fear;   20
And I could prove it too—
FRIAR   Thy blindness slays thee.
Look there, 'tis writ to thee.

Gives the letter.

GIOVANNI   From whom?
FRIAR   Unrip the seals and see;
The blood's yet seething hot, that will anon   25
Be frozen harder than congealed coral.
Why d'ee change color, son?
GIOVANNI   'Fore Heaven, you make
Some petty devil factor 'twixt my love
And your religion-maskèd sorceries.
Where had you this?
FRIAR   Thy conscience, youth, is seared,   30
Else thou wouldst stoop to warning.
GIOVANNI   'Tis her hand,
I know't; and 'tis all written in her blood.
She writes I know not what. Death? I'll not fear
An armèd thunderbolt aimed at my heart.
She writes, we are discovered—pox on dreams   35
Of low fainthearted cowardice! Discovered?
The devil we are! Which way is't possible?
Are we grown traitors to our own delights?
Confusion take such dotage, 'tis but forged.
This is your peevish chattering, weak old man.   40

---

13 poring bookmen scholars absorbed in study.   **17 on the jubilee** as I was verbally
celebrating.   **18 retired** a triple pun, meaning "delights that originally took place
secretly," "that I have been reconsidering now in seclusion," and "that have receded from
my immediate experience."   **19 prompted** reminded me of.   **20 fond** foolish.
28 factor the agent.   **30 seared** dried up.   **31 stoop** incline (your ear).

Enter VASQUES.

Now, sir, what news bring you?

VASQUES   My lord, according to his yearly custom keeping this day
a feast in honor of his birthday, by me invites you thither. Your
worthy father, with the Pope's reverend nuncio, and other
magnificoes of Parma, have promised their presence; will't please   45
you to be of the number?

GIOVANNI   Yes, tell them I dare come.

VASQUES   "Dare come"?

GIOVANNI   So I said; and tell him more, I will come.

VASQUES   These words are strange to me.   50

GIOVANNI   Say I will come.

VASQUES   You will not miss?

GIOVANNI   Yet more? I'll come! Sir, are you answered?

VASQUES   So I'll say.—My service to you.   *Exit* VASQUES.

FRIAR   You will not go, I trust.

GIOVANNI   Not go! For what?   55

FRIAR   O, do not go! This feast, I'll gage my life,
Is but a plot to train you to your ruin.
Be ruled; you sha' not go.

GIOVANNI   Not go? Stood Death
Threat'ning his armies of confounding plagues,
With hosts of dangers hot as blazing stars,   60
I would be there. Not go? Yes, and resolve
To strike as deep in slaughter as they all.
For I will go.

FRIAR   Go where thou wilt: I see
The wildness of thy fate draws to an end,
To a bad fearful end. I must not stay   65
To know thy fall; back to Bononia I
With speed will haste, and shun this coming blow.
Parma, farewell; would I had never known thee,
Or aught of thine! Well, young man, since no prayer
Can make thee safe, I leave thee to despair.   *Exit* FRIAR.   70

GIOVANNI   Despair, or tortures of a thousand hells:
All's one to me; I have set up my rest.
Now, now, work serious thoughts on baneful plots,

---

56 *gage* bet. **57** *train* lure. **61** *Yes* Yes, (I will go). **71** *Giovanni* omitted in
the quarto. **72** *set . . . rest* taken my stand.

Be all a man, my soul; let not the curse
Of old prescription rend from me the gall   75
Of courage, which enrolls a glorious death.
If I must totter like a well-grown oak,
Some under-shrubs shall in my weighty fall
Be crushed to splits: with me they all shall perish.   *Exit.*

ACT V
Scene 4   SORANZO's *house*

Enter SORANZO, VASQUES, *and* BANDITTI.

SORANZO   You will not fail, or shrink in the attempt?

VASQUES   I will undertake for their parts. Be sure, my masters, to be
bloody enough, and as unmerciful as if you were preying upon
a rich booty on the very mountains of Liguria; for your pardons,
trust to my lord, but for reward you shall trust none but your   5
own pockets.

BANDITTI OMNES   We'll make a murder.

SORANZO   Here's gold, here's more; want nothing; what you do is
noble, and an act of brave revenge. I'll make ye rich banditti,
and all free.   10

OMNES   Liberty, liberty!

VASQUES   Hold, take every man a vizard. When ye are withdrawn,
keep as much silence as you can possibly. You know the watch-
word; till which be spoken, move not, but when you hear that,
rush in like a stormy flood; I need not instruct ye in your own   15
profession.

OMNES   No, no, no.

VASQUES   In, then. Your ends are profit and preferment.—Away!

Exeunt BANDITTI.

SORANZO   The guests will all come, Vasques?

VASQUES   Yes, sir. And now let me a little edge your resolution.   20
You see nothing is unready to this great work, but a great mind

---

75 prescription   traditionally prescribed behavior (i.e. the Christian concepts advocated
by the Friar).   **76 enrolls . . . death**   will enter me among the lists of those who have
died gloriously.   **79 splits**   splinters.
🦋 **ACT V, Scene 4.   2 undertake . . . parts**   take on the responsibility of seeing that
they carry out their job.   **4 Liguria**   a region of northern Italy.   **12 vizard**   mask.

in you: call to your remembrance your disgraces, your loss of
honor, Hippolita's blood, and arm your courage in your own
wrongs; so shall you best right those wrongs in vengeance, which
you may truly call your own.   25

SORANZO 'Tis well; the less I speak, the more I burn,
And blood shall quench that flame.

VASQUES Now you begin to turn Italian. This beside—when my
young incest-monger comes, he will be sharp set on his old bit:
give him time enough, let him have your chamber and bed at   30
liberty; let my hot hare have law ere he be hunted to his death,
that if it be possible, he may post to hell in the very act of his
damnation.

Enter GIOVANNI.

SORANZO It shall be so; and see, as we would wish,
He comes himself first. Welcome, my much-loved brother!   35
Now I perceive you honor me; y'are welcome.
But where's my father?

GIOVANNI   With the other states,
Attending on the nuncio of the Pope,
To wait upon him hither. How's my sister?

SORANZO Like a good housewife, scarcely ready yet;   40
Y'are best walk to her chamber.

GIOVANNI   If you will.

SORANZO I must expect my honorable friends;
Good brother, get her forth.

GIOVANNI   You are busy, sir.   *Exit* GIOVANNI.

VASQUES Even as the great devil himself would have it; let him go
and glut himself in his own destruction. *Flourish.* Hark, the   45
nuncio is at hand; good sir, be ready to receive him.

Enter CARDINAL, FLORIO, DONADO, RICHARDETTO, *and* ATTENDANTS.

SORANZO Most reverend lord, this grace hath made me proud,
That you vouchsafe my house; I ever rest
Your humble servant for this noble favor.

23-24 *your own wrongs* wrongs done to you.   28 *turn Italian* show yourself a true
Italian (famed for their Machiavellian ways of eliminating enemies).   29 *sharp . . . bit*
rashly bent upon his old habit (of incest).   31 *law* an allowance of time or distance made to
an animal that is to be hunted.   32-33 *post . . . damnation* be hastened to hell in the
very act of incest (thus ensuring his eternal damnation).   35 *much-loved* an ironical
pun, ostensibly meaning "much-loved" by Soranzo, but actually meaning "much-loved"
by Annabella.   42 *expect* wait (here) for.   47 *grace* favor.   48 *vouchsafe* confer
the favor (of your presence).

CARDINAL   You are our friend, my lord; his holiness   50
   Shall understand how zealously you honor
   Saint Peter's vicar in his substitute.
   Our special love to you.
SORANZO   Signors, to you
   My welcome, and my ever best of thanks
   For this so memorable courtesy.   55
   Pleaseth your grace to walk near?
CARDINAL   My lord, we come
   To celebrate your feast with civil mirth,
   As ancient custom teacheth: we will go.
SORANZO   Attend his grace there! Signors, keep your way.   *Exeunt.*

ACT V

{ Scene 5   ANNABELLA's *bedchamber* }

Enter GIOVANNI *and* ANNABELLA *lying on a bed.*

GIOVANNI   What, changed so soon? Hath your new sprightly lord
   Found out a trick in night-games more than we
   Could know in our simplicity? Ha! Is't so?
   Or does the fit come on you, to prove treacherous
   To your past vows and oaths?
ANNABELLA   Why should you jest   5
   At my calamity, without all sense
   Of the approaching dangers you are in?
GIOVANNI   What danger's half so great as thy revolt?
   Thou art a faithless sister, else thou knowst
   Malice, or any treachery beside,   10
   Would stoop to my bent brows. Why, I hold fate
   Clasped in my fist, and could command the course
   Of time's eternal motion, hadst thou been
   One thought more steady than an ebbing sea.
   And what? You'll now be honest, that's resolved?   15

---

56 *near* within.
🦌 **ACT V, Scene 5. 1 *changed*** discarded me and taken another lover.   **4 *fit*** an
attack of lunacy.   ***to*** (causing you) to.   **11 *stoop . . . brows*** yield before my frowning
look.   **15 *honest*** faithful (to your husband).

ANNABELLA   Brother, dear brother, know what I have been,
    And know that now there's but a dining-time
    'Twixt us and our confusion: let's not waste
    These precious hours in vain and useless speech.
    Alas, these gay attires were not put on   20
    But to some end; this sudden solemn feast
    Was not ordained to riot in expense.
    I, that have now been chambered here alone,
    Barred of my guardian, or of any else,
    Am not for nothing at an instant freed   25
    To fresh access. Be not deceived, my brother:
    This banquet is an harbinger of death
    To you and me; resolve yourself it is,
    And be prepared to welcome it.
GIOVANNI   Well, then,
    The schoolmen teach that all this globe of earth   30
    Shall be consumed to ashes in a minute.
ANNABELLA   So I have read too.
GIOVANNI   But 'twere somewhat strange
    To see the waters burn: could I believe
    This might be true, I could believe as well
    There might be hell or heaven.
ANNABELLA   That's most certain.   35
GIOVANNI   A dream, a dream! Else in this other world
    We should know one another.
ANNABELLA   So we shall.
GIOVANNI   Have you heard so?
ANNABELLA   For certain.
GIOVANNI   But d'ee think
    That I shall see you there?—You look on me?
    May we kiss one another, prate or laugh,   40
    Or do as we do here?
ANNABELLA   I know not that.
    But good for the present, what d'ee mean
    To free yourself from danger? Some way, think
    How to escape; I'm sure the guests are come.
GIOVANNI   Look up, look here; what see you in my face?   45

---

17 dining-time the time it takes Soranzo and his guests to dine. **18 confusion** ruin.
30 schoolmen church scholars. **31 Shall . . . minute** See Deuteronomy 32:22.
42 good now (?).

ANNABELLA   Distraction and a troubled countenance.

GIOVANNI   Death, and a swift repining wrath—yet look,
    What see you in mine eyes?

ANNABELLA   Methinks you weep.

GIOVANNI   I do indeed; these are the funeral tears
    Shed on your grave. These furrowed up my cheeks   50
    When first I loved and knew not how to woo.
    Fair Annabella, should I here repeat
    The story of my life, we might lose time.
    Be record all the spirits of the air,
    And all things else that are, that day and night,   55
    Early and late, the tribute which my heart
    Hath paid to Annabella's sacred love
    Hath been these tears, which are her mourners now.
    Never till now did Nature do her best
    To show a matchless beauty to the world,   60
    Which in an instant, ere it scarce was seen,
    The jealous destinies require again.
    Pray, Annabella, pray; since we must part,
    Go thou white in thy soul, to fill a throne
    Of innocence and sanctity in heaven.   65
    Pray, pray, my sister!

ANNABELLA   Then I see your drift—
    Ye blessèd angels, guard me!

GIOVANNI   So say I.
    Kiss me. If ever aftertimes should hear
    Of our fast-knit affections, though perhaps
    The laws of conscience and of civil use   70
    May justly blame us, yet when they but know
    Our loves, that love will wipe away that rigor
    Which would in other incests be abhorred.
    Give me your hand; how sweetly life doth run
    In these well-colored veins! How constantly   75
    These palms do promise health! But I could chide
    With Nature for this cunning flattery.

---

47 *repining* discontented.   **51** *woo* The quarto reads "woe."   **54** *record* witnesses.
62 *destinies* According to classical mythology, the three Fates controlled men's lives;
they were represented as old women spinning the thread of life and then cutting it off.
64 *white* cleansed.   **70** *civil use* social custom.   **72** *that rigor* the severity (of the
crime).

Kiss me again—forgive me.
ANNABELLA   With my heart.
GIOVANNI   Farewell.
ANNABELLA   Will you be gone?
GIOVANNI   Be dark, bright sun,
And make this midday night, that thy gilt rays   80
May not behold a deed will turn their splendor
More sooty than the poets feign their Styx!
One other kiss, my sister.
ANNABELLA   What means this?
GIOVANNI   To save thy fame, and kill thee in a kiss.

Stabs her.

Thus die, and die by me, and by my hand!   85
Revenge is mine; honor doth love command.
ANNABELLA   O brother, by your hand?
GIOVANNI   When thou art dead
I'll give my reasons for't; for to dispute
With thy (even in thy death) most lovely beauty,
Would make me stagger to perform this act,   90
Which I most glory in.
ANNABELLA   Forgive him, Heaven—and me my sins; farewell.
Brother unkind, unkind!—Mercy, great Heaven—O!—O!—
                                                          Dies.

GIOVANNI   She's dead, alas, good soul! The hapless fruit
That in her womb received its life from me   95
Hath had from me a cradle and a grave.
I must not dally. This sad marriage bed,
In all her best, bore her alive and dead.
Soranzo, thou hast missed thy aim in this;
I have prevented now thy reaching plots,   100
And killed a love, for whose each drop of blood
I would have pawned my heart. Fair Annabella,
How over-glorious art thou in thy wounds,
Triumphing over infamy and hate!
Shrink not, courageous hand, stand up, my heart,   105
And boldly act my last and greater part.   *Exit with the body.*

---

82 *feign* present. **Styx** in classical mythology, the principal river of hell. 84 *fame*
reputation. 93 **unkind** both "harsh" and "unnatural." 100 *reaching* scheming.

ACT V

{ Scene 6   SORANZO's *banquet hall* }

A banquet. Enter CARDINAL, FLORIO, DONADO, SORANZO, RICHAR-
DETTO, VASQUES, *and* ATTENDANTS; *they take their places.*

VASQUES Remember, sir, what you have to do; be wise and resolute.
SORANZO Enough—my heart is fixed.—Pleaseth your grace
    To taste these coarse confections. Though the use
    Of such set entertainments more consists
    In custom than in cause, yet, reverend sir,   5
    I am still made your servant by your presence.
CARDINAL And we your friend.
SORANZO But where's my brother Giovanni?

Enter GIOVANNI *with a heart upon his dagger.*

GIOVANNI Here, here, Soranzo; trimmed in reeking blood,
    That triumphs over death; proud in the spoil   10
    Of love and vengeance! Fate or all the powers
    That guide the motions of immortal souls
    Could not prevent me.
CARDINAL What means this?
FLORIO Son Giovanni!   15
SORANZO Shall I be forestalled?
GIOVANNI Be not amazed: if your misgiving hearts
    Shrink at an idle sight, what bloodless fear
    Of coward passion would have seized your senses,
    Had you beheld the rape of life and beauty   20
    Which I have acted? My sister, O my sister!
FLORIO Ha! What of her?
GIOVANNI   The glory of my deed
    Darkened the midday sun, made noon as night.
    You came to feast, my lords, with dainty fare;
    I came to feast too, but I digged for food   25
    In a much richer mine than gold or stone
    Of any value balanced; 'tis a heart,
    A heart, my lords, in which is mine entombed.
    Look well upon't; d'ee know't?

ACT V, Scene 6.   **10** *spoil* both "what I have plundered for myself" and "what I
have spoiled for you."   **20** *rape* murder.   **27** *balanced* that can be weighed in a scale.

VASQUES   What strange riddle's this?   30
GIOVANNI   'Tis Annabella's heart, 'tis.—Why d'ee startle?
    I vow 'tis hers: this dagger's point ploughed up
    Her fruitful womb, and left to me the fame
    Of a most glorious executioner.
FLORIO   Why, madman, art thyself?   35
GIOVANNI   Yes, father; and that times to come may know
    How as my fate I honored my revenge,
    List, father: to your ears I will yield up
    How much I have deserved to be your son.
FLORIO   What is't thou sayst?
GIOVANNI   Nine moons have had their changes   40
    Since I first throughly viewed and truly loved
    Your daughter and my sister.
FLORIO   How!—Alas,
    My lords, he's a frantic madman!
GIOVANNI   Father, no.
    For nine months' space in secret I enjoyed
    Sweet Annabella's sheets; nine months I lived   45
    A happy monarch of her heart and her.
    Soranzo, thou knowst this; thy paler cheek
    Bears the confounding print of thy disgrace—
    For her too fruitful womb too soon bewrayed
    The happy passage of our stol'n delights,   50
    And made her mother to a child unborn.
CARDINAL   Incestuous villain!
FLORIO   O, his rage belies him.
GIOVANNI   It does not, 'tis the oracle of truth;
    I vow it is so.
SORANZO   I shall burst with fury;
    Bring the strumpet forth!   55
VASQUES   I shall, sir.   *Exit* VASQUES.
GIOVANNI   Do, sir! Have you all no faith
    To credit yet my triumphs? Here I swear
    By all that you call sacred, by the love
    I bore my Annabella whilst she lived,
    These hands have from her bosom ripped this heart.   60

    Enter VASQUES.

---

47 *paler* paling.   **49** *bewrayed* disclosed.   **57** *credit* believe.

Is't true or no, sir?

VASQUES   'Tis most strangely true.

FLORIO   Cursèd man!—Have I lived to—   *Dies.*

CARDINAL   Hold up, Florio.
Monster of children, see what thou hast done—
Broke thy old father's heart! Is none of you
Dares venture on him?

GIOVANNI   Let 'em! O, my father: 65
How well his death becomes him in his griefs!
Why, this was done with courage; now survives
None of our house but I, gilt in the blood
Of a fair sister and a hapless father.

SORANZO   Inhuman scorn of men, hast thou a thought   70
T'outlive thy murders?

GIOVANNI   Yes, I tell thee, yes!
For in my fists I bear the twists of life.
Soranzo, see this heart, which was thy wife's—
Thus I exchange it royally for thine,

[*Stabs him.*]

And thus and thus! Now brave revenge is mine.   75

VASQUES   I cannot hold any longer.—You, sir, are you grown
insolent in your butcheries? Have at you!

[*They*] *fight.*

GIOVANNI   Come, I am armed to meet thee.

VASQUES   No, will it not be yet? If this will not, another shall. Not
yet? I shall fit you anon.—Vengeance!   80

Enter BANDITTI [*and all fight* GIOVANNI].

GIOVANNI   Welcome! Come more of you whate'er you be,
I dare your worst—

[*He is wounded.*]

O, I can stand no longer! Feeble arms,
Have you so soon lost strength?

---

61 *strangely* astonishingly.   **67** *this*   this (whole affair of Annabella's murder and
Florio's death).   *with courage*   with a great intensity of feeling.   **72** *twists* threads
(again an allusion to the destinies mentioned in V.5.62).   **74** *royally* gloriously.   **75** *brave*
splendid.   **79** *will . . . yet*   Will your end not come yet?   *If . . . not*   if this (particular
bit of swordplay) will not kill you.   **80** *fit*   "punish," with a conscious echo of *The
Spanish Tragedy,* IV.1.67.   *Vengeance*   the code word that summons the bandits.

VASQUES Now you are welcome, sir!—Away, my masters, all is   85
  done; shift for yourselves! Your reward is your own; shift for
  yourselves.
BANDITTI Away, away!   *Exeunt* BANDITTI.
VASQUES How d'ee, my lord; see you this? How is't?
SORANZO Dead; but in death well pleased that I have lived   90
  To see my wrongs revenged on that black devil.
  O Vasques, to thy bosom let me give
  My last of breath: let not that lecher live—O!—   *Dies.*
VASQUES The reward of peace and rest be with him, my ever dearest
  lord and master.   95
GIOVANNI Whose hand gave me this wound?
VASQUES Mine, sir, I was your first man; have you enough?
GIOVANNI I thank thee: thou hast done for me but what I would have
  else done on myself.—Art sure thy lord is dead?
VASQUES O impudent slave! As sure as I am sure to see thee die.   100
CARDINAL Think on thy life and end, and call for mercy.
GIOVANNI Mercy? Why, I have found it in this justice.
CARDINAL Strive yet to cry to Heaven.
GIOVANNI   O, I bleed fast.
  Death, thou art a guest long looked for; I embrace
  Thee and thy wounds. O, my last minute comes!   105
  Where'er I go, let me enjoy this grace:
  Freely to view my Annabella's face.   *Dies.*
DONADO Strange miracle of justice!
CARDINAL Raise up the city; we shall be murdered all!
VASQUES You need not fear, you shall not; this strange task being   110
  ended, I have paid the duty to the son which I have vowed to
  the father.
CARDINAL Speak, wretched villain, what incarnate fiend
  Hath led thee on to this?
VASQUES Honesty, and pity of my master's wrongs: for know, my   115
  lord, I am by birth a Spaniard, brought forth my country in
  my youth by Lord Soranzo's father, whom whilst he lived I
  served faithfully; since whose death I have been to this man as I
  was to him. What I have done was duty, and I repent nothing
  but that the loss of my life had not ransomed his.   120

---

97 *first man* vanquisher. **111–12** *I . . . father* I have faithfully served Soranzo, as I
promised his father I would. **115** *master's wrongs* wrongs done to my master.

CARDINAL   Say, fellow, knowst thou any yet unnamed of counsel in
    this incest?
VASQUES   Yes, an old woman, sometimes guardian to this murdered
    lady.
CARDINAL   And what's become of her?   125
VASQUES   Within this room she is; whose eyes, after her confession,
    I caused to be put out, but kept alive, to confirm what from
    Giovanni's own mouth you have heard. Now, my lord, what I
    have done you may judge of, and let your own wisdom be a
    judge in your own reason.   130
CARDINAL   Peace! First this woman, chief in these effects:
    My sentence is, that forthwith she be ta'en
    Out of the city, for example's sake,
    There to be burnt to ashes.
DONADO   'Tis most just.
CARDINAL   Be it your charge, Donado, see it done.   135
DONADO   I shall.
VASQUES   What for me? If death, 'tis welcome; I have been honest
    to the son as I was to the father.
CARDINAL   Fellow, for thee: since what thou didst was done
    Not for thyself, being no Italian,   140
    We banish thee forever, to depart
    Within three days. In this we do dispense
    With grounds of reason, not of thine offense.
VASQUES   'Tis well; this conquest is mine, and I rejoice that a Spaniard
    outwent an Italian in revenge.   *Exit* VASQUES.   145
CARDINAL   Take up these slaughtered bodies, see them buried;
    And all the gold and jewels, or whatsoever
    Confiscate by the canons of the Church,
    We seize upon to the Pope's proper use.
RICHARDETTO   [*Uncovering his disguise.*] Your grace's pardon! thus long
    I lived disguised   150
    To see the effect of pride and lust at once
    Brought both to shameful ends.
CARDINAL   What, Richardetto, whom we thought for dead?
DONADO   Sir, was it you—
RICHARDETTO   Your friend.
CARDINAL   We shall have time

---

123 *sometimes* previously.   **143** *With . . . offense* on the basis of reason, rather than
on the basis of your offense.

To talk at large of all; but never yet   155
Incest and murder have so strangely met.
Of one so young, so rich in nature's store,
Who could not say, 'tis pity she's a whore?   *Exeunt.*

The general commendation deserved by the actors in their presentment
of this tragedy may easily excuse such few faults as are escaped in the
printing. A common charity may allow him the ability of spelling
whom a secure confidence assures that he cannot ignorantly err in the
application of sense.

Printer's Note   *are escaped*   appear accidentally.

8880

DATE DUE

JUN 0 1 1995

Husto

Classics of the Renaissance theater; seven
English plays. Edited by J. Dennis Huston [and]
Alvin B. Kernan. New York, Harcourt, Brace &
World [1969]
vii, 735p. illus. 21cm.
Bibliographical footnotes.
291149 Contents.-Tamburlaine the Great, by C. Marlowe.-
The Spanish tragedy, by T. Kyd.-Volpone, by B. Jon-
son.-The revenger's tragedy, by C. Tourneur.-The
Duchess of Malfi, by J. Webster.-The changeling,
by T. Middleton and W. Rowley.-'Tis pity she's a
whore, by J. Ford.
1. English drama-Early mo   lern and Elizabethan. I.
Kernan, Alvin B., joint   author. II.Title.